WITHDRAWN BY THE
UNIVERSITY OF MICHIGAN

D1713958

CHINA REVIEW 1996

Related titles already published

China Review (1991)
Edited by Kuan Hsin-chi
and Maurice Brosseau

China Review 1992
Edited by Kuan Hsin-chi
and Maurice Brosseau

China Review 1993
Edited by Joseph Cheng Yu-shek
and Maurice Brosseau

China Review 1994
Edited by Maurice Brosseau
and Lo Chi Kin

China Review 1995
Edited by Lo Chi Kin, Suzanne Pepper
and Tsui Kai Yuen

China Review
1996

EDITED BY
Maurice Brosseau,
Suzanne Pepper
AND
Tsang Shu-ki

The Chinese University Press

© **The Chinese University of Hong Kong** 1996

All Rights Reserved. No part of this publication may
be reproduced or transmitted in any form or by any
means, electronic or mechanical, including photocopying,
recording, or any information storage and retrieval
system, without permission in writing from
The Chinese University of Hong Kong.

ISBN 962–201–735–5

THE CHINESE UNIVERSITY PRESS
The Chinese University of Hong Kong
SHA TIN, N.T., HONG KONG

Printed in Hong Kong

grad
4005019l
prob
06/26/01
add

Steering Committee

Maurice Brosseau
Hsi-sheng Ch'i
Kuan Hsin-chi
Y. Y. Kueh
Suzanne Pepper
Yun-wing Sung
Tsang Shu-ki
Paul S. L. Wong

Contents

Preface

The multifarious events of the past year seriously tested the wisdom, deftness and stamina of the various generations of Chinese leaders. The following chapters attempt to elucidate the spectrum of possible factors affecting the evolution of society and some of the challenges the decision makers were forced to face. Other sectors were also reviewed which are necessary to sustain or harness the momentum of change in this populous country. Some authors, in addition, thought necessary to record their concern regarding the uncertain stability and functionality of the present institutions and organizations, a measure of speculation on long-term consequences and the pathway of institutional evolution.

Be they the internal politics of succession, the obstinacy over foreign policy and trade, the strategy quandaries over the national reunification of Hong Kong and Taiwan, the uncertainty inherent to the massive undertaking of the economic reforms, the growing and perplexing evidence of the impatient sway of the yearning masses... the questions and topics treated below kept the contributing analysts at the edge of intellectual understanding and creativity.

It is certainly tantalizing to try to measure and appreciate the evolutionary path and direction that China has been following in the recent past. This sixth volume of the *China Review* series bears witness to the scholarly interest thus encouraged and again contributes judiciously to the chronicle of the unfolding national metamorphosis.

The editors wish to express their deep appreciation to the contributors for their meticulous research and writing. They also acknowledge the highly regarded service rendered by the academic referees who graciously gave of their precious time to read the early drafts and offer their valued assistance to the authors. Warm thanks are, lastly, extended to the editing staff of The Chinese University Press for their professionalism in the pursuit of the highest quality.

The Editors
April 1996

Contributors

CLAUDE AUBERT received his education in agronomy. Currently he is Director of Research at the French National Institute of Agricultural Research (INRA) where he is conducting studies on Chinese rural economy and society. He has done several field surveys both in Taiwan and the People's Republic of China and has written extensively on Chinese agriculture.

MAURICE BROSSEAU is Research Officer at the Hong Kong Institute of Asia-Pacific Studies, The Chinese University of Hong Kong. He co-edited the first four volumes of *China Review*.

ALBERT H. Y. CHEN is a graduate of the University of Hong Kong (LL B, 1980) and Harvard University (LL M, 1982), and qualified as a solicitor in Hong Kong. He has taught at the University of Hong Kong since 1984 and is currently Reader in Law. He has written five books and over forty articles in English and Chinese in the areas of Hong Kong law, Chinese law and legal theory.

FANNY CHEUNG (Ph.D., Minnesota) is Dean of Social Science and Professor in the Department of Psychology, The Chinese University of Hong Kong. She is currently the co-editor of *Psychology and Health*, and consulting editor for *Applied Psychology: An International Review and Culture, Medicine, and Psychiatry*. Her research interests include personality assessment, clinical psychology, somatization and gender issues.

HIM CHUNG graduated in China Studies from the Hong Kong Baptist University and received his M.Phil. in Geography from The Chinese University of Hong Kong. He is currently the Research Assistant of the Universities Service Centre at The Chinese University of Hong Kong.

HANS HENDRISCHKE is Director of the Access China Research Centre at the Macquarie Graduate School of Management, Macquarie University, Sydney. He has lived and worked in China. His research and publications are in the areas of political and economic reforms in China. He is also the editor of the Australian China business journal *Access China*.

PAUL CHUN-KUEN KWONG is a Harvard trained demographer who teaches Asian populations and social science methods at Griffith University (Australia) where he is Deputy Head of the School of Modern Asian Studies. He has taught sociology at The Chinese University of Hong Kong, population statistics both at the Chinese Academy of Social Sciences and, for the United Nations, at the State Statistical Bureau.

LAU PUI KING, PRISCILLA is Associate Professor and Associate Head of the Department of Business Studies, Hong Kong Polytechnic University. She was appointed Hong Kong representative to the Guangdong Provincial People's Congress from 1988 to 1998. Her research interests are land-use problems, foreign investment and regional studies of the PRC. Her recent publications include *Zhongguo jingji daqushi, 1994, 1995 and 1996* (Economic Trends of the PRC, 1994, 1995, 1996) (editor), published in Hong Kong, mainland China, Taiwan, and Japan; *The Fifth Dragon* (co-author); and *Guangdong jingji touzi zonglan* (Economic and Investment Profile of Guangdong).

CHI-WEN JEVONS LEE is Professor of Accounting at Hong Kong University of Science and Technology, and Freeman Professor of Business and Associate Dean at Tulane University. He received a Ph.D. from the University of Rochester and has taught at the Graduate School of Business, University of Chicago, and the Wharton School, University of Pennsylvania. He has published more than 100 articles, some in the *Journal of Business*, *Journal of Accounting and Economics*, *Journal of Accounting Research*, *Accounting Review*, *Journal of Finance*, and *Review of Economics and Statistics*. He has served as consultant to the US Department of Commerce, US Department of Energy, PRC Ministry of Finance, ROC Ministry of Finance, ROC Central Bank, United Nations, World Bank, and many of China's state-owned enterprises.

KWOK LEUNG (Ph.D., Illinois) is Chairman of the Department of Psychology of The Chinese University of Hong Kong. He is currently an associate editor of *Journal of Cross-Cultural Psychology*. He co-edited *Innovations in Cross-Cultural Psychology* and co-authored *Methods and Data Analysis for Cross-Cultural Psychology*. His research interests include justice and conflict resolution, organizational psychology and cross-cultural psychology.

S. M. LEUNG lectures in Organizational Behaviour and Business Strategy at the Hong Kong Baptist University. She has an MBA from Birmingham University and is currently a Ph.D. candidate at Lancaster University where she is pursuing research on women in management in the PRC. Her other research interests include gender issues and feminist methodology, negotiation behaviour and strategic management in the Asian context.

CHU-CHENG MING is Professor in Political Science at the National Taiwan University. He holds a Ph.D. in political science from the University of Notre Dame. Author of *Change of the International Political System: Collapse of the Bipolarity and the Coming of New World Order* (in Chinese). He has published articles on Chinese politics, international relations and cross-Straits relations.

JEAN OI is an Associate Professor of Government, currently on leave from Harvard University, and Visiting Associate Professor in the Division of Social Science, Hong Kong University of Science and Technology. She is the author of *State and Peasant in Contemporary China* (University of California Press, 1989) and *Rural China Takes Off: Incentives for Industrialization* (University of California Press, forthcoming).

SUZANNE PEPPER holds a Ph.D. in Political Science from the University of California, Berkeley, and is a Hong Kong-based American writer. Her most recent publication is, *Radicalism and Education Reform in 20th Century China* (Cambridge University Press, 1996).

REN YUE (Ph.D., Columbia) is a University Lecturer in the Department of Politics and Sociology, Lingnan College, Hong Kong. He taught previously at Virginia Polytechnic Institute and State University. His research interests include international organization, international law and comparative foreign policy.

SONG WEIZHENG (MS, Beijing Normal University) is Professor at the Institute of Psychology, Chinese Academy of Sciences, leading the research team for personality study. Her major academic interests are in personality psychology, adolescent psychology and clinical psychology. She coordinated the adaptation of the Chinese version of the Minnesota Multiphasic Personality Inventory (MMPI) and the development of the CPAI in China.

TSANG SHU-KI is Associate Professor in Economics at the Hong Kong Baptist University. He is the author of four books on Hong Kong and China and a number of journal papers and book chapters on comparative economic systems, monetary economics, disequilibrium econometrics, China's reforms and the country's external economic relations.

ANDREW WEDEMAN is Assistant Professor of Political Science at the University of Nebraska, Lincoln. He holds a Ph.D. in political science from the University of California, Los Angeles. Mr Wedeman is the author of *The East Wind Subsides: Chinese Foreign Policy and the Origins of the Cultural Revolution*. His current research focuses on local protectionism, governmental malfeasance and corruption in post-Mao China.

BOB WESTWOOD was educated in the United Kingdom, receiving BA and MA degrees in Psychology and a Ph.D. in Management. He has worked in the Asia-Pacific region since 1983 and in the Department of Management at CUHK, where he is currently a Senior Lecturer, since 1988. He intends his research and writing to engage with the issues of power and resistance, persistence and change, difference and similarity, and coherence and fragmentation in organizational contexts — often within a comparative frame.

WOO TUN-OY is Associate Professor of Economics at Hong Kong Baptist University. His research interests are economic development theory, transition economics and the Chinese economy.

XIE DONG (BS, MS, Beijing University) is Assistant Professor of the Institute of Psychology, Chinese Academy of Sciences. He is an active member of the personality research team and contributed to the development of the CPAI in China. His major interests are in personality and clinical psychology.

YOU JI is a Lecturer in the Department of Political Science, University of Canterbury, Christchurch, New Zealand. He has published widely on China's political, economic and military affairs. He is the author of *Dismantling the Party/State: China's Enterprise Reform* (Routledge, forthcoming), and *Winning the Next War? The PLA in Quest of High-tech Military Power* (Allen & Unwin, forthcoming).

ZHANG JIANXIN (BS, Beijing University, M.Phil., CUHK) is a Ph.D. candidate in the Department of Psychology, The Chinese University of Hong Kong. He worked in the Institute of Psychology, Chinese Academy of Sciences for ten years. His major interests are in personality psychology, cross-cultural psychology and social psychology. He played an active role in developing the CPAI and revising the MMPI-2 in mainland China.

Abbreviations

ADB	China Agricultural Development Bank
APEC	Asia-Pacific Economic Cooperation
ARATS	Association for Relations Across the Taiwan Straits
ASEAN	Association of Southeast Asian Nations
CASS	Chinese Academy of Social Sciences
CCP	Chinese Communist Party
CDIC	Central Discipline Inspection Commission
CITMS	Chinese Individual Traditionality/Modernity Scale
CMC	Central Military Commission
CNS	China News Service
CPAI	Chinese Personality Assessment Inventory
CPI	Consumer price index
CPSU	Communist Party of the Soviet Union
DPP	Democratic Progressive Party (Taiwan)
EEZ	Exclusive Economic Zone
FEC	Foreign exchange certificates
FIE	Foreign invested enterprises
GDP	Gross domestic product
GNP	Gross national product
GPCL	General Principles of Civil Law
GVIO	Gross value of industrial output
HB	Hospital-delivered births
HKSAR	Hong Kong Special Administrative Region
ICBC	Industrial and Commercial Bank of China
IEB	China Import and Export Bank
IPO	Initial public offerings
IPR	Intellectual property rights
LLC	Limited liability company
MAC	Mainland Affairs Council
MMPI	Minnesota Multiphasic Inventory
MOWIRT	(Meaning of work) International Research Team

NGO	Non-government organizations
NP	New Party (Taiwan)
NPC	National People's Congress
NUC	National Unification Council
PBOC	People's Bank of China
PLA	People's Liberation Army
PRC	People's Republic of China
PWC	Preliminary Working Committee
RMB	*Renminbi* (Chinese dollar)
ROC	Republic of China
ROK	Republic of Korea
RPI	Retailed price index
SA	Selective abortion
SAEC	State Administration for Exchange Control
SDB	China State Development Bank
SEF	Strait Exchange Foundation (Taiwan)
SEZ	Special economic zone
SFPC	State Family Planning Commission
SOE	State-owned enterprises
SRB	Sex ratio at birth
SSB	State Statistical Bureau
TFR	Total fertility rates
TVE	Township and village entreprise
UN	United Nations
US	United States
USD	Ultrasound determination
USSR	Soviet Union
VAT	Value-added tax
WTO	World Trade Organization

Major Statistics of the PRC, 1995

	Unit	1995	Growth rate (%)
(1) Year-end total population	million persons	1211.2	1.1
(2) Gross domestic product (GDP)	billion RMB	5773.3	10.2*
GDP — primary sector	billion RMB	1136.5	4.5*
GDP — secondary sector	billion RMB	2827.4	13.6*
GDP — tertiary sector	billion RMB	1809.4	8.0*
(3) Grain production	million tons	465.0	–4.5
(4) Cotton production	million tons	4.5	3.7
(5) Industrial value added	billion RMB	2471.8	14.0*
(6) Total investment in fixed assets	billion RMB	1944.5	11.0*
State sector		1082.2	16.1**
Collective sector		297.8	11.8**
Urban and rural residents		238.1	20.8**
Others		326.4	35.3**
(7) Growth of money supply (M2)	% change		29.5
(8) Consumer price index (CPI)	% change		17.1
Urban CPI			16.8
Rural CPI			17.5
(9) Total value of exports	billion US dollars	148.8	22.9**
(10) Total value of imports		132.1	14.2**
(11) Foreign capital actually utilized	billion US dollars	48.4	11.0**
(12) Primary school net enrolment rate	%	98.5	
(13) Drop-out rate of primary school students	%	1.49	
(14) Hospital beds	thousand beds	2836	0.2
(15) Per-capita expenditure of residents in cities and towns	RMB	3893	4.9*
(16) Per-capita net income of peasants	RMB	1578	5.3*
(17) Unemployment rate in cities and towns	%	2.9	

Notes: * the growth rate is in real terms.
           ** the growth rate is in nominal terms.

Sources: "1995 nian guomin jingji he shehui fazhan de tongji gongbu" (1995 Statistical Communiqué of Economic and Social Development of the PRC), *Renmin ribao* (People's Daily), overseas edition, 7 March 1996.

Chronology of 1995

Him Chung

JANUARY

Foreign exchange certificates (FEC) were withdrawn from circulation from the **1st**. This was a major reform step of the foreign exchange control system. According to the reform plan, China aimed to make the *Renminbi* (RMB) convertible by the year 2000. The next step would be the reduction of restrictions on the use of foreign exchange in the country.

Ten cities were approved as "financially open city" by the State Council on the **10th**. They were Beijing, Hangzhou, Wuhan, Chengdu, Xian, Shenyang, Shijiazhuang, Suzhou, Chongqing and Hefei. Foreign banks were allowed to establish a representative office in these cities.

A new round of Sino-Amercian negotiations on intellectual property rights (IPR), which had stopped after the two countries had issued their proposed lists for trade retaliation and counter-retaliation at the end of last year, was resumed on the **18th**. The talks lasted for a total of nine days with a two-day adjournment on the **22nd** and the **23rd**. No agreement, however, was reached. After the meeting, United States (US) trade representative Mickey Kantor once again threatened that, if the two countries failed to reach agreement, the US would carry out trade retaliation against China.

The 5th Plenary Session of the Central Discipline Inspection Commission (CDIC) was held in Beijing from the **20th** to the **23rd**. The meeting, chaired by Wei Jianxing, secretary of CDIC, studied and worked out arrangement for deepening the anti-corruption drive in 1995. Objectives of the year included: (1) promoting honesty and self-discipline among leading cadres, especially for those at county/department level or above; (2) making further efforts to investigate violations of laws and discipline in leading party and government organs; (3) rectifying unhealthy tendencies in departments and among trades.

China's nuclear power industry entered a new stage when the Qishan nuclear power plant, the first of its kind designed and constructed by China, went through its trial operation successfully on the **30th**. This showed that China had a complete mastery of nuclear power technique in design, construction, safety operation and raffling.

The continuous increase in food prices prompted China to reintroduce government coupons in urban areas **this month**. More than 35 of China's large and medium-sized cities reintroduced grain coupons so as to curb the soaring of staple food prices. Migrant workers and those without permanent residence in urban areas, however, were excluded from such protection.

FEBRUARY

Sino-Amercian IPR negotiations continued this month. On the **2nd**, the US government imposed a 100% punitive tariff on 1.08 billion US dollars worth of imports from China after the two countries had failed to reach an agreement on the protection of US intellectual property rights. The US trade representative, Mickey Kantor, said that the sanction would automatically become effective if no acceptable agreement were reached by the **26th**. China responded by a list of counter-retaliation measures. This included a 100% tariff on all kinds of game cards, cassette tapes, compact discs, cigarettes and the suspension of imports of video products and of applications US audiovisual manufacturers to set up branches in China. Fortunately, a "common understanding" was finally reached on the **25th**, averting a trade war between the two countries.

On the **8th**, the State Economic and Trade Commission announced a "modern system" had been introduced. The system would be implemented in 100 selected companies as a major part of the government's plan for restructuring state-owned enterprises in 1995. According to the plan, a responsibility system for the management of state-owned assets in enterprises would be instituted nationwide to make sure that the value of state-owned assets would be maintained or even increased. Other key measures of the plan included: increasing enterprises' funds for production via a variety of channels, trying bankruptcy on financially unsound enterprises, adopting measures to relieve the enterprises' debt burdens, increasing investment in advanced technology and readjusting industrial and enterprise structures.

On the **14th**, the day China reached 1.2 billion population, the State Council announced the Programme for the Work of Family Planning in China (1995–2000). The programme called upon family planning departments at all levels to give top priority to propaganda and education in their work. It also required the nationwide family planning services network to improve their personnel and equipment to provide better contraception and related services. The target of the programme was to limit China's total population within 1.23 billion by the end of 1995 and 1.3 billion by the year 2000. Rural areas were still the major concern, and the national natural growth rate would be controlled at 10‰ or below.

On the **13th**, China and the Republic of Korea (ROK) reached an agreement to help China develop her nuclear industry. Both countries will cooperate until 2010, and the ROK will build 40 light-water nuclear power reactors with a capacity of one million kW each in China's coastal areas. The two countries will also jointly develop and manufacture a special model of reactor for exports.

MARCH

The Ministry of Agriculture on the **4th** mapped out a detailed plan to increase the countries' annual grain output by 50 million tons in the coming six years. The objective was to maintain self-sufficiency in grain production under the unfavourable conditions of rising population and decreasing arable land. Efforts would be made to build 378 state grain-producing counties, to expand irrigated farmland by four million ha, to open up wasteland and to introduce new farming methods.

Two new vice-premiers, Wu Bangguo and Jiang Chunyun, were elected at the 3rd Session of the 8th National People's Congress (NPC) held in Beijing from the **4th** to the **18th**. The appointment of these two sole candidates, however, met an unprecedented opposition from the assembly on the **17th**. With 210 (7.6%) of the members voting against Wu and 391 (14.2%) against Jiang. Jiang's record was the poorest among all the vice-premiers. Moreover, two new NPC Standing Committee members, Zhang Yumao and Pu Chaozhu, were elected.

On the **6th**, the Agricultural Bank of China, one of China's four largest commercial banks, launched its first overseas bond issue in Tokyo. A total of 15 billion yen (about 159 million US dollars) was raised. The bond carried an annual interest rate of 4.3% and would mature in five years. The funds raised by the issue would be used to finance a key state project designed to produce colour TV glass screens which would essentially make China less dependent on foreign inputs for the glass. Until then, a total of 1.1 billion US dollars had been raised by the Agricultural Bank of China.

China's first set of detailed regulations on the management of state property in administrative departments and institutions were issued on the **10th**. It clearly defined what state properties were and set rules to improve management in all organizations so that property would not be lost during the process of economic reform.

The Standing Committee of the 8th National Chinese People's Political Consultative Conference (CPPCC) on the **15th** held its 12th meeting in Beijing. The meeting decided to reduce the National Committee's fourteen special committees to eight. After the reorganization, the eight special committees were: the Motions Committee; Economy Committee; Committee on Science and Technology, Education, Culture, Health and Sports; Women, Youth and Law Committee; Nationalities and Religions Committee; Culture, Historical Data and Study Committee; Committee for Liaison with Taiwan, Hong Kong and Macau Compatriots, and Overseas Chinese; and Foreign Affairs Committee. Zhou Shaozheng, Fang Weizhong, Qian Weichang, Qian Zhengying, Zhao

Puchu, Yang Zhengmin, Dong Yinchu and Qian Liren were appointed as the chairmen of the above committees, respectively.

APRIL

New regulations on the mailing of state information went into effect on the **1st**. The regulations, *Provisions on Prohibiting the Sending by Mail or Illegally Carrying Classified State Documents, Information, and Other Materials Out of the Territory*, authorized the customs to seize materials which were suspected of containing state secrets and to send them to the relevant authorities for assessment. Violators of the Provisions would be punished in accordance with the *Rules for the Implementation of Administrative Punishments under the Customs Law of the People's Republic of China*.

Xinhua News Agency on the **4th** announced the publication of the first book series on Human Rights issues. All of the seven books of the "Human Rights Research Material Series" were published by the Sichuan People's Publishing House and contained topics on human rights development in China, the Marxist theory of human rights, human rights doctrines in the Western world and human rights in the developing countries. On the **8th**, Xinhua reported that the first publishing house for religious books was established in Beijing with the approval of the Press and Publication Administration of China. The Religious Culture Publishing House would handle publications on religious policy, theory, culture, history and doctrines.

Tensions ran high in Beijing after the vice-mayor of Beijing, Wang Baosen, committed suicide on the **4th**. The mayor of Beijing, Chen Xitong, was also implicated in Wang's corruption and economic crime. On the **28th**, an official spokesman announced that Chen "had taken the blame and resigned" from all his posts in the Municipal Party Committee. Chen was the first Politburo member to have been officially sacked for a case of corruption. His position as the secretary of the Municipal Party Committee was taken over by Wei Jianxing. Chen was finally dismissed from the Chinese Communist Party (CCP) Politburo and the Central Committee at the 5th Plenary Session of the 14th CCP Central Committee which ended on the 28th of September.

Chen Yun, China's revolutionary leader, died in Beijing on the **10th** at the age of 89. His death was announced officially on the **11th**, and two obituaries were published. One was the official copy jointly endorsed by the Central Committee, the NPC, the State Council, the CPPCC and the Central Military Commission. The other obituary, which gave more credit to his role and contributions, was published by Xinhua News Agency on Chen's cremation on the **17th**. All of these showed that there seemed to be disagreements on how to appraise Chen's role.

On the **25th**, another list of Advisers on Hong Kong Affairs was announced. The new group of 45 was the fourth batch of advisers on Hong Kong affairs. Businessmen again made up the majority in this batch and accounted for 27 of the appointments, the others included seven professionals, four academics, four former senior government officials and three from arts and entertainment. They received their letter of appointment in Beijing on the **28th**. The total number of advisers was thus increased to 186.

MAY

A new rule on 8-hour work day and 5-day work week took effect on the **1st**. The change was seen as a stimulus for the country's economy, especially for the service industry and tourism. One million new jobs would be created in the railway, air transportation and tourism sectors. Under the new rule, domestic tourists were also expected to reach 500 million, an increase of 50 million when compared with 1994.

A cooperative medical insurance system for rural areas was published on the **1st**. The objective of this system was to improve health care and medical service in the rural areas. It served mainly peasants, and an insurance fund would be built. Every farmer should contribute 2% of his annual income to the fund, whereas village and township enterprises must contribute 5% of their employee payrolls to augment the fund. With this coverage, peasants could get free preventive treatment and compensation of medical fees in case of serious illness. Education departments in rural areas were also required to organize primary and high school students to join the insurance system.

On the **18th**, the Walt Disney Company won the lawsuit that it had filed against three Chinese publishing houses and a book store, including the Beijing Agency of Xinhua Bookstore and Beijing Children's Publishing House, which had been charged with imitating the company's cartoon characters. This was the first copyright case judged by a Chinese court after China and the United States had signed the Memorandum of Understanding on Intellectual Property Rights Protection in 1992. According to the judgements of the First Inter-mediate People's Court of Beijing, the four defendants were ordered to make an apology to the Walt Disney Company via the news media and pay the plaintiff RMB 227,094.14 (about US$ 26,100) in damage.

China News Service (CNS) on the **23th** reported that China's State Council and the People's Bank of China had approved the establishment of the China

Minsheng Bank, the first private bank in China. It was to be a nationwide shareholding commercial bank in the form of a shareholding limited company and was prepared by the All-China Federation of Industry and Commerce. The new bank would be put under the supervision of the People's Bank of China but have independent legal status and accounting and assume sole responsibility for its profits, losses and risks.

JUNE

Sino-Amercian relations worsened when Lee Teng-hui began his private visit to the US on the **8th**. Li was the first incumbent president of Taiwan to visit the United States. China criticized US action for encouraging Taiwan to split from China.

The prominent dissident, Chen Ziming, was forced to return to prison on the **26th**, one year after he was given medical bail. Chen had been one of the leaders in 1989's pro-democracy movement and had been sentenced to jail for 13 years. Before he was sent back to prison, he had launched a 24-hour hunger strike on the **4th** to mark the sixth anniversary of the Tiananmen Incident and demand the release of all political prisoners.

The State Planning Commission, the State Economic and Trade Commission and the Ministry of Foreign Trade and Economic Cooperation jointly issued a set of provisional regulations on foreign investment on the **27th**. This was the first time that China had drawn legal boundaries to encourage, restrict or prohibit foreign investment. It indicated that the Chinese government wanted to adopt a long term and qualitative strategy in the use of foreign funds. According to the regulations, the country encouraged foreign investment in agriculture, energy, communications, high technology and the utilization of resources, while they were restricted in sectors where a state monopoly had existed, in projects for exploiting rare and valuable raw mineral resources.

China's first urban cooperative bank, the Shenzhen Urban Cooperative Commercial Bank, was opened in Shenzhen on the **28th**. The new bank was a local joint-stock commercial bank. It would operate independently and assume full responsibility for its profits and losses. It was a major measure to reform China's financial system and improve the managerial system of urban financial institutions.

Three years of negotiations on Hong Kong's new airport financial arrangements came to an end when a joint communiqué and agreed minutes on the issue were signed on the **30th**, eight months after China and Britain accepted an overall financial agreement on the issue in November 1994. According to the joint communiqué, both countries had reached two financial support agreements for the new airport and its rail link. Under the agreements, the Hong Kong government was allowed to inject additional equity into the Airport Authority and the Mass Transit Railway Corporation Ltd., to help cover the over-run cost that resulted from uncontrollable circumstances.

The National People's Congress on the **30th** appointed Dai Xianglong to replace Vice-Premier Zhu Rongji as the governor of the People's Bank of China. Zhu had been in this position for two years. According to Li Peng's proposal, Zhu was relieved of his post "in accordance with the needs of his work." The new governor, Dai Xianglong, had been the vice-governor of People's Bank of China. He had long worked in banking departments and participated in the formulation of China's financial and monetary policies, as well as the country's reform of the financial system. Analysts believed that Dai would follow Zhu's policy to limit economic growth.

JULY

China on the **11th** was granted the observer status in the World Trade Organization (WTO). This was a big achievement for China after nine years of negotiation to secure her return to the world trade body. China would now be able to participate in WTO meetings, though it would not have a vote. Negotiations, however, would be continued on the accession to full membership. A new round of informal talks on the issue immediately started on the **11th**. It ended on the **28th** with some progress but no major breakthrough.

Beijing on the **13th** appointed another 133 Hong Kong people as Hong Kong district affairs advisers. They were the third batch of people appointed, bringing the total number of district advisers to 670.

Following Lee Teng-hui's visit to the United States, the Sino-American relations faced another setback when Chinese American Harry Wu, a well known human rights activist, was arrested at a frontier inspection post on the **19th**. He was officially charged with entering China under a false name, illegally obtaining China's state secrets and conducting criminal activities, offences that could carry the death penalty. US government soon intervened and threatened to cancel US participation in the United Nations (UN) conference on women scheduled to be held in Beijing in September. The warning did not stop Beijing from charging Wu. On the 12th of August, the People's Procuratorate of Wuhan city initiated proceedings against Wu in the city's Intermediate Court. After confirmation that Wu had violated the *Supplementary Regulations on Punishing the Crime of Leaking State Secrets*, a judgement was reached on the

24th. Wu was sentenced to 15 years in jail and to be expelled from the country. On the 25th of August, Wu was deported from China.

Cross-Straits relations were strained when Beijing announced a series of missile tests in the East China Sea from the **21st** to the **26th**. The People's Liberation Army launched two missiles into the East China Sea, some 150km north of Taiwan, and approximately 55km from the nearest island under Taiwan control. This was understood as a reaction, stronger than expected, to President Lee Teng-hui's visit to the United States in June. Within less than one month, from the 15th to the 25th of August, another series of guided missile and artillery firing exercises were to be held in the same area.

AUGUST

The State Council on the **7th** released the Programme for the Development of Chinese Women (1995–2000), as the prelude to the 1995's Non-Governmental Organizations (NGO) Forum on Women to be held in late August. This was the country's first specific and detailed programme on women's development. Targets and policies on women's political rights, participation in political affairs, legal protection, employment, labour protection, education and health care were set up. The programme stressed that governments at all levels would have the unshakeable duty to implement the related policies, and they were requested to work out their local women's development programme.

The State Council on the **23rd** released a white paper on family planning. The 17,000 character White Paper, entitled "Family Planning in China," included seven chapters and provided answers to questions on China's overall policy on family planning, measures and policies she had implemented, her achievements and problems. It stressed that the country's family planning policy was a strategic policy that suited the national conditions.

China on the **24th** published her first White Paper on agriculture entitled "The Report on China's Agricultural Development 1995." The White Paper consisted of four major chapters, Summary, Sectors, Special Subjects and Information. According to the Ministry of Agriculture, the report was highly authoritative, authentic and accurate. It would serve as a major reference for overseas and local people who were concerned with China's agricultural development and rural economic development. An English version of this White Paper was also released on the 12th of December.

The 1995's Non-Governmental Organizations Forum on Women was held at Huairou, Beijing, from the **30th** to the 8th of September. It was the largest of its kind in terms of attendance and the number of workshops held. About 31,000 women from more than 2,000 organizations in nearly 200 countries and regions joined the forum, and 1,000 workshops were held.

SEPTEMBER

The United Nations Fourth World Conference on Women was held in Beijing from the **4th** to the **15th**. Over 10,000 delegates from 189 countries and regions attended the conference. Two important documents, "Platform of Action" and "Beijing Declaration," were passed. The former listed twelve critical areas of concern reflecting the strong desires of women in the developing countries for the elimination of poverty, the improvement of education and health care and the opposition to violence against women. The Beijing Declaration urged all governments and international communities to take action to accelerate the realization of the goals of equality, development and peace.

Taiwan's attempt to "return to the United Nations" was a failure when the UN General Assembly rejected the proposal on the **20th**. This was the third time Taiwan had had the proposal raised since 1993. On the 50th anniversary of the UN, Taiwan published a policy paper and launched a propaganda offensive with regard to entry to the UN. Taiwan authorities also openly offered to donate US$ 1 billion as the price for entering the UN.

OCTOBER

A nationwide one percent by-census was conducted on the **1st**. Over 1,000 county-level units and 12 million persons throughout the country were involved. According to Peng Peiyun, a State Councillor, the investigation was significant for assessing the impact of population on the economy, the society, the issue of resources and the environment. It would help the government work out a socio-economic development strategy for the next five years.

China's Ninth Five-Year Plan was published on the **4th**. The plan was proposed and passed in the 5th Plenary Session of the 14th Central Committee of the Communist Party of China. In the "Ninth Five-Year Plan for Economic and Social Development and the Long Term Targets for 2010," nine principles and four main tasks were highlighted for China's future social and economic development. The nine principles were: (1) to maintain a sustainable and healthy development of the national economy; (2) to take the increase of economic returns as the central task of economic work; (3) to vitalize China with science and education; (4) to take agricultural development as the primary task in promoting the national economy; (5) to make state-owned enterprises' reform the central task of economic reform; (6) to unswervingly open to the outside world; (7) to realize an organic combination of market mechanism and state control; (8) to narrow regional disparities; and, (9) to adhere to the building of advanced socialist culture and ideology. The four main tasks were: (1) to optimize the industrial structure; (2) to speed up the process of information delivery in the national economy; (3) to devote major efforts to developing science, technology and education; and, (4) to promote the rational distribution of the national economy.

The Seventh International Anti-Corruption Conference was held from the **6th** to the **10th** in Beijing. The theme was "Anti-Corruption and Social Stability and Development." More than 1,000 experts and government officials from 90 countries and regions attended the conference. President Jiang Zemin stressed that the Chinese government had always valued the anti-corruption struggle and had especially been aware of new problems in the era of economic reform. The conference ended up by calling for better international cooperation to combat corruption.

NOVEMBER

An anti-graft body under the control of the People's Supreme Procuratorate was formed on the **10th**, and Luo Ji was appointed as the head. The establishment demonstrated the country's attempt to wipe out corruption and put the work of prosecution under legislative control and regulation. The main duty of the body was to investigate and prosecute bribery and corruption, to collect information and to prevent corruption. Besides corruption and bribery, specific offences, such as misappropriation, the embezzlement of public funds, the concealment of overseas assets and related commercial crimes, would also be investigated.

The People's Liberation Army, the Nanjing Military Region's army, navy and air force conducted a joint military exercise in coastal areas in southern Fujian from the **15th** to the **25th**. This was the third military exercise with Taiwan in view since July. The exercise was the largest simulated military attack on Taiwan under battle conditions. The exercise was focused on air and naval landing and mobilized some 30,000 personnel, more than 300 naval vessels and two divisions of the Air Force to provide air cover. It was also the largest landing exercise conducted so far.

The Information Office of the State Council on the **16th** issued a White Paper entitled "China: Arms Control and Disarmament." It was the first time China made public her basic stand on arms control and disarmament in a comprehensive, detailed and systematic way. The 15,000 character White Paper consisted of six parts: (1) promoting peace and development for all mankind; (2) reducing military personnel by one million; (3) maintaining a low level of defence spending; (4) peaceful use of military-industrial technology; (5) strict control over the transfer of sensitive materials and military equipment; and, (6) actively promoting international arms control and disarmament. It refuted the "China threat theory" that was spread by some people in the world and stressed that China needed a peaceful environment in order to develop her socialist modernization programme. It emphasized that China's military policy was defensive and the basic objective was to consolidate her national defence to resist foreign aggression, safeguard national sovereignty and defend national unification and security.

Wei Jingsheng, China's most famous dissident, was officially arrested on the **21st** after he had been held in communicado since April 1994. Wei had been sentenced to 15 years in prison in 1979 on charges of providing military information to foreign nations and engaging in activities designed to overthrow the Chinese government. He had been released on parole in September 1993. According to the Beijing Municipal People's Procuratorate, Wei had, once again, engaged in activities which posed a threat to the state and attempted to overthrow the state power. A judgement was made on the 13th of December by the Beijing Intermediate People's Court. He was sentenced to another 14 years in prison and deprived of political rights for three years. Wei appealed against his sentence on the 26th of December but in vain.

Beijing announced on the **27th** that the search for the reincarnation of the tenth Banchan Lama had reached a conclusion. Gyaincain Norbu, six years of age, was determined as the reincarnation soul boy. The State Council on the same day issued a document approving Gyaincain Norbu to succeed as the eleventh Banchan. The decision, however, was deemed invalid by Dalai Lama, the exile spiritual leader of the Tibetans, who had declared on the 14th of May that another Tibetan child was the real reincarnation child. The US also intervened into the issue.

DECEMBER

An international seminar on AIDS prevention was held in Beijing from the **1st** to the **3rd**. More than 400 local and overseas representatives from 15 countries attended the conference. According to Chen Minzhang, minister of public health, cases of AIDS had spread quickly since the first instance was reported in China in 1985. A total of 820 cases were recorded across the country in the first nine months of 1995, a figure that far exceeded the 531 cases in 1994. Thus, the official number of people infected by AIDS virus in China had grown to 2,594 by September 1995.

The sixth meeting of the Preliminary Working Committee (PWC) for the Hong Kong Special Administrative Region (HKSAR) Preparatory Committee was held in Beijing on the **7th**. It was the last meeting of the PWC after its two and a half years of operation. As stated by Qian Qichen, vice-premier and director of the PWC, the work of the PWC had laid the foundations for the Preparatory Committee which would be set up in 1996. Two weeks later, on the **28th**, the list of 150 members of the HKSAR Preparatory Committee was formally announced. Among the Preparatory Committee members, 56 (37%) were from the mainland and 94 (63%) were from Hong Kong.

China released her second White Paper on human rights, "The Progress of the Human Rights Cause in China," on the **27th**, four years after the first one had been released. The paper was divided into ten chapters with focus on the progress achieved. It stressed that the human rights situation in China was improving on all fronts, and it was in conformity with the national situation and the interests of the whole population to put the rights to existence and to development in the first place. It attacked Western countries which used human rights as a pretext to intervene in China's internal affairs.

1

Jiang Zemin:
In Quest of Post-Deng Supremacy

You Ji

The year 1995 marked a turning point in Chinese élite politics. The ascendancy of Jiang Zemin and the further eclipse of Deng Xiaoping signalled the beginning of the post-Deng era. The question of whether the era that follows can be surnamed Jiang is not yet certain, as the transitional nature of the current leadership points to many trends in China's political development. Institutionally, however, Jiang had visibly enhanced his power base during the year. New personnel reshuffles in the party, government and the People's Liberation Army (PLA) accorded greater recognition to Jiang as the core of the People's Republic of China's (PRC) new generation of leaders. While factional dynamics persisted at the apex of the political pyramid, a degree of leadership stability could be detected with Jiang's consolidation of power. This chapter argues that the past year indicated a new pattern of élite interactions by contrast with the kind of stalemate that characterized post-Tiananmen succession politics and that politics seems to be moving toward a new equilibrium.

The Institutional Dynamics of Succession Politics

Institutional authority and personal authority are two preconditions underlying a leader's exercise of power in China's élite politics. However, each may not be congruous with the other. While the institutions of power provide the groundwork for the party boss to enhance his authority, it is not guaranteed that he can achieve the status of being an undisputed leader simply by heading these institutions. In addition to formal positions, a leader's power is also gauged by whether he can claim an informal network of personal associates charged with effective implementation of his orders. And the strength he derives from this network is usually based on his seniority. Both institutional and personal authority are thus key parameters for measuring a leader's profile in the hierarchy and his future. Indeed, Jiang Zemin's assertive rise in 1995 testified to the importance of combining the two in the last stage of power transfer since he took advantage of his institutional authority to recruit associates at a time when his mentors became incapacitated and his peers were not in a position to

---

I would like to thank Johnathan Unger for his valuable comments on this chapter and the Contemporary China Centre, Australian National University, for its great research help.

challenge him. This can be seen quite clearly from his handling of (1) party elders; (2) the party and government bureaucracies; and (3) his peers.

Timing the Ascension

All paramount leaders in China set out to boost their power through occupying formal institutional positions. Mao held key party and military positions to the day he died. Deng relinquished his last position — chair of the Central Military Commission (CMC) only when he was sure that his followers were strong enough to carry out his reform policies. The relationship between institutional and personal power is thus a dynamic one in analysing China's unfolding succession politics: with a possible power vacuum left by the passage of party elders, the incumbent leaders will have to head a formal institution to build up seniority. Therefore, institutional authority begins to increase its weight *vis-à-vis* personal authority, as it entails a measure of legitimacy (*zhengtong*).

The year 1995 proved the importance of the environment in which a successor can develop his power base. When party elders were around, grooming a personal following by the successor leaders could be a risky business and changing policy directions could be interpreted as opposing the mentors' will. Jiang's two predecessors, Hu Yaobang and Zhao Ziyang, were pressured by party elders who frequently intervened from behind the scene. Jiang and other third generation leaders kept low profiles until 1995 when their chance finally arrived. Chen Yun died in April and nothing but failing health was heard about Deng throughout the year. The gradual oblivion of immortals enlarged the room for younger leaders to manoeuvre in terms of policy formulation and personnel arrangement. This highlights the factor of timing that determines the outcome of a succession process.

Cooperation with Vested Interests

That Jiang was able to accumulate more power in 1995 was attributable to his going along with the previous power equation that had been shaped by a balance of several forces since June 1989. The most significant of these included the policy coordination among China's key political and economic institutions (compartmental interests); a coalition of moderate reformers and pro-*status quo* office holders (political mentality and attitudes); the tug-of-war between central and local interests, and between the first-line leaders and party elders. This institutional/personal nexus had paved the way for an uneasy equilibrium to emerge in the early 1990s under the politics of constraints and compromise when the top leaders realized that unchecked factional activities might doom them all.

So in the name of unity and stability, first-line leaders had set their minds upon the traditional rulership style of *wuwei erzhi*, or rule without upheavals, meaning no sudden personnel dismissals that could upset the existing factional line-ups; no sharp policy changes/reform measures that could substantially affect vested central interests; and no clear long-term goals (such as political reform regarding the authoritarian system) except for some abstract slogans. A number of bold policy changes and personnel reshuffles did take place, but these were due largely to Deng's personal push from behind. Since Deng's intervention became increasingly rare, however, Chinese élite politics was being directed toward maintaining the *status quo*.[1]

The conservative tendency of Jiang's leadership had its institutional sources of logic. Chinese bureaucracy is traditionally immobilist. Party and government functionaries easily embrace a pattern of behaviour conditioned by institutional compliance, enforcement, monitoring and sanctional mechanisms. For them, stepping outside the institutional structure is to step into a social void.[2] All key members of the successor leaders have been groomed through this official environment (*guanchang*) and therefore subject to its inertia. Jiang has been very aware of this unique characteristic of Chinese politics. He took great pains to handle his sudden rise in 1989. From the very beginning, he accepted the reality that his role as the core would be short-lived if he placed himself against the dominant bureaucratic interests. This could be seen from his unusual efforts to solicit support from Premier Li Peng in order to manoeuvre through the Zhongnanhai labyrinth. Indeed the latter's attitude toward Jiang was decisive in the development of his power base. So a more accurate term to describe post-June 4 politics at the apex of power is that of a Jiang/Li duality: the so-called Jiang/Li *tizhi* or Jiang/Li dual power structure. This started to change visibly only in 1995, which will be discussed later.

The Nature of the Jiang/Li *Tizhi*

That Jiang had to share power with Li Peng was attributable to his late arrival at Zhongnanhai, where Li had already built up a strong power base during factional strife with the ex-party general secretary, Zhao Ziyang.

When Jiang assumed office in 1989, the cooperation between Jiang and Li was crucial in stabilizing the precarious situation in Beijing following the Tiananmen crisis. The power of the premiership lies in its institutional authority and operational mechanism. The State Council exercises the so-called personal responsibility system (*shouzhang fuzezhi*) which gives the premier a high level of personal power to make major decisions. This contrasts with the principle of collective leadership in the party system. The State Council also has practical control over state financial resources. Taking advantage of the premier's personnel nomination system, Li has placed a fairly large following in key positions in the central government, noticeably people with a common experience of studying in the Soviet Union (USSR) during the 1950s. Also, a number of his secretaries are now holding key ministerial portfolios.[3] Moreover, the State Council had been traditionally powerful due to the personal influence of Zhou Enlai and, to a lesser extent, of Zhao Ziyang in the 1980s. It is understandable that when Zhao was instructed by Deng to move to the party headquarters in 1987, he expressed genuine reluctance. This precedent has posed a crucial question about Li Peng's future in Chinese succession politics after he fulfils the second term, the maximum according to the Constitution. Yet whoever the new premier is, in order to stay powerful, he will have to protect the two interest groups he represents: state administrators and central planners.

From an institutional point of view, the first dimension of the Jiang/Li *tizhi* was meant to harmonize the four main sources of power in the country: the party, military, state administration, and central financial and industrial interests.[4] In the Politburo Standing Committee, the party general secretary is in charge of party daily affairs, ideology, the party personnel system, law and order establishments and the military. The premier is responsible for running the central government and economic management. With their chief aids in the committee, the general secretary and the premier form the leadership core. It is through the four *xitong* (systems) that command, control and communications are channelled and distributed from the core among the power élites.[5] Generally speaking, in the post-Deng political landscape, Jiang is supposed to represent the interests of the party as its general secretary and the military as its commander-in-chief. Li Peng is to continue his control over the state bureaucracy and economy after being chosen by Chen Yun in 1987 as Chen's successor to represent the powerful interests of central planners. The extent to which Jiang and Li could work together holds the key to a smooth power transfer from party elders.[6]

The second dimension of Jiang/Li cooperation was to divide power among the four principal governing systems. This had been the design of party elders who survived Maoist domination and saw the need to prevent any high concentration of power in one particular leader.[7] It was not a coincidence that Deng groomed Hu and Zhao at the 12th Party Congress in 1982 to head the four *xitong* separately, although his design for Hu to take over the command of the PLA was never put into practice. Despite the fact that Hu and Zhao were in a kind of rivalry, both could still place reform as their priority in leadership, which was the reason why they were chosen. Ironically, however, this was also the reason why they had to go, because they could not satisfy the powerful compartmental interests by merely calling for more reforms.[8] A similar division of power arrangements was made at the 13th Party Congress in 1987, only to collapse two years later as Zhao Ziyang and Li Peng had little to agree upon. It was said that Li was not Deng's choice for the premiership from the very beginning, but Deng could not have his way with the surge of conservatism in the party following Hu's dismissal.[9] Chen Yun could give in on anything else but the premiership, since it was the main safeguard for the interests of central planners.

The third dimension of Jiang/Li *tizhi* is the convergence strategy through which Deng had tried to implement the post-Mao political and economic reforms. Convergence in a sense recognizes the key interests of the state administrative system and central planners in the process of reform and transforms them only in an incremental fashion. Therefore, the person in charge of the party hierarchy should be able not only to campaign for reforms but also to absorb the inertia of state bureaucracies and central planners. Yet the general direction of convergence should also be clear, as set out by Deng during his south China tour in 1992 — reform must prevail over inertia. Such a task is a tough one: Zhao and Li failed the test. Each of them never regarded their interactions in terms of convergence but as efforts to obtain supremacy. Jiang has so far succeeded in achieving a level of cooperation with Li, which is why there have not been major factional eruptions. Nevertheless, this is done only at the price of inhibiting the pace of change in China's political and economic systems, a phenomenon described as pro-immobilist earlier.

Jiang's institutional authority is also potentially powerful. Being the representative of the party system, he employs control over its central agenda, ideological line, personnel appointments, as well as law and security establishments. His directorship of the Party's Economic Leadership

Group gives him access to economic decision-making processes, although he has to exercise caution not to intervene too much to upset the principle of division of power mentioned earlier. Again, as chairman of the Party CMC, he has the crucial power to decide on key personnel changes and troop movements.[10] Here Jiang's institutional authority lies in the procedure to read reports and sign documents. For instance, appointments of officers at the divisional level are not valid until Jiang puts his signature to the decrees. Relocating troops in Beijing at any level above the company also has to be reported to the CMC with its chair acknowledging it. This has been the rule since the Lin Biao incident in 1970 which gives Jiang a clear advantage in positioning himself for the final takeover.[11]

Power Struggle as the Vehicle for Supremacy

The fact that Jiang needs to share his "core" position with Li Peng reflects the evolutionary process in which institutional authority promotes an informal network. Although the Chinese Communist Party (CCP) leadership stability still depends on cooperation between Jiang and Li to coordinate the four key *xitong*, 1995 saw moves toward Jiang's rising power within the Jiang/Li power structure. Institutionally, this is the result of enhanced PLA influence in Chinese politics. Moreover, Jiang started to step into the country's economic management, a departure from his largely non-interventionist posture a few years ago. At the same time, Jiang brought a number of new faces to the centre in 1995, which helped fill holes in the informal power network. The past year also witnessed Jiang's new efforts to push anti-corruption and discipline campaigns, which tightened central control over local cadres. Consequently, the post-Tiananmen balance has begun to shift toward a new equilibrium, which cannot yet be clearly defined. What is certain about the new equilibrium is that Jiang is now posturing himself as the first among equals at the apex of power. Whether this is good or bad for him remains to be seen.

Winning Increased Support from the PLA

The widely held view is that Jiang is not capable of governing China with full authority. The strongest reason for this assertion is that he has no prior experience in the armed forces, which respect only leaders with successful military careers. This is a long-standing tradition of modern

Chinese civil/military relations. Lee Teng-hui in Taiwan is the first exception to this tradition, as he is a civilian yet in firm control of the island's
armed forces. Will Jiang have the same luck? While this is a question to
which only the future can provide an answer, the current development of
the Jiang/military relationship seems to point in a similar direction, however obscure the road map.

The PLA has never challenged Jiang's position as the commander-in-
chief, although complaints were heard. Partly this is because he was
Deng's personal choice. People should not underestimate the constraining
power of the historical phenomenon of *tuogu* (entrusting close followers
with the mission of protecting the new successor) that can be brought to
bear on the top generals. Certainly, such traditional influence is a slippery
concept to measure. However, the two most powerful generals in the PLA,
Liu Huaqing and Zhang Zhen, have so far faithfully upheld Deng's will.
More important, however, is that Jiang has been accepted by the PLA due
to his extraordinary efforts to safeguard military interests. The number of
top generals who must honour Deng's request has to be small, although
they play a key role in supporting Jiang. The rank and file officers consider
their level of commitment to Jiang based on his contribution to their
well-being. They constantly compare Jiang with other party leaders in
terms of how hard he has tried to help. Indeed, in the five years since Jiang
has been commander-in-chief, he has increased the basic salary three times
for officers and men.[12] Militarily, Jiang's support for modernizing PLA
hardware at a quickened pace has also been well received. Hence, 1995
was probably the year Jiang finally passed the invisible "attitudes" test
imposed upon him by the PLA in 1989 when he became chair of the CMC.

In the last five years, Jiang has campaigned vigorously on behalf of
the PLA to enlarge military spending.[13] Although the military is never
satisfied with the amount of money it receives each year, the double
digit-growth of the military budget does distinguish the two periods between Jiang's leadership in the 1990s and that of Deng/Zhao in the 1980s.
Jiang has been very conscious to avoid a repetition of the situation in
which Zhao was made a scapegoat by emphasizing Deng's instruction:
jundui yao rennai or the PLA must restrain itself. His slogan is that the
armed forces must receive a budget growth in line with the growth of the
economy. At the same time Jiang has been said to favour the PLA as much
as possible when the CMC handles incidences of civil/military disputes.
Jiang is also trying to foster an image of a caring commander-in-chief. He
has made numerous visits to the PLA's basic units, talking to soldiers,

having dinner with them and making special promises to improve their living conditions.[14] For instance, the 1995 military housing reform allowed massive discount sales of houses to senior officers and handsome living space to active service men at the regimental level and above. This has attracted warm responses from the officers through whom Jiang exercises his military leadership.

Central to Jiang's efforts to win support from the PLA was his enthusiastic endorsement of the PLA's new grand defence strategy, passed by the CMC toward the end of 1992. This new strategy, defined as "fighting modern warfare under high-tech conditions," has thoroughly revised Mao's doctrine of people's war and Deng's doctrine of "people's war under modern conditions." Forcefully pushed by Admiral Liu Huaqing and General Zhang Zhen, the new strategy reflects the new thinking of the PLA in the post-Cold War and the information era, which would fundamentally affect the PLA's force structure, research and development programmes and deployment posture.[15] Politically, it serves as the banner of the new CMC formed at the 14th Party Congress to rectify the chaos induced by the removal of Yang Baibing and his close associates, much as Liu did in 1980 in the Navy under his active blue water defence strategy. The PLA has never appeared so united as now.[16]

The adaptation of a new defence strategy indicates the rise of professionalism championed by China's new brand of technocrats/officers who are forward looking, ready to learn western military science and technology, and increasingly more indifferent to politics. However, it has met resistance from some sectors within the PLA, notably from the Yang brothers who emphasized a more ideologically oriented line as the guide for military modernization.[17] In the policy debate, Jiang has given his firm support to Liu Huaqing. As an engineer, Jiang eagerly embraces the new ideas associated with the information age. A military strategy geared to suit modern high-tech warfare reflects Jiang's receptiveness to modern technology. Ever since the early 1980s when he was minister of electronics, he has consistently regarded electronics as holding the key to China's future. Politically, the high-tech consensus between him and the mainstream groups in the military, namely the professionally minded veterans, active serving commanders, and new military academy graduates, provides a sound base for cooperation. The new military strategy also inspires Jiang to employ science and technology as the fundamental mover to enhance China's comprehensive strength. This results in the party's science and technology strategy adopted in 1995.

Despite the positive interactions between Jiang and the top brass, one implicit reason for the PLA's acceptance of Jiang may be due exactly to his relatively weak authority over it. In a way, the easing up of Deng's personal control over the PLA and the purge of the Yang brothers have given rise to the emergence of senior officers with a distinctive career path and set of life experiences different from the civilian élites in the party hierarchy. This is reshaping China's post-Deng civil/military relations.[18] The PLA increasingly acquires a more cohesive corporate identity once it subdues overt internal cleavages. Its corporate interest is best protected when there are no destructive outside intrusions, as seen from the historical precedents of the Cultural Revolution when Mao forced the PLA into mass politics and the 1989 clamp-down when Deng ordered the tanks into Tiananmen. For the first time in many years the PLA has freed itself from a type of control best described as that of political strongmen. It will not ask for another Mao or Deng who could cause damage to its interests. So the weakness of Jiang in China's élite politics is a blessing for the PLA's search for autonomy in running its own affairs. The simple truth is that if Jiang is very nice to the PLA, and if the PLA does not want to grab power itself, why reject Jiang who is caring and protective? The replacement may not be as benevolent.

The CMC initiated in 1995 the third wave of personnel reshuffles which basically completed the power transfer from revolutionary veterans to technocratic professionals. Jiang promoted a number of influential officers to the rank of full general only to retire them later, a clever move both to consolidate his grip on the PLA and to avoid antagonism. Aged between 37 and 57 and numbering over 1,000, senior officers of the fourth generation are now in place to lead the PLA toward the post-Deng era. This has paved the way for Liu Huaqing and Zhang Zhen to retire finally with honour at the 15th Party Congress in less than two years, if not earlier. Since the promoted are fairly immune from factional entanglements at PLA headquarters, this has produced an unprecedented level of unity among the top brass, which could prove to be a great asset not only for China's political stability but for Jiang's consolidation of power. The 1995 PLA reshuffle was in the main conducted by the senior serving officers in the CMC with Liu and Zhang in charge. The whole process proceeded in close collaboration with PLA elders, like Xiao Ke and Zhang Aiping. It is said that Jiang's direct involvement was important, although modest.[19] Reign but not rule proves to be a workable formula for Jiang to win military support, although his relationship with the PLA is not hands-off.

For instance, he demanded to interview a number of the promoted before the appointments were made. This way he reduced the personal distance between him and those rising senior officers.

To what extent Jiang can count on these younger officers to deliver his "core" leadership in the years to come remains the question to be answered. But in the following respects, Jiang is now in a better position *vis-à-vis* the military than before the reshuffle. Firstly, in terms of seniority, when Liu Huaqing and Zhang Zhen retire, Jiang is at least equal to his colleagues in the CMC, who joined the revolution in the same period. And he is more senior than the commanders at and below the level of military regions. Secondly, probably with the exception of General Wang Ruilin, Deng's chief of staff, all other CMC members are professional soldiers with no visible political ambitions. Moreover, the CMC took pains to ensure that the promotion of lower-level generals was based on the principle of meritocracy in military science. Lastly, the personnel shakeup was accompanied by transferring commanders from different postings. As a rule in the national politics, this has made it easier for Jiang and the centre to control the PLA, since frequent removal of senior officers is conducive to undercutting the roots of informal networks.

The PLA's expressed allegiance to Jiang reached a high level in 1995. Vocally, all the CMC members made it a rule to sanction Jiang in their public speeches. Zhang Wannian, the designate successor to Liu Huaqing and the candidate to enter the next Politburo Standing Committee, eagerly voiced his support for Jiang's speech on politics. This speech contained Jiang's demand on senior cadres to uphold correct political attitudes, stance, style and sensitivity. The essence was political stance that a cadre had to adopt, the correct one being siding with Jiang and the centre. General Zhang's endorsement on behalf of the PLA exerted great weight in China's political arena where Jiang's speech on politics was compared with Deng's insistence on the "truth discussion" in 1978/79, which had forced all senior leaders to draw a line between Deng and Hua Guofeng, then party chairman.

Throughout the year, *Jiefang junbao* (Liberation Army Daily) ran numerous articles praising Jiang's instructions to the PLA. Unusually, it published a long series of reports by high ranking officers concerning Jiang's speech at the 5th Plenum on the 12 major economic relations in China. This honour had traditionally been reserved for people like Mao, Lin Biao and Deng. On 2 November, the *Liberation Army Daily* ostentatiously published a group of photos taken when Jiang was reviewing a naval parade. He was standing alone in the centre of one photo. Behind him stood the full line-up of CMC members, saluting; and behind them, were the commanders-in-chief of the three services and military regions. Such a portrayal of solidarity with Jiang and the top brass had never been seen before. The signal was clear: Jiang was in command with support from the PLA.

In 1995, Jiang repeatedly reviewed military exercises. Two of the most important were a large naval manoeuvre in the Bohai Sea on 18 October and the first major multi-purpose exercise of the armed police on 1 November. Both attracted media attention world-wide. The day following the naval exercise, Chinese Central Television devoted eight minutes of its daily half hour national news broadcast to highlight Jiang's appearance at the naval exercise, again an unprecedented exposure of Jiang standing shoulder to shoulder with the top military leaders. An interesting comparison can be drawn here between Jiang and Hua. In 1977, Hua, as chair of the CMC, expressed his desire to see the Navy's North Fleet on his way back from North Korea. The navy planned to organize a large naval exercise for him. But this angered Deng, who forcefully cancelled the plan. The privilege to review a military exercise has been traditionally regarded by the PLA as a symbolic expression of its allegiance to a civilian leader.[20]

The Victory over Beijing

Jiang's efforts to consolidate his power base have been two-dimensional: strengthening his institutional authority and grooming trusted associates to head key party, government and military offices. The year 1995 marked a great leap forward for him on both fronts. The ouster of Chen Xitong, Beijing's party secretary, represented a serious test for Jiang's advancement toward supremacy. In a way, exposing the appalling corruption case of key Beijing leaders presented Jiang an excellent opportunity to exert himself in the CCP's élite interactions — and at the right time, too. His victory over Beijing is another decisive sign of the post-Deng succession politics moving toward a new equilibrium.

The complicated nature of power transfer from Deng to Jiang at the last stage can be deciphered by their mutual efforts to prevent another power centre from emerging to challenge Jiang. On the other hand, Chinese succession politics is so dynamic that multi-power-centres always exist in their potential forms. This is due mainly to the presence of factional groupings or dissenting views within the party. While a mono-power centre is conducive to leadership cohesion, a multi-power centre anticipates factional conflict which may trigger social cleavages and protest movements, as seen in 1989. The ouster of Chen Xitong should be analysed against such a political background.

Since Jiang was anointed as Deng's successor, he has been under pressure from latent multi-power centres. But probably Jiang had only experienced one visible challenge prior to Chen's dissenting noises against his status as the core. This case was the Yang Baibing incident in 1992. There is a number of power holders in the CCP leadership who possess the potential to challenge Jiang's authority. People like Li Peng, Qiao Shi, Yang Shangkun and Liu Huaqing were Jiang's superiors in the past and lead enough personal followers in the party/military to form an alternative power centre. But this latent threat cannot become a real threat if they do not want to rock the boat or challenge existing political constraints, represented by the uncertain and complicated factional line-up. For one thing, Deng is still alive. For another, the returns may not be as great as accepting the *status quo*. Yang Baibing was, however, one of the leaders who could not handle his ambitions in an acceptable manner, as he demanded excessive rewards for his role in helping the party over the Tiananmen crisis. He repeatedly ignored Jiang's instructions, offended almost all his colleagues in the CMC, and did not pay due respect to his long time superiors who remained influential in the PLA. He alerted other military leaders when he promoted a number of his associates to key commanding posts.

Yet his fatal misjudgement was his zeal to lend support on behalf of the PLA to Deng's personal push for reform in 1992. When he raised the slogan of *baojia huhang*, he neither consulted the CMC and its chair, nor contemplated the serious consequences it might cause. Differences in opinion between Deng and other leaders, particularly Chen Yun, regarding the pace, depth and timing of major reforms were normal enough and allowable by the party's organizational principle. But the settlement of personal differences by thrusting the PLA into such a policy debate reminded both the first- and second-line leaders of the days when Mao had used the PLA to purge imagined opponents. This had set a dangerous precedent in the on-going succession politics and revealed that Yang would have a propensity to place himself above collective leadership in the post-Deng era. In this case, not only Jiang but also other CCP leaders would feel very uneasy about Yang's assertiveness, to put it most mildly. What was probably Deng's last major contribution to China's future was his decision to relieve the Yang brothers of military duties. This should have been much appreciated because he made the decision when his personal relations with the Yangs were still close.

Like Yang Baibing, Chen Xitong suffered a similar fatal judgement, as he had in recent years tried to arouse feelings of dissent against Jiang among some Beijing and provincial leaders.[21] It was understandable that he saw Jiang's sudden anointment as China's future leader to be a kind of unfair treatment, given their respective contributions to the party at the crucial moment in 1989. Comparing their achievement in managing China's two largest cities, Chen told his followers that Beijing was far better led than Shanghai. He openly criticized Jiang for his decision to hold the Fourth International Women's Congress in Beijing.[22] When he lost to Wu Bangguo, the former Shanghai party boss, in his bid for the vice premiership responsible for everyday running of the country's industries, he was alleged to have written to Deng, complaining about Jiang's discriminatory organizational line. The seriousness of the complaint was that he said he represented the view of other provincial leaders as well.[23] This allegation, if true, touched upon the question of organized resistance to the party leader, which went beyond the expression of his personal dissatisfaction. In CCP politics, this was a serious violation of party norms, as mirrored by challenges such as those by Gao Gang and Rao Shushi in the 1950s.[24]

Chen's challenge to Jiang's authority was neither open nor direct. Compared with the Yang case, it is even difficult to call Chen's action a challenge. However, it did represent a level of doubt among some first-line leaders about Jiang's role as the core. From Jiang's view, Chen's coalition building with other leaders in Beijing or elsewhere would threaten party leadership stability, cause cleavages in centre-province relations, and hamper Deng's deployment of an orderly power transfer. One can rest assured that Chen's dismissal was caused more by his antagonism against Jiang than his implication in the Wang Baosen scandal, although without Wang's case it would have been difficult to punish Chen.

Chen has been the first Politburo member to be purged since Hu and Zhao, and also the first in "peaceful times." Differing from Yang Baibing, he has also been the first key party leader to be dismissed by the initiative of the first-line leadership headed by Jiang. Does this signal the consolidation of power by the third generation leadership? The fact that Jiang was now confident enough to remove a Politburo member opened a new angle for us to assess his future. In analysing Chen's case, one must not overlook his powerful connections with other party leaders and elders and the implications his departure had. Hence, his ouster entailed a difficult process in which the leadership stability was at stake.

Chen's rise to prominence had been both an accident and due to his own shrewd manoeuvring, which reflected complicated cross factional activities. His origin in the old Beijing power group headed by Peng Zhen was deep and solid. This group had produced important figures including Li Ruihuan, Wan Li, Wang Hanbin and Peng Peiyun. Chen served as the secretary for a key member of the group, Beijing's second party secretary Liu Ren before the Cultural Revolution. When Peng's group was re-activated after 1978, Chen had drawn strength from the group and, as its new head, made it once again an "independent kingdom." The most crucial moment came in 1978 when Hu Yaobang discovered him in Changping county where he was the party secretary. He impressed Hu so well when briefing him on county work that Hu told Beijing leaders, "You guys ask the centre to send cadres to Beijing because the city is in need of capable leaders. How blind! There is one right at your door. I believed that Xitong is exactly the kind of cadre you need."[25] As soon as Chen was promoted to Beijing Municipality in 1978, he played the role of radical reformer. His article on the "truth discussion" fiercely attacked the "two-whatever faction."[26] As mayor of Beijing, he devoted enormous energy and money to change the city's physical appearance: high rise buildings, highways, high-priced shopping centres, something that impressed Deng who praised Chen as a hard worker. Deng's "real success" mentality was also instru-mental in Li Ruihuan's move upward.

But the real watershed in Chen's political career was his part in 1989 when he ruthlessly pursued a hardline attitude toward the students. By doing so, he tied his future to Li Peng, and this paid off with a ticket to enter the Politburo at the 14th Party Congress. However, Chen's connec-tion with Li Peng could be traced much further. He had come to know Li in the 1960s when serving Liu Ren, Li's cousin. Chen did what he could to help Li Peng in the latter's battle with Zhao Ziyang in the late 1980s. In return, Li lent Chen a helping hand in his promotion first as State Councillor and then Politburo member. It is said Li was behind Chen's bid for the vice premiership, as mentioned earlier, because Li, as the premier, held the key to the appointment. While other party leaders were silent on Beijing's work, Li Peng had always been caring, as remarked by the current Beijing party boss, Wei Jianxing.[27] It was reported that during one inspection trip to Beijing, Li was so impressed by Wang Baosen's ability to master detailed figures that he told other leaders Beijing was fortunate to have as a good house-keeper as Wang. He then asked other cadres to learn from Wang.

Therefore, the dismissal of Chen tested Jiang's search for supremacy in that it was a test for the Jiang/Li *tizhi*, the very foundation of the post-Deng élite politics. Chen's Beijing stronghold was vital to Li in many respects. The most crucial one was their shared fate concerning the June 4th tragedy. Chen's downfall might trigger a public reaction to weaken Li's authority. Given the serious implications of such a decision, Jiang took pains to deal with this delicate issue. The guiding principle can be defined as his efforts to prevent this event from being seen as a *zero-sum* game where he scored a great gain at another's expense. The following points can be detected from his handling of Chen's case.

Isolating Wang Baosen's Case

First of all, the purge of Chen was not Jiang's premeditated act to raise his profile in the party, although the event was well utilized to his advantage. Even after Chen's involvement in Wang's case was beyond any reasonable doubt, Jiang tried hard not to initiate a premature showdown with Chen and other key Beijing leaders. When the economic crimes of the secretaries of both Chen and Li Qiyan (the mayor) were exposed, Jiang instructed the Central Discipline Inspection Commission to refrain from investigating anyone with a rank above ministerial level, pending a decision by the Politburo. With pressure mounting, he adopted a phased process in handling the case. Each phase had its limited goals and implicated only a small number of people.[28] The central theme was to avoid unseemly haste in taking action against Beijing for the sake of leadership unity.

Building Party Consensus

However, when this caused social discontent and threatened stability, Chen had to be dealt with directly, and Jiang worked hard to build a leadership consensus on the case. The military offered Jiang its crucial support.[29] The powerful figures in the party's law and security establishments executed the central decision, very likely under Qiao Shi's advice.[30] Li Peng was convinced Chen had to go, otherwise it would adversely affect the party's legitimacy and his own image as well. If another Beijing Spring was caused by the party's protection of Chen, it would surely undermine unity and leadership stability. On the other hand, a consensus was reached by the powerful Beijing cluster of office holders, not to implicate too many Beijing officials. This consensus-building process was important because it showed that Jiang was not motivated by his personal dislike of Chen. Nor was his decision on Chen meant for personal gain, for he did not subsequently employ his own people to control this crucial city. This consensus was necessary for the party, as one of its major scandals was exposed to the public.

Managing the Damage

Even so, Chen's case caused uncertainty to the Jiang/Li *tizhi* and Jiang moved quickly to ease tensions. He reiterated the correctness of the 1989 action, and the city's success in reform and development.[31] He also gave Li Peng a large say in appointing Beijing's new leaders.[32] Particularly, he limited the nature of the Chen/Wang case to economic crimes and personal decadence. The political verdict was deliberately mild, although it made a case of their not obeying the party centre. Moreover, the bulk of Beijing's leadership was under a kind of protection. The reshuffle was conducted only gradually. No State Council member was harmed.

In summary, Jiang's handling of the Beijing case demonstrated a high level of political skill. His authority and core position in the party was thus enhanced. As mentioned earlier, Yang and Chen were the two leaders who did not submit to Jiang. While in 1992, Jiang was unable to touch Yang without Deng's backing, he could target Chen at his own initiative in 1995. Using his dismissal, Jiang sent out a clear signal to like-minded central and provincial leaders as to who was in charge in Beijing. For instance, one of Chen's crimes was transferring within-plan central allocations to the city for other purposes. This is a common practice in all provinces, which may or may not be punishable, depending on the centre's choice. Most importantly, despite the potentially explosive nature of the case, Jiang succeeded in maintaining the Jiang/Li coalition after Chen was purged, since both saw it as a precondition for party unity in the transitional period. On the other hand, if the dismissal of Chen marked Jiang's search for post-Deng supremacy, it may cause new strife at the apex of power. Movement from the old power balance to the new opens up crises and opportunities for leaders to jockey for power. Factional tensions never cease in the CCP, as with every political party, but the question is how to manage them. Again, at this crucial moment, the question is whether Jiang is able to manage them.

Policy Consensus as the Vehicle for Supremacy

The year 1995 could also be regarded as a successful one for Jiang and other party leaders in building a policy consensus about China's long term development. Consolidation of Jiang's power cannot be separated from a general agreement on key issues among party élites. Traditionally, CCP leadership strife has had an inevitable policy dimension. For instance, in the 1950s the clash between Mao's great leap forward mentality and the advocacy of balanced growth by Zhou Enlai and Chen Yun was viewed as a divide between revolutionaries and conservatives.[33] Due to the CCP's lack of institutionalized mechanisms to regulate policy disagreement, differences of opinion are taken personally and are potentially explosive. As a leader with no solid power base, it is even more crucial for Jiang to seek policy consensus whenever possible.

In 1995, the Jiang/Li leadership achieved consensus at the 5th Plenum over two major economic issues with lasting significance. The first was the confirmation of the market economy arrived at during the 14th Party Congress in 1992. This resolved a painful policy difference troubling the relationship between the party headquarters and the State Council for an extended period in the late 1980s. The debate between market reformers led by Zhao Ziyang and central planners represented by Li Peng had intensified over the key question of whether China's reform should establish a market economy as a final goal or retain essential characteristics of central planning as the cage to tame the bird. It became highly politicized, as Zhao and Li endeavoured to grab more political power in order to outdo one another. Eventually Zhao's market idea prevailed, but ironically he was removed from office partly because of his market idea.[34]

The second consensus was about how to manage China's economy. The buzz word was to *change* the mode of economic growth which called implicitly for effective central control (macro regulation). The idea was raised by Li Peng as his personal opinion in August 1995 when he toured northeast China and was confirmed as state policy by the 5th Plenum.[35] Consensus was easily reached as Jiang quickly supported it. He had worked for a long time in the state sector. When he took office as party boss, he made known his position by emphasizing the importance of protecting state factories, although he talked loudly about economic reform. In May and June 1995, he gave a number of instructions on the state sector which, he still believed, held the key to China's future. Ostensibly missing in his economic manifesto — the 12 Major Economic

Relations — is the word "planning" but instead the theme of macro-economic regulation dominates the paper. Again, he adapted himself well to mainstream economic thought at the centre represented by Li Peng and Zhu Rongji who preferred tight fiscal policies, a slower growth rate and a freeze on the reform of enterprise through bankruptcy.[36]

A high degree of flexibility is now accorded the centre's market/planning options. The market is seen as the way out for the economy but planning/macro regulations are still indispensable to keep it running smoothly. This dialectical combination lays out the basis for the new economic consensus regarding China's economic development strategy and management in the next decade. The spirit is carried in three major documents of the Plenum and specified in the so-called nine grand guiding principles (*jiuda fangzhen*) for China's economic take-off.[37]

The underlying emphasis of these principles is stability, but behind this emphasis is the centre's determination to enhance centralization. According to mainstream economic thought at the State Council, stability and centralization are two sides of a coin. Without one the other perishes. Reform and development both serve this overriding political objective. The dominant theme of centralization is thus to effect the transition from extensive to intensive growth.[38] This actually echoes Chen Yun's economic ideas: less capital investment, more technological improvement of the existing firms, balanced development so as to prevent overheating, and preferring construction of infrastructure to the processing sectors.[39]

What is the significance of the new economic development strategy to Jiang's search for supremacy in the post-Deng era? It is important in several respects:

1. The slogan of doubling China's gross national product (GNP) between the years 2000 and 2010 is a political landmark for Jiang to make claim to his new era. One of the hallmarks of the Deng regime was his famous promise to quadruple China's 1980 GNP by the year 2000. Now Jiang has copied Deng's governing tactics. Although it lacks originality, it does seem to turn a new page of history.

2. The new strategy reflects the post-Deng leadership's departure from Deng's great leap forward mentality in projecting economic development. Deng's tendency for fast growth had sound political justification but caused macro-instability with negative political impact, if not managed properly. The current high inflation is the direct outcome of his personal push for high speed during his south China tour and its lingering adverse effects have not yet disappeared. The new consensus on management did

not directly challenge Deng's propensity for double digit growth but through addressing the relations between speed and efficiency the message was put across. In the period of sensitive political transformation, the pace of economic growth has to serve political stability, and must be properly set.

3. The new economic strategy spells out the consensus at the party centre to tighten central/regional relations at times of political uncertainty and economic restructuring. The banner is to enhance central ability to regulate national development. The efforts include continuing tax reform in order to raise the centre's share of state revenues; checking the trend of an enlarged east/west divide in economic well-being; reconsidering policies for the special economic zones, and so on.

In the final analysis Jiang involved himself more deeply in the country's economic management in 1995. He issued his first comprehensive economic statement and went on numerous inspection tours to state factories. Although this could be viewed as a departure from his previous non-interventionist attitude, it did not fundamentally violate the principle of division of power, as mentioned earlier. Jiang's involvement was not designed to exert himself in the daily running of the economy. He played a largely supporting role to the current economic policies formulated by the State Council. By doing so he created more common ground with the mainstream economic managers at the centre and thus strengthened his ties with the powerful state administrators. At the same time, in order to minimize costs in his relations with the regions, he, as a dialectical general secretary, was careful not to be drawn into detailed policy making. On the other hand, Jiang's eagerness to have a say in the country's economic affairs was seen clearly in 1995. As the national leader, he reserved a supervisory role for himself. However, if this is not properly handled, it may sow seeds of conflict with central planners in the future.

Jiang's Prospects: 1995 and beyond

The year 1995 was unique in China's post-Deng succession politics. Both Jiang and Li announced completion of the power transfer.[40] To a large extent it is true that the first-line leadership has taken full control of daily management of the country, although completion is probably an exaggeration. But the commonly used worst-case speculation about Jiang's future after Deng's death is also exaggerated. The likelihood of a major power struggle in the CCP leadership was substantially eased with the passage of

1995. This argument is based on our assessment of the following facts: the difficulty of identifying a real challenger; the stabilizing role of the PLA; and a relative balance of power between different key interest groups. However, a leadership crisis does exist in latent form. Rampant corruption has generated enormous popular discontent, and the widening gap in the distribution of wealth is tearing at the very foundation of the social fabric. The issue of 1989 can be buried for a while but not forever. Relaxation of party/state controls breeds thirst for more freedom but at the same time puts pressure on the maintenance of law and order. The authoritarian political structure is increasingly out of step with the expansion of pluralistic interests in the social and economic realms. Jiang's consolidation of power in the CCP may delay the eruption of another round of social protest, but it cannot remove the root causes of it. Yet a major overhaul of the political structure contravenes the key goal of the Jiang/Li *tizhi*: stability. Therefore, Jiang's consolidation of power does not provide a long-term solution to China's fundamental problems.

In the short term, however, the eruption of these political-social problems can be put off by the gun, as seen from the tight police control of Tiananmen every June. In other words, as pointed out by Andrew Walder in 1989, had there not been an open division within the party leadership itself, the student movement could never have grown to the size it did.[41] This was understood well by both the party elders and the Jiang/Li coalition. In a way, Jiang is fairly safe in that, facing so many problems, the party élites have accepted him as the symbol of unity for better or for worse. Put another way, Jiang has also become the prime target if things go wrong. Under the circumstances, what challenges must Jiang answer so as to fulfil his demanding duties?

First, Jiang has to show the party that he is a capable leader and can contribute to the nation's prosperity. Many people in China and abroad think of him in terms of mediocrity. The adverse effect of such a view to his legitimacy is apparent in China, where people love or hate strongmen but despise mild, soft bookworm types. To readdress this problem, the media are now waging a mini-propaganda campaign to demonstrate Jiang's performance record. For instance, the 5th Plenum concluded that with Jiang in charge China achieved the fastest economic development during the Eighth Five-Year Plan period (1990–1995). Average annual growth was 11%, well above that of 9.5% during the entire Deng era.[42] The party is trying to show that Jiang's legitimacy does not solely rest on Deng's personal behest: his own accomplishments are on record.

Economic success notwithstanding, what Jiang needs most urgently is recognition that he is capable of handling difficult political issues as well. He claimed that he was given the helm when the party was in deep crisis after June 4th (*lingwei shouming*).[43] Six years later, the crisis situation is basically under control. Despite constant internal and external pressures to the top leadership, factional strife has not grown out of hand, mass protests have not yet erupted on a large scale, and China has again been accepted as a key player in the world. This is not what analysts had predicted when he mounted the central stage in 1989. Although there remains a question mark as to how much all this is attributable to Jiang, Chen Yun, who never easily praised anybody, once said to General Hong Xuezhi that Jiang coped with a tough job well and he had full confidence in him.[44] But Jiang has yet to convince the people as a whole to have full confidence in him.

Secondly, Jiang has to formulate sound strategies for the final take-over. The core of succession politics is power struggle. Sometimes it means a bloody showdown but more often it is just a quiet fight for acceptance. So the key is to make it seem less a *zero-sum* game and more a power sharing, although someone has to be more equal than others. Jiang will have to follow a set of sound strategies as seen below:

1. Delicate treatment of Deng. Deng's support for Jiang has been crucial for Jiang's ascendancy but as in every leader/successor relationship in the CCP, it has a downside. This is especially true when the successor has acquired a fairly high level of his own power and his policy is increasingly at odds with those of his mentor. At times usefulness can be turned into a liability. As seen from what happened in 1995 between Jiang and some of Deng's family members, such a possibility is open. Deng could still serve as a rallying point for Jiang's opponents, if he lost Deng's favour, although this would be highly unlikely. For Jiang, Deng's complete obviation is not undesirable, but he has to exercise great discretion to facilitate it.

2. The relationship with the PLA. With the retirement plan for Liu Huaqing and Zhang Zhen finalized, the power transfer in the PLA will soon be complete. It will become easier for Jiang to work with the younger generation of generals. But as the PLA strengthens its corporate identity in the post-Deng era, it is better positioned to protect its privileges. Put another way, if the PLA does not feel its vital interests to be compromised, it is unlikely to intrude into civilian politics. Jiang, as the commander-in-chief, tried to make sure that the PLA did not get hurt by the reforms in 1995 and he will have to do so in the future as well.

3. Campaign against corruption. The year 1995 witnessed the escalation of an anti-corruption drive in China. Yet this is a sensitive issue. Like a double-edged sword, it can be employed by Jiang as an image booster and power multiplier. It can also backlash, as corruption is so rampant that a large number of cadres would be implicated. A major house-cleaning would undermine the very foundation of the CCP: many party cadres would feel insecure, thus undermining Jiang's own leadership core. Selective punishment of corrupt officials is also potentially dangerous for party unity and Jiang's authority. Yet there seems to be no alternative for Jiang not to be selective. He is walking a tight rope.

4. Personnel arrangements. No leader is immune from promoting his trusted comrades into key positions. In the PRC, however, no leader has ever been able to fill key offices with only his confidants, including Mao and Deng. The country is huge, party groupings abound and one faces limits to the management of an ever expanding following. An undisguised promotion of followers by one leader will encourage other leaders to do likewise, and he loses credibility in the process. During the consolidation period Jiang is challenged by the temptation to form a power faction of his own and the wisdom not to. The year 1995 saw Jiang make some balanced moves here.[45] In the new year, however, the temptation will become more acute: preparation for the 15th Party Congress and a new round of reshuffles among central, provincial and military leaders. This will present a political and personal test for Jiang: to distribute the benefits in an even manner among top leaders or take advantage of the situation to transfer power into his own hands.

Thirdly, Jiang has to maintain his consensual leadership style. For a leader without a solid power base, observance of traditional party norms and prudential politics can be an effective weapon in dealing with difficult factional interactions because these are the bases of unity, which, as pointed out by Teiwes, is longed for by all post-Mao party élites.[46] That Chen Yun had full confidence in Jiang may be due to Jiang's readiness to cooperate with other top leaders, particularly with Li Peng. This underlined the fact that the current line-up of the 14th Politburo Standing Committee seems to have been the most stable one since 1978. But Jiang's mild personality is also a key factor, which distinguishes his leadership style from that of Hu, Zhao and Yang Baibing. So far Jiang has not been seen as a menace by other leaders at the apex of power. Tian Jiyun, for instance, repeatedly criticized the policy lines of the Jiang/Li axis but he is tolerated. The reason is that, unlike Chen Xitong, he is not involved in

coalition-building activities, nor is his criticism person-specific. Policy
disputes intensify personal/factional conflicts when they get out of control.
If Jiang is able to sustain a working relationship with his colleagues, then
his role as a policy coordinator and compromise-enforcer will help to
obtain consensus at the centre. Post-Mao élite politics has been a struggle
to build consensual politics.[47] Hu and Zhao failed the test because they
failed to do this. Jiang seems to have done better, but it is essential for
him to act continuously as a consensus-promoter in order to maintain a
level of leadership stability. Orderly succession is an unresolved problem
for China. The only way out is to institutionalize it under the rule of law.[48]
But since this will be a long and painful path, the second-best choice in the
meantime has to be the efforts to seek consensus through compromise. In
other words, succession difficulties alone do not lead to regime collapse:
undisciplined struggles for power do.

People do not believe that Jiang can prevail in the end because he is
not charismatic. Probably this is his strong point in a post-Deng élite
politics that emphasizes collective leadership rather than charisma of the
leader. Jiang is not the kind of leader imagined as doing great things
like Mao, who tried to move mountains, but he may be the kind of leader
who can help construct a suitable environment in which great things
happen, particularly at this moment when China is in a process of great
transition. He may be a transitional figure if chaos ensues after Deng's
death. But people do not want strongmen any more, so Jiang may be their
choice.

Notes

1. In terms of personnel dismissals, the only unexpected one was the removal
   of Yang Baibing from the PLA and the subsequent military leadership
   reshuffles, dictated by Deng. On the policy side, Deng's south China tour in
   1992 was a decisive push to alter the course of the first-line party leadership.
   Here the *status quo* can be better understood as the mentality of current
   Chinese power holders: changes seem to be driven more by expediency than
   by a long-term vision for change.
2. Andrew Nathan and Kellee Tsai, "Factionalism: A New Institutional Restate-
   ment," *The China Journal*, No. 34 (July 1995), pp. 157–92.
3. Since the 1950s, general secretaries of the State Council and their deputies
   have been called big secretaries of the premier (*damishu*); small secretaries

are the premiers' personal staff. Key members among them include Luo Gan (state councillor), Chen Jinhua (minister of the State Planning Commission) and Liu Zhongli (finance minister).

4. This category is somewhat different from that given by David Bachman who listed a few more interest groups, such as ideologues. See David Bachman, "Varieties of Chinese Conservatism and the Fall of Hu Yaobang," *Journal of Northeast Asian Studies*, Vol. VII (Spring 1988).

5. For the functioning of these *xitong*, see Kenneth Lieberthal and Michel Oksenberg, *Policy Making in China: Leaders, Structures and Processes* (Princeton: Princeton University Press, 1988).

6. Needless to say, there are dissenting voices within each of these four powerful groups, but the mainstream interests of the four *xitong* are fairly cohesive. Another point should be made about the National People's Congress, which is increasingly influential as a policy forum. On the whole, however, it has not fundamentally changed its rubber stamp role in national politics.

7. Huang Yasheng argued, for instance, this was a kind of political reform at the national level that diffused power among central governing institutions, often at the expense of the power of individual leaders. "Why China Will Not Collapse," *Foreign Policy*, No. 99 (Summer 1995), p. 60.

8. Ian Wilson and You Ji, "Leadership by Lines: China's Unresolved Succession," *Problems of Communism*, Vol. 39, No. 1 (1990).

9. Ruan Ming, *Deng Xiaoping diguo* (The Deng Xiaoping Empire) (Taipei: Shibao wenhua, 1992).

10. For more detailed discussion of Jiang's institutional authority, see You Ji, "Jiang Zemin's Formal and Informal Sources of Power and China's Elite Politics after 6.4.1989," *China Information*, Vol. VI, No. 2 (1991), pp. 1–23.

11. Zhao Zhenghui, "Dangdai zhongguo yulinjun" (The Contemporary Royal Guards), *Zhuiqiu* (Search), Beijing, No. 7 (1995), p. 34.

12. For instance, on 5 August 1995, Jiang wrote on the report of chief of general staff Fu Quanyou: "I endorse your advocacy that (the headquarters) must help to improve the well-being of soldiers at the grassroots and do a good job for them in terms of logistical supply." Cui Yaozhong and Meng Fansen, "Wennuan gongcheng zai pianchui" (The Sending-warmth Project at the Borders), *Renmin ribao* (People's Daily), 5 November 1995. All the sources in *Renmin ribao* are from the *guonei* (domestic) edition.

13. For instance, Jiang told PLA top officers at the 1995 armed forces conference on political affairs that he always tried to convince the National People's Congress to agree to a larger military allocation in the annual state budget. However, he also said it was difficult for him to press the matter if many PLA corruption cases were exposed. (Oral source from the PLA during my fieldwork trip in Beijing in January 1996.)

14. *Zhonghua yingcai* (China's Talents), Beijing, August 1995, pp. 4–11.

15. For a more detailed analysis of this strategic change, see You Ji, "In Quest of Military High-tech Power: the PLA's Modernization in 1990s," in *China as a Great Power: Myths, Realities and Challenges in the Asia-Pacific Region*, edited by Stuart Harris and Gary Klintworth (New York and Melbourne: Longman and St. Martin's Press, 1995), pp. 231–57.

16. View expressed by a PLA general to which this author agrees.

17. For instance, in a speech Yang Baibing made at the PLA National Defence University in 1991, Yang openly criticized Chi Haotian, defence minister, for his emphasis on technological improvement and enhanced training of the PLA. This he termed as "guojunlun." He said that he was for "dangjunlun," or placing the PLA firmly under the control of the party's ideological line. (Interview with a PLA officer in Beijing in 1992.)

18. Jeremy Paltiel, "PLA Allegiance on Parade: Civil-Military Relations in Transition," *The China Quarterly*, No. 143 (September 1995), p. 797.

19. Oral information from PLA sources in 1995.

20. Huang Yao, *Luo Ruiqing dajiang* (Senior General Luo Ruiqing) (Beijing: Zhongguo dangshi chubanshe, 1994), p. 338.

21. Among these people are, for instance, Xiao Yang, governor of Sichuan province and an old Beijing associate, and obviously Wang Baosen, executive deputy mayor of Beijing. It was alleged that another long-term associate of the "Beijing Gang," Wu Yi, minister of foreign trade, was also implicated. This would somewhat impede her chances of becoming a deputy premier. (Information gathered from cadres in Beijing Municipal Government, 1995.)

22. Central Committee (CC) Document, April 1995.

23. Oral source from the Central Organization Department, May 1995.

24. For the Gao/Rao episode in CCP history, see Frederick Teiwes, *Politics at Mao Court: Gao Gang and Party Factionalism in the Early 1950s* (Armonk: M.E. Sharpe, 1990).

25. Information from one Beijing official who worked under Chen in the 1980s.

26. Chen Xitong, "Taolun zhenli biaozhun wenti shi zhongyao de yike" (The "Truth" Discussion Is a Crucial Lesson), *Renmin ribao*, 21 August 1979.

27. *Beijing ribao*, 17 January 1996.

28. Wang was under surveillance as early as late 1994 and Chen was implicated. Subsequently, a "third force," (to be identified, but from its familiarity with those high-level classified cases, it must have had close connections with the party's law and security organs), pressured the Politburo to move further by exposing one major corruption scandal after another committed by Beijing leaders. It also spread the word to Beijing citizens so social pressure built up. For instance, many taxi drivers talked about the case and *Dazibao*, or big character posters appeared at the entrance of the Beijing Party Committee. All this forced Jiang and Li to take action or face the real prospect of another

social protest. (Information gathered in April/May and August/September 1995, in Beijing.)

29. One example was the circular of the PLA General Political Department to all officers and men that called them to study seriously the series of Jiang's speech made on the inspection tour of Beijing in November. *Xinhuashe* (New China News Agency), Beijing, 19 November 1995.

30. For instance, Qiao Shi's protégées Wei Jianxing and Ren Jianxin were charged with the task of investigation, and the former was also appointed as Beijing's new party chief.

31. "Jiang Zemin zai Beijing kaocha" (Jiang's Beijing Inspection Tour), *Renmin ribao*, 9 November 1995.

32. For instance, Li's confidant Luo Gan from the State Council was appointed as chair of Beijing Comprehensive Management Committee, a powerful agency composed of representatives from central ministries and Beijing Municipality. Traditionally, this was headed by the party boss of Beijing. Now the State Council has overriding power over it. Moreover, one of Li Peng's secretaries, Jing Renqing was made Beijing's executive deputy mayor, with a good possibility to become mayor in the future.

33. Bo Yibo, *Ruogan zhongda juece yu shijian de huigu* (Recall of Some Major Decisions and Events) (Beijing: Zhonggong zhongyang dangxiao chubanshe, 1993), chapter 24.

34. For more discussion of this debate, see You Ji, "Zhao Ziyang and the Politics of Inflation," *The Australian Journal of Chinese Affairs*, No. 25 (January 1991), pp. 69–91.

35. *Xinhuashe* (Beijing), 21 August 1995, p. 1.

36. *Wenzai xunkan* (Thrice-monthly Digest), Beijing, 8 September 1995, p. 1.

37. The three documents are the CC's recommendation of the 15-year plan, Jiang's 12 major economic relations, and Li Peng's explanation of the 15-year plan.

38. Minister Zeng Peiyan, "Guanjian zaiyu shixian liangge genbenxing zhuanbian" (The Key Link Is to Effect Two Basic Changes), *Renmin ribao*, 16 October 1995.

39. Zong Han, "Zouyitiao jiyou jiaogao sudu you you jiaohao xiaoyi de fazhan luzi" (Base the Economic Growth on Both Relatively High Speed and Relatively High Efficiency), *Renmin ribao*, 14 November 1995.

40. For instance, Jiang made such a claim to the president of Germany on 13 July 1995. *Zhongxinshe* (China News Service), Hong Kong, 13 July 1995.

41. Andrew Walder, "The Political Sociology of the Beijing Upheaval of 1989," *Problems of Communism*, Vol. 38, No. 3 (1989), pp. 37–39.

42. Shen Baonian, "Jiuwu: Zhongguo jingji he shehui fazhan de zhongyao shiqi" (The Ninth-five Year Period: The Key Era for China's Economic and Social Development), *Liaowang* (Outlook), Beijing, No. 40 (1995), p. 4.

43. Jiang's speech at the 5th Plenum of the 13th CC in November 1989.
44. Hong Xuezhi, "Nanwang de jiaohui, shenqie de sinian" (Unforgettable Teaching and Deeply-felt Longing), *Renmin ribao*, 8 September 1995.
45. There has been widespread talk about a "Gang of Shanghai." In reality Wu Bangguo and Huang Ju were favoured by Deng and Chen Yun, both of whom were taken good care of when they stayed in Shanghai. In fact, Wu and Huang belong to a tiny number of provincial leaders Deng knew personally, still a precondition for the selection of Politburo members. (Sources from the Central Organization Department, 1995.)
46. Frederick C. Teiwes, "The Paradoxical post-Mao Transition: From Obeying the Leader to 'Normal Politics'," *The China Journal*, No. 34 (July 1995), p. 82.
47. Ibid.
48. Bo Yibo, *Ruogan zhongda juece yu shijian de huigu* (see Note 34), p. 1296.

2

The Developing Chinese Law and the Civil Law Tradition

Albert H. Y. Chen

Introduction

Before the downfall of the communist regimes in Eastern Europe and the Soviet Union (USSR) several years ago, scholars of comparative law used to classify most of the legal systems of states in the modern world according to the threefold division of the Common Law family, the Continental European family (alternatively known as the Civil Law family or Romano-Germanic family) and the socialist family.[1] The infant legal system established by the People's Republic of China (PRC) in the 1950s, modelled largely on Soviet norms, institutions and practices,[2] properly belonged to the socialist family of laws. Since the Anti-Rightist Campaign of 1957, and particularly during the Cultural Revolution era of 1966–1976, China departed from the USSR's theory and practice of "socialist legality" and formal legal institutions. When socialist legality was rehabilitated in the late 1970s, the first set of major laws that emerged (such as the 1978 Constitution, the 1982 Constitution, the Criminal Code 1979, the Code of Criminal Procedure 1979, the Code of Civil Procedure [Provisional] 1982, the Law of Economic Contracts 1981, and the various organic laws for the people's congresses, people's courts and people's procuratorates) were to a large extent reproductions of legal texts enacted or drafted in the 1950s, and therefore exhibited heavy Soviet influences.

When the General Principles of Civil Law were drafted in the mid-1980s, the basic sources of reference were still from countries within the family of socialist laws — the USSR, Czechoslovakia, East Germany and Hungary.[3] It is the thesis of this chapter that a *new* trend can be observed in the 1990s. A kind of breakthrough has been achieved in the development of PRC law. The PRC legal system is now moving into the orbit of the Romano-Germanic family of legal systems. Indeed, as this chapter will seek to demonstrate, some of the fundamental concepts introduced by legislation into PRC law in recent years can only be properly understood in the context of the Civil Law tradition, and are wholly alien to lawyers and scholars trained in the Common Law tradition (i.e. the Anglo-American legal tradition). In the pages below, I shall seek to illustrate this thesis with reference to three major pieces of legislation enacted in recent years — the Guarantee Law (*Danbaofa*) 1995 (alternatively translated as the Security Law, which came into effect on 1 October 1995), the Company Law (*Gongsifa*) 1993 (effective from 1 July 1994), and the State Compensation Law (*Guojia peichangfa*) 1994 (effective from 1 January 1995). These three laws may be regarded as the most important developments in the areas of civil and commercial law and public law in mainland China in recent years.

The Development of Civil Law and the Guarantee Law

The significance of the Guarantee Law should be seen in the light of the overall development of the conceptual framework of the civil law[4] in mainland China. In this section of the chapter, we shall first explore the nature and structure of this framework with reference to the manner in which Chinese civil law is presented in standard Chinese textbooks published in recent years. This will provide the background for a discussion of the Guarantee Law itself.

Several leading textbooks on Chinese civil law published in the 1990s generally arrange their contents according to the following structure.[5] First there is a general discussion of the concept and history of civil law, the nature of civil legal relations and civil liability, the subjects of civil law (e.g. natural persons and legal persons), the concept of the civil juristic act, the topic of agency, and the limitation periods for legal actions. This general part is then followed by chapters each dealing with a more specialized component of PRC civil law. According to these textbooks, the components include rights over things (*wuquan*), obligations (*zhai*) or rights over obligations (*zhaiquan*), rights of the person (*renshen quan*), intellectual property rights, rights of inheritance, and civil liability for wrongs (*qinquan*, which is equivalent to the concept of tort in Common Law).

This structural arrangement of topics in the Chinese texts is not only consistent with the General Principles of Civil Law (*Minfa tongze*) 1986 (GPCL) — the most fundamental enactment in the area of civil law in the PRC — but also reflects clearly the Chinese reception of the Continental European legal tradition. Furthermore, it should be noted that Chinese scholars went even *further* than the GPCL in employing the concepts and doctrines of the Romano-Germanic family of legal systems. Lawyers trained in that legal tradition would find the content of these books familiar (if they can read Chinese), whereas lawyers from the Common Law tradition would probably find them less easily understandable.

Unlike the English Common Law tradition, Continental European legal systems, which emerged in the era of the formation of national states and movements for codification of laws, have been largely shaped and influenced by the law of the ancient Roman Empire, including that of the

Eastern Roman Empire (Byzantium) as crystallized for posterity in the *Corpus Juris Civilis* compiled by Emperor Justinian in the sixth century AD, and by the medieval European scholarship on Roman law. From the point of view of its subsequent development and influence, the core of Roman law was its civil law (i.e., that part of the law governing relations between private persons rather than relations between the government and its subjects). Hence the Continental European legal tradition is also known as the Civil Law tradition.

This civil law was understood as consisting of three major divisions relating respectively to persons, things (*res*) and actions. "Things" (*wu* in Chinese) may be understood either in a broad sense or in a narrow sense. "Things" in the broad sense include everything that has economic value — not only physical assets but also rights that are capable of being evaluated in money terms (e.g. right to repayment of a debt, a right of way over another's land). The law of "things" in the broad sense consisted of three further sub-divisions: the law of "things" in the narrow sense (referring to tangible assets such as land and goods, also known as the law of property), the law of "obligations," and the law of inheritance.

The law of property regulated rights over things ("things" in the narrow sense), which are also known as "real rights" ("*jura in re*" in Latin, "rights *in rem*" in English, "*dingliche Rechte*" in German, "*wuquan*" in Chinese), whereas the law of obligations regulated rights over obligations ("rights *in personam*" in English, "*zhaiquan*" in Chinese), and embraced the functional equivalents of both the law of contract and the law of tort in the Common Law tradition:[6]

> A man's assets [things in the broad sense discussed above] are either property [things in the narrow sense] or obligations. The difference between the two is the difference between owning and being owed something.... The difference between owning and being owed is expressed by the Roman lawyer in the distinction between actions *in rem* and actions *in personam*. Any claim is either *in rem* or *in personam*, and there is an unbridgeable division between them.[7]

Rights *in rem* consisted of ownership, which was a core and fundamental concept in Roman law, as well as rights of a limited nature over property owned by another (such rights being known as "*jura in re aliena*" in Latin, "*beschränkte dingliche Rechte*" in modern German law, "*démembrements de la propriété*" in modern French law, and "*xianzhi wuquan*," or "*tawuquan*," in modern pre-PRC Chinese jurisprudence).

The latter may be further sub-divided into rights of use and enjoyment ("*Nutzungsrechte*" in German, or "*yongyi wuquan*" in Chinese), and rights of security ("*Sicherungsrechte*" in German, or "*danbao wuquan*" in Chinese).

The conception of the civil law as consisting of the law of things (in the narrow sense) (alternatively known as the law of property), the law of obligations, the law of persons (including family law), and the law of inheritance, shaped the structure of modern codes of civil law in countries which inherited the Civil Law tradition. A good example is the Civil Code that is presently in force in Taiwan, which was originally enacted in 1929–1931 by the Nanking Kuomintang (Guomindang) Government of the Republic of China. The Code (hereafter called the "ROC Civil Code," ROC referring to "the Republic of China") consists of five "books," on general principles, obligations (*zhai*), rights over things (*wuquan*), family and succession, respectively.

Five books with similar titles are also contained in the German Civil Code 1896 (Bürgerliches Gesetzbuch, or "BGB") and the Japanese Civil Code 1898. It is noteworthy in this regard that Japanese legal developments in the late nineteenth century relied heavily on the German model, while much of the work of the late Qing legal reforms in China was done with the assistance of Japanese jurists. The legal system developed by the republican government in the late 1920s and early 1930s, and later transplanted to Taiwan, was partially based on the late Qing reforms, and almost completely an offspring of the Romano-Germanic family. As far as the ROC Civil Code was concerned, John C. H. Wu, a famous Chinese jurist of the republican era, pointed out that "if one studies carefully the new Civil Code from article 1 to article 1225, and compares it article by article with the German and Swiss Civil Codes, one will discover that 95% of the Chinese code is derived from the latter codes, either by direct reproduction or by modification."[8]

Although several drafts of a civil code had been produced in the PRC since the 1950s, the government decided in 1982 that, given the rapid ongoing changes in economic and property relations being generated by reforms of the economic system, the enactment of a detailed and comprehensive civil code ought to be postponed.[9] However, as it was still necessary to lay down some basic principles of civil law as a foundation for the operation of individual enactments on different areas of civil law relating to matters such as contracts, business enterprises, land, intellectual property, marriage and succession, the GPCL was enacted in 1986. This was regarded by scholars as a milestone in the development of Chinese civil law.[10]

Many of the concepts and principles in the GPCL are clearly derived from the Continental European legal tradition. For example, in respect of the provisions in the GPCL on natural persons, legal persons, "civil juristic acts" (or, in German, *"Geschäftshandlung,"* a distinctive concept in the BGB that has no parallel in the Common Law) and limitations of actions, counterparts exist in Book I ("General Principles") of the ROC Civil Code and of the BGB. The concept of "rights over obligations" (*zhaiquan*) in the GPCL is also similar to, though not identical with, the corresponding notion in the ROC Code and the BGB. However, unlike the Taiwan and German systems, there is no mention of "rights over things" (*wuquan*) in the GPCL. This suggests a major gap between PRC property law and its Taiwan or German counterpart.

The explanation for the gap lies in the Soviet communist element in the legal heritage of the PRC. Soviet jurisprudence rejected the multiplicity of "rights over things" as a feature of capitalist law. The abolition of private ownership of the means of production led to the creation of two and only two forms of ownership over the means of production — state ownership and collective ownership.[11] This system was adopted by the PRC,[12] and was indeed appropriate to the conditions of its planned economy. However, economic reforms since the late 1970s generated new forms of *de facto* property rights. These realities were not ignored by the draftsmen of the GPCL. While ideological change was not fast enough to enable "rights over things" (*wuquan*) to be fully rehabilitated, it was still possible to achieve a compromise and to erect a half-way house between the Soviet approach and the Continental European approach. The result was section 1 of chapter 5 of the GPCL, entitled "Property Ownership and Property Rights Relating to Ownership."[13]

This part of the GPCL gives legal recognition to a number of property rights other than full ownership that have emerged in the course of economic reforms. These include, for example, rights arising from *chengbao* contracts (that is, under the "contract responsibility system") to the use of land and resources under state ownership or collective ownership (articles 80 and 81 of the GPCL), and the rights of state enterprises over property which the state has given to them for the purpose of operational management (article 82). However, the exact legal status of these rights have not been well-defined, even though the obvious solution would have been to describe them in terms of the well-established Civil Law concept of *wuquan*.

Another unsatisfactory aspect of the GPCL relates to its treatment of security rights (*danbao wuquan*). As mentioned above, according to the Continental European Civil Law tradition as received by modern pre-PRC Chinese jurisprudence, those *wuquan* other than full ownership are known as *xianzhi wuquan* (or *tawuquan*) (restricted rights over things, or rights over things owned by another), which may be further divided into *yongyi wuguan* (rights of use and enjoyment) and *danbao wuquan* (security rights over things). *Danbao wuquan* include the Common Law equivalents of mortgage, pledge and lien. However, although the GPCL makes a brief mention of mortgage (*diya*) and lien (*liuzhiquan*), it does so not in section 1 ("property ownership and related property rights") of chapter V ("civil rights"), but in section 2 ("rights over obligations" [*zhaiquan*]) of the same chapter (article 89[2] and [4]). This approach has been criticized by Chinese scholars, who have also expressed dissatisfaction at the failure of the GPCL to draw a distinction between mortgage and pledge.[14]

By making these criticisms, and by employing the Civil Law concepts of *wuquan*, *xianzhi wuquan*, *yongyi wuquan* and *danbao wuquan* in presenting and discussing the property and security rights provided for in the GPCL,[15] Chinese scholars have demonstrated their acceptance of the persuasive force of the logic of the Civil Law, and their commitment to the employment of the categories and theories developed in this Continental European legal tradition for the purpose of the development and elaboration of contemporary Chinese jurisprudence. This is further evidenced by the proposals put forward by Chinese scholars in recent years[16] for the enactment of legislation, in the form of either a civil code or a less all-embracing and less ambitious law, which will formally acknowledge the existence of *wuquan* and provide an authoritative and exhaustive statement of the various kinds of *wuquan* (including ownership, *yongyi wuquan* and *danbao wuquan*) that are recognized in the PRC. For example, this law will have to define clearly the nature and status of the post-GPCL "land-use rights" which have been granted by the state in recent years to developers in accordance with a scheme of policy akin to the grant of Crown leases to developers in Hong Kong.[17]

The enactment of the *Guarantee Law* in 1995 is an important inter-mediate step between the GPCL and such eventual legislative statement of a systematic and comprehensive set of *wuquan* in the Civil Law sense. This law supplies the basic rules regulating five legal devices that can serve as security for credit — (a) guarantee; (b) mortgage (*diya*), which can also be translated as "hypothec," a term used in some English books on Continental European law to translate the Continental equivalent of the

English mortgage (*"Hypothek"* in German, *"hypothèque"* in French); (c) pledge (*zhiya*); (d) lien; and (e) deposit. Among these five, the guarantee and deposit are "personal security," whereas the mortgage, pledge and lien are "real security" (*"Realkredit"* in German). As mentioned above, the GPCL lumps together mortgage and pledge and describes both as *diya*; it is also extremely brief on this concept of *diya* and on that of lien, and places them within the framework of "obligations" (*zhaiquan*) rather than "property rights." The detailed rules in the Guarantee Law governing the creation, effect, operation and enforcement of the three types of real security rights now testify unequivocally to their nature as *wuquan* (or, more particularly, *danbao wuquan*, though neither term is expressly used in the Guarantee Law) in the Civil Law sense.

Finally, it is noteworthy that some of the concepts and principles in the Guarantee Law may seem difficult to understand from the point of view of lawyers in Common Law jurisdictions, but are easily explicable in terms of Continental European legal thinking as exemplified, for instance, in the ROC Civil Code. Three examples may be given here.

(1) The Guarantee Law (chapter IV thereof) provides for two kinds of pledges — pledge of movables (*dongchan zhiya*) and pledge of rights (*quanli zhiya*). In English Common Law, the concept of pledge (involving delivery of the pledged property to the pledgee) applies only to movables (chattels or goods). Rights ("choses in action") may be assigned by way of security for credit, but this is regarded as a mortgage (either a legal or equitable mortgage) rather than a pledge. For example, shares in a company may be the subject of a legal mortgage or an equitable mortgage. For the Common Law lawyer, therefore, the concept of pledge of rights may seem strange and alien. However, if one turns to the ROC Civil Code (book III, chapter 6), one will discover that in Taiwan, pledges also include pledges of movables and pledges of rights, the concepts being identical to those in the PRC Guarantee Law.[18] The same division into these two types of pledges applies to the pledge (*Pfand*) in the BGB.[19]

(2) The PRC Guarantee Law (article 51) in effect imposes an obligation on the mortgagor to maintain the economic value of the mortgaged property and not to cause its depreciation. An almost identical provision can be found in the ROC Civil Code (articles 871, 872).

(3) The Guarantee Law (article 55) provides that any new buildings erected on the mortgaged property after the mortgage has been created will not form part of the mortgaged property. Hence in the event of the mortgagee enforcing the security and selling the property, the mortgagee

will not be in the position of a secured creditor *vis-à-vis* that part of the sale proceeds derived from the new buildings. This provision clearly deviates from, and presents a hindrance to the creation in China of, the kind of building mortgage used to finance construction developments in Hong Kong. However, if one turns to the ROC Civil Code, one can find an identical provision (article 877). It might be noted in this regard that Japanese law also treats land and buildings as different "things," and thus a mortgage (hypothec) of land does not cover the buildings thereon.[20]

The Company Law

The enactment of the PRC Company Law at the end of 1993 represented another highly significant development in Chinese law. Consisting of 230 articles, the Company Law is one of the lengthiest pieces of legislation promulgated so far in the PRC. The drafting of a law on companies[21] began as early as 1983, and initial drafts were already produced in 1986. Pressures for the speedy enactment of the law were generated by the decision of the Central Committee of the Communist Party in November 1993 to develop a "modern enterprise system," leading to the formal adoption of the law by the Standing Committee of the National People's Congress at the end of December 1993.

Western-style companies had begun to operate in China since the nineteenth century, and they also had existed in republican China under Kuomintang rule and in mainland China under Communist rule before 1956.[22] The ROC (Republic of China) Company Law was enacted in 1929 on the basis of drafts produced with the assistance of Japanese scholars. As in the case of the ROC Civil Code mentioned above, the ROC Company Law also followed Continental European institutions. This law is still in force in Taiwan today, subject to various revisions which have introduced some elements of Anglo-American company law.[23]

At the time of the promulgation of the PRC Company Law in 1993, there were already nearly 1.3 million "companies" in the PRC.[24] Before 1993, chapter III ("legal persons") of the GPCL (1986), supplemented by the Regulations on the Registration and Management of Enterprise Legal Persons (*Qiye faren dengji guanli tiaoli*) (1988), have made provisions for the registration of various kinds of domestic and foreign-investment enterprises as legal persons.[25] There also existed separate laws and regulations on the structure, management and operation of enterprises with different sources of capital, such as state enterprises (i.e. "enterprises owned by the whole people"), collectively-owned enterprises, private enterprises, peasants' joint stock co-operative enterprises, Chinese-foreign equity joint ventures, Chinese-foreign co-operative joint ventures, and foreign-capital enterprises.[26]

One of the novel features of the Company Law is that it applies equally to enterprises irrespective of the source of their capital. This is said to be an important policy shift, consistent with the transition from a planned economy to a socialist market economy and facilitating fair competition in the market on the basis of legal equality.[27] Instead of providing for differential treatment of enterprises or companies according to the sources of their capital (i.e. their "ownership types"), the Company Law now draws a distinction on the basis of legal form between two types of companies, and establishes a regulatory regime for each of them. The two types are the limited liability company (*youxian zeren gongsi*) and company limited by shares (*gufen youxian gongsi*), which has also been translated as "joint stock limited company."

It is interesting to note that although the members of the limited liability company are called shareholders ("*gudong*"), as is also the case in the company limited by shares, the concept of shares ("*gufen*") is only applicable to the latter type of company (article 3 of the Company Law). Shareholders of a limited liability company do not own any "shares" in the company; their interest in the company, which they may, subject to certain restrictions, transfer to others, are called "capital contribution" ("*chuzi*" or "*chuzi' e*") (articles 3, 35). Lawyers trained in English law or Hong Kong law will also wonder what is the relationship or correlation between, on the one hand, the two types of companies in the PRC Company Law, and, on the other hand, the types of companies which they themselves are familiar with. However, as will be demonstrated below, lawyers in Taiwan, Japan or Continental Europe will have no difficulty whatsover in seeing that the two types of PRC companies are the exact counterparts of two particular types of companies in their own legal systems.

One may start the inquiry by looking at the ROC Company Law. That law provides a four-fold classification of companies: (a) unlimited company; (b) limited company (*youxian gongsi*); (c) company with some shareholders of unlimited liability and others of limited liability (*lianghe gongsi*); (d) company limited by shares (*gufen youxian gongsi*). The content of the provisions on (b) and (d) (which, like the PRC law, draws a distinction between *chuzi* and shares) shows clearly that they are the counterparts of the PRC limited liability company and company limited by shares, respectively. It is also noteworthy that according to mainland Chinese writers, companies of types (a) and (c) also exist in the PRC, although they are not expressly regulated by legislation and are of declining importance in practice.[28]

The limited liability company (hereafter called "LLC") in the PRC and Taiwan law is the direct counterpart of the *"Gesellschaft mit beschränkter Haftung"* (GmbH) in Germany, the *"société à responsabilité limitée"* (SARL) in France, and the *"yūgen-gaisha"* in Japan. The counterparts in these countries of the company limited by shares (hereafter called "CLS") in the PRC and Taiwan are respectively the *"Aktiengesellschaft"* (AG), *"société anonyme"* (SA), and *"kabushiki-gaisha."* The terms in German and French law corresponding to *chuzi* (capital contribution) are respectively *"Geschäftsanteile"* and *"parts sociales,"* and those for *gufeng* (shares) are, respectively, *"Aktien"* and *"actions."*[29]

The following features of the Chinese Company Law, which may seem peculiar to the English or Hong Kong lawyer, are in fact exactly or close approximations to the common features of the law relating to LLCs and CLSs in Continental European legal systems.

(1) There are minimum capital requirements for the LLC and the CLS (arts. 23 and 78), the requirements being higher in the latter case.

(2) There is no distinction as in English company law between authorized capital and issued capital. According to Chinese company law, *before* the registration and thus establishment of an LLC or CLS, the *whole* of the capital stated in the company's constitution must already have been subscribed to and paid up (arts. 25–27, 82–83, 91).

(3) Unlike the case in English or Hong Kong law, it is not possible to incorporate and register a company first (with a small number of subscribers and without any substantive capital contribution to the company) and raise the capital later; instead, the law requires a series of formal steps to be taken in the process of incorporation, such as the subscription and payment of full capital, proof of such payment, (in the case of a CLS) convening an inaugural meeting to elect directors and supervisors, and only thereafter the submission of an application for the registration of the company (arts. 27–27, 82–94).

(4) The constitution (*zhangcheng*) of the company is contained in a single document (arts. 11, 22, 79), unlike the separate documents of the English or Hong Kong memorandum and articles of association. This constitution is the equivalent of the *"statuts"* in France, and the

"*Gesellschaftsvertrag*" (in the case of a GmbH) or "*Satzung*" (in the case of an AG) in Germany.

(5) Office-holders in a company include not only directors but also "supervisors" ("*jianshi*"), who form a board of supervisors. Supervisors are elected from among shareholders and are responsible for the scrutiny of the financial affairs and business operations of the company (arts. 52–54, 124–128).

(6) The shares of the CLS include both bearer shares and nominative (registered) shares (art. 133). Bearer shares are virtually unknown in Anglo-American law.

(7) The law requires a stipulated portion of a company's annual after-tax profits to be placed in a statutory reserve fund of the company until the amount in the reserve reaches a particular level (art. 177).

In the PRC, as in other countries in the Continental European family of legal systems, the distinction between the LLC and the CLS lies mainly in the purpose for which they are designed. The LLC is designed to facilitate the operation of small and medium-size businesses in which members of the company come together to operate a business, while the CLS enables capital to be raised if necessary from members of the public and the shares of the company to be traded on a stock exchange. Hence, the law imposes an upper limit on the number of members of an LLC, provides for an initial capital requirement that is lower than that applicable to the CLS, introduces restrictions on the transfer of a member's interest (capital contribution) in an LLC, and prohibits the LLC from issuing shares generally to members of the public. These limitations do not apply to the CLS, but the procedure for its formation is more complicated, its management structure is more elaborate, and it is subject to a tighter regulatory regime for the purpose of investor protection.

These characteristics of the LLC and CLS would suggest that they are the functional equivalents of two species of companies limited by shares in English and Hong Kong law — the private company and the public company, respectively. Unlike the LLC, the private company is also "a company limited by shares," as in the case of the public company, but the private company is subject to an upper limit to the number of its members, restrictions on the transfer of its shares, and a prohibition against inviting the public to subscribe for its shares or debentures. A company limited by shares whose constitution does not contain these restrictions can be called a public company, but this does not necessarily mean that its shares or some of them are publicly held. Similarly, in the Continental European family of legal systems, not all CLS have shares that are issued to members of the public and traded on the stock exchange.

Finally, it may be noted that, although the PRC has chosen to adopt the Continental European system of company types, and enacted a Company Law which is strikingly similar to the ROC Company Law[30] (both laws use the same Chinese legal terminology and the same Continental European concepts and principles), the *purpose* that the Chinese legislature sought to achieve by legislating on companies is very different from the purpose of company legislation in capitalist market economies. Even before the enactment of the Company Law, businesses with foreign investment elements were already operating in China in the form mainly of private limited companies,[31] and the respective enterprise laws on various types of foreign-investment enterprises already provided an adequate set of norms governing their structure and operation. The Company Law 1993 is therefore designed primarily for domestic businesses, particularly state enterprises which the legislators hope to liberate from the political control of the state bureaucracy.

This is why when the Company Law was introduced, it was hailed as an important step in the development of a "modern system of enterprise" in China.[32] This is why the chapter of the Company Law on the LLC contains a set of provisions specially designed for "wholly state-owned companies" (arts. 64–72). This is also why Chinese scholars writing on this law focus their discussion on the distinction in article 4 of the law between the company's "entire legal person property right" ("*quanbu faren caichan suoyou quan*," alternatively translated as "the right to the entire property of the legal person") and the shareholders' rights to enjoy income and to participate in the making of major decisions and the selection of managerial personnel. The separation of the company's property from that of its shareholders, which is a fundamental principle in modern company law, is now seen to offer a new hope in the long and difficult battle dating back to the 1980s to wrest state enterprises from state control and to give them a new life as "subjects-actors" (*zhuti*) in the market.[33]

State Compensation Law

The State Compensation Law 1994, supplemented in 1995 by the State Council's Administrative Measures on Funds for State Compensation, is surprisingly liberal and confers on the Chinese citizen a set of rights against the state which are in certain significant respects even *more* extensive than those available under corresponding circumstances in legal systems belonging to the Common Law family. Indeed, there is no well-established concept of "state compensation" in these legal systems. The nature and characteristics of "state compensation" as recently developed in the PRC are only explicable with reference to Continental European legal theory and practice. In the following, the State Compensation Law will first be considered in the context of Chinese legal developments since the 1980s; then the Continental European background will be introduced.

One of the major provisions in the 1954 Constitution of the PRC, restored (after its disappearance in the 1975 and 1978 Constitutions) in the new and currently applicable Constitution of 1982, reads as follows:

> Citizens who have suffered losses through infringement of their citizens' rights by any state organ or functionary have the right to obtain compensation in accordance with the law (third paragraph of article 41 of the 1982 Constitution; article 97 of the 1954 Constitution contained substantially the same provision).[34]

This provision is not, however, self-executing and has been understood merely as a directive to the legislature; the right that it provides for only comes into existence when a relevant law is introduced to implement its principle.[35] Such implementing legislation was enacted in 1986 as part of the GPCL:

> Civil liability shall be borne by any state organ or state organ personnel for damage caused by the infringement of the lawful rights and interests of a citizen or legal person in the course of the execution of duties (article 121).

In practice,[36] however, legal actions against a state organ seeking compensation did not become common until the commencement of the Security Administration Punishment Regulations (*Zhi'an guanli chufa tiaoli*) 1986, which enable citizens to seek judicial review of decisions taken by public security organs regarding the imposition of "administrative punishment," as well as to obtain compensation for loss or damage caused by punishment adjudged to be unlawful. This set of regulations is considered by Chinese scholars to be an important milestone in the development of Chinese administrative law.[37]

The right of citizens to state compensation when affected by unlawful administration actions was further affirmed, expanded and consolidated in the Law of Administrative Litigation (*Xingzheng susongfa*) (1989). The law empowers citizens to bring administrative litigation proceedings to challenge the legality of a wide range of "concrete administrative actions."[38] The procedure for such proceedings is prescribed by this law, which thus stands together with the Law of Criminal Procedure (*Xingshi susongfa*) (1979) and the Law of Civil Procedure (*Minshi susongfa*) (1991) as the basic codes of Chinese procedural law.[39] Chapter 9 of the PRC Law of Administrative Litigation supplies a set of norms, relatively more detailed than the relevant provision in the GPCL, governing the right to compensation by the state in respect of violation of rights due to the concrete administrative actions of administrative organs or their personnel.

Immediately after the enactment of this 1989 law, work began on the drafting of a state compensation law which would elaborate and extend further the citizen's right to state compensation.[40] The end product is the State Compensation Law 1994. The fundamental principle of state compensation in the PRC, as set out in article 2 of the law, is that where a state organ or its official exercises its or his/her powers and functions in an unlawful manner, infringing the lawful rights and interests of citizens or legal persons and causing damage to them, the state is liable to compensate the citizen or legal person concerned. Unlike the case in the Law of Administrative Litigation, administrative actions in respect of which compensatory claims may lie extend beyond "administrative act" (*xingzheng xingwei*) and include acts such as assault, battery, and torture. The State Compensation Law also went beyond the Law of Administrative Litigation in extending the cause of action to acts done by judges and procurators in the course of their work.

More particularly, the State Compensation Law provides for two principal types of state compensation — administrative compensation (*xingzheng peichang*) (in chapter 2) and criminal procedure compensation (*xingshi peichang*) (in chapter 3). It is further provided (in article 31) that compensation may be sought, using the same procedure as that for criminal procedure compensation, in respect of unlawful or wrongful judicial actions regarding pre-trial coercive measures or execution of judgments and orders in civil or administrative litigation. The precise circumstances in which each type of compensation may be claimed, the procedure for making claims and the level of compensation payable are all regulated by the law.

Administrative compensation, which is in practice the most important and commonly claimed type of state compensation,[41] is available under two categories of situations:

(1) The first category consists of violations of the rights of the body of the person by administrative organs or their personnel in the course of the exercise of their powers and functions. Five types of situations are set out in article 3 of the law:

(a) detention in breach of the law (*weifa juliu*). Under PRC law, administrative organs (particularly, public security organs) have the power to impose "administrative sanctions" on citizens in specified circumstances, and administrative detention is one of the severest forms of such sanctions.[42] Compensation may now be claimed under the State Compensation Law where such detention is not authorized by law, or where the procedure or maximum duration stipulated by law has not been complied with;

(b) unlawful detention (*feifa jujin*). This relates to detention of citizens by organs or officials who do not have any power of administrative detention at all, but who unlawfully practise detention in connection with their official work. An example is where tax officials detain a businessman in order to compel him to pay tax;[43]

(c) battery or other acts of violence resulting in bodily harm or death. This relates to situations where such unlawful acts are committed in connection with officials' work, or as a means of achieving an objective relating to their work, or using such objective as an excuse, or during working hours or in work premises;[44]

(d) unlawful use of weapons or police equipment resulting in bodily harm or death;

(e) other acts in breach of the law resulting in bodily harm to or death of citizens.

(2) The second category of circumstances covered by administrative compensation consists of violations of citizens' property rights by administrative organs or their personnel in the course of the exercise of their powers and functions. Four types of situations are set out in article 4 of the law:

(a) imposition of fines, cancellation of permits and licences, order to cease business or stop production, and confiscation of property, where such administrative actions are in breach of the law. It should be noted that these actions all fall within the scope of administrative sanctions that may be imposed by administrative organs in PRC law, particularly, organs responsible for regulating commercial and industrial activities;[45]

(b) actions of sealing up, distraining or freezing property in breach of the law. These actions are known as "administrative coercive measures";

(c) requisitioning property or raising revenue in breach of state regulations;

(d) other actions in breach of the law and resulting in property loss or damage.

As regards criminal procedure compensation — the second most important type of compensation provided for in the State Compensation Law — this is also available under two categories of situations.

(1)The first category consists of violations of the rights of the body of the person by organs or official personnel in the course of the exercise of the powers and functions of criminal investigation, procuratorial work, adjudication and management of prisons. Five types of situations are set out in article 15 of the law:

(a) wrongful detention of a person where there is no evidence of crime or no evidence suggesting that the person may be seriously suspected of having committed a crime. Chinese commentators have pointed out that this also covers the situation where the detention may be initially justified but continues after it is known that there is no evidence warranting it;[46]

(b) wrongful arrest of a person where there is no evidence of crime. Commentators have pointed out that this also covers the situation where the arrest may be initially justified, and the suspect is not released when further investigation reveals no evidence which really justifies the arrest;[47]

(c) a verdict of "not guilty" is reached in the course of the ad-judicatory supervisory procedure regarding a convicted person, where the person has served part or all of the original sentence;[48]

(d) torture is used to extort a confession, or other acts of violence are committed, resulting in bodily harm or death;

(e) unlawful use of weapons or police equipment resulting in bodily harm or death.

(2) The second category of circumstances covered by criminal compensation consists of violations of citizens' property rights by organs or

official personnel in the course of the exercise of the powers and functions of criminal investigation, procuratorial work, adjudication and management of prisons. Two types of situations are set out in article 16 of the law:

(a) sealing up, distraining or freezing property or demanding payment in breach of the law;

(b) a verdict of "not guilty" is reached in the course of the adjudicatory supervisory procedure regarding a convicted person, where a fine has already been paid or property has already been confiscated pursuant to the original sentence.

The State Compensation Law came into operation at the beginning of 1995. The general legislative principle that a law does not normally have retroactive effect is followed in the case of this law; thus, claims cannot be brought under the law in respect of loss or damage caused by acts which occurred before the law became effective.[49] As in other legal actions, the State Compensation Law provides for a time limit (which lawyers call "limitation period"), counting from the time at which the cause of action arises, beyond which a claim can no longer be brought. Article 32 stipulates that the limitation period is two years from the time when the relevant action of the state organ or its personnel is determined to be unlawful, but any period during which the claimant has been under detention does not count for this purpose.

From the point of view of lawyers trained in the Common Law tradition, three features of the State Compensation Law are particularly interesting and foreign to the Anglo-American approach to the problem of violation of citizens' rights by state officials. First, the law does not require as a condition for compensation that the official has been at fault (in the sense of doing something intentionally knowing that it is unlawful, or being negligent in failing to take reasonable care in the discharge of official functions); the test is instead an objective one — whether the act is authorized by law or not (*weifa*).

Secondly, the state is *directly* liable to the injured citizen in respect of the unlawful acts of its officials. This contrasts with the position in Anglo-American law that the state is only *vicariously* liable to citizens in respect of torts committed by its employees in the execution of their duties (in exactly the same way as a private employer is held vicariously liable for acts done by an employee in the course of employment), and *both* the employee-tortfeasor and the state are liable to the victim. Under the PRC

State Compensation Law, where a citizen suffers damage as a result of an official's unlawful act, it is the state which is primarily liable to the citizen; it is only as a supplementary provision that the law provides that where the official deliberately does the unlawful act or is guilty of gross negligence, the state may seek to be indemnified by the official in respect of the compensation which the state has paid to the victim (articles 14 and 24).

Thirdly, the legal rights to compensation by the state itself that are conferred by the State Compensation Law on victims of wrongful arrests and detentions, torture in the interrogation process, wrongful verdicts in criminal cases, and wrongful orders made or steps taken in the course of civil proceedings or administrative litigation, are far more extensive than in English or Hong Kong law. In the latter systems, the state is not liable at all in most of these situations, and the personal liability of judges is curtailed by the Common Law doctrine of judicial immunity.

However, when one turns to the laws of Taiwan, one can find two pieces of legislation that are the counterparts of the scheme for administrative compensation and that for criminal procedure compensation in the PRC State Compensation Law. They are the State Compensation Law (1981) and the Law on Compensation for Imprisonment pursuant to Wrong Verdicts (*Yuanyu peichangfa*) (1959). The concepts and basic doctrines of state compensation in both the PRC and Taiwan are in fact both derived from the Continental European tradition.

Treatises on the PRC State Compensation Law published by mainland Chinese scholars in recent years[50] all contain enthusiastic expositions of the theories and institutions of state compensation developed in Continental European countries, particularly France and Germany, since the late nineteenth century. Such Continental jurisprudence is also extensively discussed in works produced by Taiwan scholars on administrative law.[51] In France, the law of state compensation was developed by the famous Conseil d'État (Administrative Council, a branch of which functions as an administrative court) through case law. This law embraces concepts such as "*faute personnelle*" (personal fault of state officials), "*faute de service public*" (behaviour in the discharge of public duties which is considered defective from an objective viewpoint even though the official is not subjectively at fault), and "*risque administratif*" (risks in the operation of the administrative system that may justify the imposition of no-fault liability on the state). The French law of state compensation is in some ways more sophisticated than English administrative law, and may be regarded as in a more "advanced" stage of development than the corresponding English law in the sense that the citizen's right to state compensation in different kinds of circumstances is more extensively and elaborately provided for.

The state compensation system developed by Germany has also been admired by other countries, and adopted as a model in Japan, Korea and Taiwan.[52] The BGB 1896 (article 839) has provided for the civil servant's liability to citizens for loss caused by his intentional or negligent breach of duty, and the famous state compensation law of 1910 made the state liable in place of the civil servant (*"an Stelle des Beamten"*) in these circumstances.[53] It is remarkable that the German Empire accepted this principle of the state's responsibility and liability for the behaviour of its civil servants at a time when Anglo-American law still maintained the traditional doctrine of the state's immunity. According to this traditional view, the sovereign could do no wrong; officials should themselves assume personal liability for their unlawful acts to subjects harmed by such acts (for which the government was not even vicariously liable) — a position which continued in Britain and the United States until the enactment of the Crown Proceedings Act 1947 and the Federal Tort Claims Act 1946, respectively). In Germany, the principle of state compensation received a constitutional affirmation in the Weimar Constitution (1919). The current constitution (Basic Law 1949) of Germany also contains an emphatic statement of the state's direct (and not merely vicarious) responsibility for the rights-infringing acts of its civil servants:

> If any person, in the exercise of a public office entrusted to him, violates his official obligations to a third party, liability shall rest in principle on the state or the public body which employs him (article 34).

In their books on the PRC State Compensation Law,[54] Chinese scholars also introduce their readers to the theoretical foundation underlying and justifying the Continental European state compensation systems. For example, in France, such theoretical support has been found in the French Revolution's Declaration of the Rights of Man and the Citizen 1789:

> The upkeep of the police force and the expenses of public administration necessitate public taxation. This must be borne by all citizens equally, according to their means (article 13).

Some French jurists have argued that it would be a violation of this principle if the cost of unlawful actions within the system of public administration is borne entirely by the victims themselves, whereas state compensation would enable such cost to be spread among all citizens. However, most Continental European theorists do not feel a need to refer to this article in the French Declaration, which in any event is not directly relevant to countries other than France. The most influential and plausible theories that they have developed may be summarized as follows.

(1) Those who enjoy the benefits of an activity should also bear its burdens, costs and risks. The operation of the state's administrative system benefits citizens generally. But inevitably the system sometimes malfunctions — some civil servants act unlawfully in some cases, and the burdens imposed on the victims in these cases should be borne by society at large through a state compensation system financed by general taxation.

(2) A related idea is that of social insurance. Risks (of unlawful official action resulting in loss for individual citizens) are inevitably generated by the operation of the administrative system, in the same way as a society with many automobiles produces risks of road accidents. A state which attends to the welfare of its citizens should work out the best system to handle such risks. In this regard, the fairest and most efficient way to deal with the risks of unlawful official action would be for the state to act as an insurer.

This means that the state should operate a social insurance scheme in which premiums are in effect paid by all taxpayers. The state as insurer makes compensation payments to victims in cases where the risk materializes, so that the losses suffered by the victims are re-distributed and spread among all members of the scheme. The premise of the scheme is that the state, on behalf of all members of society, accepts collective responsibility for the pooling of the risks and the sharing of the costs of the operation of the administrative system.

(3) Continental jurists point out that the principles governing the state's liability for wrongs done to citizens by civil servants in the exercise of public powers and functions need not and should not be the same as those applicable to civil wrongs done by private persons to other private persons. While private persons stand in a relationship of equality *vis-à-vis* one another, the relationship between the state and the citizen is not a symmetrical one. The state is in a position to issue and enforce orders and commands to citizens unilaterally (unlike the case of private law relationships which are governed largely by contracts entered into by mutual consent), and citizens are subject to a legal obligation to render obedience.

Given the state's powerful and superior position *vis-à-vis* the citizen, it has a more onerous responsibility to perform. In particular, it should in effect guarantee to citizens that civil servants will not act unlawfully in the discharge of their functions. The system of state compensation is, from this point of view, no more than a legal device to give effect to this guarantee.

Insofar as these theories have not gained much influence in the Common Law world and are seldom discussed in Common Law texts on administrative or public law, it might be argued that Continental European thinking on these matters is more advanced or mature than in the Anglo-American world. From this perspective, the PRC's adoption of the Continental European model of state compensation is a major legal development which may be applauded. On the other hand, there is still a long and arduous way ahead for the development of the PRC's state compensation law, although it is encouraging that a good theoretical and doctrinal foundation has now been laid. The major limitations and inadequacies in the existing state compensation system that need to be tackled in future would seem to include the following.

(1) The circumstances in which criminal procedure compensation is available are still relatively limited. For example, there is no compensation in the following types of situations:

(a) detention is justified by the evidence and circumstances but continues beyond the relevant maximum period stipulated by law;[55]
(b) the adjudicatory supervisory procedure has been invoked and the court decides not to overturn the conviction but to reduce the sentence, but the original sentence has already been served;[56]
(c) the conviction at first instance is overturned on appeal.[57]

(2) The level of compensation prescribed by the State Compensation Law (with reference to the average wage of a state employee and to maximum total amounts) is low, and certainly less generous than damages which may be claimed in ordinary civil suits.[58]

(3) The procedural details of a legal action for state compensation have not yet been elaborated.

(4) It is not clear whether neglect, omission or failure to act may give rise to a claim for state compensation, or whether the State Compensation Law is only applicable to positive acts that cause loss or damage.[59]

(5) The State Compensation Law confers a right to compensation only in respect of violations of the body of the person or property rights, and only where loss or damage has been caused as a result of such violations.

Other violations and violations of other rights (e.g. the constitutional rights to freedoms of speech, publication, assembly, association, etc.) and interests are not covered.[60]

(6) The state's "occupier's liability" in respect of state-owned premises, buildings and facilities on which accidents occur as a result of mismanagement has not yet been provided for.

(7) Nor does the State Compensation Law extend to public organizations that are not technically state organs.

(8) Loss or damage caused by activites of the military forces (e.g. during military exercises) are not covered.

(9) Neither has the law made provisions for loss or damage arising from accidents in nuclear power plants.

(10) As is admitted by Chinese scholars, weaknesses in China's existing legal institutions and legal culture may also hinder the successful implementation of the State Compensation Law.[61] On the institutional level, the main problem is that the courts only have limited authority and autonomy within the political system. In particular, judges' freedom to give judgements against administrative authorities is often constrained by the local judiciary's dependence on the executive branch of the same local or regional governmental level for their budgetary provision, and by the control over matters of appointment and transfer of judicial personnel exercised by the Communist Party committees of that local or regional level.[62] As regards legal culture, the problems are that citizens have not yet developed a strong consciousness of rights against the state, and many state officials are not willing to submit themselves to legal and judicial processes.[63]

Conclusion

Is it not ironic that after taking a zigzag path since the Communist Revolution began in China, Chinese law — four decades after the victory of the revolution — has finally settled on a direction parallel to that in which it was moving during the late Qing and early Republican period in the first four decades of this century? It was in that earlier period that China irrevocably abandoned its venerable legal tradition which, at times such as the Tang and Song dynasties, probably represented the most elaborate, sophisticated, "advanced" or "civilized" legal system in the world. The late Qing legal reformers, with the assistance of their Japanese colleagues, created an embryonic legal system which represented a kind of "wholesale Westernization" (as was the case of modern Japanese law) and was almost completely constructed on the basis of the Continental European legal model.[64] The law draftsmen, jurists and legislators of the republican government during the "warlord period" and the first decade of Kuomintang rule in Nanking carried on the work of their predecessors without any significant alteration of its basic orientation as a legal system belonging to the Romano-Germanic family. Indeed, there is a remarkable degree of continuity and similarity between the legal texts produced by the late Qing reformers and those by jurists under the "warlord" governments and the Kuomintang government. The discontinuity only came with the Communist takeover in 1949, for the new regime regarded the pre-existing laws and legal institutions as "non-heritable" because they were based on feudal, imperialist or capitalist ideology.[65]

Upon reflection, it seems hardly surprising, and, indeed, almost inevitable, that Chinese law should finally return to the orientation and direction of development that it took when it first began to respond to the challenges of the modern world. For there simply is no escape from modernity, from its markets of property exchanges (hence, modern property law), its business corporations (hence, modern company law) and its assertion of the rights of the citizen as against the state (hence, modern state compensation law). The pioneers of the modernization of Chinese law chose to mould the modern Chinese legal system according to one of the two traditions that are the legal carriers of modernity — the Continental European tradition.[66] They translated and studied the laws and jurisprudence of Continental Europe and of Japan; in the doctrinal writings and legal texts which they produced, a new universe of Chinese legal terminology and vocabulary, and of modern legal concepts, doctrines and theories expressed in the Chinese language, was born.

The official policy of the Chinese government at present is to develop a "socialist market economy," and the corresponding legal policy is to bring into existence laws that would facilitate the operation of such an economic system.[67] Officals and scholars alike have called for active borrowing from the legal systems of countries with highly developed market economies. Their experience in this regard is hailed as a common heritage of humankind with universal value. What is missing however in this discourse is the heritage of the pre-1949 jurisprudence of twentieth-century China, the practical significance of which seems to be increasing day by day in the present era. The striking similarity in language, concepts and structures between the laws discussed in this chapter and their counterparts in Taiwan testifies to the power and influence of this heritage.

In the final analysis, law is a cultural phenomenon,[68] and culture is inextricably bound to history and tradition. Thus, the following courageous words, written by two leading Chinese jurists in 1993, speak to us today with truth and insight:

> As two stages in the history of the development of Chinese law, the law of the Kuomintang period and the present law of the People's Republic of China have a necessary historical and cultural connection. This is an objective manifestation of the national character and continuity of Chinese legal development in the contemporary age. It is true that for long periods after 1949, particularly in the 1960s, Chinese legislative work and the legal system could not undergo normal development. But since the 1980s, the legislative work and legal system of contemporary China have been able to develop rapidly and to perfect themselves step by step, even though there have existed many deficiencies in this process. It may now be predicted that the rapid progress of the Chinese legal system in future is an irreversible trend of history. And in this process, the characteristics of the Civil Law tradition will continue to stamp themselves upon the Chinese legal system.[69]

Notes

1. See generally René David and John E. C. Brierley, *Major Legal Systems in the World Today* (3rd ed.; London: Stevens & Sons, 1985); K. Zweigert and H. Kötz, *An Introduction to Comparative Law*, trans. Tony Weir (2nd rev. ed.; Oxford: Clarendon Press, 1992); M. A. Glendon, M. W. Gordon and C. Osakwe, *Comparative Legal Traditions in a Nutshell* (St. Paul, MN: West Publishing Co., 1982). For the special affinity between socialist law and the Civil Law tradition from the points of view of historical development, rules, methods, institutions and procedures, see John Quigley, "Socialist Law and the Civil Law Tradition," *American Journal of Comparative Law*, Vol. 37 (1989), p. 781.
2. For a brief account of the legal history of the PRC, see Albert H. Y. Chen, *An Introduction to the Legal System of the People's Republic of China* (Singapore: Butterworths Asia, 1992), chap. 3. For the legal theory and practice of the USSR, see Harold J. Berman, *Justice in the U.S.S.R. — An Interpretation of Soviet Law* (rev. ed.; Cambridge, MA: Harvard University Press, 1963).
3. Qian Mingxing, *Wuquanfa yuanli* (Principles of the Law of Rights over

Things) (Beijing: Beijing daxue chubanshe, 1994), p. 58.

4. The term "civil law" (as opposed to "Civil Law" as used above) is used here to refer to that part of the law governing relations — such as family, property and commercial relations — between private persons, which may be distinguished from that part of the law governing the relationship between the citizen and the state. The term "Civil Law" has an entirely different meaning, referring to the Romano-Germanic legal tradition in the Continental European family of legal systems as mentioned above. For the multiple meanings of the terms "civil law" and "Civil Law," see, e.g., David M. Walker, *The Oxford Companion to Law* (Oxford: Clarendon Press, 1980), p. 222. For a Chinese scholar's views on the meanings of "civil law" and its translation into Chinese, see Wang Honglin, "Tantan 'Civil Law' de hanyi" (On the Meaning of "Civil Law"), *Zhongwai faxue* (Peking University Law Journal), No. 5 (1992), p. 78.

5. See Tong Rou (ed.), *Zhongguo minfa* (Chinese Civil Law) (Beijing: Falü chubanshe, 1990); Jin Ping (ed.), *Zhongguo minfa xue* (Chinese Civil Law Science) (Chengdu: Sichuan renmin chubanshe, 1990); Liu Jingwei (ed.), *Zhongguo minfa* (Chinese Civil Law) (Xiamen: Xiamen daxue chubanshe, 1994). These works may be contrasted with the following work, which shows the older and more conservative approach: Ma Yuan (ed.), *Zhongguo minfa jiaocheng* (Textbook of Chinese Civil Law) (Beijing: Renmin fayuan chubanshe, 1989).

6. The following discussion on Roman law draws on the following sources: William A. Hunter, *Introduction to Roman Law*, revised by F. H. Lawton (9th rev. ed.; London: Sweet & Maxwell, 1934); Barry Nicholas, *An Introduction to Roman Law* (Oxford: Clarendon Press, 1962); Fritz Schulz, *Classical Roman Law* (Oxford: Clarendon Press, 1951); Andrew Borkowski, *Textbook on Roman Law* (London: Blackstone Press, 1994).

7. Nicholas, ibid., pp. 99–100. The notes in square brackets are supplied by myself.

8. Quoted in Jiang Ping and Mi Jian, "Lun minfa chuantong yu dangdai Zhongguo falü (xia)" (The Civil Law Tradition and Contemporary Chinese Law [Part II]), *Zhengfa luntan* (Tribune of Political Science and Law), No. 3 (1993), pp. 1–8, at p. 7 (my own translation from the Chinese) (the article is also reprinted in *Faxue* [Science of Law], No. 11 [1993], p. 82).

9. Chen (Note 2), pp. 192–93.

10. For a detailed discussion in English of the GPCL, see *Law and Contemporary Problems*, Vol. 52, Nos. 2 and 3 (1989), special issue on "The Emerging Framework of Chinese Civil Law," and William Jones, "Some Questions regarding the Significance of the General Provisions of Civil Law of the People's Republic of China," *Harvard International Law Journal*, Vol. 28 (1987), p. 309. For the history of the drafting of this law, see Edward J.

Epstein, "The Evolution of China's General Principles of Civil Law," *American Journal of Comparative Law*, Vol. XXXIV, No. 4 (1986), p. 705.

11. David and Brierly (Note 1), pp. 290–95. See also Berman (Note 2), pp. 158–61.

12. See Yang Lixin and Yin Yan, "Woguo tawuquan zhidu de chongxin gouzao" (The Reconstruction of China's System of *Tawuquan* [Rights Over Other Things]), *Zhongguo shehui kexue* (Social Sciences in China), No. 3 (1995), pp. 78–93, at p. 95; Shi Haoming, "Woguo minfa wuquan zhidu de lifa wanshan" (The Perfection of the Law on the System of Rights Over Things in Chinese Civil Law), *Qinghai shehui kexue* (Qinghai Social Science), No. 1 (1994), p. 112, reprinted in *Faxue*, No. 4 (1994), p. 71.

13. See the discussion in Chen (Note 2), pp. 196–201.

14. See Yang and Yin (Note 12); Shi (Note 12); Jia Dengxun, "Chutan diyaquan de xingzhi ji xingwei" (A Preliminary Inquiry into the Nature and Acts of a Mortgage), *Lanzhou daxue xuebao: shekeban* (Lanzhou University Journal: Social Science Section), No. 1 (1994), p. 120, reprinted in *Faxue*, No. 4 (1994), p. 95.

15. See Jin (Note 5), chaps. 8 and 13–16; Liu (Note 5), part III; Tong (Note 5), part IV.

16. See, e.g., Qian (Note 3), p. 130; Shi (Note 12); Yang and Yin (Note 12).

17. See the Land Administration Law (*Tudi guanlifa*) (1986) as amended in 1988 (in accordance with the constitutional amendments introduced in 1988), the Provisional Regulations on the Grant and Transfer of the Right to Use State-owned Land in Cities and Towns (*Chengzhen guoyou tudi shiyongquan chuyang he zhuanyang zanxing tiaoli*) (1990), and the Urban Real Estate Administration Law (*Chengshi fangdichan guanlifa*) (1994). As pointed out in Zhongguo shehui kexueyuan faxue yanjiusuo wuquanfa yanjiu ketizu (Project Group of the Institute of Law, Chinese Academy of Social Science on Research on Rights Over Things), "Zhiding Zhongguo wuquanfa de jiben silu" (Basic Ideas regarding the Making of the Law of Rights over Things in China), *Faxue yanjiu* (Studies in Law), No. 3 (1995), pp. 3–10, at p. 7, it is not yet completely clear whether such land-use rights are a kind of *wuquan* or a kind of *zhaiquan*, although the better view is certainly that they are a kind of *wuquan*.

18. See Frederick Tse-shyang Chen, "Chattel Security Interests," in *Trade and Investment in Taiwan: the Legal and Economic Environment in the Republic of China*, edited by Herbert H. P. Ma (2nd ed.; Taipei: Institute of American Culture, Academia Sinica, 1985), chap. 16, pp. 622 ff.

19. See Niger G. Foster, *German Law and Legal System* (London: Blackstone Press, 1993), p. 255; E. J. Cohn, *Manual of German Law*, Vol. I (2nd rev. ed.; London: British Institute of International and Comparative Law, 1968), p. 186.

20. Hiroshi Oda, *Japanese Law* (London: Butterworths, 1992), p. 173.
21. See Gao Chengde, *Zhongguo gongsifa shiwu* (The Practice of Chinese Company Law) (Beijing: Qiye guanli chubanshe, 1994), pp. 10–16.
22. See Feng Xiaoguang, *Gongsifa* (Company Law) (Beijing: Zhongguo heping chubanshe, 1994), p. 27.
23. See Herbert H. P. Ma, "General Features of the Law and Legal System of the Republic of China," in Ma (Note 18), chap. 1, at p. 17.
24. Jiang Ping, "Gongsifa suo jianli de xiandai qiye falü jizhi" (The Legal Institutions of the Modern Business Enterprise Established by the Company Law), *Lilun xuexi yu tansuo* (Theoretical Studies and Inquiries), No. 3 (1994), p. 2, reprinted in *Jingji faxue* (Science of Economic Law), No. 2 (1995), p. 31.
25. See generally Tingmei Fu, "Legal Person in China: Essence and Limits," *American Journal of Comparative Law*, Vol. XLI, No. 2 (1993), p. 261.
26. See Chen (Note 2), p. 194.
27. See Jiang (Note 24); Li Fei, "Legislative Consideration on Company Law, PRC," *China Law* (*Zhongguo falü*, bilingual), No. 1 (1995), p. 76.
28. As pointed out in Jiang (Note 24) and Li (Note 27).
29. For the basic terms and concepts in Japanese and European company law, see generally Oda (Note 20); Haig Oghigian (ed.), *The Law of Commerce in Japan* (New York: Prentice Hall, 1993); S. N. Frommel and J. H. Thompson (eds), *Company Law in Europe* (London: Kluwer-Harraap, 1975); Julian Maitland-Walker, *Guide to European Company Laws* (London: Sweet & Maxwell, 1993); Nobert Horn et al., *German Private and Commercial Law*, trans. Tony Weir (Oxford: Clarendon Press, 1982); E. J. Cohn, *Manual of German Law*, Vol. II (2nd rev. ed.; London: British Institute of International and Comparative Law, 1971); F. H. Lawson et al., *Amos & Walton's Introduction to French Law* (3rd ed.; Oxford: Clarendon Press, 1967).
30. For the English translation of the ROC Company Law, see Law Revision Planning Group, C.U.S.A., Executive Yuan, Republic of China (trans. and compiled), *Laws of the Republic of China: First Series* (Taipei, 1961). For an up-to-date account, see Francis S. L. Wang, "Company Law of the Republic of China," in Ma (Note 18 above), chap. 14.
31. See Li (Note 27); Zeng Huaqun and Li Shufeng, *Zhongguang gongsifa falü shiwu* (Company Law and Practice in China and Hong Kong) (Hong Kong: Commercial Press, 1994), p. 11.
32. Renmin ribao pinglunyuan (commentator of the People's Daily), "Jianli xiandai qiye zhidu de zhongyao jucuo" (An Important Measure for Establishing a Modern Enterprise System), in *Zhonghua renmin gongheguo gongsifa* (The Company Law of the People's Republic of China) (Beijing: Renmin ribao chubanshe, 1994), pp. 65–67.
33. Jiang (Note 24); Wang Baoshu, "Xiandai qiye zhidu de jidian falü sikao" (Some Legal Reflections on the Modern Enterprise System), *Fazhi ribao*

(Legal System Daily), 13 January 1995. p. 6, reprinted in *Jingji faxue*, No. 1 (1995), p. 41.

34. For the text of the 1954 Constitution, see Chen Hefu (ed.), *Zhongguo xianfa leibian* (Compilation of Chinese Constitutions) (Beijing: Zhongguo shehui kexue chubanshe, 1980), p. 213.

35. See Gu Angran, "Guojia peichangfa zhiding qingkuang he zhuyao wenti" (The Circumstances of the Enactment of the State Compensation Law and Its Main Issues), *Zhongguo faxue* (Chinese Legal Science), No. 2 (1995), p. 16.

36. See Zhu Weijiu and Jiang Tianbo, "Guojia peichang yu minshi peichang chutan" (A Preliminary Inquiry Into State Compensation and Civil Compensation), *Faxue pinglun* (Law Review), No. 2 (1993), p. 10; Jiang Bixin, "Of China's Present State Compensation System," *China Law*, No. 1 (1995), p. 80.

37. For a discussion of these regulations, see Chen (Note 2), pp. 177–78; 204–5. Amendments to the regulations were subsequently introduced by the National People's Congress's Standing Committee in May 1994.

38. For a discussion of this law, see Chen (Note 2), pp. 178–80; Susan Finder, "Like Throwing an Egg Against a Stone? Administrative Litigation in the People's Republic of China," *Journal of Chinese Law*, Vol. 3. No. 1 (1989), p. 1; Song Ping, "Assessing China's System of Judicial Review of Administrative Actions," *China Law Reporter*, Vol. VIII, Nos. 1–2 (1994), p. 1.

39. It is interesting to note in this regard that Taiwan's procedural law is similarly composed of three basic codes bearing the same titles as their PRC counterparts.

40. See Jiang (Note 36); Pi Chunxie and Feng Jun (eds), *Guojia peichangfa shilun* (Commentary on the State Compensation Law) (Beijing: Zhongguo fazhi chubanshe, 1994), p. 3.

41. See Gu (Note 35), p. 18.

42. See Chen (Note 2), pp. 166–68, 204–5.

43. Pi and Feng (Note 40), p. 114.

44. Ibid., p. 115.

45. Ibid., pp. 117–18.

46. For a detailed analysis and commentary, see Pi and Feng (Note 40), pp. 198–200.

47. For the distinction between detention and arrest, see Chen (Note 2), pp. 155–57. Arrest must be based on prior approval by the procuratorate or the court, whereas detention may occur without such approval provided that there exist the circumstances specified in law as justifying detention. However, detention cannot normally last for more than three days, while the period for which the suspect may be kept in custody after arrest can be much longer.

48. For the distinction between the normal appeal procedure and the adjudicatory supervisory procedure, see Chen (Note 2 above), pp. 160–61. A convicted

person may appeal against his/her conviction or sentence within certain time limits. If the person does not appeal within the time limit, or if the person appeals but the appeal is dismissed by the higher court, then the judgement is said to be legally effective. However, there is still the possibility of it being overturned according to the adjudicatory supervisory procedure, which may be initiated by the convicted person, the president of the court that gave the judgement, a higher court, or a procuratorate at a higher level.

49. Pi and Feng (Note 40), pp. 311–12.
50. See Pi and Feng (Note 40); Huang Jie et al., *Guojia peichangfa shiyi yu jiangzuo* (Commentaries and Lectures on the State Compensation Law) (Beijing: Zhongguo renmin gong'an daxue chubanshe, 1994); Jiang Bixin, *Guojia peichangfa yuanli* (Principles of State Compensation Law) (Beijing: Zhongguo renmin gong'an daxue chubanshe, 1994); Jin Liqi et al., *Guojia peichangfa yuanli* (Principles of State Compensation Law) (Beijing: Zhongguo guangbo dianshi chubanshe, 1990).
51. See, e.g., Cheng Zhongmo, *Xingzhengfa zhi jichu lilun* (Basic Theory of Administrative Law) (Taipei: Sanmin shuju, 1980); Weng Yuesheng, *Fazhi guojia zhi xingzhengfa yu sifa* (Administrative Law and the Judiciary in a Rule-of-Law State) (Taipei: Yuedan chubanshe, 1994); Chen Xinmin, *Xingzheng faxue zonglun* (A General Treatise on Administrative Law) (5th ed.; Taipei: Sanmin shuju, 1995).
52. Weng (Note 51), p. 160.
53. Cheng (Note 51), pp. 581, 631.
54. See the works cited in Note 50.
55. See Gu (Note 35).
56. See Pi and Feng (Note 40), pp. 201–3.
57. See Note 48.
58. See Jiang (Note 36).
59. See the discussion in Wang Kewen, "Guojia peichang zhidu: Jinri Zhongguo liangzhong chuantong zhi bijiao" (State Compensation Systems: A Comparison of Two Traditions in Contemporary Chihna), in *Jiaqi faxi jian de qiaoliang* (Erecting a Bridge between Families of Legal Systems), edited by Yan Haikun (Suzhou: Suzhou daxue chubanshe, 1995), p. 180, at p. 184.
60. Ibid., p. 185.
61. See, e.g., Pi and Feng (Note 40), pp. 302–7.
62. Chen (Note 2), pp. 117–23. These problems have not been resolved by the enactment of the Law on Judges (*Faguanfa*) in February 1995.
63. See Pi and Feng (Note 40), pp. 304–7.
64. See Li Shuguang, "Zhongguo falü xiandaihua de quxiang" (The Orientation of the Modernization of Chinese law), *Faxue* (Jurisprudence) (Shanghai), No. 4 (1994), p. 2.
65. For changing views on the question of the "heritability" of pre-revolutionary

2. The Developing Chinese Law and the Civil Law Tradition

law, see Eugene Kamenka and Alice Tay, "Marxism-Leninism and the Heritability of Law," *Review of Socialist Law*, Vol. 6 (1980), p. 261; Wang Yongfei and Zhang Guicheng, *Zhongguo falixue yanjiu zongshu yu pingjia* (Summary and Evaluation of Research in Chinese Jurisprudence) (Beijing: Zhongguo zhengfa daxue chubanshe, 1992), chap. 5; Zheng Chengliang and Xu Weidong, "Lun falü de lishi jichengxing" (On the Historical Heritability of Law), *Jilin daxue shehui kexue xuebao* (Jilin University Social Science Journal), No. 5 (1991), p. 37.

66. For an attempt to explain this choice, see Li (Note 64).

67. See generally Albert H. Y. Chen, "The Developing Theory of Law and Market Economy in Contemporary China," forthcoming (chapter in book on law and market economy in China to be published by Sweet & Maxwell).

68. For a contemporary Chinese scholar's theory of law as a cultural phenomenon, see Liang Zhiping, "The Cultural Interpretation of Law," in *Chinese Social Sciences Year Book*, edited by Deng Zhenglai (Hong Kong: Hong Kong Social Sciences Service Centre, 1994), p. 196.

69. Jiang and Mi (Note 8), p. 7 (my own translation from the Chinese).

3

Corruption and Politics

Andrew Wedeman

Introduction

Corruption transformed itself from a latent, unintended consequence of reform into a manifest political variable with a bang, literally, in 1995. On 4 April, shortly after being questioned about US$37 million in financial irregularities, Beijing Vice-Mayor Wang Baosen put a pistol to his head and committed suicide. Twenty-three days later, Chen Xitong resigned from his post as Beijing municipal party committee first secretary and was placed under house arrest amid rumours that he had misappropriated US$24 million from municipal coffers. In September, Chen was expelled from the Political Bureau of the Chinese Communist Party (CCP), thus becoming the most senior victim of CCP General Secretary Jiang Zemin's six-year old "war on corruption" and the first Politburo member sacked since Zhao Ziyang.

The death of Wang and the fall of Chen triggered intense speculation. Wang, according to various sources, killed himself to protect Chen.[1] Others claimed that Chen's henchmen murdered Wang in a desperate effort to prevent him from testifying against Chen.[2] According to another rumour, after concluding that prosecutors were closing in on them, Chen ordered Wang to kill himself and even provided the gun.[3] Yet another story claimed that Wang killed himself after his confederates in the Beijing apparatus betrayed and abandoned him.[4] Wang had allegedly shared his ill gotten gains widely, building luxury villas for himself and other members of the Beijing leadership, and his suicide was a warning to others. Still other rumours hinted that Wang was assassinated in a Mafia-style hit as rival "gangs" battled for control of Beijing.[5]

Other analysts pointed to parallels between the Chen-Wang case and the opening rounds of the Cultural Revolution,[6] arguing that just as Mao had begun his attack on the "capitalist roader" faction led by Liu Shaoqi and Deng Xiaoping by first attacking Beijing vice-mayor Wu Han and then Beijing first secretary and Politburo member Peng Zhen, Jiang Zemin would use corruption in the Beijing apparatus as an excuse to open a political offensive against rival factions within the CCP leadership.[7] Chen and Jiang had clashed, it was said, earlier in the year over the appointments of Jiang Chunyun and Wu Bangguo as vice-premiers.[8] Angered by Chen's attacks on his "Shanghai clique" and efforts to rally opposition in the National People's Congress (NPC), Jiang seized the opportunities presented by Wang's suicide and Chen Yun's death six days later to purge Chen Xitong, cripple the "Beijing clique" and, thereby, pave the way for attacks on other centres of resistance, including most immediately the "regional lords" (*difang zhuhou*) led by the "Guangdong clique," but also Premier Li Peng and his conservative faction.[9]

Even though the Wang-Chen case did not trigger the long-anticipated post-Deng power struggle, the case raises anew questions about the impact of corruption on Chinese politics and the politics of Jiang Zemin's six-year old war on corruption. Political scientists tend to view corruption as a normal part of all political systems whose primary political significance derives from its negative impact on regime legitimacy. Always present, corruption only becomes politically salient when it leads to political decay, progressively undermining the regime from within, while stimulating opposition from without. Because it is assumed that quantitative and qualitative increases in corruption lead to the onset of political decay, much of the existing literature on corruption concentrates on the question of causality rather than consequence. This focus on causality has led various scholars to argue that increasing corruption in post-Mao China results from a volatile combination of (a) structural contradictions between a quasi-marketized economy and a Leninist political superstructure in which cadres operate largely outside the law, (b) macro-economic contradictions that create economic rents, (c) the displacement of revolutionary idealism by a "culture of corruption," new opportunities and increased payoffs resulting from rapid economic growth, and (d) Deng's willingness to tolerate corruption as a means of generating élite support for reform.[10]

According to conventional wisdom, the explosive growth of corruption has become a threat to the survival of the CCP. Drawing on Johnston, Sun and Meaney argue that increases in the number of officials engaged in corruption and the size of payoffs received from corrupt activity have led to the onset of "disintegrative corruption," which, as Meaney summarizes it, "engender[s] increasing disaffection among the populace, while at the same time rendering the regime incapable of effective response."[11] Holmes expands on this theme, suggesting that once the rot of corruption has set in, communist regimes become trapped. Anti-corruption clean-ups, he argues, actually accelerate the process of delegitimization and internal fragmentation by laying bare the contradictions between regime ideals and behaviour and pitting regime leaders against the rank and file of the party-state.[12]

Although it may help explain the growth of anti-government agitation during the spring of 1989, the "crisis of legitimacy" model described above proves to be of limited utility in defining the political significance of corruption in general, or explaining the political consequences of specific cases such as the Wang-Chen scandal. The model's primary shortcoming is that it is a macroscopic "punctuated equilibrium model" in which corruption is defined as an episodic and catastrophic variable. Because anti-government agitation entails high risks for potential demonstrators, even though it may fuel discontent, corruption must reach some relatively high level before the crisis of legitimacy erupts into tangible, and hence consequential, political activity. So long as it remains below that threshold, corruption remains politically dormant, a source of popular discontent but not tangible political movement. Although it is difficult to determine exactly where the threshold lies and to accurately gauge the popular mood, existing evidence suggest that at present the level of popular anger remains below the point at which mass instability is likely. From the perspective of the crisis of legitimacy model, therefore, corruption was not politically salient during 1995.

The Wang-Chen case shows, however, that corruption does influence the political process in the absence of massive anti-government demonstrations. Six years prior to Wang's suicide the regime locked itself into a protracted war against corruption, deeming it a matter of "life and death." Although this campaign is often dismissed as political window dressing, a public relations exercise in which the government periodically drags out a motley collection of small fry to prove its commitment to honest government, the regime's ongoing efforts to eradicate corruption create a potential source of political instability, not at the mass level, but rather at the leadership level. In theory, corruption is a potent weapon in factional infighting. In actuality, however, corruption is a very dangerous double edge sword. Not only might charges of high-level corruption trigger mass mobilization, more immediately they have the potential to trigger intense factional warfare.

Corruption is even more dangerous because the leadership cannot entirely control the evolution of the war on corruption. China's war on corruption has spawned a complex investigatory bureaucracy, including specialized anti-corruption bureaus within the Supreme People's Procuratorate, the Supreme People's Court and provincial-level procuratorates, as well as efforts to increase operational coordination between party and state by strengthening the links between the party's Central Discipline Inspection Commission (CDIC) and the Ministry of Supervision. Control over the pace and direction of the war, therefore, no longer resides solely at the top but is now shared between the top leadership and the anti-corruption bureaucracy. Division of control, in turn, means that the leadership cannot orchestrate the war and must cope with episodic scandal and the élite instability that they produce, with the net result that corruption becomes a constant political factor even though it does not necessarily represent an immediate threat to regime survival.

China's Protracted War Against Corruption

The current war on corruption began in July 1989, almost immediately after the violent suppression of anti-government demonstrations for which corruption was a critical rallying point.[13] The post-1989 war is, however, essentially a continuation of a fight against corruption that began with the 1982–1986 Party Rectification Campaign.[14] After slowly gaining momentum during 1986, the first phase of the war wound down when the struggle against corruption was eclipsed by the Campaign Against Bourgeois Liberalization in the early months of 1987.[15] Following a discernible lull during 1987 and the spring of 1988,[16] the war resumed in the summer of 1988 with the announcement of a new "full scale fight against corruption."[17] Despite some increase in intensity during late 1988 and early 1989, however, the war did not escalate significantly until after Tiananmen. Since then, the leadership has launched three distinct offensives, the first in the fall of 1989, the second between August and November 1993, and the third beginning in March 1995. Despite variations in intensity, therefore, the regime has been actively fighting corruption for roughly 13 years as of 1995.

The success of China's protracted war against corruption is difficult to measure. Because the parties to corrupt acts have strong incentives to hide their activities, it is inherently difficult to get reliable data on corruption. To the extent that hard data exist, they are found in the form of statistics on legal actions taken against those engaged in corruption. Assuming that one has access to time-series data, that they have not been cooked by their publishers, and that they reliably report the number of cases initiated by investigators and the number of cases actually prosecuted, such data at best measure the "revealed rate" of corruption, not the actual rate. The revealed rate equals the actual rate, times the percentage of cases detected, times the percentage of cases where sufficient evidence exists to pursue formal legal action, times the percentage of cases actually pursued, plus or minus random error.[18] Changes in the revealed rate of corruption offer one way of analysing trends in corruption, but one must be very clear about what the data mean. Increases in the revealed rate of corruption are primarily reflective of changes in the intensity of enforcement. Even though changes in enforcement may be a response to changes in the actual rate of corruption, that is increases in the actual rate of corruption may trigger anti-corruption clean-ups and hence raise the revealed rate, there will inevitably be lags between changes in the actual and revealed rates.

Quantitative data on the revealed rate of corruption in China are surprisingly robust. The available data on the number of economic crime (*jingji fanzui*) cases filed (*lian*) by the procuratorate,[19] which has primary responsibility for prosecuting legally defined cases of corruption,[20] bribery, embezzlement, copyright piracy,[21] tax evasion, and tax resistance, reveal major upswings in 1986 and 1989. The number of cases increased from 28,000 in 1985 to 49,557 in 1986, a 77% rise, and from 32,626 in 1988 to 77,432 in 1989, a 137.33% jump (see Figure 1). Although the number of cases filed in the years after the 1986 and 1989 campaigns fell, the drop off after the 1989 campaign, 7.12%, was considerably less than that after the 1986 campaign, when the number of cases filed in 1987 fell 35.96% compared to 1986. The 1989 offensive, therefore, led to significant increases in the average number of cases filed each year. Nevertheless, the early 1990s witnessed a definite downward trend, with the number of cases dropping to a low of 56,491 in 1993, a 8.03% decrease compared to 1992 and a 27.04% drop compared to 1989, this despite the announcement of a new anti-corruption drive in August 1993.

In 1994, the number of cases filed began to climb again, rising 6.76% that year. In 1995, the number of economic crime cases filed rose another 6.04%, reaching a total of 63,593, a 13% jump over 1993.[22] Trends in investigations of corruption (*tanwu*) and bribery cases (*shouhui*), which constitute a sub-category of economic crime, generally parallel the overall trends in economic crime. As a percentage of all economic crimes, however, bribery and corruption have fallen from a peak of 76% in 1989 to a low of 55% in 1993 and 60% in 1994, with most of the decline due to increases in the number of embezzlement cases.[23]

Party disciplinary commissions, meanwhile, investigated a total 429,913 cases of cadre malfeasance between August 1993 and May 1995, over 40% of them involving charges of corruption. As a result of these investigations, 237,627 cadres were punished, including 35 cadres at the provincial and ministerial levels, 546 at the prefectoral level, and 6,582 at the county level. During the first half of 1995, party discipline inspectors handled 75,445 cases, up 4.8% from the 71,994 cases handled during the first half

Figure 1. Procuratorial Investigations

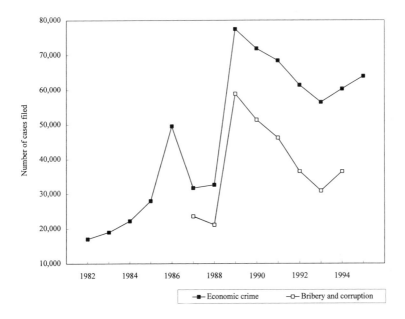

Sources: Annual report to the National People's Congress by the Supreme
Procuratorate, 1986–1992, reproduced in *Zhongguo jiancha nianjian*
(Procuratorial Yearbook of China) (Beijing: Jiancha chubanshe, 1987–1993);
1993 in *Renmin dahui gongbao* (Bulletin of the National People's Congress);
1994, No. 3 (15 April), 1994 in *BBC Summary of World Broadcasts* (*BBCSWB*),
4 April 1995. Data for 1982–1985 from "The Fight Against Economic Crime in
1985;" *Xinhua*, 6 April 1986, in *BBCSWB*, 12 April 1986; "Report of the
Supreme People's Procuratorate," *Xinhua*, 15 April 1985, in *BBCSWB*, 24 April
1985; "Report of Supreme People's Procuratorate," *Xinhua*, 6 June 1984, in
BBCSWB, 19 June 1984; "Work Report of the Supreme People's
Procuratorate," *Xinhua*, 25 June 1983, in *BBCSWB*, 29 June 1983.

of 1994. As of June 1995, 47,560 party members had been disciplined, a
15.04% increase over the 41,341 party members disciplined in the first half
of 1994.[24]

Because we cannot estimate the actual rate of corruption with any
real accuracy, it is difficult to determine exactly what these numbers mean.
We cannot, for example, determine whether the anti-corruption war has
actually reduced corruption. Recent cases suggest, at least anecdotally, that
tougher enforcement has not reduced corruption. Many of the major cases
uncovered during the 1993 and 1995 campaigns, for example, involved

criminal activity stretching back to the early 1990s, that is after Jiang escalated the anti-corruption struggle in 1989. This suggests that the post-Tiananmen escalation has failed to deter cadres from engaging in corruption, even though intuitively, by raising the risk of detection, anti-corruption clean-ups should deter rational actors from engaging in corruption. Whether the deterrent affect of the campaign has been wholly or partially offset by increases in payoffs is difficult to determine with any precision.[25]

Because raw numbers provide only a sense of the pace of the anti-corruption war, an additional analytical framework is needed to evaluate the political impact of the war. Gillespie and Okruhlik argue that corruption clean-ups should be studied in terms of (a) political context, (b) stimulus, (c) objectives, (d) strategies, and (e) consequence.[26] In their terms, the political context of China's war on corruption is a combination of "incumbent" and "post-succession" incumbent in the sense that the war has been conducted under the uninterrupted rule of the Communist Party and the guidance of party patriarch Deng Xiaoping, post-succession in the sense that Jiang Zemin is in the process of consolidating his position as Deng's *de facto* political successor.

The dual nature of the political context means that the stimulus for the war comes not from one source but rather three distinct sources. First, the war is clearly a response to "external threat," that is, threats from outside the party-state structure and specifically the negative impact on regime legitimacy caused by popular discontent with élite corruption. Second, the war is a response to "internal threat," that is, threats from within the party-state structure. Throughout the reform period, the centre has experienced difficulty maintaining control over subordinate levels of the party-state hierarchy, as evidenced by, *inter alia*, local protectionism (*difang baohu zhuyi*), arbitrary taxation and exploitation (known colloquially as the three disruptions or *sanluan*), as well as widespread misappropriation of cash allocated to purchase agricultural commodities and the illegal use of IOUs (*baitiaozi*). Abstractly, each of these represents a form of "institutional corruption" and is the same as individualized corruption in that it involves the violation of official norms and the pursuit of particularistic gain, albeit by institutions rather than individuals in the case of local protectionism, etc. Because the war on corruption seeks to increase compliance with norms defined by the leadership, it represents a response to breakdowns in hierarchical control over the party-state. Third, the war is a response to Jiang's political vulnerabilities. Thrust into the role of general secretary amid the crisis of 1989, Jiang's hold on power has, heretofore, depended heavily on the patronage of Deng Xiaoping. With Deng now politically incapacitated, Jiang has sought to strengthen his formal position by traditional factional means (i.e., the appointment of allies to key posts) and by proving to both the party-state apparatus and society that he will attack deep-seated social problems. To a not insignificant extent, in fact, Jiang has tried to build up a popular image of himself as an anti-corruption fighter.

Multiple stimuli mean that the anti-corruption effort has multiple objectives: maintaining regime legitimacy, enhancing regime cohesion, and consolidating Jiang's position as supreme leader. Given its context, stimulus, and objectives, so long as corruption continues to stimulate popular discontent and erode hierarchical control, and Jiang remains politically vulnerable, the war on corruption becomes an open-ended commitment. Quite simply, so long as he cannot produce a clear-cut victory over corruption, or at least credibly declare victory, Jiang Zemin must continue the fight, using periodic offensives and harsh rhetoric to demonstrate his commitment to the war. Oscillations in the number of cases filed by the procuratorate and tried by the courts are therefore primarily evidence of the ebb and flow of a protracted war against corruption.

There has, however, been a qualitative change in the struggle in recent years. Even though it failed to produce an increase in the number of cases filed, the 1993 offensive witnessed an intensification and escalation of the conflict. Whereas earlier drives had fallen primarily on low and mid-level cadres, since 1993 the war on corruption has fallen much more heavily on high-level cadres. Not only has the number of major cases (defined as cases involving in excess of *Renminbi* [RMB] 10,000)[27] filed increased significantly in the past three years (see Figure 2). More important, the number of cadres holding positions at the county and higher levels charged with corrupt acts has shot up dramatically, rising from just 190 in 1989 to 875 in 1990, 1,827 in 1994, and possibly 2,262 in 1995, and the number of death sentences handed down for corruption-related offenses has increased, with 375 death sentences handed down since the beginning of 1993 (see Figure 3).[28] The number of senior cadres disciplined by party disciplinary organs has also increased significantly, up 45% from 1,225 during the first half of 1994 to approximately 1,800 in the first six months of 1995.[29]

Although the war continues to concentrate on low-level corruption, this qualitative change implies a shift in strategy. Prior to 1993, the

Figure 2. Major Economic Crime and Corruption

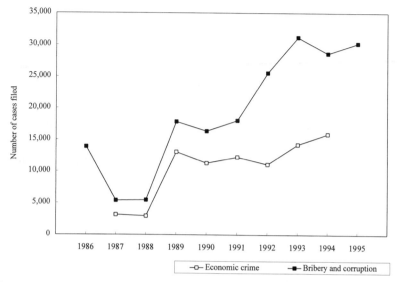

Sources: See Figure 1.

Figure 3. Severity of Anticorruption Drive

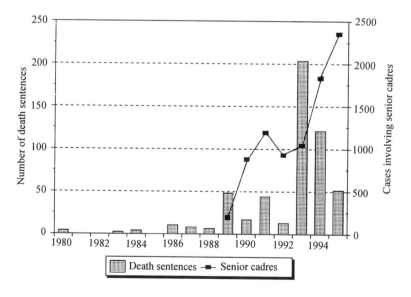

Sources: Figure 1 and author's data base.

regime's strategy for dealing with high-level corruption appears to have been one of deterrence. Instead of attacking high-level corruption directly, the leadership relied on an indirect strategy that, to use the Chinese terminology, assumed "killing the chickens would scare the monkeys" (*sha ji xia hou*). This strategy has not, however, worked satisfactorily and in recent years investigators have pursued high-level corruption more vigorously, seeking to root out corruption as well as deter it. Tiger hunting (*da laohu*) can, however, be dangerous, as Jiang Zemin discovered when investigators accidentally bagged several tiger cubs while hunting chickens in Wuxi.

The Wang-Chen Case

The Wang-Chen case came to light after the collapse of a Ponzi scheme involving the Xinxing Industrial Corporation based in Wuxi, Jiangsu.[30] Promising investors returns of up to 5 to 10% per month and offering to pay a portion of the profits in advance, Xinxing President Deng Bin, a former nurse who claimed to be in the medical supply business, raised RMB 3.2 billion from 368 state enterprises and 31 individuals in 12 provinces between August 1989 and July 1994, using a string of sub-sidiary firms in Wuxi, Jiangyang, and Shenzhen to funnel investments into Xinxing. Deng and her confederates concentrated heavily on state institu-tions and enterprises, using bribes, women, and other "considerations" to convince cadres to hand over funds from their extra-budgetary capital development accounts and monies held in off-the-books slush funds (*xiao jinku*). Cadres apparently believed that they could make quick under-the-table profits by investing in Xinxing, which they could then pocket without actually stealing public funds, a ruse that skirted criminal embezzlement. The scheme began to unravel when Deng stopped paying dividends and could not return investors' capital, at which point either some investors went to the police or auditors discovered the missing funds.[31]

At first, Deng managed to escape prosecution because of Xinxing's extensive connections (*guanxi*). Xinxing had been set up by the Ministry of State Security and had particularly close ties with its Third Bureau.[32] Xinxing established intimate ties to the Wuxi procuratorate and public security apparatus by recruiting Jin Huizhen, a retired police officer and the wife of Gao Zhenjia, the chief prosecutor. Other bureaus in Wuxi were bought off with bribes and gifts. Meanwhile, Xinxing's parent company,

Beijing Xinlong, had close ties with the Ministry of State Security, thus helping Deng to cover up the extent of Xinxing's losses and slow the investigation. As a result, it was not until July 1994, when investigators from the central government took over the investigation, that the scam finally collapsed and the principals were arrested. In November 1995, Deng, Xinlong Deputy Manager Han Wanlong, and four others (Yao Jingyi, Wang Guifeng, Jin Weichun, and Dai Baochun) were tried and convicted. Deng and Yao were executed. Wang received a death sentence with a two year stay. The others received sentences ranging from 4 to 20 years. Concurrently, 123 cadres were disciplined by the party, including 41 who were expelled from the party. Among those stripped of their party membership and sacked from their state posts were Wuxi Deputy Mayor Ding Haoxin, Wuxi Chief Procurator Gao Zhenjia, and vice-chairman of the Wuxi Chinese People's Political Consultative Conference Ni Pinliang.

In the process of sorting through the Xinxing mess, central investigators detained two members of the Beijing municipal apparatus: Chen Jian, one of Chen Xitong's secretaries, and Li Min, the deputy chief of the Beijing Security Bureau and former secretary to Beijing Mayor Li Qiyan.[33] Both Li Min and Chen Jian admitted channeling money from state units in Beijing, including the Beijing Public Security Bureau where Li Min worked, into Xinxing and accepting bribes from Deng. Both Li and Chen, however, had considerably more money than Deng had given them. Under interrogation, Li eventually revealed that he had received a bribe from Zhou Beifang, the chairman of Shougang Holdings (HK), a Hong Kong-based investment firm, in return for getting Hong Kong residency papers for Zhou's wife and daughter. Chen, meanwhile, confessed he had accepted bribes from a businessman, Wu Xiaofan, in return for helping Wu convince Beijing Vice-Major Wang Baosen to invest over US$10 million in various ventures. The collapse of Xinxing, therefore, led investigators in two directions, one toward Zhou Beifang and the other toward Wang Baosen.

Prosecutors may have been suspicious of Zhou Beifang even before Li Min confessed.[34] Shougang, a vast conglomerate of state-owned enterprises, also known as Capital Iron and Steel, had a history of corruption. In 1992, its party secretary, Guan Zhicheng, was executed for corruption.[35] Two years later, another company official was sentenced to 15 years imprisonment for accepting bribes. In January 1995, two managers of Shougang affiliates received suspended death sentences and a third was sentenced to ten years imprisonment for accepting bribes. During

1993, allegations surfaced of kickbacks paid to senior company officials in connection with the purchase of an iron mine in Peru and a steel mill in the United States. Analysts in Hong Kong, meanwhile, had begun to question the corporation's financial health, believing that even though the firm claimed profits of close to US$700 million in 1994, a three year buying spree on the Hong Kong stock exchange had left the corporation badly over extended and strapped for cash. Most observers, however, assumed that Shougang was untouchable because of the close ties between Zhou's father, Shougang Chairman Zhou Guanwu, and Deng Xiaoping and Zhou Beifang's business partnership with Deng Xiaoping's son, Deng Zhifang. Zhou Beifang's arrest for unspecified "economic crimes" in February 1995 and Zhou Guanwu's immediate retirement from Shougang, came as a shock, leading to the first round of speculation that the post-Deng power struggle had begun.[36]

The Wang case surfaced in April, although investigators had apparently been looking into possible wrongdoing for some time.[37] On 2 April, a four man team consisting of CDIC First Secretary Wei Jianxing, State Councillor Luo Gan, NPC Internal and Judicial Affairs Committee Chairman Wang Fang, and Beijing First Secretary Chen Xitong questioned Wang about a RMB 1 billion loan to a private telecommunications company.[38] Wang was also apparently asked about his role in approving the US$1.2 billion Oriental Plaza project.[39] Finally, the team may have also questioned Wang about his role in approving a massive redevelopment project in the Ritan district.[40] Two days after his meeting with investigators, Wang killed himself.

Investigators subsequently charged that Wang had (a) embezzled RMB 250,000 and US$20,000 from public coffers; (b) funnelled RMB 100 million and US$25 million from municipal accounts into corporations controlled by his mistress, his brother Wang Baochuan (an official with a Beijing bank), and others; and (c) improperly authorized bank loans to various cronies.[41] Wang was not, however, charged with accepting bribes from the main developer behind the Oriental Plaza project, Hong Kong real estate mogul Li Ka-shing, even though Wang was believed to have been paid for his help in arranging real estate deals. Investigators were unable to account for all the funds he allegedly stole. In addition to squandering considerable sums on fast living and a luxury villa in Huairou, Wang reportedly "lost" US$13 million, including US$10 million he transferred to a Hong Kong-based company some time in 1994.[42]

In the wake of Wang's suicide, the scandal spread rapidly. On 28

April, Chen Xitong formally resigned from his position as Beijing first secretary, accepting "unshirkable responsibility for Wang Baosen's case," and was replaced on an interim basis by Wei Jianxing.[43] Shortly thereafter, Chen Xitong's wife, the party secretary of the Beijing Municipal Finance Bureau, and his son, Chen Xiaotong, the manager of the joint-venture New Century Hotel, came under scrutiny for their involvement with a string of shady real estate corporations. Prosecutors also reportedly began looking into Chen Xiaotong's involvement in arms sales, illegal fund raising, and possible bank fraud, as well as links between Chen Xiaotong's real estate interests and Wang Baosen.[44] Other investigators turned up a RMB 200 million slush fund controlled by Chen Xitong's office, the origins of which Chen and his secretaries could not adequately explain. Because of his connections with Li Min, Beijing Mayor Li Qiyan came under suspicion of complicity in both the Xinxing and Wang cases. Beijing Vice-Mayor Zhang Baifa, meanwhile, was supposedly questioned about financial irregularities involving the 1990 Asian Games and the "crimes" of his son-in-law, Zhou Beifang.[45] Although both Li Qiyan and Zhang Baifa quickly returned to work, prosecutors subsequently ordered the arrest of Li Jiantong, the deputy head of one of Beijing's district governments, and detained Fang Bingsheng, public security chief of Beijing's Fengtai District, both in connection with illegal real estate deals.[46] In all, ten officials of the Beijing government were detained in connection with the Wang case.[47]

After a two month delay, the CDIC opened a formal investigation of Chen Xitong's affairs in July, looking specifically at Chen's responsibility for RMB 18 billion in financial irregularities during his tenure first as mayor of Beijing and then first secretary, the origins of Chen's RMB 200 million slush fund, and whether Chen had used Wang Baosen and Chen Jian to solicit illegal gifts and considerations from developers.[48] Investigators apparently found sufficient evidence to implicate Chen in corrupt activity and after hearing a report from Wei Jianxing in September, the Central Committee dismissed Chen from the Politburo and the Central Committee at the 5th Plenum of the 14th Central Committee. According to the communiqué announcing the Central Committee's decision, Chen had committed four "serious mistakes": (a) failing to take action against Wang Baosen, (b) leading a "dissolute and extravagant life," (c) abusing his powers "to seek illegal interests for his relatives and other people," and (d) taking advantage of his office to accept valuable gifts.[49] According to internal documents circulated soon thereafter, Chen specifically promoted

Wang despite allegations of corruption and had covered up illegal real estate deals involving his wife, his son, and Wang.[50] In return for Chen's patronage and protection, the document charged, Wang funnelled a share of his ill-gotten gains into Chen's RMB 200 million slush fund.[51] Finally, Chen was charged with having had a mistress, who apparently escaped to Hong Kong shortly after Wang's suicide, taking part of Chen's ill-gotten money with her.[52] Despite these allegations, neither Chen, his wife, or his son were formally charged with any criminal activity. Instead, Chen has ended up in the same political purgatory, at least for the time being, that Zhao Ziyang found himself in after 1989.[53]

How much of the preceding story is actually true is hard to tell. On the one hand, it reads too much like a cheap novel to be real. Yet, there is a certain logic and coherence to the plot, if not all the more racy details. Reduced to its essence, the case involved the diversion of large sums from various slush funds maintained off-the-books by a large number of governmental units and state enterprises, as well as on-the-books capital investment funds, into risky investments, including Xinxing. The collapse of Xinxing robbed these "investors" of their principal and exposed Li Min and Chen Jian, who had been acting as go-betweens. Li and Chen, in turn, led investigators to Zhou Beifang and Wang Baosen. Because Chen Xitong was part of the original team assigned to question Wang, it is possible that he was not a target of the probe during the Xinxing-Wang Baosen phase of the scandal but only came under suspicion after Wang killed himself. Because investigators already had questioned Chen's aide, Chen Jian, it is also possible that they already knew about his activities and his inclusion in the investigative team was a trick. Either way, the key event was the collapse of Xinxing because it triggered the chain of events that led to Wang's suicide and Chen's resignation.

In many ways, the Zhou Beifang case is even simpler. After running up losses speculating on the Hong Kong stock exchange, he initially tried to cover them up by diverting additional funds from Shougang Holdings (HK). Further speculation, however, resulted in further losses and ultimately Zhou, like Nick Leeson in the Barings Bank case in Singapore, could no longer prevent authorities from finding out the extent of Shougang's financial problems. At the same time, Li Min's revelation of Zhou's bribe, linked Zhou, at least tangentially, to the Wuxi scandal.

Complex though all these cases may be, ultimately they arise directly out of criminal activity and the cascading investigation into the collapse of the Xinxing Corporation. Nevertheless, the Wang, Chen and Zhou cases, and to a lesser extent the Deng Bin case, were inherently political. Chen was, after all, a member of the Politburo, the highest ranking CCP official implicated in corruption and, more important, had played a central role in the suppression of anti-government demonstrations in Beijing in 1989. Zhou Beifang, on the other hand, had connections reaching directly into the Deng Xiaoping family and into the ranks of Hong Kong's capitalists. Not only had Zhou's father served under Deng during the anti-Japanese and revolutionary wars, but Zhou and Deng had made the Shougang conglomerate a highly visible symbol of China's new socialist market economy. Zhou Beifang, meanwhile, was in business with Deng Xiaoping's son, Deng Zhifang, who managed Shougang Concord Holdings, Ltd., and Li Ka-shing, who had helped Deng and Zhou set up Shougang Concord Grand in 1993.[54] Zhou Beifang and Deng Zhifang were, in turn, part of the network of "princelings" (*taizidang*) and their murky world of Hong Kong-based "red chip" corporations,[55] many of which were managed by the sons and daughters of senior revolutionaries.[56] Deng Bin, finally, reputedly had ties to the Ministry of State Security. Though they may have been rooted in criminal activity, therefore, the twin Beijing scandals were by their very nature political.

Factional Politics and Corruption

Because of the political sensitivity of the Zhou and Chen cases, many observers jumped to the conclusion that corruption was merely a pretense. According to Gao Xin, Jiang had carefully laid the ground work for an assault on the *taizidang* and the "regional lords," using corruption to cover up what was really an effort to consolidate the position of Jiang's Shanghai clique.[57] Orchestrated by Jiang's henchman Zeng Qinghong, the director of the Central Committee's General Office, the campaign had already picked off Guizhou First Secretary Liu Zhengwei, whose wife, Yan Jianhong, was shot for corruption, and was already closing in on the Beijing and Guangdong factions when the Xinxing case broke.

Gao's argument appears to gibe with the facts, at least up to a point. Jiang had made a number of important moves to strengthen the position of the "Shanghai gang" before Wang's suicide and continued to do so afterwards. In October 1994, he transferred Shanghai first secretary Wu Bangguo and Shandong first secretary Jiang Chunyun to the Central Committee Secretariat. Soon afterwards, Jiang arranged the promotion of

Huang Ju, who replaced Wu Bangguo as Shanghai first secretary, to the Politburo. In March 1995, he nominated Wu and Jiang vice-premiers.[58] After sacking Chen Xitong, Jiang elevated Defense Minister Chi Haotian and People's Liberation Army (PLA) Chief of Staff Zhang Wannian to vice-chairmen of the Central Military Commission, thus consolidating an alliance with the PLA-based Shandong faction.[59] Jiang also moved members of his Shanghai clique into important second tier positions, appointing Ba Zhongtan, former commander of the Shanghai Garrison, commander of the People's Armed Police, and transferring Wang Liping from the Shanghai Public Security Bureau to the post of Vice-Minister for Public Security. Concurrently, he strengthened Zhu Rongji's position as economic czar by stripping the State Planning Commission, which was dominated by members of Li Peng's "conservative" faction, of its control over investment and transferring that responsibility to the State Development Bank and the State Economic and Trade Commission, which were dominated by Zhu's protégés in the central bank. Jiang also had Wu Bangguo take over Li Peng's position in the Central Committee's leading group on finance and economics.[60] Finally, Jiang replaced Yuan Mu, a close ally of Li's, as head of the State Council Research Office.[61]

The rise of the Shanghai clique and the emergence of at least a temporary alliance between it and the Shandong clique, triggered resistance from several directions. Allegedly acting with the encouragement of National People's Congress Chairman Qiao Shi, Zou Jiahua and Chen Xitong, NPC delegates staged a mini-rebellion when Jiang Zemin nominated Wu Bangguo and Jiang Chunyun as vice-premiers in March 1995. Thirteen percent of the delegates either abstained or voted against Wu, while a full third opposed Jiang Chunyun, in part, they said, because of his wife's alleged involvement in a multi-million RMB embezzlement case involving the mayor of Tai'an, Shandong. A substantial number also voted against enhancing the power of the central bank.[62] In other forums, Chen Xitong heavily criticized the Shanghai gang. Chen reportedly snubbed Jiang Chunyun when he inspected Beijing in the fall of 1994, possibly with the support of Party elders Peng Zhen and Wan Li, both of whom had served in the Beijing municipal party apparatus, and perhaps even the concurrence of Chen Yun.[63] NPC Chairman Qiao Shi and Tian Jiyun were supposedly not only stirring up opposition to the Shanghai clique in the NPC, but were also part of an evolving reformist faction including Li Tieying, Xie Fei and, possibly, Yang Shangkun.[64] Yang Shangkun, who Deng Xiaoping supposedly sacked after Yang tried to oust Li Peng and

Jiang Zemin in 1992, was rumoured to be building a southern faction with former Guangdong First Secretary Ye Xuanping.[65]

Amid all of this behind the scenes jockeying for power, it is rather easy to jump to the conclusion that Jiang either set Chen up or quickly took advantage of Chen's vulnerability after Wang had killed himself. Jiang had motive. Chen, he charged in a secret speech in July, had built an independent empire of corruption in Beijing and had defied the party leadership.[66] Chen had also made others unhappy. Senior leaders had become so annoyed by Chen's aggressive redevelopment programme, for example, that Zhu Rongji reportedly jokingly asked Chen to please let the party leadership know as soon as he had sold Zhongnanhai to the developers so they could move out before the bulldozers levelled the compound.[67] Moreover, the death of Chen Yun just a few days after Wang Baosen's suicide robbed Chen Xitong of a potential ally in his fight with Jiang Zemin.

Despite the evidence of conflicts between Jiang Zemin and Chen Xitong, it appears Jiang was caught off guard when Wang's suicide presented a golden opportunity to sack Chen and take over the Beijing apparatus on legal, rather than political, grounds.[68] All his fierce rhetoric about waging a life and death struggle against corruption aside, early in 1995 Jiang had actually called for a scaling back of the anti-corruption offensive. According to Jiang, the 1995 campaign was supposed to concentrate on ideological education, housing irregularities, illegal use of police licence plates, excessive banqueting at public expense, the use of official cars for personal purposes, and overseas junkets.[69] Pressure for a more vigorous campaign did not begin to surface until after Zhou Beifang's arrest when Li Peng, not Jiang, called for an escalation of the war.[70] Even then, Jiang continued to favour a limited intensification and rejected a request by Wei Jianxing to "chop off the heads of a dozen big tigers" because, according to Jiang, stability was more important than eliminating corruption.[71]

It was only after receiving word of Wang's suicide on 5 April and Chen Yun's death on 10 April, that Jiang actually began to move against the "Beijing clique," bringing Huang Ju, who he wanted to install as first secretary of Beijing, up from Shanghai, ostensibly on the grounds that Huang would help organize Chen Yun's funeral. Jiang, however, quickly abandoned the idea of having Huang take over as Beijing first secretary when Qiao Shi objected. Instead, Jiang agreed to let CDIC Chairman Wei Jianxing take over as interim first secretary.[72] Moreover, even after Chen's position became untenable, Jiang's initial impulse seems to have been to demote Chen and ship him off to the provinces rather than haul him out for public denunciation.[73] The evidence tends to indicate, therefore, that even though Jiang and Chen may have clashed, Jiang was caught off-guard when the collapse of the Wuxi Ponzi scheme and Wang's suicide left Chen politically exposed.

Nor does Jiang seem to have profited from Chen's fall. From a factional point of view, Wei's appointment was not advantageous for Jiang. Wei had close ties with Qiao Shi, having come up through the disciplinary apparatus. From 1984 to 1985, he served as deputy director of the Central Committee's Organization Department under Qiao. After being elected to the Central Committee in September 1985, Wei took over from Qiao as director of the Organization Department. In 1987, he became the first Minister of Supervision. Five years later, Wei replaced Qiao as chairman of the CDIC, while continuing to serve as minister of supervision until March of 1993. If, as noted above, Qiao, who some now rank as number three in the political pecking order, right after Jiang Zemin and Li Peng, was one of Jiang's most dangerous rivals, allowing his protégé to control the purge of the Beijing apparatus would have been political folly. Appointing Wei head of the clean-up put him in a position to assume a much more public role in the war on corruption, which he and Qiao have been directing since the mid 1980s, thus indirectly enhancing Qiao's visibility within the leadership.[74] Moreover, Wei, who was a member of both the Politburo and the Secretariat, and whose position as head of the CDIC gave him control of some of the most party sensitive files, was a powerful man in his own right and a potential rival for Jiang's lieutenants. If any faction came out ahead from Chen's demise, therefore, it was Qiao's, not Jiang's.

Moreover, both Zhou Beifang's arrest and Chen's dismissal put Jiang in a difficult political position. Zhou's case was a potential disaster because of his relationships with key members of the *taizidang*, including the son of Jiang's patron, Deng Xiaoping. Even if Deng Zhifang was not involved in Zhou's shady stock dealings, the fact that he was connected with Zhou and Shougang alone cast a shadow over the Deng family. Chen Xitong's son, Chen Xiaotong, meanwhile, had questionable ties with Zhou and Hong Kong real estate magnate Li Ka-shing, whose open boasting about his connections with the Dengs and other senior members of the CCP raised serious questions about how Li had acquired the rights to prime real estate in central Beijing, real estate that had only recently been leased to the McDonald's Corporation for 20 years. Chen's other son,

Chen Xiaoxi, had business ties to Deng Pufang. An attack on Zhou
Beifang and Chen Xiaotong, therefore, had the potential to mushroom into
an attack on the *taizidang* at large. And attacking the *taizidang* was a high
risk strategy, as Hu Yaobang had discovered when he had threatened to
investigate corruption among the *taizidang* and their Hong Kong confederates in 1986.[75]

Attacking Chen Xitong was also not without considerable political
risks. First, both Wang and Chen had been vocal supporters of Jiang's war
on corruption. At the time of his death, in fact, Wang had been acting as a
vice-chairman of the Seventh International Anti-corruption Conference
which was to convene in the autumn, with its headquarters in Chen
Xiaotong's New Century Hotel. Chen Xitong, on the other hand, had
publicly called on the party to "resolutely deal strict blows... and never be
soft handed" in prosecuting corrupt officials in a speech to Beijing's 1994
anti-corruption conference.[76] At a minimum, therefore, there was a risk of
exposing the regime to charges of deep-set hypocrisy. Second, attacking
Chen and the Beijing clique might also trigger the formation of a united
front among the "regional warlords," while escalating the anti-corruption
struggle in general might undermine the Shanghai-Shandong factional alliance, an alliance whose ties were already frayed by a series of investigations into corruption in Shandong. Third, because of Chen Xitong's key
role in suppressing anti-government demonstrations in 1989, sacking him
might raise anew questions about the verdict on Tiananmen and re-ignite
anti-government dissidence. Party officials were reportedly so concerned
about that possibility that they mobilized units of the People's Armed
Police and imposed a tight clamp-down in the weeks just before the sixth
anniversary of Tiananmen.

More generally, the sort of illegal activities that led to Wang's suicide
and Chen's fall was hardly unique to Beijing. On the contrary, multi-
million RMB scandals involving key insiders and public funds have become increasingly common in the past several years. The Chen-Wang case
was, in fact, representative of this new form of corruption. As noted
earlier, both Chen and Wang had siphoned off monies from their units'
small treasuries (*xiao jinku*). They were not alone. State and collective
units throughout China engage in similar practices, diverting monies allocated to them by the state budget, revenues from extra-budgetary sources,
funds raised from illegal fines and fees, and bank loans into speculative
investments. In addition to investing in schemes such as Xinxing, these
"institutional investors" frequently play the Shanghai and Shenzhen stock

markets, as well as the regional commodity exchanges. By 1995, according to the Chinese Academy of Social Sciences, between RMB 150 and 400 billion worth of "hot money" had flowed in China's capital markets. In 1995, state auditors accused state units of diverting RMB 63.5 billion to various illegal expenditures, including illegal stock and real estate speculation.[77]

Excessive demand for equities, limited regulation and leverage factors that allowed speculators to purchase futures contracts with just a 1% deposit, make playing the market a risky business, however. Just how risky became clear in early 1995. Believing that prices for treasury bond futures would fall, Shanghai International Securities Company (Sisco) went short on treasury bond contracts, only to have the price rise after the government announced it would issue a 2.5% subsidy to offset inflation for "Contract 327" bonds due to mature on 1 July. Desperate to drive prices down and cut its loses Sisco dumped bonds on the market, driving volume up to RMB 859.99 billion on 23 February before regulators suspended trading. Prices, however, continued to rise, resulting in a loss of between RMB 600 million and 1 billion for Sisco and its investors, who allegedly included units of the People's Liberation Army and a variety of state units. Sisco general manager Guan Jinsheng was subsequently arrested for his involvement in the failed attempt to manipulate bond prices and the president of the Shanghai Stock Exchange, Wei Wenyuan, was forced to resign amid charges that he had allowed Sisco to engage in illegal margin trades.[78] A second run on treasury bonds covered by Contract 317, on 12 May, prompted Zhu Rongji to suspend all bond trading on the Shanghai Stock Exchange on May 23.[79]

The Contract 327 scandal and the Wuxi Ponzi scam were in actuality just two of a growing number of spectacular scandals in recent years. In 1993, the RMB 1 billion Great Wall investment scandal hit Beijing, leading to the execution of prominent entrepreneur Shen Taifu and the jailing of vice-minister of the State Scientific and Technological Commission Li Xiaoshi for bribery, corruption and embezzlement. The following year, the managers of the Dalian Hongxiang Industrial Development Centre were charged with embezzling RMB 46.72 million and causing RMB 172.91 million in enterprise losses. Deng Ping, a credit officer with the Zhuhai municipal government was charged with embezzling RMB 1.7 million while Xiao Ling, the head of the Zhuhai Posts and Telecommunications Bureau, was charged with accepting bribes and embezzling public funds totaling RMB 3 million. In Shenzhen, Wang Jianyi, the director of the

Municipal Planning Bureau, allegedly absconded with RMB 4.8 million
and US$750,000 he had received in bribes, while Yu Qiang, the deputy
chief of the Bao'an county planning division, was sentenced to death
for accepting RMB 4.5 million in bribes. On Hainan, the former chairman
of the Qiongshan Municipal People's Congress and four officials were
arrested for accepting bribes worth RMB 1.9 million.[80]

By 1995, Shanghai had become a centre for multi-million RMB stock
frauds and, according to *Jiefang ribao* (Liberation Daily), the laundering of
corrupt monies.[81] In the first half of 1995 alone, prosecutors uncovered
economic crimes involving over RMB 90 million. Among these cases was
that of Zheng Yifan, broker for a state-owned unit in Zhejiang, who
received a suspended death sentence after he used RMB 1.07 million to
speculate in plywood futures on the Shanghai Agricultural Products and
Materials Exchange. A second case involved a broker with the Shanghai
branch of the Industrial and Commercial Bank who was shot for embezzling RMB 5.7 million and then murdering another broker in a failed effort
to cover up his theft. Another case involved a broker with the Shanghai
office of the Hainan Trust and Investment Company who received an
18-year sentence for misusing RMB 3.4 million in corporate assets to
speculate in stocks. During the months that followed, a new series of
serious stock scandals emerged. In August, the manager and two officials
of the Jiaxing Trust and Investment Company were accused of diverting
RMB 189 million in public funds to their personal stock accounts. The
general manager of Shanghai Rubber Belt Company was executed for
pocketing over RMB 800,000 in profits from insider trading. And a broker
with an un-named provincial brokerage was sentenced to 10 years for
diverting RMB 40.37 million to his own account.[82] The Shanghai clique's
base, in short, had become a hot bed of corrupt activity, a fact that clearly
compromised the clique's ability to use corruption for factional advantage.

Given the potential pitfalls, it is not surprising, therefore, that Jiang
was not well prepared to move when opportunities presented themselves
and quickly backed off from launching a full scale purge of the Beijing
apparatus or pursuing allegations of corruption among the princelings. In
fact, aside from the flurry of rumours and nervous jitters that infected
Beijing cadres throughout much of the summer, the Beijing purge fizzled
out within a matter of weeks. On 28 April, Politburo member Hu Jintao
and Wei Jianxing told cadres that the situation in Beijing must be stabilized as soon as possible. By the first week of May, most if not all senior
Beijing officials, besides Chen, had been cleared and returned to public

view. In early June, while declaring that the anti-corruption struggle must go on, Wei told the deputies of the Beijing Municipal People's Congress: "stability is Beijing's prime task." Two days later, he reassured nervous Hong Kong investors that the CDIC considered Wang and Chen's corruption an isolated problem. Soon thereafter, Wei ruled out the possibility of a politically motivated purge of the Beijing apparatus, telling a national anti-corruption conference that cases must be handled according to established legal procedures. On 23 June, he told Li Ka-shing that investigators had concluded there was no connection between Wang and the Oriental Plaza project. As a result, although Jiang and Wei may have "decapitated" the Beijing apparatus by removing Chen, they did not systematically purge either the Beijing party apparatus or the municipal government. By late autumn, it even appeared that Chen had been let off the hook when Jiang made a careful distinction between Wang's criminal acts and "comrade Chen's" serious mistakes, thus implying that Chen had been clear of criminal wrong doing.[83] Jiang's efforts to soft pedal the investigation may, however, be derailed by Wei. Wei continues to pursue the case and has publicly dismissed rumours that Chen will escape prosecution, saying that fear of the potential political fallout will not deter his investigation. Moreover, Wei has threatened to prosecute anyone who obstructs his investigation.[84]

Conclusions

Because the evidence remains circumstantial, it is still unclear whether the Zhou, Wang, and Chen cases were the result of a random intersection between corruption and factional politics caused by the collapse of Xinxing or a deliberate manoeuvre by Jiang Zemin. Given the macro-political context, the factional argument is certainly intriguing and probably at least partially valid. Yet, it is also problematic. First, even though Jiang may have wanted to punish Chen Xitong, using corruption to get at him was a very dangerous proposition. Using the arrest of Zhou Beifang to intimidate the *taizidang* was even more dangerous. Both cases could have easily hurt Jiang and the risks probably outweighed any benefits Jiang might have gained by taking a tough stance on corruption. Second, the motive factor behind the scandal was not factional politics but the corruption that led cadres to invest in shaky deals, such as Xinxing, and the on-going war against corruption that ultimately exposed them. Third, Jiang did not seem to have been prepared for Chen's fall and gained relatively little from it. If anything, Qiao Shi and Wei Jianxing gained more than Jiang and his Shanghai allies. Fourth, Jiang's reaction to the Wang suicide was essentially defensive. Rather than moving into an attack mode and using the fall of Chen as a segue for attacks on other regional power holders, Jiang immediately shifted into a damage limitation mode. Jiang's factional offensive was, therefore, either ill planned and poorly executed or simply a half-hearted afterthought. Nor did it appear that Wei and his patron, Qiao Shi, saw Chen's fall as a pretense for a factional offensive. Wei, after all, was clearly active in trying to bring the Beijing scandal to a speedy conclusion by sweeping it under the rug as quickly as possible.

Jiang's response was, however, consistent with how we would expect an incumbent leader to react when an anti-corruption clean-up threatens élite stability. Anti-corruption campaigns require that the incumbent maintain a balance. On the one hand, he needs a war that is sufficiently intense to prevent corruption from reaching levels that might trigger external threats to the regime. At the same time, the incumbent also needs to prevent the war from escalating to a point where it might destabilize the regime internally. The goal of the incumbent is, in short, to ensure that corruption remains politically dormant.

If the anecdotal data on the public's response to the Wang-Chen scandal serve as a reasonable guide to the political salience of corruption, Jiang has succeeded in shunting it to the political sidelines. Rather than respond with shock and anger, the public appears to have accepted Wang's suicide and Chen's sacking with a combination of apathy and irony. Beijing residents seem to assume that Chen and Wang were corrupt because they believe that most senior cadres and their families have dirty hands. As one person summed up this line of thought: "if you arrested half the officials above the rank of department chief, you'd still miss a few." Many treated the case as something far removed from their lives, a party problem as some put it. As a result, even though posters calling for resolute action and demanding that no tigers be spared reportedly went up on bulletin boards on several of Beijing's university campuses, the city basically remained nonplussed by the entire scandal.[85] By mid-summer, most Beijing residents seemed to have forgotten the politics of the scandal, preferring instead to dwell primarily on the more titillating details.

In conclusion, the political salience of corruption in contemporary China lies less in whether corruption has reached endemic levels and is now likely to trigger renewed anti-government demonstrations. Instead, corruption has become a source of periodic instability within the élite as the war on corruption claims an increasing number of politically sensitive victims. Although the fall of senior leaders, such as Chen Xitong, has the potential to trigger serious intra-regime crises, thus far Jiang Zemin has been able to contain and limit the damage. The danger exists, of course, that Jiang may not be able to do so in the future and it would not, therefore, be surprising if he once again sought to de-escalate the war in 1996, backing away from tiger hunting and continuing to concentrate on hunting chickens instead. Jiang does not, however, exercise total control over the anti-corruption campaign and may find himself pressured to re-escalate the drive, either by Qiao Shi, Wei Jianxing, and others seeking factional advantage, or by deputies to the National People's Congress who have reportedly lobbied hard for a more intensive and open attack on corruption.[86]

Notes

1. Reuters, Beijing, 8 April 1995.
2. Associated Press (AP), Beijing, 23 July 1995 and *The Chicago Tribune*, 29 April 1995.
3. *The Economist*, 6 May 1995.
4. *South China Morning Post* (*SCMP*), Hong Kong, 16 April 1995.
5. United Press International (UPI), Beijing, 28 April 1995.
6. Analogies to the Cultural Revolution abound. Among the more striking was a cartoon published by *Nanfang ribao* (Southern Daily), Guangzhou, showing Chen Xitong dressed in a Mao suit and wearing a Cultural Revolution-style placard around his neck, weeping over the body of Wang Baosen (*SCMP*, 21 August 1995).
7. *Los Angeles Times*, 16 May 1995; *New York Times*, 8 May 1995; and *Tangtai*, Hong Kong, 15 January 1995, in British Broadcasting Corporation, *Summary of World Broadcasts* (*BBCSWB*), 26 January 1995.
8. *Hsin Pao*, Hong Kong, 12 May 1995, in *BBCSWB*, 17 May 1995.
9. *SCMP*, 24 May 1995, 14 July 1995, 19 August 1995, 29 September 1995; and Mo Yi, "*Zhonggong san bang yanyi zheng tianxia*" (CCP's Three Cliques and Their Epic Fight for Control), *Beijing zhi chun* (Beijing Spring), November 1995, pp. 28–29.
10. See Richard Baum, *Burying Mao* (Princeton, NJ: Princeton University Press, 1994), pp. 378–79; Kenneth Lieberthal, *Governing China* (New York, NY: W.W. Norton, 1995), pp. 178–79; Ting Gong, *The Politics of Corruption in*

Contemporary China: An Analysis of Policy Outcomes (Westport, CN: Praeger, 1994); Alan P. L. Liu, "The Politics of Corruption in the People's Republic of China," *The American Political Science Review*, Vol. 77, No. 3 (September 1983), pp. 602–23; James T. Myers, "China: Modernization and 'Unhealthy Tendencies'," *Comparative Politics*, Vol. 21, No. 2 (January 1989), pp. 193–213; Clemens Stubbe Ostergaard, "Explaining China's Recent Political Corruption: Patterns, Remedies and Counter-strategies at the Local Level," *Corruption and Reform*, Vol. 1 (1989), pp. 209–33; Lynn T. White, III, "Changing Concepts of Corruption in Communist China: Early 1950s Versus Early 1980s," in *Changes and Continuities in Chinese Communism*, Vol. 2, edited by Yu-ming Shaw (Boulder, CO: Westview, 1988), pp. 319–53; Milton D. Yeh, "Modernization and Corruption in Mainland China," *Issues & Studies*, November 1987, pp. 11–27; and Hsi-sheng Ch'i, *Politics of Disillusionment* (Armonk, NY: M. E. Sharpe, 1991).

11. Connie Squires Meaney, "Market Reform and Disintegrative Corruption in Urban China," in *Reform and Reaction in Post-Mao China: The Road to Tiananmen*, edited by Richard Baum (New York, NY: Routledge, 1991), p. 138; Micheal Johnston, "The Political Consequences of Corruption: A Reassessment," *Comparative Politics*, Vol. 18, No. 4 (July 1986), p. 466; and Yan Sun, "The Chinese Protests of 1989: The Issue of Corruption," *Asian Survey*, Vol. 31, No. 8 (August 1991), pp. 762–82.

12. Leslie Holmes, *The End of Communist Power* (New York, NY: Oxford University Press, 1993), p. 5.

13. Sun, "The Chinese Protests of 1989" (Note 11).

14. For an extensive chronology of China's anti-corruption effort, see *Xin Zhongguo fanfubai tongjian* (Compilation of China's Struggle against Corruption) (Tianjin: Tianjin renmin chubanshe, 1993).

15. Ch'i, *Politics of Disillusionment* (Note 10), chapter 7.

16. After Zhao Ziyang fell from power, conservatives blamed him for the slackening of the anti-corruption campaign, claiming that because Zhao believed "corruption is inevitable at the initial stage of socialism" and members of his own family were involved in corrupt activities, he actively obstructed efforts to eradicate corruption. Although Zhao denied the charge, his "self-criticism" suggests that he was in fact slow to recognize the extent of corruption and the need to combat it. See *Hsin Pao*, 4 June 1994, in *BBCSWB*, 9 June 1994 and *Tangtai*, 15 December 1991, in *BBCSWB*, 31 December 1991.

17. Xinhua, 24 May 1988 in *BBCSWB*, 27 May 1988.

18. See David C. Nice, "Political Corruption in the American States," *American Politics Quarterly*, Vol. 11, No. 4 (October 1983), pp. 510–11.

19. The filing stage represents the point at which the procuratorate decides to formally charge a defendant. Cases may originate from three different sources. If the case involves a party member, it is generally first investigated

by a discipline inspection commission. Cases involving government personnel who are not party members would generally be handled by investigators from the Ministry of Supervision. If the charges are determined to have merit at this stage, the case may be resolved by the imposition of party disciplinary sanctions, including probation or expulsion, or administrative sanctions, including demotion or dismissal. Serious cases involving criminal acts may then be referred to the procuratorate. If the procurator decides that the case has merit, he then "accepts" it (*shouan*). Following further investigation, the case may be dismissed or filed (*lian*). Filed cases are then submitted to the court which reviews cases and decides whether to accept them or refer them back to the procurator for dismissal or further investigation. The final stage in the process is the actual trial. See *Jiancha jiandu zhineng lun* (Procuratorial and Supervisory Functions) (Beijing: Qunzhong chubanshe, 1988).

20. Sinologists tend to define "corruption" loosely. In their analyses of corruption, for example, Liu, Ting, Myers, and Oi lump over forty different activities under the heading of "corruption." Jean C. Oi, "Partial Market Reform and Corruption in Rural China," in *Reform and Reaction* (Note 11), pp. 143–44; Liu, "The Politics of Corruption" (Note 10), p. 604; Myers, "China Modernization and 'Unhealthy Tendencies'" (Note 10), p. 196; and Ting, *The Politics of Corruption in Contemporary China* (Note 10), p. 9. Many of these offences are technically violations of party or official discipline (*faji*), not corruption according to Chinese law, and are treated separately by the procuratorate, which has responsibility for investigating and prosecuting disciplinary violations, such as torture, illegal detention, criminal negligence, dereliction of duty and nepotism, as well as bribery, corruption, etc.

21. Copyright piracy amounts to a relatively minor percentage of economic crime cases handled by the procuratorate.

22. Reuters, Beijing, 12 March 1996.

23. Data on the number of cases tried in the courts reveal a slightly different pattern from that found in the data on procuratorial investigations. Although 1986 and 1989 witnessed significant jumps in the number of cases tried, 1983, the second year of the Party Rectification Campaign, also witnessed a 46.37% increase as the number of trials which rose from 35,176 in 1982 to 51,486 in 1983. In 1990, when procuratorial investigations dropped 7.17% compared to 1989, the number of cases tried rose 14.45%. The increase in 1990 can be explained in part on technical grounds because cases may not be tried in the same year they are filed by the procuratorate. The sudden drop in trials reported beginning in 1991 is, however, troubling. The number of cases tried fell from 87,846 in 1990 to 40,366 in 1991, a 54.05% drop. Concurrently, the number of defendants convicted of economic crimes, fell from 121,053 to just 33,781, a 72.09% decrease, and 22,106 in 1993. Note that data on the number of cases filed by the procuratorate and the number of

cases tried by the courts do not line up because the courts define economic crime differently from the procuratorate. In addition to corruption, bribery, embezzlement, copyright piracy, tax evasion, the court's purview includes smuggling, forgery, failure to report foreign bank deposits, illegal titles, and illegal logging, which originate with the Public Security Bureau rather than the procuratorate. "Supreme Court President on Economic Crime and Possible Remedies," Xinhua, 14 January 1986, in *BBCSWB*, 18 January 1986; 1986–1987: "Supreme People's Court Work Report," *Renmin ribao* (People's Daily), 18 April 1988, in *BBCSWB*, 3 May 1988; 1988–1992: *Zhongguo falü nianjian* (Legal Yearbook of China), Vols. 1989–1993 (Beijing: Falü chubanshe, 1989–1993); 1993: "Supreme People's Court Work Report to the NPC," Xinhua, 25 March 1994, in *BBCSWB*, 22 April 1994; and 1994: "Work Report of the Supreme People's Court Presented by Ren Jianxin," Xinhua, 22 March 1995, in *BBCSWB*, 29 March 1995.

24. Xinhua (English language service), 2 January 1996; Xinhua, 4 August 1995, in *BBCSWB*, 7 August 1995; and Xinhua, 25 September 1994, in *BBCSWB*, 19 October 1994.

25. Rational choice models of corruption assume that an individual's propensity to engage in corruption is a joint function of benefit and risk. See John Macrae, "Underdevelopment and the Economics of Corruption: A Game Theory Approach," *World Development*, Vol. 10, No. 8 (August 1982), pp. 677–87 and Melanie Manion, "Corruption by Design: Bribery in Chinese Enterprise Licensing," *Journal of Law, Economics & Organization*, Vol. 12, No. 1 (Spring 1996), forthcoming.

26. Kate Gillespie and Gwenn Okruhlik, "The Political Dimensions of Corruption Cleanups: A Framework for Analysis," *Comparative Politics*, Vol. 24, No. 1 (October 1991), pp. 77–95.

27. Because the definition of "major case" has not changed since the early 1980s, inflation and economic growth undoubtedly account for a portion of the growth in major cases. Whereas a bribe of over RMB 10,000 would have represented an extraordinary sum in 1980, by 1995 the relative value of such a bribe would have fallen dramatically, and it is not surprising that more RMB 10,000-plus cases have been uncovered.

28. Including both death sentences carried out immediately and those involving a two-year stay.

29. Xinhua, 25 September 1994, in *BBCSWB*, 19 October 1994 and Xinhua, 4 August 1995, in *BBCSWB*, 7 August 1995.

30. A Ponzi scheme is a type of investment scam in which a confidence man lures investors in with promises of high rates of return. To attract more investments and new investors, the perpetrator initially pays out dividends as promised, using part of the monies collected from the investors. Ultimately, however, he absconds with the bulk of the money. A Ponzi scheme differs

from an investment pyramid wherein the original perpetrator collects money from an initial set of "investors" who then recoup their money by bringing in additional investors, whose funds they split with the original perpetrator.

31. *Renmin ribao,* domestic (*guonei*) edition, 30 November 1995; Xinhua (English), 29 November 1995; and Reuters, Beijing, 28 July 1995. It was never entirely clear whether Deng Bin simply stole the money or whether she lost it in a series of failed real estate deals.

32. Reuters, Beijing, 25 April 1995 and *SCMP,* 30 November 1995.

33. AP, Beijing, 28 July 1995, 1 December 1995; *Ming Pao,* Hong Kong, 5 May 1995, in *BBCSWB,* 6 May 1995; *Lien Ho Pao,* Hong Kong, 10 April 1995, in *BBCSWB,* 12 April 1995; and *SCMP,* 2 June 1995.

34. It is not known, for example, whether Zhou's case was linked to an extensive investigation into Chinese corporations in Hong Kong conducted by the Ministry of Supervision in the spring of 1994. If Zhou was speculating on Hong Kong stocks, as later charged, then it is quite possible that investigators may have uncovered evidence of his activities at that time but did not take action against him until later (*Cheng Ming,* Hong Kong, 26 July 1994, in *BBCSWB,* 28 July 1994).

35. *SCMP,* 12 March 1995; *Beijing ribao* (Beijing Daily), 4 February 1994, in *BBCSWB,* 26 March 1994; *Agrence France Presse* (*AFP*), Beijing, 4 May 1995; *The Washington Post,* Washington, DC, 16 March 1995; and *Business Week,* 6 March 1995.

36. In December, Beijing Vice-Mayor Zhang Baifa told reporters that Zhou Beifang had been charged with embezzling Shougang funds to cover extensive loses he had incurred while speculating on Hong Kong stocks and bribing two city officials, one of whom was presumably Li Min (Reuters, Beijing, 28 December 1995). In February 1996, *Gongren ribao* (Worker's Daily) charged that Zhou had misappropriated US$120.5 million from Shougang and had placed his wife on the corporate payroll even though she did no work (UPI, Beijing, 28 February 1996). Other reports indicated that Zhou had lost upwards of US$107 million in bad investments (*Asiaweek,* Hong Kong, 28 April 1995).

37. According to the *South China Morning Post,* Wang's wife threatened to expose him after she found out Wang had a mistress. Wang offered her RMB 600,000 to keep quiet, but she refused and went to the police with documentary evidence of his corruption (*SCMP,* 8 July 1995). *Lien Ho Pao,* on the other hand, reported that Wang decided to kill himself after finding out that his secretary, whom prosecutors had arrested earlier in the year, had agreed to testify against him (*Lien Ho Pao,* 10 April 1995, in *BBCSWB,* 12 April 1995). Still other sources claimed the Wang's partners turned him in after he cheated them out of their shares (*Lien Ho Pao,* 2 May 1995, in *BBCSWB,* 5 May 1995). Informants in Beijing, meanwhile, claimed that Chen Xitong's wife

turned him in to prosecutors after he cheated her and Chen Xiaotong in a real estate deal.

38. *Ming Pao*, 9 May 1995 in *BBCSWB*, 17 May 1995.

39. The Oriental Plaza (also known as the Dongfang Square) Project had already generated fireworks in November 1994 when the McDonald's Corporation protested an order to demolish its recently opened restaurant on the corner of Chang'an Boulevard and Wangfujing. McDonald's reportedly appealed to party elder Wan Li, who questioned why a massive development project in the heart of Beijing had never been discussed by the central leadership, but had instead been approved by the Beijing Municipal Planning Commission, of which Wang Baosen was the director. (*The Times*, London, 26 May 1995 and *Asiaweek*, 21 December 1995).

40. *SCMP*, 30 October 1995.

41. Xinhua (English), 4 July 1995; UPI, 28 April 1995; and *The Washington Post*, 22 July 1995. To punish the dead Wang, the Central Disciplinary Inspection Commission posthumously expelled him from the party, the Beijing Municipal People's Congress stripped him of his posts as vice-mayor and director of the Municipal Planning Commission, and the Xuanwu District People's Congress recalled him from his position as deputy to the Beijing Municipal Congress (Xinhua, 4 July 1995).

42. Xinhua, 4 July 1995; *SCMP*, 8 July 1995, 13 November 1995; and *Lien Ho Pao*, 2 May 1995, in *BBCSWB*, 5 May 1995.

43. Xinhua (English), 27 April 1995, in *BBCSWB*, 1 May 1995. Chen, it was widely reported, at first sought to avoid accepting responsibility for Wang's suicide, claiming that he knew nothing about Wang's illegal activities. Nevertheless, the Politburo decided to remove Chen on 23 April immediately after Politburo Standing Committee member Qiao Shi returned to Beijing from a trip to South Korea. Three days later, Chen "asked" to resign (*Lien Ho Pao*, 29 April 1995, in *BBCSWB*, 1 May 1995 and *Ming Pao*, 9 May 1995, in *BBCSWB*, 17 May 1995).

44. *SCMP*, 3 October 1995; *Lien Ho Pao*, 2 May 1995, in *BBCSWB*, 5 May 1995; and *Lien Ho Pao*, 30 April 1995 in *BBCSWB*, 2 May 1995.

45. UPI, Beijing, 4 May 1995. Zhang allegedly also had ties to the Beijing underworld (*Asiaweek*, 28 April 1995).

46. The Economist Intelligence Unit, EIU Views Wire, 11 August 1995.

47. Reuters, Beijing, 28 February 1996. In an apparently unrelated case, Tie Ying, deputy secretary of the leading party group of the Beijing Municipal People's Congress, was expelled from the party and arrested for accepting bribes from a Hong Kong business executive (Reuters, Beijing, 8 February 1996).

48. AFP, Beijing, 14 November 1995; Reuters, Beijing, 3 October 1995, 9 November 1995; and *SCMP*, 14 July 1995.

49. Xinhua (English), 28 September 1995. Thereafter, both the National People's Congress and the Beijing Municipal Congress stripped Chen of his seats on those bodies (Xinhua [English], 29 September 1995 and Reuters, Beijing, 29 September 1995).

50. The "obstruction of justice" charge had been made publicly as early as July when *People's Procuratorial News* wrote; "If the party secretary had not given Wang Baosen protection, how would he have dared to act so fearlessly?" (Quoted in AFP, 30 July 1995). According to sources in Beijing, Chen Xitong had refused to look into charges that Wang's mistress had reaped vast profits by illegally speculating in Beijing real estate because he was romantically involved with her as well (*The Times*, 29 April 1995 and *Lien Ho Pao*, 2 May 1995 in *BBCSWB*, 5 May 1995).

51. Reuters, Beijing, 3 October 1995. Chen's wife and son supposedly claimed that they had set up the slush fund, without Chen's knowledge (*SCMP*, 14 July 1995).

52. Reuters, 3 October 1995.

53. The fact that the CDIC continues to have jurisdiction over the investigation, not the Procuratorate, means that no criminal charges have been made against him. In late December, Zhang Baifa told reporters that Chen was not under arrest. Wei Jianxing's February remarks, however, suggest that Chen may still be charged but that the investigation has perhaps bogged down. According to most sources, Chen has not been detained thus far. Taiwanese reporters have claimed, however, that Chen was under detention and was initially imprisoned in Beijing. He was later transferred to Shenzhen, according to these reports, after attempting suicide twice. Chinese officials have denied these reports (AFP, Beijing, 27 November 1995 and Reuters, Beijing, 28 December 1995).

54. UPI, 3 May 1995.

55. According to business sources, many of these red-chip companies have played an active role in helping "overseas" investors (many of whom are actually mainland-based businesses operating through shell companies based in Hong Kong) to set up profitable "joint ventures" by acquiring existing plants from state-owned enterprises at cut-rate prices or by "pocket swapping," that is transferring state-owned enterprises to privately controlled corporations. *Legal Daily* estimated the net loss to the state from these deals at US$95 billion (*Business Week*, 6 March 1995 and *Sydney Morning Herald*, 22 February 1995).

56. Other members of the *taizidang* found themselves in hot water during 1995. Ding Peng, the daughter of Deng Xiaoping's brother Deng Ken, for instance, was at the centre of a complicated case involving a naturalized Australian businessman living in Hong Kong. In 1987 James Peng, who had been a cinema projectionist in Shenzhen before emigrating to Australia, bought a

money losing textile company, Yuan Ye, and converted it into a joint venture by paring it with Hong Kong-based Panco Industrial Company, which Peng owned. Three years later and apparently in financial trouble, Peng set up a public corporation, Champaign, and then tried sell Panco to Lolliman, another Hong Kong-based corporation which was itself in the process of being bought by corporations controlled by the People's Liberation Army. When the deal fell through, Peng then tried to sell off half of Panco's stock to other concerns based in Shenzhen, only to see those deals fall through. At this juncture, the Shenzhen branch of the Bank of China froze Champaign's accounts, charging him with various financial irregularities, and the Industrial and Commercial Bank of China sued to recover RMB 20 million it had lent Champaign. In 1993, Shenzhen authorities further charged that Peng had manipulated the value of Yuan Ye's stock allowing Panco to make windfall profits while defrauding his state-owned partner, the Xinye Corporation. Mired in legal difficulties, Peng turned to Ding Peng, who worked for the PLA, hoping that she could fix things with the Shenzhen government. Rather than help Peng, however, Ding took over Champaign and accused Peng of embezzling US$10.8 million from the firm. Peng countered by suing Ding in the Hong Kong courts, who ruled in favour of Peng. Shenzhen authorities, meanwhile, opened an investigation into whether Ding Peng had embezzled US$12 million from Champaign, now renamed Shenzhen Fountain Corporation, possibility with the assistance of the China National Nonferrous Metals and Mineral Corporation and its chairman Wu Jiachang, Deng Xiaoping's son-in-law. The case became still more complex when Macau police detained Peng and then handed him over to the Chinese authorities, who immediately arrested him on charges of corruption. After a lengthy trial during which the court sent the case back to the procuratorate several times for further investigation, Peng was convicted on corruption charges in October 1994 and sentenced to 18 years imprisonment the following month. Although Ding has thus far escaped prosecution and Peng's sentencing would appear to end the case, charges that Ding railroaded Peng and used her connections to avoid prosecution on embezzlement charges continue to make the rounds (UPI, Beijing, 10 May 1995; *SCMP*, 29 September 1995; and *The Financial Times*, London, 23 July 1995). Wang Zhen's son Wang Bing, meanwhile, was implicated in the kidnapping of Chen Xianxuan, the husband of the granddaughter of former PRC vice-president Ulanfu, after Wang and Chen became involved in a RMB 10 million business dispute (*SCMP*, 5 July 1995).

57. Gao Xin, "*Jiang Zemin ruhe zhansheng Beijing bang?*" (How Was Jiang Zemin Able to Defeat the Beijing Clique?), *Zhongguo zhi chun* (China Spring), Nos. 146 and 147 (October and November 1995).

58. *SCMP*, 5 October 1994; *Hsin Pao*, 17 May 1995, in *BBCSWB*, 17 May 1995; and *SCMP*, 10 May 1995.

59. *SCMP*, 29 September 1995 and Mo, *"Zhonggong san bang yanyi zheng tian-xia"* (Note 9).

60. Inter Press Service, Beijing, 12 July 1995.

61. *Tangtai*, 15 January 1995, in *BBCSWB*, 26 January 1995; and Reuters, Beijing, 18 May 1995.

62. *Lien Ho Pao*, 8 April 1995 in *BBCSWB*, 12 April 1995; *SCMP*, 4 December 1995; *International Herald Tribune*, Hong Kong, 29 March 1995; and *Los Angeles Times*, 18 March 1995. In February 1996, the Tai'an Intermediate Court sentenced Tai'an party secretary Hu Jianxue, and Municipal Police Chief Li Huimin to death sentences after convicting them, along with five others, of bribery. Two other officials, Party Secretariat head Lu Jiaoqing and vice-mayor Sun Limin, received death sentences with two-year stays, while the manager of a state-owned petrochemical firm was sentenced to life in prison. In addition to receiving RMB 616,291 in bribes, Hu was also rumoured to be involved in heroin trafficking, although he was not convicted on drug charges (Reuters, Beijing, 27 February 1996).

63. *Ming Pao*, 28 April 1995, in *BBCSWB*, 29 April 1995; *Asiaweek*, 28 April 1995; and *Tangtai*, 15 January 1995, in *BBCSWB*, 26 January 1995.

64. *International Herald Tribune*, Hong Kong, 29 March 1995 and *SCMP*, 19 April 1995.

65. *SCMP*, 24 May 1995.

66. UPI, Beijing, 28 September 1995.

67. *The Boston Globe*, 1 October 1995.

68. *Ming Pao*, 9 May 1995, in *BBCSWB*, 17 May 1995.

69. Xinhua, 20 January 1995, in *BBCSWB*, 24 January 1995; and Xinhua, 1 March 1995, in *BBCSWB*, 4 March 1995. Procurator General Zhang Siqing, on the other hand, did appear to call for a marked intensification of the war, placing particular emphasis on the need to sternly punish "leading cadres," in his address to a national conference on procuratorial work in December 1994 (Xinhua, n.d., in *BBCSWB*, 11 January 1995).

70. Xinhua (English), 13 March 1995.

71. *SCMP*, 1 March 1995.

72. *Ming Pao*, 9 May 1995, in *BBCSWB*, 17 May 1995; and Yomiuri, 31 May 1995.

73. Jiang Zemin, Li Peng, and Hu Jintao allegedly tried to convince Chen to accept a transfer to either Fujian or Guangdong, but Chen refused (*Lien Ho Pao*, 29 April 1995, in *BBCSWB*, 1 May 1995; *Ming Pao*, 9 May 1995, in *BBCSWB*, 17 May 1995; and *Lien Ho Pao*, 26 April 1995).

74. Neither of the other two key actors in the anti-corruption effort, Procurator General Zhang Siqing, and Minister of Supervision Cao Qingze are likely candidates for membership in Jiang's Shanghai clique. Cao worked in Sichuan, where he headed the provincial Discipline Inspection Commission,

before replacing Wei Jianxing as minister of supervision. Zhang worked in the Hubei procuratorate and public security apparatus before becoming first deputy procurator in 1983.

75. *Washington Post*, 22 July 1995.

76. *Beijing ribao*, 5 April 1994, in *BBCSWB*, 4 May 1994.

77. Kyodo, Beijing, 24 December 1995 and *Beijing Review*, Vol. 39, No. 4 (22–25 January 1996).

78. *Shanghai Star*, 22 September 1995 and *SCMP*, November 7, 1995. In an apparently unrelated case, Xu Cong, an assistant manager in Sisco's Nanshi branch, was arrested for diverting over RMB 8 million in public funds to his own stock accounts (*SCMP*, 22 June 1995).

79. Kyodo, Beijing, 24 December 1995.

80. *The Straits Times*, Singapore, 10 August 1993; *Ta Kung Pao*, Hong Kong, 8 December 1994, in *BBCSWB*, 19 December 1994; Xinhua, 8 October 1994, in *BBCSWB*, 22 November 1994; Xinhua, 8 September 1994, in *BBCSWB*, 24 October 1994; *Ming Pao*, 4 August 1994, in *BBCSWB*, 22 August 1994; Xinhua, 5 August 1994 in *BBCSWB*, 22 August 1994; Xinhua, 13 July 1994, in *BBCSWB*, 11 August 1994; and *Wen Wei Po*, Hong Kong, 9 August 1994, in *BBCSWB*, 22 August 1994.

81. Reuters, Beijing, 21 June 1995.

82. Reuters, Beijing, 11 April 1995, 2 June 1995, 19 June 1995, 21 June 1995, 31 August 1995; *SCMP*, 14 July 1995.

83. *SCMP*, 10 May 1995, 24 May 1995; *Ta Kung Pao*, 29 April 1995 in *BBCSWB*, 3 May 1995; *Lien Ho Pao*, 6 May 1995, in *BBCSWB*, 8 May 1995; *Beijing ribao*, 7 June 1994, in *BBCSWB*, 22 June 1994; *Beijing ribao*, 9 June 1995, in *BBCSWB*, 22 June 1995; Xinhua, 17 June 1994, in *BBCSWB*, 20 June 1994; Kyodo, 23 June 1994; and Reuters, 9 November 1994.

84. Xinhua (English), 27 February 1996; *Ming Pao*, 29 February 1996; and *SCMP*, 29 February 1996. Wei's investigation according to some sources has been stalled by Chen's refusal to cooperate and stonewalling by members of the Beijing apparatus (Reuters, Beijing, 28 February 1996).

85. *U.S. News & World Report*, 15 May 1995 and *SCMP*, 12 July 1995, 29 September 1995.

86. *SCMP*, 17 February 1996, 25 February 1996, 29 February 1996.

4

The Chinese Discourse on Social Democracy

Hans Hendrischke

The image of China as the last bastion of Marxist orthodoxy is misleading. It is true that the Communist Party has carefully preserved the facade of orthodox ideology against the worldwide decline of socialism. But behind this facade, we find a desperate search for a new socialist ideology, often purposefully hidden from the public media. The main theme of this radical political debate has been the issue of how to adapt China's political ideologies to the changes in the socialist world and to the changing Chinese society and economy. In this process, social democracy has played a greater role than other alternatives to orthodox socialism.

The debate about social democracy marks an important breakthrough in China's ideological discourse. Never before in the history of the People's Republic of China have such broad and unorthodox views on major political questions been allowed a public airing. Admittedly, these are views expressed in specialized journals, and they are unfailingly accompanied by orthodox voices. But the fact that they could be "trialed" publicly in this way makes them more than an exercise in academic freedom. In an environment where economic reforms are justified by pragmatic reasons, social democratic ideas have been the main vehicle for preparing the ground, and discussing ideological and political reforms has contributed to reflections about domestic economic and social reform. They are possibly the last common ideological ground that China could share with the former socialist countries, especially the Soviet Union. Furthermore, social democracy opens a perspective of finding a common ground link with the economically advanced Western countries, and, more importantly, creates an appreciation of their complex social policies.

The Chinese debate on social democracy is not about imitating Western countries or learning from their mistakes, but about giving an ideological justification to China's emerging economic and political reform programme. For this purpose, social democracy is most suitable, because it is imbedded in the international workers' movement and does not require the abandonment of the notion of socialism. Another reason for focusing on social democracy is that, in the Soviet Union, Gorbachev had used social democratic ideas as an ideological basis for his reform programme. The Soviet debates had exerted a strong influence on the Chinese debates.

The author wishes to gratefully acknowledge the research support received from Macquarie University, Sydney, the Australian Research Council and the Australian Academy of Social Sciences.

In the 1980s and the early 1990s, the debate on social democracy had served to explore the spectrum of political, economic and social reforms and, at the same time, preserve common political ground with what remained of European and Soviet socialism. After the collapse of the Soviet Union, the need to preserve some common ground with the other major socialist power disappeared, and social democracy came under criticism. However, in the mid-1990s, as socialism became a new national orthodoxy for China, many of the ideas that were previously identified with social democracy found their way into "socialism with Chinese characteristics." This debate illustrates how China has modified its understanding of modern capitalism and created the ideological basis for adopting many of its features. In addition, it provides important glimpses on how far the ideological preparation for further reform has gone and, especially, where further political reform might be heading. The redefinition of socialism for China has gone a long way but is far from being finalized.

The first part of this chapter is concerned with the emergence of a Chinese debate on social democracy as a response to reforms in China, and an attempt to join an international ideological discourse. Social democracy opened the way for an understanding of many features of modern capitalism that had previously been overshadowed by the over simplifications of orthodox ideology.[1] The second part will consider how this debate was influenced by the transformation of Eastern Europe and the end of Soviet socialism. The fact that from a Chinese viewpoint, the Soviet Union had essentially embarked on a social democratic reform course, proved to be both a challenge as well as a disincentive for the Chinese reform debate.[2] Finally, the third part will trace the debate into the mid-1990s when commitment to ideologies is waning, and China is reaffirming its national identity as the last major socialist country. This part will look at the lasting influence of social democratic concepts on China's new socialist orthodoxy.

A short comment is necessary on where such debates take place, and why they are rarely mentioned in official media and the press. Ideological debate usually takes place at three levels. One level is the formulation of official ideology. Official ideology is contrasted with different deviating opinions and defined and interpreted through party channels and official party organs. The Communist Party finds theoretical justification for its leading role in these formulations and tends to preserve them as official orthodoxy. Changes occur slowly, and official ideology is quite often allowed to be at variance with actual policies, as has been the case during most of China's reform period.

At the opposite end of the ideological spectrum, there can be debates that contain hardly any references to the official language, at least not in the formal sense of clinging to prescribed formulations. The relaxed political control during the late 1980s, for example, allowed for intellectual debates "along a far-flung fringe area of permissible contention."[3] Bill Brugger and David Kelly, in their book *Chinese Marxism in the Post Mao Era*, see these debates as being far removed from the "core region of the ideology." These debates are of little political relevance, since they do not feedback into the political process. They also may be terminated at any time, as happened after the events of 1989.

In secondary literature on the Chinese reform debates of the mid and late 1980s, social democracy received less public attention and was a less spectacular topic than the fringe debates. Yet, in contrast to the latter, it remained the vehicle for continuous debate on national and international ideological issues that became more sensitive after 1989. Research on social democracy was then removed from the public agenda of the Chinese Academy of Social Sciences (CASS) in Beijing and confined to the Central Party School and other more secluded research institutes. Still, in late 1990 and early 1991, the Chinese Academy of Social Sciences held two internal conferences on social democracy for a very select circle of scholars.[4] From 1992 onwards, social democracy has been on a more public agenda again and has remained there since.

The discussion of social democracy has been part of what may be called a semi-official debate and is of greater practical relevance than the purely intellectual debate along the political fringe. This semi-official or hidden discourse differs from the political fringe debates in that there is official approval and encouragement for arguments brought forward, irrespective of the fact that they may actually contravene official ideology. Issues are open for discussion as long as no official "conclusion" (*zongjie*) has been reached on them. Participants from academic and party institutions conduct these debates in internal publications where contents are less strictly controlled and authorship of dissenting articles carries fewer sanctions. When these debates reach into external publications, the presentation of viewpoints which contradict official ideology follows certain conventions, especially if foreign countries are concerned. Authors cannot make openly dissenting statements and, instead, have to rely on quotes, often from foreign sources, to present their views. In this way, they can make indirect statements on sensitive issues, provided that they refrain from any overt personal judgment. This was the way in which the topic of social democracy was introduced. Many of the articles quoted below are from central and provincial party journals. It would take a separate enquiry to determine why certain provincial journals participate in these ideological debates and why their views can differ so much. While some provinces lead the debates,[5] others only occasionally intervene with strongly conservative arguments.[6] This indicates that there are broader political concerns that structure such debates, an observation supported by the fact that there seems to be little debate between individual authors, but rather an exchange of arguments between people and institutions adopting different positions.

The "Discovery" of Social Democracy

Research on social democracy began in the mid-1980s and led to numerous articles in academic and party journals[7] and book publications.[8] In a climate of prevailing orthodoxy, interest in this topic was justified by the election victories of socialist and social democratic parties in France, Spain and Greece in the early 1980s. Another source of inspiration for this debate was the reform debate in the Soviet Union, but during the 1980s this link between the Chinese debate on social democracy and Soviet reform debates was never made public. Instead, social democracy was introduced into the Chinese discourse at two levels. The first was in the form of academic research on socialist alternatives as well as on capitalist countries, starting in the late 1970s. The second was a public media campaign on the reassessment of capitalism during the second half of the 1980s.

Research on social democracy culminated in a national key research project "Research on contemporary schools of socialism"[9] under the 7th Five-Year Plan (1985–1989), headed by Yin Xuyi of the Bureau for Translation of Marx-Engels-Lenin-Stalin's Works. Such national key projects occupy the highest rank in research funding. Unlike smaller research projects organized by individual researchers or by institutes, key projects involve whole academies and are much more generously endowed. They receive the highest level of funding available for social science projects, including expenses for overseas travel and hard-currency allocations for library purchases. Such projects go ahead only with high-level political support, and generally have some impact on political decision making through internal policy recommendations and alternatives presented to the political leadership. A key project, for example, was organized on the "one country-two systems" policy regarding Hong Kong and Taiwan.[10] In the public domain, the project on contemporary socialism resulted in three research volumes,[11] the most important of which was devoted to the theory and practice of West European social democratic parties.[12] The published results of the key research project on contemporary socialism are an indication of how thoroughly the traditional assessment of social democracy had been revised.

There are two Chinese terms for social democracy. Works written after the late 1970s generally use "democratic socialism" (*minzhu shehui zhuyi*), although the earlier term "social democratism" (*shehui minzhu zhuyi*) is also still referred to.[13] This change is not based on a systematic differentiation between the two terms, but marks the move away from the previous radically negative view of social democracy. By using the term "democratic socialism" Chinese authors follow the terminology of the social democratic movement,[14] as well as Soviet terminology under Gorbachev. Changes in the usage by the Socialist International have been closely followed[15] and the two terms have come to be used interchangeably.[16]

The Re-evalution of Social Democracy

What did social democracy mean to Chinese authors? What were their areas of interest? What were the signs to indicate that they wanted to apply social democratic concepts and policies to China? The main issues raised in the late 1980s were the question of the socialist character of social democracy, the links between social democracy and the workers' movement, the role of the state in social democratic policies and last, but not least, the role of the party.

The first question concerned the old controversy about the political nature and consequences of reformism. The Chinese orthodox attitude toward social democracy was informed by the traditional hostility of the communist parties toward the social democratic movement, that dated back to the split of the socialist movement into the Second Socialist International and the Communist International. Social democratic reformist policies in the communist view had always contributed to maintaining the capitalist system. Social democratic parties were, therefore, traditionally regarded as allies of the bourgeoisie and not as socialist allies. In the terms of the 1980s, this question was now newly raised: did social democracy or "democratic socialism" qualify as socialism? The answer this time was positive.

Social democracy, as a non-Marxist-Leninist form of socialism,[17] became acceptable on the basis of a new pluralistic concept of socialism which allowed for the coexistence of ethical and scientific socialism. In the past, ethical socialism had been set apart from orthodox scientific socialism on the ground that it was based solely on the conscious realization of basic values such as democracy, equality, freedom, justice and solidarity,[18] while disregarding the economically determined inevitability of socialism postulated by orthodox views. In order to explain that the realization of basic human values and economic determinism were both equally important aspects of socialism, Yin Xuyi referred to Engels on the need to emphasize the role of the superstructure and also cited Engels' own regret that the constant need to argue against 19th century idealist schools of thought had prevented Marx as well as himself from accentuating the ethical position.[19]

It sufficed that social democratic parties in capitalist countries were claiming to rid capitalism of unfair and irrational elements to find the approval of Chinese academics. "The Socialist International as well as the different socialist parties in their programmes and declarations proclaim their intention to transform the capitalist system according to socialist principles (as they understand them) and to establish a new social order. Whether in government or in opposition, they have been working a lot to realize this aim. Although there are many shortcomings and mistakes, we have no reason to deny that democratic socialism is a brand of socialism."[20] In this view, the socialist nature of social democratic parties was upheld on the grounds of its commitment to social fairness as exemplified by progressive policies aimed at reducing unemployment, improving living standards and raising the social status of the working population in their respective countries.

The social composition of social democratic parties was seen as additional proof of their progressive political character. In view of the relative decline of workers among party membership, Chinese researchers followed the argument of social democratic parties who argued that dependent employed labour in various forms still constituted a majority of party membership and that traditional links with the trade union movement had always been maintained.[21] Social democratic parties in Western Europe were depicted as representing a loosely defined "proletariat" or working population, comprising social and occupational groups such as workers, employees, technicians and scientists, middle-level managers and the less well-off self-employed.[22] The arguments used to prove the socialist nature of social democracy were based on statistics put forward by these parties, and their use by Chinese scholars seems to have been guided by the intention to accept their results, rather than by a desire for meticulous inquiry.

The orthodox view that social democracy with its reformist tendencies was a tool of the exploiting class was now reversed. Research on the Western European social democratic parties concluded that they were an integral part of the workers' movement as much as were the communist parties and, in fact, to a greater extent than many socialist parties of Asian countries with a more nationalist background.[23] The anti-fascist tradition of social democracy was recognized as a further proof of its progressive historical role.[24] The social democratic view that a peaceful transition from one historical stage to the next was possible, including a peaceful change from capitalism to socialism, was no longer rejected.

New research on the impact of social democracy on the development of capitalism came to several previously unthinkable conclusions. It was proposed that in the early developed capitalist societies, through both violent and nonviolent means, the bourgeoisie had achieved political and economic rights for the working class; that in societies which entered industrial development at a later stage, the parties of the working class were able to achieve workers' rights through democratic means; and that to undertake a violent revolution was only unavoidable in societies where feudal and bureaucratic traditions had brought violent suppression of the working class.[25]

As a result, the history of the working class became the history of social democratic parties and communist parties gaining predominance in turn, dependent on the historical circumstances of their societies. The Second International was no longer perceived as marking a decisive split in the history of the working class. The post Second World War period in Western Europe was now seen as being characterized by the achievements of social democracy in improving the social and economic situation of the working population, while the communist movement in the West was acknowledged to have committed serious mistakes and to be facing relative decline.[26]

While the role of social democracy in socialist tradition and the history of the workers' movement were more of academic interest, there were other topics that had a direct bearing on China's reform policies. One of them was the role of the state. The post-war shift of all major social democratic parties to accept and utilize the capitalist state was justified by the changed role of the state in controlling the economy and in providing social and economic welfare. Chinese researchers did not go so far as to deny the notion of the "bourgeois nature" of the state, but at the same time they accepted that the state was accessible to democratic control and political pressure from social forces, including social democracy.[27] Proof of the positive role of the state was seen in the success of social democratic parties in creating comprehensive state-run welfare systems and implementing reformist policies regarding state enterprises, state planning and employment as well as social and political participation. Anti-hegemonist and anti-nuclear policies and support for the Third World by Western European social democratic parties and governments were seen as further evidence for a positive role of the state. Welfare policies became the major area for which a positive role of the state could be demonstrated, reversing the traditional socialist view of the bourgeois state as a tool of suppression. Many articles appeared on welfare systems and welfare policies. Sweden was a most prominent example,[28] but other countries, such as France and West Germany, were also mentioned for specific issues. Social democratic welfare concepts inspired Chinese reforms plans in these areas, and research on social democracy for the first time allowed a factual assessment of the positive role of social welfare policies and of the state in general in Western countries.

Another point of interest was the role of the party in social democracy. Chinese observers were fascinated by the observation that inner-party democracy,[29] coexistence of differing opinions and non-dogmatic flexibility in changing party programmes seemed to be no apparent impediment to unity of action.[30] A whole chapter of *Theory and Practice of West European Social Democratic Parties*[31] was devoted to a discussion of how social democratic parties under changing economic and social conditions had managed to broaden their popular support, even among the rural population and the self-employed. The main reason was seen as their flexibility in responding to social change without insisting on dogmatic positions.

An extremely positive view of social democracy thereby emerged, which was based on the areas for which common points between social democracy and orthodox scientific socialism could be constructed. They included the commitment to building a socialist society, the common historical background in the workers' movement and the emphasis on the party as the main political actor. In particular, social democratic policies toward the state were shown to have been a major contributing factor to the development of capitalist societies since the 1950s. Areas where there were essential differences between social democracy and scientific socialism, such as their position toward parliamentarianism and multiparty systems, received less attention. The similarity of social democratic and liberal or conservative positions, and the broad consensus in Western societies regarding these policies, were generally disregarded.

In conclusion, academic research had turned social democracy into "a theory and model proposed by social democratic parties to realize socialism in developed capitalist countries,"[32] comparable to what the Chinese Communist Party had set out to achieve for China. There is no reason to suggest that this research was intended to provide a blueprint for a future party programme of the Chinese Communist Party, but there can also be no doubt that it enabled the party to adopt major elements of social democracy into its programme, without necessarily losing its identity and having to deny its socialist tradition.

The Reassessment of Capitalism

What was the impact of these academic results? To what extent were they made public and was social democracy presented to a wider audience? To answer these questions we have to turn to the debate on the reassessment of capitalism between 1987 and 1989, in which social democracy was a major issue.

The reassessment of capitalism had been on the agenda and had been discussed in scholarly journals since the late 1970s when reform policies began in China. After the 13th Party Congress in 1987, when China was declared to be in the primary stage of socialism, reassessment of capitalism developed into a political campaign. At the Party Congress, due to the political stalemate between conservatives and reformers, no agreement could be reached on the definition of this primary stage of socialism. Instead it was agreed that socialism needed to be reassessed and that, for historical reasons, a reassessment of capitalism would be the first logical step. Reassessment of capitalism, therefore, went ahead without a parallel debate on socialism. It entailed a drastic revision of all previously held official positions on Western post-war capitalism and presented a radically positive image of capitalism in Western Europe, North America and Japan. Social democracy was an essential element in this reassessment.

Economically, capitalism was now seen to be able to control the contradictions between productive forces and the relations of production, while in traditional Marxist terms they had been said to lead to its collapse. Regarding productive forces, it was stressed that capitalism had achieved the technological revolution and created conditions for stable development. Capitalism was assumed to be able to maintain a steady organizational development through new forms of management, macro-economic measures and social policies, among other factors. These were areas where social democratic policies had played a major role.

Socially, the traditional Marxist view of two major antagonistic classes gave way to an image of a predominantly middle-class society with a materially satisfied working class on a path of upward social mobility, largely through intellectualization of labor. It was recognised that the working class lived under largely improved circumstances, although sometimes the notion of relative pauperization was still brought into the debate. But, even after 1989 in articles criticizing an overly positive view of the West, workers in Western countries were described as living in material stability in spite of decreasing working hours, insured against social and health risks and spending holidays abroad. Social democracy was again seen as the proponent of all these policies, especially of the welfare state.

A third point raised in the debate on the reassessment of capitalism was the transition from capitalism to socialism. A violent revolution was no longer deemed necessary, the transition was expected by way of "an orderly, peaceful, democratic and gradual readjustment and structural reform."[33] Some authors even denied that capitalism had to pass through a stage of socialism at all. The merits of social democratic policies were that they created elements of such a transition already in capitalist society, the so-called "seeds of socialism," enabling them to move directly to socialism or to an undefined higher stage of social development without violent revolution. Such elements were health and social insurance combined with stable living standards for the working population. On the policy level, further socialist elements or seeds were identified in state planning, macro-economic control, state ownership, in workers' participation in management and in a changed attitude toward the human factor in production as well as in socially widespread shareholding.[34]

What was characteristic about this revision of the traditional view on the capitalism debate was its syncretism. This popular presentation of modern capitalism blurred the distinction between capitalism and socialism and came close to postulating an intermediate system between the two. The clearest expression of this was the frequent reference to "convergence" and "convergence theory." The arguments for convergence were the similarity of technical developments, the co-existence of planning and market mechanisms and the growing equalization of incomes. The concept of convergence also hinged on the role of social democracy in bridging the gap between capitalism and socialism.

By 1989, Chinese ideologists had made social democracy politically acceptable by crediting it with the economic, political and social achievements of advanced Western nations. Social democracy became accepted as one form of socialism, and a particularly successful one at that. In this sense, social democracy was used to defend the viability of socialism in general. More specifically, social democracy could be used politically to legitimize China's market reforms, and the social reforms that had started to take shape during the late 1980s.

The gap between social democracy as a market-oriented ideology and Marxist ideology was narrowed to the extent that a communist party would not face insurmountable difficulties in adopting social democratic positions. Social democracy was not so much presented as an alternative to orthodox Marxist ideology, but rather gave sufficient flexibility to the concept of socialism that it could incorporate important elements of capitalist societies. What is striking for the Western observer about this new positive evaluation of social democracy is the limited account that was taken of critical Western voices. For example, the view most poignantly expressed by Dahrendorf[35] that social democracy was obsolete, because its policy aims had long been incorporated into the programmes of all middle-of-the-road parties in the West, was not considered at all.

Social Democracy with Soviet Characteristics

The Chinese ideological response to the 1989 Tiananmen incidents put an immediate end to the positive rendering of capitalism, and criticized it as part of a Western conspiracy to undermine socialism in China and worldwide. In June 1989, a propaganda campaign against "peaceful evolution" (*heping yanbian*) was started which took an extreme cold-war attitude toward the West, with attacks against détente and cooperation between socialist and Western states. Social democracy was an obvious target for this campaign due to its role in the ideological liberalization in the late 1980s. However, while the campaign with its attacks on liberalization and social democracy dominated the general public media, the debate and reporting on social democracy continued in more academic publications.[36] The reason for this was that Gorbachev at the same time was propagating social democracy as part of his reform programme and Chinese propaganda had to take care not to rashly condemn ideological reforms in the Soviet Union in order to avoid alienating their last major socialist ally. Thus, while Chinese propaganda was attacking social democracy, China's reporting on the Soviet Union after 1989 continued to involve China in the Soviet attempts to bring social democracy into the mainstream of socialism.

In retrospect, for Chinese readers the continued reporting on Gorbachev and his reform programme showed the degree to which earlier debates in China had been indebted to Soviet debates in the 1980s.[37] For the first time, extensive reference was being made to Soviet sources, and Soviet views were openly quoted and presented at length. They revealed that Soviet views on socialist reforms had been much more radical than the debate in China, and that they had inspired many of the topics of the Chinese reform debates during the 1980s. Arguments that had been more implicit than explicit in the Chinese debates became now directly ascribed to Soviet scholars and politicians. For example, the notion of convergence between capitalism and socialism, which in China in the late 1980s had been presented as a Western inspired concept, was now ascribed to Sakharov and elevated to the status of a respectable academic and political contribution.

Many elements of the debate on social democracy that were attacked in the campaign against "peaceful evolution" were at the same time shown to have been influenced by the reform debate in the Soviet Union. Such points were, for example, the view that social democratic parties should be regarded as parties of the working class, albeit with "right opportunistic and social reformist views."[38] Another such point was that Western post-industrial information society had in fact reached the primary stage of communism and that Sweden and Austria could be regarded as socialist countries with the many features of socialism in their societies.[39] The Chinese fascination with the Swedish model in the 1980s became linked to the popularity it had gained in the Soviet Union, following a visit to Sweden by one of Gorbachev's economic advisers.

But, beyond showing the Soviet influence on previous Chinese debates, the reporting on Soviet ideological developments exposed Chinese scholars to the "social democratization" of socialism. These ideas were of interest to Chinese scholars, because they were reflections on issues that had come up in the course of Chinese reforms as well, but simply had not been allowed to be formulated in China's more restricted political climate. For example in 1990, the journal *Guoji zhengzhi yanjiu* (International Political Studies) reported in detail on a conference on modern socialism held by the Soviet Academy of Sciences in June 1989.[40] It described a spectrum of Soviet views on the Stalinist model, in terms that would have been completely unacceptable in the Chinese context of the time because of their often stated disregard for the tenets of Chinese socialism, such as the unquestioned authority of the party and of Marxism-Leninism. The Soviet views presented a much more differentiated and complex understanding of the socialist past and the reform process than the propagandistic Chinese representation with its dogmatic emphasis and enforced "unified thinking."

One Soviet view reportedly held that the merits of socialist construction in the Soviet Union were undeniable in spite of Stalin's crimes, and that the Soviet Union had either reached socialism or was at least in a transitory stage toward it. "Transition" was explained in political terms as leading from bureaucratic to humanitarian socialism, economically as from a mandatory command system to a system managed by economic and legal mechanisms, and in industrial structure as moving from traditional manufacture to science and technology based industries. A more orthodox view held that Stalinism should not be attacked as it would implicitly be directed against Marxism-Leninism as a whole and that, instead, the achievements of socialism should be emphasized. A third, radically different, view was quoted as saying that Stalin had replaced socialism by his own creed and that, consequently, socialism had never existed in the Soviet Union. According to this view, only the most recent Soviet reforms had been a step toward the establishment of socialism. The fourth view quoted by the Chinese observer stated that the attempt to separate socialism and Stalinism was futile, as in all socialist countries there was no other model than the Stalinist one for the building of socialism. Reforms in the Soviet Union would, therefore, have to chart their own, new course.

Among these diverging opinions, Chinese observers could find surprisingly pragmatic arguments in favour of socialism; for instance, the point that it provided a sense of security, because people had become accustomed to it and had pinned their hopes on it. One reason given for preserving a socialist system was that its abolition would result in instability. Quoting the Soviet debate, Chinese observers discovered socialist elements in capitalist countries in state enterprises, economic planning and the practice of remuneration according to work. In regard to the socialist world, a need was expressed to eliminate obsolete elements from Marxism-Leninism in order to bring it in line with contemporary circum-stances. According to a more radical view, Marx, and to a lesser degree Lenin, had only limited notions of socialism, and socialist theory would need to incorporate ideas taken from Christianity, Bernstein's reformism and the value system of social democracy.[41]

A decisively reformist approach was reflected in Soviet ideological debates on economic issues; and yet, despite the radical nature of these arguments, they were quite similar to Chinese reform concepts in a practical policy sense. The difference was that Chinese scholars were not able to voice concerns and alternatives as freely. The majority of Soviet scholars saw state ownership as a continuation of exploitation and criticized the state bureaucratic system as having replaced but not improved the system of private ownership. While Chinese scholars could not take their theoretical criticism that far, the actual Chinese reform programme did not differ much from the suggested Soviet reform agenda that at this stage proposed mixing state ownership with individual, share-holding and cooperative forms of ownership.[42]

The strongest contrast between official Chinese propaganda positions at the time and what could be published in an academic journal such as *Guoji zhengzhi yanjiu* manifested itself in the area of political reforms. The Soviet arguments presented here were in total opposition to the dogmatic Chinese view on its one-party rule. As far as Soviet arguments were in favour of the one-party system, they were conditional on inner-party democracy. The proponents of a multiparty system were cited with their claim that present economic and social reforms necessitated a multiparty system. Socialism in their view was safeguarded as long as there were different socialist parties competing for voters' support. They suggested that communist parties relinquish their hold on state power and participate in the political process through propagating their programmes and ideas in the public media. Democratization was another area where Soviet ideas had moved far away from Chinese orthodoxy. The view was that democracy transcended specific political systems and that democratic reforms would bring the Soviet Union back into the mainstream of universal political culture.[43]

For all these points, continuous reference was made to the programmes of social democratic parties. The resulting Chinese view was that Gorbachev's reform programme in practical as well as ideological terms owed much to social democracy and that he had also encouraged Eastern European countries to adopt social democratic policies. Chinese sources even revealed a concern about China being excluded from this emerging socialist relationship between the Soviet Union, Eastern Europe and Western European social democratic parties. They specifically pointed to an initiative by the President of the Central Committee Social Science Research Institute who in 1988 had suggested organizing a conference in 1989 on the occasion of the 125th anniversary of the First International, and the 100th anniversary of the Second International, with participation from communist and social democratic parties in West Germany to promote the "common socialist tradition." In his comment, the Chinese reporter added in brackets: "So far, the CPSU (Communist Party of the Soviet Union) has not even suggested to all communist parties to commemorate the 70th anniversary of the Third International in 1989."[44] Chinese scholars also took more direct notice of the ongoing debates in Western social democratic parties and the Socialist International.[45] The degree to which social democracy (used interchangeably with the term "democratic socialism") had gained public attention and become part of public discourse in China, could be seen from statements such as the one made in 1992 that "in recent years, the ideas of democratic socialism have gained some influence in our country. Some people assume that democratic socialism represents the mainstream and method of socialism."[46]

For Chinese intellectuals, this debate provided an opportunity to rethink orthodox positions and gain argumentative diversification. The Soviet debate about social democracy widened the ideological choices available to Chinese ideologists. The debate laid an argumentative basis for future reforms by making social democratic concepts acceptable in a socialist context. For over a decade, Chinese reform ideas had been unable to derive direct inspiration from the West whether intellectual or political. With the Soviet Union as an intermediary, the hurdles were lower and the potential for a practical outcome higher. In spite of all the disagreements and reservations at the official level, the Soviet Union for some time again became China's closest ideological partner. The debate on social democracy was a case in point, but it remained an ideological debate which continued to approach ideology from a normative perspective rather than from the practice of actual Chinese reforms.

The Critique of Social Democracy

After the 1991 August *coup* and the dissolution of the Soviet Union, China became the only remaining major socialist country. The common socialist heritage that it had shared with the Soviet Union was no longer a reason to show concern for alternative forms of socialism. Moreover, the Soviet reform experiment had failed, and China now distanced itself from the ideological reform that was seen at the root of the collapse of Soviet communism. This was the close identification of Gorbachev's reform programme with social democracy. The ensuing critique was to draw a dividing line between Chinese "scientific socialism" and social democracy as a capitalist ideology opposed to socialism. One aim was to show that social democracy had contributed to the downfall of socialism in Eastern Europe and the Soviet Union as part of a Western conspiracy. Another was to critically assess the role of social democracy in Western societies. This critique allowed Chinese scholars to make their independent assessment of social democracy. As they became more familiar with its actual role and policies in Western market economies, the focus of their debate shifted from ideological to more practical concerns.

The first reason for the Chinese disenchantment with social democracy was the end of socialist regimes in Eastern Europe. By the end of 1991, the expectation or at least hope expressed earlier that social democracy might play a positive role in transforming Eastern Europe[47] had vanished. The public recognition that Western European social democracy had failed to preserve some form of socialism in Eastern Europe[48] was at the same time an indirect admission that this possibility had not been excluded earlier. In a first explanatory attempt, it was claimed that this did not amount to a defeat of socialism, because socialism had in fact never fully grown roots in Eastern Europe. The reason given was that the Eastern European communist parties had nearly all grown out of former social democratic parties[49] and had been more social democratic than socialist anyway. It was argued that their socialist system had been imposed on them by the Soviet Union without consideration of their national characteristics: "… the communist parties of all Eastern European countries were either merged with social democratic parties or developed from social democratic parties. Ideologically and organizationally, they have therefore been broadly and deeply influenced by social democratic parties. Because of the external influence of the Red Army and the CPSU, Marxism as the ideological basis of the Eastern European communist parties has not been fully consolidated. The communist parties of all Eastern European countries neglected their own organizational build-up and were lax in the Marxist education of their people."[50]

In regard to the Soviet Union, the situation was different, as there was no doubt that the Soviet Union had been a socialist country. The Chinese evaluation gave very little consideration to why the changes in the Soviet Union happened and, instead, concentrated more on the personal responsibility of Gorbachev. The general view was that, up to 1988, Gorbachev's reforms had still been in a socialist framework, although his policies of class-independent democratization and glasnost were already no longer socialist. In the second stage from 1988 to 1991, Gorbachev's proclamation of humanitarian socialism, together with his abolition of the leadership of the communist party, the dictatorship of the proletariat and the leading ideological role of Marxism-Leninism, were seen as strongly influenced by social democracy.[51] The final abandoning of socialism was seen in the CPSU's draft party programme of August 1991.[52] Social democratic ideology and the support from Western social democratic leaders were depicted as the driving forces that had turned Gorbachev away from socialism. This evaluation concluded the Chinese debate about the Soviet model which had lasted throughout the 1980s and even in its last stages had followed the lead of the debates within the Soviet Union. As a sign of emancipation, the Chinese Communist Party in 1993 finally omitted the reference to proletarian internationalism from its party statutes, following the lead of most other remaining communist parties.[53]

The personalization of the argument around Gorbachev was a sign that China at the time was not able to discuss the real causes for the collapse of the Soviet Union in a more general manner. The political and economic reasons for the collapse of the Eastern European regimes were simply explained away with relative ease. The use of the person of Gorbachev as a scapegoat and the construed identification of social democracy with the strategic and commercial interests of Western European countries toward Eastern Europe were convenient distractions from the economic and political causes of the breakdown of the Soviet Union. This identification led to the final geographic and political localization of social democracy as the leading ideology of Western Europe. In this context, the Socialist International was attacked for the support its leaders had given to Gorbachev, and for its hostile statements and policies toward communist parties.[54] An additional reason for perceiving the Socialist International as hostile was its condemning statements concerning the Chinese handling of the

Tiananmen incident.[55] Chinese observers stated that the Socialist International had become anti-communist in 1989, after decades of increasing cooperation with communist parties.[56] This assertion was based on its programme of ideological pluralism, parliamentarianism and economic policies as expressed in communiqués and statements made by the various congresses of the Socialist International and on other occasions. Specific mention was made again of the danger that China faced from the social democratic threat to its one-party policy and its ideological commitment to the "four ideological principles."[57] These Chinese statements identified the Socialist International not just as irrelevant, but as an active hostile force.

The final step was the demarcation of social democracy from Chinese socialist orthodoxy. An article entitled, "Analysis of Democratic Socialism," published in 1991, gives a representative overview of the major ideological objections against social democracy. The authors began with the warning that "democratic socialism is an ideological fashion that in recent years has rapidly spread and become rampant. It is distantly linked with the Western bourgeois peaceful evolution (campaign) and has played a most pernicious role in pushing the dramatic changes in Eastern Europe and the Soviet Union. Its influence is not to be underestimated in China, where it has led to considerable ideological confusion."[58] The article went on to list the usual theoretical and political objections against social democracy from a general Marxist perspective, before pointing out that it was specifically unsuited for China on the basis of China's national characteristics. This was explained by three simple points. Firstly, political pluralism was not acceptable, as it would undermine the role of the Communist Party. Secondly, China would not aim for a mixed economy based on private ownership, as it would endanger the people's livelihood. Thirdly, ideological pluralism was rejected on the ground that it would eventually lead to corruption and negative attitudes.[59]

In the final conclusion, this criticism contributed to a more realistic view of social democracy. It recognized that social democracy was not able to cooperate with communist parties within a socialist system and that its role was that of a pragmatic and reformist political force confined to instigating reforms within a capitalist system. While it was admitted that social democracy was able to implement positive reforms in the context of a capitalist economy,[60] in the context of a socialist economy its commitment to a multiparty system and a private economy would necessarily lead to the restoration of capitalism.[61] In the Chinese interpretation, this meant that social democracy posed an imminent threat to their socialist system. This served to draw a sharp dividing line to separate it from orthodox socialism. As social democracy had proven to be such a danger to Soviet socialism, the Chinese discussants now formulated Chinese special characteristics in a way that would prevent the same from happening in China.

Parallel to the assessment of the role of social democracy in the collapse of the communist systems in Eastern Europe and the Soviet Union, a more pragmatic evaluation of social democracy policies in their own right began to take shape after 1992. Now, the social democratic welfare state was criticized not only because of its role in stabilizing capitalist exploitation, but also because in countries such as Sweden it placed too great a burden on public funding and proved to be economically inefficient. At this point, more sceptical Western views of social democracy were borrowed from Western sources and reflected in the Chinese debate.[62] The new argument was that social democracy in Western Europe had reached its peak in the 1970s and that its political relevance had in fact started to decline during the 1980s and might continue to decline for another two or three decades.[63]

The practical evaluation of social democracy, while ending its role as a contender for orthodox approval, created new interest in the functioning of social democratic institutions. This led to the discussion of issues which were much closer to the concerns of Chinese economic reforms than the previous ideological considerations. One such issue was the role of the state. As the Chinese state assumed more new functions under reform policies, the strong role of the state postulated by social democracy was now recognized to be much more appropriate than the Marxist paradigm of its withering away. It was also recognized that this would necessitate political reforms as state and Communist Party became more closely intertwined.[64] The consideration of these aspects even led to the conclusion that the failure of Soviet socialism was due to the mismanagement of these issues.[65] Other issues included specific labour policies under social democratic parties,[66] social policies and the function of social democratic parties in opposition and their relationship with conservative parties.[67]

In the end, this produced a much more pragmatic understanding of Western societies and their interplay of political, social and economic forces. After 1992, ideological restrictions on borrowing from the West had been relaxed to the extent that it was possible to argue for any kind of Western economic and social policy to be adopted in China.[68] There was no need to justify such borrowing from the West with the social democratic origins of certain policies. Consequently, in areas such as social welfare, where Western concepts were introduced into China, they were acknowledged to come from other countries, including the United States.[69] A specifically social democratic inspiration for Chinese reforms was the depth of social welfare systems and the involvement of the state: "The most outstanding characteristic of the nordic welfare model is its 'social, universal and institutional system.' This means that society is in charge of all kinds of social guarantees for the citizens, from 'cradle to grave,' including everything."[70] As to the role of this concept of social democratic welfare system for China, the same author concluded: "Even if the nordic welfare system is facing a challenge and needs to undergo adjustments and reforms, this does not mean that there is nothing to learn or borrow for our usage. For instance, we can learn a lot from the historical development and perfection of the nordic welfare system, and also we can gain a lot of experience from the conflicts and problems that are now besetting the nordic welfare system."[71]

In summary, the sudden disillusionment with social democracy resulting from the collapse of the Soviet Union led to a bedeviling of what previously had seemed to be a potential model for the reform of socialism. Exaggerated expectations of social democracy as an ideology combining socialism and capitalism were replaced by a more realistic assessment of its historical and practical merits and demerits that proved to be of more relevance to China's practical concerns.

Socialism with National Characteristics

In the ideological debate in the mid-1990s, "socialism with Chinese characteristics" emerged as a notion that combined market-oriented economic policies with a continued role for the Communist Party and its ideology. By 1995, reference to social democracy and other foreign concepts of socialism had become increasingly sparse. Instead, newly coined terms such as "special characteristics theory" (*tese lilun*) and "socialism with special characteristics" (*you tese de shehui zhuyi*) aimed at giving "socialism with Chinese characteristics" a theoretical relevance.[72] China was now the only remaining major socialist country and regarded itself as the guardian of orthodox socialist tradition.[73] However, social democratic concepts continued to be discussed, albeit without reference to their origins, whenever ongoing reforms raised issues such as the role of the state and social fairness. While social democracy as such was no longer a topic to be discussed, its ideas continued to make an indirect impact on the reform debate that arose, out of practical needs. During 1995, several bold reform initiatives were made that were either inspired by democratic ideas or were put forward by scholars who had previously played a prominent role in the social democracy debate.

As China's economy continued to grow, so did ideological self-confidence. Chinese scholars comparing reforms in China and the Soviet Union now claimed that China had followed superior strategies in every aspect.[74] National characteristics served to emphasize national independence in light of the Chinese experience with the Soviet model. Beyond that, the notion of national characteristics also served to hold other potential models at bay. The emphasis on national characteristics did, however, not preclude the study of capitalist countries for specific purposes. The borderline was drawn where China would again follow a model, as it had with the Soviet Union.[75] The emphasis on national characteristics became a defence of the pragmatic nature of Chinese reforms against ideological interference. As the primary task of socialism in China was defined to be developing the productive forces and the economy, the previous political obstacles to borrowing from the West disappeared. The warning of the danger that capitalist ideas could lead China onto the road of capitalism, was ridiculed in one article as reflecting the mentality of a cave man.[76] In line with this view, social democracy began to loose its significance as a potential model for China. It was now merely regarded as an ideology representing the national characteristics of specific Western European countries.

As calls for a reinterpretation of Chinese Marxism were voiced openly and were supported by people as prominent as Hu Sheng, the president of the Academy of Social Sciences in Beijing,[77] social democratic arguments as a cover for the debate of ideological reforms were replaced by those taken from Marxist classics. Chinese scholars working on ideology became more adventurous in advocating political reforms. Instead of having to turn to social democracy in order to introduce new concepts, they could now draw their arguments from the Marxist-Leninist tradition of which they had become the only guardians. Gao Fang, for example, a prominent scholar who had published widely on social democracy, argued in an article published in 1995 that Lenin had proposed a multiparty system for the Soviet Union. With veiled reference to China's present situation, Gao Fang wrote that in Lenin's view a multiparty system guaranteed a better political representation of social interests as well as a separation of government and party functions.[78] What was new about this was not the content of the proposed reforms, but the reference to orthodox sources. In previous years, similar arguments would most likely have been made by referring to social democracy.

The issue of social fairness and the role of the state, traditional topics of Western social democracy, came to the fore in 1995 as a result of the social changes induced by economic reforms in China. This was another example of how social democratic concepts continued to inform the Chinese reform debate. By 1995, China had begun to introduce a broadly based system of social insurance to cover unemployment, old age pensions and other areas. The result of these reforms was that the Chinese state acquired a whole range of new functions in providing these services. In fact, the role of the state expanded even further, to include safeguarding a socially tolerable distribution of income and wealth and equality of opportunity in gaining access to them.[79] The issues that arose of the policies were new in the Chinese context, but they were exactly the same issues that had been raised in Chinese debates in previous years, when the dilemma of social democratic parties[80] had been raised in respect to combining a market economy with social and regional income equalization, equality of opportunity and social fairness in general. The issue of social fairness was now discussed in terms that had been regarded as social democratic.[81] As with Western social democracy, Chinese scholars found their answer in the role of the state and its ability to create appropriate taxation and insurance systems, protect the socially weak,[82] and promote social ethics as well.[83]

In summary, China's ideological debate in recent years has had two separate aspects that have been connected in a syncretistic fashion. "Socialism with national characteristics" was a response to the worldwide collapse of socialist states and supported above all a commitment to the leading role of the Communist Party and its ideology. Social democracy was no longer part of this socialist ideology. Parallel to this, there was another debate going on that was inspired by China's pragmatic reform policies and reflected their ideological consequences. Social democratic concepts have played a major role in this debate, not because they have been consciously adopted, but because the results of the Chinese mixture of market policies with social components so closely resembles the situation in which social democracy has historically developed.

Conclusion: The Issue of Social Democracy and Its Impact

In spite of the limited public attention it has received in official Chinese media, social democracy has played a central role in the contemporary Chinese ideological discourse. It has linked China with the reforms in the Soviet Union, when it was seen as an alternative and attractive option to combine reform and socialism. After the events of 1989 in China and Eastern Europe and finally after the collapse of the Soviet Union, the Chinese rejected social democracy as an ideological threat to their political *status quo* and accused it of being the cause for the collapse of communism in Eastern Europe. The Chinese saw social democracy much more through Soviet than through Western European eyes. They turned away from it as soon as the Soviet Union had ceased to exist.

For the Chinese ideological discourse in a wider sense, the importance of the social democratic interlude lay in the fact that it integrated China's intellectuals into a larger Western, albeit Euro-centred, discourse. As these ideas gained increasing publicity, the Chinese world-view became more differentiated and political reform less unthinkable than official party slogans would indicate. In the course of their critique of social democracy, Chinese scholars dismantled much of the orthodox Leninist ideology that prevented them from gaining a deeper understanding of the West. Since the mid-1990s, it has been recognized that social democracy had provided useful concepts for a reforming economy faced with radical social and economic change and the need to balance the demands of the market with a commitment to social fairness. Under the eclectic concept of socialism with Chinese characteristics, social democratic ideas have reemerged in a practical sense.

At present, the emphasis on national characteristics allows Chinese ideologists to justify China's pragmatic policies and to reinterpret Marxism and Leninism to suit their purposes. However, in this pursuit they are isolated and have moved outside of the spheres of international political discourse. Whether social democracy will gain new importance in the future depends more on China's international than on its domestic policies. China has turned away from social democracy, not only because of the events in Eastern Europe and in the former Soviet Union, but also because of the diminishing role of Western Europe as compared to the United States.[84] Should China decide to revive ideological links with Western countries, or should social democracy in Western Europe experience a revival, China might well rediscover an interest in social democracy.

Notes

1. The first part is taken with minor alterations from my previous article "Chinese Interest in Social Democracy," in *Market Reform in the Changing Socialist World*, edited by Hans Hendrischke (Sydney, Macquarie Studies in Chinese Political Economy, 1992), pp. 70–85.

2. A detailed analysis of the political background to these developments is contained in Hans Hendrischke, "China's Lessons from the Collapse of the Soviet Union" (unpublished paper presented at the Contemporary China Centre, Australian National University, 16 July 1994).

3. Bill Brugger and David Kelly, *Chinese Marxism in the Post-Mao Era* (Stanford: Stanford University Press, 1990), p. 4.

4. Information from interviews by the author in Beijing in 1990 and 1991.

5. For example, the journal *Dangdai shijie shehui zhuyi wenti* (Problems of the Contemporary World Socialism Quarterly) published by Shandong University.

6. For example, the journal *Lilun tantao* (Theoretical Enquiry), published by the Party School of Heilongjiang Provincial Committee of CPC.

7. For example, Yin Xuyi, "Xi Ou shehuidang de minzhu shehui zhuyi guojia xueshuo chutan" (Preliminary Study of the Theory of the State in Western European Social Democracy), *Xi Ou yanjiu* (Western European Studies), No. 5 (1987), pp. 1–9.

8. Su Shaozhi and Cai Shengning (eds), *Shehui zhuyi zai dangdai shijie shang* (Socialism in the Contemporary World) (Beijing: Guangming ribao chubanshe, 1985); Guowai shehui zhuyi wenti jiaoxuezu (Study Group for Problems of Foreign Socialism)(ed.), *Shehuidang zhongyao wenjian xuanbian* (Anthology of Important Documents of Social Democratic Parties) (Beijing: Zhonggong zhongyang dangxiao yanjiu bangongshi, 1985); Jiang Shilin and Guo Dehong (eds.), *Dangdai shehui minzhudang yu minzhu zhuyi zhengdang luncong* (Studies on Contemporary Social Democratic Parties and Social Democracy) (Beijing: Zhongguo zhanwang chubanshe, 1986).

9. Yin Xuyi (ed.), *"Dangdai shijie shehui zhuyi yanjiu" congshu* (Collection of "Studies on Contemporary World Socialism") (Harbin: Heilongjiang renmin chubanshe, 1988).

10. Key project organized by Li Honglin of the Fujian Academy of Social Science, see Zhang Weiguo, "Li Honglin tan dui shehui zhuyi zairenshi" (Li Honglin on the Reassessment of Socialism), *Shijie jingji daobao* (World Economic Herald), Shanghai, 11 April 1988.

11. See Yin Xuyi (ed.) (Note 9); the three books under this series comprise a volume on theory and practice of West European social democratic parties, one volume on important personages and one volume containing a collection of social democratic party documents.

12. Li Xinggeng (ed.), *Dangdai Xi Ou shehuidang de lilun yu shijian* (Theory and Practice of Contemporay Social Democratic Parties) (Harbin: Heilongjiang renmin chubanshe, 1988).

13. Li Can, "Cong shehui minzhu zhuyi dao minzhu shehui zhuyi" (From Social Democracy to Democratic Socialism), *Zhonggong Zhejiang shengwei dangxiao xuebao*, Hangzhou, No. 2 (1990), 75–80.

14. Yin Xuyi, "Xifang fada guojia de 'minzhu shehui zhuyi'" ("Democratic Socialism" in Western Developed Countries), in *Dangdai Xi Ou shehuidang renwuzhuan*, edited by Yin Xuyi (Biographies of Contemporary Western European Social Democrats) (Harbin: Heilongjiang renmin chubanshe, 1988), p. 3; see also Lu Ren, "Shilun Xi Ou shehui minzhu dang de minzhu shehui zhuyi" (Essay on the Democratic Socialism of Western European Social Democratic Parties), in Jiang Shilin and Guo Deheng (eds) (Note 8). In a Soviet book publication of 1979, published in Chinese translation by CASS in 1984, the term democratic socialism is only used in quotation marks to indicate that it is not accepted as a form of socialism, see P. H. Fedoceev, *Shto takoe "Democratcieski Socialism"?* (What Is "Democratic Socialism"?) (Moscow: Political Books Publishing House, 1979); translation by Shi Jian et al. *Shenme shi "minzhu shehui zhuyi"?* (What Is "Democratic Socialism"?) (Beijing: Zhongguo shehui kexue chubanshe, 1984).

15. Yin Xuyi, "'Minzhu shehui zhuyi' haishi 'shehui minzhu zhuyi'?" ("Democratic Socialism" or "Social Democracy"?), *Dangdai shijie yu shehui zhuyi* (The Contemporary World and Socialism), No. 3 (1994), pp. 31–35.

16. Wang Fengwu and Lin Hekun (eds.), *Shehui zhuyi redian wenti zonghenglun* (Reflections on Popular Issues of Socialism) (Beijing: Jingji xueyuan chubanshe, 1990), p. 113.

17. Yin Xuyi, "Xifang fada guojia de 'minzhu shehui zhuyi'" (Note 14), p. 6.

18. Ibid.

19. Ibid., p. 11.

20. Ibid., p. 6.

21. Huang Ansen, "Guanyu shehuidang de xingzhi he zuoyong de chutan" (Form and Function of Social Democratic Parties), in *"Dangdai shijie shehui zhuyi yanjiu" congshu*, (Note 9), pp. 16–25, pp. 21ff.

22. Li Yongqing, "Lun Xi Ou shehuidang qunzhong jichu de guangfanxing ji qi yuanyin" (On the Extent of the Mass Basis of Contemporary World Socialism and the Reasons), in *'Dangdai shijie shehui zhuyi yanjiu' congshu* (Note 9), pp. 46–65, 53.

23. Huang Ansen (Note 21), p. 24.

24. Ibid., p. 17.

25. Yin Xuyi (Note 14), p. 7.

26. Li Yongqing (Note 22), pp. 56–57.

27. Yin Xuyi, "Minzhu shehui zhuyi de guojia xueshuo" (The Theory of the State

in Social Democracy), in *Dangdai Xi Ou shehuidang renwuzhuan* (Note 14), p. 40.

28. Pan Peixin, "Tantan Ruidian moshi de youlai, yiyi he jidian sikao" (On the Origin and Meaning of the Swedish Model and Some Considerations), *Dangdai shijie shehui zhuyi wenti*, edited by Yin Xuyi, No. 2 (1989), Issue 20, pp. 52–55.

29. Guo Weimin, "Xi Ou shehuidang de dangnei minzhu" (Inner Party Democracy in Western European Socialist Parties), *Guangming ribao* (Guangming Daily), 10 April 1989.

30. Li Yongqing (Note 22), pp. 57–59.

31. Ibid.

32. Yin Xuyi (Note 14), p. 15.

33. Liu Shihua, "Capitalism Reconsidered: A Review of Views," *Social Sciences in China*, No. 1 (March 1991), pp. 9–33, 28.

34. Ibid., p. 19.

35. R. Dahrendorf, *Betrachtungen ueber die Revolution in Europa* (Considerations about the Revolution in Europe) (Stuttgart: Deutsche Verlagsanstalt, 1990).

36. Example of such publications are the essays collected in Zhou Xincheng, Ren Dakui et al. (eds.), *Dangdai minzhu shehuizhuyi pingxi* (An Analysis of Contemporary Social Democracy) (Shenyang: Liaoning renmin chubanshe, 1991) and Lin Tai (ed.), *Dangdai sixiang zhengzhi jiaoyu redian wenti sikao* (Thoughts on the Popular Issues of Contemporary Ideological and Political Education) (Beijing, Jiancha chubanshe, 1991). In addition, a large number of articles on the topic appeared in journals such as *Shehui zhuyi yanjiu* (Socialist Studies).

37. Le Xiong, "Zhanhou Xi Ou shemindang yu Sugong guanxi de yanbian" (The Changing Relationship between Post-War Western European Social Democratic Parties and the Soviet Communists), *Dangdai shijie shehui zhuyi wenti*, No. 3 (1990), Issue 25, pp. 41, 60–63.

38. Ibid., p. 63.

39. Ye Zicheng, "Sulian lilunjie guanyu shehui zhuyi wenti de zhenglun" (The Debates about Problems of Socialism among Soviet Theoreticians), *Guoji zhengzhi yanjiu* (International Political Studies), No. 2 (1990), Issue 36, pp. 13–18.

40. Ibid.

41. Ibid., p.15.

42. Ibid., pp. 15–16.

43. Ibid., pp. 16–17.

44. Le Xiong (Note 37), p. 63.

45. This included historical accounts and current events. For party histories, see Ma Ju, Yu Qingtian and Wang Jucai (eds.), *Minzhu shehui zhuyi de youlai he*

yanbian (Origins and Evolution of Democratic Socialism) (Beijing: Beijing gongye daxue chubanshe, 1992).

46. Wang Xintang, "Ping minzhu shehui zhuyi de minzhuguan" (Critique of the Concept of Democracy of Democratic Socialism), in Lin Tai (ed.) (Note 36), p. 2.

47. Pan Peixin (Note 28), pp. 52–55.

48. Ma Zhiliang, "'Di santiao daolu' yu Dong Ou shibian" (The "Third Way" and the Changes in Eastern Europe), *Dangdai shijie shehui zhuyi wenti*, No. 2 (1991), pp. 61–64.

49. Xu Fujun, "Dong Ou jubian yu minzhu shehui zhuyi" (The Dramatic Changes in Eastern Europe and Democratic Socialism), *Dangdai shijie shehui zhuyi wenti*, No. 1 (1992), pp. 51–54.

50. Ibid.

51. Xu Wenze, "Sulian de jieti yu rendao zhuyi de minzhu de shehui zhuyi de pochan" (The Dissolution of the Soviet Union and the Bankruptcy of Humanitarian Democratic Socialism), *Sulian wenti yanjiu ziliao* (Soviet Studies Research Materials), No. 4 (1992).

52. Dai Longbin, "Sugong de zuihou yige danggang caoan" (A Last Draft of the CPSU's Last Party Statutes), *Guoji gongyun shi yanjiu* (Studies on the History of the International Communist Movement), No. 4 (1992).

53. Xiao Feng and Ma Zhiliang, "Guanyu 'wuchan jieji guoji zhuyi' de jige wenti" (Some Problems of "Proletarian Internationalism"), *Guoji gongyun shi yanjiu*, No. 1 (1993), pp. 1–5.

54. Chang Xinxin, "Jian ping shehuidang guoji shiba da 'yuanze shengming'" (A Brief Comment on 'the Principle Statement' of the 18th Congress of the Socialist Party International), *Dangdai shijie shehui zhuyi wenti*, No. 3 (1991).

55. Xu Fujun (Note 49), p. 54.

56. Yang Zhangming, "Shi xi shehui dangren dui gongdangren zhengce de bianhua" (Trying to Analyse the Change in the Policies of the Socialists toward the Communists), *Dangdai shijie shehui zhuyi wenti*, No. 1 (1991), pp. 60–64.

57. Ni Baozhi, "Shi xi shehuidang guoji dui gongchandang de zhengce" (Trying to Analyse the Policy of the Socialist Party International toward the Communist Party), *Dangdai shijie shehui zhuyi wenti*, No. 3 (1991), pp. 53–56.

58. Wei Cizhu and Sun Fengzhi, "Minzhu shehui zhuyi pouxi" (Analysis of Democratic Socialism), *Dangdai shijie shehui zhuyi wenti*, No. 4 (1991), pp. 16–19.

59. Ibid.

60. Ma Zhiliang (Note 48).

61. Wei Cizhu and Sun Fengzhi (Note 58); see also Xi Tiewang, "Dong Ou gongchandang minzhu shehui zhuyi hua tedian chu xi" (Preliminary Analysis

of the Characteristics of Social Democratization of the Eastern European Communist Parties), *Dangdai shijie shehui zhuyi wenti*, No.4 (1991), pp. 46–47.

62. For example, Tang Haijun, "Minzhu shehui zhuyi yu Ouzhou shehuidang mianlin de kunjing ji yuanyin jianxi" (Brief Analysis of the Difficulties Faced by Democratic Socialism and European Socialist Parties and Their Reasons), *Jiaoxue yu yanjiu* (Teaching and Research), No.3 (1994), p. 70–73.

63. Shi Huiye, "Qiantan Xi Ou shehuidang de xianzhuang ji qianjing" (Talk on the Present State and Future Perspectives of Western European Social Democratic Parties), *Dangdai shijie shehui zhuyi wenti*, No. 1 (1992), pp. 55–60.

64. Wu Jiang, "Ershi shiji shehui zhuyi de xin fazhan" (New Developments in 20th Century Socialism), *Tong zhou gong jin*, No. 7, quoted in *Xinhua wenzhai* (Xinhua Digest), No. 11 (1994), pp. 3–6.

65. Ibid.

66. Zhang Peihang and Chen Lin, "Minzhu shehui zhuyi de minzhu moshi zhi yi" (One Model of Democracy of Democratic Socialism), *Guoji gongyun shi yanjiu*, No. 2 (1993), pp. 3 and 23–28.

67. Tang Haijun (Note 62).

68. Qiu Zhaorong, "Dadan liyong ziben zhuyi — jianjue bu gao ziben zhuyi" (Courageous in Using Capitalism — Determined in Not Practicing Capitalism), *Dangdai shijie shehui zhuyi wenti*, No. 2 (1993), pp. 25–27.

69. Yi Bocheng, Xu Wenhu and Cao Hengchun (eds.), *Zhongguo shehui baoxian zhidu gaige* (The Reform of China's Social Insurance System) (Shanghai: Fudan daxue chubanshe, 1993).

70. Zhang Yunling (ed.), *Bei Ou shehui fuli zhidu ji Zhongguo shehui baozhang zhidu de gaige* (Nordic Social Welfare System and Reform of China's Social Security System) (Beijing: Jingji kexue chubanshe, 1993), p. 5.

71. Ibid., p. 5.

72. Su Changpei (ed.), *Te se lun* (The Theory of Special Characteristics) (Beijing: Shehui kexue wenxian chubanshe, 1992); Gao Fang, "Jianshe you Zhongguo tese shehui zhuyi de shijie yiyi" (The International Significance of Socialism with Chinese Characteristics), *Lilun tantao* (Theoretical Investigation), No. 6 (1994), pp. 5–8.

73. Zhang Hanqing, "Lue lun shijie shehui zhuyi yundong de muqian xingshi yu qianjing" (Brief Discussion of the Present Situation and Outlook for the World Socialist Movement), *Shehui zhuyi yanjiu* (Studies in Socialism), No. 6 (1994), pp. 6–10.

74. Xue Dezhen, "Zhongguo yu Sulian gaige de bijiao" (Comparing the Chinese and the Soviet Reforms), *Xiandai zhexue* (Contemporary Philosophy), No. 2 (1995), quoted from *Xinhua wenzhai*, No. 10 (1995), pp. 5–12.

75. Hu Sheng, "Makesi zhuyi shi fazhan de lilun" (Marxism Is a Developing

Theory), *Renmin ribao* (People's Daily), 27 December 1994, quoted in *Xinhua wenzhai*, No. 2 (1995), pp. 5–8.

76. Wu Jiang (Note 64).

77. Hu Sheng (Note 75).

78. Gao Fang, "Liening guanyu shehui zhuyi minzhuzhi de lilun yu shijian" (Lenin on Theory and Practice of Socialist Democracy), *Nanjing shehui kexue* (Nanjing Social Sciences), quoted in *Xinhua Wenzhai*, No. 4 (1995), pp. 2–4.

79. Li Peilin, "Shi xi xin shiqi liyi geju bianhua de jige redian wenti" (Tentative Analysis of Some Current Issues regarding the Changes in the Structure of Benefits in the New Era), *Renmin ribao*, 12 April 1995, quoted in *Xinhua wenzhai*, No. 6 (1995), pp. 9–12.

80. See Zhou Yongliang, "Xi Ou shehui minzhudang: liang nan xuanze de kunjing" (The Socialist Parties in West Europe: Being on the Horns of a Dilemma), *Dangdai shijie shehui zhuyi wenti*, No. 4 (1990), pp. 61–65.

81. Li Fengsheng, "Lun shehui gongping de sanji neihan" (On the Three Levels of Meanings of Social Fairness), *Guangming ribao*, 19 March 1995, quoted in *Xinhua wenzhai*, No. 5 (1995), pp. 53–54.

82. Li Peilin (Note 79).

83. Guo Xuejian, "Shichang jingji tiaojian xia renmen jiazhi guannian de bianhua yu duice" (Changes in the Values of People under Conditions of a Market Economy and Respective Policies), *Qiye da shijie* (The Big World of Enterprise), No. 3 (1995), quoted in *Xinhua wenzhai*, No. 7 (1995), pp. 33–35.

84. Li Cong, "Dangqian fada ziben zhuyi guojia jingji de zhongda bianhua" (Major Economic Changes in Contemporary Developed Capitalist Countries), *Jingji xuejia* (The Economist), No. 1 (1995), quoted in *Xinhua wenzhai*, No. 4 (1995), pp. 43–47.

5

Economic Development, Stability and Democratic Village Self-governance

Jean C. Oi

Introduction

While successful rural industrialization has occurred under the leadership of local governments in some of China's villages,[1] other villages remain poor, mostly agricultural and run by ineffective, sometimes corrupt, leaders who are neither willing nor able to rule the community. Despite more than a decade of economic reform, many problems that plagued China's peasants in the late 1980s continue in the mid-1990s. In addition to suffering under the weight of village fees, peasants receive IOUs instead of payment for their deliveries,[2] wait for promised supplies of inputs, suffer as officials demand advance payment of grain sales quotas and taxes,[3] and endure unexpected increases in procurement targets.[4]

These problems have been made more urgent because of the recent occurrence of peasant protests and demonstrations.[5] Peasants have always had the means to show their unhappiness with government policies and local officials. Even during the Maoist period peasants could engage in resistance.[6] What has changed in the 1990s is that peasants have different means of articulating their interests. In many cases, they are now resisting openly. The violent demonstrations and destruction of property in Renshou county, Sichuan is one example. Many other types of political actions have been undertaken. Officials are being beaten, their property is damaged, or they are simply ignored, if not actually thrown out of office.[7]

Officials, both at the national and local levels, are sensitive to the destabilizing effect of peasant disturbances. A cursory glance at the press makes clear that this has become an issue of major concern for top policy-makers in Beijing as well as in provincial capitals. Jiang Zemin explicitly addressed this issue and its importance for China's reform and stability in his speech to the 14th Party Congress.

Central authorities acknowledge the problems of poor villages and the inequalities they represent. Authorities have attributed the economic backwardness to lack of proper leadership following introduction of the household responsibility system in agricultural production. Officials readily admit that decollectivization has left some villages "paralysed" or "partially paralysed" because of a lack of economic resources that underlies the lack of effective leadership.[8]

Equally worrisome is the ageing of the current village leadership and lack of interest by talented individuals to serve in their place.[9] Village officials have had difficulty implementing unpopular policies, such as family planning; some are simply ignored; taxes and fees go unpaid; village coffers stand empty, and nothing gets done. In other cases, unpopular village officials have been beaten and their property has been destroyed in retaliation by disgruntled villagers. Safety is no longer assured as robbery and other crimes, including banditry, have become major problems in parts of the Chinese countryside.

New leaders are needed for the backward villages. The problem is that there is disagreement on how the right man should be chosen. One set of answers discussed in literature on the subject calls for improving the quality of the village party secretary — a familiar and not surprising solution that relies on appointment by higher levels of authority or selection limited to party members within a village. The second is an unexpected call for competitive *democratic* elections to select village leaders. Both solutions see leadership as the key to achieving the ultimate goal of village economic prosperity. The difference lies in who should lead — the party secretary or the village committee.

This chapter will examine the two diverse sets of solutions to the leadership problem in China's poor villages. It will pay particular attention to why China is advocating village democracy in light of its resistance to democratic movements in the urban areas. One could argue that the existence of these two sets of antithetical solutions points to divisions within the central leadership — democratic reformers versus party hard-liners. Certainly, one can identify distinct sources of support for the competing solutions, and there are differing views about the role that more participatory forms of government should play in rural China, but I want to caution that one should not overdraw the analysis of differences. As will be evident in the sections that follow, although the solutions are radically different, the ultimate goal of the two sets of solutions are not that divergent.

While the full agenda that lies behind the policy of promoting democratic village self-rule is no doubt multi-faceted, one clear objective is a strategic concern about *stability and economic development* in China's countryside. Undoubtedly, some within the bureaucracy who are promoting democratic self-rule as the solution to the problems of China's villages may fervently believe in the value of participatory government. Nevertheless, the selling point of this policy that has allowed broader official support may be premised on less democratic ideals. For many, direct elections of village government is a limited experiment in democracy that is a *means* to stability and economic development, rather than an end in itself.

Village self-rule has been embraced as a viable, relatively low-cost answer to the many problems that have developed in the wake of economic reform in the countryside. As reports of peasant burdens continue to accumulate and as the lists of peasant disturbances grow, village self-rule is grasped as a way to maintain order and build the legitimacy of village cadres, upon whom the upper levels depend for completion of state-set quotas and effective rule at the local levels. The hope is that self-rule will be the answer to the problems of economic development in those villages that have failed to advance in the reform period.

Rather than seeing this difference of views as representing radically divergent views about democracy, it may be more useful to interpret this as reflecting a more basic and long-standing disagreement about where power lies in today's villages given the system of dual decision making where there is both a party and a government leader. The two views mirror the contradiction between theory and practice regarding the proper role for the party after the dissolution of the communes. Decollectivization has in any case so far failed to take the party out of economic decision making since that role does not yet belong to the government, i.e., the village committee. Let me begin by looking first at the more familiar call to improve the quality of the village party secretaries.

Upgrade Party Leadership

As might be expected, local party committees and organization (*zuzhi*) departments at different levels of government have put forth the position that upgrading village party leadership will solve the problems of China's backward villages. With new, better qualified cadres, poor villages can be led out of poverty. Party committees and organization departments at provincial or county governments are frank about the shortcomings of the current party leadership in China's poor villages. They admit the need to "bring up to speed" the party leadership in politically backward villages.[10] Increased educational levels and decreased age rank high on the list of needed innovations. The right man now must possess certain technical skills and ability to operate in a market environment.

The need for a more democratic process in the selection of the village party secretary, rather than simple appointment by the party at the township or county levels, is acknowledged in some of the articles. While the meaning of "democratic" is left vague, it is clear that only party members can elect the village party secretary. Most articles stress the role of the upper levels in selecting promising and talented individuals as the new party secretaries to run China's villages. In most cases, those appointed will be from the village itself. Talented villagers should be persuaded to return and use their superior skills to lead their villages to economic prosperity.[11]

In some villages, outsiders must be brought in because of a lack of local talent. When this is necessary, then the upper levels could tap those currently working in rural enterprises or those working at higher levels of government to take charge of the most troubled villages. To ensure sufficient personnel for the task of village leadership, a third echelon of leaders are being groomed for future positions as village cadres. Not all of these people will actually be appointed village leaders. Those who show themselves to be deficient are dropped, while new recruits are selected to take their place.[12]

Little mystery surrounds such proposals. They represent efforts to keep the *status quo* in the distribution of power in the Chinese countryside. The party secretary is assumed to be the leader whose actions determine the course of the village. No reference is made to village committees or the law authorizing them. One would never know from this discussion that such a law exists. What is new is the recognition that old policies and tactics for selecting local leaders are unsuited to the post-decollectivized, market environment.

Democratic Village Self-rule

An unexpected turn of events in light of the crackdown on the various democracy movements, most notably the 1989 Tiananmen demonstrations, that developed in the urban areas is the call for direct, competitive election of village committees. Beginning in 1988, with the trial implementation of the Organic Law on Village Committees (*Cunwei hui zuzhi fa*), competitive, democratic elections have been promoted to ensure the rule of law and village self-rule.[13] These elections differ from those held during the Maoist period.[14] Instead of the slate of candidates being pre-selected by the upper levels, candidates are now nominated by the villagers themselves. Instead of a simple ratification of a predetermined slate, there are now more candidates than seats. Candidates campaign to curry favour among voters. Some village elections have become hotly contested, democratic affairs.

Unlike the past, peasants take an active interest in the outcome of these local elections. Reportedly, peasants who have gone out of the village to find work, return to vote in close races. International organizations have helped teach officials and peasants about secret ballots and electoral procedure, ranging from when campaigning should stop to the erection of proper polling places and secret ballots.[15] Perhaps, equally important, the existence and promulgation of the village Organic Law has empowered peasants to use it to protect themselves against local officials and illegal practices.[16] Some, when they find out about the law, demand elections to get rid of corrupt officials.

According to the Organic Law on Village Committees, the village committee, is the governing body of the village. The entire registered adult population is entitled to vote for the village committee, which consists of the committee chairman (village head), vice-head and 3–5 committee members. The frequency that the committee as a whole meets varies from village to village. In one Hunan village it met formally either once or twice each month. The village committee chairman along with his vice-chairman are the key decision-makers, who run the village on a day-to-day basis. Those elected as head of the village committee may or may not be party members. Increasingly, the criterion for election is success in economic work. More than a few former private entrepreneurs have been elected in the hopes that they can teach others and lead the village down the road to economic prosperity.

Some villages have gone a step further to elect democratically villagers assemblies or villagers representative assemblies (what some have called village councils) to oversee the work of the village committee. The villagers assembly consists of a representative from each household in the village. The villagers representative assembly consists of representatives from small groups of families. In practice, these often correspond to the small groups (*xiaozu*), which were the predecessors of the former production teams. This smaller assembly is now advocated as a more practical legislative body.

In one 420 household Hunan village, every 10–15 households elect one representative, for a three-year term of office. The village representative assembly has a total of 22 representatives, with a representative from each of the 12 village small groups (*xiaozu*). An effort is made to ensure that different interests are represented in the assembly. Of the 22 members, there are 4 members over 40, one factory manager, 4 women, and 4 younger people who represent the interests of youth.[17] This assembly meets every two to three months or as necessary to discuss and approve the work of the village committee. The village committee reports to the village representative assembly plans for agricultural production, industry, and use of village funds.[18] In another Hunan village with 525 households, there is a 5 person village committee and a 52 member representative assembly, with approximately three representatives from each of the village's 17 small groups. The village representative assembly meets each quarter, and the entire village once a year.

The most visible promoter of democratic village self-rule and the government bureau responsible for village self-governance is the Ministry of Civil Affairs. The ministry has within it a special section, the Department of Basic-Level Governance, which actively leads day-to-day affairs, does investigations in the countryside, writes reports, and generally tries to draw as much attention as possible to the Organic Law. The work is under the direction of a core group of ministry officials, most notably Bai Yihua and Wang Zhenyao.[19] They, along with a limited but energetic staff, supplemented by others outside the ministry, traverse the Chinese countryside to investigate problems and help localities implement the Organic Law. This work has received international attention, as this small group has mounted an almost evangelistic campaign to promote this law.[20]

The Benefits of Village Self-governance

Promoters of democratic elections and village self-rule would like to see this system in place in all villages, rich and poor. But, the need is most urgent in poor, underdeveloped villages. It is noticeable that most articles and writings on village democracy refer to poor and underdeveloped villages. This is where concerns about stability and economic development result in the adoption of village self-governance as a possible solution. If the peasants do not want to listen to leaders that the upper levels appoint, then maybe they will listen to the leaders that they themselves elect. It puts the burden directly on the villagers. The hope is that this will alleviate the paralysis that has struck poor villages and get them moving on the road to development.

Villages which have succeeded in instituting democratic self-rule proudly proclaim that where there was once chaos, there is now order, and quotas set by higher levels are met. The agricultural tax gets paid, and the voluntary labour responsibilities (*yiwu gong*) are fulfilled. The role of the elected representative is to convince those hesitant households to pay.[21]

Casual observers might assume that peasant burdens are simply caused by corrupt local officials; those familiar with the context of post-Mao China realize that the situation is much more complex. The fees may be unpopular, but they are necessary for effective local government. Villages, unlike the townships or counties, receive no budget from the upper levels, nor are they allowed to keep any portion of the tax revenues. They must be totally self-financed. The abolition of the collective system of agricultural production has meant that village government no longer automatically receives the income from the sale of the agricultural products. With the household responsibility system, the income belongs to the individual households. Taking the income from the sale of the agricultural products from village government and returning it to the individual households is not only an economic fact, it has significant political consequences. In those villages that have no effective means of generating revenue, there are few viable alternatives to asking peasants for more fees.

Unfortunately, poor villages must both demand high fees (*tiliu*) and face disgruntled peasants who resist giving up what little they have. One can see why cadres in such villages would not want to serve and why some might resort to coercive and oppressive measures; one can also understand why peasants subject to such administrative coercion would accuse their cadres of abuse of power and corruption. Thus, the reasons for "excessive peasant burdens" are fiscal in origin, but the problem is how to break the vicious cycle. For poor peasants, any levy, regardless of how legitimate, would be viewed as a burden. To use R. H. Tawney's analogy, poor peasants are like a man already up to his neck in water, "so that even a ripple is sufficient to drown him."[22] If levies are simply assessed by cadres who use administrative fiat, it is not surprising that some peasants are beginning to protest. In the West, there would be a similar response but in the West, citizens can vote the officials out of office. More than one politician has fallen due to tax increases. At issue in China, especially in the poor areas, is how to convince peasants to pay taxes and other levies.

In some villages, there may simply not be enough for levies, regardless of who sets them. In those instances, outside assistance is needed. In other villages, it is hoped that democratically elected village leaders will provide a viable solution. Left to themselves, poor peasants might be more inclined to protest and withhold revenues than to pay taxes and levies. The hope is that the democratically elected officials will have sufficient vision and be able to convince fellow villagers of the merits of contributing to the community good.

Similarly, democratic elections and village self-rule are being pushed where the collective is poor but individuals are wealthy. These are villages that have private entrepreneurs or individual peasants who are rich from the sale of their own agricultural produce. Village leaders control little revenue, command little respect and, therefore, are capable of little in the way of governance, much like the situation where everyone is poor. In villages with privately held wealth, the problem is to convince the individually successful peasants that they should give up part of their time and, thus, sacrifice some of their wealth to tend to collective affairs. This problem is evident in village assemblies — the most successful of the members cannot make meetings because they are too busy making money. There are funds and talented individuals in these villages; the issue is how to bring the village together as a community and establish a government able to function as an administrative body.

Democratic village rule is also being pursued to improve security in China's villages and ensure general stability. Village security has become a major issue, especially in poor areas. In some locations, bandits stand in wait at the roadside to rob trucks and cars. In the context of limited budgets and fiscal constraints, localities are looking for ways to cut costs. Without sufficient funds to increase the official police force in the countryside, officials are encouraging villages to take on the responsibility and costs directly. Villages are to establish voluntary security patrols to ensure the safety of the village members and their property. The problem is that this is not being done in all villages.[23]

Village self-government charters (*Cunmin zizhi zhangcheng*) are handbooks distributed to all village households. They resemble mini-constitutions which stipulate the rights and responsibilities of the villagers, as well as those of the village government. Included in these charters are provisions for the establishment of security within the village. The hope is that if villagers elect their own government and write their own village charters, then, they will also be more responsible in the implementation of the laws contained in them.

Villages that are seen as models have set up rotating security patrols. In one village in Henan, the village, as a whole, has hired a five-person security team (*zhi'an dui*) and each small group has its own special security guard. To supplement this professional force, within each small group, each 10 households takes turns to act as a joint defense force (*lianfangzu*) that stands guard at night. Once this system is instituted, the trouble makers are targeted and watched closely, whereupon there is a substantial decrease in the village crime rate.[24]

The state has no guarantee that democratically-elected leaders will faithfully implement the regime's goals and ensure that quotas will be fulfilled, but for the moment, the authorities seem to be willing to give this system a try. The role of the Ministry of Civil Affairs and its subordinates at each level is to help villages find capable leaders, give them training to effectively lead a village in an increasingly marketized economy and develop village enterprises. To further this goal, the ministry is considering setting up a school for local cadres to better prepare them for the tasks of leadership in today's market economy.

The Evolution of the Organic Law on Village Committees and Democratic Village Self-rule

Winning adherents to democratic village self-government has been slow. The role of village committees was first laid out in the 1982 Constitution of the People's Republic of China (item 111), which established that "the neighbourhood committees and villagers committees established in the cities and villages … are the self-government organizations of the people at the basic level."[25] The process of decollectivization was then underway. The Ministry of Civil Affairs was assigned to write a draft of what would eventually become the Organic Law on Village Committees to formally stipulate the basic law in the new institutional context of post-Mao China.[26] According to ministry records, this was not an easy task. It required not only investigation by the ministry officials of conditions in villages, but many rounds of negotiations and changes before an acceptable draft was produced. Only after a three-year battle and as many as 40 revisions did the State Council in 1986 approve the "Organic Law of the Villagers Committees of the PRC (draft)" and send it to the Standing Committee of the National People's Congress, which did not give final approval until November 1987.[27] Even then, the law was only for trial implementation, which began on 1 June 1988.[28]

The legalization of the 1987 Organic Law on Village Committees started efforts to establish democratic elections in China's villages, institute democratic oversight of the ruling village committee, and to codify local laws on village self-rule.[29] Villagers committees throughout the country were ordered to undergo elections in 1988. A second round of elections was called in 1992 in 20 provinces. But, as the ministry itself admits, not all villages have fully implemented the law and not all elections have been democratic or competitive.

Progress in the election of villagers assemblies has also been slow. As of the end of 1993, only about 50% of the villages had set up a villagers representative assembly system. Some provinces have done better than others. Liaoning, Jilin, Fujian, Shandong, Hubei, and Sichuan already have over 85% of their villages with villagers representative systems.[30] About 5% have villagers self-rule charters.[31]

In the last few years, however, momentum has been building up to fully implement the village organic law by having each province pass specific rules known as "The Implementation Methods of the Organic Law on Village Committees." As of 1994, 24 out of 30 provinces, autonomous regions and municipalities had formal implementation measures.[32] International conferences were held in the summers of 1993, 1994, and 1995 to highlight the importance of village committees, villagers representative committees, and the laws surrounding the institutionalization of these organizations. Foreign scholars as well as representatives from each provincial office of the Ministry of Civil Affairs were invited to attend.[33]

In an attempt to promote the proper implementation of the law and show others the way to democratic village rule, the Ministry of Civil Affairs has created a system for verifying whether a village, township or county has correctly implemented the village Organic Law. When a locality meets minimum requirements, it is given the status of a "demonstration point." As of the end of 1993, nationally there were 63 demonstration counties, 3,930 demonstration townships and 82,024 demonstration villages.

In the fall of 1995, the ministry ranked 30 of the best counties to put forth as national models for the implementation of village self-rule.[34] This ranking was determined after teams of investigators, mostly from the Ministry of Civil Affairs, aided by provincial personnel, went on extended field investigations lasting more than a month during the fall of 1995. These teams assessed the way that localities implemented the law. Among other things, they checked whether the elections were competitive and whether secret balloting was correctly implemented during voting. Aware of the problem of feigned compliance, the teams thoroughly investigated the different sites and found, in a few cases, that the localities had embellished records of "democratic" assembly meetings. Immediately after their return to Beijing in October, the teams met in the ministry compound to make their reports and determine the rankings. After spirited debate about the strengths and weaknesses of the performance of different localities, a ranking emerged of the 30 counties. Lishu county, Jilin, ranked first in this competition.

To further raise the importance of democratic village self-rule, the Ministry of Civil Affairs convened in Beijing 20–21 November 1995, the first national work conference to honour the model counties that had implemented well the Organic Law. The November conference received wide coverage in the major national papers, including a *People's Daily* editorial, on the importance of this work.[35] Its increased importance and legitimacy was signalled by the speech given at the conference by the vice-premier of the State Council, Jiang Chunyun. His attendance was in line with the increasing attention national leaders had been giving village political reform and restructuring. In 1994, there was a Chinese Communist Party directive on the importance of strengthening the work of grassroots organizations. The importance of this work was stressed by both Jiang Zemin and Li Peng. A final benchmark was reached when, in the summer of 1995, after eight years of trial implementation, revisions to the Organic Law of village self-governance were completed, and the law was sent to the State Council for final approval.

The Economic Basis of Village Political Power

What should we make of the two sets of solutions? Which is the decision making body in China's villages? At this point in our understanding of the countryside, there is no simple answer. The passage of the Organic Law on Village Committees and the continued existence of village party secretaries has resulted in a variety of outcomes. Sometimes, the village committees actually have power. In other cases, especially in rich, industrialized villages, the party secretary remains the undisputed decision maker. In some developed villages where the party secretary has the final word, the organic village law has been implemented and village committees are democratically elected, but in such cases, the power of these committees is limited. In a number of cases, the village committee is given control of the civil and social welfare functions and, maybe, control over agriculture, but the important revenue generating economic affairs remain in the hands of the party secretary. This leaves the village committee with control over an empty shell (*kong jiazi*) while the real power remains in the hands of the party secretary who makes the key economic decisions regarding industry, which generates the bulk of the collective income.

Which the decision making body is in China's villages boils down to who controls the economic resources. There is an economic basis of village political power. As one article states explicitly, effective village government must be able to provide benefits to its members.[36] Under the reformed economic structure, this is only possible when the village is capable of developing collective wealth, which provides jobs for its members and money for the collective coffers. This may be the party secretary, but in villages with newly developing economies, this growth could take place under the auspices of the village committee.

One can find examples where the democratic elections of new leaders and the establishment of a villagers representative assembly has improved a village economy. Yet, there are also numerous examples of highly industrialized villages, aside from the notorious Daqiuzhuang village, which suggest that high levels of economic development do not necessarily bring enthusiasm for implementing democratic reforms. Some of the most economically advanced areas lag behind in carrying out village political reform. On the contrary, there is often one-man authoritarian rule. Rich Guangdong province is notable for its unenthusiastic response to carrying out the Organic Law.

In many of China's industrialized villages, key economic decisions are being made by a non-democratically elected official — the party secretary. Some rural party officials at the village level and, for that matter at the township and county levels, have adapted well to the economic reforms and lead local development.[37] Economic decision making is left to a body that specializes in economic matters, such as the industrial management committee (*gongye guanli weiyuan hui*), with the party secretary at the head. This may result in the economy doing better, but this also reduces the power of the village committee. If one took a broader, longer-run perspective, one could argue that, by allowing a more specialized body to run the economy, the village committee may be able to do more in the provision of services by having a larger budget derived from the profits of efficiently managed village industries. How this issue should be resolved remains a topic of debate among top policy makers.

In practice, in developed areas village committees seem to have only veto power to decide the general use of village resources — what might be called macro-economic control — that is exercised through the right to guide, rather than direct management of the village economy. Interestingly, even in those less developed villages which seem to be taking seriously the democratic election of village committees and villagers representative assemblies, once the number of enterprises increases, a special economic or industrial council is set up, often with the party secretary, as its chairman of the board.[38]

The power of the village party secretary is acknowledged in a recent ministry report on village self-rule. In the few references to the party secretary, it complains that, in some villages, "the functions of the party and the government agencies are still combined ...."[39] Later in the same report it is noted that, "the management of the party branch and party members is given prominence whereas the role of the other village organizations such as the village committee and the village assembly is put into the shade."[40] The recommendation of the report is that, "the functions of the party organizations and government agencies shall be strictly divorced, the functions and emphases of the different levels of government agencies in formulating rules shall be made distinct and clear, and the functions of the lower levels of government shall be made more and more specific and detailed."[41]

To understand the power of the party secretary or village committees, one must again return to the fiscal consequences of the household responsibility system for village government. Village governments are not provided budgets by the upper levels, the revenue of village government is entirely dependent on the income that the village government can generate. In those villages where there is only agricultural production and no collectively-owned village enterprises, the village government is left with little or no revenue. This lack of funding, as the authorities recognize, is the underlying reason for the paralysis in China's poor villages. When there is income from village industry, who decides how much funding should be redistributed by the village committee? What can a democratically elected government do in such a situation? Funding for village governments is a problem that remains to be solved if democratically elected bodies, such as the village committees, are to be effective and independent.

A north China village party secretary, who runs a very successful village economy with a number of industrial enterprises, has not paid much attention to elections or village assemblies. He is not opposed to elections but simply indifferent. When asked about elections, he said that he did not want to participate because he wanted to attend to more substantive matters. He had been too busy developing the economy of his village, building new houses for village members and setting up schools.

In spite of the current lack of interest, the prospects for a more participatory style of village rule are not completely bleak in those developed villages with strong party secretaries. Economic development makes effective village rule easier to achieve and peasants are usually more content. But party secretaries who have successfully led their villages to economic wealth may find it in their interest to pay attention to the Organic Law and make use of the village representative assemblies.

The Ministry of Civil Affairs' recent report on the village representative assemblies noted the increasing complexity and changing nature of peasants and villages in China.[42] As a result of the reforms, diverse interests are developing within China's villages as different peasants pursue different means of livelihood. In such an increasingly diverse setting, the potential for divergent and conflicting interests is greater. Even for a capable village party secretary, it is increasingly difficult to please everyone. The village party secretary, cited above, complained that, as peasants get rich, they are more difficult to rule. For the first time, he has feelings of frustration and thinks the job of village party secretary may be a thankless one. No matter what he does for villagers, they still complain. Those who have made it rich, especially the private entrepreneurs, are unhappy. Interestingly, the reason why the private entrepreneurs are unhappy is that the party secretary has refused to name them as the factory managers of the *collective-owned* village factories. Regular village representative meetings to explain and discuss what is being done and also to let those who are discontent air their views may alleviate such problems.

Conclusion

The village Organic Law, the holding of democratic elections and the creation of village representative assemblies have the potential to serve an array of functions in different types of villages. For now, the emphasis is on poor villages where democratic rule is seen as a possible key to successful economic development — sense of community, common purpose, sacrifice for the collective good — even when there is little individual wealth. For those villages where there is individual but no collective wealth, the village assemblies may be a way of re-establishing the sense of community. For rich villages, where there is still a strong sense of the collective, it eventually may be an effective way to promote stability and harmony, both of which are important for further economic development. The precise role and power of these democratically elected bodies are likely to vary with economic structure and level of village development.

The relationship between economic development and political change remains a puzzle. Economic development is linked with good leadership, but economic development is not necessarily linked with democratic rule. The experience of highly industrialized villages suggests that there may be an inverse relationship between level of economic development and progress in the implementation of democratic village rule. How generalizeable such a characterization is remains a question for future research. At minimum, such examples caution that there is no concomitant rise in the democratic process with economic growth. This is not to say that democratic elections cannot be implemented in rich villages, only that the concern about these elections is less in villages already on the road to prosperity.

The Organic Law on Village Committees may soon be codified law at both the national and the local levels, but democratic self-rule in all of China's villages will be a much lengthier process. The experience of developing countries, such as those in Latin America, cautions that, while laws are very important and while it is important to have them clearly written and comprehensive, one cannot assume that laws democracy make. There are countries that have constitutions that provide broad protection of the rights of citizens, they have volumes and volumes of laws and regulations, yet once one gets out away from the capital, especially in poor remote areas, all these beautifully written laws are relatively meaningless.[43] The situation in China is further complicated by the existence of a dual decision making structure — the party and the government.

The writings on the organic law leave the relationship between the party and the village committee vague, although in places there is acknowledgment that the party should remain the core (*hexin*). If the party is to remain the core, then the law contains within it a major inconsistency that will become manifest in those circumstances where there is already a powerful party secretary who has developed and controls the village enterprises. When this power is in the hands of the party secretary, then democratically elected village committees will still only have limited power, at best. Under those circumstances, to strictly implement the law and force the party out of economic decision making would risk undermining the incentive for the party secretaries who have been doing a very good job of leading village industrial development. The lack of clarity surrounding this issue limits the power of democratically elected bodies and threatens the existing power of incumbent party secretaries.

Whether the party secretary or the village committee is the decision making body is relatively unimportant. More important is whether there is *democratic accountability* of local officials to the peasants. The current village Organic Law provides for this in the case of the village committees, but the weakness of this law is that it does not include the accountability of the party secretary to the villagers. In a system with a dual structure of party and state, steps still need to be taken to allow villagers a voice in deciding who is to be their key decision makers, regardless of whether it is the party secretary or the head of the village committee.

Notes

1. See, for example, Jean Oi, "Fiscal Reform and the Economic Foundations of Local State Corporatism," *World Politics*, Vol. 45, No. 1 (October 1992), pp. 99–126; and Oi, "The Role of the Local State in China's Transitional Economy," *The China Quarterly*, No. 144 (December 1995), pp. 1132–49.

2. See, for example, An Shuyi, Wong Xueshi, Lin Xingting, "Siqian nonghu zhuanggao 'baitiao'" (Four Thousand Households Lodge a Complaint Against 'White Slips'), *Zhongguo nongmin* (Chinese Peasantry), No. 3 (1995), pp. 45–47.

3. See, for example, Zhong Yan, "Zhixing xiashou he shuishou zhengce yao kaolü nongmin liyi" (Peasant Interests Should Be Considered When Implementing Policies regarding the Summer Harvest and Tax Collection), *Zhongguo nongmin*, No. 10 (1995).

4. See, for example, Guan Defeng, "Laizi nongcun jiceng ganbu de husheng" (An Appeal from Rural Cadres at the Grassroots), *Nongcun zhanwang* (Rural Prospect), No. 10 (1995).

5. For a useful discussion of the different types of protests see, Lianjiang Li and Kevin O'Brien, "Villagers and Popular Resistance in Contemporary China," *Modern China*, Vol. 22, No. 1 (January 1996), pp. 28–61.

6. See Oi, *State and Peasant in Contemporary China: The Political Economy of Village Government* (Berkeley: University of California Press, 1989), especially chapter 5.

7. Li and O'Brien, "Villagers and Popular Resistance" (Note 5).

8. See, for example, Wang Qinglin and Fan Wenke, "Jiaqiang nongcun jiceng dang zuzhi jianshe shi dangwu zhi ji" (Strengthening the Construction of Rural Party Organizations at the Grassroots Is a Pressing Task), *Hebei nongcun gongzuo* (Hebei Rural Work), No. 12 (1994), pp. 7–8.

9. See, for example, Zhang Guoqing, Fan Zhiyong, and Yan Xinge, "Zhuazhu sange huanjie, gaohao cunji ganbu guifanhua guanli" (Concentrate on the Three Steps, Standardize the Supervision of Cadres), *Hebei nongcun gongzuo*, No. 5 (1994), pp. 40–41. Also see an account written by a county

vice-party secretary, Chen Yuming, "Diaodong cunji ganbu gongzuo jiji xing zhi wojian" (My Opinion on the Enhancement of the Work Enthusiasm of Village Cadres), *Xiangzhen jingji yanjiu* (Rural Economy Study), No. 4 (1995), p. 42, on the difficulties of being a cadre.

10. See, for example, Gao Dechun, "Cunmin zizhi de quxiang yu jianshe" (The Direction and Construction of Village Self-rule), *Shehui gongzuo yanjiu* (Social Work Studies), No. 5 (1994), pp. 27–28; also Wang Xuejun, "Jingxin xuanpei zhishu, jiasu houjin zhuanhua" (Careful Selection of the Party Branch Secretary Speed Up the Transformation from Backwardness), *Hebei nongcun gongzuo*, No. 12 (1994), pp. 6–7.

11. For the different methods see Wang Xuejun, "Jingxin xuanpei zhishu" (Note 10); and Zhang Guoqing, et al., "Zhuazhu sange huanjie" (Note 9).

12. Zhang Guoqing, et al., "Zhuazhu sange huanjie" (Note 9).

13. This law was passed on 24 November 1987 by the 23rd Session of the Standing Committee of the National People's Congress. It went into trial implementation on 1 June 1988. Research Group on the System of Village Self-government in China, China Research Society Basic Governance, "Research Report on the System of Village Self-government in China (1995 Volume): Legal System of Village Committees in China (Draft)," (hereafter cited as Legal System of Village Committees), 10 June 1995, pp. 19–21.

14. See John Burns, *Political Participation in Rural China* (Berkeley: University of California Press, 1988).

15. In the summer of 1994 during an international conference on Villagers Representative Committees, one of the invited foreign speakers, a representative from the Republican Institute in the United States, demonstrated and taught provincial officials how secret voting was supposed to work. Since then, literature, graphics and illustrations have been provided to help the ministry explain the process of secret ballot voting to peasants.

16. This is what Li and O'Brien term "policy based resistance." Li and O'Brien, "Villagers and Popular Resistance" (Note 5).

17. Unfortunately, it is not known to this author how these representatives of special interests are selected.

18. China Interview (CI) 81694.

19. Yan Mingfu, linked with the more reformist faction in China, is a vice-minister of the Ministry of Civil Affairs and has taken an active role in promoting this work. He has been the presiding official at the last two international conferences organized by the Ministry of Civil Affairs on village self-government.

20. Wang Zhenyao among others has also been speaking on this subject to the international press and at conferences outside of China.

21. CI 82494.

22. R. H. Tawney, *Land and Labour in China* (New York: Harcourt, Brace, 1932), p. 77.

23. When officials responsible for village self-rule from the ministry go to the counties, townships, and villages, they expect detailed reports on crime and security in the area. CI 82594.

24. CI 82494.

25. *Study on the Election of Villagers Committees in Rural China* (China Rural Villagers Self-Government Research Group, China Research Society of Basic-Level Government, December 1, 1993), p. 1.

26. For a chronology of events and developments see "Legal System of Village Committees" (Note 13).

27. Peng Zhen was one of the earliest supporters of this move and helped to push through the initial draft version of the law in the 1980s. See "Legal System of Village Committees", (Note 13), p. 19 for excerpts of his speech at the session where the draft law was passed in 1987.

28. For a history of the passage of the bill see, "Legal System of Village Committees" (Note 13), pp. 12–34.

29. There have been a number of articles on the work of villagers representative assemblies and village committees. See, for example, Kevin O'Brien, "Implementing Political Reform in China's Villages," *Australian Journal of Chinese Affairs*, No. 32 (July 1994), pp. 31–59; Susan Lawrence, "Villagers Representative Assemblies, Democracy Chinese Style," *Australian Journal of Chinese Affairs*, No. 32 (July 1994), pp. 61–68; and also Kevin O'Brien, "Agents and Remonstrators," *The China Quarterly*, No. 138 (June 1994), pp. 359–80.

30. Descriptions of the situation in different provinces is found in "Legal System of Village Committees" (Note 13).

31. Shandong seemed to be in the lead in this respect. It reported that 30% of its villages already accomplish this task.

32. Beijing, Shanghai, Guangdong, Hainan, Guangxi, and Hunan still are without such rules. "Legal System of Village Committees" (Note 13), p. 2.

33. The author participated in both the 1994 and 1995 conferences.

34. CI 241095.

35. See, for example, *Renmin ribao* (People's Daily), domestic edition, 21–23 November 1995; *Nongmin ribao* (Peasants' Daily), Beijing, 21–22 November 1995; and *Jiefang ribao* (Liberation Daily), Shanghai, 21 November 1995. The editorial is "Qieshi jiaqiang cunmin weiyuanhui jianshe" (Conscientiously Strengthen the Construction of Villagers Self-Rule), *Renmin ribao*, 21 November 1995.

36. Xu Shaowei, "Qiantan nongcun dangzhibu de ningjuli" (A General Discussion of the Cohesion of Rural Party Branches), *Nongcun zhanwang*, No. 9 (1995), pp. 6–7.

37. A description is contained in my "The Role of the Local State" (Note 1).
38. CI 82394.
39. "Legal System of Village Committees" (Note 13), p. 70.
40. Ibid., p. 81.
41. Ibid., p. 70.
42. Ibid.
43. Guillermo O'Donnell, "On the State, Democratization and Some Conceptual Problems: A Latin American View with Glances at Some Postcommunist Countries," *World Development*, Vol. 21, No. 8 (August 1993), pp. 1355–69.

6

Sovereignty in Chinese Foreign Policy: Principle and Practice

Ren Yue

Introduction

In comparison with the radicalism evident during the 1970s, it is fair to say that current Chinese foreign policy is by and large friendly in nature. Students of China's foreign policy note that it is now based on Deng Xiaoping's pragmatism. Ideology, as used in Mao's time to draw the line between China's friends and enemies, has been long abandoned. This is not surprising: China's economic reconstruction requires a peaceful environment and the priority of Chinese diplomacy is to ensure and enhance its economic reforms. Thus, China's foreign policy is said to serve primarily its domestic economic needs. This is true, however, only if we take for granted one very important ingredient in Chinese foreign policy, namely, state sovereignty.

Over time, the well-known "Five Principles of Peaceful Coexistence" have changed little. These have been the cornerstones of foreign policy since the early years of the People's Republic of China (PRC). Of the five, the core principle is mutual respect for sovereignty and territorial integrity. Where China's sovereign right is at stake, the economic component of its foreign relations may well be treated with less priority. Recent developments in cross-Taiwan Straits relations which began last year, therefore, suggest a need to re-evaluate guiding principles.

In this chapter, I begin with a review of the major events in China's foreign relations during 1995. The discussion focuses on Chinese arguments about state sovereignty. In a given foreign policy context, the following questions are asked: to what extent does the Chinese government feel its sovereignty is at stake? How does the Chinese government handle the issue? Is the way the Chinese government deals with the issue consistent with its declared principles of sovereignty? For the purpose of this analysis, I do not discuss in detail China's relations with those countries which do not involve the sensitive issue of sovereignty. Except in discussing Sino-American relations, the cross-Taiwan Straits relationship *per se* will also be excluded since it is not, at least from the Chinese government's point of view, a "foreign" policy issue. Instead, the focus will be on China's bilateral and multilateral relations with the United States (US) and Southeast Asian countries, with which Beijing has sovereignty or territorial disputes.

China's Foreign Relations in 1995: A Brief Review

Chinese foreign relations in 1995 witnessed impressive challenges. First,

Sino-US relations fell to the lowest point since *rapprochement* occurred in 1971, precipitated by the US President Clinton administration's granting an entry visa to Taiwan President Lee Teng-hui. Second, for the first time in over two decades, China found itself confronting a united Association of Southeast Asian Nations (ASEAN) (Vietnam included) over territorial disputes in the South China Sea. Finally, although the Fourth United Nations (UN) Conference on Women was held according to schedule in Beijing, some of the guests seemed less than grateful in speaking of their host country's human rights record.

Yet diplomatic achievements were also impressive. The year 1995 was a very active one in Chinese diplomacy. Bilateral relations reached an all-time high: China's principal leaders paid state visits to over 60 countries on five continents. Over 40 foreign heads of state and government visited Beijing. These visits enhanced mutual understanding and strengthened amicable relations and cooperation between China and other countries. The UN Conference on Women attracted an unprecedented number of celebrities from all over the world. China's relations with its neighbouring countries also improved considerably. Some border issues with India, the central Asian republics, Vietnam, and Russia were resolved. Most important, the Chinese government seemed to be shaking off the shameful image cast upon it by the 1989 Tiananmen incident.

In 1995, China generally maintained and, in some cases, improved its relations with all its neighbours. President Jiang Zemin visited South Korea in November, the first visit to that country by a Chinese president in PRC history. He also participated in the 50th anniversary of V-E Day in Moscow and the informal Asian Pacific Economic Cooperation (APEC) summit in Osaka. On each occasion, he met with various heads of state and government of China's neighbouring countries. In addition, other principal Chinese leaders paid official visits to 11 neighbours, including Russia, Japan, South Korea, Pakistan, India, and most of the ASEAN countries. Heads of state or government from many of these countries also visited China. Japanese Prime Minister Tomiichi Murayama's visit in May was considered, among other things, a gesture to quell China's bitter war memories. Through these high-level contacts, diplomatic ties were strengthened and economic cooperation enhanced. Last year, trade with these countries and regions accounted for 60% of the PRC's total import and export volume.[1] To promote the spirit of free trade, Jiang announced in his APEC summit address that China would reduce its tariffs by 30% on more than 4,000 items starting in 1996. This would be

welcomed by all countries that have trade with China and bring it one step
closer to joining the World Trade Organization.

Continuing the healthy trends of recent years, the PRC either settled
or agreed to put aside for the time being practically all remaining land
border disputes with its neighbours in 1995. Sino-Russian border talks
made substantial progress with both countries assuring one another that the
development of friendly bilateral relations would be given top priority.
Since 1993, the Sino-Vietnamese land border has been basically normal-
ized, as cross-border trade has flourished. Prior to Vietnamese Communist
Party Chief Do Muoi's visit to China last December, the two countries
had achieved remarkable progress on land and water border demarcations
in three previous rounds of border talks. India and China agreed to
pull back troops from the disputed Sumdurong Cho sector on India's
northeastern border where the two nations almost went to war in 1986–
1987.[2] Also improved were China's bilateral relations with other border
countries such as Myanmar (Burma), Laos, Nepal, Kazakhstan, Kirghistan,
and Tadzhikistan.

China's relations with African and Latin-American countries were
also very active in 1995. Starting with Foreign Minister Qian Qichen's
visits to five African countries, top Chinese leaders visited almost all the
countries in the two continents that have diplomatic relations with the
PRC. Heads of state or government from over a dozen developing countries
visited Beijing, often with their pledge to support China's effort in keeping
Taiwan out of international organizations, such as the United Nations.
Even without excessive foreign aid like that during Mao's time, China has
managed to have stable and positive relations, and expanded economic and
trade cooperation with these countries.

Top officials from countries like Spain, Austria, Portugal, the
Netherlands, Norway, New Zealand, as well as Romania, Ukraine, and
Yugoslavia visited China in 1995. President Jiang Zemin and other top
Chinese leaders also visited many European countries. Most noticeable of
these high-level contacts was German Chancellor Helmut Kohl's five-day
visit in November, during which four intergovernmental agreements were
signed and 12 business contracts were made totalling US$2.18 billion.
Through Kohl's visit, China strengthened its economic ties with Germany
as well as the European Union (EU). Though still critical of China's
human rights record, the EU expressed its support for China's accession to
the World Trade Organization.

This examination of China's foreign relations in 1995 has revealed a new pattern of Chinese diplomacy: Beijing's "all-round" diplomacy has managed to maintain good and healthy relations with all those countries which have no sovereign or territorial disputes with China. On the other hand, Beijing would not hesitate to take an antagonistic stand against any country that might harm Chinese sovereignty.

We will now turn to China's concept of state sovereignty and how it is applied in diplomatic practice, illustrated by some of the major events in China's foreign relations during 1995.

State Sovereignty and the Chinese Context

In modern diplomacy, sovereignty is central to the building of nation-states. Sovereign power within a given territory is one essential requirement for any political entity to qualify as a nation-state. Hence, the fundamental objective of diplomacy is to maintain a state's independence within the international community.

Sovereignty is a very old concept. Its use can be traced back to Aristotle's time.[3] According to one well-known source, sovereignty in its original meaning suggests the "supreme, absolute, and uncontrollable power by which any independent state is governed." It is the "power to do everything in a state without accountability."[4] This definition gives no clue to the legitimacy of the sovereign. As it turns out, this omission has invited controversial interpretations of sovereignty among past and contemporary nation-states.

Until medieval times, sovereigns were kings, emperors, and occasionally religious leaders. Powerful individuals gained legitimacy to rule territory from divine right or historic authority. There was no need for them to ask for the consent of their subjects. Later, with the emergence of nation-states, the concept changed gradually. Sovereignty began to rest on the national government, which derived its legitimacy from a constitution or other legal sources. Though the people's will would be taken into consideration in making laws, the state sovereign did not have to ask its citizens' consent to exert power.

A revolutionary change in the concept came by the end of World War II, when in most democracies "popular sovereignty was firmly rooted as one of the fundamental postulates of political legitimacy."[5] This change is directly at odds with the traditional usage of state sovereignty. According to those who argue for popular sovereignty, it is the people's will, not the will of rulers, that makes up the contemporary content of sovereignty. Traditionally, only outside invaders violate sovereignty in international law. Today, many believe that actions of domestic authority may also breach sovereignty if such actions are against the will of the people. Decisions of government must have the consent of the governed. Thus, to usurp or overthrow a legitimate government, or deprive citizens of their freedoms, could well be regarded as violations of sovereignty in the same fashion as an invasion by a foreign country. This conceptual change, however, has brought more confusion than clarity to the community of nations.[6] Different political systems tend to have different processes to legitimate power. Different political cultures tend to introduce different value criteria to measure the degree of freedom citizens may enjoy. As will be examined later in this chapter, contradictory views on sovereignty could explain many contemporary conflicts in state-to-state relations between China on one side, and the United States and several other countries on the other.

The Conceptual Development of Sovereignty

The power distribution of a bipolar or multipolar global political structure, the interdependence of the world economy and trade, and the rapid development of science and technology make the medieval concept of sovereignty obsolete. A number of international legalists also found the term, state sovereignty, "murky and ambiguous," claiming it is "out of fashion," and declaring it "a dead concept."[7] To them, the conventional understanding of state sovereignty — namely, that the state government has freedom to do whatever it wants within its own territory — simply does not fit today's situation. With these caveats stated, one should know that sovereignty is still an active concept, rooted in the theories and practices of international relations. Nation-states attempt to choose the interpretation of this concept that fit their national interests.

For example, one could argue that the concept of sovereignty is interpreted by China in a different way than by Western countries, and that many of the sovereign disputes China has with other nations are attributed to the Chinese interpretation of the concept. This argument is true only when we recognize the fact that the concept has varied in its historical development. Beijing often claims that the Western powers, led by the United States, interfere with China's domestic affairs and thus infringe upon Chinese sovereignty. Yet, from the former's point of view, acts such as supporting human rights struggles in a foreign nation do not damage that nation's sovereignty, since the legitimacy of a sovereign government should be based on its people's consensus. Apparently the two sides hold different views on what sovereignty means.

The Chinese government uses the term sovereignty in its original context to mean "state sovereignty." Mutual respect of state sovereignty is at the core of China's Five Principles of Peaceful Coexistence. To the PRC, it is also the foundation upon which the new world order will be built. In this regard, the Chinese understanding is similar to that of many developing countries. These countries believe state sovereignty is one of the fundamental principals of international relations and its violation by any nation requires the condemnation of the community of nations. For them, the inviolability of state sovereignty is clearly articulated in documents of international law, such as the UN Charter. Any foreign intervention, even if it is for humanitarian reasons, is a violation of international law. As the Nicaraguan Permanent Representative to the United Nations stated in a 1989 UN debate over the US action in Panama, "No argument can possibly justify intervention against a sovereign state."[8] By consistently casting votes of abstention in the UN Security Council on issues such as the Gulf War resolutions, China also let the world know its firm stand on state sovereignty.

This is not, of course, what many Western legalists would argue. They deem that state sovereignty is *passé*, calling for the abandonment of this concept and the beginning of a "post-sovereignty" era, in which individual states can no longer claim exclusive sovereignty over such matters as security, trade, and human rights. The new concept, based on popular sovereignty, gives rise to many actions that would traditionally be considered erosions of sovereignty such as the humanitarian intervention in Somalia and the dismemberment of Yugoslavia. They advocate that human rights are more important than state rights. They argue that "one can no longer simply condemn externally motivated actions aimed at removing an unpopular government ... as *per se* violations of sovereignty without inquiring whether and under what conditions that will was being suppressed, and how the external action will affect the expression and implementation of popular sovereignty."[9] Here the major difference between China and many developing countries on the one hand, and Western countries on the other, lies in that the former takes sovereignty to mean legitimacy of the national government's power over its own territory, while the latter use it to mean popular sovereignty. Such a difference inevitably invites controversy in many disputes China has with other countries.

One essential element the state sovereignty school stresses is the equality of independent nations in terms of their authority within their respective territories. No nation can legitimately meddle in anothers' domestic affairs. Again, though the theory of equal sovereign states was developed by Western nations, it is interesting to note that the Chinese government now seems to be its firmest defender. Ironically, the concept of equal sovereignty is relatively new to Chinese decision-makers. For centuries, Chinese rulers viewed the rest of the world as both inferior and barbarous. The "one-hundred-year humiliation" since the Opium War in 1840 gradually shattered their feelings of superiority. Then, the opposite feeling, that worships blindly anything foreign, prevailed among many Chinese rulers. There is no lack of historical evidence in this regard. Thus, it is fair to say that for Chinese rulers the concept of equal nation-states has never been rooted in their minds. Changes came after the 1911 revolution and especially since the establishment of the People's Republic of China. The traditional Chinese concept of hierarchical order within the country may still be there, but its equivalent, the hierarchical order between countries, has been largely abandoned by Beijing, at least in its declared policies.

What I have argued above is that China's understanding of sovereignty is not a new or peculiar one. Rather, the Chinese government holds the classic definition of the term: the state has legitimate authority over its territory and that this authority is supreme, indivisible, and absolute. In short, China insists on state sovereignty and is very skeptical of the concept of popular sovereignty. As Deng Xiaoping points out, state sovereignty is far more important than anything else in terms of regime survival: "To do things in China should be based on the circumstances in China, and to rely on our own strengths.... Any foreign country should not expect China to be its dependency, nor should it expect China to swallow any consequences that hurt her national interests."[10] To counter-argue with the universality of human rights, Deng suggests that there are "national rights" based on state sovereignty, which are much more important than human rights.[11]

The Declared Policy

China's declared foreign policy guidelines have remained unchanged in the past four decades. What Zhou Enlai said at the first anniversary of the PRC is being reiterated by current Chinese foreign policy-makers.

Zhou pointed out that the "principle of the PRC's foreign policy is to ensure the country's independence, freedom and the integrity of territorial sovereignty."[12] This is exactly what the concept of state sovereignty would emphasize. A couple of years later, the PRC formally adopted the Five Principles of Peaceful Coexistence as its foreign policy guideline. Again, mutual respect of sovereignty was being stressed.

Based on the Chinese government's interpretation of state sovereignty, several principles can be noted. First, China's territorial integrity is not a matter subject to negotiation. China is determined to defend its perception of its territory by any means. Second, the Chinese government is the supreme authority in its territory and takes exclusive responsibility to oversee China's internal affairs, including China's human rights record. No foreign government or organization may make indiscreet remarks or criticisms on matters the PRC considers falling within its domestic jurisdiction. Finally, every nation, no matter large or small, strong or weak, rich or poor, has equal sovereignty in the community of nations. No nation has the right to bully others and force them to accept its own value system.

China is unusually insistent on absolute state sovereignty as the foundation upon which to conduct international relations. For the Chinese leaders, "sound state-to-state relations can be established and developed *only* when countries, in recognition of the diversity of the world, observe such norms governing international relations as mutual respect for sovereignty and territorial integrity ..."[13] "For the Chinese people who suffered grievously from aggression and bullying by foreign powers throughout modern times, state sovereignty and territorial integrity are of paramount importance."[14] For instance, almost every diplomatic communiqué Beijing signs with other nations includes a clause that recognizes the PRC's sovereignty over Taiwan, a territory that has never been administered by the regime. As far as territorial disputes are concerned, Beijing is particularly defensive toward anything that it sees could put its territorial integrity in danger. This attitude, coupled with its long history, has at one time or another enmeshed China in disputes with almost every country on its borders. In the past, China was involved in at least three border wars with India, the former Soviet Union, and Vietnam. Though there were other considerations in the minds of Chinese decision-makers, each time China's official justification for the wars was that its territorial integrity had been infringed upon and its sovereignty over these territories had been violated.

In addition to insisting on China's territorial integrity, Chinese leaders are particularly vigilant concerning what they see as a trend led by the United States to internationalize China's internal affairs. From their viewpoint, issues such as human rights conditions in China, China's weapons sales, and its nuclear tests should not be subject to foreign influence. Foreign pressure on Beijing may only irritate its leaders to adopt more hostile attitudes in handling these issues. For instance, the Chinese government regards it an infringement of its sovereignty when foreign governments condemn China's policies toward minorities and prisoners. For Chinese leaders, some foreign governments simply ignore historical precedents in the reincarnation process of the Banchan Lama and accuse Beijing of violating the Buddhist rules. What makes Beijing more angry is that, while foreign governments and the press did not condemn the illegal actions of Chinese-American Harry Wu in collecting evidence of China's human rights violations, they put pressure on the Chinese government by demanding his release once he was caught. The Chinese government feels particularly offended that some foreign governments are blind to its improvements and achievements regarding human rights. They ignore the fact that, in recent years, Beijing has published two major documents on the improvements of China's human rights conditions.[15] Yet some foreign governments and the press concentrate on digging up biased and negative stories about human rights in China, including the Chinese government's alleged mistreatment of Tibetans, prisoners, and children. This could only leave the Chinese government with one conclusion, namely, that it would be useless to try to accommodate foreign demands.

As a consequence, more stern attitudes are taken by Beijing on this issue to demonstrate that it is not others' business to meddle in China's internal affairs. For example, after the United States House of Representatives adopted a resolution on 12 December 1995, to condemn China's trial of political dissident Wei Jingsheng and his return to jail, China's officials did not even try to hide their aversion to such foreign pressure. Foreign Ministry spokesman Chen Jian rebuked it immediately, claiming such moves "constitute a serious infringement upon China's sovereignty and interference in China's internal affairs." The spokesman reiterated China's firm stand on state sovereignty:

China is a sovereign state. It is its sovereign right to bring law-breakers to trial according to its law, and handle religious affairs in Tibet in line with religious rituals. China's sovereignty and territorial integrity brook no interference.[16]

The Chinese government reasons that the only purpose of some Western governments in criticizing China's human rights situation is to weaken China. Accordingly, those foreign governments want to use human rights and democratic values as a pretext to "bully" Asian nations into allegiance to their interests. China would of course resist such efforts "as long as such hegemonism and bully-politics exist."[17]

Another issue which concerns the Chinese government is nuclear testing. Despite the positive responses from Beijing to nuclear disarmament movements in recent years, including the willingness to sign a comprehensive test ban treaty in 1996, other nations seem to be very picky about China's "restrained" nuclear tests and often make a big fuss over them. The Japanese government had been relatively mute on the many nuclear tests conducted by the two superpowers in the past, yet when the Chinese detonated an underground nuclear explosion, the Japanese government warned that such testing could "negatively affect" Japanese public support for loans as well as aid. The Diet passed a resolution on 4 August denouncing the test. Later that month, Japan suspended its grants to China for the rest of the year.[18] As the Chinese saw it, these tests in Chinese territory should be part of China's defense policy over which they have unquestionable sovereignty. Again, from the Chinese government's viewpoint, China has been making great efforts to accommodate people's anti-nuclear sentiments and is willing to cooperate with other nations on this issue.

Taking the Chinese understanding of state sovereignty into account, the various kinds of foreign pressure have only convinced the Chinese that some vicious countries want to plot an international conspiracy against China. Beijing was eager to let its people know this. Last year, there was a resurgence of nationalism in China, especially among Chinese intellectuals who would otherwise be quite critical of the government.

One final aspect of the Chinese concept of state sovereignty manifested in its declared foreign policies is the equal status of sovereign states. Beijing claims that all nations, no matter large or small, rich or poor, should be treated equally. From official statements, "The basic starting point for China's foreign policy has always centred on consolidating unity and cooperation with developing countries."[19] In the international arena, China has always tried to speak for the developing countries and claims that China is one of them. As the only non-white permanent member of the United Nations Security Council, China certainly has some advantages in this regard.

Yet despite Beijing's constant claims to uphold the principles of state sovereignty in conducting its foreign policy, discrepancies between China's declared policy and its contemporary practice are equally obvious and reflect on all the above-mentioned principles. Flexibility can be found in China's negotiations over territorial disputes with its neighbouring nations. What the Chinese government considers within its domestic jurisdiction is not immune from foreign pressure. Although contemporary Chinese leaders stress equal sovereignty among nation-states, their diplomatic behaviour in the past reveals a gap between China's declared policy and its practice.

With regard to the equality of sovereign nation-states, current Chinese leaders actually pursue a policy of equal sovereign status among the *great* powers. The relatively poorer developing countries are important in Chinese foreign relations only with regard to China's claim that it belongs to the developing camp. A quick glance at Chinese foreign relations activities in 1995 could not fail to indicate that Beijing spent most of its resources in dealing with its major counterparts. Trade with developing countries continues to fall proportionally in comparison with trade with industrialized and newly industrialized countries. *Realpolitik* is certainly no stranger to Chinese decision-makers. Beijing can choose to ignore criticism and complaints from smaller and weaker powers as to its external and internal policies. Yet it does not tolerate similar attacks from great powers. China watches closely the rise of militarism in Japan and demands the Japanese government apologize for the latter's war crimes. But what makes Chinese leaders really furious is American foreign policy (e.g., on trade and human rights), which constantly belittles China's importance.

China is very sensitive to being bullied or treated unfairly by the great powers. Qian Qichen, the Chinese foreign minister, pointed out quite frankly, "The United States is a major power and has its own dignity, and so is China."[20] One finds that Beijing often deliberately chooses a *different* foreign policy to distinguish itself from other great powers of the world. This approach is very similar to that of France. They both want to prove one point: they have the ability to carry out an independent foreign policy. Of course, there are differences between the two nations' foreign policy objectives. Though both are considerable regional powers, it seems that what France wants is to be "first among equals" while China tries to reach "equal status among the firsts." Beijing's leaders know that only when China becomes economically prosperous and militarily powerful will they be able to carry out a genuinely independent foreign policy. In this sense, equal status among all sovereign states is beneficial to Chinese national interests only when China can say "no" to other great powers.

On the issue of territorial integrity, the official Chinese stand is that, "When it comes to acts of encroachment upon China's sovereignty and obstructing its peaceful reunification, the Chinese government has no choice but to react strongly." Yet, as pointed out earlier, on many similar occasions Beijing's reactions are rather flexible. It is worth noticing that the friendly relations China has managed to maintain with some countries suggest territorial disputes *can* be negotiated and China *can* make certain concessions to win the trust of its neighbours.

The next section uses Chinese foreign relations with the United States and the ASEAN countries in 1995 as case studies to further illustrate how the concept of state sovereignty is practised in China.

State Sovereignty: Chinese Foreign Relations in Practice

By 1995, China had improved its negative image created by the 1989 Tiananmen incident. Beijing had managed to maintain good relations with an unprecedented number of nations. Nevertheless, Chinese foreign relations faced two severe challenges. One challenge came from the United States. The primary task for Chinese foreign policy-makers was how to break what they perceived as a new "containment" policy plot hatched by Washington against China. The other challenge was a relatively new one: for the first time in well over a century, China's economic and military strength might well cause its smaller neighbours to see it as a threat.

The "Chinese threat" arguments started around early 1993, when the International Monetary Fund, based on purchasing-power parity calculations, quadrupled China's gross domestic product (GDP), making it the world's third largest economy. Some experts even suggested that China's economy would surpass that of the United States by 2010.[21] Matching its rapid economic growth, China had in recent years been trying to modernize its military force. Its defence budget had been steadily increasing in the 1990s, and the Chinese navy was very active during the past year. Recent nuclear tests would only reinforce the world's impression that China's strategic forces had been transformed into combat readiness. Changes like these, coupled with China's territorial claims, made some strategic analysts conclude that China was not a *status quo* power.[22]

The two challenges require the Chinese government to handle its foreign relations with great caution, especially when the issue of sovereignty is involved. It seems that a new pattern has emerged in China's foreign relations practice in the past year: on the issue of Taiwan, Beijing has proved to be firm and non-retrogressive, no matter how much it wishes to have good relations with Washington. On the other hand, in the territorial disputes in the South China Sea, it appeared to be quite acquiescent and flexible.

Sovereignty in Sino-US Relations

In the 1970s and 1980s, the Sino-US relationship had gradually developed toward a quasi-strategic partnership. Since 1989, relations had steadily deteriorated over the Tiananmen incident, human rights, Tibet, and Taiwan. The climax came in 1995, when bilateral relations spiralled down to the lowest point, leading toward what one prominent American called "a collision course."[23] Stanford University China scholar Michel Oksenberg summarized it this way:"Clearly, this is not a healthy situation. Emotion, rather than reason, dogma rather than realism, are beginning to dominate both capitals."[24]

In the intellectual property rights (IPR) issue early that year, China was forced to reach an eleventh-hour agreement with the United States, or face severe economic retaliation. The Harry Wu incident showed that China's human rights record is frequently scrutinized by American politicians and the general public, often putting the Chinese government on the defensive. In June, the granting of a visa by the Clinton Administration to Lee Teng-hui, president of Taiwan, to visit his Alma Mater — Cornell University — so infuriated Chinese leaders that they took a number of retaliatory measures. Bilateral talks and visits between Beijing and Washington were cancelled. The Chinese ambassador to the US was called back for prolonged "consultations." And the Chinese showed no interest in welcoming the new American ambassador, Jim Sasser. Insidious comments were directed at Lee personally, with explicit condemnation of American connivance. The suspension of cross-straits talks and especially China's decision to conduct missile "tests" in waters off the Taiwan coast sent out clear and strong signals that the PRC was determined to oppose any attempt at Taiwan independence.

The Taiwan issue has been a "time bomb" in bilateral relations between China and the United States since the *rapprochement* in the 1970s. Mr Lee's US visit was only the immediate cause of the deterioration in Sino-American relations. Ironically, both the American and Chinese governments invoked their sovereign rights to defend their positions. For the Americans, visa granting was perfectly within the power of a sovereign state. Lee's visit to Cornell was regarded as of a private nature. For the Chinese, "The question of Taiwan is the most important and sensitive issue in China-US relations," claimed China's President Jiang Zemin. "This is an issue of vital principle with a bearing on China's sovereignty, territorial integrity, national unity, and the national sentiments of the Chinese people."[25]

Lee's Cornell visit was a personal victory for the Taiwanese president. Beijing may have been unfair in blaming the Clinton Administration for this offensive behaviour, because diplomatic manoeuvres at the time indicated that Washington, like Beijing, was only reacting to Taipei's diplomatic initiative. In a sense, Lee adroitly played the "American card" to broaden Taiwan's "living space" in the world. At the same time, he increased his domestic support for the presidential election in 1996.

Indeed, both Washington and Beijing knew Lee's visit was not a purely private one: it was part of Taiwan's initiative to gain recognition in the community of nations. For Beijing, however, the Taiwanese president's move was a direct threat to its claim of sovereignty over the island province. No matter from what point of view, geographic, strategic, emotional, or practical, Taiwan was extraordinarily important to regime survival in the PRC.

From the Chinese side, the American visa for Lee Teng-hui was not an isolated event. Rather, it was an integral part of a series of deliberate actions the US had been taking to sabotage the existing agreements and understanding between Beijing and Washington. The feeling among Beijing's policy-makers is that since the end of the Cold War, Washington finds itself for the first time in history having to conduct an inter-nationalist foreign policy without a clearly identified opponent. It needs a re-definition of American national interests and their major challenger. The Gulf War proved that countries like Iraq could not become a serious challenge to the United States. China, due to its size, population, growing economy, and huge military forces, may well become one. As such, the United States needs to keep it in check. Moreover, even if China believed that Lee's visit was not an American initiative, the United States could not shirk its responsibilities for recent acrimonious relations. Washington's permit to Lee's entry set a bad example and might cause "domino" re-actions in other countries. Tiny changes may eventually lead to an upset of the current international *status quo* between the PRC and Taiwan. In this regard, no one remembers better than Beijing what happened in the early

1970s, when Washington started the normalization process with the PRC. Quite a number of countries followed the United States and established diplomatic relations with China. In addition, Chinese leaders might have personal reasons to feel insulted and angry since the US government did not even bother to brief them on Lee's visit. Jiang Zemin was said to have learned of it from the newspapers.[26]

Besides the issue of Taiwan, Beijing is also annoyed by its feud with Washington over China's human rights record. The Chinese believe that the Americans have always tried to impose their own value criteria on China. Beijing feels strongly that Washington singles out China as a human rights target for malicious purposes. In recent years, China has published two major official documents on human rights conditions in the country. While letting the world know the achievements the Chinese government has made in past decades, Beijing does not try to conceal the differences between itself and the West. Chinese leaders feel they know more than foreigners about the situation in China and are especially resentful of those nations which try to put their noses into others' business.

As mentioned earlier, the Chinese government holds to what may be regarded as a traditional conception of its sovereign rights whereby the state has the ultimate legal right to decide its own policy and jurisdiction in its territory. This means that "the government, the official voice of the state, indicates in a legal sense what should be public policy within the domestic jurisdiction of the state."[27] From Beijing's point of view, the West, especially the United States, uses human rights as a pretext to interfere in China's domestic affairs and encroach upon China's sovereignty.

To be fair, many of the US attacks on China are not initiated from the White House. From time to time, the Clinton Administration has reiterated that the United States would like to adhere to the spirit of the Sino-American communiqués that brought the two giant nations together diplomatically, if not strategically. However, the White House's "one China" policy has recently been interrupted by pressure from the US Congress, where conservative Republicans consider Clinton's "kowtow" diplomacy intolerable. For them, the United States should be much tougher in handling bilateral relations with China, especially on issues like China's human rights conditions, alleged intellectual property violations, increasing tension across the Taiwan Straits, and expansive behaviour in the South China Sea.

The key to a successful foreign policy is compromise. In a confrontation, each side should seek compromise while at the same time minimizing damage to its own national interest. Yet in the eyes of Chinese leaders, the US government in recent years has forced China to give in repeatedly. Though Beijing made several eleventh-hour concessions, such as the intellectual property rights agreement and the release of Harry Wu, Washington seemed to remain unimpressed. The danger of this kind of unilateral concession, especially in a game where two powerful nations are involved, is that the one party may eventually feel cornered and obliged to take revenge. As Henry Kissinger pointed out, "China's leaders have frequently taken into account the special needs of their counterparts provided such an action also served Chinese interests. What they will not accept, or will accept only under extreme duress, is the implication that America bestows its cooperation as a special favour without reciprocity to be withdrawn at will."[28]

There is already a growth of nationalism in China, particularly among the intellectuals and the military who think China should be much tougher in facing hostility from the United States. Ironically, among those who argue for China's stronger stand *vis-à-vis* the United States are those who have either been educated in the Western countries or participated in the pro-democracy movements in China a few years ago.[29]

It seems that the American public and government alike lack an understanding of the different interpretations of sovereignty between them and the Chinese. This may well be the main cause for the deterioration of Sino-American relations last year. In his testimony before the US Senate Foreign Relations Committee on 13 July 1995, Dr Kissinger talked about how the Americans' perception of foreign policy might be different from that of other countries: "Populated almost exclusively by immigrants, ours is the only country that has never experienced a powerful neighbour along its borders, and therefore has never had to face the security issues confronted by less favoured nations."[30] The United States, because of its geographic location, could engage and disengage in an international event fairly easily, without worrying much about its own security. Thus, it may not be easy for Americans to understand why state sovereignty is so sensitive to the Chinese, who in the past 150 years have suffered from numerous invasions, threats, and exploitation by other powers.

The Chinese view of Lee Teng-hui's visit to the United States was understandably quite different from American domestic perception. While to many Americans it was a US sovereign right to determine the entry of visitors, the Chinese saw it as a provocation; if China bowed, it could bring a disastrous "snowball" reaction and damage its position internationally.

China's past experiences no doubt underpin its current strategic calculations. Chinese leaders believe that alliances and tight alignments would jeopardize China's security and endanger its sovereignty. Beijing is particularly on guard against a post-Cold War tendency toward US dominance. China also views the US military presence in Asia as a potential destabilizing factor and even a threat to China's strategic leverage in the region. Although China has managed to maintain relatively good relations with its neighbours, the sense of insecurity is clearly seen in Chinese government statements and the speeches of Chinese leaders.

Unless the American government understands China's concerns over its state sovereignty, the protracted quarrel between China and the United States is likely to continue. It will also be virtually impossible to achieve a breakthrough on China's missile sales or nuclear testing in the way Washington hopes. Fortunately, political differences did not affect bilateral economic relations that much. China enjoyed a lucrative trade surplus worth some US$30 billion last year, and saw an increase of American business investment. By the end of 1995, there were also signs that bilateral political relations were on an upturn. The release of Harry Wu paved the way for Hillary Clinton to be at the Fourth World Conference on Women, and the Jiang-Clinton summit held in New York further relaxed the tension between the two countries.

The South China Sea Territorial Disputes

In February 1995, China was found to have built some structures on Meijijiao (Mischief Reef), in the Nansha (Spratly) Islands. This action prompted a strong protest from the Philippines, also a claimant to the disputed region. In March, Manila took retaliatory measures against Chinese activities in areas which it claimed to be part of Philippine territorial waters. A number of Chinese markers on Jackson Reef (Wufangjiao) and Half Moon Reef (Banyuejiao) were dismantled by Philippine authorities. Also, some Chinese fishing boats were seized on charges of illegally fishing.[31] The significance of this new round of sovereign disputes between China and the Philippines went far beyond these barren rocks in the South China Sea. It caught international attention and stirred up fears in Southeast Asian countries about China's intent.[32]

Until the early 1970s, those islands, islets, atolls, shoals, and banks in an area 500 nautical miles from north to south and 400 nautical miles from west to east in the South China Sea were hardly noticed. In recent years, however, the Nansha Islands, the largest among the four South China Sea archipelagoes, have become an international hot spot. The islands are claimed by six governments, either wholly or in part. Malaysia, Brunei, Vietnam, and the Philippines each claim part of the Spratlys. China and Taiwan, on the other hand, declare the whole archipelago to be Chinese territory.

Claimant states justify their titles to these islands based on various sources of international law: claims by China and Taiwan are based mainly on historical discovery and uncontested (until recently) occupation by its fishermen. China was the first to exercise administration and sovereignty over the Spratlys.[33] Vietnam's claims are on similar grounds and, in a weaker sense, on cession derived from the French occupation. Philippines' claims derive from the method of prescription, that is, continued occupation of the abandoned foreign territory. Malaysia and Brunei joined the chorus with something relatively new: the continental shelf and Exclusive Economic Zone (EEZ), as defined by the United Nations Convention on the Law of the Sea. Strictly speaking, none of the claimants can fully justify their demands, given the vagueness of international law on this matter.

Until recently, China had not paid much attention to its territorial waters claims. In the past decades, Beijing had basically followed the principle of "shelving the differences and seeking the common interests" in handling disputes over South China Sea islands with other claimants. This was not surprising because the Chinese government had been engaged in border disputes with almost all of its neighbours, which made it less eager to be involved in the islands disputes where the question of national security was not at stake. Also, the Chinese navy had not had a deep-water capability, limited both by financial constraints and strategic considerations of the Chinese leadership.

This situation has now changed dramatically. Signs show that, as Beijing is becoming a global power, China's territorial waters have been given ever more attention. First, the Chinese government began to popularize the idea of "oceanic territory." For a long period, all Chinese textbooks stated China's total territory as 9.6 million square kilometres. This calculation did not count its territorial seas. Recent articles in authoritative Chinese journals and newspapers have tried to "correct" this misperception by telling their people to focus on the "ocean," "because the territorial seas are also our inalienable territory." By the new calculation, China's total territory should also include over 3 million square kilometres of oceanic territory.[34] Premier Li Peng also stressed in his government work report to the National People's Congress in 1995 that China should "strengthen ... coastal construction, maintain national territorial integrity and the rights of the seas."[35] To reinforce its citizens' awareness of territorial claims, China's television weather forecasting programme also includes the weather in the South China Sea, even though few in the audience are concerned.

Secondly, the Chinese have become very active in the South China Sea area. Fishing activities have been noticeably increased. Naval bases have been established. China even built a weather station, claiming to do so under the auspices of the World Meteorological Organization, which subsequently denied the authorization.[36] With the prospect of rich oil deposits in the region, China was reportedly engaged in drilling, seismic surveys, and negotiations with foreign oil companies for the development of Nansha's natural resources.

Finally, legal measures have been endorsed by the Chinese government to back up its activities in that area. In February 1992, China's National People's Congress passed the Laws of Territorial Waters and Contiguous Zones, making it clear that the Spratlys belonged to China.

> The land territory of the People's Republic of China consists of the mainland and its offshore islands, Taiwan and various affiliated islands including Diaoyutai Island, the Penghu Islands, the Dongsha Islands, the Xisha Islands, the Zhongsha Islands, the Nansha Islands and other islands ...

In addition, the islands have appeared in all related laws, rules, and regulations promulgated in recent years. The administrative power over the South China Sea territories was given to a provincial government (Hainan) to demonstrate China's sovereignty.

China's stand on the South China Sea region has inspired research on China's activities in and attitudes toward the South China Sea. The tension there has been a matter of concern to all nations in the area, as well as the major global powers. One significant development of the territorial disputes between China and these nations last year was that China, so far, had tried to avoid a united front against it. In the past, China had only taken actions against Vietnam. Now, with the Philippines involved, it is more difficult for China to seek a peaceful solution, unless some sort of compromise is reached on the question of sovereignty. During Qian Qichen's visit to Brunei, China for the first time indicated that it was willing to negotiate a peaceful solution with concerned parties based on the United Nations' Convention on the Law of the Sea, to which it has not yet attached its signature. Facing a possible coalition of ASEAN countries against its claims, Beijing also showed signs of relaxation of its previous position that insisted on bilateral but not multilateral talks over the Spratlys.

In the past, the Chinese government was quite tough in defending its oceanic territories. It resorted to military conflicts twice with Vietnam over the South China Sea islands. When Japan and South Korea signed an agreement for joint development of the East China Sea continental shelf — another area claimed by the Chinese — Beijing issued a strong protest against it, warning that the two nations should bear all the consequences resulting from this serious encroachment of Chinese sovereignty.[37]

Such attitudes inevitably caused fears among the other parties, whose military forces are not comparable to China's. Therefore, China was depicted by many foreign commentators as an aggressive power, expanding its territories at a time when there is a military vacuum left by the Americans and Russians.[38] However, if Chinese claims are carefully examined, it becomes apparent that despite the verbal protests and some activities of a non-military nature, China has acted in a remarkably restrained way, favouring peaceful negotiations with the governments concerned over military means. The Chinese government has repeatedly appealed for peaceful solutions to disputes over sovereignty and, where that is not possible, to shelve them for the time being. Beijing has also encouraged joint development of the resources in the Spratlys and acquiesced to the other claimants' exploration of the area.

What makes the Chinese government exercise restraint in handling territorial disputes in the South China Sea? Besides the obvious concern of the Chinese government that in order to ensure smooth domestic reforms, China needs a peaceful external environment, there are at least three major reasons: the importance of maintaining friendly relations with ASEAN countries (including Vietnam); the need to have Taiwan's engagement in that area; and the limits of China's military capacity.

China has a vital interest in maintaining peace and stability in East Asia. First, to have constructive relations with Asia Pacific countries has great economic importance for China. Its trade with Asia Pacific nations took a significant 62% of the total trade in 1994.[39] With a decline of European and North American economic influence in ASEAN nations, and with a large overseas Chinese population engaged in business in Southeast Asia, China expects to gain great benefits from these booming economies.

Economic interests aside, the more subtle issue is China's security. Though the South China Sea islands are scattered in strategically important seaways, China views its strategic relationship with ASEAN countries as more important. To have healthy relations with the Southeast Asian countries would ensure China a peaceful environment to accelerate its domestic economic growth, stabilize its border areas, break any united front against it, and enhance China's influence in the region as well as the world.

ASEAN countries traditionally have had good relations with the other great powers in the Asia Pacific. Chinese leaders know that in case of severe conflicts with ASEAN, they would risk the danger of confronting directly the United States, and possibly Japan. They also know that tension in the area may well invite the return of US military force, thus changing the current strategic equilibrium to their disadvantage.

On 30 July 1995, Chinese Vice-Premier and Foreign Minister Qian Qichen assured the seven ASEAN countries, during his visit to Brunei at an ASEAN-China consultative session of the Southeast Asian organization's ministerial meeting, that China and ASEAN would be good neighbours and friends forever. He stressed that equal treatment, respect, trust, mutual benefit, and cooperation between China and the Southeast Asian nations would be a model for international relationships in the changing post-Cold War world situation. He said the first goal of Chinese foreign policy was to maintain a stable periphery in order to ensure smooth development of economic construction at home. To achieve this goal, China needed stable and lasting good-neighbourly relations and friendly cooperation with ASEAN countries. Maintaining peace and stability in the region and promoting economic prosperity and cooperation were the common interests and goals of both ASEAN and China.[40]

On the other hand, China realizes the danger a united ASEAN could do to its own national interests. ASEAN has already made a statement showing considerable solidarity even though there are different claimants within ASEAN itself. Other powers are also likely to join in the quarrel, on the ASEAN side. These have made Beijing reconsider its position, mending its endangered relationships with the Southeast Asian countries before irrevocable consequences occur. During his stay in Brunei, Qian Qichen agreed for the first time that the Law of the Sea was applicable and multilateral discussion of this issue might be accepted.

Though never indicated publicly, Taiwan could also be a concern that led to China's "soft" position in the South China Sea disputes. Since

Taipei's claims over the area are solely based on its legitimacy as *the* government representing all of China, it would be one motive for the Kuomintang (KMT) government not to divorce from China if it wishes to keep the islands. In addition, both governments' engagement in the area may create opportunities to enhance mutual understanding, even coopera-tion. If China adopts a more threatening policy, Taiwan would be forced to choose sides. That could change its current status and decrease China's chance for a peaceful unification.

China's limited naval capabilities may also contribute to its less asser-tive attitude toward territory in the South China Sea. Experts believe that China does not yet have a real blue-water naval capability. According to the then US Assistant Defense Secretary Joseph Nye, the Chinese "have very severe limitations in command-control communications and logistics which prevent them from operating at a distance from their shores. They have some improvements in indigenous improved destroyers and frigates, but not a true blue-water navy."[41] Though there are indications that China has accelerated its pace to build a modern navy, it will be years before the Chinese navy can achieve its full potential.

To sum up, although China has recently been quite active in the South China Sea, its basic tone in the sovereignty disputes is rather restrained. Because of China's needs for a good relationship with ASEAN, engage-ment with Taiwan, and the modernization of its navy, the Chinese govern-ment has adopted a relatively "soft" position on sovereignty in this area, a sharp contrast to its uncompromising stand on Taiwan.

Why Is Sovereignty So Important?

Some Western observers describe Chinese foreign policy as "that of a nineteenth century, mercantile power in a twenty-first-century, 'post-modern' region where state sovereignty is a 'Victorian value'."[42] To a large extent, this is true. China is a developing country and needs to protect its sovereignty from the encroachment of great powers. Chinese leaders have reasons to be very tough toward the United States over Lee Teng-hui's US visit. Any "soft" stand on issues like this may well en-courage Washington's pro-Taiwan politicians to push for the recognition of Taiwan as an independent political entity. What Chinese leaders cannot forget is that after the US established contacts with the PRC, a wave of nations established diplomatic relations with China. Beijing also has reasons to believe that Lee's "personal diplomacy," with the support or at least acquiescence of the US government, may encourage other countries to explore the possibility of establishing relations with Taiwan.

Beijing faced a dilemma in conducting its foreign policy in 1995. On the one hand, China could not tolerate various attempts to encroach on its sovereignty. On the other, it was on constant guard against a tendency to regard China as an aggressive power. The former required a firm stand, the latter called for a "softer" peace-loving image. As a result, Chinese foreign policy-makers had to be flexible in dealing with sovereignty issues.

Leadership Succession

One of the most commonly mentioned reasons for the Chinese government's paradoxical attitudes toward sovereignty, at least from the viewpoint of the West, is that China is at the major juncture of leadership change. With Deng Xiaoping, China's "paramount leader" reaching the age of 91, power succession is imminent. The current leader, Jiang Zemin, lacks both Mao's charismatic leadership style and Deng's pragmatic political experience. He also has little previous experience either in governing a region (except briefly in Shanghai) or commanding the military, which are the conventional paths to power for Chinese leaders. To ensure a smooth transition, Jiang has much to do in a short time. He must win the support of both local officials and the military, and his success to date is uncertain. In any case, whoever leads China into the twenty-first century should be able to maintain domestic stability as well as a peaceful international environment. To do so, diplomacy and military force become vital.

The post-Deng leadership wants to prove to the world that China will continue to carry out Deng's foreign policy even after the patriarch is gone. Beijing is eager to convey the impression that the Chinese government is stable, united, and ready to deal with any possible uncertainties after Deng's death. To ensure continuous reform and economic growth, the last thing the Chinese government wants to see is a chaotic international environment. This requires the Chinese leadership to handle sovereignty issues with great caution, as manifested in the two examples mentioned above.

Related to the succession struggle, one factor that has caught the attention of western observers is the role of the People's Liberation Army (PLA). Study of the PRC's political culture has clearly indicated that whoever controls the military controls the nation. The tension across the Taiwan Straits gave a new prominence to the PLA in Chinese politics. China's 1994 state budget saw a sharp increase of 25% in military spending.[43] Currently, PLA members account for about 20% of the Chinese Communist Party's Central Committee. General Liu Huaqing is a member of the CCP Politburo's Standing Committee, the highest decision-making institution in China.

The current military leadership is so strong that no Chinese leader can afford to neglect it. Even if Jiang's own style in dealing with issues like Taiwan is cautious, it is doubtful whether he wants to put his will against the generals. Evidence shows that Jiang has been trying to emphasize his military connections. Last year, he made several trips to military bases to enhance his role as the chairman of the Central Military Commission. Moreover, in his other visits to the provinces, there have always been local military or military police officers accompanying him.

As a result of this military resurgence, China's position on the Taiwan question has become tougher than ever. Chinese Defence Minister Chi Haotian's recent speech may well illustrate this point. He warned that Beijing would not "sit idle" should Taiwan "attempt" independence.[44] The quite visible military exercises begun last year are also a sign of the military's strong stand.

Rising Nationalism

Nationalism calls for the independence of a nation. For Beijing, nationalism is an effective adhesive to unite the huge population under its control. Since Deng's reform, regional conflicts have been growing at a unprecedented speed in China, due largely to the gap between the more economically liberalized coastal provinces and the relatively backward and conservative interior. For the Chinese leadership, the best way to mobilize its people's nationalist feelings is to make full use of sovereignty conflicts with other nations.

Sovereignty implies equality, and China is very sensitive about equal treatment. Humiliating past experiences have contributed to Chinese leaders' determined attitudes to restore the "lost dignities" of the Chinese nation. One way to do so is to hold a strong position on issues concerning China's sovereignty. On the Taiwan issue, this is exactly what Chinese leaders are supposed to do: be tough and uncompromising. They know that nationalist feelings in China could topple any government, should it "lose" Taiwan.

In handling Lee Teng-hui's US visit, Chinese leaders adroitly cultivated an impression that, after the collapse of the communist regimes in East Europe and the Soviet Union, the United States' true intent was to undermine China's economic achievements by keeping China weak and divided. To a large degree, Beijing's strategy was successful. Said Michel Oksenberg, testifying at a US Congressional Committee on International Relations hearing, "Many Americans are beginning to think that China, an emerging economic and perhaps military giant, may be America's next enemy. Meanwhile, many on the Chinese mainland think the real intent of the United States is to isolate and split China."[45] Another US China expert, Donald Zagoria, warned that US domestic pressures on China could only help China's growing nationalism adopt a strong anti-Western tone. To minimize the detrimental consequences to American interests, Zagoria suggested the US should strengthen and expand both official and unofficial ties with China, and encourage more extensive and durable economic links that promote moderate Chinese growth.[46]

The "Sino-phobia" Syndrome

Traditional balance of power theory would predict that when a power becomes dangerously dominant in a region, the region's other powers would come together to hold the dominating party at bay. This is something Chinese leaders worry about. From their viewpoint, there is already a conspiracy to weaken China's economic strength by the West, as reflected in placing China as the world's third (or even second!) economy and thus depriving it of favourable loan terms from the World Bank and other international organizations.

While Sino-phobia might be felt among several of China's neighbours, the Chinese see things differently. For more than two thousand years, China dominated East Asia in terms of cultural influence and technology. That sense of superiority was smashed by the gunboats of Western powers in the mid-nineteenth century. The Chinese were defeated and invaded by Western powers and Japan. The lessons drawn from these invasions and defeats are that China should be strong: weak nations are bullied by the powerful. This realistic assessment of the international system makes for an unusually stubborn position when the matter of sovereignty and territorial integrity is concerned.

However, given the fact that China does not want to alert its neighbours, one would also expect Beijing to adopt a cautious foreign policy toward the surrounding countries, especially when delicate issues of sovereignty are concerned.

One thing the Chinese government hates to acknowledge is radical changes in its foreign policy. Thus, Beijing has repeatedly emphasized that China will hold to its principles on sovereignty issues. Meanwhile, it constantly reminds its neighbours of the fact that China has never been an expansionist nation in the past, that no matter how powerful China may become, its peaceful policy will remain unchanged. By doing this, Beijing hopes to dispel the fears of the smaller countries. However, it remains to be seen whether the Chinese effort can bring about fruitful results.

Conclusion

Ideas about national sovereignty have undergone dramatic changes since World War II. Many Western countries have shifted their focus to popular sovereignty, which stresses that the state derives its authority and should be responsible to the will of the people. Therefore, the actions taken by a foreign government or governments to help people challenge their oppressive government do not violate sovereignty. However, China, like many developing countries, still holds to the concept of state sovereignty which stresses national territorial integrity based on historical possession and national independence.[47] For Beijing, to talk about popular sovereignty is to split the country. An obvious example is its sovereign claim on Taiwan which is genuine and tenacious. On this issue, the Chinese have repeatedly declared that there is no room for negotiation. This is clearly revealed in the unprecedented personal attacks on Lee Teng-hui. From the reasons analysed above, it is not hard to conclude that such a firm stand is inevitable: no one in the current Beijing leadership could afford to have Taiwan cut off from China.

Clearly, for Chinese leaders, it is not what to govern, but how to govern that matters most. The Chinese government is particularly enraged by American interference in what China sees as its domestic affairs, such as human rights issues, Tibet and Taiwan. On the other hand, because of the strategic significance of China's relations with ASEAN countries, the need for domestic construction, and the concern for national unification, territorial disputes with China's neighbours will take a secondary position in Chinese foreign policy.

Notes

1. *Beijing Review*, Vol. 38, No. 1 (2–8 January 1995), p. 9.
2. *The Economist*, London, Vol. 336 (26 August 1995), p. 30.
3. For a review of the historical development of the concept of sovereignty, see Daniel Philpott, "Sovereignty: An Introduction and Brief History," *Journal of International Affairs*, Vol. 48, No. 2 (Winter 1995), pp. 353–68.
4. *Black's Law Dictionary* (6th ed.; St. Paul: West Pub., 1990), p. 1396.
5. W. Michael Reisman, "Sovereignty and Human Rights in Contemporary International Law," *American Journal of International Law*, Vol. 84 (October 1990), p. 867. For a detailed discussion of the changing norms of sovereignty, see Samuel Barkin and Bruce Cronin, "The State and the Nation: Changing Norms and the Rules of Sovereignty in International Relations," *International Organization*, Vol. 48, No. 1 (Winter 1994), pp. 107–30. See also, Gene Lyons and Michael Mastanduno, "International Intervention, State Sovereignty, and the Future of International Society," *International Social Science Journal*, Vol. 45 (November 1993).
6. Lassa Oppenheim commented that it is "doubtful whether any single word has caused so much intellectual confusion." See Lassa Oppenheim, *International Law*, Vol. 1 (London: Longman, 1905), p. 103. Quoted in Daniel Philpott (Note 3), p. 354.
7. Oyvind Osterud, "Sovereign Statehood and National Self-Determination," in *Subduing Sovereignty*, edited by Marianne Heiberg (London: Pinter, 1994), p. 19. Lee C. Buchhieit, "The Sovereign Client," *Journal of International Affairs*, Vol. 48, No. 2 (Winter 1995), p. 527. Ole Waever, "Identity, Integration and Security," *Journal of International Affairs*, Vol. 48, No. 2 (Winter 1995), p. 416.
8. *United Nations Document, S/PV. 2902* (23 December, 1989), p. 7.
9. W. Michael Reisman, "Sovereignty and Human Rights" (Note 5).
10. *Deng Xiaoping wenxuan, 1975–1982* (Selected Works of Deng Xiaoping, 1975–1982) (Beijing: Renmin chubanshe, 1983), p. 372.
11. See *Deng Xiaoping wenxuan*, Vol. 3 (Beijing: Renmin chubanshe, 1993), pp. 331, 345.
12. *Zhou Enlai waijiao wenxuan* (Selected Works of Zhou Enlai on Diplomacy) (Beijing: Zhongyang wenxian chubanshe, 1990), p. 20.
13. "Jiang Reviews China-US Relations," *Beijing Review*, Vol. 38, No. 47 (20–26 November 1995), p. 9.
14. *Beijing Review* Vol. 38, No. 43 (23–29 October 1995), p. 13.
15. See "Human Rights in China," *Beijing Review*, Vol. 34, No. 44 (4–10 November 1991); "The Progress of Human Rights in China," *Beijing Review*, Special Issue (January 1996).
16. *Beijing Review*, Vol. 39, No. 1 (1–7 January 1996), p. 13.

17. *Japan Economic Newswire* (15 December 1995).
18. *The Guardian*, London, 23 May 1995; *Beijing Review*, Vol. 38, No. (16–22 October, 1995), p. 22.
19. Tian Zengpei, "1994: A Victorious Year for China's Foreign Relations," *Beijing Review*, Vol. 38, No. 1 (2–8 January 1995), p. 9.
20. See Note 14.
21. Nicholas R. Lardy, *China in the World Economy* (Washington: Institute for International Economics, April 1994), pp. 14–18, cited in Paul Dibb, "Towards a New Balance of Power in Asia," *Adelphi Paper* 295 (London: The International Institute for Strategic Studies [IISS], 1995), p. 27.
22. See Paul Dibb, "Towards a New Balance" (Note 21), p. 26.
23. Henry Kissinger, "Heading for a Collision in Asia," *The Washington Post*, 26 July 1995, p. A23.
24. Ibid.
25. Note 13, p. 8.
26. US Senator Dianne Feinstein was surprised when Jiang Zemin told her that "he actually read about Lee Teng-hui's visit to the United States in the newspapers and felt a sense of betrayal because the Chinese government had been assured as late as May 22 — or at least what it interpreted as an assurance — that there would be no visit." *Federal News Service* (Washington: Federal Information System Corporation [FISC], 11 October 1995).
27. Kelly Pease and David P. Forsythe, "Human Rights, Humanitarian Intervention, and World Politics," *Human Rights Quarterly*, Vol. 15 (May 1993), p. 291.
28. Henry Kissinger, "U.S. Foreign Policy Goals in the Near Future," *Federal Document Clearing House Congressional Testimony*, 13 July 1995.
29. This observation was based on the author's conversations with scholars in various Chinese academic institutions, and interviews with graduate students for research on Chinese foreign policy last year.
30. Note 28.
31. *Window*, Hong Kong, 31 March 1995, p. 4.
32. For a recent summary of this incident, see Mark J. Valencia, "China and the South China Sea Disputes," *Adelphi Paper* 298 (London: IISS, 1995), pp. 6–7.
33. For a brief account of the legal basis of China's claims over the Nansha Islands, see Pan Shiying's report for *Window* (3 September 1993), pp. 23–37.
34. Lin Mu and Jin Yan, "Zhongguo guotu you duo da?" (How Big Is China's Territory?), *Xinhua wenzhai* (New China Digest), Beijing, August 1995, pp. 11, 13.
35. Ibid., p. 13.
36. See Mark J. Valencia (Note 32), p. 9.
37. See Chen Degong, *Xiandai Zhongguo haiyangfa* (Contemporary International

Law of the Sea) (Beijing: Zhongguo shehui kexue chubanshe, 1988), p. 460.

38. See, for example, Eric Hyer, "The South China Sea Disputes: Implications of China's Earlier Territorial Settlements," *Pacific Affairs*, Vol. 68, No. 1 (Spring 1995), pp. 34–54. Michael G. Gallagher, "China's Illusory Threat to the South China Sea," *International Security*, Vol. 19, No. 1 (Summer 1994), pp. 169–94; Mark J. Valencia (Note 32).

39. Compiled from *China Statistical Yearbook 1995* (Beijing: China Statistical Publishing House, 1995), pp. 543–45.

40. *Xinhua News Agency*, Beijing, 30 July 1995.

41. See Joseph Nye's testimony before the US Senate Foreign Relations Committee in *Federal News Service* (Washington: FISC, 11 October 1995).

42. Gerald Segal, "China Changes Shape: Regionalism and Foreign Policy," *Adelphi Paper* 287 (London: IISS, 1994), p. 34.

43. Jack A. Goldstone, "The Coming Chinese Collapse," *Foreign Policy* (Summer, 1995), p. 45.

44. Yojana Sharma, "China: Military Looms Large Over Foreign Policy," *Inter Press Service*, Beijing, 6 September 1995.

45. *Congressional Testimony* (Washington: Federal Document Clearing House, Inc., 20 July 1995). Also see, *Federal News Service* (Washington: FISC, 20 July 1995).

46. Donald Zagoria, *China: Domestic Change and Foreign Policy* (Santa Monica: RAND, 1995).

47. See Samuel Barkin and Bruce Cronin (Note 5), p. 112.

7

Political Interactions Across the Taiwan Straits

Chu-cheng Ming

For relations between Beijing and Taipei, 1995 was the most dramatic year since 1987. Throughout the entire year, we saw events that might lead to great advances in bilateral relations and we also witnessed events that seemed to lead in the opposite direction.

In the second half of 1994, the Straits Exchange Foundation (SEF) of the Republic of China (ROC) and the Association for Relations Across the Taiwan Straits (ARATS) of the People's Republic of China (PRC) met and talked three times, once in Nanjing and twice in Taipei, trying to reach a consensus on three important issues, namely, aircraft-hijacking, illegal immigration, and fishing disputes. Since discrepancies persisted between the two sides, little progress was made. In January 1995, the two agencies picked up where they had left off the year before and met in Beijing again with the hope that they could resolve the problems. After several days of negotiation, the two delegations reached only preliminary agreement on the first two issues. As for the third, on fishing disputes, the two sides first argued over the definition of "official ships" then they could not agree on the related concept of "jurisdiction," which eventually ended the meeting without signing any agreement.

If China watchers anticipated that the bilateral relationship would continue in this vein, they were in for a big surprise. Since politics dominated the scene, we review in this chapter only political issues and events that occurred during 1995: the issuance of Jiang Zemin's eight-point proposal concerning the promotion of China's reunification; Taipei's responses to Jiang's overture, including Lien Chan's speech which called for an era of negotiation in cross-Straits relations and Lee Teng-hui's six-point statement; the preparation for the second Koo-Wang meeting; and Taipei's newest round in the diplomatic offensive which triggered the heavy-handed retaliation from Beijing. Our analyses lead us to conclude that although political relations across the Taiwan Straits experienced a low ebb after June, signs of flow still exist, and bilateral relations have become a triangular interaction with the United States (US) playing an increasingly important role.

Jiang Zemin's New Overture toward Taipei

On 30 January 1995, the eve of traditional Chinese Spring Festival, Jiang Zemin, on behalf of the Central Committee of the Chinese Communist Party (CCP) and the State Council, made a speech entitled "Continue to

Promote the Reunification of the Motherland." The speech had a long "preface," tracing the history of Taiwan's cession to Japan in 1895, reiterating Deng Xiaoping's reunification formula, "one country, two systems," and advocating that under the ever-growing trend of exchanges across the Taiwan Straits direct "three links," namely, direct sea and air transportation, mail, and trade, will benefit both the mainland and Taiwan.

Following the preface, Jiang put forward an eight-point opinion regarding the development of bilateral relations and the promotion of China's reunification:

1. Adherence to the principle of one China is the basis and premise for peaceful reunification.
2. We (the CCP and the PRC) oppose Taiwan's activities in "expanding its living space internationally," which is aimed at creating "two Chinas" or "one China, one Taiwan." ... Such acts can only help the forces working for the independence of Taiwan and undermine the process of peaceful reunification.
3. It has been our consistent stand to hold negotiations with Taiwan authorities on the peaceful reunification of the motherland.... By "on the premise that there is only one China, we are prepared to talk with the Taiwan authorities about any matter," we mean, naturally, that all matters of concern to the Taiwan authorities are included.... Here again I solemnly propose that such negotiations be held. I suggest that, as the first step, negotiations should be held and an agreement reached on officially ending the state of hostility between the two sides in accordance with the principle that there is only one China. On this basis, the two sides should undertake jointly to safeguard China's sovereignty and territorial integrity and map out plans for the future development of their relations. As regards the name, place and form of these political talks a solution to both sides can certainly be found so long as consultations on an equal footing can be held at an early date.
4. We should strive for the peaceful reunification of the motherland since Chinese should not fight Chinese. Our undertaking not to give up the use of force is not directed against our compatriots in Taiwan, but against the schemes of foreign forces to interfere with China's reunification and to bring about the independence of Taiwan.
5. We hold that political differences should not affect or interfere with the economic cooperation between the sides.... (I)t is absolutely necessary to adopt practical measures to speed up the establishment of such direct links (postal, air and shipping services and trade).
6. The splendid culture of 5,000 years created by the sons and daughters of all ethnic groups of China has become ties keeping the entire Chinese people

close at heart and constitute an important basis for the peaceful reunification of the motherland.

7. We should fully respect their (the Taiwanese') lifestyle and their wish to be the masters of their own affairs (*dangjia zuozhu*) and protect all their legitimate rights and interests.... We also hope that all political parties in Taiwan will adopt a sensible, forward-looking and constructive attitude and promote the expansion of relations between the two sides. All parties and personages of all circles in Taiwan are welcome to exchange views with us on relations between the two sides and on peaceful reunification and are also welcome to pay a visit and tour.

8. Leaders of the Taiwan authorities are welcome to pay visits in appropriate capacities. We are also ready to accept invitations to visit Taiwan. We can discuss the state affairs or exchange ideas on certain questions first. Even a simple visit to the other side will be useful. The affairs of the Chinese people should be handled by us, something that does not take an international occasion to accomplish.[1]

Taiwan has long been a very important and sensitive issue to the People's Republic of China. Since the day of China's division in October 1949, Beijing had declared its firm resolution to achieve reunification. Nowadays, reunification to the PRC leaders is not only a matter of nationalism, which is considered by most Chinese to be the utmost cause, but an issue of practical significance. Since the demise of the Soviet Union and the Eastern European regimes, Beijing has found itself caught in a situation with mixed implications. On the one hand, it has become the arch enemy of the Western "capitalist" states, with no one else but itself to lean on. On the other hand, no longer being threatened by the Soviet Union from the north, it now enjoys the "best and safest" strategic environment since its establishment. Thus, Taiwan becomes even more relevant in determining its future strategic security. Should Taiwan become independent or even worse, fall into the hands of an enemy, its security and ambition of outward development would be jeopardized. Besides, if Taiwan independence is not curbed, a chain reaction of separatist movements may emerge inside China which poses a real strategic threat to the PRC's security, but would also confront any ruling faction in Beijing with a fundamental power challenge, not to mention the historical indictment of humiliation.

Beijing's policy toward Taipei has undergone changes but the current policy is "peaceful unification through 'one country, two systems'," an idea originating with Deng Xiaoping in the early 1980s. Underneath the slogans, or the so called "peaceful hand," lies Beijing's "coercive hand," which is used to compel Taipei to comply, if necessary. In the past, Beijing had almost no means of working with Taiwan. Since 1987, however, economic, cultural, athletic and personal exchanges across the Straits have provided numerous ways for Beijing to woo Taipei. Jiang Zemin's new overture represented yet another wave of Beijing's Taiwan policy.

As the cross-Straits political relations reached a deadlock following the unsuccessful negotiations between the ARATS and SEF, Jiang Zemin's speech was certainly helpful and timely. Even Lee Teng-hui later admitted that there were some new ideas contained in Jiang's "old tune."[2] What then, are the new ideas in Jiang's old tune? The first impression that strikes readers is its tone. Although the proposal still holds to the standard phrases of "one China," "peaceful reunification," and "one country, two systems," the entire speech was presented in a very mild tone, much more so than ever before.

Second, different from all the past practices, Jiang for the first time is not opposed to the arrangement of "one country, two governments."[3] In the past, the PRC's position on the issue has been very consistent. For example, in the Shanghai Communiqué between the PRC and the US issued on 28 February 1972, we read the following position statement: "The Chinese government firmly opposes any activities which aim at the creation of 'one China, one Taiwan,' 'one China, two governments,' 'two Chinas,' and independent Taiwan, or advocate that 'the status of Taiwan remains to be determined'."[4]

In the more than two decades that followed, the PRC never deviated from this position.[5] Following Jiang's speech, however, when referring to this particular issue, PRC leaders and spokesmen never mentioned a word about "one China, two governments" but simply repeated the formula offered by Jiang. Since the mainland is very strict on "matters of principle," this is no accident. Considering the words and tone of the speech, our interpretation of this omission is that Beijing was sending a signal to Taipei, hinting that if the latter was willing to accept the propositions made by Jiang, that is, entering into negotiations on ending the state of hostility between the two sides, establishing the direct three links across the Straits, and exchange of visits by both sides' leaders, Beijing was ready to accept "one China, two governments" as the new arrangement for the cross-Straits relations.

The most important message Jiang tried to convey, according to Beijing officials, was the call for bilateral negotiations on the matter of reunification and "as the first step, negotiations should be held and an agreement reached on officially ending the state of hostility between the two sides in accordance with the principle that there is only one China." This must be where Jiang wished to make an immediate breakthrough in cross-Straits political relations. After the speech was made public, the ROC side made several official responses, but few seemed to have taken this proposition seriously, which caused different personages from the PRC side to come forward to "further explain" the point and asked the ROC leaders to respond. Aside from the more indirect occasions, the following are those when Taiwan's attention was directly invoked. On 6 March 1995, the first day of the 3rd Plenum of the 8th National People's Congress (NPC), the PRC held an unusual press conference. It was pointed out that, since Taiwan had not fully understood the most important message contained in Jiang's speech, the PRC wanted to take the opportunity to clearly reiterate it, the message being to end the state of hostility across the Straits through negotiations based on equal footing.[6] Similar messages were repeatedly sent by both Tang Shubei, vice-chairman of the ARATS, and Wang Zhaoguo, head of both the CCP's United Front Work Department and the Taiwan Affairs Office under the State Council.[7] Wang even went so far as to say that, "The essence of Jiang's eight-point proposal is to enter into negotiations with Taiwan on the question of ending the state of hostility under the principle of 'one China,' and to reach an agreement. We can talk about anything concerning each other. As for reunification, that is for the next step."[8] If the PRC leaders meant what they said, their message was rather clear: let us sit down to talk about how to end the state of hostility. As for reunification, that can wait until time is right in the future. In other words, on the part of the PRC there was no sense of urgency for reunification, but the rhetoric must be kept. This observation is par- tially supported by the fact that Deng Xiaoping's favourite unification formula, "one country, two systems" was never mentioned in Jiang's eight points; it appeared only in the "preface" where Jiang had to pay due respect to Deng.

One can only speculate as to why Beijing handled the matter in this manner. For example, Beijing was keenly aware that it posed a deadly threat to Taipei. Ever since Lee Teng-hui took office in 1988, he had been proclaiming that Beijing must relinquish its hostility by denouncing the use of force against Taipei as a prerequisite for the normalization of rela- tions between the two sides. Jiang's proposal was a direct reply to Taipei's major concern. The latter, of course, may very well perceive this as another tactical move by Beijing. But if Taipei perceived sincerity in Jiang's invitation and accepted it to enter into negotiations, this was to be a major victory for Jiang's Taiwan policy. Moreover, should an agreement be reached, the structure of cross-Straits relations was to be stablized, and the PRC's nightmare of an independent Taiwan manipulated by "foreign forces" was to naturally disappear. In terms of strategic calculations, this new bond established between Beijing and Taipei strengthened its power position against Japan, Russia and, to some extent, the United States. Jiang was to then enjoy an almost unchallengeable position in the possible power competition after Deng's passing.

In short, the PRC had come to admit that reunification was to be a matter of "the next step," and their current policy toward Taiwan could best be described as "prevention of Taiwan independence taking priority over the promotion of reunification."

On the other hand, did the Taiwanese leaders correctly understand Jiang's message? There were signs to indicate that they did. On 3 March, responding to the questions raised by a Legislative Yuan member, Premier Lien Chan said that a non-aggression treaty would be meaningful only when there existed mutual trust between the signing parties. Otherwise, any formal arrangement would be no more than a piece of paper.[9] Apparently, Lien utilized the question and answer session in the Legislative Yuan to respond indirectly to the burning question raised by Beijing, and Taipei has never touched upon the question since.

Lastly, Jiang took the opportunity to extend an invitation to the Taiwanese leadership to visit the mainland and expressed his wish to be invited to visit Taiwan. Several points deserve further consideration here. (1) Jiang pointed out that Taiwanese leaders could come to the mainland only "in appropriate capacities." This implied that should Lee Teng-hui visit the mainland, at best he could expect to be received as the "head of Taiwan." The title "president of the ROC" would be out of the question. (2) Should the mutual visit materialize, again, Jiang's power position in the CCP was to be strengthened. (3) Jiang reminded his Taiwanese counterpart that this was a "family matter" among Chinese and it was inappropriate for them to meet on an international occasion, which was a direct rejection of Taiwan's position. (4) According to the ROC's Guidelines for National Unification adopted in February 1991, leadership from both sides can meet only when cross-Straits relations reach the second stage, namely, that of mutual trust and cooperation. This invitation put forward by Jiang was another way of responding to the guidelines.

In summary, we can say that behind Jiang Zemin's eight-point proposal there lay his calculations concerning: Beijing's power position in a changing international system; Beijing-Taipei relations; and his own preparation for the possible power competition after Deng. Still, it is fair to say that Jiang Zemin had advanced Beijing's Taiwan policy, and the ball was now in Taipei's court.

Taipei's Reactions

Lien Chan's Response and the Ensuing Interactions

On 3 February, the first day back to work after the Spring Festival, Lee Teng-hui met with the Central Committee members of the Kuomintang (KMT) and said: "Mr Jiang Zemin, the CCP's secretary-general, has expressed his views and propositions concerning cross-Straits relations at the present stage. This is an important matter. We must pay attention to it and exchange views with people from various circles in society. Those party members who are also responsible for governmental works, please make an in-depth study and propose plans for reaction."[10] This, in fact, should be interpreted to mean that Lee attached great importance to the speech and he wished Beijing to know it.

In the following weeks, Taiwanese society was flooded with so many roundtables, meetings, conferences, newspaper and magazine articles and special TV reports that almost no one could possibly escape being overexposed to the topic. Oddly enough, the first reactions from Taipei's political circles were not as negative as in the past when similar moves were made by Beijing. Hsu Shui-teh, the KMT's secretary-general, admitted the significance of Jiang's talk and proposed that the two leaders meet in June during the Asia-Pacific Economic Cooperation (APEC) meeting to be held in Japan.[11] Shih Ming-teh, chairman of the Democratic Progressive Party (DPP), Taiwan's largest opposition party, argued that the DPP was not opposed to conducting negotiations with the PRC, but the prerequisite for such contact must be consensus among the Taiwanese people. In addition, the negotiations must be conducted in the forms of either "government to government" or "political entity to political entity."[12] Chao Shao-kang, secretary-general of the New Party (NP), the second largest opposition party, urged people on Taiwan not to "dance to the tune of the mainland," and that Taiwan's future would be determined by its own unity rather than Beijing's policy.[13] Being with the ruling party, Hsu Shui-teh's reaction was understandable. But the reactions of Shih Ming-teh and Chao Shao-kang were interesting. In the past, the DPP had been opposed to any form of contacts with the mainland, especially by the KMT, and had repeatedly warned the public of a possible sell out of Taiwan by the KMT. In short, it had to highlight its opposition role by criticizing whatever the ruling party might do. But now, Shih sounded almost like Hsu which indicated that the DPP was becoming a more mature opposition party. By contrast, the New Party, still new to its opposition role, was eager to show its uncompromising "radicalism."

By 9 February 1995, the ROC government seemed to have made some preliminary decisions about how to respond to Jiang's speech. The Executive Yuan had reportedly decided upon two principles. First, the ROC would make different responses "with different stages (at different points of time), according to different issues, and according to the differing nature of the issues." Second, the ROC would respond passively to Jiang's political propositions, but positively to the economic and trade proposals.[14]

On the whole, the preliminary official responses from the ROC side were cautiously positive and pragmatic.

The PRC side, of course, expected more. Premier Lien Chan's response partially fulfilled this expectation. On 21 February, facing the shouts and demands for his resignation from some opposition legislators, Lien calmly read his biannual report of state affairs. In response to Jiang's eight-point statement, Lien said that "in terms of bilateral relations what both sides ought to do is to face the present status, increase exchanges, respect each other and pursue reunification."[15] These words were later termed "Lien's four-point proposal." Toward the end of his hour-long report, he concluded his observation of cross-Straits relations with anticipation:

> In future negotiations on practical issues between the SEF and ARATS, we hope the two parties will start as soon as possible discussions of the signing of agreements on the protection of investment from Taiwan, of the protection of intellectual property rights on both sides of the Straits, and of arbitration on cross-Straits trade disputes. It is also time for topics of cultural and educational exchanges to enter the negotiation agenda. In addition, the two parties must conduct negotiations on the three current topics, aircraft-hijacking, illegal immigration, and fishing disputes, in a practical fashion so as to reach agreements as soon as possible. Looking to the future, we can say that cross-Straits relations have entered an "era of negotiation." We believe negotiations that

are based on an equal footing, pragmatic and rational, will not only help establish orderly exchanges, but also strengthen the foundation for mutual trust and for a win-win situation. Convening of the Koo-Wang talks will be an important link in this negotiation process. An adequate adjustment of the SEF's negotiation function will also strengthen our capability to welcome this new challenge.[16]

Lien Chan's words were in line with Taipei's mainland policy. Being the smaller entity in the dyad, Taipei had been cautious, sometimes conservative, in making any move concerning cross-Straits relations. The mounting demands and pressure derived from exchanges since 1987, led it to adopt the Guidelines for National Unification which have been the primary reference in dealing with affairs relating to the mainland. In the guideline, the process of China's unification is divided into three phases: exchanges and reciprocity; mutual trust and cooperation; consultation and unification. For the time being, we are in the first phase, a phase of exchanges and reciprocity.[17]

With this design, Taipei wishes to counter Beijing's unification pressure, to build internal consensus, and hopefully to bring about a positive change in the mainland's political, economic and social structure so as to make unification possible. Hence exchanges across the Straits become a feasible mechanism.

Lien's words, however, carried some "new ideas" too. In addition to the three current topics requiring negotiations and agreements between the SEF and ARATS, he anticipated more issues receiving attention, such as the protection of Taiwanese investment on the mainland, the protection of intellectual property rights on both sides of the Straits, arbitration on bilateral trade disputes, and issues concerning cultural and educational exchanges. Consequently, he had high hopes for the next Koo-Wang talks, not only for their convention in the near future, but also for their role in shaping cross-Straits relations. In accordance with the design of the guidelines, both the SEF and ARATS were created to promote exchanges. Now that the mechanism did not work properly, the only alternative was to conduct the Koo-Wang talks with the hope that delegates of higher ranking from both sides re-establish the goodwill needed to make negotiations proceed. As a result, although never publicly mentioned, the possibility of a change in the SEF's definition, from a non-governmental private organization to a politically authorized one, always exist. In fact, the PRC side had been urging this change almost since the SEF's inception. Lien's remark about the "adequate adjustment of the SEF's negotiation function" may thus be interpreted as a strong hint of this possibility. Last but not least important, Lien announced in his speech the coming of the "negotiation era" in cross-Straits relations. Although negotiations across the Straits had been going on for more than nine years since the 1986 negotiations on Taiwan's defected China Airline B-198, and despite the SEF and ARATS having negotiated more than 13 times in the past four years, this was the first time either of the two sides had made such announcement. Lien's conception had greater weight since Lee Teng-hui himself later reiterated the idea.[18]

How then was this era of negotiation related to the ROC's Guidelines for National Unification? Another passage contained in Lien's report provided the answer: "In terms of cross-Straits relations, in the past six months, both sides have conducted several negotiations on practical issues, and exchanges in economic and cultural aspects are increasing steadily, but it (cross-Straits relations) basically remains in the short-term stage, namely, the stage of non-governmental exchanges."[19] It appeared that the ROC leaders had as yet no intention of deviating from the guideline and they were determined to handle most, if not all, cross-Straits affairs through negotiations.

In less than one week, the Mainland Affairs Council (MAC) adopted the "Programme for the Strengthening of Cross-Straits Non-Governmental Exchanges at the Present Stage," indicating that their work would focus on economic exchanges, cultural exchanges, negotiations on practical issues, and review of related laws and regulations. Substantive plans for implementation of each area were also made. Lien's announcement was no doubt important, but the fact that the MAC could put forward its first implementation programme at such short notice indicated that the ROC was serious about this conception of the negotiation era and some preparatory work had been done prior to its publicity.[20]

Lien Chan's words were well received in Beijing, yet in the latter's eyes Taiwan still ignored some very important messages Jiang had delivered. As discussed in the last section, different figures from the PRC then came forward to remind Taiwan about what they considered important in Jiang's statement. In sum, four points were repeatedly mentioned: Jiang's call for negotiations and agreements on ending the state of hostility between the two sides; Taiwan ought to enter into political negotiations with the PRC; the content of "one China" is discussable; and reunification of China will be a matter of the next step. In an attempt to respond and to cultivate goodwill, ROC leaders kept sending signals back to their mainland counterparts. On 10 March, when asked about the ROC's South China Sea policy, Lien Chan replied in the Legislative Yuan that the South China Sea had been the traditional territory of the ROC and the government had sound policy guarding its security. In case of a dispute, Lien added, the ROC would resort to peaceful means first. Moreover, joint exploration and development of oil deposits, and other natural resources with neighbouring countries, including the PRC, would be acceptable.[21]

Four days later, while offering his own assessment of the post-Deng situation on the mainland to several lawmakers, Lien indicated that the ROC government did not want to see chaos on the mainland after Deng's passing and the ROC would not take any irrational action to irritate the PRC. If opportunities arose, the leaders from both sides could meet and chat on international occasions, so special arrangements would not be necessary.[22]

Soon thereafter, the MAC relaxed previous bans restricting visits to Taiwan by PRC economic affairs officials. On the whole, Taiwan's re-actions during this period can be summarized as "promoting economic exchanges and cultivating goodwill while remaining conservative in politi-cal exchanges," just as expected by the PRC.

In early April, however, Taipei's pragmatic diplomacy struck again. Being curbed by Beijing, Taipei's diplomacy for a long time has ma-noeuvred in very limited scope. Many countries in the world, including the powerful ones, being concerned about Beijing's protests, deal with Taipei only in a non-governmental fashion. Lee Teng-hui, the president of the ROC, has often been received by different countries as an "expert in agricultural economics," as "Dr Lee," or even "Mr Lee." In an attempt to operate diplomatically, Taipei has to accommodate, hence, the name of pragmatic diplomacy. This time, President Lee paid "private" visits to several Arabian states. But for Beijing's interference, he would have been welcomed by Saudi Arabia, although Beijing acted with self-restraint. After Lee's visits, the PRC Foreign Ministry spokesman accused Lee of political motivation in making them. Lee's purpose, according to the spokesman, was to create "two Chinas" or "one China, one Taiwan." But compared to past practice, Beijing's reaction this time was rather mild.[23] The rationale behind this low-profile protest is easy to grasp: they did not want to ruin the goodwill across the Straits and the best was yet to come, so they tolerated Lee.

Lee Teng-hui's Response and the Ensuing Interactions

After returning from the Middle East, Lee turned to the task of reshuffling the members of the National Unification Council (NUC). On 8 April, the new NUC met for the first time and listened to Lee Teng-hui's report on his mainland policy. He began with a reiteration of the ROC's determination to seek national unification through peaceful means, then moved on to discuss the goal and principles of unification stated in the Guidelines for National Unification, the mushrooming exchanges in recent years, and the coming era of negotiation. These words were followed by his six-point proposal:

1. Only by respecting the fact that Taiwan and the mainland have been governed by two different political entities since 1949 can the ways to achieve unification be sought. Consensus on the content of "one China" can be built across the Straits only by treating the reality with objectivity.
2. Chinese culture has been the pride of all Chinese people. Both sides should therefore cherish this brotherhood and enhance bilateral exchanges in the cultural area.
3. Bilateral trade is mutually beneficial. In developing its economy, Taiwan must regard the mainland as its market and a place which provides both raw materials and labour, and the mainland must look to Taiwan as an example. Taiwan is willing to help the mainland improve upon its agriculture, economy, and living standard. Preparations for exchange in business and shipping services should be planned, so that negotiations can be made in the future when the time is ripe.
4. Leaders from both sides meeting on international occasions can help reduce hostility across the Straits. More equal participation in international organizations for both sides will facilitate the development of bilateral relations and the process of peaceful unification.
5. The ROC has unilaterally denounced in 1991, the use of force as a way to achieve unification, while the mainland authorities have not reciprocated the ROC's goodwill by denouncing the use of force against Taiwan which has caused the state of hostility to linger until now. As soon as the PRC does so, the ROC will come forward, at an appropriate time, to engage in preparatory negotiations.
6. The ROC government is deeply concerned with the future of both Hong Kong and Macau. We hope that both sides can join efforts in keeping the prosperity and stability of both Hong Kong and Macau.[24]

In conclusion, Lee promised that Taiwan would help the mainland to develop in stability. He wished the mainland would become economically prosperous and politically democratic, so that the 1.2 billion Chinese compatriots would enjoy freedom and affluence. This, Lee contended, would be the true solution to the question of China's unification.[25]

Lee's words constituted the ROC's major response to Jiang. In an attempt to clarify Beijing's suspicion of Taiwan independence, Lee held high the banners of Chinese nationalism and national unification. He not only reiterated the principles of the Guidelines for National Unification, but also accused the PRC of ignoring and distorting the ROC's national spirit, namely, to build China into a strong, democratic, prosperous and unified country. To Jiang's call for negotiations on ending hostility, the focal point in his opinion, Lee argued that Taipei had already unilaterally denounced the use of force as a way to achieve national unification, but Taipei's goodwill had not been reciprocated by Beijing. Should the latter do so, Lee said that peace negotiations would soon be in order. In other words, he spelt out the prerequisite for such negotiations. To the question of the three direct links with which the PRC was much concerned, Lee promised, in a somewhat indirect way, to study the possibility. Lastly, Lee raised the question of the prosperity and stability of both Hong Kong and Macau. This time, he was self-assertive enough to demand joint efforts with the PRC to accomplish these goals. On the whole, one can say that except for the point on Hong Kong and Macau few new ideas were contained in Lee's speech, but what it tried to convey was goodwill.

The mainland side remained silent on the matter for more than ten days. First to break the ice was Qian Qichen, vice-premier and foreign minister of the PRC. Speaking at an international occasion, he offered a stern remark on some of the points. The second response from the mainland was made in late April by an anonymous official from the ARATS. Following a polite but uneasy compliment on Lee's speech, the mysterious ARATS official proposed that various exchanges, especially concerning the three direct links, ought to be further promoted. Thus, a second Koo-Wang meeting, including dialogue of a policy (political) nature, was in order.[26]

From this anonymous response, one could detect that mainland authorities were disappointed by Lee's response, because he could find only very limited points worth citing from his speech as proof of agreement. Besides, the mainland side responded only twice, both with levels much too low in comparison with both Lee and Lien from the Taiwan side. We may conclude that in Beijing's eyes, Taipei had not changed its basic political position concerning bilateral relations. There was, however, a bit more goodwill than before. Therefore, any real thaw on the political front was still not in sight, but they could engage in further exchanges with the hope that these would eventually lead to a major breakthrough. On the other hand, Taiwan may have come to a parallel conclusion about the mainland. Hence, the second Koo-Wang meeting became the only realistic next step for both sides.

The Chain Reactions Following Taipei's Pragmatic Diplomacy

Prelude: Preparations for the Second Koo-Wang Meeting

The SEF and ARATS had been established to resolve questions arising from bilateral exchanges since 1987, when Taipei allowed its people to visit their mainland relatives. Yet, during their negotiations distrust and political considerations interfered, leading the two sides to conclude that only a high-level meeting could help relieve the dilemma. Hence the first Koo-Wang meeting took place in 1993. During the meeting, the two sides purposely cultivated an atmosphere of goodwill, and four agreements were signed: the Agreement on Document Authentication Between the Taiwan Area and the Mainland Area; the Agreement on the Tracing of and Compensation for Lost Registered Mail Between the Taiwan Area and the Mainland Area; the Agreement on the Establishment of Systematic Liaison and Communication Channels Between the SEF and ARATS; and the Koo-Wang Talks Joint Agreement.[27] These agreements looked good on paper but were not faithfully implemented. Hence, the need for a second Koo-Wang meeting.

In mid-April 1995, Mr Koo Chen-fu broke the impasse by suggesting that the meeting could be held before August. He added that since Taiwan-Hong Kong relations after 1997 would be of vital importance to Taiwan's future economic development, the topic deserved further discussion in the meeting.[28] On 30 April, the MAC announced its decision to permit PRC Taiwan Affairs officials to enter Taiwan in the capacities of advisers to the ARATS, sending a message of goodwill to the mainland. Accepting the gesture from Taipei, Beijing formally agreed that the second Koo-Wang talks be held in Beijing during the latter half of July, and there would be three rounds of preparatory negotiations between Mr Tang Shubei, vice-chairman of the ARATS, and Mr Chiao Jen-ho, vice-chairman of the SEF, aimed at ironing out differences prior to the actual Koo-Wang meeting.

Taipei's Diplomatic Moves and Beijing's Retaliation

While the SEF and ARATS were busy preparing for the coming meeting, two events occurred which affected the Koo-Wang talks. In early May, the MAC announced the establishment of the Offshore Transshipment Centre which was essentially an introductory step for the direct sea link across the Straits. Kaohsiung, the largest city and port in southern Taiwan, applied for the status, which was granted the next day. A week later, sensing Taipei's true intention, the Taiwan Affairs Office in Beijing responded favourably yet claimed that they were more in favour of direct air and sea links.

The second issue was the controversial American decision to allow President Lee Teng-hui to visit Cornell University, his Alma Mater. Beijing responded with fury and then adopted a series of retaliatory measures. On 23 May, the PRC's Foreign Ministry issued a protest claiming the United States should be held responsible for all the damage done to Sino-American relations. Yu Zhenwu, commander of the People's Liberation Army (PLA) air force, abruptly cut short his visit to the United States and returned home. A similar visit to the United States by State Councillor Li Guixian, originally scheduled for late May, was also cancelled. PRC Minister of Defense, Chi Haotian, declared that his visit too would be postponed. On 28 May, negotiations on guided missiles and control techniques between Chinese and American experts were also cancelled.[29]

In contrast with the measures taken against the United States, Beijing's initial response toward Taipei was primarily verbal and surprisingly low-key considering what was to come. Between 23 May and 5 June, Beijing made only one verbal attack on Taipei, accusing Lee Teng-hui of harming the interest of all Chinese and advising him to return to the "one China" position.[30] More importantly, with the knowledge that Lee was going to visit Cornell University, Tang Shubei flew to Taipei on 26 May, as originally scheduled, to start negotiations preparatory to the Koo-Wang talks. During the session, Tang even suggested that the ARATS could arrange for Koo Chen-fu to meet with someone of vice-premier rank or higher.[31] The differences in Beijing's reactions toward Taipei and Washington revealed that, although Beijing was very angry at both, Washington bore the brunt of its wrath. Since Koo-Wang talks were imminent and Lee's visit would be no more than an "alumni diplomacy," far from a state visit, preservation of goodwill seemed to be both important and in Beijing's interest.

On 30 May, a consensus between Chiao Jen-ho and Tang Shubei was reached and an agreement signed, stating that the Koo-Wang meeting would be scheduled around 20 July and the topics as well as the agenda were all set. On the same day, Chen Yunlin, deputy director of Taiwan Affairs Office, announced in Beijing that both the ARATS and SEF had successfully reached an agreement and the Koo-Wang meeting would be held in late July.[32]

Despite Beijing's annoyance, President Lee Teng-hui's trip to Cornell went smoothly. He toured the campus, met with people, both academic and political, and most importantly he gave a speech, entitled: "Always in My Heart," to an invited audience. He said that, since the ROC had been successful in both economic and political development, it intended to make its contribution to the international community. In this respect, a proper recognition of the ROC's international status would be of great significance. The Xinhua News Agency issued several commentaries criticizing Lee's speech but generally exercised self-restraint. On 13 June, Shen Guofang, spokesman of the PRC Foreign Ministry, came forward to attack the US again but when asked about cross-Straits relations, he replied that exchanges and negotiations continued and there was no sign of change.[33] It was at this time that Premier Lien Chan was found to have gone to Europe, almost secretly, paying visits to several countries. Rumours had it that one of his stops had been Germany with the hope that Germany would follow the US in changing their attitude, or even policy, toward the ROC. ROC Foreign Minister, Frederick Chien, paid a low-profile visit to the US. And in Taipei, President Lee was rumoured to be interested in visiting Japan to attend the coming APEC meeting.

Suddenly, however, Beijing realized that it could no longer tolerate Taipei's moves to "expand its international space." On 16 June, the Taiwan Affairs Office and ARATS jointly declared that the second Koo-Wang meeting would be indefinitely postponed because "Taiwan had recently taken a series of actions which were harmful to the cross-Straits relations."[34] The mainland escalated its attacks against Lee from then on. Jiang Zemin, who had rarely made any personal attack in public, made a public criticism accusing both Lee and the US of having ruined the positive relations they each enjoyed with the mainland.[35] Even more surprisingly, the Xinhua News Agency announced on 18 July that, from 21 to 28

July, the Second Artillery of the PLA would launch a surface-to-surface missile test at a target area 80 miles north of Taiwan Island and warned all ships and aircraft to stay away from the area during that period.[36] The news dealt a heavy blow to Taiwan, its stock market dropped hundreds of points in one week, and the PLA missile test became a topic of much concern. But, Taipei's political circles could do little besides express feelings of frustration and anger.

In response to the news, some contended that Beijing conducted the missile test mainly to intimidate Taiwan. The true reason behind it, however, was much more complicated. Judging from the situation in Beijing and messages made public, when launching the test Beijing had at least three targets in mind. Beijing was furious at Taipei this time because it felt that Taipei had deceived it with the coming Koo-Wang talks while making several moves in pragmatic diplomacy. Had Germany and Japan followed the American precedent, Beijing might have faced a diplomatic debacle, much as Taipei had suffered in 1971 when a *rapprochement* was reached between the PRC and the US, only this time Beijing would be the loser. A change of this nature, as Beijing saw it, would be a gigantic step toward Taiwan's independence even if not its actual realization. As for international circles, especially the United States, Beijing sensed the initial intention of deviating from the traditional "one China" policy, leading to possibly "two Chinas," "one China, one Taiwan," or even Taiwan independence. What happened now was by no means Beijing's bottom line, but it had to react as if this was. If it did not do so, next time when its bottom line was challenged, it might be too late to respond. Furthermore, since the collapse of the Soviet Union, Beijing had developed an unspoken ambition to become one of the major powers. To respond to this possibility, some westerners had proposed a theory of "containing China." Launching the missiles could be seen as an act of self-assertiveness. There were, of course, internal reasons, too. In recent years, since communism as an ideology had lost its charm, Beijing had to turn to nationalism, patriotism as they called it, as a means to mobilize and bring society together. But nationalism was a dangerous weapon and once fervently launched, it must march on. Whoever retreated would be severely condemned. At present, nationalism on the Chinese mainland had not been mobilized to this level, but in the presence of possible Taiwan independence, Beijing could not retreat to the point of doing nothing. Firing missiles would make an acceptable gesture of response. Finally, the risk of power competition could not be readily dismissed. Any Beijing leader, especially Jiang

Zemin, who wished to survive the post-Deng struggle would have to demonstrate his firm resolution by fighting any "counter-revolutionary enemies," be they American imperialists, Taiwan independence elements, or bourgeois liberalists inside the CCP. All in all, Beijing's leaders had to act tough to show their resolution to these three targets.

Beijing, meanwhile, heightened tensions further by issuing four consecutive commentaries on Lee's Cornell speech. Written jointly by the *Renmin ribao* (People's Daily) and the Xinhua News Agency, these commentaries appeared on 23, 24, 25 and 26 July while the missile tests were under way. The first commentary, "A Self-Vindication of Advocacy for Splitting the Motherland," argued that, "Having now embarked on the road of 'Taiwan independence,' Lee Teng-hui has betrayed the great reunification cause of the Chinese people including the Taiwan compatriots.... Should Lee Teng-hui continue to follow that dangerous road in defiance of the will of the people, he certainly will be utterly discredited and stand condemned by the Chinese nation through the ages."[37]

The second commentatary, "Absolutely No Space for the Existence of 'the Independence of Taiwan' in the International Community," proclaimed that "Lee's 'expanding living space internationally' obviously runs counter to the principle of 'one China,' to the goal of the two sides of the Taiwan Straits moving toward a peaceful reunification, and to people's hopes of maintaining peace in Asia and the rest of the world. Of course, we are firmly opposed to this kind of 'expansion of international living space'."[38]

The third commentary, "Political Hallucinogen for 'Taiwan Independence'," suggested that, "Under the name of 'democracy,' Lee Teng-hui has wantonly encouraged and cultivated the forces of 'Taiwan independence.' Thus Lee is responsible for the expansion of Taiwan independence forces on Taiwan."[39]

The fourth commentary, "Lee Teng-hui Is Guilty of Damaging Relations Between the Two Sides of Taiwan Straits," contended that, "Not long ago, however, Lee Teng-hui took his activities to the United States in an attempt to create 'two Chinas' or 'one China, one Taiwan,' and made relations between the two sides of the Straits, which had become more relaxed, retrogress, casting a shadow over the great cause of reunification of the motherland.... Lee Teng-hui also has placed many obstacles in the way of contacts between people on the two sides of the Straits and on economic and trade exchanges.... Facts have shown that expecting a person such as Lee Teng-hui who 'does not know what China is' to improve and develop cross-Straits relations is nothing less than climbing a tree to catch fish. All Chinese should definitely not cherish any illusions about Lee Teng-hui'."[40]

In the PRC's history, using consecutive commentaries for an attack of this magnitude against an external political enemy happened only twice. The only other instance had occurred between 1963 and 1964, when the Chinese Communist Party (CCP) issued its famous Nine Commentaries to engage in theoretical struggles against the "Revisionists of the Communist Party of the Soviet Union." The debates ran for less than two years but the deadlock between the two states lasted for more than two decades. The difference between these two cases lay in the fact that in 1964 only commentaries were used as weapon, while in 1995, the commentaries were accompanied by missiles. The target of the commentaries was very clear, namely, Lee Teng-hui. And, the purpose was clear too — Beijing tried to force Taiwan to knock down Lee Teng-hui.

To further tighten the rope, Beijing repeated the exercise in August. On 2, 4, 6, and 8 August, the Xinhua News Agency again issued four consecutive commentaries attacking Lee Teng-hui's "words and deeds" for Taiwan independence.[41] In these commentaries, the words were even harsher, but the target was still Lee Teng-hui. Moreover, the Xinhua News Agency announced on behalf of the Ministry of Communications that from 15 to 25 August, the PLA would conduct an exercise of missiles and shelling at an area in the East China Sea. The location was again quite close to Taiwan, and Beijing's message was rather clear. Taipei reacted to the new challenge in a similar way. Mr Su Chi, vice-chairman of the MAC, pointed out that "it takes two to tango. While Beijing was acting irrationally, we should not react in an equally irrational manner. We should, rather, continue to conduct our mainland policy in a rational way, that is, to enhance exchanges in various aspects and to re-open channels of negotiations so as to eliminate the misunderstanding."[42]

On 19 August, Qian Qichen said that tension had arisen because Taiwan was engaged in activities leading to "one China, one Taiwan," or "Taiwan independence" and was supported by the US. But, if Taiwan authorities gave up the ideas of Taiwan independence and of splitting the motherland, things would be easier to manage.[43] Qian's message was later reinforced by Qiao Shi. Qiao told guests from Singapore, Lee Kuan Yew and Wang Ding Chan, that Beijing would maintain its peaceful reunification policy provided Taipei stopped seeking Taiwan independence.[44] In late August, PRC Foreign Ministry spokesman, Shen Guofang, was reported to have indicated that according to the mainland's assessment,

Lee Teng-hui would defeat all other candidates and be elected president in March 1996. Until then, cross-Straits relations would remain in a state of "waiting in peace."[45] Taken together, these statements could be interpreted as Beijing's "peaceful hand" raised once its "coercive hand" had been shown.

Beijing's peaceful hand was well received by Taipei. On 1 September, in an interview with the *New York Times*, President Lee said: "You can see that I have not uttered a word even though they (the PRC) attacked me so fiercefully. I can assure you that we will handle the matter with patience, reason and calm instead of emotion. Our doors are wide open, waiting for the other party to return to the (negotiation) table." He also talked about the possibility of a summit meeting with Jiang. He said: "After the dust of power transition settles on the Beijing side and after Taiwan's election is over next March, perhaps we can get together to consider the possibility of meeting. At present, Jiang Zemin is caught in a very delicate position. Therefore, we have to wait awhile until the sensitivity is toned down."[46] Beijing reciprocated to Taipei's new gesture by repeatedly sending the same message: Jiang Zemin's eight-point proposal remained effective in handling cross-Straits relations. By early October, the message became even more optimistic. In an interview with both the *Washington Post* and *Newsweek*, in addition to reiterating the eight-point proposal, Jiang was reported to have said: "I welcome Lee Teng-hui to visit Beijing. If he invites me to visit Taipei, I am ready to go any time."[47] By now, we can say that tensions across the Straits seemed almost to have disappeared.

For Beijing's part, however, the issue was not quite over. As suggested, to Beijing, the question of Taiwan was not considered only from the perspective of bilateral relations but had to be placed within Beijing's international strategy. Beijing had to prevent other countries from utilizing the Taiwan issue as a leverage against itself. In other words, Beijing had to make sure that no major countries would support Taiwan independence, "two Chinas," or "one China, one Taiwan." This purpose was accomplished when Jiang met with President Clinton in late October. On 24 October, Clinton and Jiang met when they attended the 50th anniversary commemorations of the United Nations in New York. During the meeting, Jiang was personally assured by Clinton that the US was against Taiwan independence and opposed the admission of Taiwan into the United Nations.[48] By mid-November, Beijing was relieved to learn that Lee Teng-hui would not attend the APEC conference in Japan. Koo Chen-fu went on behalf of Taipei, and he met with Jiang at a dinner party.

They shook hands and exchanged social greetings which marked the highest-level personal contact across the Straits so far since the two sides had separated in 1949.[49]

After the atmosphere in cross-Straits relations improved, Taiwan devoted most of its attention to domestic affairs, since this was an election year for Legislative Yuan members. The three major parties, the KMT, the DPP and the NP, plus a good number of independents were competing for 164 assembly seats. Concerned with both the future distribution of political forces on Taiwan and the development of Taiwan independence, Beijing paid close attention to the elections. Rumours of its interference abounded, but little hard evidence was found prior to election day, 2 December. Still, Beijing must have been satisfied with the results: KMT-85 seats, DPP-54 seats, NP-21-seats, and 4 independents. Beijing made no official comments because it was regarded as a "regional election." But, Shen Guofang did point out that the Taiwanese people were against Taiwan independence because many advocating independence had lost to other candidates.[50]

For Beijing, 1995 ended in a somewhat satisfactory manner when Lien Chan made an announcement at a cadre-training programme demonstrating further goodwill. On 6 December, while addressing participants in the programme, Lien stressed that since the ROC government was opposed to "one China, one Taiwan," "two Chinas," and Taiwan independence, Beijing's use of nationalism as an excuse to threaten Taipei was absolutely inappropriate. In cross-Straits relations, the question lay in the "principle of democracy," rather than in the "principle of nationalism." Looking ahead, Lien pointed out that Beijing would soon start working on its Ninth Five-Year Plan and Taipei would be happy to assist in all ways possible. But, he also reminded his audience that the ROC was a country with independent sovereignty and would continue to seek international living space in the future.[51]

Concluding Remarks

While the excitement in cross-Straits relations was concentrated on the political front, bilateral exchanges in other areas continued. Statistics for the entire year are not available at the time of writing, but it seems safe to say that steady growth was maintained in most areas. According to the MAC statistics, the total amount of trade across the Straits during the first eight months of 1995 was US$15 billion dollars. The full-year figures for 1991, 1992, 1993, and 1994 were $8.6 billion, $11.6 billion, $15 billion, and $17.8 billion, respectively. Taiwan's trade dependence upon the mainland during the first eight months of 1995 was 10.48%, and the figures for the past four years were 6.2%, 7.6%, 9.32%, and 10.02%, respectively. On the other hand, the mainland's trade dependence upon Taiwan was 8.64% for the first 8 months of 1995, and 6.35%, 7.05%, 7.71%, and 7.55%, for the past four years, respectively.[52] Figures for telephone calls, mail and visitors either dropped slightly or remained much the same. Taken together, they seem to demonstrate that despite the political unrest exchanges in other areas thrived in 1995.

Tang Shubei expressed a similar view of cross-Straits relations in 1995. He concluded that the development of bilateral relations had suffered a major setback due to the political tensions, but economic cooperation, cultural exchanges, and personal visits had continued with some improvement.[53]

By year's end, however, the worst of the political tension seemed to be over, Beijing's response to the March 1996 Taiwan presidential election to the contrary notwithstanding. The result is an ostensible stalemate, but signs of goodwill have also been in evidence for some time. After the moves and countermoves made by both sides and by the US, the three parties fully realize that there exists a bottom line and no one is ready to cross it. The bottom line for Taipei is that Taiwan independence or even anything that might trigger Beijing's suspicion in this respect will be hazardous to its stability and security. For Washington, "one China" policy is still its basic position and it has taken note of Beijing's extreme sensitivity on this issue. As for Beijing, it reaffirms its policy of "peaceful reunification," although it understands that its realization will take some time. So long as Taiwan does not embark on the road to independence, a military invasion of Taiwan will remain nothing more than a contingency plan.

Notes

1. *China Daily*, Beijing, 2 February 1995.
2. *Lien Ho Pao* (United Daily News), Taipei, 10 March 1995.
3. Gao Xin has a similar observation, yet he considers that the PRC treats the omission of the "one China, two governments" formula as a tacit understanding between the two sides instead of a bargaining chip. Gao Xin, *Haixia*

wu zhanshi (No Warfare in the Taiwan Straits) (Taipei: Chouchi Culture, Co., 1995), pp. 208–26.

4. For the Shanghai Communiqué, see *Department of State Bulletin*, Vol. LXVI, No. 1708 (20 March 1972) (Government Printing Office: Washington, DC, 1972), pp. 435–38.

5. For example, in the report Jiang delivered to the CCP's 14th Party Congress, it reads: "we firmly oppose 'two Chinas,' 'one China, one Taiwan,' or 'one China, two governments' of any sort, and we firmly oppose any attempts or activities aiming at the creation of independent Taiwan." One year later, to counter the international pressure Taipei's pragmatic diplomacy had brought about, the PRC issued a white paper on "The Taiwan Question and Reunification of China," reassuring that: "The Chinese government firmly opposes any words and deeds aiming at splitting China's sovereignty and territorial integrity, we oppose 'two Chinas,' 'one China, one Taiwan,' or 'one China, two governments,' and we oppose any attempts and activities that might lead to 'independent Taiwan'." One notices that except for some variations in wording, the PRC's position remained unchanged over time.

6. *United Daily News*, 6 March 1995.

7. *Chung-kuo shih-pao* (China Times), Taipei, 3 March and 1 April 1995.

8. *China Times*, 9 March and 1 April 1995.

9. *Tsu-yu shih-pao* (The Liberty Times), Taipei, 4 March 1995.

10. *Chung-yang jih-pao* (The Central Daily News), Taipei, 4 February 1995.

11. *China Times*, 6 February 1995.

12. *United Daily News*, 6 February 1995.

13. Ibid.

14. *United Daily News*, 10 February 1995. The two "principles" were not officially released but were synthesized by this author from two separate reports in the newspapers.

15. *United Daily News*, 22 February 1995.

16. Chu-cheng Ming, "Our Strategy for the Era of Negotiation," in *Grand Strategy for National Development*, edited by Tsai Cheng-wen (Taipei: Foundation for the Study of National Development, 1996), pp. 119–20.

17. Ma Ying-jeou, *Retrospects and Prospects of Cross-Straits Relation* (Taipei: Mainland China Affairs, 1992), pp. 71–73.

18. Lee Teng-hui, "Speech Delivered to the National Unification Council," in *Studies on Chinese Communism*, Vol. 29, No. 4 (Taipei: Weng Yen-ching, 1995), p. 17.

19. Chu-cheng Ming, "Our Strategy for the Era of Negotiation" (Note 16), pp. 137–41.

20. *Central Daily News*, 28 February 1995.

21. *The Liberty Times*, 11 March 1995.

22. *China Times*, 15 March 1995.

23. *Tsu-li Tsao Pao* (The Independence Morning Post), Taipei, 6 April 1995.
24. Lee Teng-hui (see Note 18), pp. 17–19.
25. Ibid., p. 19.
26. *China Times*, 29 April 1995.
27. Ibid., p. 40.
28. *K'ung-shang shi-pao* (Commercial Times), Taipei, 14 April 1995.
29. *United Daily News*, 17 June 1995.
30. *United Daily News*, 27 May 1995.
31. Ibid.
32. *United Daily News*, 29 May 1995; *China Times*, 29 May 1995.
33. *China Times*, 14 June 1995; *United Daily News*, 14 June 1995.
34. *China Times*, 17 June 1995; *United Daily News*, 17 June 1995.
35. *United Daily News*, 1 July 1995.
36. *Studies on Chinese Communism* (Note 18), Vol. 29, No. 8 (1995), monthly chronology on cross-Straits relations, pp. 149–50.
37. *China Daily*, 24 July 1995.
38. *China Daily*, 25 July 1995.
39. *China Daily*, 26 July 1995.
40. *China Daily*, 27 July 1995.
41. *Renmin ribao* (People's Daily), Beijing, 3, 5, 7, and 9 August 1995.
42. *United Daily News*, 21 August 1995.
43. *China Times*, 20 August 1995.
44. *United Daily News*, 23 August 1995.
45. *The Liberty Times*, 1 September 1995.
46. *United Daily News*, 4 September 1995.
47. *United Daily News*, 16 October 1995. The story did not end here. A few days later, the Xinhua News Agency issued the "official" version of the interview with some modifications on the key words. The new version read: "We welcome the leaders of the Taiwan authorities to visit (the mainland) in appropriate capacities; we are willing to accept invitations from Taiwan to visit Taiwan." In the modified version, the subject of the conversation is changed from "I" (Jiang) to "we" (a collective body), and the target person is changed from "Lee Teng-hui" to "leaders of the Taiwan authorities." It is generally believed that the modifications meant neither a change of mind on the part of Jiang, nor a denial of Jiang's authority inside the PRC. Rather, it meant to conceal the fact that Beijing had already considered Lee Teng-hui the winner of Taiwan's presidential election in next March. Undoubtedly, Taipei was much happier to see the version in which Jiang mentioned Lee by name, but either way it would mean that the worst between the two sides was over.
48. *Beijing Review*, 13–19 November 1995.
49. *Exchanges*, No. 25 (Taipei: SEF, January 1996), pp. 4–8.

50. *United Daily News*, 3 December 1995.
51. *United Daily News*, 7 December 1995.
52. MAC, *Statistical Monthly on Cross-Straits Economies*, No. 38 (Taipei: MAC, 1995), pp. 23–27.
53. *Wen Wei Po*, Hong Kong, 21 December 1995.

8

The Economy

Tsang Shu-ki

After the reform euphoria of 1994, the year 1995 was not expected to be very eventful. However, while the macroeconomic situation seemed to have improved, various microeconomic tensions were building up. On the other hand, crucial strategic and policy decisions, both short run and long run in nature, were made. The year could hardly be described as a lacklustre one for the Chinese economy.

Short-Run Issues

Landing: Hard or Soft?

Inflation soared in 1994, and all eyes were on whether a soft landing was possible in 1995 for the overheated economy. I had predicted such a possibility, on the simple grounds that a number of the key factors that had pushed up inflation in 1994 were reform-related and, therefore, one-off in nature. In other words, they would not be repeated in 1995, barring further reform initiatives. Moreover, there were no signs of any serious supply-demand imbalance.[1] As it turned out, there was some form of landing for the economy, which represented notable improvements over recent trends in the country.

As can be seen from Table 1, the trends for output growth and inflation were mainly downward during the year, but both the gross domestic product (GDP) and industrial production showed a rebound in the fourth quarter.[2] Preliminary figures for 1995 as a whole show that GDP grew by 10.2%, compared with 11.8% in 1994 and 13.4% in 1993, while the growth of industrial value-added for all levels slipped to 14.0% from 18%

Table 1. Growth and Inflation in 1995

	Jan.	Feb.	Mar.	Apr.	May	June	July	Aug.	Sept.	Oct.	Nov.	Dec.
GDP		11.2			9.4			8.8			11.4	
IP	11.4	15.5	16.3	15.4	13.1	13.9	13.6	11.8	11.1	12.9	12.1	14.9
RPI	21.1	19.7	18.7	18.0	17.6	16.0	14.6	12.3	11.4	10.3	9.2	8.3
CPI	24.1	22.4	21.3	20.7	20.3	18.2	16.7	14.5	13.2	12.1	11.2	10.1

Notes: All figures are year-on-year growth rates. GDP: gross domestic product; IP: industrial value-added at the level of *xiang* and above; RPI: retailed price index; CPI: consumer price index.

Sources: CERD Consultants Ltd., *China's Latest Economic Statistics*, various issues.

a year ago. Inflation, meanwhile, declined to 14.8% in terms of the RPI and to 17.0% in terms of the consumers price index (CPI), compared with the respective rates of 21.7% and 24.1% in 1994. The record harvests in the agricultural sector, pushing up food supplies, had apparently helped. According to preliminary estimates, the net value of agricultural output amounted to RMB 1,100 billion in 1995, up 4.5% in real terms, as grain production reached a historical record of more than 460 million tons.[3] So had continued administrative control measures.[4] The government had vowed to keep real growth within 10% and push retail inflation from the peak of 21.7% in 1994 to below 15%. Hence some degree of success could be claimed.

Behind the growth-inflation picture was a change in the expenditure mix, as testified by Table 2. While investment expansion showed signs of further restraints in 1995, at least up to the summer time, consumption staged a moderate rebound from the doldrums of 1994. Overall, the *real* rate of investment in fixed assets by state-owned enterprises fell from 16% in 1994 to about 11% in 1995, while the real growth of retail sales of consumer goods rose from 7.2% to 10.1%.

In any case, both aggregate growth and inflation rates were still high; so were those of investment and consumption expansion. The rebound in output and expenditure in the last few months of the year was already characterized by some economists as a kind of "gentle take-off." The possibility that the cyclical adjustment has been a fragile one cannot be ruled out, and any resurgence of inflation could jeopardize economic stability. As yet, though, there is not too much cause for alarm.

Table 2. Investment and Consumption in 1995

(Unit: Percentage)

	Jan.	Feb.	Mar.	Apr.	May	June	July	Aug.	Sept.	Oct.	Nov.	Dec.
IV	—	31.3	37.2	31.5	28.1	22.2	14.0	16.8	17.6	18.0	17.5	19.0
RSC	10.8	9.0	9.5	10.2	10.4	10.4	10.8	11.1	11.1	11.4	11.5	10.1

Notes: IV — *nominal* growth rate of investment in fixed assets by state-owned enterprises; RSC — *real* growth rate of retail sales of consumer goods. Monthly deflators for investments are not available. The figure for a month in the table represents the *cumulative* year-on-year growth rate up to the month, e.g. the nominal growth rate of IV in January–May 1995 over the same period in 1994 was 28.1%.

Sources: CERD Consultants Ltd., *China's Latest Economic Statistics*, various issues.

Performance of the External Sector

For the whole of 1995, China's exports grew by 22.9% over 1994 to US$148.77 billion, while imports expanded by 14.2% to US$132.08 billion. A trade surplus of US$16.69 billion was registered, which was US$11.34 billion higher than that of 1994.

The government implemented two measures that would have different impacts on trade. First, the rate of export rebate was cut from 17% to 13% on 1 July 1995 and further reduced to 9% at the beginning of 1996. Secondly, in the Asia Pacific Economic Cooperation (APEC) Leaders' Conference in November 1995, President Jiang Zemin announced that in 1996, China would reduce import tariffs to an average of 22–23% from the existing 35.6% level (by cutting tariffs over 4,000 categories out of the total of 6,000) and to liberalize some non-tariff trade barriers including quota, licencing and market restrictions. The package was obviously intended to help China's application to become a member of the World Trade Organization (WTO). Cynics would however argue that *effective* tariff collection was at a much lower level than that indicated by the average nominal tariff rate.[5] Hence, if the reduction of the nominal rates is offset by a vigourous enforcement of collection, some traders may not necessarily end up better off.

The first measure, which seemed to have arisen from fiscal revenue as well as trade considerations, has already generated some dampening impact on export growth. The growth rate of exports was 8.8% in the second half of 1995, markedly lower than the 44.2% in the first half. Indeed, in December 1995, total exports were RMB 1.56 billion less than total imports, creating the first monthly trade deficit since May 1994. It should also be noted that both domestic and foreign companies in China faced the same disincentive. The second package, on the other hand, is likely to stimulate imports. Hence, their combined effect may reduce China's trade surplus in 1996.

With regard to the capital account, contracted foreign direct investments amounted to US$90.29 billion in 1995, 3.7% less than 1994. The actual utilization of foreign direct investments, on the other hand, amounted to US$37.7 billion, up 11.7% from 1994.[6] Such a yearly growth rate was however significantly down from the 22.7% registered in 1994 and the 150% in 1993.

In the course of the year, there was quite a lot of discussions about giving "national treatment" to foreign investors in China, which may be a two-edged sword. While some market barriers will be lifted when such a policy is enforced, it will also mean that tax concessions and other preferential treatments that foreign invested enterprises (FIEs) have enjoyed will be abolished. There are also many press reports that China has become more demanding with regard to technology transfer from foreign investors.[7]

In any case, these changes seem to reveal that, while China is committed to a policy of gradual liberalization and the creation of a "level playing field," she has also embarked on a course to adjust the structure of her external trade and the policy of absorbing foreign investments. I shall come back to this issue when I discuss the Ninth Five-Year Plan and the long-term economic strategy.

Controversy about the Monetary Stance

The government had made it clear from the beginning that its monetary policy had to be "suitably tight" in order to bring down inflation. However, a view that was frequently aired during the course of the year alleged that the "landing" of the economy was achieved through an "excessively tight" monetary policy.[8] The issue became a constant focus of controversy and debate. A prima facie piece of evidence supporting the "excessive" view was that the growth of monetary aggregates went below recent trends, as testified to by Table 3.

On the surface, the growth of M0, M1 and M2 was all substantially

Table 3. Monetary Expansion in China: 1989–1995

(Unit: Percentage)

Year	M0	M1	M2
1989	9.84	5.71	18.32
1990	12.82	19.68	27.99
1991	20.17	23.58	26.52
1992	36.45	38.18	31.28
1993	35.26	24.50	24.01
1994	24.30	26.80	34.40
1995	8.23	16.69	29.44

Note: Annual growth rates in the table are based on year-end figures calculated against those of the previous year end. There are inconsistencies in the statistics provided by *China's Financial Outlook* in 1994 and 1995 due to the restructuring of the financial system under the 1994 reforms. The numbers for 1994 are taken from the 1995 edition.
Sources: *China's Financial Outlook*, 1994, 1995; *Wen Wei Po*, 1 February 1996, p. A8.

below that of 1994. But then, 1994 was an unusual year when the cumulative effect of credit expansion in 1992–1994 was coupled with the monetary effect of huge capital inflow which the government failed to sterilize.[9] Indeed the expansion of all *M's* was quite extraordinary in 1992–1994. As far as 1995 is concerned, one has to note that, although the growth of M0 and M1 were below trend, M2 still expanded at a rate of 29.5%, which was *above* the annual average compound rate of 27.3% for the period of 1989–1995.

According to the spokesman of the People's Bank of China (PBOC), Ma Delun, the base money of the central bank increased in 1995 by RMB 360.3 billion, which was RMB 39.1 billion less than the growth in 1994. So, the intention of the PBOC to be cautious, particularly to more effectively sterilize the monetary impact of capital inflow and the cumulative growth in base money in 1992–1994, was clear. However, Mr Ma also revealed that loans by all financial institutions rose by RMB 933.9 billion in 1995, RMB 212.3 billion more than in 1994.[10] It is not clear whether Ma was talking about the amount of newly increased loans or the growth in *outstanding loan balances*, although another report led one to believe that he was referring to the change in loan balances.[11] That implied a growth of 22.9%, compared with 23.9% in 1994, and the average of 23.2% in 1990–1994. Such an expansion rate could hardly be regarded as "excessively low." The trouble is that if we assume the figure of RMB 933.9 billion to be the increase in outstanding balances, then the figure of RMB 212.3 billion does not square with the increase in the changes of those balances between 1994 and 1995.[12] It appears that, because of the financial restructuring and the emergence of new banks and non-bank financial institutions since 1994, Chinese financial statistics have undergone some modifications which have not been made clear to outside commentators. In any case, the standard of financial reporting by Chinese press has not been very impressive.

Ma Delun also revealed that *newly increased loans* of the state banks were RMB 638.7 billion in 1995, a figure confirmed in many reports.[13] Compared with the figure of RMB 514.8 billion in 1994,[14] it would mean a growth rate of 24.1%, up from that of 19.5% for 1994.[15] In another development, the PBOC President, Dai Xianglong, revealed that the original credit target for 1995 was RMB 570 billion, but was raised by RMB 70 billion in September in the light of changing situations.[16] It therefore appears that the Chinese authorities did maintain flexibility over credit control, and the view of "excessive tightness" of the monetary stance in China is exaggerated. There were also reports that credit expansion by other financial institutions was as high as 53.7% in 1995,[17] and that black market interest rates declined during the year.[18] The most damning piece of evidence against the "excessive" view is that, despite all the doomsday talk about an imminent financial crisis, enterprise deposits at all financial institutions amounted to about RMB 1,700 billion at the end of 1995, up 30% from 1994.[19] That was hardly a meagre growth.

At the other end of the spectrum of opinions, some commentators criticized the Chinese monetary authority for being too "loose" in its policy, if only by default rather than by design. The money multiplier, defined as the increase in M2 divided by the growth of the monetary base, was reported to be 3.8 in 1995, way above the figure of 3.0 in 1994.[20] Some have taken that as an indication that the PBOC's control was deteriorating. However, the situation may be more complicated. A mechanical relationship between base money and a monetary aggregate, such as M2, is jeopardized by the existence of "excess reserves" even in a market economy. It appears that the huge capital inflow under the new foreign exchange settlement system significantly inflated the monetary base in 1994, a phenomenon which the authority tried hard to rectify in 1995. Despite some success, banks and financial institutions were able to use their accumulated liquidity in the form of excess reserves to extend credit. The PBOC did try to address this problem by raising the excess reserve ratios for the state banks from the range of 5–7% fixed under the 1994 reform[21] to that of 5–11% in late 1995.[22] Given that there are time lags between the increase in the monetary base and credit extension, as well as the ultimate deposit creation, the situation in 1994 and 1995 should be analyzed together rather than separately.

It should be noted that M2 may have increased not just because of loan growth, but also, and indeed more directly, as a result of balance of payments surplus (in both the trade and the capital accounts). The surplus was to the tune of US$30 billion (RMB 255 billion) in 1994 and US$22 billion (RMB 180 billion) in 1995, on the basis of the changes in China's foreign exchange reserves, compared with the size of RMB 4,693.33 billion of M2 at the end of 1994. Under the settlement system of 1994, foreign exchange earned or accrued would immediately be translated into RMB deposits of the units concerned, boosting M2. The designated banks and financial institutions which bought the foreign currencies had to turn them over to the PBOC, but their reserves, in the form of "position for foreign exchange purchases," would also increase. They could then extend more loans using the reserves as base money, thus creating more deposits which form M2.[23]

All in all, there are more than one channel through which M2 could increase in China. Other factors that have also boosted M2 in the past two years include the interest payments on bank deposits which have been indexed to inflation and the impressive hike in national savings. On the other hand, the rise in doubtful and bad debts in the financial system, with their counterparts in the form of inter-enterprise payment arrears, would also underpin the size of M2, as loan repayments are equivalent to the destruction of deposits.

From this perspective, one could argue that credit expansion by banks and financial institutions have not been excessively loose, given the huge increase in deposits. From the statistics revealed by Ma Delun and netting out M0 (currency in circulation), the marginal loan/deposit ratio for all financial institutions in the year of 1995 turned out to be 63.8% (i.e. {9,339/[60,749 – 600 – (46,933.3 – 600 – 825)]} = 0.638), if we take the figure of RMB 933.9 billion as the amount of newly increased loans rather than the outstanding balances. The marginal loan/deposit ratio for the state banks was 68.1% (i.e. (6,387/9,375)=0.681). Both ratios were well within the 75% loan/deposit ratio imposed under the "asset and liability ratio management system" of the 1994 reform.[24] Chinese financial institutions on the whole could not be accused of being "unscrupulous" this time round, as was the case in the first half of 1993.[25]

On the other hand, the significant fall in the growth rates of M0 and M1 in 1995, as shown in Table 3, might have represented a restructuring of monetary behaviour as inflationary pressure showed some signs of being alleviated. One has to remember that M0 (currency in circulation) and M1 (M0 plus demand deposits) are only definition subsets of M2 (M1 plus savings, time and other deposits). The relative growth rates, therefore, could indicate a tendency on the parts of money holders and depositors to opt for higher returns at the expense of lower liquidity. In other words, they were less worried about inflation.

These developments — the widening deposit-loan gap and the shift toward more stable money — have resulted in a slow, but steady, "cleaning up" of the mess in the financial system in China. If they persist, there may be light at the end of the tunnel.

Debt Trap, Policy Dilemma and Structuralism

In any case, complaints about the lack of credit funds became increasingly vocal. One main reason has been the worsening of the liquidity and solvency problems of the state-owned enterprises (SOEs). According to the spokesman of the State Statistical Bureau of China, Qiu Xiaohua, the situation was quite serious.[26] In 1995, four notable developments were:

1. More than 40% of SOEs reported losses in 1995, up 4–5% from 1994. Total losses went up by more than 20% to over RMB 40 billion, while realized profits fell by about 20%. One worrying feature was that the coverage of loss-making SOEs extended from the industrial sector to commerce, trade and finance. "This has not been observed in recent years."

2. Inter-enterprise arrears in payments increased in 1995 by more than RMB 140 billion.

3. Weak sales led to inventory accumulation. In January-October 1995, the sales-output ratio of SOEs averaged only 94%, which was 1% below that of 1994 and 2–3% below the normal level.

4. Enterprises with insufficient production orders reached one-third while official unemployment rate was 3%. The effective unemployment situation was nearing the "alarm level."

Here lies the dilemma facing the Chinese authority. If the monetary policy is not further relaxed, many of the SOEs will allegedly slide into financial crisis. But, if the monetary stance is loosened, there is no guarantee that their problems can be quickly solved. The decline in the sales-output ratio shows that many of the SOEs have not put forth their best efforts in adjusting to the rapidly changing market situation. In the past five years, for every RMB 100 input of funds, only about RMB 50 of GDP was produced in China.[27] Such fund-intensive mode of growth simply cannot continue. Moreover, to the extent that inflation is re-ignited by a much looser monetary stance, another form of crisis may occur in the fiscal and banking systems.

According to one source, fiscal expenditure in the form of price subsidies grew at an average annual rate of 46% in the past few years. At the same time, since bond rates were indexed with the inflation rate from July 1993 onwards, inflationary pressure had aggravated the domestic debt situation. Domestic debt retirement amounted to RMB 75.67 billion and was expected to rise above RMB 100 billion in 1996. Total (domestic and external) debt issues reached RMB 153.0 billion in 1995, yielding a debt ratio (debt issues as a percentage of total fiscal expenditure) of 52.8% for the central government. That was already near the internationally recognized "alarm level."[28] Similarly for the banking system, the indexation of deposit rates with inflation had also exerted pressure on their financial position. One estimate put it that losses from interest subsidies alone amounted to over RMB 20.0 billion in 1994.

It appears that the Chinese authority has been walking on a tightrope, trying to balance two difficult considerations. While it seems unlikely that China's monetary stance will be significantly relaxed in 1996, a "top authority" has indicated that the stance would not be "tighter than 1995," and there would be some "slight loosening."[29] Another report had it that the new loan scale for the state banks in 1996 had been set at RMB 700 billion, up 9% from the level of RMB 640 billion in 1995.[30]

In any case, the "top authority" emphasized that aggregate credit had actually not been "contractionary." What had been significant was a "structural adjustment" through which funds were concentrated on infrastructure. The growth in the construction of railways, roads, ports and telecommunications was "historically unprecedented."[31] Hence, the squeeze on some of the SOEs had largely been "structural." The selective nature of credit expansion by the state banks in 1996 was reiterated in the national banking conference held in January. Agriculture, heavy industry and infrastructure were reportedly given priority,[32] while no new loans would be extended to enterprises which insisted on increasing production despite piling up inventories and delayed repayments to other enterprises and the banks. On the other hand, credits would only be granted to firms which could come up with concrete plans to turn around their losses and repay debts, but approval would have to be granted by the authority one level up in the banking hierarchy.[33] As far as the Industrial and Commercial Bank of China (ICBC) was concerned, special emphasis would be placed on the large and medium-sized SOEs, in particular the "1000 key enterprises, the 56 enterprise conglomerates, and the three national holding companies."[34]

Aftermath of the 1994 Reforms

Taking a longer view, one has to say that the reforms of 1994 were significantly different from past attempts. Much greater emphasis was placed on achieving a breakthrough in key areas, on top of, or even at the expense of, macroeconomic balancing. The launching of reforms which had obvious inflationary impact at a time of already high inflation was the clearest indication of a notable shift in strategy. It was partly a result of greater confidence after a period of relatively successful reforms; but, on the other hand, the leadership had few choices if it did not want to repeat the past cycles. The problems arising from procrastination had become too pressing.

As I have analyzed elsewhere,[35] useful building blocks for a modernized financial system were put in place in 1994 although there were many observable imperfections. As there remains a great deal of work to be achieved, the possibility of bolder attempts cannot be ruled out if the macroeconomic atmosphere and the external environment are to improve.

The year 1995 bore evidence to both the imperfections and their consequences as well as the commitment to push reforms wherever they could go. There were blatant setbacks, but also courageous initiatives to go forward.

Foreign Exchange: Full Speed Ahead?

The foreign exchange reform was the most progressive among the various reforms of 1994, in both conception and practice.[36] It also turned out to be the most successful so far, helped by a huge capital inflow that has kept the exchange rate of the *Renminbi* firm.

Defying pessimistic forecasts, the *Renminbi* showed remarkable strength under the new system. On 4 April 1994, the first trading day of the China Foreign Exchange Trade System (CEFTS) in Shanghai, the Chinese currency was sold at RMB 8.6967/US$. It later continued to strengthen and ended 1994 at 8.4462. In the course of 1995, the steady arrival of funds from the 1992–1993 peak of contracted investments continued to underpin the *Renminbi* (see Table 5). The currency was quoted at 8.3174 at the end of the year.[37] The rates offered by banks and financial companies in Hong Kong were very close to these prices, indicating that the Chinese rates were accepted as reasonable by the offshore free market.

The stability of the *Renminbi* in the new system is a testimony to the success of the reform. There are various explanations.[38] The most important one has been the very impressive rise in the foreign exchange reserve, which went up from US$20 billion at the beginning of 1994 to US$51.62 billion by the year end. The rise continued in 1995, albeit at a lower rate, to reach US$73.6 billion by the year end (see Table 6).

Such a satisfactory result has apparently encouraged the Chinese government. Top officials seem to have been increasingly optimistic about the prospect for the convertibility for the *Renminbi*. In early 1993, Vice-Premier Zhu Rongji had argued that the *Renminbi* could become fully convertible only when China's foreign exchange reserve had reached the US$100 billion level. Many had held the view that a 10-year transition was needed. Then, the pace quickened. In March 1994, the then director of the

Table 5. Monthly Movements of the *Renminbi* in 1995

(Unit: RMB/100US$)

Month	Quotation at the end of month	Average quotation in the month
January	8.4384	8.4413
February	8.4316	8.4354
March	8.4269	8.4276
April	8.4102	8.4225
May	8.3077	8.3180
June	8.3011	8.3009
July	8.3003	8.3007
August	8.3193	8.3075
September	8.3189	8.3188
October	8.3149	8.3156
November	8.3120	8.3135
December	8.3174	8.3156

Sources: Various local newspaper and magazine reports in Hong Kong.

State Administration for Exchange Control (SAEC), Zhu Xiaohua, said that "China will strive to achieve the full convertibility of the *Renminbi* in the current account within six years." In late 1994, a vice-president of the PBOC, Chen Yuan, "optimistically estimated" that the *Renminbi* could be turned into a "convertible" currency by 1998, "two years ahead of the schedule."[39] In summer 1995, the newly appointed president of the PBOC, Dai Xianglong (who took over from Zhu Rongji), floated the idea of achieving "current account convertibility" by 1997. Finally, Zhu Rongji

Table 6. China's Gold and Foreign Exchange Reserves

Year	(1) Gold reserves (10,000 ounces)	(2) Foreign exchange reserves (US$ billion)	Growth of (2) (%)
1986	1,267	2.072	−21.6
1987	1,267	2.923	41.1
1988	1,267	3.372	15.4
1989	1,267	5.550	64.6
1990	1,267	11.093	99.9
1991	1,267	21.712	95.7
1992	1,267	19.443	−10.5
1993	1,267	21.199	9.0
1994	1,267	51.620	143.5
1995	1,267	73.597	42.6

Sources: The People's Bank of China, *China Financial Outlook '95*, Tables 3–13; *Wen Wei Po*, 1 February 1996, p. A8.

said in December 1995 that such convertibility could be realized "sooner than planned."[40] Such a statement was widely interpreted to mean that 1996 would be the year.[41] It appears that success breeds confidence.

The Chinese government did implement some measures in that direction. The intention to let the FIEs join the bank-based foreign exchange market (instead of being confined to swap centres) some time in 1996 was frequently reiterated. In February 1996, the State Council promulgated a new set of regulations on foreign exchange control. One key feature was to further enhance current account convertibility by exempting the repatriation of profits by FIEs from any approval procedure by the SAEC from 1 April 1996 onwards.[42] There were reports that the FIEs would be the first to enjoy "full convertibility in current account" in 1996, ahead of domestic enterprises.[43]

However, one should note that the foreign exchange control regime is closely related to the trade control system, as far as convertibility is concerned. It will mean little if the government pays lip service to current account convertibility while significant trade restrictions in the form of licencing, quotas, canalization and registration requirements still persist. To be fair, China has been making simultaneous efforts to reduce the latter barriers.

Banking: Persistent Reform Attempts Despite Severe Limitations

By most recognitions, the banking reform was the least successful among the macroeconomic reforms of 1994. The key reason was that given the prevailing state of the Chinese economy, the reform of the banking system was simply the most difficult among the major macro mechanisms. The fact that a muddled financial state could exist was a testimony to the lack of economic reorganization that clearly defined rights and responsibilities, backed by genuine sanctions. Chinese banks and their clients were not particularly bothered by the implications of credit risks, because they knew that the consequences of any failure or default would not really bite. Top leaders certainly wanted to change the situation, but also realized that no overnight solutions were available. In 1995, various attempts to improve the legal, institutional, and operational systems were pushed through. Although their immediate relevance was undermined by the harsh reality of the debt mess, the necessity of administrative intervention to preserve stability, and the lack of much needed progress in enterprise reforms, these new building blocks did represent important benchmarks to assess performance and officially endorsed goals to strive for.

Three "policy banks" were established in 1994. They were: (1) The China State Development Bank (SDB); (2) The China Import and Export Bank (IEB); and (3) The China Agricultural Development Bank (ADB). I commented last year that their planned capital bases and loan scales were not large enough to make a significant impact on the restructuring of the banking system, in terms of shouldering the policy loans of the state banks.[44] There was not much progress in 1995. Total loans extended by the SDB, the largest among the three, were reported to be RMB 87.3 billion,[45] hardly different from the total of RMB 86.2 billion targetted for 1994. The ADB, on the other hand, planned to increase its lending to the agriculture sector to RMB 16 billion in 1996, which would be 47.2% above that in 1995.[46] These amounts pale in comparison with the total increased loans of RMB 638.7 billion by the state banks and the rise in outstanding loan balances of RMB 933.9 billion by all financial institutions in 1995.

Besides the policy banks, other forms of commercial banks have been on the drawing board for some time. The idea of establishing rural and urban cooperative banks had been floated in 1993. In 1995, experiments were carried out in five major cities (Beijing, Shanghai, Shenzhen, Shijiazhuang and Tianjin) to set up the urban versions, and the Shenzhen Urban Cooperative Bank was the first one to start operation in mid-October. It was constituted under a shareholding system, with the local government having a "relative controlling share" among the founding 165 shareholding companies. At the start of its operation, the bank had a total asset of RMB 11.5 billion with a network of 15 branches. Outstanding loans amounted to RMB 4.9 billion and total deposits reached RMB 6.7 billion.[47] The second one to begin operation was the Shanghai Urban Cooperative Bank, which formally opened on 29 December 1995. Its capital was supplied by more than 40,000 individuals and over 2,400 *legal-person* shareholders. Overall, individual shares represented 30% of the total stake, medium and small-sized enterprise 30%, city and district-level fiscal authorities 30% and 12 large enterprises in Shanghai 10%. It had a total asset of about RMB 30, including outstanding loans of RMB 9.6 billion which was supported by a deposit base of RMB 25 billion. A network of over 220 branches and "operation points" was already in place.[48]

On the other hand, the State Council formally had approved in June 1994 a plan by the All-China Federation of Industry and Commerce to set up a shareholding commercial bank, the Mingsheng Bank. It started operation on 12 January 1996, with an initial capital of RMB 1.38 billion supplied by 59 shareholders. Over 80% of the equity funds were reported to come from non-state owned or citizen-operated (*minying*) companies. Without any direct state stake, it was the first of its kind in the country.[49]

Foreign banking and financial institutions continued to make inroads into China. In the course of 1995, China admitted 18 foreign banks, 1 Sino-foreign joint-venture investment bank, 2 foreign insurance companies, 82 representative offices of foreign financial institutions. At the end of the year, there were a total of 117 foreign bank branches, 5 joint-venture banks, 5 wholly foreign-owned banks, 5 wholly foreign-owned or joint-venture finance companies, 4 foreign insurance companies, 1 joint-venture investment bank and 519 representative offices in the country. The combined assets of foreign banks and finance companies had reached US$18.33 billion by the end of November, with outstanding loans at US$12.05 billion and total deposits at US$3 billion.[50] However, as to the involvement of foreign banks in *Renminbi* business, no firm decision had been made other than a declaration of intention. Top officials have in the meantime reiterated the familiar difficulties of the lack of progress in domestic financial reforms and the pre-conditions for creating a level playing field in terms of taxation and related operational matters.[51] It seems unlikely that any major breakthrough will occur in 1996.

In any case, given the worsening debt situation of the SOEs, domestic banks and financial institutions in China face considerable risk of "poor-quality assets" (*buliang zichan*) and illiquidity. The hardest hit seems to have been be the Industrial and Commercial Bank of China (ICBC). Chairman and President Zhang Xiao admitted that because of the increased provisions for bad debts, ICBC's net profit was expected to fall from RMB 4.2 billion in 1994 to about RMB 3.6 billion in 1995, which would be a far cry from the average of about RMB 13.5 billion in the last ten years.[52] A vice-president of the PBOC, Chen Yuan, disclosed in mid-1995 that the ratio of problematic debts in the four state banks was about 20%, but actual bad debts constituted only 3%. On the other hand, another survey published by *Guangming ribao* put the ratio of loans in arrear in the banking system at more than one-third.[53] Unless huge amounts of new capital and funds can be raised or massive write-offs be acceptable, the only choice is to proceed gradually. In this context, there was a report at the end of 1995 that a department in the PBOC had proposed to set up a special bank to take over 20% of the bad loans of the four state banks.[54] The PBOC refused to comment on the report. Nevertheless, it appeared that the debt mess was still far from being resolved. International credit rating companies, the Moody's Investors Services and Capital Intelligence, both downgraded the rating of key Chinese state banks, because of the perceived difficulties in the course of their commercialization. Such moves met strong repudiations by the Chinese side, which insisted that the state banks were fully backed by the government and credit risks were, therefore, minimal.[55]

With regard to the commercialization of the state banks, an "asset and liability ratio management system" was launched in 1994, which showed a high degree of "softness" with "Chinese characteristics." However, because of the need to control inflation, loans for fixed asset investments was put explicitly under mandatory plans.[56] In his interview granted to the pro-China press in Hong Kong in early 1996, the "top authority" also admitted that such a management system, which was a norm in the West, could function effectively by itself "when conditions in all aspects are ripe." In the transition process, credit plans were still necessary to ensure stability. He also stressed that it did not mean that nothing needed to be done to push forward the implementation of such a system. The reforms in the legislative framework, operational system, as well as personnel and quality management had to go on.[57]

Two of the most important pieces of legislation enacted in 1995 were the PBOC Law and the Commercial Bank Law. The Law on the People's Bank of China, passed at the 3rd session of the 8th National People's Congress in March 1995,[58] further clarified the functions of the central bank and pushed its de-commercialization to its logical conclusion. Under the law, the PBOC was prohibited from lending to non-financial institutions, giving overdrafts to the Treasury, underwrite or subscribe to any state bonds or debt instruments. Moreover, the law also stipulated that the regional setup of the PBOC should be based on "economic regions" rather than "administrative regions." This would imply a major reshuffle in the admin-istrative system of the central bank, one of whose goals was to further severe the link between its regional offices and the local governments, so as to strengthen the independence of the monetary authority.[59]

The Commercial Bank Law came into effect on 1 July 1995. A key provision was that banks should be responsible for the security, liability and efficiency of their own capital. This was to ensure that political authorities of different kinds could not exert influence on banks to obtain funds against the will of the banks. Critics said that such a law went against the dominant mode of monetary policy in 1994–1995 which had relied on a mixture of economic and non-economic measures (including aggregate credit targets and plans on loans for fixed asset investments), with a rather heavy dose of administrative micro-management (on the channelling of loans), on top of the leverage of the reserve requirements and relending through the newly imposed "asset and liability management system." However, its supporters argued that the main purpose of the law in the short run was again to maintain the independence of the commercial banks at the local levels, against the intervention of cadres and powerful enterprises. Overall, though, the long-term effectiveness of the law remains to be seen.

Other than the legal framework, the Chinese government also took measures to build a foundation for a more flexible monetary control. A system of "open market operation" based on the trading of state bonds was actively prepared. From 1994 onwards, the government's fiscal deficit had to be covered by bonds instead of borrowing from the PBOC. As a result, total state bonds issued in 1994 amounted to RMB 102.0 billion, about RMB 64.0 billion more than in 1993. At the end of 1994, the outstanding balance of state bonds was RMB 230.0 billion (about 6% compared with the total assets of all financial institutions), while the transaction of state bonds in the secondary market in the year reached RMB 2,300.0 billion, which was 2.3 times the transaction in stock shares (mainly in Shanghai and Shenzhen). The increasing stock of state bonds may provide a key instrument for open market operation and a basis for monetary fine-tuning.

While the outstanding balance of state bonds at the end of 1994 was RMB 230.0 billion, the value of bonds (not necessarily all Chinese state bonds) in the hands of all financial institutions was RMB 185.87 billion and that in state banks 180.29 billion. The amounts constituted 4.6% and 5.6% of total assets, respectively. They look relatively small, and trading in them may not generate significant impact on liquidity. The PBOC started experimenting with "monetary bonds" (bonds issued to provide liquidity in the financial system rather than for covering budget deficits) from 1993 onwards, but without much success. The major stumbling block was the lack of alternative investments to finance these non-fiscal bond issues. In any case, as a result of fiscal pressure and the prohibition of the monetization of deficits, total (domestic and external) debt issues reached RMB 153.0 billion in the year, adding significantly to the liquidity of the market. Transactions in the secondary market apparently increased by leaps and bounds, e.g., the average daily volume of the repurchases of treasury bonds in the national centre in Shanghai went from RMB 128 million in February to RMB 624 million in June 1995. The expansion and the related irregularities were so large that the authorities had to clamp down on the submarket in August.[60]

There has been a related difficulty about interest rates, which have been heavily manipulated by administrative measures in China. The PBOC is caught in the dilemma of finding a middle ground for the rates so that both the banks and the enterprises can be kept afloat. Hence, it still cannot afford the risk of letting them be fully determined by the market. A tricky issue for open market operation is the relationship between the interest rates formed in the operation and the administered rates which are still rather rigid and highly differentiated. In a process of a "gradual" reform to liberalize them, the key is to start with a prototype inter-bank market, which will probably be contained initially, before spreading the extent of liberalization to the deposit and loan markets.

An interbank market was indeed established, and it started operation on 4 January 1996 in Shanghai. Initially, 27 members, including all the state banks and commercial banks, plus 15 funding centres in major cities ranging from Beijing to Liaoning, constituted a market where funds of six different maturities (7 days, 20 days, 30 days, 60 days, 90 days and 120 days) were traded. The weighted averages of the interest rates of funds so traded in the centre would be adopted by the PBOC as interbank rates for the whole financial system in the country.[61]

Overall, despite all the institutional limitations and economic setbacks, some progress has still been achieved in the reforms of China's monetary framework. Top officials have hinted that a basic structure of a modernized central and commercial banking system based on indirect and flexible control could be in place by the year 2000.

The Fiscal Front: Difficulties Ahead

In 1994, China pushed through major taxation reforms which covered three major aspects: (1) central-local fiscal arrangements in the form of a *fen shui zhi* (tax assignment system); (2) the rationalization of the direct taxation system and the abolition of fiscal contracts for SOEs; and (3) the streamlining of indirect taxes and the enhanced roles for value-added tax (VAT) and the consumption tax.[62]

These were relatively bold attempts, driven by necessity or confidence. Despite official pronouncements of success, there have been some signs of troubles. The revamping of central-local fiscal relations, a cornerstone of the 1994 reforms, has turned out to be a compromise solution. The "double-track" arrangement, where rebates to local governments are based on the growth rates of the VAT and the consumption tax, is intended to ensure that the shift in central-local ratio is achieved through the growth in tax revenue, while the stock of revenue distribution is kept intact. It is unclear when the target ratio of 60:40 for central-local tax revenue (in contrast to the pre-reform ratio of 40:60) will be realized and the rebate arrangement abolished under such a programme although some have mentioned the possibility of year 2000. A World Bank projection, however, estimates that only 52% of fiscal revenue would accrue to the centre in that year.[63]

The problem actually goes deeper than the superficial division of revenue between the central and local authorities. On the surface, central revenues amounted to RMB 290.65 billion in 1994, the first year after the launching of the tax assignment system, while local revenues were RMB 231.1 billion. The central-local share, therefore, worked out to be 55.7:44.3, a big improvement over the pre-reform ratios. However, after intergovernmental transfers, disposable revenue in the hands of the central government was only RMB 108.746 billion, while the local governments' summed up to RMB 413.064. Hence the central's share in disposable income was a mere 20.84%,[64] which was markedly below the 25.08% budgetted for 1994 and below the ratios in the preceding years. It was caused by the larger-than-budgetted central-to-local transfers of RMB 238.909 billion (which consisted of the rebates under the assignment system, as well as various kinds of subsidies) and a less-than-budgetted remittance of RMB 57.005 billion from local authorities to the central government.[65] With these figures, it is hard to say whether and how the tax assignment system has helped to boost the fiscal resources of Beijing.

Moreover, in its rush to push through tax assignments to alleviate its fiscal problems, Beijing has side-stepped the long-term objective of clearly defining rights and responsibilities. The system has not been augmented by any clear demarcation of the responsibilities of the central and the local governments.[66] Such an asymmetry between rights (tax assignments) and responsibilities (expenditures) may lead to instability in the system, as different parties could contest the tax assignments in the future, when problems and arguments arise on the expenditure side.

Related to this incompleteness of the fiscal reform of 1994 are two important issues: (1) The reform of subprovincial public finance has lagged behind. The tax assignment system applies largely to central-provincial fiscal relations, while at the subprovincial level, various forms of fiscal contracts persist.[67] (2) The inter-governmental transfer system (which operates at a secondary stage compared with the original tax assignments) between the central and the local authorities has not been rationalized. Despite various proposals by the World Bank, including formula-based and need-based versions,[68] the transfer system remains *ad hoc* and subject to bargaining. The decline in the post-transfer share of the central government in disposable revenue in 1994, discussed above, might or might not have been the result of irrational transfers. These two factors, taken together, are also blamed by some economists as an important reason behind increasing regional disparities.[69]

As far as 1995 is concerned, there were many reports that the central government had to twist the arm of local authorities to ensure plan fulfillments of revenues, especially with regard to the revenue targets of the VAT and the consumption tax, the key variables in the rebate system. An official report noted that, by October 1995, only 77.4% of the planned amount of the two taxes had been collected, which was "6 percentage points less than that on time schedule."[70] Near the end of 1995, the State Taxation Bureau found it necessary to require local bureaus to make frequent, even daily, reports on the progress of tax collection. A vice-minister even threatened that, if fiscal revenues were below targets and the planned deficit of RMB 66 billion was exceeded, Beijing might have to rethink the tax rebate system.[71] Despite such moves, a report had it that by 25 December 1995, the cumulative amount of the VAT and the consumption tax collected was RMB 299.8 billion, which represented only 94.7% of the target for the whole year, although the plan for total collection of industrial and commercial taxes was 100.2% fulfilled.[72] The worsening of the financial position of enterprises also had its impact. The Finance Minister, Liu Zhongli, revealed that overdue tax payments by enterprises had reached RMB 21 billion by August 1995.[73]

There were some problems with the collection mechanism of the tax assignment system, which could be classified into two kinds: (1) the design of planned targets: the establishment of two parallel collection agencies and the existence of central-local shared taxes have given rise to "soft" targets (guidance plans) for the national and local tax bureaus as there are overlapping functions. The result could be either vicious competition for tax resources or negligence. (2) Actual collection: the detailed regulations on collection authority and responsibility are either not clear enough or not followed. There were anomalies where local authorities "usurped" central taxes, if only temporarily to gain a better tax base.[74]

Under pressure, the Chinese government had to seek various means to enhance revenue and reduce expenditure. The reduction of tax rebates for exports, discussed above, was one indication. Another was the plan in the course of 1996 to scrap tariff-free imports of investment goods by FIEs. Both could be justified on grounds of trade liberalization, but few would deny their fiscal connotations.

In the meantime, the government expressed its intention to bring the fiscal system to order. According to press reports, the target for the Ninth Five-Year Plan was to reduce the fiscal deficit progressively, so that by the year 2000 it could be eliminated. Given that the planned deficit was RMB 66 billion for 1995, it would mean an annual decrease of about RMB 13 billion in the coming years.[75] Experts predicted that the deficit could only be depressed to about RMB 60 billion in 1996. Hence, the pressure on the remaining four years of the century would be quite great.[76]

Under-capitalization, the Debt Chain and Behavioural Changes

The intertwined nature of the fiscal-monetary-debt dilemma has prompted some to probe the crux of the complex phenomenon and seek a comprehensive solution. One emerging view is that the syndrome has as its source a fiscal mess. Given the fiscal decline of the central government and the restructuring of the funding for the SOEs by replacing fiscal allocations with bank loans (the so called *bo gai dai* reform), the SOEs have been significantly under-capitalized. The state, as the rightful owner of the SOEs, has not put into them enough money. As a result, they have to depend increasingly on bank loans to sustain their operations.

A recent survey by the PBOC put the problem into focus. The survey covered 248 representative large- and medium-sized SOEs in eight provinces. The aggregate ratio of total liabilities/total assets was 68.9%, while that of total liabilities/liquid assets was 98.1%. One compounding problem was the deteriorating quality of their assets, with rising receivables and inventories. The survey report pointed out that the main causes for the "excessively low level of self-owned funds" included "*insufficient input from the state* and the lack of effective capital accumulation mechanism on the part of the SOEs" (our emphasis).[77]

According to one view, that set of conditions started the debt chain. Under-capitalized SOEs that failed to repay bank loans had been a major cause of the financial fragility of state banks, which in turn had had to depend on "re-lending" from the central bank, the PBOC, to maintain balance.[78] The PBOC was then forced to monetize the shortfall by issuing currency or expanding the monetary base, thus generating inflation. The fiscal problem had become a monetary problem.

So, theoretically, the debt chain can be broken by reversing the process. Instead of the PBOC lending to the state banks which then lend to the SOEs, creating all the debt problems, the PBOC may extend a massive loan to the Treasury, which then injects capital into the SOEs, redressing their precarious equity base. The SOEs can, therefore, repay the state banks, which will reduce their financial dependency on the PBOC.

Such a relatively radical proposal was put forward by Wu Xiaoling and Xie Ping in a number of recent papers.[79] At the end of the process, the "policy-induced debt problem" of both the enterprise and the banking sectors would be transformed into a huge and *explicit* liability of the Treasury against the PBOC. Wu and Xie argued that such a transfer would not create much additional inflationary pressure because the implicit fiscal deficit had already been monetized and the inflationary consequences already borne by society. They also stressed that there were debt problems which were not policy-induced but created by inefficiency and excessive social burdens on the part of the SOEs, which could only be cured by commensurate reforms.

In any case, the macroeconomic implications of such a proposal in terms of inflation or financial stability on policy-induced debts are controversial and should be debated.[80] For one thing, it goes against the policy of de-linking fiscal deficits from the monetary regime adopted in 1994. This kind of recommendations is actually in line with that of *dai gai tou* (turning bank loans to enterprises into equity investments), which has lately become popular within China. Nevertheless, even for this limited form of reform, there are already many problems involving the transformation of SOEs into proper shareholding companies so that banks can hold a well-defined equity stake, as well as the proper evaluation of the assets without which banks may suffer big losses. A milder version advocates the turning of poor-quality debts into bonds, which is again constrained by the underdeveloped state of China's financial market.[81]

The outstanding feature of the radical proposal is that it pushes the argument to its logical conclusion: the state, rather than the banks, should become the investor. So, we are back to square one: after all, SOEs are *state-owned enterprises*. The trouble is that, even if the analysis of the formation of the debt chain is correct, a simple one-off reversal would not necessarily produce beneficial results, as economic agents along the chain have reacted in vastly different ways, formed various "bad habits," and got into all kinds of financial and operational traps.

Hence, the key weakness of the radical proposal is its ambiguous microeconomic implications. There is no guarantee that a one-off cleaning of the slate (even of only policy-induced debts) would induce significant changes in the *behaviour* of all the parties concerned, in particular the enterprises. In other words, the revamp in the *stock* variable does not necessarily lead to improvements in the *flow* variable. This is a key argument against one-off type of "big bang" adventurism in economic transition.[82] To be fair, Wu and Xie did insist that complementary reforms must be implemented together with the financial restructuring, but then there is a problem of *time consistency* among reforms which can only proceed at different speeds. On the other hand, if the one-off solution fails to produce marked improvement in the operational efficiency of the enterprise and banking sectors, from which the Treasury could benefit through buoyant fiscal revenues, how would its huge liability against the PBOC be progressively reduced is a big uncertainty.

The alternative is a more gradualist, eclectic approach which involves a degree of *dai gai tou*, the transformation into bonds of a certain amount of loans, the rescheduling of some doubtful and bad debts, as well as the selling off or merger of some SOEs.[83] Such an approach has the merit of sharing the burden among all parties, while at the same time exerting pressure on them to reform. At the end of the day, to prevent the debt problem from re-emerging, genuine reforms, particularly in the enterprise sector, is a crucial pre-condition.

The Ninth Five-Year Plan and Long-term Strategy

In September 1995, the 5th Plenum of the 14th Central Committee passed an important document on economic strategy, which would have to be endorsed by the National People's Congress in March 1996. It contained the proposals for the Ninth Five-Year Plan (NFYP) for 1996–2000 and the long-term development strategy up to the year 2010.[84]

Easy Quantitative Targets

At the beginning of the economic reforms in 1980, the Chinese government had vowed to quadruple real GNP before 2000, a task which was achieved in 1995. Under the proposed NFYP, a new target of quadrupling per capita GNP by 2000 (compared with 1980) was put forward.[85] This seems easily achievable, barring major disasters. In 1994, the per capita GNP was already 316% of that in 1980 in real terms.[86] To reach the new target, it needs only to grow at an annual real rate of 4.8% in the period of 1995–2000, which is substantially below the average rate of 8.6% per year in the preceding 14 years.

Taking the Socialist Market Economy Seriously

As can be seen from Table 7, the share of state-owned enterprises in GVOI fell from 77.6% in 1978 to 34.1% to 1994, while the shares of collective-owned and individual-owned enterprises rose from 22.4% and 0% in 1978 to 40.9% and 11.5% in 1994, respectively. The latter two sectors combined started to exceed the output value of the state-owned sector in 1993, while the collective sector outdid the state-owned one in 1994. However, in terms of overall employment and fixed asset investments, the state-owned sector still dominated. In 1994, 66.7% of urban employees worked in it, while 71.3% of all fixed asset investments were made by state-owned enterprises and units.

As far as the published guidelines of the two proposed plans can tell,

Table 7. Distribution of Gross Value of Industrial Output

(Unit: RMB billion)

Year	Total	State-owned	Collective-owned	Individual-owned	Other ownership
1978	423.700	328.918	94.782	0.0	n.a.
1980	515.426	391.560	121.336	0.081	2.449
1983	646.100	473.940	166.314	0.075	5.040
1984	761.730	526.270	226.309	1.481	7.670
1985	971.647	630.212	311.719	17.975	11.741
1986	1,119.426	697.112	375.154	30.854	16.306
1987	1,381.299	825.009	478.174	50.239	27.877
1988	1,822.400	1,035.128	658.749	79.049	49.532
1989	2,201.706	1,234.291	785.805	105.766	75.844
1990	2,392.436	1,306.375	852.273	129.030	104.756
1991	2,824.801	1,495.458	1,008.475	160.910	159.958
1992	3,706.571	1,782.415	1,410.119	250.680	263.358
1993	5,269.199	2,272.467	2,021.321	440.205	535.206
1994	7,690.946	2,620.084	3,143.404	885.323	1,042.135

Sources: *China Statistical Yearbook*, various issues.

they would represent a further step toward defining the "socialist market economy" and rectifying some of the emerging socioeconomic problems and difficulties. It has been confirmed that the large and medium-sized state-owned enterprises will remain the pillar in the Chinese economy, so as to show "the superiority of the socialist system."[87] These enterprises serve as a key leverage of socialist planning and control, which is supposed to be modernized and focussed on long-term and macro issues, leaving the routine allocation of resources and price-setting to the market mechanism. At the same time, the party stresses that the other socialist aspects of the system, including a well funded social security network, must be established or strengthened.[88] From these angles, China is apparently taking the concept of "socialist market economy" seriously.

Such a concept, however, is not much more "socialist" than the Northern and Western European social-democratic systems, *minus* all the politics of course. There has been a debate in China on how many large and medium-sized state enterprises (which number about 14,000) should remain under state ownership. The answers from various camps range from a few hundred to a few thousand, and it looks as if the authority is inclined toward a more cautious stance.

Other than holding to the "main pillar," though, the government seems to be relatively flexible with regard to the other medium and small-sized state enterprises. While no massive selling off of the Russian or East European types is conceived, a creeping process of privatization or semi-privatization in non-strategic sectors, provided it is done without fanfare, appears to be within tolerance limits. As far as *new* enterprises (including domestic collective, domestic private and foreign-invested enterprises) are concerned, the government is again open-minded as long as they do not challenge the strategic positions of the large and medium-sized state enterprises in key economic sectors.

Intensive and Balanced Growth

Another key idea which has emerged from the guidelines and the following official discussions is that the mode of economic growth should be changed from that of "extensive" into "intensive" growth, meaning that efficiency enhancement should become the focus of effort.[89] The party has recognized that, in the past one and a half decades, growth was promoted mainly by increased capital and labour input, rather than improvement in productivity. One manifestation of such a shift in focus is the emphasis on technology transfer from FIEs as well as domestic investments in high-tech industries and education.

A more balanced pattern of economic development is stressed, with priority given to agriculture, as well as a regional economic policy that aims at gradually narrowing disparity. As far as promoting economic development in the middle and western parts of the country is concerned, the guidelines propose to increase budgetary input, giving "key national project" status to infrastructural and natural resource exploitation projects in these regions, encouraging domestic and foreign investments there, and rationalizing the price of basic commodities.

There has been speculation that preferential policies for the coastal region may soon be eliminated, leading to a heated debate on whether the Shenzhen SEZ should remain "special," pitting the economist Hu Angang from the Academy of Sciences against SEZ officials and supporters. The flare-up ended when the central government re-affirmed the special status of the SEZs, not so much by reiterating that preferential financial policies would last, but that they should concentrate on utilizing foreign capital, developing high-technology and less resource-consuming industries as well as high value-added services, and opening overseas markets.

Hence, the authorities are keen to implement a more rational division of labour between the coastal region and inland China. In the past, industrial development was concentrated in the east while resources and raw materials were extracted in and transported from mid-land and the west. Given the unfavourable price structure, the latter were not getting much benefit. Moreover, such long-distance movement of production inputs put a huge burden on the transportation system, which was relatively under-developed.[90] Therefore, for the consideration of both economic rationality and regional equality, such an anomaly had to be rectified.

Moreover, the authorities seem to be re-orientating their policy toward foreign investment. On the one hand, plans for the continuing absorption of huge amounts of foreign capital are on the drawing board. According to an official at MOFTEC (Ministry of Foreign Trade and Economic Cooperation), the amount of FDI that China intends to utilize in the five years of the NFYP would amount to US$150 billion, which would equal the cumulative total of actual FDI funds already in the country.[91] On the other hand, though, the authorities also want to strengthen guidance over the direction of foreign investments. Two sets of regulations on such "directional guidance" were issued by the government in 1995, and Wu Yi, the Minister heading MOFTEC, stressed that they should be followed by future policies.[92] It was also revealed that, in the NFYP, the sectors in which the government would encourage foreign capital input would be: agriculture; infrastructure; machinery, electronics, petrochemicals, auto-mobile, and construction; high-technology and energy and resource-saving items; investments that raised enterprise efficiency and opened up new markets; investments that enhanced foreign exchange earning capabilities; environmentally friendly projects; as well as investments that helped to effectively use the comparative advantages of the middle and western parts of the country in manpower and natural resources.[93] The list seems to be quite consistent with the thinking behind the proposed NFYP and the Long-term Development Strategy.

While demanding more contribution from FIEs, China also intends to create a fair competition framework between foreign and domestic enterprises. Duty-free exemption for imports of capital equipment and raw materials by FIEs as part of their total investment would be abolished from 1 April 1996 onwards, as the overall level of import duties would be reduced to 23%, causing some resentments within the circle of foreign investors.[94] There are also various speculations that other tax benefits for FIEs may soon be phased out in the name of giving them "national treatment."

Implications for Hong Kong

The intensive and balanced growth strategy seems to have inspired not only regional policy, but also intra-regional measures. An interesting ex-ample is those adopted by the Guangdong province. The newly elected provincial governor, Lu Ruihua, urged Hong Kong investors to invest in the mountainous areas of northern Guangdong, which are relatively poor and underdeveloped.[95] This is in line with the re-orientation of economic development in Guangdong, which I have discussed elsewhere.[96] Whether Hong Kong investors will opt for that is another story.

On the other hand, Wang Changyao, economic research manager of the Hong Kong and Macau Regional Office of the Bank of China, has said that the Ninth Five-Year Plan would mean good and bad news for Hong Kong investors. As the plan envisages greater emphasis on pillar sectors, such as agriculture, energy, transport and heavy industry, which are not in Hong Kong's comparative advantage, and "as China continues to raise its demand for technology from foreign companies, some Hong Kong inves-tors would encounter problems."[97]

In an related development, it was reported that investors from Hong Kong, along with those from Macau and southeast Asian countries would be barred from further joint ventures in retail business during the NFYP, as they are already too strong a presence. Priorities would be given to partners form Europe, the US and Japan.[98]

It appears that Hong Kong may have to undergo adjustments in catering for the changing structure and orientation of the Chinese economy. "Windfall profits" that were easily earned in the earlier years of economic reforms through outward processing across the border would become increasingly hard to come by.

Potential Implementation Problems and Geopolitical Sea Changes?

The NFYP and the Long-term Development Strategy, as far as the published proposal can tell, would, if effectively implemented, represent a significant change in China's economic policy. They aim at moulding a "socialist market economy" whose growth is to be more quality-oriented than before. A more balanced developmental trajectory is also planned for efficiency as well as equity considerations.

Details of the actual socioeconomic plans beyond the published proposals of principles and guidelines have yet to appear at the time of writing. While the general stance seems to be natural or justified given the progress, on the one hand, and the cumulative problems, on the other, of the past 15 years, some possible contradictions in the conception and design of strategies can already be detected. For example, it is not clear how the shift to "intensive growth" and the likely rise in unemployment are to be harmonized. The increased utilization of foreign funds and the more stringent demands on them may also create some conflicts.

Finally, one big uncertainty hanging over the future of China's economic development and reform is her relations with the outside world after the euphoria of 1992–1994, which ironically contrasted sharply with the post-1989 doldrum. The change of fortune could not have been more dramatic between those two periods, when many of those who predicted the imminent death of the Chinese economy reversed their view within a very short time and endorsed its prospects enthusiatically. From 1995 onwards, the mood has however changed again, as political tension concerning the leadership succession in the post-Deng era as well as the confrontation with Taiwan and the US has cast a long shadow. A "new

cold war" might emerge, pitting China against the US over Taiwan independence, in which case the trajectory of the Chinese economy would be
quite different from the one conceived one or two years ago.

In a way, though, the proposal document on the NFYP and the
2010 targets already contained an element of caution. The emphases on
"socialist market economy," intensive and balanced growth, as well as
regional re-orientation could be regarded as a relatively more inward-
looking strategy that pays greater attention at consolidation and internal
strengthening, in contrast to the more outward-looking and optimistic posture of 1992–1994. Further down the road, geopolitics will probably play
an increasing role in determining the course of the Chinese economy.

Notes

1. See Tsang Shu-ki, "Financial Restructuring," in *China Review 1995*, edited
   by Lo Chi Kin, Suzanne Pepper and Tsui Kai Yuen (Hong Kong: The Chinese
   University Press, 1995), chapter 21.
2. The growth rate of GDP for the fourth quarter of 1995 has not been officially
   announced. It is computed from the published figures for the first three
   quarters and for the year as a whole. Finalized numbers may differ somewhat
   from those presented here.
3. CERD Consultants Ltd., *China's Latest Economic Statistics*, January 1996,
   Part I.
4. This point was admitted by nearly all top officials when they reviewed the
   "economic success" of 1995.
5. The ratios that Jiang Zemin referred to in the APEC Conference were
   arithmetic-average rather than weighted-average ones. It is not clear what the
   gap between the nominal and effective arithmetic-average ratios is. But, for
   the weighted-average ratios, the gap has been quite striking. According to one
   source, the nominal weighted-average ratio of import tariffs in 1994 was
   16.7%. See Wang Xinhuai, *Zhongguo waimao tizhi gaige yu fazhan* (The
   Reform and Development of the Foreign Trade System in China), Working
   Paper Series No. 2, China Business Centre, Hong Kong Polytechnic, March
   1994. However, on the basis of the figures in *Zhongguo tongji nianjian, 1995*
   (China Statistical Yearbook, 1995), total tariffs collected were reported to be
   RMB 33.0 billion, while total imports amounted to RMB 996.69 billion. It
   implies an effective tariff rate of only 3.3%!
6. See the report in *Ta Kung Pao*, Hong Kong, 31 January 1996.
7. See, for example, "Global Tremors from an Unruly Giant," *Business Week*, 4
   March 1996, pp. 15–18.

8. See, for example, *The China Analyst*, November 1995, p. 10: "The Chinese economy is clearly in a pre-recession mode, with some sectors already into a sharp downturn. China's austere monetary policy has been long and brutal and as a result, forced the demonetization of a large proportion of business transactions because of a lack of money and credit."

9. See my previous discussion in Tsang Shu-ki, "Financial Restructuring" (Note 1).

10 *Wen Wei Po*, Hong Kong, 1 February 1996, p. A8.

11. See the interview of PBOC President Dai Xianglong published on *Jingji ribao* (Economic Daily), 22 January 1996, p. 1. In answering the reporter's first question, Dai referred to the amount, RMB 934.0 billion, as the increase in outstanding loan balances for all financial institutions in 1995, then in his answer to the fourth question, he used the term "newly increased loans" to describe the amount but gave a growth rate of 23%. That growth rate is consistent only if the figure of RMB 934.0 billion had been the outstanding loan balances, on the assumption that the number for such balances at the end of 1994 in Tables 3–7 of *China Financial Outlook '95* is accurate.

12. From Tables 3–7 of *China Financial Outlook '95*, p. 95, the increase in loan balances of all financial institutions was RMB 786.7 billion in 1994. If the growth in these balances was RMB 933.9 billion in 1995, it would have been RMB 147.2 billion more than that in 1994, rather than the figure of RMB 212.3 billion stated by Ma Delun.

13. Including the interview of Dai Xianglong referred to in Note 11.

14. See Tsang Shu-ki, "Financial Restructuring" (Note 1), p. **21**.12.

15. *China Financial Outlook '94*, Tables 1–3.

16. See the interview report in *Ta Kung Pao*, 18 January 1996.

17. *South China Morning Post*, Hong Kong, 15 February 1996, Business 4.

18. See Joe Zhang, "China's Credit Is Easing at Last," *Asian Wall Street Journal*, 4 January 1996, p. 6. According to the author, black market interest rates fell "from about 25% in January to between 18% and 19% in November."

19. Same source as Note 11.

20. *South China Morning Post*, 15 February 1996, Business 4.

21. See Tsang Shu-ki, "Financial Restructuring" (Note 1), Table 2.

22. *Southern China Economic News*, 23 October 1995.

23. These probably have been the major factors behind the 30% growth in enterprise deposits in 1995 discussed above.

24. Tsang Shu-ki, "Financial Restructuring" (Note 1), Table 2. For the state banks, the 75% limit was to be the incremental (margin) ratio (i.e. new loans divided by new deposits), while it was meant to be the overall upper limit (total loans over total deposits) for the other financial institutions.

25. For an analysis of the latter case, see Tsang Shu-ki, "Financial Restructuring" (Note 1).

26. *Wen Wei Po*, 9 January 1996, p. A6.
27. *Ta Kung Pao*, 26 January 1996.
28. *Zhongguo jingji shibao* (China Economic Times), 5 January 1996, p. 1.
29. The remarks were made in an interview granted to the pro-China press in Hong Kong. *Ta Kung Pao*, 15 January 1996, pp. 1–2. The "top authority," who was anonymous in the initial report, was widely speculated to be Vice-Premier Zhu Rongji.
30. *Hong Kong Economic Times*, 17 January 1996, p. A2.
31. *Ta Kung Pao*, 15 January 1996, pp. 1–2.
32. *Hong Kong Standard*, 16 January 1996.
33. *Hong Kong Economic Times*, 17 January 1996, p. A2.
34. Ibid.
35. See Tsang Shu-ki, "Inertia, Resistance and Forced Innovation: A Longer View of China's Recent Financial Reforms," *International Journal of Public Administration*, 1996, forthcoming.
36. For a historical analysis of China's foreign exchange system up to the reform of 1994, see Tsang Shu-ki, "Towards Full Convertibility? China's Foreign Exchange Reforms," *China Information*, Vol. IX, No.1 (Summer 1994), pp. 1–41.
37. *Wen Wei Po*, 4 January 1996.
38. Tsang Shu-ki, "Financial Restructuring" (Note 1).
39. Ibid.
40. *Wen Wei Po*, 10 December 1995, p. A2.
41. See, for example, *United Daily News*, Hong Kong, 14 November 1995.
42. For the full text of the Regulations, see *Wen Wei Po*, 6 February 1996, p. B5.
43. See for example the analysis in *Wen Wei Po*, 25 November 1995, p. C3. The message was allegedly passed by Vice-Premier Zhu Rongji to a delegation of Hong Kong businessmen.
44. Tsang Shu-ki, "Financial Restructuring" (Note 1).
45. *Ta Kung Pao*, 24 January 1996.
46. *Hong Kong Standard*, 16 January 1996.
47. See the interview with the bank's president in *Renmin ribao* (People's Daily), 8 November 1995.
48. *Ta Kung Pao*, 4 January 1996.
49. *Hong Kong Standard*, 13 January 1996.
50. *Wen Wei Po*, 12 January 1996, p. A6.
51. Ibid.; and Ma Delun, *Wen Wei Po*, 1 February 1996, p. A8.
52. See the report in *South China Morning Post*, 21 December 1995. Another major reason for the ICBC's profit decline which was not discussed was the rising amount of interest rate subsidies for indexed deposits. Holding the largest amount of savings deposits in China, the ICBC's burden has been the heaviest.

53. For Chen Yuan's figures, see *Hong Kong Economic Times*, 21 June 1995. For the report on the survey published by *Guangming ribao* (Guangming Daily), see the extract in *Ta Kung Pao*, 30 June 1995. According to the author's source, Chen's figures were from the reporting statistics of the PBOC, while the latter report was from a sample survey of the four specialized banks and the nine smaller commercial banks.

54. *Hong Kong Economic Times*, 28 December 1995.

55. See the reports in *Hong Kong Economic Journal*, 7 December 1995; *Hong Kong Economic Times*, 8 December 1995; and *South China Morning Post*, 21 December 1995.

56. See Tsang Shu-ki, "Financial Restructuring" (Note 1); and Mao Hungjun, *Zhongguo jinrong tizhi gaige xin jucuo* (New Measures in the Financial System Reform in China) (Beijing: Beijing daxue chubanshe, 1994), pp. 109–25.

57. *Ta Kung Pao*, 15 January 1996, pp. 1–2.

58. See "Law Gives Central Bank Some Teeth," *China Daily Business Week*, 26 March 1995.

59. *Renmin ribao*, overseas edition, 27 March 1995.

60. See Hongkong Bank China Services Ltd., *China Monthly Report*, November 1995.

61. *Wen Wei Po*, 4 January 1996.

62. For a summary of the reform measures and a preliminary assessment, see Tsang Shu-ki and Cheng Yuk-shing, "China's Tax Reforms of 1994: Breakthrough or Compromise?" *Asian Survey*, Vol.XXXIV, No.9 (September 1994), pp. 769–88.

63. The World Bank, *China: Macroeconomic Stability in a Decentralized Economy* (Washington, DC, 1995), pp. 69–70.

64. See the summary of the report on execution of the 1994 budget by the Finance Minister, Liu Zhongli, in *Caizheng* (Public Finance), No. 8 (1995), p. 2.

65. For the budgeted amounts and ratios for 1994, as well as the actual figures for the preceding years, see Tsang Shu-ki and Cheng Yuk-shing, "China's Tax Reforms of 1994" (Note 62).

66. See Tsang Shu-ki and Cheng Yuk-shing, "China's Tax Reforms of 1994" (Note 62). The same view is expressed by The World Bank, *China: Macro-economic Stability in a Decentralized Economy* (Note 63).

67. For a discussion of subprovincial public finance in China, see Christine P. W. Wong, Christopher Heady and Wing T. Woo, *Fiscal Management and Economic Reform in the People's Republic of China*, published for the Asian Development Bank by Oxford University Press, 1995, chapter 3; and Christine P. W. Wong, "Caizheng gaige yu shengji yi xia de caizheng" (Fiscal Reform and Subprovincial Public Finance), *Jingji shehui tizhi bijiao* (Comparative Economic and Social Systems), No. 6 (1994), pp. 35–41.

68. See The World Bank, *China: Revenue Mobilization and Tax Policy*, 1990; and Ramgopal Agarwala, *China: Reforming Intergovernmental Fiscal Relations*, World Bank Discussion Papers, China and Mongolia Department, 1992.

69. See Christine P. W. Wong, "Caizheng gaige yu shengji yi xia de caizheng" (Note 67).

70. *China Economic News*, 1 January 1996, p. 2.

71. See the report in *Ming Pao*, Hong Kong, December 1996.

72. *Renmin ribao*, 30 December 1995.

73. *Ming Pao*, 22 September 1995.

74. Guo Jiangang, "Xin shuizhi tiaojian xia zuzhi shuishou zhong de maodun" (The Contradictions in Tax Collection under the Conditions of the New Taxation System), *Jianghan luntan* (Jianghan Forum), No. 6 (1995), pp. 90–91.

75. *Ming Pao*, 25 October 1995.

76. See the analysis in *Wen Wei Po*, 25 February 1996, p. 1.

77. See the report in *Wen Wei Po*, 5 December 1995, p. B4.

78. For a discussion of the financial fragility of the banking system, see Tsang Shu-ki, "Financial Restructuring" (Note 1).

79. Wu Xiaoling and Xie Ping, "Zhongguo guoyou qiye-yinhang zhaiwu chongzu de shexiang" (Thoughts on the Debt Restructuring between SOEs and Banks in China), *Caimao Jingji* (Finance and Trade Economics), No. 12 (1994), pp. 13–17; Wu Xiaoling, "Zhongguo guoyou qiye-yinhang zhaiwu chongzu wenti" (The Problems of the Restructuring of SOE-Bank Debts in China), *Jingji shehui tizhi bijiao*, No. 3 (1995), pp. 2–9.

80. For a skeptic view and more gradualist proposal, see Zhou Tianyong, "Jiuwu qijian zhaiwu chongzu de mubiao suliang he fangshi zuhe" (The Targets, Quantities and Patterns of Debt Restructuring in the Ninth Five-Year Plan), *Gaige* (Reform), No. 5 (1995), pp. 30–36.

81. See, for example, the discussions in Yin Mengbo and Li Ding, "Dui jiejue zhuanye yinhang buliang zichuan wenti de tantao" (An Investigation of the Solutions to the Problems of Poor-Quality Asset Rights of Specialized Banks), *Jinrong yanjiu* (Financial Research), No. 10 (1994), pp. 63–68.

82. See Tsang Shu-ki, "Against Big Bang in Economic Transition: Normative and Positive Arguments," *Cambridge Journal of Economics*, March 1996.

83. See the reference in Note 81.

84. The document was published in the overseas edition of *Renmin ribao* on 5 October 1995.

85. Item 5 of the document, ibid.

86. *Zhongguo tongji nianjian, 1995*, Tables 2–10.

87. Item 12, reference in Note 84.

88. Item 35, reference in Note 84.

89. Item 9, reference in Note 84.

90. See Wang Jian, "The Issues concerning China's Regional Structure Following the Open-Door Policy", in *The Long-term Prospects of the Chinese Economy*, edited by Kyoichi Ishihara et al. (Tokyo: Institute of Developing Economies, 1993), chapter 2.

91. See the report in *Ta Kung Pao*, 24 February 1996, p. 1. According to the official, the cumulative total of FDI was about US$110 billion at the end of September 1995.

92. *Ta Kung Pao*, 24 January 1995.

93. See the reference in Note 88.

94. See for example Nigel Page, "China's Level Playing Field," *Financial Times*, 30 January 1996.

95. See *Ta Kung Pao*, 11 February 1996, p. 2.

96. See Tsang Shu-ki, "The Economic Link-up of Guangdong and Hong Kong: Structural and Developmental Problems," BRC Papers on China, No. CP95003, Business Research Centre, School of Business, Hong Kong Baptist University, January 1995.

97. See the report in *South China Morning Post*, December 1995, Business 4.

98. *Ming Pao*, 6 January 1996.

9

The Land and Real Estate Management System

Lau Pui King

The land and real estate market is a new economic sector in the Chinese economy. Legislation on land-use rights in 1986 transformed the allocation of land system in the country. In order to develop a land and real estate market, China needed to break away from traditional and Marxist ideological barriers and revamp the institutional set-up. In less than 10 years, a market with Chinese characteristics for a population of 1.2 billion has been built. Similar to the situation in other socialist planned economies, the urban land-use system had produced inefficiences and spatial anomalies in the country.[1] Rural land for agricultural production has been threatened by the rapid development and the transformation of the economy. A major concern of the Chinese government was to establish a pricing system for land use and real estate development. It was too soon to consider clarification and protection of property rights for existing users. The first step was to provide a legal framework, administrative bodies and procedures, and incentives for the efficient and effective adjustment of land use and property development by the government at various levels and locations.[2] In fact, the government has been a major player in the reform of the Chinese land and real estate market.

Land-Use Rights Reform

Land was an immobile factor under the planned economy. Land-use rights were appropriated free of charge and the transfer of land use was prohibited. The planning system in the urban sector undermined the value of land as a production factor. Planning units, including enterprises and other organizations, tended to maximize their budget, by the expansion of production and the improvement of welfare benefits for the staff. In order to achieve higher growth rates in gross output value, planning units tried to increase the free appropriation of capital, raw materials, labour, and land. Once land was appropriated to a unit or an enterprise, its usage could not be changed. In the rural areas, arable land was distributed to peasant households based on the head count and the labour force of the household in order to guarantee the production of food grains and the distribution of income on an egalitarian basis.[3] The household responsibility system reinforced the land-use rights to guarantee self-sufficiency and the provision of food and raw materials for the urban sector. But the peasants were given certain cropping freedoms in the use of the land to achieve better market returns. The transfer of land for non-agricultural purposes and the transaction of land-use rights were prohibited. The emergence of a free market for rural produce in the early 1980s increased the peasants' revenue from the sale of agricultural output. As the income and savings of the peasants increased, their first desire was to build new homes for their families. Adult peasants have a legal right to build new houses on their agricultural land.[4] As a result, rural residential houses are scattered in the fields and occupy portions of the sowed land. The industrial development of the rural areas is also a threat to the environment, producing poor spatial planning and an acute decrease in arable land.

The rapid industrialization and economic transformation of the Chinese economy required a more efficient allocation and management of the land system. The former land-use allocation system inhibited economic development. In 1986, the Land-Use Law was promulgated and the State Land Administration Bureau was established under the State Council. A series of laws and regulations on land-use were adopted by the central and local governments. State Land Administration Bureaux were established at the central to the township levels. The new institutions govern the transfer of land-use rights between different administrative or business units for various uses. Most important, there is now a mechanism for the government to collect revenue from the transfer of land use and to use this revenue to finance infrastructure and economic development. The Chinese land and real estate market is a monopoly market. Local government organizations are the major suppliers and controllers of the market. The large-scale involvement in land and real estate investment projects by the public sector, especially in the coastal and the large cities, has been a major cause of the inflationary pressures on the Chinese economy since 1993. According to the *China Statistical Yearbook*, the price index of building materials jumped from 111.1 in 1992 to 142.8 in 1993, one of the highest increases in industrial products, which resulted in a rise in the Industrial Producer Price Index from 106.8 to 124.0. Urban and rural retail price indices for building and decoration materials in 1993 reached an unprecedented high of 134.2 and 128.2 respectively, much higher than the overall retail price indices of 114.2 and 112.6.

Competition among government organizations and between different regions led to a readjustment of the sector, especially under the macroeconomic control policy since mid-1993. In 1995, the Chinese legislature promulgated the Guaranty Law (*Danbaofa*) which provided a legal framework for bank mortgages to final buyers for real estate sales, which encouraged real estate developers to turn to local residents to develop a residential housing market. This move will increase the private ownership of residential housing units and lay the foundation for a mature secondary real estate market and a rental market.

Constrained Rural Land-Use Rights under the Household Responsibility System

The household responsibility system had two functions: to contract responsibility for food grain production and to distribute land according to population as a means of income distribution in terms of food supply. In this respect, the two- field system (*liangtian zhi*) fulfilled these objectives. Under this system, peasant households were allotted both subsistance fields (*kouliang tian*) and responsibility fields (*zeren tian*). The subsistence fields were allotted based on a principle of equity among all the members of the rural organization and the responsibility fields were allotted by contracts, based on a consideration of the number and the skill of the labourers in the household. Subsistence field allotments were a proxy for income distribution in rural China.

Under the household responsibility system, farmers possessed residual rights for arable land and residual claims for improved agricultural output value as a result of substantially improved output per hectare. Between 1979 and 1984, output value of grain and other economic crops increased as a free market for agricultural produce grew. With limited rights for the appropriation of land use, farmers managed to shift their efforts from grain to economic crop production in response to the changing price levels.

Efficiency of agricultural land use improved due to the relaxation of price controls over agricultural products and the emergence of a free market. But it was constrained by the immobility of land use for other purposes. Under the system, local governments played a passive role in the adjustment of land use allocation on a yearly basis or for longer periods. Through the agricultural procurement, cadres guaranteed a food supply for the urban areas.

In short, the first stage of the agricultural reform did not provide an incentive to the local governments to improve the efficiency of rural land use. Land-use efficiency was constrained by limited freedoms in agricultural production.

Economic development in the coastal cities, especially in the Pearl River Delta, has been characterized by industrialization — which was triggered by the influx of industrial processing from Hong Kong investors. Foreign investors were not subject to the land utilization restriction. The rapid changes in the use of agricultural land and the resultant problems raised the concern of the Chinese government.

Land Registration and Ownership

In 1984, China launched a nationwide rural land-use survey as a foundation for setting up a system of land registration. The survey was not completed until the State Land Administration Bureau was established in 1986. Primary land registration with the county bureau was finally completed in the early 1990s, based on the assignment of land use during the Land Reform in the 1950s and the implementation of the household responsibility system in the early 1980s.

During the 40 years of state planning, most of the urban land was appropriated to government administrative, social service, and business units. Under central planning, the central government could appropriate land to bureaux and enterprises in the urban areas. Village and township authorities controlled the majority of the unreclaimed land reserves in the rural areas. The new Land-Use Law and the economic reform put an end to the old system. Land-use appropriations are now subject to approval and to the payment of land-lease fees. The new system provides incentive to local governments to charge differentiated land-lease fees to different users.

Arable rural land was allocated to farmers under the household responsibility system. All rural land was collectively owned. In other words, the village government had major control over rural land use.

To clarify land ownership and use rights, the Land Administration Bureau issued guidelines for the implementation of the land registration in 1989:[5]

State-owned Land

1. Urban land, rural land which was not distributed to peasants during the Land Reform in the 1950s, such as arable land, waterways, mountains, etc.
2. Repossessed collectively-owned rural land used for state construction work;

3. Land used for public works, such as railways, highways, electricity, communication, and navigation projects;
4. Land leased for development uses;
5. Collectively-owned land after repossession and termination of use rights that was assigned to rural administrative institutions;
6. Properties on collective-land sold to state-owned units;
7. Collectively-owned land used for non-agricultural purposes and for which land-lease fees are paid;
8. Land taken from the peasants in 1962 and not yet returned to them;

Collectively Owned Land

1. Land distributed by land certificates issued to the peasants during the Land Reform;
2. Land utilized collectively in the village;
3. Collectively owned land which was utilized by other collectives for more than 20 years. In cases of less than 20 years, if the request comes from the original owner, the ownership is subject to a decision of the county government;
4. Land utilized for public infrastructure and facilities;
5. Land appropriated to collectives before 1962 and transferred between 1962 and 1982, with the transfer procedures properly completed and registered.

Use Rights of State-owned Land

In principle, land-use rights are assigned to the actual user, either the individual, unit, or collective, such as peasants, the army or the village. In the 1980s, overseas Chinese and religious units could request the return of land and properties which were confiscated or transferred without compensation. Landlords could maintain land-use rights even though the buildings on the land were occupied by tenants. Use rights do not change as long as the actual utilization remains the same. After 1988, use rights of state-owned land could be obtained by anyone after repossession and appropriation, by negotiation, by tender, or by auction, at a price charged by the government. Use rights of state-owned land can be extended up to 20 to 70 years.[6]

Use Rights of Collectively Owned Land

The difference between state-owned and collectively owned land is that collectively owned land is rural land mainly used by peasants or collective organizations for farming, for construction of public works and facilities, and for rural housing. The owners of properties on collectively owned land may have their land repossessed and re-distributed, with the compensation stipulated by law. If the land is re-allocated among members or organizations of the rural collective for agriculural purposes or for the construction of public works, no charges are levied on the transfer. When land-use rights are granted for non-agricultural use by non-members of the collective, such as for public construction by the state or for real estate development, the rural entitlement to the land must be surrendered to the State Land Bureau by repossessing the land from peasants. The collective must get approval and pay the bureau a land-lease price which is set at a rate according to the development plan.

The new Land-Use Law recognizes and authorizes the local government bureaux to exercise land appropriation rights. The land supply is thus in the hands of the local governments.

Real Estate Development

In the urban areas, land is appropriated by the state to public organizations or for the construction of buildings for administrative, economic, and social activities, or for staff housing. All buildings on the land appropriated free-of-charge through the state planning organs are owned by the state or state-owned institutions or business organizations. Housing provided by the institutions and organizations to their employees is also owned by the state. The institutions, business organizations, and residents have rights to the use of these business properties and residential housing units, but they do not have rights of transfer, of use of the properties for rental income or mortgage loans.

Economic reform and development have created excessive demands for property for various uses. Economic rents have emerged in prosperous locations. The Land-Use Law which prohibited the transfer of use rights cannot cope with this new development. As a result, an underground land and property market has developed.[7] Many government organizations and local administrations have breached this law, although the Ministry of Construction has firmly prohibited any illegal transfers. In 1989, the Ministry issued many decrees regarding the conditions and procedures for land-use transfer as temporary control measures.

In 1990, the Provisions on the Leasing and Transfer of State Land-Use Rights were implemented.[8] According to the provisional regulations, organizations and individuals with the right of use may be granted by the local governments the right to lease, to transfer, to let, or to mortgage their properties, subject to a tax payment to the State Land Administration Bureau. But these legal provisions have not stopped illegal market transactions because the government has placed controls on the transfer prices and rental rates. The real prices and rentals for transactions are much higher and flexible.

Economic growth has created a potential market for land and real estate development. The Chinese government strongly believes that economic rents should be levied by the government through taxation. In order to capture the yields, land and property development is monopolized by government enterprises. In 1990, state-owned urban construction enterprises were included under the control and management of state plans and budgets. The income tax from development enterprises is listed separately in the government revenue. Taxes and revenue from land and property development have become a major financial resource for the government. The proceeds are re-invested in the economy, resulting in an unprecedented increase in aggregate demand in the overheated economy.

The Land and Real Estate Management Structure

Before the economic reform, land-use planning was subordinate to production planning by government departments, social services organizations and state-owned enterprises. The Planning Commission approved the annual plan and appropriated land to different organizations for various uses. The recipients had land-use rights based on the plan. Land could not be transferred for alternate uses, nor could it be sold, or leased to other people or units. Once land was appropriated, it became an immobile factor.

In the late 1980s, both the Land-Use Law and the City Planning Act were implemented. To correct the problem of the immobility of land use, a land price was charged by the government for the transfer of land-use rights in lease contracts with a duration of up to 70 years. This replaced the prior free appropriation. In 1991, the "Ten-year Plan and the Eighth

Five-year Plan Outline for National Land Management (1991–2000)" was adopted. The outline laid down the principles for the land management system and the reform of the land-use system. It was planned that a five-level unified land management system would be established within 10 years. Land management administration bureaux were to be set up at the national, provincial, city, county, and village(township) levels. The Outline emphasized that the establishment of bureaux at the county, village, and township levels was crucial to the management system. They must maintain a standard number of engineers and a scale of investment capital to carry out co-ordination functions in planning, financing, and operations for development.

In 1994, a nationwide long-term general land-use plan was completed. At the same time, most of the urban areas had a city plan. Land was to be appropriated for public construction according to the City Outline Plan (*Chengshi zongti guihua gangyao*).[9]

The major government organizations in charge of land and real estate development are the Ministry of Construction, the State Land Administration Bureau, and the City Planning Bureau. The State Land Administration Bureau is responsible for land registration, land-use planning, land management legislation, and the administrative bureau for land repossession, land appropriation and land lease. In practice, the bureau represents the government in the collection of the land-lease and land-use fees. The proceeds are shared among the central, provincial, and local governments.

Since 1990, a Construction Land-Use Plan, which is part of the National Economic and Social Development Plan, has been prepared and implemented at four levels: state, province, city, and county. The plan was drafted by the State Land Administration Bureau and is approved by the State Planning Commission. Government organizations, central and local investing bodies involved in large projects, and military units may draft plans separately, and report to the Land Administration Bureau and Planning Commission. Repossession of arable land for construction is subject to direct planning controls. Other repossessions are subject to indicative planning. Construction land is defined as land assigned for the construction plans of the state, village, and township collective economic bodies, joint venture enterprises, and rural individuals, either for production activities, infrastructure, social services, or residential housing.

The functions of the Ministry of Construction include policy making, city planning, and oversight of the construction industry, the real estate industry, and public works. The Ministry is the major land management organization and developer. The City Planning Bureau, which is under the Ministry of Construction, was set up in 1990, after the implementation of the City Planning Act (Chengshi guihua fa) at the end of 1989. City outline plans are drafted by city, county, and township government bureaux and submitted and approved by the Standing Committee of the People's Congress at the same level. A City outline plan includes short-term plans of three to five years duration and long-term city development plans of up to 20 years. The annual Land-Use Plan of a city is required to conform with the approved city outline plan.[10]

The multi-agent structure in the management of land use and overall city planning has caused disputes among decision-making bodies. To co-ordinate the different bureaux, many local governments have combined the City Planning Bureau with either the State Land Administrative Bureau or the Construction Bureau. In practice, the local senior officials are the major decision makers for land and real estate investment projects of state-owned and collectively owned enterprises.

In the Land-Use Law, the village and township governments are given responsibility for the protection of land ownership, the prohibition of the illegal transfer of land-use rights, and the protection of arable land, especially for grain production. The land management institutes established in the village and township governments are responsible for the management of the land-use system, including land-use surveys on the area, quality, distribution, and appropriation of land in the region. Land-use rights, land valuation, and land-use transfers all fall under the land registration system.[11]

The village and township governments are responsible for the protection and utilization of natural resources. They must guarantee agricultural output, especially the food supply for the region, and protection of the environment. On the other hand, the overall economic achievement of the region is the major indicator by which the performance of the cadres is judged. Industrial and commercial development by enterprise investment and the transfer of arable land into non-agricultural uses, such as real estate development, may produce much more revenue than agricultural development. This revenue has greatly improved the public financial situation of the local governments. Cadres in the rural areas are under pressure to speed up the transfer of land use for industrial and real estate development because job opportunities in the non-agricultural sector improve the income level of the people. Since the early 1990s, China has experimented with more democratic elections for local government administrations. The political reform from below has reinforced the economic reform and development in the rural areas by majority voting.

In Guangdong province, an estimated 112,000 hectares of land were reclaimed and developed between 1988 and 1995. Since 1992, income derived from land and property development has accounted for 42.3% of the government revenue, and more than 10% of the provincial gross domestic product (GDP).[12]

Land and real estate development enterprises must be approved and registered with the government administration. The majority of domestic enterprises are either state-owned or collectively owned. In the transitional Chinese economy, there were no private developers because capital investment in the planned economy was impossible for private investors. Land was appropriated according to the state plan. Land and real estate enterprises are classified according to their capital outlay and the strength of their organizational structure and management, such as the number of engineers. For joint ventures with foreign capital, most are granted land and real estate development rights on a project basis. The success of land and real estate development enterprises depends on the availability of land. In other words, government organizations at the various levels with land ownership and land-use rights are the major land and real estate developers. Local enterprises are encouraged to form their own real estate firms in order to speed up development (Table 1).

Local governments are constrained by the scale of each development project and by the Land-Use Plan approved by the State Land Administration

Table 1. Real Estate Development by Ownership (1994)

Ownership		No. of firms (%)	Floor space completed (1,000,000m^2)	Residential housing (1,000,000m^2)
State-owned		11,939 (49.0)	304 (21.1)	172 (18.0)
Collective-owned	urban	5,478 (22.5)	44 (3.0)	21 (2.2)
	rural		252 (17.5)	42 (4.4)
Foreign-funded		1,231 (5.0)	17 (1.2)	7 (0.7)
Hongkong, Macau, Taiwan		3,456 (14.2)	8 (0.6)	42 (4.4)
Private and Others	urban	2,268 (9.3)	163 (11.3)	98 (10.2)
	rural		654 (45.4)	576 (60.1)
Total		24,372 (100)	1,442 (100)	958 (100)

Source: *Zhongguo tongji nianjian, 1995* (China Statistical Yearbook, 1995), pp. 138, 184.

Bureau. A project which requires a large area of land must be approved by higher authorities. This regulation allows the central and provincial governments to keep a check on the spatial development of the region.

In the rural areas, cadres of township and village governments actually possess allocative and distributive land rights. Based on the Constitution and the Land-Use Law, land which has already been owned and managed by rural residential committees or rural cooperatives can be *collectively* owned by the peasants. In principle, cadres in charge must reach a collective consensus for any change in land allocation and land use. In reality, through the process of land repossession, *individual* peasants or the land users surrender their land to the cadres in charge, and the cadres are authorized to appropriate land on behalf of the peasants in the collective. Rural cadres thus play two roles; they are in charge of all residents in the rural collective body, and therefore they are the decision makers for the repossession and appropriation of land for agricultural and non-agricultural use. In addition, they are land and real estate developers. In the repossession and development of land, government revenue from the leasing of land and real estate sales has increased while only negligible compensation has been paid to the peasants according to the law and local regulations.

Revenue Distribution and Pricing

The various fees, taxes, and charges for land and real estate development fall under four categories:

— land-lease price (*tudi chuzu jia*);
— taxes;
— fees;
— compensations to tenants or landlords, and peasants for land repossession.

Land-Lease Price

The price for land-use transfer from the state to the user, or the land-lease price, is subject to the identity of the land-use unit or person and the distribution of revenue among different government administrations.

The rationale for charging a lease price is to collect economic rent from land users. The charge includes a land development fee before the leasing and the expected economic rent derived from the development.

The revenue is distributed among governments at various levels — usually the central, provincial, city, and local governments. Land can be leased out for development by negotiation, by tender or by auction. In the past, negotiation was the major form of transfer of land-use rights. Tender and auction were not widely used. Transfer by negotiation allows for the assigning of land to desired users at discounted prices.

One of the explanations for the transfer of land use by negotiation and for charging a discounted price is that the payment from the state-owned land-use unit to the State Land Administration is actually an internal transfer of accounts. The low land-lease price may lower the costs of the land transfer and that means an increase in the revenue and profits for the development enterprises. A higher price for the land transfer means less working capital available for enterprises in the construction and development of the project. As a result, it may reduce the quality of the construction project and lower the market price of the property in the open market. In some cases, land and real estate development has been used to release state-owned enterprises and units from financial difficulties. The free appropriation of land or a low land-lease price can be regarded as a government subsidy to those units. It is a measure to relieve the government budget of its financial burdens[13] (Table 2).

The Guangdong experience of the past few years shows that land and real estate development has provided extra-budgetary revenue to senior local administrators, while the land-lease price has been shared by different levels of government and used for investment in the infrastructure. Restrictions in the distribution and utilization of revenue from land and real

Table 2. Revenue from Real Estate Development

(Unit: RMB 1,000,000)

Year	Total Revenue			Taxes	Profits
	Total	Land transfer fee	Property sales and rental		
1988	16,212	786	15,426	—	1,304
1989	17,951	747	17,204	—	786
1990	21,871	871	21,000	—	1,793
1991	28,403	1,538	26,865	2,055	2,752
1992	52,856	4,274	48,582	4,144	6,351
1993	113,591	8,392	105,199	9,659	15,592
1994	128,819	9,594	119,225	9,510	16,743

Source: *Zhongguo tongji nianjian, 1995*, p. 185.

estate development has resulted in land-use transfers by private negotiation instead of by open market tender and auction.

Taxes

There are many taxes charged for land and real estate development projects. The taxes can be divided into two types, i.e. economic rent for land use; and taxes applicable to all enterprises. Taxes imposed on land and real estate transactions are the land-lease price for land-use transfer and the capital gain tax for land and property sales. When land users are not local government units but investors from abroad, they are required to pay market prices. Profits from the resale of the land and property is subject to a capital gain tax at progressive rates. Land developers are not permitted to put undeveloped land on the market for resale. The objective is to prohibit speculation in land and property development. In practice, it is difficult for the government to implement this law and to define the capital gain from land and property transactions.

Land and real estate development enterprises are subject to other taxes, such as a sales tax, stamp duties, contributions to the infrastructure investment fund, state budget surcharges, city maintenance fees, and other taxes to be paid by all enterprises.

Fees

The Chinese government charges various specific and burdensome fees for services provided, such as a property registration fee, a notary fee, and a land-lease management fee, etc. The transaction costs in the collection of these services charges are high in terms of the time costs to the businessmen and administrative bureaux. At the same time, there are many government agencies involved in the process. These include bureaux in charge of foreign trade and economic cooperation, land administration, construction, industrial and commercial administration, and utilities, such as water and electricity suppliers. Any one of these units can create red tape to hinder efficient transactions.

Compensation to Tenants or Landlords, and Peasants

The repossession of urban and rural land for re-development is much more expensive as compared with the development of newly reclaimed land. If the developer is responsible for the compensation to the tenants and landlords of the urban land, or to the peasants in the rural areas, it may take a long period of time for the negotiations. There are many compensation fees to be levied, based on different categories of land use:

— land-use compensation fee
— plantation compensation fee
— labour resettlement fee
— rural household resettlement fee
— rural enterprise resettlement fee
— rural land facility compensation fee
— grain reduction compensation fee
— arable land repossession fee
— land reclamation fee
— vegetable land construction fee
— public housing construction fee for peasants

Disputes over compensation between land developers and occupants in the repossession of urban land are common due to differences between the existing rents and the expected returns on the land for alternative uses after re-development.

For the developer, compensation costs for land repossession can increase the total costs and delay the development project. In most cases, the local governments settle the compensation costs and transfer the collectively owned land into state-owned land by paying a land-use tax to the Land Administration Bureau. Land is then transferred to the investor for development.

Local Governments and the Evolution of Rural Land Use

After the promulgation of the Land-Use Law in 1986 and the amendments to the law and the Constitution in 1988, local government cadres interpreted the meaning of "collective ownership" to be allocative and distributive rights to land. In the Constitution and the Land-Use Law, land which was already owned and managed by residential committees or agricultural cooperatives was collectively-owned by the peasants. In the cooperative, cadres in charge of the local organizations were authorized the right of land appropriation. There are two stages involved in the process of changing the land use. First, the local governments repossess the land from the farmers and pay a land-use tax to the government land administrative body and pay compensation to the farmers. These two sums can be regarded as fixed costs, usually accounting for a negligible percentage of the value of the returns from the land after development. There are no barriers to land repossession, except that the area for each land development project is restricted by law by the local governments at different levels. Each land project for a village government cannot be larger than three *mu* (= 0.20 hectares). If a project requires a larger area, approval must be sought from higher authorities as stipulated by law. In the experience of the past few years, this law has not obstructed land and property development projects. In fact, the central government has issued orders prohibiting the violation of land-use approval procedures by local authorities.[14]

The first stage of land repossession is called the change in the land ownership. After the settlement of the taxes and other compensations, the rural land is transferred from the collective to the state. By law, the local government maintains power over the management of the use of the land. However, peasants in rural bodies cannot claim ownership, nor can they claim the rights of appropriation and a share of the returns.

After the payment of the taxes, the local government is empowered to lease out the land for development. At this stage, the local governments play a different role — that of forming real estate development enterprises. These enterprises are registered either as state-owned or collectively owned or in some cases, as joint ventures. Their capital is the repossessed land. They may lease out the land at market prices or at negotiated prices. Many of these enterprises develop the property for sale on the market. Profits are the margin between the market return from the newly developed project and the repossession costs. If the enterprise is state- or collective-owned, proceeds from the land and property development are turned over to the treasury of the local government. If it is an extra-budgetary unit or project, the local government is not required to share the proceeds with the central government. Many local authorities have "off-the-account" funds (*xiao jinku*). These are the major source of local capital funds for investment in industry, infrastructure, commerce, and property development. In return, cadres involved in the management of these newly formed state- or collective-owned enterprises receive relatively higher income and fringe benefits. This explains why local officials in the coastal cities refuse to be promoted to higher ranks or to be transferred to central government units. They prefer to be managers of local collective enterprises. Many of these land and property development enterprises are autonomous and have separate accounts which are not subject to surveillance and auditing by leading units in the budgetary process. In reality, only the mayor and a few senior officials in the hierarchy of the local governments have access to information about these accounts.

In estimating the revenue from land and property development in China, one has to take into account the taxes (value- added tax, income tax, etc.), the revenue from the leasing of land, and the profits from land and property enterprises. In 1994, the tax revenue from property development accounted for about 10% of the total revenue in Guangdong Province. Income from land and property development accounted for about 40% of the total local government revenue in the Pearl River Delta.

Under the new institutional structure for land use, local government officials have every incentive to speed up land and property development in order to skim the cream of the economic rent from improved land-use efficiency. From 1988 to 1993, the Pearl River Delta developed 88,000 hectares of land. Capital investment in land and properly development accounted for 20% of the total fixed capital investment in Guangdong province.

Decrease in Arable Land

Since the mid-1980s, agricultural production has been squeezed out of the Pearl River Delta. The area of arable land dropped from 2,750,000 hectares in 1980 to 2,320,000 hectares in 1994. Actually, many fertile areas have been turned into non-agricultural areas and, arable land has been replaced by newly reclaimed land and less fertile land. Yet, total agricultural output has increased, except for that of grain production. Total output value has increased because of the efficient use of arable land by farmers, who are now guided by market information.

Legal and administrative institutions have assigned rights of land appropriation, land repossession, and claims for residual revenue to local governments. The institutional setting indicates that the reduction of arable land in the Pearl River Delta has been inevitable.

At the national level, an absolute decrease in the area of arable land has been the result of distorted agricultural prices which are set by government policy. The drastic change in land use has been the result of a widening spread in the difference of returns from alternate land uses. The opportunity costs are too high for local governments to ignore them.

With the intervention of the central government, Guangdong is required to take measures to guarantee grain production. In 1994,

Guangdong passed a Basic Farmland Protection Law (*jiben nongtian baohu fa*) to safeguard 2,000 million hectares for agricultural production in the province. Of course, as long as price controls for food grains remain, the trend of shifting land use from grain crop to economic crop production cannot be reversed.[15]

The Emergence of Rural Share-holding Cooperatives

Rapid land and property development has produced conflicts between cadres and farmers regarding compensation and the distribution of proceeds from land repossession. Since 1991, small-scale riots and fights have been reported between rural residents (including farmers who surrendered their land) and cadres in charge of rural organizations, such as township governments, village residents' committees, and villagers' cooperatives. Peasants have accused the cadres of a lack of transparency in the accounts of the collectives. They have complained of no say in decision-making, no role in supervision, and the lack of an effective auditing system. Cadres are tempted by corruption throughout the entire land leasing and real estate development process. Most important, many villagers believe that they own the property rights of the rural land and are entitled to share the residual returns from development. Their claims have no legitimate grounds, yet their concerns have alarmed the local and central governments.

In 1988, there were experiments with a new form of rural administrative organization in a small village in Shenzhen. It was called a rural share-holding cooperative system (*nongcun gufen hezuo zhi*). The new system was tentatively adopted by the Ministry of Agriculture in 1990.

In 1993, some villages in Guangdong cities, such as Nanhai, Dongguan, and Panyu, and in Shandong were chosen to organize and implement the new rural administrative organization and management system.[16] These villages were more developed and industrialized. Most of the residents have become workers and businessmen. They have hired immigrant labour to do the farming for them. With the formation of the new share-holding economic cooperatives, all local residents are shareholders. Their holdings depend mainly on family head counts and age. In some cases, the amount of arable land originally allocated under the household responsibility system is taken into consideration. However, the direct conversion of land into shares is prohibited by the government.

Under this system, rural residents are given the choice to do farming on contracted areas by negotiation. Or they can hire workers to do the farm work. Those residents who work for village and township enterprises may surrender their land to the collective. Cadres in collectives may re-allocate land for alternate uses, such as for infrastructure, for the building of industrial plants, or for real estate development, according to the city plan. Farm land can be re-distributed to other farmers in order to achieve economies of scale, or can be leased out to people from other parts of China and overseas. Proceeds from changes in land use are put into the cooperative pool. Shareholders receive dividends from the total revenue of the cooperative. Income for the collective, and thus dividends for the members, increases as the property price goes up. Under this organizational structure, farmers are alienated from the land which was originally appropriated for farming. Yet all members of the village have a claim over the returns, according to their shares. The new system pacifies peasant discontent in the collective and avoids the "hold-out" problem, i.e. a refusal to surrender land. For the local governments, officials who are appointed as executive members in the cooperatives are given a free hand to re-allocate land resources for more efficient use.

There are several advantages to this organizational structure and its management. First, land appropriation is more efficient. With the shortage of labour in the industrialized and urbanized Pearl River Delta, the cooperative recognises the property rights of local residents and farmers concerned in the distribution system. A lack of confidence regarding political and policy stability is common among the rural population. Farmers tend to protect their land and rural membership by the household registration system (*hukou zhidu*), although they no longer work in the fields and their land is underutilized or idle. In the new rural cooperative, land is pooled together for leasing, either to local or to immigrant farmers — in many cases, to Hong Kong investors to grow vegetables for the Hong Kong market. Second, land-lease contracts encourage large-scale production and modern management farming methods. Productivity and economic efficiency can be improved under this new arrangement. Management by the cooperative allows for more efficient planning and investment in the infrastructure, such as irrigation and transportation. The spatial re- allocation of land use and the city plan are beneficial to environmental protection. In addition, the new rural organization may speed up an adjustment in land use for the economic transformation from agricultural production to industrialization and urbanization.

The new rural share-holding co-operative has settled the disputes between the rural government officials and the peasants over compensation for land repossession, and over the distribution of income from land and property development. By holding shares instead of arable land, peasants are entitled to returns from the overall performance of the investment by the cooperative. With rapid economic growth, villagers receive relatively high dividend payments which are based on the total profits of the collectively owned business. The new system allows rural cadres more freedom and reduces barriers to land development, including real estate development.

In the new rural organizational structure, local government officials play the role both of government and of manager of the rural share-holding cooperative. The operation of the cooperative is subject to supervision by the government at a higher level. This new relationship between peasants and the cooperative represents progress in clarifying the rights of land use. For the local government officials, the new cooperative provides them with more resources for appropriation, including land and capital. A very large proportion of the returns from their investments are re-invested, mainly in the infrastructure. In 1994, infrastructure investments accounted for 40% of the gross fixed capital investment in Guangdong. This explains the dramatic improvement in the provincial infrastructure.

The rural institutional experimental reforms in the Pearl River Delta can only be implemented in developed regions of the country. In the remote areas, the unemployment of the rural surplus labour, due to the change in the relationship between land and farmers — from actual cultivators to shareholders entitled to returns — may cause instability.

Financing Urban Land and Real Estate Development

The pressure for urban renewal and development due to the success of the economic reform and development increased in the mid-1980s, especially in the coastal and major cities of China. Shenzhen Special Economic Zone was the first city to institutionalize an organizational structure for land and real estate development. In addition to the free appropriation of land through economic planning, negotiated land-leasing was widely used. Tender and auction were introduced with some reservations. The reason for this was that the government units were the major land users. High land-lease prices reduce the operating funds available for the government to implement their projects.

After the free appropriation of land in the planned economy for more than 40 years, most, if not all, land in the major cities had been allocated to different parties, government bureaux, social and business organizations. The use of the appropriated land was restricted by state regulation. Organizational and individual occupants were not required to pay for the land or for property-use rights by leasing. There were no financial channels for capital accumulation for on-going development.

The economic reform brought about a demand for land, offices, factories, and residential housing for investors and households. Restrictions in the transfer of land-use rights forced people to resort to the underground market for land sales and rental arrangements.

The Land-Use Law legally recognized land and property transactions and rental markets. Assets and revenue of land-holding organizations and local authorities immediately increased through land and real estate development. The performance of land and real estate enterprises relied on the supply of land by the local governments. In return, local governments could finance investment in the infrastructure with receipts from this sector.

At first, land and real estate development projects began in the Pearl River Delta as a means of attracting foreign capital. This was a major economic activity in the region during the 1990s' real estate market boom in Hong Kong. The increase in demand for property for industrial, commercial, and residential uses was due to the economic surge after Deng Xiaoping's visit to the south. Local cadres discovered that it was easy to derive revenue from land sales and real estate development and this revenue was significantly higher than that from any other activities. In some areas, such as Wenzhou, Shenzhen, and Zhuhai, land and real estate development has become the major financial source for the local governments. Hong Kong investors who cannot afford the high prices in the Hong Kong market, have invested in the Pearl River Delta instead. Thus capital has poured into the region. Local governments which have been the major developers have re-invested the revenue from land sales into the further development of land repossession and real estate projects.

In order to encourage land and property development, the People's Construction Bank of China started to extend bank loans to development projects of up to 30% of their total investment. In 1992, the State Council issued a circular on the management of land and real estate markets. Investment capital for land and real estate development was included in the total fixed capital investment planning quota. Foreign capital for real estate projects was not restricted and local authorities were given autonomy to approve self-financed projects. Specialized banks were given authority to extend land and real estate development funds, within the credit control quotas. Bank loans, and security and bond issues were required to be listed in government credit control plans, subject to the macro control policy of the State Council.

In 1993, the macro control policy did not affect the total investment in land and real estate development in the major cities in China as foreign capital kept pouring into the country. Hong Kong financial institutions and individuals were the major sources of this funding. Other measures were borrowed from Hong Kong, such as sales arrangements before completion to boost demand for properties located in the Pearl River Delta and Shanghai. But the People's Bank of China imposed further stringent control quotas on financial institutions, including all specialized banks, regional banks, commercial banks, and city credit cooperatives. Shortages of working capital caused setbacks for many development projects, including joint ventures.

The macro control policy has not only reduced the investment capital in land and real estate development, but has also reduced the purchasing power for property. In China, most of the domestic buyers and tenants of real estate are institutional organizations, mainly state-owned and collective-owned enterprises. Their planning, and investment activities are under the surveillance of their supervisory bodies and co-ordinating organizations, such as the State Planning Commission and the central bank. Many of their projects have been frozen; land and real estate development has topped the list of those projects to be adjusted.

The slide in the market demand for property in China has also been affected by the downward adjustment of the property market in Hong Kong. The upward trend of the international interest rate since early 1994 has pulled international capital away from Hong Kong and China.

Demand for Housing

In 1985, an urban housing survey projected the total urban population would reach 351,971,000 by the year 2000 and the projected increase in the urban housing area was around 200 million square metres per year.[17] The total urban population had reached 343,010,000 by the end of 1994, according to the State Statistical Bureau. In other words, the actual growth of the urban population had been greater than the 1985 projection. The proportion of the urban population has increased from 23.71% to 28.62% of the total population in the past 10 years.

The household registration system collapsed after the economic reform and the development of the rural economy. The surplus labour from the agricultural sector became workers in the industrial and service sectors, by migrating into cities within or outside their provinces. The migrant population added to the growth of the urban population and increased pressure for housing in the cities.

The success of the rural reform led to the construction boom in the 1980s. The government does not provide rural housing. Local rural residents may build their own housing. In 1994, more than 64% of the total completed residential floor space was privately owned housing for rural residents. State and collective development firms provided about 25% and foreign investors provided about 11% of the housing development (see Table 1).

Urbanization and industrialization in the Pearl River Delta has led to a demand for housing in suburban areas and in new towns. Many rural residents have obtained urban citizenship (*nongzhuanfei*) and they prefer urban flats with modern facilities and convenient locations over their rural residences by the farming land (*zhaijide*). In the 1990s, a demand for township flats has replaced that for rural farm houses in rich villages. Housing policy has become one of the concerns of the village and township governments.

When residents are required to buy their own flats at full price, their demands for residential units have been limited by their purchasing power.

The new Land-Use Law which recognized free land and real estate transfer rights provided an incentive to invest in real estate. People in coastal and urban areas have increased their per capita income and savings and thus have become potential buyers in the new real estate market.

Urban Housing Reform

In 1988, China experimented with an adjustment in the rental of urban housing. Several approaches were adopted in experimental cities. The first step of the reform was to provide in-kind housing benefits to employees with their wages. The second step was to pay rental subsidies and other cash subsidies as part of their wages. The objective was to put the housing subsidies on to the payroll. Another approach was to encourage employees to purchase their living quarters at a discount. This approach was limited by the availability of land and capital for the building of staff quarters.

According to the survey on the demand for urban housing, China must build over 200 million square metres of floor area per year. In 1994, an average building cost about RMB800/m². The annual investment fund required was RMB 160 billion, which accounted for 10% of the total fixed capital investment. In 1994, total investment in fixed assets by urban state-owned and collectively owned units was RMB 43.3 billion, of which only 30% was invested in the building of 293 million square metres of housing area. In addition, floor space supplied by private and external capital reached 765 million square metres. In 1993 and 1994, investment in land and real estate development had absorbed the major share of the capital funds (see Table 1).

Most of the residential housing supplied by the state-owned and collective-owned firms was purchased by state-owned and collective-owned units for their own staff. In fact, the state-owned and collective-owned units have been the major sources of development funds and there have been limited financial options available. The purchase of residential housing by instalment has not been widely practised due to credit controls by the central bank. Private investment provided for about 80% of the residential space in 1994. In 1995, the new Guaranty Law made the purchase of residential housing by mortgage possible in the future.

Regional Commodity Housing Development

The supply of commodity housing accompanied the emergence of the real estate market. The major investors were Hong Kong individuals and local governments. For Hong Kong investors, the real estate supply in the Pearl River Delta was a supplement to or an extension of the Hong Kong market. The local governments in the coastal cities also found that the sale of land for development was easy money to improve the investment environment. In 1994, government revenue from land and real estate development reached RMB 128 billion, accounting for 25% of the total revenue of China (Table 3). In Guangdong, land and real estate development made up 42.3% of the total government revenue in 1992, or 10% of the total GDP of the province.[18] In fact, income from real estate development has been a major source of extra-budgetary revenue for the local governments. Many

Table 3. Real Estate Development by Region (1994)

Region	No. of Firms	Total revenue (real estate development) (RMB1,000,000)	Floor space sold (commodity housing) (1,000 m²)	Sales value (commodity housing) (RMB1,000,000)
National	24,372	128,818	72,303	101,849
Guangdong	4,080	34,459	10,299	26,882
Shanghai	2,081	11,354	1,656	3,461
Jiangsu	1,629	10,843	7,960	9,589
Liaoning	1,127	8,976	5,677	7,733
Zhejiang	1,166	8,613	6,977	7,734
Beijing	81	7,640	1,686	6,038
Shandong	1,465	7,446	7,080	6,772
Fujian	1,279	5,315	2,413	4,463
Sichuan	1,502	4,287	4,018	3,546
Heilongjiang	345	2,757	1,677	2,702

Source: *Zhongguo tongji nianjian, 1995*, pp. 184–86.

local governments in the hinterland have followed the example of the coastal cities by establishing development zones. But because of logistic and locational barriers, the move has led to financial difficulties.

In 1995, the development of the real estate sector was still under the strict control of the central government. At the same time, efforts have been made with respect to the institutional set-up of the real estate market for efficient and fair operations. During the year, the Chinese government established a qualification system to govern real estate appraisers and official translation issued regulations governing real estate transfers in urban areas. The Guaranty Law provided legal support for future real estate mortgages. These are important moves which lay the foundation for the development of a secondary real estate market in China.

Conclusion

Since 1986, China has successfully revamped the institutional structure and the management of the land and real estate sector. Land has been mobilized as a factor of production and its development has strengthened local public finances for economic growth. In the process of the reform, the Chinese government has built up a mechanism to assure the efficient use of land for various purposes, i.e. agricultural production and food supply, infrastructure, and housing construction. Land and real estate development organizations are owned and managed mainly by government organizations. Laws, regulations, and policies have been enacted to enable the government to re-allocate the efficient use of land and to impose macroeconomic control measures on the growth rate of the sector.

The Chinese government has taken advantage of the property market boom in Hong Kong in the early 1990s. This has enabled the government to accumulate development funds to finance public sector operations by developing a land and real estate market without rapid ownership reforms. The banking laws which aim at transforming the specialized banks into commercial banks and allowing home mortgage bank loans have provided a mechanism for bank financing and have encouraged real estate transactions among developers, business organizations, and individuals. As urban housing reforms expand, there will be more supplies on the primary and the secondary real estate markets. As long as the economy maintains its growth momentum and as labour mobility increases, the Chinese land and real estate market will mature and become more competitive, thus playing an important role in the economy.

The Chinese objective of building up a real estate market under government control has been achieved. The leasing of land and real estate development have created a market environment for the free transfer of property rights. When the market has sufficient institutional and financial support, private development and transactions will emerge as a significant force in the sector.

Notes

1. Alan Bertaud and Bertrand Renaud, *Cities Without Land Markets, Lessons of the Failed Socialist Experiment*, World Bank Discussion Paper, No. 227 (1994), pp. 1–8. Because China has a shorter history of a socialist economy, major cities, such as Shanghai, have been able to build on their market bases. Since the reform, the population density at the city centre has produced constraints for economic development.

2. The World Bank, *China: Urban Land Management in an Emerging Market Economy* (Washington DC: The World Bank, 1993), p. xi. This author agrees with the following from the World Bank report: "Control, rather than the introduction of market mechanisms, became a primary driving force behind urban land 'reform'."

3. According to Huang Qinghe and He Daofeng, in their papers on the evolution of the rural land system and policy in *Zhongguo tudi zhidu de biange* (Evolution of the Rural Land System in China), 1993, pp. 17–18, 33–37, survey results show that rural land was equally distributed on head count basis in about 70% of the villages; in less than 5% it was distributed based on to the labour force, and 25% it was distributed based on both the head count and the labour force. Land of different grades was distributed separately to ensure that every member or household had arable land of both good and poor quality.

4. According to Clause 38 of the Land-Use Law and the regulations regarding the requirements for application: children of rural households who have reached marriage age and who do not have a separate room and where the building of an addition is impossible. Approval of the application must comply with the annual town planning quota. Also see Chen Shunzeng (ed.), *Nongcun zhaijidi guanli shouce* (Rural Residential Land Management Handbook) (Beijing: Zhongguo laodong chubanshe, 1992), pp. 13, 65–66.

5. According to the decree of the State Land Administration Bureau, *Guanyu queding tudi quanshu wenti de ruogan yijian* (Opinions on the Identification of Land Ownership Rights), No. 73 (1989).

6. The regulation was first spelled out in Clause 12 of *Chengshi guojia tudi shiyongquan zulin he zhuanrang zhanxing tiaoli* (Provisions on the Leasing and Transfer of Urban State Land-Use Rights, (1990).

7. Institute of Finance and Trade Economics, Chinese Academy of Social Sciences, and Institute of Public Administration, New York (ed.), *Zhongguo tudi shiyong yu guanli* (Urban Land Use and Management in China (Beijing: Jingji kexue chubanshe, 1994), pp. 154–211.

8. See Note 5.

9. According Order No. 14 by the Ministry of Construction, *Chengshi guihua bianzhi banfa* (City Planning Guidelines, 1991).

10. Clause 29 of the City Planning Act, 1989.

11. Chang Xuenian, *Xiangzhen xingzheng guanli* (Village and Township Administrative Management) (Beijing: Jingji kexue chubanshe, 1990), p. 114.

12. Y. W. Sung, P. W. Liu, Richard Y. C. Wong and P. K. Lau, *The Fifth Dragon: the Emergence of the Pearl River Delta* (Singapore: Addison Wesley, 1995), p. 164.

13. See Note 7, pp. 73–75.

14. For example, in January 1990, the State Council issued a decree from the State Land Administration Bureau on "*Guanyu bufen difang zhengfu yuequan pidi qingkuang baogao*" (Report on Land-Use Approval Violations by Some Local Governments). In the report, a survey of 24 provinces and regions showed that there were 97,000 cases of land-use approval violations in 1987 and 1988.

15. See Note 7, pp. 154–211.

16. Zhang Tingyan and Liao Fuzhou (eds.), *Gufen hezuo jingji de lilun yu shijian* (Theory and Practice of the Share-holding Cooperative Economy) (Henan: Henan renmin chubanshe, 1994). The book includes elaborate details about the new rural system. Model and sample texts of regulations and statutes from local governments in Guangdong are presented.

17. World Bank Report, *Zhongguo chengzhen zhufang gaige de wenti yu fang'an* (China: Problems and Scenario for Urban Housing Reform) (Beijing: Zhongguo caizheng jingji chubanshe, 1992), pp. 24–25.

18. Sung, et al. (Note 11), p. 164.

10

The Reform of
the State-owned Enterprises

Chi-Wen Jevons Lee

Introduction

Although their importance in the national economy has been declining over the past two decades, state-owned enterprises (SOEs) still play a crucial role in China's economy. In 1995, 17% of all industrial firms were SOEs. About 60% of profit taxes collected by the Ministry of Finance come from SOEs. China has 77,000 state-owned business organizations which are independent accounting and legal entities. Of these, 14,000 units are large and medium-sized enterprises.

Restructuring SOEs is a critical part of the economic reform in China. One of the burning issues related to restructuring SOEs is their widespread haemorrhaging losses. According to the State Statistical Bureau, 42.2% of SOEs were in the red. Losses in the frist 11 months of 1995 for all SOEs amounted to RMB 40 billion, which was about 25% of the net output of the industrial sector. Premier Li Peng mentioned in his report to the People's Congress in March 1995 that restructuring SOEs was the most important task of his economic policy.

In this chapter, we will first illustrate the characteristics of China's SOEs. A brief survey of history can shed light on the evolution of SOEs since 1949. Based on the characteristics of China's SOEs and their history, I will analyse three important issues related to the reform of SOEs in China: their haemorrhaging losses, corruption, and the financial crisis.

China's State-owned Enterprises

China's state-owned enterprises have many special characteristics primarily arising from the transition from a centralized planned economy toward a socialist market economy.

Ageing Facility

Under the planned economic system, most large SOEs are virtual monopolies. They are protected from international as well as from domestic competition. Ageing facility may produce low quality output, but it may not affect SOE's survival. On the other hand, most operation surplus is extracted by the central government. Even though SOEs would like to renovate and expand, they may not be able to find necessary resources to do so.

Ageing Workers

For the past half century since the People's Republic of China (PRC) was established, labour mobility has been essentially nil. The socialistic system requires SOEs to take their workers from cradle to grave. The recent economic boom in the far less regulated and less protected non-SOE sector attracts young workers straight out of schools. The stagnant SOEs have no capacity to hire the young. Consequently, the increasingly ageing labour force in the SOE sector in comparison to the non-SOE sector is inevitable.

Heavy Burden of Social Services

SOEs' cradle-to-grave responsibility for their workers implies the heavy burden of social services. Many large SOEs act the dual role of government and enterprise in company towns. To play the role of government, the SOE meets the social need at the cost of profit-seeking. To play the role of enterprise and to succeed in the increasingly competitive market place, the SOE must concentrate on profit-maximization. Separating the role of providing social services from normal business operation is an important step to modernize SOEs.

An Important Part of Labour and Management Compensation Is Implicit in Nature

A major part of social services is the implicit compensation to labour and management. Due to its unobservability, the implicit wage is usually unfair, inefficient, and trouble-prone. The implicit labour and management compensation is part of the cost of running normal business. We need to estimate these numbers and incorporate them into the costing process. Without a formal accounting system to take account of these implicit items, distortion of resources allocation is inevitable.

Decision Flow: Top to Bottom

In a planned socialist economy, the flow of economic decision is from the top to the bottom. The economic information generated at bottom is *ex post* in nature, a simple record keeping. Since this information is often used for performance evaluation, the *ex post* information generated at the bottom may be distorted by low level managers. The economic decision made at the top, which is based on the distorted information, can be misguided. Because the low level managers are required to follow the order from the top, managers at the bottom do not use available information in managerial decision. Information collected by the managers at the top is useless for performance evaluation and policy making.

Monitoring and Control: Centralized, Inefficient and Ineffective

The organization in China's SOEs is highly hierarchical.[1] Monitoring and control are centralized at the top. Due to the heavy loss of information as a result of multi-layer communication in a hierarchical structure, for a monitoring and control system to be effective, they have to be rigid and tight. The tight and rigid control leads to inefficient production/investment decisions. If the monitoring system gives low level managers flexibility and independence, the control cannot be effective.

Transition from a Factory in a Planned Economy to a Modern Business in a Market Economy

Before 1979, most SOEs were single-product factories under tightly controlled central planning. Labour costs were fixed. No migration was allowed. All raw materials were allocated by a central planning agency and all output were distributed by government-specified quota. Most operating funds were budgeted from the top. The chief executive officer (CEO) of an SOE was simply a factory foreman/engineer in charge of delivering the output according to quota. The acquisition of raw materials, the marketing of the output and the securing of the financial resources for operation were not the CEO's primary concern. In a modern business, marketing and financing play a central role in strategic management. Most CEOs of SOEs are ill-equipped to handle this task.

A Brief History of Enterprises' Reform

Before the economic reform initiated by Deng Xiaoping in 1978, SOEs were the core of the Chinese economy, especially in the industrial sector. In 1978, SOEs represented 24% of all manufacturing firms in China and produced 80.8% of national industrial output. The typical problems of pre-reform SOEs can be summarized in a few memorable metaphors: "Iron

Rice Bowl," "Big Rice Pot," and "No Matter What You Do, You Get 36 (RMB per month)." The manager had no managerial discretion, the worker had no incentive to work, and the production was at the technical minimum. Under the leadership of Deng Xiaoping, the 3rd Plenum of the 11th Central Committee of the Chinese Communist Party took a series of sweeping reform measures.[2]

The series of economic policies to adjust the relationship between the government and the enterprises can be essentially summarized as "let power go and set profit free," that is, in a more professional terminology, decentralization and incentive enhancement. The experiment of enterprise autonomy began in Sichuan. By 1979, the experiment was extended to 4,200 enterprises in the whole country. The experiment allowed enterprise autonomy on implementing the economic plan set by the central government, marketing and sales, and reinvestment. Moreover, each enterprise was allowed to keep a given percentage of profits for reinvestment.

The Chinese State Council initiated the "economic responsibility system" in 1981. State administrative agencies set a profit target for each enterprise to submit to the Ministry of Finance. For profits above this target, the SOE could keep the majority (often all) for reinvestment and employee benefits. The other important new economic policy in 1981 was the introduction of a taxation system, the so-called "converting the profit submission to taxation" policy. Under this policy, the SOE needed to pay a fee for the use of financial capital and to pay sales tax.

In 1983, the State Council introduced the "uniform income tax." All profits were taxed at a 55% rate. Part of the after-tax profits were submitted to the government for its role as the owner of the enterprise. In 1985, the State Council established a new policy to rationalize the use of state financial resources — "converting fund allocation to bank loans." Before 1978, all SOE's working capital and investment funds had been allocated by the government. After 1978, the SOE gradually took the full responsibility for working capital. After the policy of "converting fund allocation to bank loans," the SOE needed to borrow from banks for long-term and infrastructural investments. Although these loans were often highly subsidized, the cost of capital became an important consideration in the SOE's investment decision.

During the first decade of economic reform, the SOE went through various types of restructuring to adjust to the new economic environment. The most successful and widely adopted restructuring model was the "contract responsibility system." Under this system, the government and the

SOE found a way to define the new relationship in terms of rights, responsibilities and economic interests. A primitive enterprise autonomy took hold. A typical contract responsibility system took the form of "two guarantees and one link." The SOE guaranteed to submit the contracted amount of profits to the government and guaranteed to implement the contracted level of reinvestment and technological improvement. After fulfilling these contracted obligations, the manager of the SOE had the autonomy to operate the firm. Moreover, the government encouraged the linking of the SOE employee compensations and benefits to the enterprise's profits. By 1987, 90% of SOEs' operations had adopted some sorts of contract responsibility system. In 1991, most SOEs took the second contract with the government under the contract responsibility system.

In August 1991, the Ministry of Finance and the State Economic Reform Commission jointly announced the policy of "separation of taxes and profits," following the modern practice that the SOE needed to pay tax first and then use the after-tax profits for reinvestments, loan payments, and returns to the ownership. In 1994, the People's Congress passed the Corporation Law. The State Council selected 87 SOEs as restructuring experiments under the Corporation Law.

The policy of "let power go and set profit free" gradually allowed the enterprise to pursue market opportunities, while fulfilling the assigned obligation under the central economic plan. A dualistic market system grew out from the old socialistic system. The number of product items completely under the control of State Planning Commission was reduced from 120 in 1979 to about 50 in 1995. The number of products and materials items allocated by the central government was reduced from 125 in 1979 to about 20 in 1995. The share of planned economy in the total economic system fell to below 30%.[3] The rise of the market sector and the decline of the planned sector created several problems for SOEs:

1.   The dualistic price and market system created arbitrage opportunity, which led to rampant corruption.
2.   The new market opportunities were quickly seized by the township and village enterprises (TVEs) and foreign-invested enterprises. The industrial output share of SOEs fell from 77.6% in 1979 to barely 40% in 1994.
3.   For reasons analysed above, many SOEs faced losses. About 40% of SOEs reported losses in October 1995.

In March 1995, the 3rd Meeting of the 8th National People's Congress elected the former mayor of Shanghai, Wu Bangguo, as the vice-premier in charge of industry. China's industry policy made a subtle turn. During 1991–1994, some SOEs went through drastic restructuring and transformation under the leadership of Vice-Premier Zhu Rongji. Many SOEs took inital public offerings (IPO) and listed their stocks in Shanghai, Shenzhen and Hong Kong. In a public interview on 18 January 1995,[4] Zhu announced that he planned to implement a large scale lay-off and bankruptcy policy to shake off those hopeless SOEs. Wu took a more careful and slower approach to economic reform. As 1995 came to an end, the focus of policy moved away from lay-off and bankruptcy toward strengthening the current organization structure and finding a way for survival. In 1995, the government chose 161 SOEs in 18 cities to go through a bankruptcy process, which involved 50,000 workers, RMB 1.8 billion in assets and RMB 3.2 billion in liabilities. This policy of "let small fries go, hold big fish tight" will continue in 1996.

As a part of the Ninth Five-Year Plan, China initiated a "hundred, thousand, ten-thousand" plan to restructure SOEs. In 1994, the State Council identified 100 SOEs for restructuring experimentation. This experiment will be expanded to 10,000 SOEs toward the end of the decade. The four guiding principles of restructuring and reform are: (1) to clarify the property rights; (2) to specify rights and responsibilities; (3) to separate the government and the enterprise; and (4) to introduce scientific management methods.

Haemorrhaging Losses of SOEs

The mounting losses of SOEs became the most troublesome economic issue in China in 1995. It was so important and dangerous that President Jiang Zemin visited northeast provinces and southern provinces in summer to reiterate the central government's resolution to face this issue head on and shore up support for necessary SOE reform. At the National Economic Reform Conference in December 1995, the reform of SOEs was listed as the most important task of economic policy.

Table 1 provides a few aggregate statistics to illustrate the severity of SOE losses. The inflation rate, according to the consumer price index (CPI) for the first 11 months of 1995 was 17.7% and the inflation rate according to the retail price index (RPI) was 15.4%. The net industrial output grew only 12.1%, a decline of 5.6% if adjusted by CPI and a decline

Table 1. Key Statistics on China's Industrial Enterprises at the End of October 1995

Items	Amount (RMB billion)	Annual change rate (%)
Industrial value-added	164	12.1
Consumer price index	—	17.7
Retail price index	—	15.4
Fixed asset investment	909.1	17.5
Infrastructure investment	513.2	19.5
Account receivable	773.8	25.1
Inventory	470	38.2
Number of industrial enterprises	378,000	—
Percentage of industrial firms in loss	24.1%	6.2
Percentage of state-owned enterprises in loss	42.2%	2.7
Loss of industrial enterprises	79.1	32.2
Loss of state-owned enterprises	40	14.7

Source: State Statistical Bureau of China.

of 3.3 % if adjusted by RPI. While fixed asset investment and infrastructure investment stayed essentially flat in real terms, account receivable increased by 25.1% in nominal terms and increased by 7.4% in real terms adjusted by CPI. Inventory increased by 38.2% in nominal terms and increased by an alarming 20.5% in real terms adjusted by CPI. Officially, 42.2% of SOEs reported losses. Many unofficial sources indicate that about one-third of SOEs that reported profits were actually in the red.

The State Council conducted a large scale survey about the SOEs and reported the results on 11 November 1995. They sent out 9,000 questionaires to all types of enterprises and got 2,752 returns, with an effective return rate of 30.5%. The questionaires were answered by the representatives of the legal entity (i.e., the CEOs). Table 2 lists the justification of losses given by the CEOs of SOEs. The State Council asked each CEO to identify three major reasons for losses. Of the CEOs, 59.6% pointed the finger to the heavy burden of social services; 50.5% blamed the failure on poor internal organizaton structure; 36.4% thought the heavy historical burden might be a major problem. The major historical burdens were surplus labour and retired workers. Most of the Western scholars, including those in Hong Kong, have suggested that the core of SOE problems in a socialist country like China is the ambiguous property rights and the lack of enterprise autonomy.[5] Interestingly, only 25% of CEOs of China's SOEs agreed with this diagnosis.

Table 2. Manager's Justification of Losses in State-owned Enterprises

Justification	Percentage of managers naming it as one of top three reasons
Heavy burden of social services	59.6
Poor internal organization structure	50.5
Heavy historical burden	36.4
Bad management	31.1
Heavy tax burden	27.6
Ambiguous property rights	25.2
Lack of autonomy	24.3
Obsolete technology and equipment	23.4
Poor employee structure	13.7

Source: China Enterprises Survey System, State Council.

The monitoring and control system of the SOEs in a socialist country is costly and ineffective. The manager of the SOE is an agent of the administrative department. The officer of the administrative department is an agent to the State Council. Without a democratic balloting system, the only monitor and control mechanism at the State Council level is the political infighting and rivalry among the big-wigs. Even without "letting power go and setting profit free," the monitoring and control mechanism cannot assure an efficient operation of SOEs. Once autonomy is given to SOE managers, it becomes very difficult to prevent managerial rent-seeking behaviour.[6] A major reason of mounting SOE losses is this rent-seeking behaviour. Naturally, the manager would never admit such behaviour. However, I have an interesting piece of evidence.

The data in Table 3 were collected from the same State Council survey as that in Table 2. The SOEs reported a 28.7% increase in employee compensation in 1995, a growth of 10% in real income adjusted by CPI. In

Table 3. Annual Increase Rate of Employee Income Reported at the End of October 1995

Type of enterprises	Increase rate (%)
State-owned	28.7
Collectives	27.3
Private	18.2
Foreign capital (*sanzi* enterprises)	17.5
Mixed	26.0
87 state-owned enterprises on reform experiment	26.9

Source: China Enterprises Survey System, State Council.

the highly competitive and efficient sector of the Chinese economy, the private and the foreign-invested enterprises, the nominal income increase was about 18%, and the real income increase was about zero. It is obvious that SOE managers tried very hard to improve their employees' as well as their own welfare at the expense of the state.[7]

Corruption and State Assets Drain

An obvious and ruthless rent-seeking behaviour is corruption. Most of the corruption can be classified into six categories.

1. Use insider's information to speculate on real estate and stocks.
2. Turn state-owned assets into collective assets. Turn collective assets into private assets. Then, find a way to transfer these assets outside China.
3. Use family connection (that of parents, spouse or relatives) to get special business licenses or privileges.
4. Cover-up for each other, suppress complaints and plug the leak.
5. "Eat the state." Use state funds for luxurious meals, travels and entertainment.
6. Manipulate financial reports and create false performance so as to get career promotion.

China's judicial system reported 94,785 cases of corruption and economic crimes in 1994, which involved 131,703 government (including SOE) employees.[8] The corruption was so widespread that President Jiang Zemin himself took charge of this issue to make sure that corruption would not bring down the regime.

The two most famous SOE managerial corruption cases in 1995 were the Shougang Holdings (Hong Kong) Ltd. and the Guizhou International Trust Investment Corporation. The former is a good example of how a son used his father's position and influence for rent-seeking, and the latter of how a wife used her husband's position for self enrichment.

Shougang Holdings (Hong Kong) Ltd. is a subsidiary of Shougang Corporation in Beijing. The president of Shougang Holdings, Mr Zhou Beifang, is the son of the CEO of Shougang Corporation, Mr Zhou Guanwu. In May 1979, Deng Xiaoping visited Beijing's Shougang and authorized the experiment with the contract responsibility system with three important authorizations of rights — the right to conduct long-term investments, the right to make international deals and transactions and the right to make autonomous financial decisions. Under the contract responsibility system, Shougang gradually became one of the biggest and most profitable SOEs in China.

In 1992, Zhou Guanwu sent his son Beifang to set up a subsidiary in Hong Kong. Quickly, it became one of the largest China-capital companies in Hong Kong. By 1994, Shougang Holdings had five publicly listed companies under its control with market capitalization of HK$ 5.8 billion. Deng Xiaoping's youngest son, Deng Zhifang, became the president of one of Shougang Holdings' subsidiaries, Shougang Concord Grand (Group) Ltd. On 13 February 1995, Zhou Beifang was held by Beijing Investigators' Office and, on 17 February, Zhou Guanwu was removed from his job. The extent of Zhou Beifang's charge is still unclear. But, Shougang in Beijing faced huge asset write-off.

The CEO of Guizhou International Trust Investment Corporation, Yang Jianghong, is the wife of the governor of Guizhou province, Liu Zhengwei. The "first lady" of Guizhou province was an able party member and powerful bureaucrat in herself. She joined the Communist Party at a tender age of nineteen in 1952 and had moved up the ladder to become the vice-chair of Guizhou Discipline Inspection Commission. In 1992, she set up the Guizhou International Trust Investment Corporation and appointed herself as the chairperson of the board. She initiated a few joint venture projects with Hong Kong businessmen that involved her son, Liu Bo, as a "foreign investor." This corruption case may have involved a few hundred million of *Renminbi*. Guizhou is a province with 30 million population living at subsistence levels; this level of corruption is truly incredible.[9]

In an illustrious scheme, she set up a subsidiary in Shenzhen and provided a loan of RMB 70 million. The subsidiary used the fund for real estate speculation in Shanghai, to buy shares from Liu Bo's company and to "bribe" her. The central government spent a year to investigate this case and sent in a high-power investigation team. She was convicted on 3 January and executed on 16 January 1995 in Guiyang, the capital city of Guizhou.

A common and often legal form of corruption is to cause a state asset drain. It is sophisticated rent-seeking cloaked in modern accounting and finance. It is legal simply because there is no clear legal code against it and the SOE managers do not directly pocket the "grease." There are seven major sources of state asset drain:

1. Not assessing fair value for state assets while negotiating a joint venture contract or issuing new stocks.
2. Withholding dividends from state-owned shares.
3. Selling state assets to private individuals at below fair value during the process of clarifying property rights.
4. Avoiding the liability to state bank loans by hiding assets and equipment.
5. Keeping assets off the balance sheet.
6. When an SOE sets up a collective enterprise, the SOE tranfers the state assets to a collective enterprise without compensation.
7. When an administrative office sets up a sideline business unit, the administrative office tranfers the state assets to the business unit without compensation.

These activities are so common they are referred to as "digging the house foundation of the Communist Party."

Triangular Debts, Bankruptcy and Potential Financial Crisis

Before 1985, the SOE's financial needs for long-term and infrastructure investment were met by state allocation. The cost of capital was not an issue on capital budgeting. Personal connection and the senior official's favourable opinion were the major factors to win approvals of investment projects. The policy of "converting fund allocation to bank loans" in 1985 has changed the rule of the game on capital budgeting. Due to the heavily subsidized bank loans, whose approvals were still based on the old tradition of connection and favour, the SOEs did not feel the pinch at the beginning. As the economic reform deepened, competing demand for financial resources from the non-SOE sectors increased drastically. Under the tough "cold shower" economic policy of Zhu Rongji, bank loans became increasingly difficult to get and the market interest rates increasingly reflected the real cost of capital. Even before Zhu Rongji was appointed vice-premier in April 1991, SOEs had started feeling the financial pressure in the late 1980s. This pressure, which became suffocating to many SOEs after 1993, gave rise to a new wave of "triangular debt" problems.[10]

The "triangular debt" problem indicates a debt chain in which firm A is indebted to firm B, firm B to firm C, and firm C to firm A. In reality, triangular debts involve SOEs and state banks.[11] Table 4 provides a rough

Table 4. Triangular Debts Estimates for Year End 1994

(Unit: in RMB billion)

Panel A: Aggregate balance sheets of SOEs		
Total assets of SOEs		2,800
Total equities of SOEs		650
Total liabilities of SOEs		2,150
Bank loans to SOEs	1,500	
Account receivables among SOEs	450	
Debts to other enterprises	200	
Panel B: Aggregate balance sheets of state banks		
Net foreign assets		448
Total loans and credits outstanding		4,310
Loans and credits to SOEs	1,500	
Claims on central government	133	
Loans to others	2,677	
Estimated bad loans	1,250	
Money		2,054
Time and saving deposits		2,638
Bonds		21
Equities of state banks		370

Sources: The balance sheet of the banking sector is from *The People's Bank of China Annual Report*, 1994. Other data are the author's estimates.

estimate of triangular debts for SOEs. At the end of 1994, the total assets of SOEs were estimated to be RMB 2.8 trillion and the average debts/ assets ratio was 0.8. The total debts of SOEs were RMB 2.15 trillion, among which 70% (RMB 1.5 trillion) came from bank loans.[12] The account receivables among SOEs were about RMB 450 billion.

Until now, most of the state bank loans have been policy driven. Since the acquisition of bank loans has to go through many layers of administrative offices, most SOE managers still view bank loans as essentially equivalent to old-fashioned fund allocation. Hence not too many SOE managers have a clear idea of how to pay back these loans.[13] Many economists in China estimate that about one-third of state bank loans may be bad. With this ratio, the estimated bad loans could be as much as RMB 1.25 trillion. The Panel B of Table 4 shows that the equities of state banks at the end of 1994 were barely RMB 370 billion, which represented 8.5% of total loans and 30% of estimated bad loans. Even with a much lower estimate of the bad loan ratio, the financial position of China's state banks may still be rather shaky. Moreover, the average debts/assets ratio of SOEs is estimated to be 0.8. Hence, most SOEs will not be able to borrow additional capital in open, free financial markets and will face bankruptcy if the creditors have the power to call in their credits and loans.

The State Council introduced the Bankruptcy Law in November 1988, but few enterprises took that course in the beginning. Without a relatively clear definition of property rights and financial claims, the Bankruptcy Law was simply not functional. The 3rd Plenum of the 14th Central Committee accepted the policy of "socialist market economy with Chinese characteristics" and outlined the structure of a "modern enterprise system." These changes in the political and economic environment set bankruptcy processes in motion in 1993. Before 1993, the court had processed 600 bankruptcy cases. In 1993 alone, the court processed 900 bankruptcy cases. In 1994, under the leadership of Vice-Premier Zhu Rongji, the State Council selected 18 cities to conduct large scale experiments with bankruptcy. However, in the spring of 1995, Vice-Premier Wu Bangguo replaced Zhu Rongji as the industry policy-maker and slowed down the implementation of the bankruptcy law.

A major reason for slowing down the bankruptcy process has been the thorny issue of property rights. An SOE cannot go through a proper bankruptcy procedure without touching the issue of property rights. The central government is not ready to face this issue squarely. Another major reason is the unemployment and social issues. China has not established a well-functioning social welfare system. The SOEs as a whole employ about 300 million workers. But 42.2% of them are currently in the red. About another 30% of SOEs face *de facto* losses. Just letting 5% of SOEs declare bankruptcy would send 15 million workers on to the street. After visiting SOEs in several provinces, a respected member of the Politburo nervously pointed out: "The situation is so dire that it only waits for Chen Sheng and Wu Guang (to set off a rebellion)."[14] The consideration of political stability makes the slow-down of the bankruptcy process an imperative.

Table 5 reports the SOE manager's perspective on the resistance to bankruptcy filing. As can been seen, 62.9% of the managers pointed out that the administrative government agency would not want to see a bankruptcy. The reason is rather clear — the administrative government agency does not want to bear the responsibility for the political and social consequences of a bankruptcy process. And, 51.7% of managers thought that the state banks would also be against the filing for bankruptcy. Without a proper legal protection, the bankruptcy process would definitely lead to asset loss for the state banks. Interestingly, only 23.6% of managers were against bankruptcy. We can see that many intelligent managers might

Table 5. Percentage of Managers Identifying a Given Source of Resistance to the Bankruptcy Filing of SOEs

Sources of Resistance	Percentage
Administrative government agency	62.9
Banks	51.7
Employees	46.0
Managers	23.6
Other creditors	19.7
Others	8.9

Source: China Enterprises Survey System, State Council.

even stand to gain handsomely from the bankruptcy process.

The issues of mounting SOE losses, triangular debts, bankruptcy and potential banking crisis are all entangled. This entanglement makes the reform of SOEs an extremely difficult task. The central government has to face clearly the difficulty and the danger associated with it. The current thinking of policy-makers in Beijing is to slow down and be careful. The reform of SOEs will be a long, dragging, painful process for many years to come.

Concluding Remarks

Without a clear delineation of property rights, without an efficient and effective monitoring and control system, without a functional legal system, and without fair and square market competition, SOEs will continue to be in a mess. The mounting losses, the rampant corruption, the triangular debts and the looming financial crisis are symptoms of rent-seeking activities through the transition from a socialist economy to a market economy. No quick fix really works, and no miracle drug can cure the disease arising from the economic transition. Only time, patience and painful work will do.

In 1994, the 3rd Plenum of the 14th Central Committee set the policy of "clarifying the property rights, specifying the rights and responsibilities, separating the government and the enterprises and introducing scientific management methods." The State Council identified 100 SOEs for reform experiments and named 1995 as the year of enterprise reform. Almost right from the beginning of 1995, the government officials and enterprise managers quickly realized the difficulty and danger associated with this task. In March, Vice-Premier Wu Bangguo took charge and switched gear on this economic policy. The year of 1995 turned out to be a year of reflection, not a year of action for SOE reform.

Reflecting on the difficulty of reforming SOEs, we can gain some insight from SOE managers' opinions. Table 6 lists the top three causes for managerial difficulties as identified by the managers of 87 SOEs which were chosen for the reform experiments in 1994. These 87 SOEs are large firms with good performance. Their managers are industry leaders and some may become political leaders in the future. The two most cited causes of managerial difficulties are lack of knowledge and skill regarding financial management and surplus labour. The traditional function of SOE managers is to carry out the orders from above. Most top managers are engineers in training with little knowledge of modern business. In a market economy, production seems to be a secondary problem in comparison with the complex and complicated issues of financial management. Most SOE managers are ill-equipped for their new responsibilites. So are the middle level managers, as exemplied by the fact that the low quality of management staff is viewed as the fourth most frequently cited source of managerial difficulties.

Although separating the government bureaucracy and the enterprise is a core of the new economic policy, government interference is still a major source of frustration. As shown in Table 7, the 87 SOEs under reform have acquired a bit more autonomy on appointment of top and middle level managers (hence, fewer complaints on this issue). Meddling from the top and policy-driven production decisions are still common place in SOEs. These phenomena will not disappear in the short run.

The economic reform in China for the past 15 years basically followed Deng Xiaoping's strategy of "crossing the river by feeling for the stones."

Table 6. Managerial Difficulties: The Top Three Causes for Managers

Causes of difficulties	Percentage of managers viewing it as one of top three causes
Lack of knowledge and skill on financial management	62.5
Surplus labour	61.7
Government interference	43.0
Low quality of management staff	42.8
Ignorance of modern management methods	33.6
Lack of autonomy on personnel	31.7
Low employee morale and loyalty	9.5

Source: China Enterprises Survey System, State Council.

Table 7. Managers' Perspective on the Three Most Troublesome Government Interferences

(Unit: Percentage)

Government interferences	All SOEs	87 SOE under reform
Appointment of top managers	67.4	52.6
Policy-oriented operation directives	57.3	40.0
Meddling in daily operation	53.8	62.5
Appointment of middle-level management	50.4	39.0
Ambiguous operation rights between the government and the enterprises	45.2	59.7
Preventing the board of directors from exercising their rights	12.2	16.0
Others	13.6	30.0

Source: China Enterprises Survey System, State Council.

The essence of this strategy is the incremental approach to economic reform: while holding the old system under tight control, let a new system sprout up. For example, the town and village enterprises are essentially family-owned entrepreneurial firms. The new system, which is rational, efficient and adaptable, gradually cannibalizes the old system. The current crisis of state-owned enterprises can be viewed as a result of this cannibalization. Many state-owned enterprises will die, through bankruptcy, merger, selling off and spinning off. It is only a matter of how painful and how long the process will be.

Notes

1. For a theoretical discussion of monitoring and control, see R. Antle and J. S. Demski, "The Controllability Principle in Responsibility Accounting," *Accounting Review* (October 1988), pp. 700–18; S. J. Grossman and O. D. Hart, "An Analysis of Principal-Agent Problem," *Econometrica*, Vol. 51, No. 1 (1983); B. Holmstrom, "Moral Hazard and Observability," *Bell Journal of Economics* (Spring 1979), pp. 74–91; B. Holmstrom, "Moral Hazard in Teams," *Bell Journal of Economics* (Autumn 1982), pp. 324–40.
2. Kao and Zhou provided a good survey of the evolution of China's SOEs from planned economy to market economy. See Kao Xincai (ed.), *The Grand Trend of Chinese Economic System* (Lanzhou: Lanzhou University Press, 1993); Zhou Shulian, *From Planned Economy to Market Economy* (Beijing: Economic Management Publisher, 1994).

3. See John McMillan and Barry Naughton, "How to Reform a Planned Economy: Lessons from China," *Oxford Review of Economic Policy*, Vol. 8 (Spring 1992), pp. 130–43; John McMillan and Barry Naughton (eds), *Reforming Asian Socialism: The Growth of Market Institutions* (Ann Arbor: University of Michigan Press, 1995).

4. *Hong Kong Economic Journal*, 20 January 1995.

5. Cheung is an early advocate of the importance of property rights on economic behaviour. See Steven N. Cheung, *Theory of Share Tenancy* (Chicago: University of Chicago Press, 1969). Also, see Masahiko Aoki and H. K. Kim (eds), *Corporate Governance in Transitional Economies* (Washington, DC: World Bank, 1995).

6. See Lin Yifu, Fan Cai and Zhou Li, "The Core of Enterprise Reform Is to Create a Competitive Environment," Working Paper, Peking University, 1995.

7. Lee Chi-Wen Jevons, "Financial Assessment of State-owned Enterprises," Working Paper, Hong Kong University of Science and Technology, 1995.

8. *Hong Kong Economic Journal*, 6 April 1995.

9. *Renmin ribao* (People's Daily), various issues in February 1995.

10. In the second half of 1991 and the early part of 1992, Zhu had largely succeeded at solving the previous triangular debt quandary.

11. Lawrence Lau and Yingyi Qian, "Suggestions on China's Banks and Enterprise Financial Restructuring," *Reform*, 1994; Ming Qi, "Can We Find a One-Shot Solution to the Huge State Owned Bad Debts?" *Jingjixue xiaoxi bao* (News in Economies), 14 January 1995.

12. According to the data of the State Assets Administration Bureau, 150,000 SOEs were under asset revaluations in 1994; the average debt/asset ratio was 74%, and the average equity/asset ratio was 26%. The interest payments in 1994 was RMB 148.8 billion. My estimates are based on publicly available data and my consultancy for several SOEs.

13. For the economic analysis of agency cost and financial decisions, see M. C. Jensen and W. H. Meckling, "Theory of Firm: Managerial Behavior, Agency Costs, and Ownership Structure," *Journal of Financial Economics* (October, 1976), pp. 305–60. For a classical financial decision theory, see J. Williams, *The Theory of Investment Value* (Cambridge, MA: Harvard University Press, 1938).

14. Chen Sheng and Wu Guang were two peasant leaders who led the first rebellion against the Qin dynasty around 200 B.C. Obviously, this quote is not documentable in the secretive society of China. However, it was quite well circulated in the inner political circle in Beijing in the early spring of 1995.

11

Regional Economic Development and Disparities

Woo Tun-oy

Introduction

China is a large country both in terms of the size of the territory and the population. With a land area of 9.6 million square kilometres, stretching over thousands of kilometres from east to west and north to south, the climatic conditions, resource endowment, and even the traditions of the inhabitants, vary enormously among the various geographical regions — the East, the Middle, and the West regions.[1] Due to historical reasons (the opening up of "old" China by the western imperialists) as well as due to differences in natural conditions economic activities, especially "modern" activities and productive capability, are concentrated in the East, especially in the coastal areas. Thus, people in the East enjoy a much higher living standard and quality of life. Yet, the land area of the interior regions (the Middle and West regions) is much larger. Nearly all the mineral ores and significant raw materials are found in the interior regions; more important-ly, a predominant proportion of China's minorities are native inhabitants of the interior regions. Such a mismatch between the spatial distribution of productivity and higher living standards in one region and resource endow-ment in the other has overloaded China's transportation facilities, thus disrupting material supplies and production. A continual and substantial decrease in productivity and income relative to the East will exacerbate the discontent of the inhabitants in the Middle and West regions. As a result, they may attempt to protect their own interests via the practice of economic protectionism, that is, by blocking the inter-regional flow of materials and products between the East and the interior regions. In the worst case scenario, racial problems may be intensified and national unity would be threatened. In fact, before 1978, the Chinese authorities under Mao Zedong felt uneasy about the above pattern of regional economic distribution inherited from the Nationalist regime, not only for economic, but also for strategic and ideological reasons.[2] To rectify this irrational pattern of regional distribution (before 1978), the Chinese authorities pur-sued regional development strategies aimed at relocating production capacity, channelling relatively more (material and human) resources to the interior areas, and granting these areas more autonomy to diversify their economic activities. The most dramatic strategy was the large-scale construction and development of the third-front industries, from the mid-1960s to the mid-1970s, as a means of war preparation against possible military invasion by the United States (US) or even the Soviet Union (USSR). Accordingly, the investment and output shares of the interior regions increased, while the income gaps among the East, the Middle, and the West regions were reduced.[3] Furthermore, economic activities in the relatively backward areas became diversified and more balanced, resulting in higher productivity growth. The cost was, as expected, some decrease in the static allocative efficiency at the national level.

After 1978, with the replacement of the ideological-inclined Maoist line of socialist construction by Deng Xiaoping's efficiency-centred modernization drive and the waning of war panic, the Chinese authorities altered their regional development strategy. Preferential policies to foster industrial growth in the interior regions were phased out. Instead, special privileges were granted to the coastal regions. Such a change was inevitable, given the post-1978 efficiency/profit-oriented development goals and the decentralized administrative institutions. In fact, with the decrease in direct control over resources and fund allocation, the Chinese central authorities found it increasingly difficult to realize the planned delivery of resources to the interior regions. Thus, starting in 1979, the pattern of spatial resource allocation was reversed. Nevertheless, it was not until 1985 that the central authorities officially announced a three-tier gradated regional development strategy for the Seventh Five-Year Plan period (1986–1990).

The underlying rationale for the three-tier gradated regional development strategy is the law of comparative advantage. The East would serve as the growth pole specializing in the production of products that are relatively technology-intensive and export-oriented. An outward-oriented development strategy, which included the granting of preferential policies, tax concessions, and administrative autonomy to promote exports, especially high-tech products, and to absorb foreign investment would be implemented. The remaining two regions would cooperate with and help the East achieve the above objectives. The interior regions are relatively well-endowed with mineral ores and natural resources. They would concentrate on producing agricultural products, industrial raw materials, energy, and some select manufacturing industries for which they enjoy resource advantages. It was believed that this strategy would enhance substantially the economic growth of the "high-productivity" region. In the second phase, via the powerful linkage and multiplier effects generated by the growth poles in the East, the growth momentum would be transmitted to the interior regions step by step in accordance with productivity differentials and the law of comparative advantage; that is, first to the Middle region, then to the West. Initial income and productivity disparities would be contained and reduced, while the whole nation would enjoy much more rapid growth.

In late 1988, the Seventh Five-Year Plan was abandoned and replaced by retrenchment-cum-readjustment policies to combat inflation. Like other policies, the three-tier gradated regional development strategy had not been strictly enforced. Beginning in the mid-1980s, the Middle-West regions engaged in economic protectionism to press for better terms of trade with the coastal areas, and various local authorities in the East engaged in illegal practices to seize resources. Furthermore, most authorities in the East used the privileges, concessions, and autonomy granted in accordance with the gradated regional development strategy to expand existing activities with unchanged production techniques, for rent-seeking purposes; not to upgrade products and enhance efficiency.[4] Since the economic strength, especially the financial strength, of the East was much greater than that of the interior regions, and without the blessing of the central government, the interior regions failed to halt the deterioration of their relative strength. The ratio of average national per capita income in the East to that in the Middle and the West regions changed from 100:68.76:54.74 in 1985 to 100:63.82:52.61 in 1989, indicating a widening of income disparities to the advantage of the East. Only by 1990, when the retrenchment-cum-readjustment policies were implemented, were the inter-regional income disparities narrowed. In that year the ratio of average national per capita income in the East to that in the Middle and West regions changed to 100:65.53:55.79.[5] The increase in the income share of the West was spectacular. As a matter of fact, the retrenchment-cum-adjustment policies not only aimed at repressing aggregate demand and freezing price increases, but also emphasized a reshuffling of the output and investment structure, enlarging the shares of agriculture and basic industries, and repressing the growth of consumer goods, especially the output of small rural enterprises. Since the output of agriculture and basic industries accounted for a major proportion of the total domestic output in the Middle and the West regions, while consumer goods and rural industries were relatively more important in the East, the retrenchment-cum-readjustment policies definitely were advantageous to the Middle and West regions. Furthermore, tighter control over the administrative economic autonomy of various authorities retarded income growth in the East.

Originally, the Eighth Five-Year Plan was formulated in line with the spirit of the retrenchment-cum-readjustment policies: stability and structural balance over growth rate of output; and emphasis on a lax economic environment to launch economic institutional reform. However, in mid-1991 Deng Xiaoping and his associates insisted that the Chinese economy was in the prime of its growth and that such a rare opportunity should not be lost. China could and should strive for rapid economic growth, via comprehensive economic liberalization and especially via a fully-fledged opening up to the outside world. The climax was Deng's visit to South China in early 1992. Then, the tide turned. Once again, the "speed" of income growth and institutional reform was of utmost importance. The retrenchment-cum-readjustment policies were officially abandoned, and the Eighth Five-Year Plan was drastically revised. Notably, the planned average annual growth rate for the real national product was raised from the original 5%–6% to 8%–9%. Most importantly, the so-called socialist market economy was to replace the planned socialist commodity economy as China's (future) basic economic system. Accordingly, some compre-hensive financial and price reforms were launched to accelerate the construction of socialist markets. Local authorities and enterprises were given a free hand to conduct reform experiments and to engage in economic relations with overseas agents. The reforms of 1992–1993 had a "big-bang" and even a "Great-Leap Forward" flavour. As a result, the gradated regional development strategy was abandoned *de facto*. Instead (guided by Deng's call to "grasp the development opportunity") simultaneous rapid growth and liberalization in all sectors and regions became the rule.

The growth and liberalization drive ignited by Deng's visit to South China did result in very dramatic income growth — since 1992 double-digit growth in the real gross national product for four consecutive years, and a very spectacular upsurge of foreign investment. However, once again, rapid economic growth and liberalization triggered and intensified inflation and generated chaos in the financial sector. Thus, since mid-1993 the central authorities have launched a so-called macro economic regulatory policy to counteract these problems. In addition, in response to the very drastic widening of the income gap between the East and the interior regions since 1991 which had accelerated during the "growth and liberalization drive," the central authorities have adjusted the regional development strategy. Apparently, the central authorities have decided to resume a biased regional development strategy, but this time to the advantage of the interior regions.

Inter-regional Income Disparities, 1990–1994[6]

The Facts

The launching of a gradated regional development strategy biased toward the coastal regions during the Seventh Five-Year Plan period widened the income gap between the East and the interior regions. This showed (in contrast to the belief of the proponents of the gradated regional development strategy) the expected trickle-down effects generated by the growth poles in the East could not counteract the combined backward and cumulative causation effects which led to a continual net outflow of productive resources, including manpower, from the interior regions to the East, thus further enlarging the productivity differentials and the income gap to the detriment of the interior regions. Such an outcome was not unexpected because this regional development strategy enabled the East to enjoy additional policy privileges in addition to its original productivity advantages. In theory, the *de facto* abandonment of the coastal-region-biased regional development strategy accompanied by the pursuit of a "comprehensive, fully-fledged liberalization and growth in all regions" should have narrowed the policy gap between the East and the interior regions so that the East, the Middle, and the West regions could compete on a more equal basis. Thus, many pro-liberalization, pro-market commentators, including central officials, expected that the development gap between the East and the interior regions could be narrowed via the free play of market forces guided by the profit motive. The reality was, however, just the opposite.

As shown in Table 1 and Table 2, during 1991–1994 (with 1990 as the base year) the average annual compound growth rate of the real per capita gross domestic product (GDP) in the East had been 15.51%, substantially higher than that attained in the Middle and West regions during the same period — 10.264% and 9.15%, respectively. As a result, the ratio of the average real per capita GDP in the Middle region to that in the East had declined from 0.6383:1 in 1990 to 0.53:1 in 1994. Similarly, the corresponding ratio for the West to the East had dropped from 0.5582:1 to 0.445:1. Note that the decrease in the relative income of both the Middle and West regions as a proportion of per capita GDP in the East during 1991–1994 amounted to more than ten percentage points. In 1986–1989 (during the coastal-region-biased regional development strategy), however, the decrease in the relative income of the Middle and the West regions (as a proportion of the national per capita income in the East) had

Table 1. Real Per Capita GDP by Province 1990–1994

(Unit: RMB)

Province	1990	R	1991	R	1992	R	1993	R	1994	R
Shanghai	6241.74	1	6669.93	1	7635.24	1	8746.92	1	9946.09	1
Beijing	5036.28	2	5474.41	2	6065.06	2	6737.86	2	7559.02	2
Tianjin	3657.81	3	3770.63	3	4161.41	3	4624.78	3	5246.52	3
Liaoning	2851.27	4	3007.77	4	3349.88	4	3824.25	5	4226.43	6
Guangdong	2391.98	5	2565.27	5	3329.17	5	4021.04	4	4726.39	4
Zhejiang	2203.19	6	2574.37	6	3038.91	6	3681.40	6	4388.87	5
Jiangsu	2103.52	8	2339.83	7	2919.61	7	3495.64	7	4041.66	7
Shandong	1860.21	10	2112.65	10	2458.21	9	2902.20	10	3361.08	9
Fujian	1790.32	11	2020.20	11	2401.44	12	2974.16	8	3584.95	8
Hainan	1581.90	14	1787.98	13	2462.97	8	2913.98	9	3214.77	10
Hebei	1568.16	16	1723.59	14	1975.00	14	2302.92	13	2623.69	13
Guangxi	1079.91	29	1199.33	26	1400.66	26	1675.42	21	1919.70	19
East <15.51>	2194.30	9.08	2441.64	8.5	2865.08	8.08	3382.68	7.42	3906.33	7.25
Heilongjiang	2176.21	7	2305.54	8	2439.80	10	2602.14	12	2803.87	12
Jilin	1762.59	12	1847.23	12	2053.75	13	2295.81	14	2604.74	14
Hubei	1575.34	15	1657.08	15	1867.69	15	2107.20	15	2401.56	15
Shanxi	1550.95	17	1592.45	18	1789.70	17	1986.06	16	2143.28	17
Inner Mongolia	1546.79	18	1646.80	17	1808.88	16	1978.23	17	2151.06	16
Hunan	1260.26	23	1342.08	23	1494.54	21	1678.55	20	1850.28	21
Anhui	1179.97	25	1151.88	29	1328.57	28	1590.39	25	1899.33	20
Jiangxi	1162.84	26	1240.29	25	1406.39	25	1577.69	26	1838.95	23
Henan	1131.03	27	1193.35	27	1341.84	27	1538.56	27	1735.75	27
Middle <10.264>	1400.60	18.89	1464.48	19.33	1633.72	19.11	1839.26	19.11	2070.38	18.33
Xinjiang	1920.41	9	2160.19	9	2403.00	11	2610.90	11	2847.55	11
Qinghai	1601.12	13	1654.19	16	1749.68	18	1892.93	18	2017.93	18
Ningxia	1457.23	19	1495.42	19	1600.62	19	1733.94	19	1842.46	22
Tibet	1353.60	20	1350.89	22	1434.21	23	1525.00	28	1733.05	28
Shaanxi	1302.56	21	1388.43	20	1483.76	22	1662.53	22	1785.81	25
Yunnan	1300.94	22	1368.09	21	1497.42	20	1633.54	23	1798.05	24
Sichuan	1187.42	24	1269.12	24	1415.90	24	1597.35	24	1761.96	26
Gansu	1129.00	28	1187.70	28	1288.94	29	1419.45	29	1545.29	29
Guizhou	829.16	30	892.61	30	951.71	30	1031.20	30	1101.97	30
West <9.15>	1224.77	20.67	1308.16	21	1434.58	21.78	1591.17	22.67	1738.33	23.67
National <12.96>	1688.83		2832.67		2096.49		2418.67		2749.84	

Table 1 (Continued)

Notes: Real per capita GDP of the relevant province or city in year t–1 = Y_{t-1}/Pop_{t-1} = $[Y_t/(1 + g_t)]/Pop_{t-1}$ where Y_{t-1} is real GDP in year t-1, Pop_{t-1} is the population size in t-1, Y_t is real GDP in year t with t starting from 1994, g_t is the growth rate of real GDP in year t; real

per capita GDP of a region in year $t = \dfrac{\sum_i y_{it}}{\sum_i Pop_{it}}$ where y_{it} is real GDP of province i or

city i of the relevant region in year t, Pop_{it} is the population size of province i or city i of the relevant region in year t; the real national average per capita GDP =

$\dfrac{\sum_j \sum_i Y_{ijt}}{\sum_j \sum_i Pop_{ijt}}$ where Y_{ijt} and Pop_{ijt} are the respective real GDP and population size of

province i or city i of region j in year t.

East: the East (region) includes Beijing, Tianjin, Hebei, Liaoning, Shanghai, Jiangsu, Zhejiang, Fujian, Shandong, Guangdong, Guangxi, and Hainan.

Middle: the Middle (region) includes Shanxi, Inner Mongolia, Jilin, Heilongjiang, Anhui, Jiangxi, Henan, Hubei, and Hunan.

West: the West (region) includes Sichuan, Guizhou, Yunnan, Tibet, Shaanxi, Gansu, Qinghai, Ningxia, and Xinjiang.

RMB: *Renminbi*

< >:   average annual compound growth rate of real capita GDP of the relevant

region or the national economy during 1991–1994 = $100 \cdot \left(\sqrt[4]{\dfrac{Y_{1994}}{Y_{1990}}} - 1 \right)$

where y_{1994} and y_{1990} are the real per capita GDP of the relevant region or the national economy in 1994 and 1990, respectively.

R: the rank order of the relevant province/city in terms of the size of real per capita GDP among all provinces and directly administered cities in mainland China, with "1" as the highest; the "R" for the relevant region is the arithmetic mean of the 'R's of all provinces/cities within its jurisdiction.

Source: State Statistical Bureau, People's Republic of China, *China Statistical Yearbook, 1995* (Beijing: China Statistical Publishing House, 1995), pp. 33, 60.

been equivalent to only 4.93 and 2.13 percentage points respectively. Based on other measures of income disparities, such as the weighed coefficient of the variation of per capita income, and a comparison of the average per capita GDP rank of all provinces within each region, we can conclude that after 1990 the income gap between the East and the interior regions had widened (to the advantage of the East) at a faster rate. The weighed coefficient of variation of per capita real GDP among the East, the Middle, and the West regions increased from 0.2544 in 1990 to 0.3547 in 1994. The average per capita GDP rank of the East improved consistently after 1990, surging up from 9.08 in 1990 to 7.25 in 1994. In 1994, China's top ten richest (in terms of per capita real GDP) provinces or directly-administered cities were all in the East. Even the rank of the poorest province (Guangxi) rose substantially from number 29 (out of thirty) in 1990 to 19 in 1994. The average rank of the Middle region fluctuated, and deteriorated somewhat in 1991, but improved to 18.33 in 1994. On the other hand, the average rank of the West continued to deteriorate, from 20.67 in 1990 to 23.67 in 1994. As a matter of fact, in 1994, out of nine provinces in the Middle region, only Heilongjiang attained a per capita real GDP (RMB 2,803.87) on par with (or higher than) the national average (RMB 2,749.84). Similarly, in the West, only Xinjiang succeeded in maintaining an average per capita real GDP (RMB 2,847.55) at or above the national average. Furthermore, the income polarization continued. In 1990, the ratio of the highest to the lowest per capita real GDP (on a provincial basis) was 7.528 (RMB 6,241.74 in Shanghai *vis-à-vis* RMB 829.16 in Guizhou). The corresponding ratio increased to 9.026 in 1994. Actually, over the period 1991–1994, no province in the interior region, attained a per capita real GDP growth rate on par with the national average (12.96% per annum). As for the inter-regional income distribution in the rural areas, in 1980 the ratio of rural household per capita net income in the East to that in the Middle and the West regions was 1:0.80:0.7194. This changed to 1:0.654:0.5424 in 1990. In 1994, the ratio was 1:0.664:0.357[7] which indicated a very slight improvement in the peasants' per capita net income in the Middle region, but a substantial decrease (in peasants' per capita net income) in the West relative to that in the East, compared with 1990. In the same year, the ratio of the highest (RMB 3,437 in Shanghai) to the lowest (RMB 724 in Gansu) rural household per capita net income reached 4.75, larger than that in 1990 (4.43). As a matter of fact, in 1995 there were still 592 poor counties in China, 90% of which were in the interior regions. With respect to urban households, the distribution of the inter-regional per capita disposable income followed that of the average rural households, but with less disparity. In 1994, the average per capita income of all urban residents in the East, the Middle, and the West regions was RMB 4,294, RMB 2,883, and RMB 3,045, respectively. The corresponding ratio was 1:0.674:0.709, which in comparison to that in 1993 (1:0.679:0.73) indicated some widening of income disparities to the advantage of the residents in the East. In the interior regions, only two provinces, one in the Middle region (Hunan) and one in the West (Tibet), attained a per capita urban household disposable income at least on par with the national average. In the same year, the ratio of the highest (RMB

Table 2. Inter-regional Income Disparities 1990–1994

Year	E:M:W	E^X:M^X:W^X	IRV	IRV*
1990	100:63.84:55.82	100:64.35:54.89	0.2544	0.2559
1991	100:59.98:53.58	100:59.98:53.58	0.2807	0.2807
1992	100:57.00:50.10	100:56.46:50.05	0.3094	0.3124
1993	100:54.37:47.04	100:54.07:46.31	0.3360	0.3408
1994	100:53.00:44.50	100:53.57:44.19	0.3547	0.3581

Notes: E:M:W is the ratio of real per capita GDP in the East to that in the Middle and that in the West of the relevant year with that in the East = 100; E^X:M^X:W^X is the same as E:M:W but the income variable is in current prices.

IRV: the weighed coefficient of variation of regional real per capita GDP =

$$\frac{1}{\bar{y}_t} \sqrt{\sum_j (y_{jt} - \bar{y}_t)^2 \frac{Pop_{jt}}{\sum_j Pop_{jt}}}$$ where $\bar{y}_t$ is the national average real per capita GDP in year t, y_{jt} is the average real per capita GDP of region j in year t, Pop_{jt} is the population size of region j in year t.

IRV*:   the same as IRV but the income variable is in current prices.

Source: See Table 1.

6,367, in Guangdong) to the lowest (RMB 2,498 in Inner Mongolia) per capita urban household disposable income was 2.55, larger than that in 1991 (2.15).

The Causes

The income gap between the East and the interior regions can be attributed primarily to differences in the output/employment structure and labour productivity. For instance, in 1993, the share of net output from primary, secondary, and tertiary industry in the total domestic product in the East was 16.45%, 50.07%, and 33.48%, respectively; whereas the corresponding shares in the Middle and West regions were 24.22%, 45.50%, 30.28% and 25.91%, 42.04%, 32.05%, respectively. With respect to the per capita GDP gap between the East and the Middle region, the contribution rate[8] of the difference in per capita output from primary, secondary, and tertiary industries was 7.29%, 55.46%, and 37.25%, respectively. As for the gap between the East and the West, the respective contribution rate was 8.29%, 57%, and 34.71%. In 1993, the (labour) employment share of primary, secondary, and tertiary industry in the East was 49.38%. 28.34% and 22.28%, respectively, whereas the respective share in the Middle and in the West regions was 59.52%, 20.81%, 19.67% and 69%, 14.67%, 16.33%.

The average labour productivities of the secondary and tertiary industries were usually much higher than that of the primary industry. In addition, the average labour productivities for all industries (primary, secondary, and tertiary) in the East were higher than the corresponding counterparts in both the Middle and West regions. Thus, the per capita GDP differential between the East and the interior regions can be explained both by the differences in the employment structure and by the labour productivity. It can be shown that if the West in 1993 had adopted the same employment structure (in terms of primary, secondary, and tertiary industries) and had achieved the same labour productivity as those industries in the East, its GDP could have increased by RMB 587.57 billion, or by 115.2%. Moreover, differences in the employment structure contributed directly to 38.49% of the per labour GDP gap between the East and the West in 1993.[9] Similarly, the employment structure directly explained 23.09% of the per labour GDP gap between the East and the Middle region in the same year. The use of a more disaggregated activity classification scheme (compared with our three-sector classification) definitely would have increased the contribution rate of the difference in the employment structure. Note that, if we take into consideration the income effect of the difference in the unemployment rate and assume that the West could lower its unemployment rate in the urban areas to the same level as that in the East, and that, if the structure and productivity of this hypothetical additional employment in the West were to be the same as that in the East, then the GDP in the West would have risen by RMB 2.18 billion.[10] Under the same assumptions, the GDP in the Middle region would have increased by RMB 0.57 billion. To conclude, if in 1993 the West had adopted the same employment structure and had achieved the same labour productivity, while maintaining the same unemployment rate (in the urban areas) as in the East, its per capita GDP would have risen by RMB 2,185.5. Similarly, in the same year, the per capita GDP in the Middle region would have increased by RMB 1,565.4. Thus, in order to narrow the per capita GDP gap between the East and the interior regions, the interior regions must lower their unemployment rate, increase the (labour) employment share of the secondary and tertiary industries and enhance the (labour) productivity at rates higher than those in the East.

Similarly, per capita rural household income disparities between the East and the interior regions can be largely attributed to the very unequal distribution of rural enterprises (especially rural industries) between the East and the interior regions as well as to the relatively lower (labour) productivity of the rural enterprises in the interior regions. In 1994, the output value of (rural) township and village enterprises (TVEs) amounted to RMB 4,264.36 billion (far exceeding that of farming, forestry, animal husbandry, and fishery — RMB 1,575.047 billion) of which those TVEs in the East accounted for the lion's share — 69.28% followed by the Middle region (23.09%) and the West (7.63%). As a matter of fact, in the same year, township and village enterprises in Shandong (in the East) alone turned out an output value of RMB 680.39 billion, more than double that of all provinces in the West (RMB 325.4 billion). At the same time, the industrial output value accounted for more than 75% of the total output value of all township and village enterprises. The East contributed 74.76% of this industrial output value, while the Middle and the West regions shared the remaining 19.08% and 6.16%, respectively. In 1994, employment in township and village enterprises accounted for 34.55% of total rural employment in the East, as opposed to the corresponding 27.29% and 14.24% realized in the Middle and the West regions. The average labour productivity of township and village enterprises is always much higher than that of farming, forestry, animal husbandry, and fishery. For instance, in 1994, the average national labour productivity of township and village enterprises was RMB 35,484.3, very much higher than that in farming, forestry, animal husbandry, and fishery (RMB 4,818.1). In addition, the average labour productivity of township and village enterprises in the East had been higher than that in the Middle and the West regions. In 1994, the ratio of that in the East to the Middle and the West regions was 1:0.5093:0.4264. Obviously, a relatively smaller employment share and a lower labour productivity in township and village enterprises in the interior regions "contributed" substantially to the output gap between the East and the interior regions.

Since 1991, more resources had been allotted to the East, which had thus further strengthened the relative competitiveness of the East. As shown in Table 3, in 1990, in terms of value, 58.994% of China's total fixed assets investment took place in the East, with the remaining 25.886% and 15.12% absorbed by the Middle and the West regions, respectively. The per labour fixed assets investment in the East, the Middle, and the West regions was RMB 1,046.59, RMB 573.0, and RMB 487.9, respectively. After 1990, the share of the East continued to rise. In 1994, it rose to 65.826%, while that in the Middle and the West regions dropped to 21.664% and 12.51% respectively (see Table 3). The corresponding per labour fixed assets investment was RMB 3,982.75, RMB 1,618.68, and

RMB 1,373.58, respectively. The investment gap grew as indicated by the change in the ratio of fixed assets investment in the East to that in the Middle and the West regions from 1:0.4388:0.2563 in 1990 to 1:0.3291:0.1900 in 1994. With respect to the regional distribution of capital construction investment, similar changes occurred. The share of capital construction investment in the East increased from 55.96% in 1990 to 60.39% in 1994, while that in the Middle and the West regions declined from 25.58% and 18.46% to 24.40% and 15.21% during the same period.

Table 3. Total Investment in Fixed Assets and Capital Construction by Region 1990, 1992–1995

		1990	1992	1993	1994	1995[+]
East	IFA	2525.68	4689.55	7688.78	10370.12	5433
		(58.994)	(61.903)	(64.106)	(65.826)	(63.20)
	ICC	867.53	1513.42	2383.69	3459.80	4008.88
		(55.96)	(54.95)	(57.045)	(60.39)	(60.62)
Middle	IFA	1108.22	1799.75	2684.15	3412.86	2024
		(25.886)	(23.757)	(22.38)	(21.664)	(23.55)
	ICC	396.6	742.73	1087.47	1397.84	1725.56
		(25.58)	(26.968)	(26.024)	(24.40)	(25.58)
West	IFA	647.32	1086.32	1620.88	1970.84	1193
		(15.12)	(14.34)	(13.514)	(12.51)	(13.25)
	ICC	286.19	497.97	707.48	871.28	1011.20
		(18.46)	(18.081)	(16.931)	(15.21)	(14.99)
Unclassified	IFA	168.08	279.37	464.08	616.51	495
	ICC	153.49	258.56	436.86	302.82	619.07
National*	IFA	4449.3	7854.99	12457.89	16370.33	9091
Total	ICC	1703.81	3012.68	4615.5	6031.74	7364.71

Notes: IFA: value of investment in fixed assets, in RMB100 million.
ICC: value of investment in capital construction, in RMB100 million.
( ): the share of the value of investment realized in the relevant region, as a percentage of the national total (excluding investment unclassified by region).
1995[+]: January–December for ICC; January to November for IFA.
*: National total: sum total of the investment value of all regions plus investment unclassified by region.
( )*: the percentage share of the relevant item during January–December 1994.

Sources: State Statistical Bureau, People's Republic of China, *China Statistical Year-book*, various issues (1991–1995) (Beijing: China Statistical Publishing House); Zhongguo Tongji Xinxibao (ed.), *Chinese Latest Economic Statistics Confidential Monthly Report* (Beijing: China's Statistics Information Consultancy Service Centre), February 1996 (Part 1), p. 14; *Ming Pao*, 19 December 1995, p. C2.

Note that the share of state-owned investment in the interior regions was larger than that of the total investments. It decreased from 43.95% in 1990 to 40.93% in 1994, compared with a decrease from 41.01% to 34.17%, respectively, for total fixed assets investment. This indicated the relative concentration of state-owned economic units in the interior regions. Since China's economic growth still relied heavily on increasing the intake of capital goods and intermediate inputs to expand production, more rapid growth of fixed assets investment in the East (which was already relatively endowed with capital goods) would increase the productive capacity gap between the East and the interior regions.

In addition, the sources, and thus the quality, of investment varied between the East and the interior regions. Most notably, during 1990–1994, over 85% of the foreign investment in China was utilized in the East (see Table 4). In 1990, about US$4.864 billion of foreign investment was utilized in the East (accounting for 88.55% of the national total). This increased to US$31.149 billion in 1994 (87.35% of the total). As for the Middle and the West regions, the corresponding amount and percentage share of the national total was US$0.442 billion (8.058%) and US$0.1865 billion (3.395%) in 1990; US$2.873 billion (8.057%) and US$1.638 billion (4.594%) in 1994. In 1994, the total amount of foreign investment in the Middle and the West regions was still much less than that in Guangdong province in the East — US$4.51 billion compared with US$10.928 billion. Note that, although measured in terms of RMB, utilized foreign investment did not constitute a very substantial proportion of China's total fixed assets investment (23.64% in 1994 measured in terms of the 1994 exchange rate of the US$ or 15.8% measured by the 1993 exchange rate). And an increase in the share was always exaggerated by the drastic devaluation of RMB against the US$ over time. Nevertheless, foreign investment played a very vital role in fostering the economic development of the host localities. In addition to the positive effects of foreign investment as noted by the Chinese authorities, foreign investment utilization in China had always been accompanied by administrative autonomy, policy privileges and tax concessions which allowed for exemption (or evasion) from the state's regulatory economic policies and law enforcement.[11] In fact "to let foreign investors earn profits in order to promote opening to the outside would" had successfully been used by the Special Economic Zones and other open areas as an excuse to maintain and even to increase privileges relative to the "non-open" areas. To a certain extent, foreign trade, especially the promotion of exports, had played a similar role. Unfortunately (for the interior regions), the East accounted for the lion's share of China's total exports. Its share increased from 82.48% (of the national total), based on the source of the goods, in 1992 to 86.71% in 1994, while that of the Middle and the West regions declined from 13.32% to 9.57% and from 4.2% to 3.72%, respectively (see Table 4). Thus, such a regional distribution pattern of foreign-involved economic activities, based on the pursuit of open-door policies had in effect, worsened the competitiveness of the interior regions relative to the East. Also, since the 1980s, China's economic policies, especially those regarding administrative autonomy and tax burdens, had on balance been unfavourable to state-owned economic units relative to those with non-state ownership. However, the output value of state-owned units in the interior regions accounted for a large proportion of the total output value compared with that in the East, although the output shares of state ownership in all regions had declined. For instance, in 1993, the industrial output value

Table 4. Utilized Foreign Investment and Commodity Exports by Region 1990, 1992–1995

		1990	1992	1993	1994	1995
East	FI	48.64	120.09	265.66	311.49	
		(88.547)	(91.957)	(87.869)	(87.35)	
	X		700.62	770.72	1049.50	1311.13
			(82.484)	(84.008)	(86.708)	(88.137)
Middle	FI	4.42	7.855	26.42	28.73	
		(8.058)	(6.015)	(8.738)	(8.057)	
	X		113.15	109.41	115.86	111.48
			(13.321)	(11.926)	(9.572)	(7.494)
West	FI	1.87	2.65	10.26	16.38	
		(3.395)	(2.028)	(3.393)	(4.594)	
	X		35.63	37.31	45.02	64.99
			(4.195)	(4.067)	(3.72)	(4.37)
National*	FI	102.89	192.02	389.6	432.13	
	X	620.90	849.4	917.4	1210.4	1487.60

Notes: FI: value of foreign investment, in US$100 million.
        X: value of commodity exports, in US$100 million.
        ( ): the share of the relevant item realized in the concerned region as a percentage of the sum total of the three regions.
        *:   the national total for FI includes investment unclassified by region.
Sources: State Statistical Bureau, People's Republic of China, *China Statistical Yearbook*, various issues (1991–1995) (Beijing: China Statistical Publishing House); Zhongguo Tongji Xinxibao (ed.), *China's Latest Economic Statistics Confidential Monthly Report* (Beijing: China's Statistics Information Consultancy Service Centre), January 1996 (Part 2), pp. 52–54.

of state-owned enterprises contributed 33.58%, 54.05%, and 59.79% of the gross industrial output value in the East, the Middle and the West regions, respectively. In 1994 the corresponding shares dropped to 28.09%, 43.15%, and 52.87%. Neverthe-less, policies discriminating against state ownership should have lowered the relative competitiveness in the Middle and the West regions. Furthermore, the economic policies, particularly the price and output sales policies were unfavourable to heavy industry, especially mining, energy and other raw material production industries (relative to light industry, especially that of consumer goods). As a result, the average profit rates of these basic industries were always below average. However, the basic industries were largely concentrated in the Middle and the West regions, so the average profit rates of the industrial enterprises and, accordingly, the accumulation rate in the interior regions tended to be lower.

People in the East in general are better educated and relatively better trained to upgrade economic activities and to rationalize the economic structure in favour of high-tech and higher value-added activities. Indeed, in 1994 the number of students enrolled in colleges, universities, and specialized secondary schools in the East constituted 47.7% of the national total and accounted for 0.584% of its population. The corresponding shares in the Middle and in the West regions were 33.389%, 0.47% and 18.91%, 0.415%. Furthermore, as general living conditions and job prospects are better in the East, there has been a continual outflow of well-educated and well-trained administrative and technical personnel from the Middle and the West regions to the East which has improved the quality of the labour force in the East at the expense of the areas where they were educated and trained. Thus, if the practice of "peacocks flying (from the interior regions) to the South-East" cannot be contained, the relative competitiveness of the interior regions will be further lowered. In sum, since 1991, the productivity and structural advantages of the East which prevailed in the 1980s had been reinforced and fuelled by the relatively more rapid growth of per labour investment; by an improvement in labour quality; and more importantly by the perpetuation of policies favouring foreign-involved economic activities, non state-owned enterprises, and light industries. The outcome had been obvious — a further widening of the income disparities between the East and the interior regions which had begun in the 1980s. However, unlike the situation in the 1980s, after 1990 the Middle region had improved its position relative to that of the West.

Remedial Measures

The rapid increase of inter-regional income unequalities after 1990 had alarmed the Chinese central authorities. As a result, since 1992 some measures have been taken to contain this disparity. They aim at reducing policy differences between the East and the interior regions; increasing investment in the interior regions; and enhancing the central government's capacity to redistribute income and allocate resources among various regions and sectors. In 1992, the central government extended the open economic areas to include cities along the Yangtze River in the Middle region, and to the capital cities of all provinces in the Middle and the West regions, except for Lhasa in Tibet (Taiyuan, Hohhot, Changchun, Harbin, Hefei, Nanchang, Zhengzhou, Wuhan, Changsha, Chengdu, Guiyang, Kunming, Xi'an, Lanzhou, Xining, Yinchuan, and Urumqi) and to cities on the borders (in Inner Mongolia, Heilongjiang, Jilin, Xinjiang, Yunnan, and Guangxi). It is expected that with the opening up of the above cities in the interior regions, policy differences between the East and the interior regions will be reduced. With these open cities as the growth poles, the economic growth of the interior regions will be accelerated so as to contain the income gap between the East and the interior regions. Furthermore, and more importantly, the central government has launched a tax reform in 1994 whereby all domestic enterprises, regardless of the ownership structure or of the region in which they operate, are subject to the same income tax rate and must adopt similar cost accounting methods. In addition, for some taxes, such as the value-added tax, unlike the pre-reform practice, there are no exemptions for foreign-involved enterprises. Finally, taxes are allotted to the central government and to the local authorities for their own purposes or are shared between them according to prearranged distribution rates. Note that, with the exception of ocean oil-drilling, all tax revenues from the exploitation of natural resources are allotted to local authorities. Although under the new tax system the central government must remit part of the increase of the value-added tax and the consumption tax (over the previous year) to the local governments, the taxes allotted solely or predominantly to the central government account for a large proportion of the total tax revenues and have relatively higher growth potential. Thus, it is expected that the central government's share of the national tax revenue will rise. Finally, the local authorities are not allowed to grant additional tax concessions beyond what is permitted by the tax law without approval from the State Council. The new tax system equalizes the tax burden of domestic state-owned and non state-owned enterprises, raises the tax revenue for provinces with substantial mining and natural resource exploitation activities, and in the longer run reduces the privileges enjoyed by foreign-involved enterprises and reduces the autonomy of the coastal provinces to grant concessions to foreign-involved or non state-owned enterprises. Thus, in theory, the tax reform should be advantageous to the interior regions. Furthermore, as it tends to enlarge the revenue share of the centre, it could enhance the central government's capability to regulate the national economy, especially to redistribute income and to allocate resources to the advantage of the interior regions.

The Chinese central government has earmarked funds to combat poverty in the poorest localities (predominantly in the interior regions). Also, it has decided to accelerate the growth of township and village enterprises in the interior regions. Among other practices, in 1993 the central government extended RMB 5 billion in loans to the interior regions to develop township and village enterprises, and since this figure has been increased to RMB10 billion. It is hoped that the rapid expansion of township and village enterprises in the interior regions will accelerate the growth of peasants' income and narrow the per capita rural household income gap between the East and the interior regions. The central government has also encouraged the authorities and enterprises in the coastal provinces to invest in the interior regions, to establish joint-ventures to exploit resources, to construct a socio-economic infrastructure, and to transfer some of their manufacturing activities to the interior regions. In theory, all of the above measures may help enhance the relative competitiveness and accelerate income growth in the interior regions. However, empirical evidence shows that these measures have failed to contain the growth of the income inequalities. This is not surprising because, under the "liberalization and growth" craze, the need to reduce inter-regional income disparities was not regarded urgent relative to the "growth" objective, especially from the position of the officials in the East. Even the central authorites did not have a well-designed comprehensive programme to contain the inter-regional disparities. They pursued piecemeal measures which were not strictly followed by the local authorities. Specifically, the increase in inter-regional factor mobility (due to reforms of financial and commodity circulation) intensified the backward effect. For instance, in 1994, because of profit motives, over 40% of the loans earmarked (by the central government) to finance the development of township and village enterprises in the poorest localities of the interior regions flowed back to the well-developed localities in the East, where the rate of return from investment was higher.[12] Of course, because the development gap between the East and the interior regions is already quite large, it will take time for the above measures (which have only been implemented in the last one or two years) to be effective. Nevertheless, interior provinces within the Yangtze River economic region, such as Anhui, Jiangxi, Hubei, and Sichuan, did experience relatively more rapid economic growth during 1991–1994. Their average annual compound growth rate of per capita real GDP during 1991–1994 was 12.64%, 12.14%, 11.12%, and 10.37%, respectively, higher than the corresponding average growth rate for the Middle (10.264%) and the West regions (9.15%).

Regional Economic Development in 1995

The Policies

According to the outline of the Ninth Five-Year Plan, it appears that the central government will attach much greater importance to reducing the income disparities between the East and the interior regions during 1996–2000.[13] Indeed, the acceleration of economic development in the Middle and West regions, so as to rationalize the economic relationship between the East and the interior regions, constitutes one of the main goals of the Ninth Five-Year Plan. To achieve this, the state will increase its share of investment in the interior regions. In addition, it will grant policy privileges and concessions to authorities and enterprises in the East and to overseas investors for investment and for economic activities in the interior regions. Various industrial ministries, the Ministry of Finance, the Ministry of Foreign Economic Relations and Trade, and the banking system have been instructed to concentrate on serving the interests of the interior regions. Specific plans to assist the relevant sectors and/or localities in the interior regions have been formulated by the ministries concerned. Based on the above plan and on the central government's practices in 1995, it can be said that China has launched a biased regional economic development strategy to the advantage of the interior regions — as opposed to the "East-biased" gradated regional economic development strategy which was launched during the Seventh Five-Year Plan period. Some economic policies which are by nature sector-, activity-, or ownership-biased affect the pattern of inter-regional income distribution. Thus, the strengthening of basic industries, pure agricultural production, and state-owned enterprises — which is an important objective of the Ninth Five-Year Plan — could indirectly help to contain the growing income disparities between the East and the interior regions.

Since 1995, the Chinese central authorities have implemented some policies in line with the regional development strategy for the 1996–2000 period. They have encouraged and facilitated the transfer from the East to the interior regions of equipment for light manufacturing industries. For instance, the textile industry has adopted a strategy of "transferring spindles from the East to the West" during the Ninth Five-Year Plan period. It is planned that during 1996–2000, more than 500,000 cotton yarn spindles will be transferred from Beijing, Tianjin, Shanghai, Guangdong, and other coastal cities to Xinjiang so that by the end of this century the total number of cotton yarn spindles in Xinjiang will rise from 1.14 million to 3 million. During 1996–2000, a total of 2 million cotton yarn spindles will be transferred to the interior regions.[14] In 1995, the Chinese Textiles Association selected the first transfer project which involved a total of 0.206 million spindles (0.075 million of which came from Shanghai) for Xinjiang. Unlike the practice during the Third-Front Construction Campaign, this transfer campaign will be conducted on a voluntary basis and with due compensation. The projects selected to be transferred will require a total investment of RMB 0.52 billion. Nevertheless, this will definitely strengthen the textile industry in Xinjiang and will lower national production costs (including transport costs) for cotton textiles because Xinjiang is already the largest base of cotton production (for commercial purposes) in China. In August 1995, a contract was signed between the textiles bases in Shandong and in Xinjiang to transfer 0.17 million cotton yarn spindles to Xinjiang. Thus, by that time (August 1995), 0.6 million cotton yarn spindles had been transferred to the interior regions. Similarly, arrangements have been made for authorities and enterprises in the East to explore investment as well as other economic cooperation opportunities in the interior regions. They have been persuaded to transfer their resource-processing and/or labour-intensive manufacturing activities to the interior regions. Credit and tax concessions are to be extended to support such investment efforts.

In addition to encouraging domestic agents to invest in and to transfer manufacturing activities to the interior regions, for the first time the Chinese authorities in 1995 issued regulations steering the structure of foreign investment.[15] According to these (provisional) regulations, foreign investment projects are classified into three explicit categories: those which are encouraged, and thus subject to preferential treatment; those subject to restrictions; and those which are prohibited. All others implicitely fall into the "permitted" category. Those investment projects which utilize the resources and manpower of the interior regions and which conform to the state's sectoral priorities are to be encouraged. Furthermore, even if they fall under the category of "restricted projects" (due to the nature of their activities) normal restrictions may be relaxed if they fulfil the above conditions. Foreign investors will be allowed to extend their business (in China) to include "related activities" if their principal investments are in basic industries and in transportation facilities which require huge overhead investments but have long gestation periods. Most foreign investment at present is in the East and falls under the category of restricted projects. At the same time, the central government has reduced tax concessions to foreign-involved enterprises in line with the spirit of the 1994 tax reform. The tax rebate rate for exports has been lowered and tax exemptions which were previously granted to foreign-involved enterprises for the purchase of China's domestic inputs to produce exports abandoned. Furthermore, it has been decided that with the decrease in the general tariff rate to 23% starting from 1 April, 1996, generally there will be no tariff exemptions for foreign-involved enterprises to import equipment and raw materials.[16] The tightening of control and the reduction of privileges for foreign investment will enhance the relative competitiveness of China's domestic enterprises and (more importantly) motivate foreign investors to concentrate on activities and localities favoured by the Chinese authorities where concessions and privileges are still granted. In theory, the interior regions should benefit from these policy changes. In addition, more economic activities have been opened to foreign investors. In 1995, in addition to the 13 cities in the coastal areas or along the Yangtze River, 11 other cities in the interior regions were open for foreign financial institutions to establish offices and conduct business. Basic industries, agriculture, transportation and communication facilities, and even gold mining, were opened for foreign investment. To attract foreign investment, the central government increased the power of the authorities in the interior regions to approve on their own foreign investment projects. The central authorities will serve as the guarantor to back up foreign investment in the basic industries. Foreign-involved agents are given price and fee concessions for land use. Above all, priority is given to the interior regions in the use of loans from the Asian Development Bank, the World Bank, and foreign governments — which are usually soft loans with very favourable terms. It is hoped that via the above measures, the share of foreign investment in the interior regions will increase from 8% to over 20%.[17] Certainly, if foreign investment in the interior regions increases more quickly than that in the East and if it is technology-oriented and used in appropriate ways (to improve the economic infrastructure) the productivity disparities between the East and the interior regions may be contained to a certain extent.

In 1995, construction of the Three Gorges Project began in Hubei. This should have given rise to relatively higher growth rates in capital construction and industrial output in Hubei and in the Middle region. At the same time, the contractionary or (at least) non-expansionary macro economic regulatory policies which lowered the growth rate of credit and strengthened financial discipline continued, but with a slight relaxation in the second half of the year. The impact of the economic regulatory policies on the inter-regional income disparities is complex. In general, if the "cooling down" effect is non-discriminatory to all activities and regions, the foreign-involved and non-state-owned business (thus the East) benefit relatively, because they have more autonomy and resources to evade the regulatory policies, or at least to tide over the difficult times. On the other hand, if the "cooling down" effect is discriminatory, targeting mainly non-state-owned agents and the consumer goods industries, then the interior regions could fare better — as was the case in 1990. On balance, the regulatory economic policies pursued in 1995 were selective, to the advantage of agriculture, and basic industries and, thus, to the interior regions. However, as the state still sought to achieve a "reasonably high" national economic growth rate, no effort was made to depress the absolute output/income level in the East. Because of the existing large productivity/income gap, there should not have been a substantial reduction in the income inequality gap between the East and the interior regions in 1995. Probably, the growth rate of the inter-regional income inequalities in 1995 (over that of 1994) could have been lower than that realized during 1991–1993. But due to the launch of the Three Gorges Project, the on-going acceleration of economic growth within the Yangtze River economic region, which was propelled by Shanghai, as well as due to a relatively better socio-economic infrastructure compared with that of the West, the Middle region, especially Hubei, Anhui and Jiangxi, the three provinces along the Yangtze River, should have performed better than the West.

Table 5. Real Gross Value of Industrial Output by Province January–December 1995

Province	Value (RMB100 million)	Growth rate (%)
Beijing	1164.66	4.70
Tianjin	1158.74	16.3
Hebei	1535.27	14.6
Liaoning	2027.54	6.50
Shanghai	3332.64	15.50
Jiangsu	6380.16	21.20
Zhejiang	3285.79	19.80
Fujian	1109.82	17.00
Shandong	3948.11	14.10
Guangdong	4550.13	16.30
Guangxi	787.07	17.30
Hainan	102.77	17.70
Shanxi	686.41	12.00
Inner Mongolia	423.06	11.30
Jilin	857.69	13.70
Heilongjiang	1075.25	14.00
Anhui	1358.54	23.20
Jiangxi	833.92	10.30
Henan	1737.48	21.70
Hubei	1887.7	18.00
Hunan	1148.24	12.80
Sichuan	2221.03	15.80
Guizhou	349.58	13.70
Yunnan	553.6	20.30
Tibet	—	—
Shaanxi	670.95	11.80
Gansu	399.87	9.90
Qinghai	86.37	10.70
Ningxia	105.2	13.00
Xinjiang	385.52	14.50
National[+]	44163.11	16.05
East	29382.7	16.02(66.532)(66.546)*
Middle	10008.29	17.31(22.662)(22.419)*
West	4772.12	13.64(10.806)(11.035)*

Notes: Growth rate: percentage change of the gross value of industrial output (produced by industrial enterprise of township level and over) of the relevant province/city; region or the nation during January–December 1995 over that of the same period in 1994.

( ):   the percentage share of the gross value of industrial output (produced by industrial enterprises by township level and over) of the relevant province/city; region or the nation in national total during January–December 1995.

( )*:   the same as ( ) but the time period covered is January–December 1994.

—:   not available.

+:   excluding the output value of Tibet.

Sources: Zhongguo tongji xinxibao (ed.), *China Latest Economic Statistics, Confidential Monthly Report* (Beijing: China's Statistics Information Consultancy Service Centre), December 1995 (Part 1), p. 7; January 1996 (Part 1), p. 7.

Performance

Industrial Output

As a result of the macro economic regulatory policies, the average quarterly growth rate (compared to the same period of the previous year) for China's real industrial output of enterprises at township and higher levels declined from January to October 1995, from 17.114% from January to March, to 14.675% from July to September. The average monthly growth rate during January — December was 16.05%. During January — December, the average monthly growth rate in the Middle region exceeded the national total, which was in turn higher than that realized in the East and in the West. As a result, compared with the previous year, during the same time period the share of real industrial output produced by enterprises at township and higher levels in the Middle region rose from 22.419% to 22.662% . On the other hand, the share of the East declined from 66.546% to 66.532%, while that in the West fell from 11.035% to 10.806%. As expected, the three provinces along the Yangtze River in the Middle (region) (Anhui, Jiangxi, and Hubei) did achieve growth rates higher than the national average. Note that the two other provinces along the Yangtze River in the East region (Jiangsu and Zhejiang) achieved above-average growth rates as well, higher rates than Guangdong and Guangxi in the Pearl River Delta area. With respect to the West, the growth rates of Xinjiang and Sichuan were the highest within the region. This was expected because Sichuan should have benefitted from the opening up of the areas along the Yangtze River as well as from the "Three Gorges" project and, as discussed above, Xinjiang had gradually emerged as a key textile production base by "absorbing" textile production equipment transferred from the coastal cities. However, on the whole, it appears that the discriminatory regional development policies pursued in 1995 were still insufficient to uplift the relative industrial production performance of the West (region), despite some improvement in the performance of the Middle region relative to the East.

Industrial Production Efficiency

With respect to the efficiency of industrial production, as measured by the combined index of six efficiency indicators (output-sales ratio, capital-tax ratio, cost-profit rates, labour-productivity ratio, circulation of capital flow, and net-productivity ratio), it declined by 2.52% during January–December 1995 (over the same period of the previous year) compared with some increase in 1994. This confirms that the economic efficiency (as measured by the above indices) of industrial enterprises in China is speed-propelled, highly dependent on the growth rate of industrial output/sales. Nevertheless, with the implementation of discriminatory policies to the advantage of the interior regions, the deterioration of the efficiency of the industrial enterprises in the Middle region was less severe. In the West, three provinces, Gansu, Ningxia, and Xinjiang, experienced a deterioration rate (-0.7%, 3.29%, and 2.84%, respectively) lower than the national average. In the Middle region, only three provinces, Heilongjiang, Jiangxi, and Hubei, experienced a rate of deterioration which was above the national average (−4.53%, −4.92% and −3.16%, respectively). In the East, however only four provinces or cities, Tianjin, Jiangsu, Shandong, and Hebei, had a rate of deterioration below the national average or some positive growth (3.46%, 4.22%, 4.25%, and −1.59%). The rate of deterioration in Beijing, Liaoning, Guangxi and Hainan was as high as −7.73%, −9.68%, −16.13%, and −21.49%, respectively. Thus, it appears that in 1995 with respect to industrial production, the growing disparities in the rate and efficiency of the output growth (measured by the above indices) between the East and the Middle regions were retarded. The westward-biased economic policies should have had a substantial effect. However, the relative performance of the West remained disappointing.

Investment

The macro economic regulatory policies succeeded in depressing the growth rate of fixed assets investment from 31% in 1994 to 19% in 1995. The regional distribution followed the pattern of industrial output. During January–November, the Middle region experienced the most rapid growth (23.4% over the same period of 1994) followed by the East (17%) and the West (15.3%). As a result, the share of completed fixed asset investment in the Middle as part of the national total (including investments unclassified by region) increased from 21.2% to 22.3%, while that of the East and the West declined from 60.02% to 59.86% and 12.77% to 12.55%.[18] Excluding investments unclassified by region, the respective share for the East, the Middle, and the West regions during January–November 1995 should be 63.2%, 23.55%, and 13.25% compared with the corresponding 65.83%, 21.66%, and 12.51% during 1994 (see Table 3).

As for investment in capital construction, (see Table 6) in 1995, the national total grew by 22.10% (including investments unclassified by region) or 17.75% (excluding investments unclassified by region) which was surpassed by that realized in the Middle region (23.4%, excluding investments unclassified by region). The East, however, achieved a much lower growth rate (15.90%). As a result (compared with the same period in 1994), in 1995 the share of the national total capital construction investment completed in the Middle region (excluding investments unclassified by region) increased from 24.4% to 25.58%, while that of the East and the West declined from 60.39% to 59.43% and from 15.21% to 14.99%, respectively. Including investment in technical innovation and trans- formation, the combined investment shares of the Middle, East, and West regions changed from 24.27% to 25.44%, 61.09% to 59.61%, and 14.64% to 14.94%, respectively. This indicates a relatively lower growth rate of investment in technical innovation and transformation in the East (7.84%) compared with that realized in the Middle region (17.76%) and the West (23.57%) in 1995. As expected, the provinces and cities along the Yangtze River, Shanghai, Jiangsu, Zhejiang, Anhui, and Hubei, achieved spectacular growth in capital construction investment.

Commodity Exports and Foreign Investment

In brief, 1995 policies failed to reduce the value share of commodity exports contributed by the East because the Middle region continued to suffer a significant decrease in its export share. In 1995, the national growth rate of commodity exports was 22.90%, which was surpassed by that achieved in the East (24.93%) and in the West (44.36%). The Middle region, however, attained a negative growth rate of −3.78%. As a result, the export share of the East continued to rise from 86.71% in 1994 to 88.14%, although the share of the West increased from 3.72% to 4.37%. The share of the Middle region decreased from 9.57% to 7.49%. It might be that the rapid increase in capital construction in the Middle region "crowded out" exports. With respect to foreign investment, utilized foreign investment in 1995, in the Middle region and in the East, increased by 9.6% and 6.4%, respectively, while that in the West decreased by 30%.[19] In the entire year, foreign investment utilized in the East amounted to 12 and 42.6 times that realized in the Middle and in the West regions, respectively. The per item foreign investment in the West in 1995 was only about US$1.2 million, substantially lower than the national average of US$2.02

Table 6. Investment in Capital Construction by Province, January–December 1995

Province	Value (RMB100 million)	Growth rate (%)	Share[+](%)
Beijing	268.20	–5.90	
Tianjin	160.27	37.30	
Hebei	295.70	29.90	
Liaoning	321.56	–3.40	
Shanghai	658.73	29.50	
Jiangsu	333.12	30.70	
Zhejiang	280.11	34.70	
Fujian	204.43	23.10	
Shandong	358.12	17.10	
Guangdong	868.06	8.30	
Guangxi	144.87	6.40	
Hainan	115.72	–0.80	
East	4008.88<5917.24>	15.90<13.15>*	(59.43)(60.39)* [59.61][61.09]*
Shanxi	130.00	–3.10	
Inner Mongolia	118.88	–6.10	
Jilin	151.94	12.50	
Heilongjiang	199.99	20.20	
Anhui	158.73	33.20	
Jiangxi	100.29	18.50	
Henan	310.42	32.60	
Hubei	349.44	41.00	
Hunan	205.86	37.50	
Middle	1725.56<2525.47>	23.49<21.58>*	(25.58)(24.40)* [25.44][24.27]*
Sichuan	344.06	15.30	
Guizhou	64.04	21.20	
Yunnan	144.33	19.30	
Tibet	35.00	90.70	
Shaanxi	114.02	11.50	
Gansu	78.14	29.10	
Qinghai	30.91	10.80	
Ningxia	25.86	4.40	
Xinjiang	174.84	5.80	
West	1011.20<1483.27>	16.10<18.38>*	(14.99)(15.21)* [14.94][14.64]*
National**	7364.71<10563.21>	22.10<18.62>*	

Notes: < >:   the value of investment in capital construction and technical innovation and transformation.

Growth rate: percentage change of the investment value of the relevant province/city; region or the nation during January–December

Table 6. (Continued)

1995 over that of the same period in 1994; without < >* is for investment in capital construction only, with < >* for investment in both capital construction and technical innovation and transformation.

National: includes investment unclassified by region.

+: the value of investment of the relevant region as a percentage of the sum total of the East, the Middle, and the West (excluding investment unclassified by region); with ( ), for investment in capital construction only and for the period January–December 1995; with ( )*, the same as ( ) except that the period concerned is January–December 1994; [ ], for investment in both capital construction and technical innovation and transformation for the period January–December 1995; [ ]*, the same as [ ] except that the period concerned is January–December 1995.

Source: Zhongguo Tongji Xinxibao (ed.), *China Latest Economic Statistics, Confidential Monthly Report* (Beijing: China's Statistics Information Consultancy Service Centre), February 1996 (Part 1), pp. 14, 18.

million. The disappointing performance of the West can be attributed to inadequate supplies of basic facilities, including electricity, telecommunication, and transportation. Certainly, as foreign investors are free to decide where they will invest, they are inclined to be more cautious, and in view of the huge differences in the investment environment between the East and the interior regions, especially the West, it will take time to achieve a significant reshuffling of the regional distribution of China's foreign economic activities to the advantage of the West.

Inflation and Market Sales of Consumer Goods

The continuation of the macro economic regulatory policies succeeded in repressing the inflation rate (in terms of the retail price index of commodities) from 21.7% in 1994 to 14.8% in 1995. As the structural rigidities in the interior regions were more severe and as the central authorities applied less-stringent credit controls on basic industries and infrastructure construction and financed the relocation of light industries from the coastal areas to the interior regions — which sustained relatively rapid growth of aggregate demand in the interior regions — the inflation rates in the Middle and especially in the West regions in 1995 were higher than those in the East. During January–November, the average national inflation rate was 15.4%. Out of the 12 provinces and cities in the East, only two, Hebei and Guangxi, experienced an inflation rate higher than the national average. On the other hand, only three provinces in the Middle region (Anhui, Jilin, and Heilongjiang) and none in the West (excluding Tibet) had inflation rates lower than or equal to the national average. The highest inflation rates were recorded (in ascending order of severeness) in Shaanxi, Sichuan, Guizhou, and Yunnan — all in the West. A similar pattern occurred in December, except that Shanghai and Beijing experienced much higher inflation rates (13.2% and 11.9%, respectively) relative to the national average (8.3%). A higher inflation rate together with relatively lower income indicated a further deterioration of the living standard of the poor people in the interior regions, especially in the West, relative to the residents in the East.

With respect to the retail sales of consumer goods, the national total increased by 23.63% in 1995 (in current prices, compared with the same period in 1994) of which, sales in the East grew by 24.37%, while those in the Middle and the West regions increased by 24.57% and 18.68% respectively. As a result, during the same period, the sales share of the East expanded from 59.10% to 59.45% of the national total and that of the Middle region increased from 26.89% to 27.10%. On the other hand, the share of the West declined from 14.01% to 13.45%. In fact, since the inflation rate in the East was lower than that in the Middle and the West regions, in real terms the increase of the sales share of the East should have been larger. Thus, in 1995 the biased economic policies in favour of the interior regions did not bring about any significant change in the regional distribution of commodity retail sales. Market sales (of commodities) in the East remained most important and continued to increase faster than the national total. This may indicate that there were no substantial changes in the regional per capita income distribution. Nevertheless, it is likely that the performance of the Middle region improved relative to the national average.

Concluding Remarks

Based on the outcome of the experiments in the 1980s and early 1990s, the Chinese central government has recognized that neither the discriminatory regional development policies, which are biased in favour of the East, nor the non-discriminatory comprehensive liberalization programme can accelerate economic growth in the interior regions sufficiently so as to narrow the growing income/development gap between the East and the interior regions. In order to accelerate income growth in the interior regions and to narrow the alarming inter-regional income disparities, the Chinese central government has adopted some discriminatory regional economic development policies which are biased in favour of the Middle and the West regions. In fact, some such policies have been pursued since 1995; for instance those involving the relocation of some light industries from the East to the interior regions, preferential treatment for foreign investment in the interior regions, the opening up of more cities in the interior regions, and increasing investment in the interior regions via the use of soft loans from foreign governments, the World Bank, and the Asian Development Bank. These policies have been implemented together with macro economic regulatory policies. As expected, the policies have failed to bring a substantial upsurge in the economic strength of the interior regions relative to the East. Yet, it is too early for any conclusive judgements regarding this new regional development strategy. Most of the policies have yet to be launched. With regard to those which have been nominally implemented, "transitional measures" are often offered to the concerned agents (especially the foreign-funded economic units) in order to minimize the "damaging" effects. However, this reduces the effectiveness of the policies. Furthermore, it will take time for the policies to become effective, especially if they are pursued, as is the case in China, via the manipulation of financial levers. In general, the share of the East in most economic activities has continued to rise. However, it appears that the growth rates of the disparities in some important activities, such as industrial output and fixed assets investment, between the East and the interior regions, especially the Middle region, have been reduced. The encouraging performance of the Middle region may be attributed to the biased regional policies which enhance its competitiveness *vis-à-vis* the East as well as to its stronger and more efficient economic infrastructure (which can generate a higher rate of return from investment) relative to that of the West.

With the launching of the Ninth Five-Year Plan, the above discriminatory policies (in favour of the interior regions and basic industries) will be strengthened and will include a much larger scope. However, this does not necessarily imply that the income/development gap between the East and the interior regions will be narrowed as the Chinese central government hopes. It depends largely on whether the central authorities will be able to control and (even) to lower the expected average effective rate of return from investment in the East relative to that in the interior regions because the planned westward transfer of resources and production activities is mainly based on profit motives rather than on the central authorities' administrative directives. As the existing productivity gap between the East and the interior regions, especially the West, is quite large, it will take time for the interior regions to raise their relative rate of return from investment via productivity improvement. Thus, at least in the short run (at least several years), the central government should on the one hand try to repress the growth rate of the rate of return in the East, propably by imposing a more stringent credit policy — especially on activities in which the interior regions have potential advantages — and, on the other hand, by subsidizing investment in the interior regions. Subsidies to the interior regions must be for projects essential to enhancing productivity and to encouraging the re-investment of profits earned in the interior regions so as to minimize a backward effect: the outflow of resources from the "backward" interior regions to the relatively better developed coastal region. Most likely, the above measures will lower the economic growth in the East and depress the static allocative efficiency of resources which may in the short-run retard the growth of the national economy. Furthermore, relatively stagnant income growth in the East, plus subsidies to encourage investment in the West, will probably intensify the centre's fiscal problems. Thus, the central government has to strike a balance between short-run national economic growth and fiscal balance on the one hand and, on the other, regional income/development distribution equity, national unity, and long-run steady economic growth which cannot be decided purely on grounds of economic efficiency.

Whether the centre has the determination and capability to contain possible opposition from the East to a reduction in its concessions and privileges remains to be seen. With a continual decrease in the share of resources (both physical and financial) at its disposal, its capability is dubious. It may be helped if the East were to have easy access to the opportunities and to share the benefits of the "westward" policies, probably moderated by the central government. But the centre must restrain as much as possible the practice of "offering (privileged) policies but not money." If this cannot be avoided, it should be pursued with utmost care, otherwise it will not only violate the principle of equalizing opportunities for all agents, it might also be used by some self-interested agents as loopholes to evade other policies. The social opportunity costs thus incurred could be larger than the subsidies thus saved. Certainly, an enhancement of the centre's credibility and authority over the local governments and ministries and a significant increase in the centre's capability to redistribute income and regulate resource flow would be most effective in implementing the discriminatory policies at low costs. These should be realized as quickly as possible.

Notes

1. The constituent provinces or directly administered cities of the three regions are enumerated in the note to Table 1 in this chapter.

2. For a discussion as to why Mao Zedong wanted to narrow the development gap between the coastal and the interior regions, see Hsueh Tien-tung and Woo Tun-oy, "Regional Disparities in the Sectoral Structure of Labour Productivity, 1985–1989" in *Productivity, Efficiency and Reform in China's Economy*, edited by Tsui Kai-yuen, Hsueh Tien-tung, and T. G. Rawski (Hong Kong: Hong Kong Institute of Asia-Pacific Studies, The Chinese University of Hong Kong, 1995), pp. 56–57.

3. For instance, the ratio of national per capita income in the East to that in the Middle and the West changed from 1:0.7761:0.5544 in 1953 to 1:0.8293:0.7278 in 1965. Ibid., p. 64, Table 1B.

4. By applying the "shift-share Model," Hsueh and Woo find that the relative net productivity competitiveness in the East accounted for 10.99% of the real increase in average labour productivity during 1985–1989, only marginally larger than that of the West (10.02%). Ibid., pp. 83–98.

5. Ibid., p. 64, Table 1B.

6. Unless specified, statistical data for the quantitative analyses in this chapter are from various issues of State Statistical Bureau, People's Republic of China, *China Statistical Yearbook* (Beijing: China Statistical Publishing House) (for annual data); Zhongguo tongji xinxibao (ed.), *China's Latest Economic Statistics Confidential Monthly Report* (Beijing: China's Statistics Information Consultancy Service Centre), (for monthly data) and *China Economic & Trade News Digest* (Hong Kong: Cerd Consultants Ltd.).

7. *Zhongguo xiangzhen jinrongbao*, 25 November 1995, p. 3.

8. The contribution rate of the difference in per capita output from industry i in region $j = \left(\dfrac{y_{iE} - y_{ij}}{y_E - y_j} \right) \times 100\%$ where y_{iE} is the per capita net output of industry i in the East, Y_{ij} is the per capita net output of industry i in region j; y_E and y_j are the per capita GDP in the East and the per capita GDP in region j respectively.

9. The hypothetical increase in GDP in region j in the case where region j has

adopted the same employment structure and has achieved the same labour productivity as that in the East

$$= \Delta EDP_j = E_j \left(\sum_i S_{iE} q_{iE} - \sum_i S_{ij} q_{ij} \right)$$

where Ej is the labour employment in region j; S_{iE} and S_{ij} are, respectively, the proportion of employment in industry i in the East and region j; q_{iE} and q_{ij} are, respectively, the average labour productivity of industry i in the East and in region j.

The direct contribution of the change in the employment structure in region j to the hypothetical increase in

$$GDP = \left[\sum_i q_{ij}(S_{iE}-S_{ij}) \bigg/ \left(\sum_i S_{iE} q_{iE} - \sum_i S_{ij} q_{ij} \right) \right] \times 100\%$$

10. The hypothetical increase in GDP in region j due to a reduction in its unemployment rate down to that in the East $= L_j \cdot (\mu_j - \mu_E) \cdot q_E$

where Lj is the labour force available for employment in region j; μ_j and μ_E are, respectively, the unemployment rate in region j and in the East; q_E is the average labour productivity of all sectors in the East $= \sum_i S_{iE} q_{iE}$

11. For a more detailed discussion of the undesirable effects from undue preferential treatment for foreign investment in China, see Woo Tun-oy, "Opening Up to the Outside World: Myth and Reality," *Hong Kong Journal of Social Sciences*, Special Issue (Hong Kong: Oxford University Press, July 1995), pp.124–48.

12. See Note 7.

13. "The Central Committee of the Chinese Communist Party's Proposal on the Ninth Five-Year Plan for National Economic and Social Development and the Long-Term Goals in 2010," *Ta Kung Pao*, Hong Kong, 5 October 1995, pp. A5–A6.

14. *Xinjiang jingjibao*, 2 June 1995, p. 1.

15. *Xinxi shibao*, 29 June 1995, p. 1.

16. *Ming Pao*, Hong Kong, 11 November 1995, p. C2.

17. It is planned that in 1996 foreign investment in the interior regions will reach US$8 billion, out of a national total of US$39 billion, *Ta Kung Pao*, 19 December 1995, p. B8.

18. *Ming Pao*, 19 December 1995, p. C2.

19. *Ming Pao*, 12 January 1996, p. C2; *Ta Kung Pao*, 13 February 1996 p. B8.

12

The Chinese Rural Economy in 1995

Claude Aubert

Introduction

The recurrent plagues in the Chinese countryside — sluggish investments, output fluctuations, low prices and low incomes, etc. — seem to necessitate the strong medicine of deeper reforms.[1] Strangely enough, at a time when the agricultural reforms are getting paralysed, or are regressing, agricultural output is reaching still higher levels and the peasant revenues are on the increase. According to the preliminary figures from the Chinese authorities, the grain harvest was at an all time record in 1995, while, for the first time, peasant income progressed in real terms at a higher rate than the urban residents'. One may wonder if this is not a miracle, and whether it may last long.

Actually, to a certain extent, these results were engineered by the very return to administrative planning methods, principally relating to cropped areas, together with higher prices given to the farmers by a state anxious to get the necessary deliveries to the cities. The apparent strength of the agricultural performance of the year would therefore underscore the intrinsic weakness of the state, unable to deliver the long expected reforms, and forced to surrender to the short-term peasants' interests.

One may consider that the temporary relief obtained from these retreating policies cannot solve the long term challenges faced by agriculture in the context of a fast developing economy. Beyond the presentation of the economic results of the past two years in the Chinese countryside, we will precisely focus our attention on these challenges which, to be met, will require more ingenuousness from the authorities than the return to the old recipes of the past.

Is There a Grain Problem in China?

With an increase of more than 20 million tons to a total of 465 million tons (or more, on the basis of provisional figure), China achieved a record harvest of grain in 1995, despite rather bad weather conditions. The heavy floods in June and early July of the previous year affected the rice basins of Hunan and Jiangxi, after a severe drought had plagued the north China wheat areas of Henan, as well as the loess region in the northwest. In 1994, floods had devastated the Guangxi province while drought was already well installed in northern China.[2]

As usual the drought had a longer and deeper effect on crops than the floods. In 1994, the wheat harvest dropped by 7.1 million tons, whereas it recovered barely in 1995 with a gain of 2.7 million tons only. On the other hand, corn, which had also declined in 1994, benefited from better summer conditions and increased its output, probably by about 10 million tons last year (see Table 1).

The fluctuations of these two crops reflect the fragile environment of

Table 1. Agricultural Output 1984–1995

(Unit: millions of tons)

Year	Grain	Paddy	Wheat	Corn	Oilseeds	Cotton	Meat	Eggs
1984	407.3	178.3	87.8	73.4	11.91	6.26	n.d.	4.32
1985	379.1	168.6	85.8	63.8	15.78	4.15	19.27	5.35
1986	391.5	172.2	90.0	70.9	14.74	3.54	21.12	5.55
1987	403.0	174.3	85.9	79.2	15.28	4.25	22.16	5.90
1988	394.1	169.1	85.4	77.4	13.20	4.15	24.80	6.96
1989	407.6	180.1	90.8	78.9	12.95	3.79	26.29	7.20
1990	446.2	189.3	98.2	96.8	16.13	4.51	28.57	7.95
1991	435.3	183.8	96.0	98.8	16.38	5.68	31.44	9.22
1992	442.7	186.2	101.6	95.4	16.41	4.51	34.31	10.20
1993	456.5	177.7	106.4	102.7	18.04	3.74	38.42	11.80
1994	445.1	175.9	99.3	99.3	19.90	4.34	44.99	14.79
1995	465.0	180.0	102.0	110.0	22.50	4.50	50.00	15.00

Sources: 1984–1994: *China Statistical Yearbook, 1995*, pp. 347–48, 354–55.
1995: estimates.

north China's agriculture, where water resources are limited and constrain any further progress.[3] The problem here is that wheat and corn have displayed the higher rates of growth in the last decade (respectively, more than 2 and 3% annual growth of yields), whereas average grain yields increased at a very slow speed (with a low 1.5% annual increase, out of which less than 1% for paddy). The resulting shift of the growth in grain from the south to the north renders the harvests highly sensitive to climate conditions and casts doubts on the sustainability of future grain production.[4]

After a drop of two consecutive years, in 1993 and 1994, paddy production gained some 4 million tons in 1995 (Table 1). As the (official) yield had stabilized to the level of more than 5.8 tons per cropped hectare, the previous drop in output was the result of the decrease of cropped areas from 32 million hectares in 1992 to a low of 30 million in 1993 and 1994. The decrease partly reflected a readjustment of the cropping pattern, underlined by a lack of interest on the part of the peasants for the low-priced early paddy; it was, moreover, the consequence, as exemplified in the Guangdong province in 1993, of huge reduction in paddy-fields in favour of more lucrative agricultural activities.[5]

Actually, this trend had already been present since 1990 in the basins of the middle and lower Yangzi (Yangtze), as well as in the coastal areas of the southeast. Whereas this decline in grain cropped areas had been checked in the north plain, it was aggravated in the fast developing provinces of the south by the shrinking of cultivated surfaces giving way to industrial sites or urban constructions. For the whole of China, the net decrease in cultivated area was 300,000 hectares (0.3% of the total) in 1993 and again 200,000 hectares in 1994.[6]

To counter this trend, the Chinese government resorted to authoritarian measures, at least as concerns the planning of grain cropped surfaces. Particularly demonstrative of these efforts was the recovery of paddy production in Guangdong province. Whereas the drop in output had been of no less than 2 million tons in 1993 (10% of the provincial grain harvest), the paddy output was 1 million tons up in 1994, and the whole grain production was back to its 1992 level, in 1995, with an 8% increase.[7] The same recovery was true for Jiangsu (another fast growing province), the drop of 2.5 million tons of grain from 1992 to 1994 being followed in 1995 by a 2.5 million tons increase.[8]

Despite these recoveries, the China north of the Yangzi River was still the main source of grain growth in 1995 with 7% increases in output for the centre north region (Hubei to Jiangsu) and the north plain.[9] Will that pattern affect durably the future of grain production?

Actually, huge potential for growth is still present for paddy production in south China. New hybrid varieties of good quality late rice have been developed which, overtime, should push up again the harvests in the following years (hybrid rice accounts now for 50% of the paddy-fields and 65% of rice production).[10] Hence the levelling off of the yields observed in the last decade may be reversed.[11]

Still, the official objective of a 500 million ton grain harvest in the year 2000 will be difficult to reach with a necessary annual growth of near 1.6% during the next five years, against the 1.4% achieved in the last decade (calculation based on two year mean output from 1985 to 1995).[12] Moreover, it is not sure that such a growth will be enough to meet the growing requirements of husbandry.

The real challenge, actually, will not only be to ensure the continuity of the past pattern of growth (which does not seem out of reach given the diverse and huge resources of the Chinese mainland) but to modify it in order to provide enough feed grain for the fast developing animal productions.

In 1995, the output of meat and eggs, at 50 and 15 million tons (preliminary estimates) respectively, reached, five years in advance, the targets originally fixed for the year 2000 (cf. Table 1).[13] Indeed, the growth of meat output, and more generally of all animal products, has been impressive in the last ten years, with a steady annual increase of 10% (red meat) to 13–18% (eggs and poultry). These high rates, resulting in a quasi exponential pattern of growth, are in contrast with the modest increases already noted in grain (1.4% per year in the last decade) (see Graph 1). It is clear that such a huge difference between these growth rates will not be maintained for long. Sooner or later, therefore, a grain problem will appear if China is to maintain the present trend of fast growing meat consumption.

Up to now this problem, however, failed to materialize. Actually, the husbandry benefited in its past growth from hidden, or undeclared, resources. First, in all likelihood, the official grain output is under-estimated by 30 to 50 million tons. The under-reporting of cultivated areas (133 million cultivated hectares according to the land census figures revised in 1989, against 96 million reported by the State Statistical Bureau) is of such magnitude (about 30% in comparable terms) that one may wonder how best to assess the official claims of grain output and yields. Probably, we are faced with both an underestimation of output and an overestimation of yields.[14]

Whatever the proper assessment to be made, it is clear that without these unreported grain output capacities, a huge deficit in feed grain would have already happened. Our estimates of the requirements for feed grain, based on the official amounts of animal products, seem to indicate that these requirements have quadrupled since 1978, from 35 million tons to 140 million tons in 1994 (see Graph 2). If we were to add the direct consumption by rural and urban residents, 270 million tons in 1994, and the industrial uses (30 million tons), we would get a total amount of 440 million tons actually used that year, whereas the net availability (after deduction of seeds, losses and net balance from external trade) was probably less than 400 million tons.

The deficit has also been avoided due to the use of huge quantities of milling sub-products which do not appear in the global grain balances. About 50 million tons of bran, broken rice, etc. (counted within the gross

Graph 1. Population, Grain and Meat Indexes (1952 = index 1)

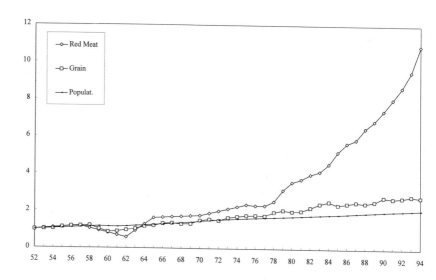

Graph 2. Grain Uses

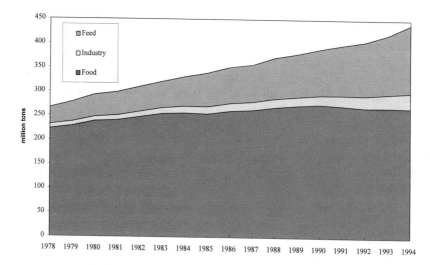

food grain amounts) are, therefore, to be added to the 140 million tons of feed grain proper. The use of these sub-products, together with green fodder, explain the apparently low ratios of grain conversion, observed in particular in traditional pig raising, that we used in our estimates.[15]

One may consider that the hidden resources of unreported grain production have already been used up, while the turn to modern methods of husbandry (for the production of lean meat) will increase the use of feed grain. So that further growth in meat and egg production will have to rely on much higher resources in feed grain. These higher demands, combined with the decline of agricultural land, were among the main reasons for the gloomy projections made by Lester Brown in his last controversial book, predicting massive imports of grain by the year 2030: more than 200 million tons that year, about the equivalent of the total world trade of 1994.[16]

Of course, this kind of scenario (based on questionable hypotheses about the future of Chinese grain production) is absurd as corrective mechanisms will have to occur before the catastrophe happens. These mechanisms could be a levelling off of the meat consumption (already higher in China than in Japan with a per capita gross availability reaching 40 kilograms)[17] triggered by massive price hikes. This already occurred in 1994–1995 in China, when the high price of meat in cities somewhat froze the urban demand (cf. *infra*). Nonetheless, the "warning call" of Lester Brown is to be taken. And, sizeable net imports of grain (up to 30–40 million tons, mainly feed grain) are not out of order for the year 2000. In that (limited) way, China may have a real grain problem in the near future.

Whither the Trade Reforms in Agricultural Products?

For the time being, the problem of peasants' incomes is for sure more pressing than the prospects of future grain supply and demand. These incomes are related, apart from the fluctuations of the harvests,[18] to the prices paid to the farmers and are, therefore, highly dependent on current agricultural trade policies.

After the reforms which, since the mid 1980s, have largely liberalized the trade of animal products and other "secondary" foodstuffs, the last years have witnessed the decisive (and failed) turn toward the abolition of the mandatory delivery quota in grain sales, together with the scuttling of food rationing in the cities.[19]

We will see that these reforms did not have the expected results. But, at least, and for the first time in a decade, the peasants were not the main losers in the process. According to official figures, their per capita net income, reaching RMB 1,550 in 1995, increased by 5% in real terms, whereas urban incomes, at RMB 3,855, progressed only by 4%.[20] Actually, an analysis of the peasants' incomes, computed in real terms (cf. Table 2), shows that the upturn dates back to 1992 when higher rates of increase were observed (up to 7.4% in 1994), contrasting with the low, or negative, rates of the previous years.[21]

What changed then? On the one hand, non-agricultural revenues rose more vigorously (more than 50% increase, in real terms, from 1991 to 1995) and constitute now about 40% of total income (only 30% in the mid 1980s). On the other hand, and still more significantly, there has also been a steady increase of crop incomes since 1993, after more than five years of continuous decline (20% drop in real terms from 1986 to 1992, more than 35% increase from 1992 to 1995).

This recent increase in crop revenue is at odd with the grievances of the peasants always complaining about low agricultural prices. It is, nonetheless, verified by our estimates of grain net incomes based on the actual figures from the Price Bureau rural surveys (cf. Table 3). In these estimates,

Table 2. Rural Per Capita Net Income

(Unit: RMB)

Year	Official Current RMB	Rectified RMB in 1985	Growth (%)	Of which Crops	Other agr.	Non-agr.	Non-agr/tot(%)
1985	397.6	441.6	—	235.5	64.2	141.9	32
1986	423.8	443.8	0.5	237.7	60.2	146.0	33
1987	462.6	452.8	2.0	226.8	73.9	152.2	34
1988	544.9	450.2	-0.6	206.4	85.2	158.5	35
1989	601.5	415.9	-7.6	187.1	76.5	152.4	37
1990	686.3	415.7	-0.1	199.9	69.7	146.1	35
1991	708.6	419.5	0.9	191.6	74.3	153.6	37
1992	784.0	443.4	5.7	191.1	77.1	175.2	40
1993	921.6	458.5	3.4	218.1	60.9	179.5	39
1994	1,221.0	492.3	7.4	238.1	56.9	197.4	40
1995	1,550.0	516.9	5.0	261.9	50.0	205.0	40

Note: Rectified revenues: deflated with the index of rural consumer prices, with readjustment, before 1990, of the crop revenues, using average procurement prices for the self-consumed part.
Sources: 1985–1994: *China Statistical Yearbook, 1995*, p. 279.
1995: *Renmin ribao* (People's Daily), 6 January 1996, and estimates.

Table 3. Grain Income

(Unit: RMB per cropped hectare)

Year	Price Bureau Survey*			Estimates[†]		
	Gross inc.	Mater. cost	Net inc.	Gross inc.	Mater. cost	Net inc.
1985	1,545	506	1,039	1,545	506	1,039
1986	1,758	537	1,221	1,618	506	1,112
1987	1,842	615	1,227	1,648	540	1,108
1988	2,148	747	1,401	1,620	554	1,066
1989	2,721	950	1,770	1,661	599	1,062
1990	2,693	1,036	1,656	1,631	639	992
1991	2,538	1,065	1,473	1,519	638	880
1992	2,811	1,102	1,710	1,623	627	996
1993	3,706	1,548	2,158	1,862	778	1,085
1994	n.a.	n.a.	n.a.	2,313	799	1,514
1995	n.a.	n.a.	n.a.	2,665	1,042	1,623

* Current RMB.
[†] RMB in 1985.
Sources: Price Bureau Survey, *Quanguo nongchanpin chengben shouyi ziliao huibian* (Compendium of Materials on Costs and Benefits of Agricultural Products of All the Country) for 1985–1993 (three grains average).
1994–1995: estimates, based on increases of, respectively, 25% and 50% for the materials costs for these two years (in current RMB).
Rectified: gross income computed on the basis of average yields in China, incomes deflated by the overall retail price index.

we have deflated all the reported figures (material costs and net incomes) according to the overall retail price index and corrected the sample's observed yields in order to adjust them on the national averages.[22] The results show that, after a drop in 1990 and 1991, substantial gains were made afterwards. The net income per hectare of cropped grain, in 1985 constant RMB, increased from less than RMB 900 to about RMB 1,100 in 1993 (deduced from the survey) and more than RMB 1,600 in 1995 (estimated).

This trend in grain incomes is, therefore, coherent with the overall crop revenues (the low levels of these crop revenues in 1992 are to be explained by the drop in cotton production and prices, offsetting the gains in grain incomes).[23]

Generally speaking, the rises in grain net incomes, as well as the increases in agricultural net revenues, were the direct result of the big price hikes in agricultural products which took place during the past years. These price increases have been tremendous, much faster than those of the prices of the industrial products sold in the countryside: 64% increase from 1991 to 1994 (agricultural prices) against 35% (industrial prices).

They permitted the peasants to make up for their agricultural losses of the previous years (see Table 4).[24] One may say that this big rise in agricultural prices has been the main achievement of the failed liberalization of the grain trade, attempted in 1993.[25]

This liberalization had been well prepared, however, with the raising of retail urban ration prices in 1991 and 1992. The increases (RMB 0.20 per kg in 1991, RMB 0.22 in 1992) more than doubled the average price of subsidized grain rations (from RMB 0.314 per kg of "commercial grain" to RMB 0.734). The price paid by the urban dwellers for wheat flour or white rice in state retail shops was then very close to the market price (there was only 10% difference on average).[26]

In 1993, the conditions seemed then ripe for extending to the whole country the experiments in total liberalization already made in a few localities the previous years, particularly in Guanghan county, Sichuan (as soon as in 1991) and in the whole of Guangdong in 1992. As a matter of fact, following a decision issued in February (Document No. 9, 1993), the grain trade had been freed in 94% of the counties by the end of the year.[27]

The results were not exactly those expected by the authorities. The mandatory procurement quotas were abolished, and the State Grain Bureaux were to buy "fixed quantities at market prices" (*baoliang fangjia*). Actually they tried to buy the peasants' surpluses at the previous year's market prices, whereas the current market prices were pushed up by the competition from private traders. The peasants, therefore, waited before selling to the state and often preferred to sell their grain to the merchants

Table 4. Agricultural and Industrial Price Index

Year	Agricultural procurements prices		Annual growth (%)	Industrial products rural retail prices		Annual growth (%)
1985	100.0	—	—	100.0	—	—
1986	106.4	—	6.4	103.2	—	3.2
1987	119.2	—	12.0	108.2	—	4.8
1988	146.6	100.0	23.0	124.7	100.0	15.2
1989	168.6	115.0	15.0	148.0	118.7	18.7
1990	164.2	112.0	−2.6	154.8	124.2	4.6
1991	160.9	109.8	−2.0	159.5	127.9	3.0
1992	166.4	113.5	3.4	164.4	131.9	3.1
1993	188.7	128.7	13.4	183.9	147.5	11.8
1994	264.0	180.1	39.9	215.5	172.9	17.2

Source: *Zhongguo tongji nianjian, 1995* (China Statistical Yearbook, 1995), p. 233.

who came into their courtyards to take the deliveries, and paid cash (contrary to the Grain Bureaux which waited for the peasants to come and were well known in the past for frequently issuing IOU instead of cash).[28] As a result, the state procurements dropped by about one third, from 97 million tons in 1992 to an estimated 65 million tons (see Table 5).[29]

The peasants gained from the competition between the Grain Bureaux and the private merchants, with an increase of about 17% in the average price paid for their grain (see Table 6). The rise was higher for rice, due to the drop in production, with the average price increasing by more than 35% to RMB 810 per ton, whereas the average price of wheat rose by only 10% to RMB 730 (the market price, RMB 800 in November 1993, being kept down by the record harvest of 1993).[30]

These gains, however, were dwarfed by the huge hikes in cities' retail prices which occurred at the end of 1993. This sudden inflation was triggered by a rice shortage in south China (particularly in Guangdong), not alleviated by neighbour provinces which were themselves fighting to supply their own granaries from reluctant peasants. The inflationary pressure in China at that time added to the speculative behaviour of both private traders and grain bureaux, and transformed this local crisis into a

Table 5. Grain Commercialization

(Unit: millions of tons)

	1978	1984	1985	1990	1991	1992		1993
								official estimate
Total output (gross grain)	305	407	379	446	435	443	456	456
Commercialization rate	0.20	0.35	0.31	0.37	0.37	0.35		(0.34)
Total sales ("commercial grain")	52	117	108	140	136	132		(130)
of which state procurement	51	112	91	124	99	97	90	(65)
% of total sales	98%	95%	84%	88%	73%	73%		50%
out of which quotas	38	24	60	51	47	43	51	
	73%	20%	55%	36%	34%	33%		
out of which negotiated	13	88	31	44	52	51		
	25%	75%	29%	31%	38%	39%		
out of which special reserves				28				
				20%				
of which market	1	6	17	6	37	36		(65)
and direct sales	2%	5%	16%	12%	27%	27%		50%

Sources: *Zhongguo shangye nianjian* (China Commerce Yearbook), 1991 to 1993; *Zhonguo guonei maoyi nianjian* (China Domestic Trade Yearbook), 1994.

Table 6. Grain Producer Prices

(Unit: RMB per ton of "commercial grain")

Year	General index (last year = 100)	Quota	% of Market	Procurement	% of Market	Market
1985	101.8	382	66	416	72	578
1986	109.9	390	56	466	67	697
1987	108.0	406	49	509	62	823
1988	114.6	419	41	564	55	1,022
1989	126.9	475	34	750	54	1,396
1990	93.2	489	54	716	79	908
1991	93.8	485	59	677	83	820
1992	105.3	555	69	706	87	810
1993	116.7	637	64	830	83	1,000
1994	146.6	1,014	56	1500	83	1,800
1995	n.a.	1,106	48	1850	80	2,300

Note: The official figures of the general index are not necessarily consistent with the quota, procurement and market prices quoted in the table.

Sources: General index of commercialized grain prices: *China Statistical Yearbook*, 1995, p. 24; procurement prices, 1985–1992: ibid., 1993, p. 273; quota prices, 1985–1995: estimate market prices; 1985–1990: Institute of Rural Development (CASS), *Zhongguo nongcun* (Chinese Rural Economy), October 1992, p. 11.

nationwide inflation of food prices. The price of rice (at RMB 1.2 per kg on average in December 1992 after the programmed retail prices increases) was up 40% in December 1993 at RMB 1.69 (for good quality rice, the standard wheat flour reaching also the high level of RMB 1.59 per kg).[31]

This inflation persisted on for the whole of 1994, despite the selling of state stocks in the cities' markets. In December 1994, the price of good quality rice reached RMB 2.95 per kg (75% increase in one year), and the standard wheat flour RMB 2.31 (45% increase).[32] On average, retail grain prices, throughout China, went up by 48% from 1993 to 1994. This price hike of grain induced similar increases for all foodstuffs, with 37% increase for meat products, 36% for vegetables, etc.[33] The pork price, in particular, followed the prices of feed grain and gained 50% from December 1993 (RMB 9.7 per kg) to December 1994 (RMB 14.47; the price was only RMB 7 in 1992).

No doubt that these unprecedented rises in urban food prices scared the Chinese authorities, who were also deeply worried by the drop in their commercial grain stocks. Actually, no general deficit in supply was involved in that situation, as, in spite of the rice shortage, 1993 had been a surplus year for grain, and 1994 witnessed a huge increase in meat production.

But, the supply to the cities had been disrupted by the grain trade reform, while the inflationary pressures on the whole economy (as a result of the big upsurge in the supply of money) prepared the stage for the general price hikes.[34] In that situation, the Chinese government took the quickest solution for the replenishment of the state stocks and reinstated the mandatory quotas for grain procurements in the spring of 1994. Later, grain rationing was also back in most large cities, in order to help the poorest of the urban dwellers.[35]

That quick retreat from the liberalization attempt had a price. In order to convince the peasants to sell again to the state organs, the quota prices of grain had to be raised in 1994 by an unprecedented margin, up to 40% on average.[36] The actual increase of average prices paid to the farmers, including quota and negotiated purchase, was eventually 60% for paddy rice and 80% for wheat (up to RMB 1,300 per ton for both products, the market prices at the end of 1994 nearing RMB 1,500).[37]

We still do not know if the objective of the government, which was to regain control of 70 to 80% of the grain trade, was achieved in 1994. But, as already demonstrated, peasants were the short-term winners of this year of commercial turmoil with the big gains in revenues already noted (cf. *supra*). It is not sure whether this victory would serve their long term interests. The result of this aborted reform was also to reinstall the "double track" of quota and negotiated prices. Despite the rise in quota prices in 1994, the gap between these prices and the market ones began again to grow (the market prices being more than 75% higher than those of the quota at the end of the year). It has been calculated that this price differential (cotton included) implied a cost of up to RMB 76 billion to the peasants in 1994, more than offsetting the state's investments in agriculture (on the increase to RMB 53 billion, accounting for 9% of total expenditures).[38]

During 1995, this gap widened as it was decided not to increase the quota prices.[39] Fuelled by the high inflation of last year, with a 50% upsurge in fertilizers' costs, the market prices of grain reached record levels: about RMB 2,200 to 2,700 per ton for paddy, RMB 1,800 for wheat, and RMB 1,700 for corn.[40] Actually, provincial authorities had to increase, at their own costs, the procurement prices in order to get the surplus grain from the peasants,[41] with an estimated increase of more than 20% in average price paid to the farmers (personal estimate, cf. Table 6).

If peasants seemed to have further increased their profits last year, the Chinese authorities were back to their old dilemma, having to heavily subsidize the retail prices. Due to these costly efforts, the price of rice and flour increased only moderately in 1995, 15% for flour (up to RMB 2.69 per kg in October 1995), 20% for rice (RMB 3.55 for good quality rice).[42]

The wild price hikes in grain had also perverse effects last year. In particular, intensive pig breeders suffered from the high cost of feed grain. On the one hand, the retail price for pork levelled off, after the boom of 1994, and the festive consumption of the Lunar New Year, and fell to RMB 14.17 per kg in October. As butchers kept their profits high, the price of live hogs fell by a higher proportion (almost 20% from RMB 8.4 per kg to a low of RMB 6.8). On the other hand, the market price of corn had increased by 75%, leading, therefore, to a widespreading crisis in husbandry.[43]

The price of cotton, still an administrative one, had also to be increased. In 1994, the official price was raised by no less than 60% in order to keep cotton growing competitive against grain cultivation. At RMB 10,900 per ton, this price was, however, lower than the one offered (illegally) by local enterprises, and the traditional "cotton wars," usual when supply is short, went on pushing the average price to RMB 13,000 per ton. In 1995, in spite of a new increase of state official price up to RMB 14,000 per ton, cotton growing was still at a disadvantage compared to grain, while massive imports were necessitated to make up for the inadequacy of output.[44]

The decision not to liberalize cotton trade and the return to the mandatory procurements of grain quota at fixed price, implying some planning of cropped areas, are clear signs that agricultural trade reforms are at a standstill in China. More than a political comeback to conservative politics (real enough in other fields), these decisions mean principally that the state commercial organs (especially for grain) are not ready to assume the new roles that a true liberalization would imply for them. The current reform trying to separate in their accounts the policy tasks of the Grain Bureaux (the costly ones of regulating the market through grain reserves and funds) from their purely commercial activities (trade and processing for profit)[45] underline more than resolve the funda-mental ambiguity and weakness of these bureaux, speculating instead of fighting the inflation, but otherwise unable to compete efficiently with private traders when markets are really open.

However, if peasants are to adjust their production to fast changing consumption demands, an efficient trading network will have to be installed, sooner or later, in China. And, reforms will undoubtedly come back right at the top of the authorities' agenda.

From the Countryside to the Cities

The challenges of agricultural production (grain self-sufficiency) and reform (grain trade reform) are only a part of a more comprehensive challenge, which is to achieve a balanced transition from a predominantly agrarian economy to an industrial state. What kind of price policy will be necessary to ensure a level of peasant income high enough to provide a sizeable market in the countryside for industrial products? What kind of income differential is nonetheless necessary to sustain the transfer of labour from the primary sector to the rest of the economy?

For certain, this income differential, or gap between the standards of living of the peasants and of the urban dwellers, is already quite large and, up to 1994, increasing. The ratio of urban living expenses to the rural ones (cf. Graph 3), which had decreased from 2.4/1 in 1978 to 2.2/1 in 1984 (measured in constant RMB), increased again afterwards and reached 3.2/1 in 1994.

This fact may be unfortunate, and peasants have some reason to rejoice if the reversal in 1995 is confirmed. But, all the same, the fast rise

Graph 3. Urban/Rural Living Expenses (constant yuans 1985)

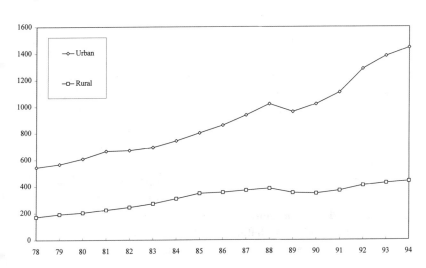

incomes permitted the urban population to absorb the huge price increases in foodstuffs of the last two years. The reported figures of the budgets of urban households (cf. Table 7) indicate that, in spite of these price hikes, the proportion of food expenses within the overall budget continued to decrease (from 54% in 1990 to 50% in 1994), with the respective proportions of grain and secondary food (meat, vegetables, etc.) remaining unchanged.

This trend is consistent with the Engel Law, and the general evolution of China follows the classical pattern of development with the growing importance of industry, and the corresponding differential between industrial and agricultural growth (cf. Table 8). If industry displayed some disproportionately high rates of growth during the early 1990s (up to 21%), which could be cooled off last year to a more reasonable rate of 14%, one may say that agriculture enjoyed quite a robust growth with rates of 4 to 5% a year.

The problem is that the corresponding decline of the share of agriculture in the GDP (particularly fast for the a drop from 27% in 1990 to 19% in 1995) was not accompanied by a decline of similar amplitude in the agricultural employment (decreasing only from 59% of total labour to 53%, cf. Table 9). Hence, the challenge faced by China will be to speed up this transfer of activities, both within the countryside and toward the cities.

One key factor will be the capacity of rural industries to absorb the surplus labour from agriculture. In the past ten years, about 50 million non-agricultural jobs were created in the booming sector of rural enterprises (the so-called "township and village enterprises" or TVEs, *xiangzhen qiye*). With an estimated 120 million people employed in 1994, these TVEs constituted no less than 27% of all rural labour, against less than 20% in 1985 (cf. Table 9). However, during the same period, the total number of active persons in the countryside had increased by 75 million, to 447 million. Therefore, despite the impressive performance of the TVEs, the number of agricultural workers had still gone up by about 25 million persons in the last decade, adding to the already pervasive agricultural under-employment.

The uncertainty about and the lack of coherence in the available figures make difficult a precise assessment of this race between the agricultural and non-agricultural workforce in the countryside for the last years.[46] It would seem that, during the four years from 1990 to 1994, rural enterprises had absorbed 27 million persons, the same number as the

Table 7. Urban Budgets

Items	1990				1992				1993				1994				94/93 (%)
	Quant jin	Price ¥/jin	Total RMB	%	Quant jin	Price ¥/jin	Total RMB	%	Quant jin	Price ¥/jin	Total RMB	%	Quant jin	Price ¥/jin	Total RMB	%	(%)
Total expenses			1,279	100			1,672	100			2,111	100			2,651	100	35
Food			594	54			864	52			1,058	50			1,422	50	34
Grain	26	0.32	85	7	200	0.55	110	7	196	0.66	130	5	185	1.10	204	7	57
Op	13	1.60	20	2	4	2.60	36	2	16	2.66	41	2	16	4.00	62	2	51
Secondary food			401	31			481	29			616	29			807	28	31
of which pork	30	2.70	81	6	30	2.80	84	5	25	3.50	88	4	25	5.00	125	4	43
Year pork	7	3.50	27	2	10	4.00	40	2	15	4.50	68	3	15	6.50	98	3	44
beef and mut.	7	3.30	22	2	7	4.00	28	2	10	4.50	45	2	10	6.50	65	2	44
poultry	7	3.75	26	2	11	3.80	42	3	12	4.00	48	2	12	5.00	60	2	25
eggs	5	2.40	35	3	20	2.40	48	3	20	2.40	48	2	20	3.00	60	2	25
fish	5	2.55	39	3	17	3.50	50	4	18	4.00	72	3	18	5.00	90	3	25
vegetab. 1	180	0.05	27	2	160	0.15	24	2	140	0.25	35	2	140	0.30	42	1	20
vegetab. 2	100	0.55	55	4	100	0.60	50	4	120	0.555	78	4	100	0.90	90	3	15
fruits	45	1.20	54	4	45	1.30	50	3	45	1.50	68	3	45	2.00	90	3	33
other			36	3			37	2			67	3			87	3	30
Tobacco, Beverages			76	6			9	5			114	5			50	5	31
Other			2	9			146	9			157	7			200	7	27

Notes: jin: 0.5 kilogram;
vegetab. 1: cheap vegetables (cabbages, etc.);
vegetab. 2: other vegetables.

Sources: *China Statistical Yearbook, 1991 to 1995*, for total amounts of living and food expenses.
Estimates for the details of food consumption, based on the urban surveys in *Zhongguo chengzhen jumin jiating shouzhi diaocha ziliao* (Materials on Chinese Urban Households Survey of Incomes and Expenses), 1990, 1994.

Table 8. Gross Domestic Product, Industrial and Agricultural Output Values

(Unit: millions of current RMB, annual growth in real terms)

Year	Gross Domestic product (GDP)	Growth (%)	Industry (added value)	Growth (%)	Agriculture (added value)	Growth (%)	Agricult./ GDP
1990	1,853.1	3.8	685.8	3.4	501.7	7.3	0.27
1991	2,161.8	9.3	808.7	13.8	528.9	2.4	0.24
1992	2,663.5	14.2	1,028.5	21.8	580.0	4.7	0.22
1993	3,451.5	13.5	1,414.4	21.0	688.2	4.7	0.20
1994	4,500.6	11.8	1,835.9	18.0	943.8	4.0	0.21
1995	5,770.0	10.2	2,300.0	14.0	1,100.0	4.5	0.19

Sources: 1990 to 1994: *China Statistical Yearbook, 1995*, p. 32.
1995: *Renmin ribao*, 6 January 1996.

increase in the total rural labour force (cf. Table 9). On the other hand, official figures show a decrease in the absolute number of agricultural workers since 1991, which would imply that a turning point has been reached where the ratio between labour and land in Chinese agriculture may begin to improve.

Whatever of the future trends with these respective numbers, one must notice that the level of agricultural employment (53% of total labour force, cities included) is still very high, considering the stage of development already reached by China. The same is true of the high proportion of the rural population which still constitutes more than 70% of the Chinese total (see Table 9). The urban transformation of China is clearly lagging behind the industrialization process, and some studies have suggested that, by international standards, the urbanization rate should be more than ten points higher than the present one.[47] As a matter of fact, the official rural exodus, as estimated from the urban population figures, is very slow with only 5 to 7 million net new migrants every year into the cities since 1985.[48] This limited exodus seems to correspond mainly to the progressive absorption by the large cities of their agricultural suburbs.

On this background of still insufficient, and uneven, absorption of the surplus agricultural labour by rural enterprises and sluggish overall urbanization process, one may better understand the new phenomenon which appeared in the past years: the huge migration of temporary peasant workers into the towns and cities.

In 1995, these migrations were increasing fast with 80 million officially reported as leaving their villages at least for a few months and seeking outside jobs, out of which 30 million changed administrative regions

Table 9. Rural Population and Labour

((Unit: millions of persons)

Year	Population			Labour					Labour of rural entreprises
	Total	Rural	% Rural	Total	Rural	(%)	Agricultural	(%)	Rural (%)
1985	1059	808	76	499	371	82	304	61	70	18.8
1986	1075	811	75	513	380	80	305	59	79	20.9
1987	1093	816	75	528	390	79	309	58	88	22.5
1988	1110	824	74	543	401	79	315	58	95	23.8
1989	1127	832	74	553	409	79	324	59	94	22.9
1990	1143	841	74	567	420	79	333	59	93	22.1
1991	1158	853	74	584	431	79	342	59	96	22.3
1992	1172	848	72	594	438	78	340	57	106	24.2
1993	1185	852	72	602	443	75	333	55	123	27.9
1994	1199	855	71	615	447	73	327	53	120	26.9

Source: *China Statistical Yearbook, 1995*, pp. 59, 83, 329–30, 364.

or provinces.[49] In 1994, on the basis of local surveys, these respective numbers were only 60 and 20 million.[50]

These "tides of peasant workers" (*mingong chao*) are probably the rational response of the peasantry to the income differentials both between cities and countryside and between different regions. Most of the migrants crossing borders are from the poor provinces of Sichuan, Henan, Anhui and from the agricultural basins of Hunan and Jiangxi. They go east and south toward the most developed regions of coastal China (see Map 1). They may find work in the booming rural industries of these advanced regions (see Map 2). They fill mostly the dirty or hard jobs of the large cities (e.g. the 3 million migrant workers in the municipality of Beijing). This flux of migrants meets the need for skilled workers in the construction sites of the growing cities, and for female workers in the labour intensive industries of the coastal area, etc. They also alleviate the poverty of their places of origin. It has been estimated that the 6 million migrant workers from Sichuan sent back home more than RMB 10 billion in 1994, i.e., the equivalent of RMB 100 per rural person in the province.[51]

Sure enough, these migrants do not come from the poorest provinces, such as Yunnan (19 million persons, 59% of the rural population, with per capita income less than RMB 500 in 1994) or Guizhou (12 million persons, 43% of the population).[52] Actually, the 70 million persons living in the pockets of poverty of rural China (mainly in the southwest and in the arid areas of Ningxia and Gansu) are clearly left out in the present developing process. But, the other regions, even backward by the standards of the coastal areas, participate in the overall economic development through the rural industries when present, or through the remittances of their migrant workers.

Conclusion

The dichotomy between the countryside and the cities, real enough if standards of living are to be assessed, is not so meaningful when the

Map 1. Peasant Incomes 1994

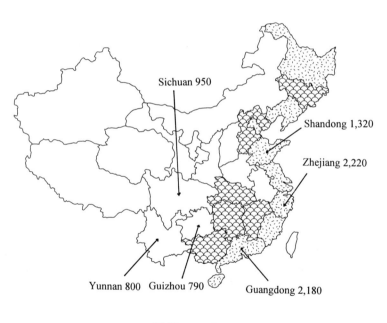

Sichuan 950

Shandong 1,320

Zhejiang 2,220

Yunnan 800   Guizhou 790   Guangdong 2,180

RMB per capita

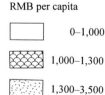

☐ 0–1,000

▨ 1,000–1,300

▨ 1,300–3,500

Map 2. Rural Entreprises Labour Force, 1994

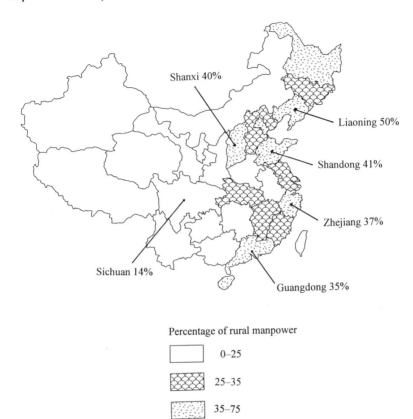

Shanxi 40%

Liaoning 50%

Shandong 41%

Zhejiang 37%

Sichuan 14%

Guangdong 35%

Percentage of rural manpower

    ☐   0–25

    ▨   25–35

    ▨   35–75

whole process of development is addressed. The "poles of development" of the coastal areas and of their rich cities have repercussion well beyond the immediate surroundings of their own hinterland. Farmers of the south Jiangxi small rice basins sell their live pigs to Guangzhou, small furnaces in deep rural Hunan hill country prepare construction materials for Shenzhen buildings … and Sichuan farmers sell their workforce in Beijing during the agricultural slack season. In that respect, the challenge will be to open still more the urban jobs to the "peasant workers" in spite of all the turmoil that their arrival provokes in the cities. As urban privileges will be therefore directly questioned, this opening, in the long run, may have deeper effects than the nonetheless necessary reform in grain trade or the improvements in agricultural production.

Notes

1. See Liu Yunhua, "The Rural Economy in China," in *China Review 1995*, edited by Lo Chi Kin, Suzanne Pepper and Tsui Kai Yuen (Hong Kong: The Chinese University Press, 1995), pp. **22**.1–**22**.22.

2. For the general weather conditions at the beginning of the summer 1995, see *Nongmin ribao* (Farmers' Daily), 23 June 1995; floods in Hunan, ibid., 4 July 1995, in Jiangxi, ibid., 18 July 1995. There have been also summer floods in the northeast (Liaoning, ibid., 5 August 1995). In Shanxi, floods and frost followed the previous long drought (*Shanxi ribao*, 12 October 1995, translated in BBC, *Survey of World Broadcast*, Far East, W-0413). In 1994, the natural disasters had been more widespread, with a total of 31 million hectares devastated (out of which 17 million by drought), compared to only 23 million in the good year of 1993 (cf. *Zhongguo tongji nianjian 1995* [China Statistical Yearbook 1995], p. 361.) In Guangxi, one million hectares (half of the paddyfields) were flooded in the early summer 1994 (ibid. and *Nongmin ribao*, 9 August 1995). For a general assessment of the disasters in 1994, see *Renmin ribao* (People's Daily), 25 December 1994.

3. See Liu Jiang on the problem of the lack of water resources and the necessity of dry farming in North China, *Nongmin ribao*, 30 September 1995.

4. In a paper revised in 1995, we have presented a regional analysis, disaggregated by types of grain, of the past and current trends in grain production, in relation to the improvements in irrigation facilities. See Claude Aubert, "Before and after the Green Revolution, Irrigation and Grain Yields in China," *Giessen*, 1995.

5. *Zhongguo tongji nianjian 1995*, p. 344. On the fall in paddy crops in 1993, see *Nongmin ribao*, editorial, 12 August 1993; situation in Guangdong, ibid. 21 December 1993; same early trends noticed in Zhejiang, ibid., 18 February 1993.

6. *Zhongguo tongji nianjian 1995*, p. 377.

7. The planned minimum grain area to be cropped had been fixed at 110 million hectares for 1995 (*Nongmin ribao*, 13 January 1995), with corresponding provincial planned figures. Detailed indicators of this "indicative plan" (*zhidao jihua*) were to be applied in each province. See National Work Conference for the Autumn Sowings, *Nongmin ribao*, 17 October 1995. In Guangdong, the recovering in grain output was obtained through tighter control on cultivated areas and the announcement of particularly high quota prices for early paddy, cf. *Nongmin ribao*, 25 January 1995. These measures were successful enough, yielding an output of 18 million tons in 1995, compared to 16 million tons in 1994 (*New China News Agency*, 4 December 1995).

8. Deduced from *New China News Agency*, 27 November 1995, and *Zhongguo tongji nianjian 1995*, p. 347.

9. Grain output rose only 1% in Hubei, but 8% in Jiangsu and 14% in Anhui (*New China News Agency*, 6 January 1996, 27 November 1995 and 20 December 1995). Increases of 6% in Hebei, 7% in Shandong (ibid. 23 November 1995 and 25 October 1995), and 7% in Henan were observed (despite a slight drop in wheat production due to the continuation of the previous year's drought, cf. *New China News Agency*, 23 July 1995, and *Nongmin ribao*, 7 July 1995, more than offset by good autumn harvests, ibid. 6 January 1996).

10. *Nongmin ribao*, 20 May 1995.

11. For a general assessment of future grain yield capacities see Lin Yifu et al., *Zhongguo nongcun guancha* (China Rural Survey), No. 3 (1995), pp. 1–14.

12. Liu Jiang in *Nongmin ribao*, 27 October 1995, and ibid. 10 November 1995. Discussion of possible sources of increased grain productivity in *New China News Agency*, 26 May 1995; general discussion of economists on long term grain strategy in *Zhongguo nongcun jingji* (China Rural Economy), August 1995, pp. 3–18.

13. The output of red meat increased by 18% during the first nine months of 1995. Estimates for 1995 were of 15 million tons of eggs, 6 million tons of milk and 23 million tons of aquatic products (*Nongmin ribao*, 26 December 1995).

14. Revised figures of the Land Census for 1989 were published by the Institute of Agricultural Zoning (Chinese Academy of Agricultural Sciences) and the Station of Soil Fertilization (Ministry of Agriculture), in *Zhongguo gengdi ziyuan ji qi kaifa liyong* (Resources of Cultivated Land in China and Their Developmental Utilization) (Beijing: Cehui chubanshe, 1992). See discussion in Aubert, "Before and after the Green Revolution" (Note 4). The Chinese mass media recently admitted a 20% gap only between reported State Statistical Bureau figures and Land Census data, with 120 million hectares cultivated, see *Nongmin ribao*, 9 March 1995.

15. For more details, see our report for the OECD, "Politiques, marchés et échanges agricoles en Chine," *Politiques, marchés et échanges agricoles dans les pays d'Europe Centrale et Orientale, dans certains nouveaux états indépendants, en Mongolie et en Chine, suivi et perspectives 1995*, OCDE, Paris, pp. 201–202.

16. Lester Brown, *Who Will Feed China? Wake-up Call for a Small Planet* (New York: W. W. Norton & Co., 1995), p. 97.

17. Computed on the basis of output and population figures, this per capita gross availability was 38 kilograms of (total) meat in 1994. See *Zhongguo nongye nianjian 1995* (China Agricultural Yearbook 1995), p. 320. The corresponding consumption figures published by the State Statistical Bureau (13 kilograms per capita for peasant households and 24 kilograms, purchased, for urban ones) (*Zhongguo tongji nianjian 1995*, pp. 263, 287) clearly do not fit

with the reported outputs. These low consumption levels observed in the surveys actually under-report (by a big margin) the real quantities consumed, as they do not take into account the consumption out of the family (canteens, restaurants, etc.) for the urban sample, peasant migrants consumption for the peasant one, etc. See Zhang Cungen, *Nongye jingji wenti* (Problems of Agricultural Economy), May 1995, pp. 43–47.

18. On the influence of the weather on Chinese crops, see the study of Y. Y. Kueh, *Agricultural Instability in China, 1931–1991* (Oxford: Clarendon Press, 1995), p. 387.

19. For a general overview, see Terry Sicular, "Redefining State, Plan and Market: China's Reforms in Agricultural Commerce," *The China Quaterly*, December 1995, special issue "China's Transitional Economy," pp. 1020–46.

20. *Renmin ribao*, 6 January 1996.

21. The official figures of peasants' incomes in current prices have been deflated by the index of rural consumer prices (*Zhongguo tongji nianjian 1995*, pp. 233, 279). For the years before 1990, the total income has been rectified by multiplying the crop revenues by a constant ratio of 1.23, in order to take into account the fact that the self-consumed parts of these revenues were counted at quota prices, whereas they were computed at average sales prices for the following years (for the year 1990, the crop income computed in the former way was RMB 269, cf. *Zhongguo tongji nianjian 1991*, p. 295, and RMB 330, 23% higher, in the present method of computation, cf. ibid., 1992, p. 307).

22. Overall retail price index, in *Zhongguo tongji nianjian 1995*, p. 233. The adjustment to average national yields has been made using the year to year changes reported by the State Statistical Bureau's yields figures, from the base figure, for 1985, of the average yields of the three grains (rice, wheat, corn) published by the Price Bureau.

23. The purchase price for cotton, by and large an administrative one, was reduced by 5% in 1992, following the surpluses of the previous year's record output, at the very time when the output fell by more than 20%, then resulting in huge losses for the cotton growers (see *Zhongguo tongji nianjian 1993*, p. 273). For the bad timing of cotton pricing policies, see Wang Qinggong and Liu Fali, in *Zhongguo nongcun jingji*, August 1995, pp. 36–40.

24. *Zhongguo tongji nianjian 1995*, p. 233. For this reversal in the price scissors, see Han Zhirong, in *Zhongguo nongcun jingji*, July 1995, pp. 9–12.

25. For a detailed analysis of this trade reform, see Claude Aubert, "Consommations alimentaires et libéralisation du commerce agricole en Chine," in *Les paysans peuvent-ils nourrir le tiers-monde?*, edited by Maxime Hambert (Paris: Publications de la Sorbonne, 1995), pp. 121–41.

26. See *Zhongguo shangye nianjian 1992* (China Trade Yearbook 1992), p. IV–5, 1993, p. IV–2, *Zhongguo shichang tongji nianjian 1993* (China Market Statistics Yearbook 1993), p. 445. "Commercial grain" (*maoyi liang*) is the

measure unit used by the Ministry of Domestic Trade for the average grain it handles, corresponding to semi-processed grains (mixing for example wheat counted at gross weight with milled rice).

27. *Zhongguo guonei maoyi nianjian 1994* (Almanac of China's Domestic Trade 1994), p. IV–3.

28. The active competition of private merchants, contrasting with the clumsy business policies and general apathy of the State Grain Bureau, has been well described in surveys made in Hunan, cf. *Nongye jingji wenti*, March 1994, pp. 38–43. See the same kind of reports in Hubei (*Nongmin ribao*, 3 July and 28 September 1993), Henan (ibid., 10 June and 12 August 1993), etc.

29. The official figures for grain procurements indicate a drop of only 7 million tons in 1993. However, this figure is contradicted by the fact that commercial stocks were down by 30% while retail sales by the State dropped by 23 million tons that same year (to a low 67 million tons) (*Zhongguo guonei maoyi nianjian* 1994, p. IV–1). The official survey made by the State Statistical Bureau in 1993 indicate on the contrary a sharp drop in the peasants' sales to the State (93 kilograms per capita in 1992, only 66 kilograms in 1993), cf. Zhu Xinwu, *Zhongguo nongcun jingji*, February 1995, pp. 21–25. This general survey is confirmed by alarming local reports at the end of 1993 (Hunan, *Nongmin ribao*, 15 and 20 October 1993, Hubei, ibid. 20 October 1993, Jiangsu, ibid. 16 and 29 November 1993, etc.).

30. See *Zhongguo wujia tongji nianjian 1994* (China Statistical Yearbook of Material Prices 1994), p. 55. Average prices paid for paddy rice and wheat in Price Bureau, *Quanguo nongchanpin chengben shouyi ziliao huibian 1994* (Compendium of Materials on Costs and Benefits of Agricultural Products of All the Country 1994), p. 1. Wholesale market price (Zhengzhou) of wheat in *Zhongguo wujia* (China Prices), December 1993, p. 35.

31. *Zhongguo wujia*, January 1993, p. 60, January 1994, p. 45.

32. *Zhongguo wujia*, January 1995, p. 39.

33. *Zhongguo tongji nianjian 1995*, p. 236.

34. On the end of 1993 price hikes, see Yu Xian, *Zhongguo nongcun jingji*, July 1794, pp. 3–7.

35. See details of the rationing in Harbin, *Heilongjiang ribao*, 1 September 1994 (translated in *SWB, FE*, weekly, W-0350).

36. Quota price increases at 10 June 1994, up to RMB 950 to 1,050 per ton for paddy, and RMB 1,000 to 1,080 per ton for wheat, cf. *Nongmin ribao*, 19 October 1994, and 6 January 1995.

37. Personal trip notes, October 1994, and *Nongmin ribao*, 17 January 1995 (Shanghai futures market).

38. Guo Shutian, *Nongye jingji wenti*, October 1995, pp. 2–7. State investments in agriculture, cf. *Zhongguo tongji nianjian 1995*, p. 231.

39. Guo Wei, *Zhongguo nongcun jingji*, September 1995, pp. 23–28.

40. Prices in September 1995, see Survey of the Ministry of Agriculture, *Nongmin ribao*, 1 November 1995, and prices at Zhengzhou wholesale market, ibid., 8 November 1995.

41. Li Shutian, *Zhongguo wujia*, August 1995, pp. 16–18.

42. *Zhongguo wujia*, November 1995, p. 39.

43. See example in Jiangxi, *Nongmin ribao*, 30 May 1995.

44. See prices, in *Jingji ribao* (Economic Daily), 7 July 1995, and *New China News Agency*, 16 August 1995. Comparative incomes in Shandong, see Wang Fuli et al., *Zhongguo nongcun jingji*, August 1995, pp. 36–40. The policy of State monopoly on cotton trade was reiterated in the autumn of 1995, before the harvest. See the "san bufangkai" in *Nongmin ribao*, 5 September 1995.

45. See work conference of grain departments in *Nongmin ribao*, 19 July 1995.

46. Some uncertainty surrounds the exact figure of employment in the TVEs for 1994. *Zhongguo tongji nianjian 1995*, p. 364, indicates 120 million persons, whereas *Zhongguo xiangzhen qiye nianjian 1995* (China Yearbook of Township and Village Enterprises 1995), p. 88, gives the number of only 113 million (for 1995, a preliminary estimate put it at 125 million workers, "five million more than in 1994," cf. *Renmin ribao*, 8 January 1996). These numbers of employees of the TVEs, and their respective distribution among different sectors, do not coincide with the distribution otherwise indicated for the total rural manpower.

47. Yu Depeng, *Renkou yanjiu* (Studies in Population), No. 16 (1995), pp. 17–21.

48. We have computed this estimate from the difference between the reported growth of the total urban population and its natural increase; see detailed analysis and estimates for the rural exodus from 1952 to 1992 in Claude Aubert, "Exode rural, exode agricole en Chine, la grande mutation?", *Espace, Populations, Sociétés*, Université de Lille, No. 2 (1995), pp. 231–45.

49. See *Nongmin ribao*, 22 September 1995 (general description) and 24 November 1995 (interview Wu Bangguo).

50. A survey by the Ministry of Agriculture, made at the level of villages in May 1994, indicated that 14% of the local rural population migrated during the year, out of which 36% crossed the border of their province of origin to find an outside temporary job; 84% of the migrants were employed for more than three months in these temporary jobs. See *Zhongguo nongcun jingji*, January 1995, pp. 43–50. A similar previous survey at the end of 1993 indicated only 11% of locals as migrants; cf. Han Xiaoyun et al., ibid., August 1994, pp. 10–14, September 1994, pp. 31–35.

51. *Nongmin ribao*, 10 November 1995.

52. *Zhongguo nongye nianjian 1995*, p. 453. In 1994 a total of 69 million persons had an income of less than RMB 500; this number can be compared to the 70 million persons declared as living under the threshold of poverty by the

Chinese authorities in 1995 (cf. Chen Junsheng, quoted in *Nongmin ribao*, 7 June 1995).

13

Chinese Personality and Social Change

Fanny M. Cheung, Kwok Leung,
Jianxin Zhang, Weizheng Song and Dong Xie

Studies on Personality and Social Change

Studies of personality in non-Western countries have often considered the context of the rapidly changing social conditions in these countries as possible influence on the individual's personality development or on the cohort differences in modal personality profiles. There are a few important psychological studies on the influence of social changes on individual lives in Western societies,[1] including the impact of the Great Depression, the Second World War, or the Vietnam War. In non-Western societies, studies of social change have focussed on economic development and societal modernization. In these studies, personality is viewed both as determinant and behavioural consequence of the social changes.[2]

The concept of modernization in particular has been the subject of active research by contemporary Chinese psychologists who have tried to adapt Western psychology to the Chinese context. Earlier examinations of the Chinese personality have focussed on the national character, often based on philosophical, particularly Confucian thoughts. In this paradigm, a person's character is conceptualized in a moral domain. More recent attempts to explain the historical genesis of the Chinese national character have pointed to the importance of the Chinese agricultural economy in fostering the familial organization of society and the national personality.[3] With the influence of the twentieth century Western epistemological paradigm of empiricism, personality variables have been studied descriptively to delineate the characteristics of people who espouse individual modernity as well as to examine the outcomes of societal modernization.[4] Kuo-shu Yang, a social psychologist who has advocated the indigenization of social sciences, has highlighted the cultural-ecological factors that have

Research projects conducted on the CPAI in Hong Kong and the PRC were supported by the following grants: Hong Kong Government Research Grants Council (RGC) Earmarked Grant Project #CU89106, RGC Earmarked Grant Project #CU911113, research grant from the South China Programme of the Hong Kong Institute of Asia-Pacific Studies, CUHK, and the PRC National Science Foundation research grant. We would also like to acknowledge the research support of the Department of Psychology, CUHK, and the Institute of Psychology, Chinese Academy of Sciences, Beijing, as well as the assistance of Ruth Fan, Josephine Law, Florence Yip, Bill Lau, Eliza Lau, Eric So, Zhang Jianping, Mok Wenbin and Sun Haifa at different stages of the research projects.

affected the socialization of personality and behavioural traits in the changing Chinese society in Taiwan. He and his associates have developed the Chinese Individual Traditionality/Modernity Scale (CITMS) to measure the degree of individual modernization. They have studied the antecedent determinants, personality correlates and behavioural consequences as a basis for inferring the effects of societal modernity.

In his 1985 chapter, Kuo-shu Yang summarized the empirical studies of Chinese personality change which had previously been published mainly in Chinese. He concluded that, under the influence of societal modernization, "Chinese people have been becoming higher in their sociability (extroversion), dominance (ascendance), flexibility, tolerance, and masculinity; and lower in their emotionality (anxiety), self-restraint (cautiousness), friendliness (harmonious relationship), conscientiousness, perseverance, and femininity."[5] In these studies, however, most of the personality correlates were measured using Western-based personality instruments which had been translated into Chinese. In studies of personality changes during the process of modernization, it is particularly important to consider traditional Chinese personality characteristics, many of which are not covered in Western personality measures.

Development of an Indigenous Chinese Personality Measure

The problems of using translated personality tests for Chinese people have been thoroughly discussed by Fanny Cheung and her associates.[6] In the early psychological studies of Chinese personality, Western personality tests were translated and used directly without following the rigorous procedures of testing the cross-cultural equivalence of the instruments. The cultural validity, i.e., whether the translated instrument actually measured what the original instrument purported to measure, was not demonstrated. Even if the cross-cultural equivalence of the translated instruments were established through validation studies, the question still remained as regards the coverage of the personality domain included in these personality inventories. The fundamental issue lay in the cross-cultural similarities and differences in defining and describing people's personality. Some of the personality dimensions covered in the inventories developed in Western countries may be irrelevant to the Chinese in their conceptualization of a person's personality. At the same time, these inventories may not include important considerations of person-descriptions indigenous to the Chinese cultural context. Based on her earlier research experience with translated instruments, Cheung and her associates developed the Chinese Personality Assessment Inventory (CPAI).[7]

The CPAI was constructed on the basis of an empirical inductive approach. The personality dimensions included in this broad-spectrum personality inventory were derived from concepts of person descriptions used in Chinese societies to ensure cultural relevance. The sources of these constructs included adjectives describing the major characters in contemporary Chinese novels, attitudes and behaviours identified in books of Chinese proverbs, self-statements collected from people in informal street surveys in Hong Kong, other-descriptions by professionals in the People's Republic of China (PRC) and Hong Kong and the psychological literature on Chinese personality. The personality adjectives and descriptions generated from these sources were integrated according to their similarity in meaning to remove redundancy. Researchers from Hong Kong and the PRC used a consensual method to select the personality dimensions to be included in the CPAI scales. The researchers agreed on 22 normal personality dimensions and 12 clinical dimensions which they believed to be important aspects of personality and psychopathology among the Chinese people. Scales to identify and screen out those individuals who deliberately faked their responses or were careless in filling out the inventory were also designed. These validity indicators were important for personality assessment because response styles could bias the true responses and distort the assessment results or research findings.

In preliminary studies, items written for each scale were carefully tested for readability, cultural relevance and internal consistency. Respondents in the PRC and Hong Kong were asked to rate each item in terms of their ability to understand the statement and the relevance of the item content to their cultural experience. The items of each scale were analysed in terms of their correlations with the other items as well as with the total score on that scale. Items which had low or negative correlations were considered to be measuring a different dimension from what had originally been intended for that scale. These poor items were deleted or rewritten. On the scale level, the pattern of intercorrelations among the scale scores of the CPAI were examined. Scales which were highly correlated, and were therefore assumed to be very similar, were combined.

In order to establish a basis for comparing individuals' scores in an objective personality test, norms have to be developed for each scale by using the score distribution of a general population as the reference or norm. The usefulness of the norm depends on the extent to which the test sample represents the general population. In the case of the CPAI, a standardization study was conducted in Hong Kong and the PRC in 1992 to develop the national norms for the scale scores. After screening out invalid protocols, the normative sample consisted of 441 adults from Hong Kong and 1884 adults from the PRC. The Hong Kong sample was based on a random sample of residents aged 18 to 65. The PRC sample was drawn using a quota sampling method to represent the demographic characteristics of the national population for the same age range. Except for the requirement that the respondents had at least primary education in order to comprehend the paper-and-pencil test, the other demographic characteristics of the CPAI samples were consistent with the general population in Hong Kong and the PRC. The average scores of these normative samples would serve as the bench mark to compare the scores of an individual or a specific group of individuals on the CPAI.

The final form of the CPAI consists of 33 personality and clinical scales to assess normal and abnormal personality. In addition, three validity index/scales are designed to screen out individuals who are faking good, faking bad, or are careless in responding. The design of the CPAI has borrowed from Western methodology of psychological testing.[8] The selection of scales for the CPAI has integrated the knowledge base of Chinese and Western personality. In addition to the personality dimensions which are common across cultures, several other scales are included because they are deemed to be of specific interest to the Chinese culture. Although similar concepts may have been studied in other cultures, these personality dimensions have been highlighted with special reference to the Chinese culture in previous studies. Examples of these scales are:

Harmony — one's inner peace of mind, contentment and avoidance of interpersonal conflict;

Renqing (Relationship Orientation) — social favours that are exchanged in the form of money, goods, information, status, service and affection according to an implicit set of rules which is dependent upon the category of social ties between the individuals involved in the interaction;[9]

Modernization — attitudes toward traditional Chinese beliefs and values in the areas of family relationships, materialism, hierarchical order, rituals and chastity;

Thrift vs. Extravagance — the tendency toward and the Confucian virtue of saving rather than wasting, and carefulness in spending, as opposed to the willingness to spend money for pleasure and entertainment;

"Ah-Q" Mentality (Defensiveness) — a pattern of defence mechanisms depicted in Lu Xun's famous caricature of Ah-Q, a fictional character satirizing the personality shortcomings of the Chinese people;

Graciousness vs. Meanness — a Confucian virtue characterized by patience, forgiveness, acceptance of self and others and self-sacrifice, as opposed to the mean and calculating characteristics of cynicism, vindictiveness and negativism;

Veraciousness vs. Slickness — a dimension of trustworthiness exemplified by being loyal and honest, keeping one's feet on the ground, working hard without pretence, upholding one's principles and sacrificing one's personal interests for the group, to the extreme of being inflexible or unadaptable;

Face — maintaining social behaviours which enhance one's face and avoiding losing one's face;

Family Orientation — the strong sense of family ties which provides emotional support and economic security;

Somatization — the tendency to present one's emotional distress in the form of somatic complaints instead of directly expressing them.[10]

Results of the factor analyses of the CPAI produced four factors among the personality scales and two factors among the clinical scales. The four normal personality factors may be labelled as *Dependability,*[11] *Chinese Tradition, Leadership,*[12] *and Individualism.*[13] The two clinical factors are *Emotional Problems*[14] and *Behavioural Problems.*[15] The *Chinese Tradition* factor is characterized by high positive loadings on the *Harmony, Renqing, and Thrift vs. Extravagance* scales and by high negative loading on the *Flexibility* and the *Modernization* scales. In our preliminary studies comparing the CPAI to another major personality measure which purports to encompass the universal structure of personality,[16] scales on the Chinese Tradition factor were found to be distinct from the so-called Big Five personality structure. This culture-specific factor supports the need for using an indigenously constructed personality inventory in measuring Chinese personality.

In addition to the *Chinese Tradition* factor, it is interesting to note that some of the other "culture-related" scales are included in the *Dependability* factor, including *Graciousness vs. Meanness, Veraciousness vs. Slickness, Family Orientation and Face.* These characteristics are considered to be as important to defining the characteristics of a dependable person in the Chinese culture as other culturally common dimensions as *Emotionality, Responsibility, Practical-mindedness, Inferiority vs. Self-acceptance,*

Table 1. Mean Raw Scores and Standard Deviations for the Final Form of CPAI in Hong Kong (N = 441) and the PRC (N = 1884)

Scale	Hong Kong Mean (S.D.)	PRC Mean (S.D.)
Self-Social Orientation (S-S)	6.64 (2.70)	6.94 (2.80)
Graciousness-Meanness (G-M)	11.53 (2.61)	10.73 (2.83)
Introversion-Extraversion (I-E)	7.10 (3.27)	7.19 (3.32)
Harmony (HAR)	11.11 (2.17)	11.33 (2.41)
Leadership (LEA)	6.27 (3.56)	4.71 (3.49)
Face (FAC)	6.11 (3.21)	7.45 (3.44)*
Renqing (Relationship Orientation) (REN)	12.18 (2.02)	12.65 (2.01)
Family Orientation (FAM)	10.75 (2.88)	10.40 (2.87)
Optimism-Pessimism (O-P)	10.10 (2.71)	9.48 (2.83)
Flexibility (FLE)	6.39 (3.03)	5.66 (2.94)
Logical-Affective Orientation (L-A)	9.00 (2.93)	9.23 (2.96)
Modernization (MOD)	9.65 (2.75)	9.93 (2.62)
Emotionality (EMO)	4.15 (2.78)	4.75 (2.90)
Thrift-Extravagance (T-E)	9.28 (2.57)	8.55 (2.94)
Responsibility (RES)	9.93 (3.17)	9.63 (3.10)
Adventurousness (ADV)	7.69 (2.74)	7.90 (2.96)
Meticulousness (MET)	9.99 (2.82)	9.70 (2.90)
Ah-Q Mentality (Defensiveness; DEF)	4.47 (2.62)	5.97 (3.00)*
Veraciousness-Slickness (V-S)	11.70 (2.43)	11.75 (2.65)
Practical Mindedness (PRA)	11.30 (2.31)	10.06 (2.61)*
External-Internal Locus of Control (E-I)	6.66 (2.67)	7.35 (2.93)
Inferiority-Self-acceptance (I-S)	4.56 (3.45)	4.76 (3.57)
Somatization (SOM)	5.17 (2.52)	5.11 (2.68)
Depression (DEP)	3.92 (2.77)	4.47 (3.06)
Physical Symptoms (PHY)	3.49 (2.38)	3.38 (2.56)
Antisocial Behaviour (ANT)	2.26 (2.03)	2.81 (2.29)
Anxiety (ANX)	3.63 (2.75)	3.57 (3.07)
Sexual Maladjustment (SEX)	1.98 (1.60)	2.28 (1.85)
Distortion of Reality (DIS)	2.36 (1.95)	2.44 (2.12)
Paranoia (PAR)	1.54 (1.82)	1.80 (1.93)
Need for Attention (NEE)	2.55 (2.31)	2.74 (2.51)
Hypomania (HYP)	3.89 (2.48)	4.06 (2.82)
Pathological Dependence (PAT)	1.02 (1.58)	1.28 (1.77)
Infrequency Scale (INF)	1.48 (0.73)	1.38 (0.72)
Good Impression Scale (GIM)	4.95 (2.51)	4.73 (2.30)

* T-test significant at < .01 level.

Optimism, External vs. Internal Locus of Control, and *Meticulousness.*
Results from the standardization study demonstrate that the psychometric properties of the CPAI are good. Table 1 lists the name of the scales and the mean scores for the Hong Kong and PRC normative samples. The

internal consistency coefficients (Cronbach's alpha) of the scales were mostly in the .70s range. Studies with college students in Hong Kong and the PRC show that the test-retest reliability of the personality and clinical scales (excluding the validity scales) lies between .71 and .94 for a one-week interval and from .59 to .81 for a one-month interval. The test-retest reliability results indicate that scores on the CPAI scales are stable and not random responses. A number of studies are now underway to establish the validity of the CPAI personality and clinical scales, i.e., to show that the CPAI scales do indeed measure what they purport to measure.

Regional Differences in Personality

In the development of the national norms for the CPAI, the empirical question is whether the average scores of the Hong Kong and the PRC samples are significantly different to warrant the development of different regional norms. The explicit assumption behind this question is that Hong Kong and the PRC are two distinct social systems which have had divergent historical developments in the past 100 years. The two will remain two separate social and administrative systems under one country after 1997. It has often been claimed that people in Hong Kong have been exposed to Western influence both in school and in popular culture and are, therefore, more "Westernized" in values and behaviour. The urbanized Hong Kong society is also more modern in its socioeconomic development. The influence of traditional Chinese culture on social life and interpersonal relationships is expected to have been curtailed. On the other hand, Chinese in the PRC have undergone fundamental cultural changes fostered by the Communist form of government and economy. The extent to which the traditional Chinese culture is shaping human behaviours and practices is also being queried. While it is not the intention of this chapter to resolve the more fundamental issue of Chinese culture in modern society, there is a general consensus that, despite the geopolitical boundaries, it seems that a common cultural identity exists among the Chinese of the diaspora.[17] We shall direct our attention here to the empirical question whether there are any major group differences in the personality make-up of Chinese living in Hong Kong and the PRC.

Since the samples collected for the CPAI standardization study were intended to be representative of the populations of Hong Kong and the PRC, the two samples were directly compared on the basis of their group means of each scale on the CPAI. The results showed very similar scale scores and test statistics on most of the scales. Statistically significant differences were found on only three of the 22 personality scales and on none of the clinical scales. The three scales with significant differences were: *Face, Ah-Q Mentality (Defensiveness)* and *Practical-mindedness.* The PRC sample scored higher on the *Face* and the *Ah-Q* scales which had high loadings on the *Chinese Tradition* factor. The Hong Kong sample, on the other hand, scored higher on the *Practical-mindedness* scale which may reflect the stronger emphasis on productivity and efficiency in both working style and interpersonal relationships in the Hong Kong society. Other than these three scales, there was no significant regional difference in the average scale scores.

On the basis of the overall similarity of the Hong Kong and the PRC results, a combined national norm was developed for the CPAI. However, given the significant gender differences found on many of the scales within both the Hong Kong and the PRC samples, separate norms for males and females were developed for the national norms.

The limited differences found between the Hong Kong and PRC samples on the CPAI were corroborated by results in other personality inventories. For example, the mean scores of the Hong Kong and the PRC normal samples on the Chinese Minnesota Multiphasic Inventory (MMPI) and its revised version (MMPI-2) were also found to be very similar,[18] whereas distinct differences were consistently found between the Chinese samples and the American samples on some of the clinical scales.

Age Trends in Personality

Age patterns in personality may sometimes be attributed to shifting psychosocial factors of social change over cohorts. It is assumed that group differences among age groups or cohorts reflect the particular social pressures during the maturational process or the social changes experienced by different generations. In Western studies of personality differences across age, the focus has often been placed on adolescents or the elderly, with particular concern with psychopathology.[19] A paradoxical theory of personality continuity and individual differences by Caspi and Moffitt[20] which states that potentially disruptive transitions produce personality continuity instead of change has provoked controversial reactions. They argue that characterological continuity will emerge during periods of social discontinuity. Behavioural changes take place during the transition to a new situation only when previous responses are actively discouraged and information is provided on new adaptive behaviour.

Given this context, one would expect longitudinal continuity in personality. Observed group differences in age trends may be attributable to social changes across cohorts. On the other hand, if we consider age trends across the adult lifespan, maturational factors should also play a role in personality differences among younger and older age groups. These age differences in personality were explored in the CPAI standardization sample.

Due to the large sample size, results for the total sample of 2,444 respondents in the PRC and Hong Kong showed that age was significantly correlated with most of the personality and clinical scales except for *Logical vs. Affective Orientation, Ah-Q Mentality, External vs. Internal Locus of Control, Somatization, Physical Symptoms, Sexual Maladjustment* and *Pathological Dependence.* Only those scales with correlation coefficients over .25 will be discussed here (see Table 2). These include the personality scales of *Practical-mindedness* (.39), *Thrift vs. Extravagance* (.30), *Responsibility* (.30), *Modernization* (–.26), *Veraciousness vs. Slickness* (.26), and *Emotionality* (–.25), and the clinical scales of *Hypomania* (–.32), and *Need for Attention* (–.27). These characteristics reflect a trend toward stability, responsibility and conservatism with increasing age. The age trends for the male and the female samples are basically similar with the exception of much higher correlations with *Practical-mindedness* (.43),

Table 2. Correlations between Age and CPAI Scales*

Scales	Total sample	PRC	HK	Male	Female
Family Orientation (FAM)	.17	.14	.29	.20	.15
Flexibility (FLE)	–.18	–.16	–.30	–.19	–.17
Modernization (MOD)	–.26	–.26	–.23	–.25	–.27
Emotionality (EMO)	–.25	–.24	–.31	–.24	–.25
Thrift-Extravagance (T-E)	.30	.31	.24	–.36	.24
Responsibility (RES)	.30	.29	.33	.31	.29
Adventurousness (ADV)	–.18	–.19	–.14	–.26	–.16
Meticulousness (MET)	.20	.19	.26	.26	.15
Veraciousness-Slickness (V-S)	.26	.26	.24	.32	.21
Practical Mindedness (PRA)	.39	.39	.39	.43	.34
Need for Attention (NEE)	–.27	–.27	–.23	–.26	–.27
Hypomania (HYP)	–.32	–.35	–.16	–.31	–.33

* Only the scales with correlations ≥ .25 are reported here.

Veraciousness vs. Slickness (.32), *Adventurousness* (–.26) and *Meticulousness* (–.26) for the males. The pattern of correlations for the PRC and the Hong Kong samples is also very similar, except for higher correlations with *Family Orientation* (–.31), *Flexibility* (–.30), and *Meticulousness* (.26) for the Hong Kong sample. This reflects greater differences between the younger and the older age groups in Hong Kong on these personality characteristics.

The interactions among these age differences, gender and the geographical location (PRC vs. Hong Kong) were further examined by running three-way analyses of variance on each of the CPAI scales. Five age groups were defined: Age 25 and below, 26–35, 36–45, 46–55, and over 55. No significant three-way interaction effect was found. Significant two-way interaction effects (at p ≤ .01 level) between Age and Gender were found on the personality scales of *Meticulousness, Veraciousness vs. Slickness* and the clinical scale of *Pathological Dependence*. On the *Meticulousness* scale, younger females scored higher than younger males, but the pattern was reversed among the older respondents. On the *Veraciousness vs. Slickness* scales, younger males scored higher than younger females, but little gender difference was found among the older age groups which in general had much higher scores than the younger counterparts. On the *Pathological Dependence* scale, female respondents generally scored very low, except for a slight increase among those older than age 55. On the other hand, male respondents scored much higher, especially

Table 3. Mean Scores on CPAI Scales with Significant Two-way Interactions between Age and Gender

CPAI Scale	Gender	Age Groups					F	p-value
		1	2	3	4	5		
Meticulousness	M	8.47	9.54	10.16	10.80	10.60		
(MET)		(N=287)	(N=345)	(N=297)	(N=129)	(N=118)	3.87	.00
	F	9.02	9.85	10.40	10.03	9.78		
		(N=363)	(N=363)	(N=298)	(N=124)	(N=60)		
Veraciousness-	M	10.24	10.76	11.76	12.41	12.93		
Slickness		(N=290)	(N=344)	(N=293)	(N=133)	(N=116)	3.34	.01
(V-S)	F	11.34	11.79	12.22	12.85	12.68		
		(N=355)	(N=360)	(N=294)	(N=130)	(N=63)		
Pathological	M	2.04	2.43	2.07	1.98	1.51		
Dependence		(N=274)	(N=327)	(N=280)	(N=129)	(N=111)	6.26	.00
(PAT)	F	0.60	0.58	0.56	0.63	1.13		
		(N=338)	(N=344)	(N=280)	(N=120)	(N=60)		

Table 4. Mean Scores on CPAI Scales with Significant Two-way Interactions between Age and Location

CPAI Scale	Location	Age Groups					F	p-value
		1	2	3	4	5		
Self vs. Social	PRC	7.41	7.00	6.90	6.70	6.58		
Orientation		(N=577)	(N=542)	(N=453)	(N=213)	(N=158)	3.34	.01
(S-S)	HK	6.71	6.36	6.83	7.93	7.16		
		(N=78)	(N=162)	(N=133)	(N=45)	(N=25)		
Graciousness	PRC	10.31	10.25	10.66	11.08	11.44		
vs. Meanness		(N=563)	(N=534)	(N=466)	(N=211)	(N=154)	3.35	.01
(G-M)	HK	11.13	11.79	11.32	10.87	11.36		
		(N=78)	(N=165)	(N=133)	(N=45)	(N=25)		
Family	PRC	9.50	10.35	10.79	10.68	10.53		
Orientation		(N=574)	(N=544)	(N=465)	(N=219)	(N=154)	4.02	.00
(FAM)	HK	8.54	10.77	11.25	11.07	11.88		
		(N=78)	(N=164)	(N=131)	(N=45)	(N=25)		
Flexibility	PRC	6.32	5.60	4.92	5.20	5.03		
(FLE)		(N=566)	(N=535)	(N=452)	(N=211)	(N=155)	3.90	.00
	HK	8.14	6.72	5.90	4.67	4.92		
		(N=78)	(N=165)	(N=133)	(N=45)	(N=25)		
Defensiveness	PRC	5.83	6.43	6.30	5.91	5.96		
(DEF)		(N=567)	(N=534)	(N=452)	(N=207)	(N=150)	3.19	.01
	HK	3.91	4.74	4.70	5.73	5.92		
		(N=78)	(N=164)	(N=133)	(N=45)	(N=25)		
Practical-	PRC	8.86	9.46	10.65	11.37	11.77		
mindedness		(N=569)	(N=543)	(N=458)	(N=217)	(N=159)	5.09	.00
(PRA)	HK	8.97	11.12	11.50	12.22	12.16		
		(N=78)	(N=165)	(N=133)	(N=45)	(N=25)		
External vs.	PRC	7.28	7.70	7.64	7.34	6.86		
Internal Locus		(N=566)	(N=533)	(N=449)	(N=215)	(N=152)	4.12	.00
of Control (E-I)	HK	7.81	6.87	6.51	7.11	5.84		
		(N=78)	(N=164)	(N=132)	(N=44)	(N=25)		

among the younger age groups. The scores for the older males were much lower than those of the younger males, and the gender difference for the over 55 age-groups became minimal.

More significant interaction effects were found between Age and Geographical Location: *Self vs. Social Orientation, Graciousness vs. Meanness, Family Orientation, Flexibility, Ah-Q Mentality, Practical-mindedness* and *External vs. Internal Locus of Control* on the personality scales. None of the interaction effects on the clinical scales was significant at $\leq .01$ level.

On the *Self vs. Social Orientation* scale, the younger PRC respondents scored higher than the young Hong Kong respondents as well as their older PRC counterparts. The trend for the Hong Kong respondents was reversed. The older Hong Kong respondents had a higher inclination toward self-orientation than the younger Hong Kong respondents and were even more so than the PRC respondents.

On the *Graciousness vs. Meanness* scale, the younger PRC respondents scored much lower than the young Hong Kong respondents, but there was an increasing trend toward more gracious attributes with older age. The difference between the PRC and Hong Kong respondents was removed among the older age groups with increasing scores among the PRC older respondents and decreasing scores among Hong Kong older respondents.

For the *Family Orientation* scale, there was a much sharper increase in scores across the Hong Kong age groups whereas the increase for the PRC respondents reached a ceiling at the 26–35 age group. Whereas the youngest age group in Hong Kong scored lower than its counterpart in the PRC, the oldest age group in Hong Kong scored much higher than its PRC counterpart.

For the *Flexibility* scale, there was a much sharper decrease in score across the Hong Kong age groups. Although the younger Hong Kong respondents scored significantly higher than the PRC respondents, these differences became minimal among the older groups who generally scored much lower in both locations.

The score levels of PRC respondents on the *Ah-Q Mentality (Defensiveness)* were generally high across all age groups. The younger Hong Kong respondents, however, scored much lower on this scale, although the two older age groups were much more similar to their PRC counterparts.

On *Practical-mindedness*, there was an increasing age trend for both samples. Although there was no difference between the PRC and Hong Kong samples among the under 25 age groups, there were significant differences between the two samples among the older age groups when the increase in scores was more pronounced among the Hong Kong sample, especially among the middle-aged respondents.

Results on the *External vs. Internal Locus of Control* scale showed that the younger Hong Kong respondents tended to adopt more external attributions while the older respondents would adopt more internal locus of control. For the PRC respondents, there was much less difference across the age groups.

The age trends on the CPAI scales generally fit the pattern of maturation across the adult lifespan in which one would expect older people to become more stable, dependable and traditional. One would also expect that younger people exposed to modernization influences would be more self-directed and less externally-focussed. However, the divergent patterns of age differences in the PRC and Hong Kong samples suggest that the context of social changes in the two societies may also account for the cohort changes. For example, with the recent expansion of individual enterprise in the PRC, the younger age groups may have a stronger individualistic orientation whereas their older compatriots would be more inclined toward a collectivistic orientation. This pattern of personality characteristics is reflected by their scores on the *Self vs. Social Orientation* scale. As shown by their scores on the *Graciousness vs. Meanness* and *Ah-Q Mentality* scales, the young PRC age cohort may also be more scrupulous and less accepting of others than its Hong Kong counterpart. However, this pattern of age differences is not shared by the age cohorts in Hong Kong. One may speculate that with increasing affluence in Hong Kong, the self-reliant, logical and down-to-earth styles needed for economic survival for the older generation are less prevalent among the young, based on the results on the *External vs. Internal Locus of Control* and *Practical-mindedness* scales. The younger generation may, however, afford to be more flexible and open to new ideas, as seen from their higher scores on the *Flexibility* scale. Alternatively, the pattern of personality characteristics of the elderly in Hong Kong may reflect the social isolation and cynicism that this generation may be feeling when faced with the decreasing respect, attention and support they receive from the younger generation. With nuclear families replacing the extended or the stem families in Hong Kong, the older residents have to count on themselves more than their PRC counterparts to survive. These possible explanations remain speculations and are worth a further examination in future studies.

Significant two-way intereaction effects between gender and location were found on only two CPAI scales (Table 5). On *Introversion vs. Extraversion*, PRC males were found to be less introverted than females, whereas Hong Kong males were more introverted than females. On the clinical scale of *Pathological Dependence*, while males generally scored much higher than females, the gender difference was more pronounced in the PRC than in Hong Kong. Whereas PRC males scored higher than Hong Kong males, PRC females scored slightly lower than Hong Kong females.

Table 5. Mean Scores on CPAI Scales with significant Two-way Interactions between Gender and Location

		Gender			
CPAI Scale	Location	M	F	F	p-value
Introversion-Extraversion (I-E)	PRC	6.92 (N=924)	7.46 (N=996)	11.79	.00
	HK	7.47 (N=240)	6.79 (N=205)		
Pathological Dependence (PAT)	PRC	2.20 (N=881)	0.57 (N=936)	19.42	.00
	HK	1.75 (N=240)	0.83 (N=206)		

Economic Development and Personality Adjustment

Rapid economic development is taking place in China, especially in the coastal area. It has brought along major social changes in the social environment, including material standard of living, higher employment rates and broader educational and cultural exposure. These coastal cities are more open to outside contacts leading to societal modernization. On the one hand, one may expect that economic development would bring about better living conditions and, therefore, better adjustment. On the other hand, others may argue that economic development also brings with it social ills associated with industrialization, urbanization and depersonalization and, therefore, leads to poorer psychological well-being.

Using the CPAI, a small study[21] was conducted in three locations in China varying in degree of economic development: the city of Guangzhou, the city of Xian, and the rural county of Rongyuan in Guangdong. Guangzhou is one of the earliest coastal cities to have been opened to the outside world, and its economic development far supersedes that of the more inland city of Xian as well as the more remote rural region of Rongyuan. A small stratified sample was collected after screening out invalid responses on the CPAI. The sample consisted of 117 respondents (58 males and 59 females) from Guangzhou, 107 respondents (50 males and 57 females) from Xian and 82 respondents (40 males and 42 females) from Rongyuan. The average age of the samples was 33.8, 33.9 and 32.5, respectively. The educational and occupational levels of the three samples were balanced.

Table 6. MANOVA for Five CPAI Personality Scales and Seven Clinical Scales[a]

	Guangzhou (n=117)		Rongyuan (n=82)		Xian (n=107)		
	M	SD	M	SD	M	SD	F
Personality Scales							
Graciousness-Meanness (G-M)	11.13	2.53	9.94	2.87	9.73	3.07	6.76**
Flexibility (FLE)	6.38	2.95	5.44	2.34	4.96	2.80	8.48**
Emotionality (EMO)	4.22	2.34	4.93	2.33	5.66	2.84	10.41**
Responsibility (RES)	8.92	2.59	9.73	3.03	8.98	2.74	4.64 *
Defensiveness (DEF)	5.49	2.15	6.32	2.09	6.67	2.90	4.68 *
Clinical Scales							
Somatization (SOM)	5.56	2.86	6.62	2.44	5.54	2.52	4.95 *
Antisocial Behaviour (ANT)	2.18	2.11	3.46	2.24	5.07	2.99	16.45**
Anxiety (ANX)	3.38	2.60	5.81	2.76	4.28	3.45	11.30**
Sexual Maladjustment (SEX)	2.09	1.87	3.35	2.01	3.13	2.10	11.61**
Paranoia (PAR)	1.65	2.02	2.78	2.01	2.51	2.38	5.99 *
Hypomania (HYP)	3.82	2.48	5.68	2.70	4.90	3.17	7.38**
Pathological Dependence (PAT)	0.87	1.23	1.72	1.85	1.56	2.09	7.42**

[a] This table displays only the scales with significant differences.
* $p < .01$;
** $p < .001$.

The average scale scores on the CPAI for the three samples were compared using multivariate analysis of variance (MANOVA) with the age, gender and educational levels of the respondents controlled. Significant differences at the p .01 level were found among the three samples on five personality scales and seven clinical scales (Table 6). *Post hoc* multiple comparison tests showed that on the personality scales of *Graciousness vs. Meanness* and *Flexibility,* Guangzhou respondents scored higher than both Xian and Rongyuan respondents. On the *Emotionality* and the *Ah-Q Mentality (Defensiveness)* scales, Guangzhou respondents scored lower than both Xian and Rongyuan respondents. Xian and Rongyuan respondents did not differ significantly on the mean scores of these four personality scales.

Guangzhou respondents also differed significantly from the other two samples on six clinical scales, including *Antisocial Behaviour, Anxiety, Sexual Maladjustment, Paranoia, Hypomania* and *Pathological Dependence.* On all of these scales, Guangzhou respondents scored lower than the other two groups. The Xian and the Rongyuan samples did not differ in their mean scores on the above scales except for the *Anxiety* scale. On the *Somatization* scale, Guangzhou respondents were not significantly different from Xian respondents, but both scored lower than the Rongyuan villagers.

These preliminary results supported the hypothesis related to the positive consequences of economic development on psychological adjustment. The Guangzhou respondents had more positive personal attributes which were conducive to better interpersonal relationship, social adjustment and emotional stability. They tended to be more flexible in problem solving and gracious in their interpersonal relationships. They also exhibited less psychological distress associated with emotional and behavioural problems, including anxiety, hypomania, paranoia, antisocial behaviour, sexual maladjustment and pathological dependence. This finding was consistent with the results of Diener and Diener[22] who reported that financial satisfaction was a significant predictor of life satisfaction across 31 nations. One should caution, however, that the small sample size and the lack of representativeness of the respondents in this study precluded overall generalization of the results to the rest of China.

Personality Correlates of Individual Modernity

In previous studies of personality and modernization of the Chinese people,[23] individual and societal modernity were often assumed to be closely related. The premise that individual psychological modernity directly affects behaviour related to societal modernity has been refuted by Armer and Issac.[24] They have found large individual differences within societies varying in levels of modernity. The personality variable of psychological modernity has had only negligible effects in predicting modern behaviour and is more useful as an interpretative construct than as a predictor.

In the small-scaled study involving three locations differing in modernization level mentioned in the previous section, the individual's personality dimension of modernization was analysed in the context of other personality and adjustment characteristics. Contrary to our expectations, it was noted that Guangzhou, Xian and Rongyuan respondents did not differ in their average scores on the *Modernization* scale. There were more individual differences within each of these locations despite their variations in the level of economic development.

Attention was then directed to the personality characteristics associated with the individual's level of modernity in these locations. Using multiple regression to predict scores on the *Modernization* scale, it was found that the respondents' education level, scores on the *Flexibility* and the *Logical vs. Affective* scales were included as positive predictors while scores on the *Thrift vs. Extravagance, Ah-Q Mentality (Defensiveness), Practical-mindedness, Family Orientation* and *Sexual Maladjustment* scales were negative predictors. This suggested that, although individual modernity was not directly related to the level of economic development of the environment, a more complex relationship would be expected. On the individual level, modernity is related to the deviation from traditional Chinese orientations associated with the agricultural economy, such as emphasis on thrift and close family relations. On the other hand, individuals with more modern orientations would tend to be less defensive and more logically minded and flexible, characteristics which may be fostered by education.

Using the data from the CPAI standardization study, the individual *Modernization* scale scores were correlated with all of the other scales. These other scales were also used to predict *Modernization* in multiple regression analyses. Given the large sample size, the majority of the scales were significantly correlated with the *Modernization* scale, even though the value of the correlation coefficient might be low. Therefore, only those scales with a correlation coefficient of at least .25 were retained for discussion (Table 7).

For the total sample of PRC and Hong Kong respondents, *Modernization* has the highest correlation with the personality scales of *Flexibility* (.36), followed by *Thrift vs. Extravagance* (–.30), *Adventurousness* (.27), *Harmony* (–.26), and *Face* (–.25), and the clinical scales of *Sexual Maladjustment* (–.31) and *Somatization* (–.27). These personality scales have

Table 7. Correlations between Modernization and Other CPAI Scales*

Scales	Total sample	PRC	HK	Male	Female
Harmony (HAR)	–.26	–.26	–.22	–.25	–.27
Face (FAC)	–.25	–.25	–.31	–.23	–.27
Relationship Orientation (REN)	–.20	–.19	–.28	–.19	–.22
Flexibility (FLE)	.36	.36	.36	.39	.32
Thrift-Extravagance (T-E)	–.30	–.31	–.25	–.29	–.30
Adventurousness (ADV)	.27	.28	.23	.28	.25
Defensiveness (DEF)	–.24	–.22	–.36	–.24	–.24
Somatization (SOM)	–.27	–.29	–.23	–.28	–.26
Sexual Maladjustment (SEX)	–.31	–.30	–.37	–.31	–.30

* Only the scales with correlations ≥ .25 are reported here.

high loadings on the *Chinese Tradition* factor and are closely related to traditional Chinese values and practices as well as to the willingness to change or try out new ideas. Individuals with more modern orientations are less likely to follow the traditional Chinese practice of frugality, face-saving or maintaining harmony. They would also tend to be more open about expressing their emotional concerns as well as about sex and less likely to experience difficulties with sexual adjustment. While results for the PRC sample mirrored that of the total sample, slight variations were found in the pattern of correlations for the Hong Kong sample. *Modernization* was most highly correlated with *Ah-Q Mentality* (−.36) and *Flexibility* (−.36), followed by *Face* (−.31), *Renqing* (−.28), and *Thrift vs. Extravagance* (−.25). Its correlation with the clinical scale of *Sexual Maladjustment* (−.37) was the highest among all scales. For the Hong Kong respondents, individual modernity was more distinctly distanced from traditional Chinese behavioural orientations and more related to openness about sex. No significant difference was found between the male and female respondents in the overall pattern of correlations between *Modernity* and the other personality characteristics.

The results of the multiple regression analyses for the total sample produced similar pattern of predictors of individual modernity (Table 8). The personality scales which significantly predicted *Modernization* for the total samples included *Flexibility, Thrift vs. Extravagance, Logical vs. Affective Orientation, Face, Practical-mindedness* and *Ah-Q Mentality*.

Table 8. Multiple Regression of Modernization on other CPAI Personality and Clinical Scales

	Beta	Cumulative Multiple R^2
Personality Scales		
Flexibility (FLE)	.26*	.13
Thrift-Extravagance (T-E)	−.14*	.17
Logical-Affective Orientation (L-A)	.20*	.19
Face (FAC)	−.23*	.21
Practical Mindedness (PRA)	−.25*	.24
Defensiveness (DEF)	−.14*	.26
Clinical Scales		
Sexual Maladjustment (SEX)	−.26*	.09
Somatization (SOM)	−.25*	.12
Depression (DEP)	.22*	.14
Anxiety (ANX)	−.16*	.15
Antisocial Behaviour (ANT)	.13*	.16

* $p < .001$.

The multiple correlation coefficient based on these six predictors was .51, which meant that, together, these personality variables would explain 26% of the variance on *Modernization*. Five clinical scales best predicted scores on *Modernization*, including low scores on *Sexual Maladjustment, Somatization* and *Anxiety*, and high scores on *Depression* and *Antisocial Behaviour*. The multiple correlation coefficient was .40, with 16% of the variance being explained. The results corroborated the correlational analyses in forming the pattern of personality characteristics of individuals who were more modern in their orientation. These individuals would be more pragmatic, rational and less bound by traditional values and practices. They were likely to be flexible and open to new experiences. They would tend to be less defensive and more willing to express their feelings or act out their frustration and anger rather than to use indirect means to address their psychological distress.

Conclusion

Studies on Chinese personality using the CPAI have shown robust similarities between the modal personality of people from the PRC and Hong Kong, despite the apparent differences in the social systems and economic development between the two geographical locations. The only differences in modal personality have been found in characteristics related to more Chinese traditional orientations among the PRC sample and more pragmatic orientations among the Hong Kong sample. The lack of major discrepancies in the average personality profiles of the two representative samples may argue for the strong cultural roots and identity among the Chinese diaspora. Gender and age pose as more important social variables than geographical location in differentiating groups of Chinese in their personality dispositions.

Age differences may reflect to a large extent developmental maturation across the lifespan with older people assuming greater stability, responsibility and conservatism with increasing age. This pattern of age difference is consistent for both Chinese males and females. However, the age trends for the PRC and Hong Kong samples diverge on a number of personality characteristics, suggesting that the context of social changes in different age cohorts in the two societies may account for the interaction effects. On a number of scales related to traditional Chinese values and working styles, there is a steeper rate of difference between the young and the old in Hong Kong than in the PRC. The different patterns of age trends suggest that greater exposure to Western influence in Hong Kong may accentuate the generation gap. However, the personality characteristics of the young Hong Kong respondents are not entirely consistent with the expected patterns associated with modernization in Western studies. The local sociocultural context should be further explored in the future.

Rapid social changes are also taking place in China, especially in the coastal regions where economic development has been transforming the social environment. A small-scale study comparing samples from two Chinese cities and one village fails to demonstrate that economic development is related to more psychological distress. The results support the alternative hypothesis that economic improvements associated with development would lead to a better quality of living and more life satisfaction. The Guangzhou sample, compared to their economically less developed counterparts in Xian and Rongyuan, shows more positive personal attributes in interpersonal relationship, social adjustment and emotional stability, and less psychological distress associated with emotional and behavioural problems. The three samples, however, do not differ in their average level of individual modernity. Individual modernization is independent of societal modernization, and there are great individual differences in modernity level within the same society. Societal modernization *per se* does not necessarily lead to individual modernization.

On the CPAI, individual modernity is delineated by a cluster of other personality characteristics which are associated with willingness to change or try out new ideas, and deviation from the traditional Chinese values and practices. It is likely that individual modernity is an important moderator variable in predicting the individual's adaptation to the social changes in the environment. Particularly in situations of rapid social changes, individuals who are more pragmatic, rational, flexible and open to new experiences would be more likely to adjust than those who are defensive and rigid in their adherence to traditional practices.

The CPAI has demonstrated its usefulness as an indigenous personality instrument in assessing a broad range of personality dispositions which have relevance to the Chinese culture. In the context of social change, the personality scales associated with the *Chinese Tradition* factor illustrate the complex interactions between the individual and the social environment. These complex relationships are worth closer examination in future studies.

Notes

1. Abigail J. Stewart and Joseph M. Healy, Jr. "Linking Individual Development and Social Change," *American Psychologist*, Vol. 44, No. 4 (1989), pp. 30–42; G. H. Elder, *Children of the Great Depression* (Chicago: University of Chicago Press, 1974); G. H. Elder, "Military Times and Turning Points in Men's Lives," *Developmental Psychology*, Vol. 22 (1986), pp. 233–45.

2. Michael Armer and Larry Isaac, "Determinants and Behavioral Consequences of Psychological Modernity: Empirical Evidence from Costa Rica," *American Sociological Review*, Vol. 43, No. 3 (1978), pp. 316–34.

3. W. La Barre, "Some Observations on Character Structure in the Orient: The Chinese, Part One," *Psychiatry*, Vol. 9 (1946), pp. 215–37.

4. Kuo-shu Yang, "Social Orientation and Individual Modernity among Chinese Students in Taiwan," *Journal of Social Psychology*, Vol. 113 (1981), pp. 159–70; Kuo-shu Yang. "Chinese Personality and Its Change," in *The Psychology of the Chinese People*, edited by Michael H. Bond (Hong Kong: Oxford University Press, 1985), pp. 106–70.

5. Kuo-shu Yang (Note 4), p. 159.

6. Fanny M. Cheung, Leung Kwok, Ruth M. Fan, Song Weizheng, Zhang Jianxin and Zhang Jianping, "Development of the Chinese Personality Assessment Inventory (CPAI)," *Journal of Cross-Cultural Psychology*, in press; Fanny M. Cheung, Zhang Jianxin, and Song Weizheng, "Cong xinli ceyan kan huaren de xingge: (1) liangbiao de yunyong" (Chinese Personality as Seen from Personality Tests: I. Use of Inventories), in *Huaren de xinli yu zhiliao* (Chinese Psychology and Therapy), edited by Wen-shing Tseng (Taipei: Kuei Kuan Books, in press).

7. Cheung et al., "Development of the Chinese Personality" (Note 6). Readers who are interested in more details on the development and the psychometric properties of the CPAI may refer to this article.

8. Readers who are unfamiliar with psychological testing may refer to Anne Anastasi, *Psychological Testing*, (6th ed.; New York: Collier Macmillan, 1988) and James N. Butcher, John R. Graham, Carolyn L. Williams and Yossi Ben-Porath, *Development and Use of the MMPI-2 Content Scales* (Minneapolis, MN: University of Minnesota Press, 1990).

9. Kwang-kuo Hwang, "Face and Favor: The Chinese Power Game," *American Journal of Sociology*, Vol. 92 (1987), pp. 944–74.

10. F. M. Cheung, "Facts and Myths about Somatization among the Chinese," in *Chinese Societies and Mental Health*, edited by Tsung-yi Lin, Wen-shing Tseng and En-kung Yeh (Hong Kong: Oxford University Press, 1995), pp. 156–66.

11. The *Dependability* factor is characterized by loadings on the following

personality scales: high positive loadings on *Responsibility, Practical-mindedness, Graciousness-Meanness, Family Orientation*, and *Meticulousness*; high negative loadings on *Emotionality, Inferiority vs. Self-acceptance, External vs. Internal Locus of Control*, and *Face*.

12. The *Leadership* factor is loaded positively on the *Leadership* and *Adventurousness* scales, and negatively on the *Introversion-Extraversion* scale.

13. The *Individualism* factor is loaded on the *Self vs. Social Orientation, Logical Orientation*, and *Defensiveness* scales.

14. The *Emotional Problems* factor is characterized by loadings on the following clinical scales: *Depression, Inferiority, Physical Symptoms, Anxiety, Somatization* and *Need for Attention*.

15. The *Behavioural Problems* factor is characterized by loadings on the following clinical scales: *Hypomania, Antisocial Behaviour, Paranoia, Pathological Dependence, Distortion of Reality* and *Sexual Problems*.

16. The NEO-PI is the personality measure used to demonstrate that the basic personality structure across cultures may be grouped into five underlying dimensions. The description of the NEO-PI is found in Paul T. Costa, Jr. and Robert R. McCrae, *NEO-PI/NEO-FFI Manual Supplement* (Odessa, FL: Psychological Assessment Resources, 1989).

17. See the "Special Issue: Identity in Comparative Perspectives," *The Humanities Bulletin, Volume 4* (Hong Kong: Faculty of Arts, The Chinese University of Hong Kong, December 1995) for a fuller discussion of the cultural identity among the Chinese diaspora.

18. Fanny M. Cheung, "Cross-cultural Considerations for the Translations and Adaptation of the Chinese MMPI in Hong Kong," in *Advances in Personality Assessment, Volume 4*, edited by James N. Butcher and Charles D. Spielberger (Hillsdale, NJ: Lawrence Erlbaum Associates, 1985), pp. 131–58; Fanny M. Cheung, Song Weizheng and Zhang Jianxin, "The Chinese MMPI-2: Research and Applications in Hong Kong and the People's Republic of China," in *International Adaptations of the MMPI-2: A Handbook of Research and Clinical Applications*, edited by James N. Butcher (Minneapolis, MN: University of Minnesota Press, in press).

19. For example, see Peter M. Koeppl, Karen Bolla-Wilson and Margit L. Bleeker, "The MMPI: Regional Differences or Normal Aging?," *Journal of Gerontology*, Vol. 44, No. 4 (1989), pp. 95-99; Michael K. Zuschlag and Susan K. Whitbourne, "Psychosocial Development in Three Generations of College Students," *Journal of Youth and Adolescence*, Vol. 23, No. 5 (1994), pp. 567–77.

20. Avshalom Caspi and Terrie E. Moffitt, "Individual Differences Are Accentuated during Periods of Social Change: The Sample Case of Girls at Puberty," *Journal of Personality and Social Psychology*, Vol. 61, No. 1 (1991), pp. 157–68; "When Do Individual Differences Matter? A Paradoxical

Theory of Personality Coherence," *Psychological Inquiry*, Vol. 4, No. 4 (1993), pp. 247–71.

21. Dong Xie, Weizheng Song, Fanny M. Cheung, Kwok Leung and Jianxin Zhang, "Bu tong xiandaihua chengdu diqu jumin de xingge chayi" (Personality Differences of Residents from Regions Differing in Levels of Modernization), Manuscript under review by the *Acta Psychologica Sinica*.

22. Ed Diener, and Marissa Diener, "Cross-cultural Correlates of Life Satisfaction and Self-esteem," *Journal of Personality and Social Psychology*, Vol. 68, No. 4 (1995), pp. 653–63.

23. See Kuo-shu Yang (Note 4).

24. Armer, Michael and Larry Isaac (see Note 2).

14

Work under the Reforms:
The Experience and Meaning of
Work in a Time of Transition

R. I. Westwood and S. M. Leung

Introduction

Whilst the macro-level political, economic, legislative and institutional aspects of the post-1978 reforms in China have been well documented, the more micro-level implications for the meaning and experience of work of people functioning in the reform environment have been less well attended to. This chapter reflects on those implications by exploring the perceptions, interpretations and responses of working people to the new work environment. In doing so it draws illustratively on recent research by the authors which has, in one way or another, dealt with the lives of working people as they respond to the new opportunities, constraints and ambiguities of the work context in the ever changing circumstances of a transitioning economic and social system.[1] The link between those personal experiences and the wider situation of institutional change and development is facilitated by drawing on additional material from secondary sources.

The meanings people attach to work and their experiences of working are shaped by a complex set of factors. These incorporate the individuals' background and past experiences; the wider socio-cultural context, including cultural norms and values associated with work; the economic environment; the political environment; the organizational context; and, factors in the immediate work environment.[2] It is also apparent that the meaning and experience of work is not universal but is highly variable around the world due to differences in these factors.[3] Furthermore, the meanings of work held by people, especially common patterns within a society, have important consequences both for the work-related attitudes, motivations and calculations of individuals, and hence their work performance, but also collectively and reflexively on the societal and institutional factors that continue to shape work practices and meanings.

The nature, meaning and experience of work in China is subject to a particularly complex admixture of deep-rooted cultural traditions and values, more recent politico-ideological proclivities and structurings, and particular practical and economic exigencies, all of which have shaped it in distinctive ways. The work system in China has been singular at least since the Communist Revolution, and possibly before. We do not intend here to provide a full historical analysis of the shaping and content of the work context in China, but rather to articulate some of the experiences and meanings associated with it through the voice of working people and to use those accounts to reflect on the wider shaping context. In particular, we seek to anchor the experience and meaning of work to aspects of the post-1978 reform process that impinge most directly upon people's working lives. Space will not permit a full account, either, of the full sweep of the economic reform process in China since 1978, which has, in any case, been adequately covered elsewhere, not least in past and present issues of the *China Review*. It is necessary, however, to discuss aspects of the reform process in order to contextualize our discussion of the meaning and experience of work in the contemporary environment.

What is apparent is that the context and nature of work in China is changing rapidly and looks likely to continue to do so. Many of the macro-societal level factors that directly or indirectly impinge on the world of work and have a determining effect on work meanings have been subject to quite radical change in recent years. In particular, those aspects of the reform process that deal with enterprise governance and the employment relationship are having an especially acute effect. These are complemented by other changes in the wider social formation, such as welfare reforms, rising costs of living and radical alterations in the functioning of the labour market. Additional changes at the organizational level, such as those associated with staffing policies and decisions, job security, leadership style and altered reward mechanisms, add to the complexity of the situation and are of further significance in changing work, work relationships and the values associated with work. Inevitably, such changes serve to re-shape and re-configure the meanings work holds for people and has consequences for work attitudes, actions and performance.

The Meaning of Work

The meaning of work has been a woefully neglected topic in organization and management theories, where they have preferred to focus more narrowly on constructs like motivation. This despite the fact that the meaning of work has highly significant implications for motivation and other issues, such as job satisfaction and job design. It has been left primarily to the sociologists to more fully explore the notion of the meaning of work.[4] The most significant comparative, empirical study to date of the meaning of work that is from more of a management/organization theory perspective was undertaken by a cross-national team which was referred to collectively as the MOW (meaning of work) International Research Team (MOWIRT).[5] It developed a conceptual model based on a thorough review of the literature and undertook an extensive empirical investigation in eight countries (Belgium, Great Britain, Germany, Israel, Japan, the Netherlands, United States and the former Yugoslavia).

The model related a set of core meaning of work variables to sets of antecedent or conditional variables and consequent variables. The antecedent conditions included aspects of the macro socio-economic environment, personal and family situation factors and issues relating to the present job and career history. Consequences were conceptualized in terms of certain objective outcomes of working (such as the number of hours worked, work continuity, the type of jobs undertaken) and subjective expectations about future working situations (such as the future importance of working to workers, the recommendations they would make to their children about jobs and careers). The model depicts five central meanings of work variables: centrality of working as a life role, societal norms about working, valued working outcomes, the importance of work goals and work role identification). We will elaborate somewhat on these variables later in the chapter.

The authors recognize the dynamic nature of what work means to people and the interrelationship between the central variables. They therefore talk about the meaning of work patterns since that "provides a more ideographic and holistic view of individuals in terms of the interrelated meanings they assign to work."[6] The central variables should not be treated in isolation, but holistically as a complex of attitudes, values and responses that people hold about working. There is also a dynamic relationship between the work meanings that may have developed in commonality among a group of people and the contingent situational variables. In other words, a simple, linear causal model is not implied. Antecedent conditions, such as aspects of the economic environment may help to shape the meanings about work people hold, but the meanings about work held by the collective may have a reciprocal impact upon the form and development of the wider economic system. As the authors say "Work meanings are both affected by and affect social, work and societal factors. Cultural conditioning, learning and development, and socialization are important processes which influence the meaning of work. Self-selection, the formation of groups, organizational and societal change are processes affected by meanings assigned to working."[7] We concur with those sentiments and note that they elevate the significance of the meaning of work since meanings held by groups and other impactful collectives in a society can help shape the wider social formation and facilitate change. It is this that makes the issue of the meaning of work of such critical importance in the Chinese context.

Whilst applauding the efforts of the MOWIRT and agreeing with much of their conceptualization, we find that the model could be extended, modified and refocused. Although they identify the macro socio-economic environment as an important antecedent factor, the discussion of it is extremely restricted. They give more emphasis to the personal, family and job/career history and experiences as determining factors. This reflects a tendency of Western management/organization theorists, perhaps influenced by cultural individualism, to locate explanations at the individual level and to relatively underplay structural and more macro issues. It is our contention that it is exactly the macro-societal level factors, and particularly those associated with the political and ideological environment, that have been especially relevant to the shaping of work meanings in China. Their model also almost completely neglects organizational-level factors. This may result from their concern not to deal with people's work meanings in relation to particular contexts and experiences, but the meanings and values attached to working *per se*. This approach is correct, but it leads to the neglect of organizational-level factors that are general and typical in a society and not confined to the specificities of a particular organization. We also feel that there are more immediate and pragmatic consequences that derive from people's meanings about working. The meaning of working patterns affect future work calculations, evaluations of work experiences and certain psycho-social responses. Such factors as generalized job satisfaction, alienation, organizational and career commitment, and motivation may all be affected and, in the end, will impact upon job performance and productivity.

In the light of these additional concerns and modifications to the model based upon aspects of the MOWIRT's own discussion of the issues, we reconfigure the model into a new form as shown in Figure 1 below. We have divided the antecedent/contingent variables into the broad categories of "macro-societal" and "micro-psycho-social." We have more fully delineated the former by identifying three sub-factors: economic, political/ideological and socio-cultural. The next most significant change is to introduce "organizational-level" factors as mediating between the first order antecedents and the central MOW variables. Note again that we are not concerned with the specific organizational features of individual employing organizations, but with the typical types of organizational forms and processes found within a given culture or society. In the case of China, there are some distinctive, commonly occurring types of employment practice, typical forms of management/leadership style, and

Figure 1. Meaning of Work Model

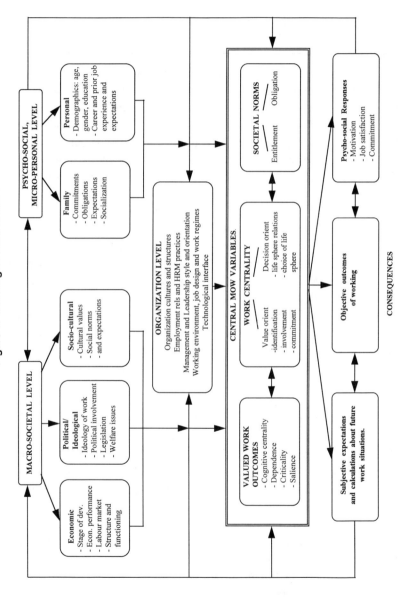

frequently encountered organizational cultures and structural configurations. We contend that exposure to and experience of such organizational level factors has a strong and immediate effect on how people experience their working lives and shapes the meaning patterns they develop with respect to working. We still allow for the first order antecedents to have a direct effect upon work meanings, unmediated by the organizational level.

In sum, the meanings associated with working are shaped by a complex combination of macro-societal factors; people's personal background, socialization and particular past and present job/work experiences; and by the common forms of structures, practices and values that they typically encounter at the organizational and work-place level. It should also be noted that, whilst the overall pattern of experience and meanings development within one culture or society may have sufficient commonality for it to be distinctive in relation to other cultures or societies, there will be considerable heterogeneity within a culture/society. The work meanings of different sectors of society will show significant variance.

We have collapsed the central MOW variables into three, largely following the discussion by the MOWIRT themselves which appears to deviate from the graphical depiction of their model. The three variables of "work centrality," "societal norms" and "valued work outcomes" are interrelated and should be thought of holistically, as making up variable patterns of response. These will be elaborated upon subsequently. Finally, we have also extended the consequences that we feel follow from the meaning of work patterning. The important point here is the link with motivation and performance: something of acute significance in the China context.

It is not our intention to test this model and explore all aspects of it in this chapter: we have neither the data nor the space to do so. We will use it as a framework for discussing some important aspects of the meaning of work in the Chinese context, and in those areas where we have some supporting evidence. That evidence comes from a partial replication of the MOWIRT empirical study as well as data from other research studies in which we have been involved. We will be giving particular emphasis to the macro-societal and organizational level factors as they relate to the central MOW variables and speculating somewhat on the consequences, both personal and societal, for China's continuing reform process.

The Macro-Societal Environment: Working in the Context of Reform

More so than in other countries, the macro-political/ideological context of work in China has a profound effect upon work, working and work meanings. The *foundational* basis for that difference, naturally, is a Marxist-Leninist-Maoist conceptualization of the economic system, production and labour in a socialist state. That ideological edifice places work and working on a significantly different footing than pertains in capitalistic systems. It may not entail major differences in the nature of work, but it does re-position work in terms of rationale, value and function as well as its organization and administration. In a dictatorship of the proletariat, working and the worker take on a different location in the social formation and hold different significances. Most saliently, the extent of individual calculations with respect to work is minimized, and the whole organization and administration of work is subject to centralized control. Work allocation, values, methods and rewards are all determined by government bodies guided more by political-ideological considerations rather than those of the market, efficiency and productivity. In China, the control, organization and administration of work systems has been tight and monolithic ever since the communist revolution. These broad aspects of the political-ideological determination of work forms only the base background to the more specific and dynamic macro-level machinations that have continued to mould the world of work in China in recent decades.

The contemporary context of work in China has been variously shaped since 1949 by a succession of policy initiatives, adaptations and reform measures of economic and enterprise management, often with sharp reversals and radical shifts of direction. The roots of the work system can be said to reside in the adoption of many aspects of the Soviet system of economic and industrial management in the early 1950s.[8] The legacy of that system continues to be a manifest force: "... the features of inflexibility, arbitrariness, impracticality, and over control in workshops have remained virtually unchanged... and have even been exacerbated...."[9] It was partly as a reaction to the increasingly recognized deficiencies of that base system that the current round of reforms were directed.

Since then, and until the 1978 reform initiative, various periods of change and adjustment have had a shaping influence which Child summarizes in terms of four, widely recognized phases:[10]

Phase 1: the period of rigid, tightly centralized command economy from 1953 to 1956.
Phase 2: the period of the Great Leap Forward (1957–1961).
Phase 3: "the period of readjustment" (1962–1965).
Phase 4: the Cultural Revolution (1966–1976).

At the enterprise level, the first phase entailed the so-called "one director (or 'one man') management system," intensive divisions of labour, "scientific" job design, limited worker participation, and diverse material incentives, particularly piece rate systems. Each phase that followed can be seen primarily as successive reactions to and reversals of the perceived failures of the preceding one, largely in terms of the selective centralization-decentralization of control of the economy and enterprise governance, and differences in the extensiveness of the vertical, bureaucratic linkages enterprises were tied to. Typically this was accompanied by variations in the level of political/ideological and party influence relative to the responsibilities and autonomy of enterprise managers and directors. The nature and extent of direct worker participation in the decision making and other affairs of the enterprise also shifted in each phase. Additional changes of emphasis centred on reward and motivation regimes ranging from reliance on moral/ideological incentives to a focus on material incentives.

An important legacy of this historical turbulence is the perception of a very unstable, uncertain and complex work environment. A perception which continues and impacts upon workers' attitudes, making them hesitant and uncertain about approaches and attitudes with respect to work. However, throughout, principles of egalitarianism in reward distribution, controlled work allocation, firm job security and extensive, paternalistic employment relationships and management orientations persisted.

The more recent reform-orientated changes that have impacted upon work and working began with the end of the Mao era as the new leadership responded to the country's badly declining economic situation. The signal for this was the "Four Modernizations" initiative announced at the 3rd Plenum of the 11th Central Committee meeting of the Chinese Communist Party (CCP) in 1978. There was open recognition of failures in the previous systems at both the macro-economic and enterprise management levels. These shortcomings, and the resultant economic malaise, are well documented.[11] The introduction of "responsibility systems," first in the agricultural and then the industrial sector, set the pattern for what was to follow. At the same time collectives and limited private enterprises were encouraged. The third major component of the reform thrust was the "open-door policy," which itself has had profound enterprise-level implications, not least through the increasing presence of joint ventures (JV) and foreign management.

The main thrust of the post-1978 reforms, as they bear on enterprise governance and management, can be divided into four phases (the first three taken from Hussain, and a fourth derived from collapsing two phases provided by Child):

1979–84 Permitting enterprises to produce outside the plan, to retain depreciation allowances and a portion of profits; a shift in the financing of working capital and investment from the government budget to enterprises' own funds and bank loans; discretion over the recruitment of workers and the introduction of performance-linked wage bonuses.

1984–86 Letting enterprises sell above-plan output at negotiated prices and to plan their output accordingly; new procedures for the appointment of enterprise directors; the replacement of remittances with profit taxes; a diversification of the sources of finance; leasing of small state-owned enterprises to managers.

1987 Formalisation of the role of enterprise directors, their methods of appointment and criteria for the evaluation of their performance; the introduction of performance targets for directors (the system of management contracts); introduction of bankruptcy law; formalisation of the main provisions into the 1988 Enterprise Law.[12]

1988 Periods of adjustment with successive austerity measures — including selective recentralisation and economic tightening to control inflation and an "overheating" economy, curtailment of investment, control of money supply, credit restrictions, price control and selective subsidies — followed by an easing of restrictions. Relaxation has included an easing of money supply, release of prices to the market and reduction of subsidies, some bankruptcies allowed to proceed, ease on credit and borrowing, increased share issues.[13]

This latter cycle looks set to continue as the government seeks to prevent the economy from overheating and keep inflation at tolerable levels whilst pressing on with the economic reforms and sustaining growth. The adoption, at the 14th Party Congress in 1992, of the principle of a "socialist market economy" reaffirms and consolidates the general direction of the reform process.

These broad aspects of reform have had both an indirect and direct impact on the work context, representing some radical changes. At the enterprise level, these have included: shifts in enterprise management responsibility, with greater decentralization and more discretion for enterprise directors, and a diminishing of party and bureaucratic control; alterations in the nature and extent of worker participation; an increased focus on performance and productivity, guided more by market-sensitive indicators than by centrally imposed production quotas; a change in the incentive environment with a clearer linkage between performance, reward and responsibility via the use of material incentive schemes and responsibility systems; alterations in employment terms with an erosion of "lifetime employment," the use of contracts, and more open recruitment and selection.[14]

There were other changes, in enterprise governance and management, employment relations and welfare, that have had a more direct impact on the work context. The most significant has been the gradual introduction of the principle of contract systems. As Howard suggests, the assumption has been made that "the key to raising labour productivity and improving enterprise efficiency lies in developing contractual relations between the enterprise and the government and between management and labour."[15] A set of contract responsibility systems were progressively introduced which radically altered the whole basis of the employment relationship and the relationship between enterprises and central government, particularly by shifting control, linking reward to performance and altering job security.

It is the systems of *labour contracting* that have had the most profound impact upon the working context, although related enterprise and management responsibility/contract systems are also of significance. Howard points out that contract labour had been part of the work scene since the inception of the People's Republic, but the form and intent of such systems have been radically altered.[16] Until the present reform process, labour contracts were largely confined to providing temporary employment to the urban unemployed or as temporary measures for peasants brought into urban industrial work. The government has been at pains to differentiate this old type of labour contract (*hetong gong*) from the new type (*hetongzhi gong*). The new form began as experiments in Shanghai and the Special Economic Zones (SEZ) in 1980. By 1983, Ministry of Labour temporary regulations and circulars set guidelines for contract systems and called for their universal extension to all new workers in state-owned (SOE) and collectively-owned enterprises. Early assurances that employees employed under old "permanent worker" conditions soon came under threat.[17] Almost in parallel, early experiments in management and enterprise responsibility contracting were significantly strengthened through 1984 State Council directives and the Central Committee document "China's Economic Structure Reform" which introduced the "direc tor responsibility system." These changes were extended and more explicitly formalized in the 1985 State Council regulations and the beginnings of a more extensive and formalized "Contractual Responsibility System."

By October 1986, State Council temporary regulations further fleshed out aspects of labour contract systems. This was a significant watershed in terms of the conditions of work and had a profound impact on what work would now mean in China. It was fundamental primarily because it began to dismantle the "iron rice bowl." The core principles of this reform were to (1) introduce a labour contract system by which workers were employed on a contractual basis and no longer as "permanent" employees with virtual lifetime guarantees, (2) establish a more open and rational recruitment system and dissolve the system of giving recruitment priority to the children of existing work unit members, (3) give enterprises the right to terminate the employment of inadequately performing workers, (4) establish systems of social security and old age pension schemes that were, at least partly, contributory, (5) allow non-profitable enterprises to be declared bankrupt.[18] Notably though, "cadres and intellectuals" were exempt from these rules.

This was a radical and controversial step challenging basic and deeply cherished principles of the old order and effectively created a two-tier employment system.[19] It has, in practice, been slow to take full effect — for instance by 1992 only about 16% of employees were on labour contracts[20] — and has been applied with caution and variability. Similarly, bankruptcy and worker dismissals have been extremely sensitive and relatively rare. Nonetheless, unemployment has become a fact of life and is officially recognized as an inevitable feature of the new order, despite the disquiet it generates. As Leung comments "… the Chinese government has partially abandoned its commitment to full employment and the strategy of job creation through administrative procedures."[21]

Many of the provisions, policies and guidelines relating to enterprise management were collected, codified and given the full force of law with the passing of the *Law concerning Enterprises Owned by the Whole People* which came into effect on 1 August 1988. There was little new in this legislation, it basically confirmed and concretized the measures discussed above. More importantly, the new employment relationships, particularly the use of contracts, were extended and fully cemented most recently and potently in the *Labour Law of the People's Republic of China* adopted at the 8th Session of the Standing Committee of the 8th NPC on 5 July 1994, coming into effect on 1 January 1995. It covers most aspects of the employment relationship, and its overall aim is summarized in Article 1: "This law is formulated... in order to protect the lawful rights and interests of workers, to regulate labour relations, to establish and safeguard a labour system that suits the socialist market economy and to promote economic development and social progress."[22] It extends employment contracts, affirming that "A labour contract shall be entered into whenever a labour relationship is established" and should cover the term of the contract, a job description, labour protection and labour condition clauses, labour remuneration, discipline matters, conditions for contract termination and liabilities. They may be either fixed or open terms, or terms that expire on completion of certain work, thus introducing considerable flexibility. The law makes clear provision for contract termination — for example, contracts can be terminated with 30 days notice if workers are incompetent and remain so after training or reassignment — and guidelines for staff layoff.

There are also provisions that amount to a form of collective bargaining. Article 13 states that "Enterprise employees, as one party, may enter into a collective contract with the enterprise on matters such as labour remuneration, working hours, rest, holidays, labour safety and hygiene, insurance, welfare, etc."[23] Such collective agreements entered into by the labour union, on behalf of the staff, with the enterprise are binding, and labour contracts cannot offer terms less favourable than those contained in the collective agreement.

Other important aspects of the law deal with wages and social insurance. Article 46 affirms the broad policy of the statute and reflects the general momentum of the reform process: "Wage distribution shall conform to the principle of distribution according to work. Equal pay shall be given for equal work. Wage levels shall be gradually increased on the basis of economic development. The state shall adjust the total amount of wages at the macroscopic level."[24] The last phrase hints at state wage control and is a little at odds with the following Article: "Employing units shall autonomously determine their own methods of wage distribution and wage levels in accordance with the law, on the basis of their own production and operation characteristics and economic benefits."[25] The mode of central control is unclear, except for a state-implemented minimum wage. The social insurance provisions are also still rather vague and have the appearance of an interim set of measures. They declare that eventually all funds for social insurance "shall be raised by society," but that "Employing Units and workers must participate in social insurance and pay social insurance fees according to law."[26] The aspiration clearly exits to develop a full-scale, national social insurance scheme that will remain, at least partially, contributory. It will cover assistance and protection with respect to retirement, illness or injury, invalidity through work-related injury or disease, job loss and maternity. The law also encourages employing units to set up supplementary insurance of their own.

The reforms of the employment relationship, particularly the contract system, the possibility of becoming unemployed and the dismantling of the "iron rice bowl," represent the most significant areas of change in the work context in contemporary China. But, they are compounded by other changes in the socio-economic order. There are, for example, related shifts in welfare policy (which we will discuss in more detail subsequently) that devolve responsibility from the central government to more localized terrains including the individual and his/her family. These have a significant bearing upon job security and alter the conditions of protection should that be threatened. Such matters affect how people perceive their work context, affect the calculations they make with respect to working and, ineluctably, impinge on the meanings they construct about work and working.

At the same time, there are changes in the level of wealth and its distribution. There is official encouragement of personal acquisitiveness, and the disposable income and living standards of certain sectors of the population have risen dramatically. The average per capita urban income in 1993 was RMB 2,335 (a 10% rise, after inflation, on 1992), and incomes are considerably higher in some of the wealthiest cities.[27] Furthermore, most SOEs and government bodies reverted to a five-day week in 1994. A consequence is that people have more free time and more money to expend on leisure activities. It has been estimated that Chinese households now spend about a fifth of their discretionary income on recreational activities.[28] There has been a boom in television sales, and even the karaoke and compact disk markets are expanding quickly. China now has about 1,000 radio stations, and there have been significant changes in content. Domestic tourism has also shown marked growth in recent years.[29] These new options affect the work-leisure relationship, provide a different kind of motivational factor for working and, again, further alter the meaning framework with respect to work.

However, there are also growing disparities in earnings and wealth which look set to continue.[30] Whilst some of the so-called "new rich" are enjoying the new opportunities for earning and consumption, others are struggling with sustained low earnings and severely restricted opportunities, whilst still others suffer the deprivations of unemployment and a restructured welfare system. The changes have fomented a new environment with the complex motivations of new opportunities for material advancement together with the fear of falling out of the system into isolation and poverty. This situation cannot but affect people's assessment of the work environment, their motivational calculations and response strategies.

Another important change is a general broadening of work options. Outside of the agricultural sector, SOEs, although still the major employer, are no longer the only choice available. There are collective and private enterprises, and increasing numbers are pursuing the entrepreneurial track, with, as we have seen, government encouragement. Furthermore, employment opportunities exist in Sino-foreign JVs or wholly-owned foreign companies. Here earning potentials may be greater[31] and certainly many see better opportunities for training, development and career advancement, as we shall see shortly. However, there may be less security and welfare provision.

In the work place itself, there is a sharper emphasis on performance and productivity, and on linking rewards more directly to performance. Material incentives are now very much in vogue, even if their group basis weakens the impact on individual motivation. How hard and well people work now matters. Jobs are less secure, and there is always the possibility, in theory, of being laid-off or even dismissed. Management and leadership styles are altering as a result of the changes in enterprise governance and increased management autonomy. There is also less party influence at the enterprise level, and the role of the Trade Unions and Worker's Congress has shifted.[32] Skill shortages persist, with competition now to secure and hang-on to those with scarce skills and abilities. This is recognized, and people are very keen to secure training and development opportunities. It is to these organizational-level issues that we now turn in detail. It should be noted that the distinction between macro-societal factors and organizational ones is purely an analytic device, there is a fundamental interpenetration between levels, and this is particularly acute in the PRC context.

The Organizational Level: Life in (and out) of the "*Danwei*"

The Demise of the *Danwei* and the Breaking of the "*Iron Rice Bowl*"

The economic and political/ideological macro-societal factors have a determining effect on work meanings, largely by framing the context of work, defining viable work options, and moderating the calculations people make with respect to work and in relation to other aspects of their lives. They are also determining through their direct and indirect impact on the organizations and work environments in which people actually work. Theoretically, organizational-level factors are multiple, complex and interrelated. Our model identifies broad ones such as organizational cultures and structures; employment relations and human resource practices; management/leadership styles and orientations; the working environment, job design and work regimes; and technological interface issues. Remember that we are not dealing with specific manifestations of these factors in particular organizations but with the typical forms they take across organizations within a social system. In China, given the centralized control of the economic system and the whole organizational and employment system, such commonalities are perhaps more pronounced than in other countries.

The central feature of Chinese organizations of most direct relevance to people's work experience is the work unit, or *danwei* system. The reforms outlined in the last section, particularly the 1988 and 1995 laws on employment relations, have had the most direct and profound impact upon the working lives of people in China today, especially when considered in conjunction with welfare reforms and other changes in the socio-economic system. The significance is that they represent a breaking of the "iron bowls" and fundamentally alter the *danwei* system which had been at the heart, not only of peoples' basic work life, but also of broader aspects of their social and community life. Indeed, Howard has been moved to suggest that the whole thrust of the contract labour and other reforms has been "the elimination of the 'iron rice bowl' and its replacement with a 'clay rice bowl' (*cifanwan*) system."[33]

China's extensive post-revolutionary industrial social welfare system had always been concentrated at the level of the individual work unit. The *danwei* was the key element of the country's welfare system, and remains very significant.[34] As Leung puts it, "Functioning as a self-sufficient 'small society' or 'mini-welfare state', the state-owned enterprises provided comprehensive, non-contributory, and from-cradle-to-grave welfare services to their employees… [including] … a social security programme, various allowances, and personal and collective welfare services."[35] The state made all work assignments and did so under the assumption that the state's economic needs took precedence over individual choice or family concerns, even to the extent of separating families.[36]

Members not only received a secure job for life and a basic wage, but also a whole series of "benefits," facilities and welfare support, including subsidized housing, health care, education, transportation, utilities, food, and even bathing and haircuts. In the work community, in addition to educational, health and housing provision, would be cinemas, recreational centres, libraries and other facilities. Social security included benefits for sickness, maternity, work injury compensation, invalidity allowances and pensions. The work unit, then, took comprehensive responsibility for the well-being of the individual and the community. This type of all-embracing and paternalistic work environment entailed that it "(was) organized as much as a security system as it (was) a social or economic system … the essence of the Chinese system… was the individual's ties to his *danwei*, a kind of industrial feudalism."[37] To get married, visit relatives, buy a bicycle required permission from the *danwei*. The so-called *dingti* system also meant that children of retiring members would be given preference in recruitment. Such a system meant that enterprise managers "must take an holistic approach to looking after employees and their families; managers get involved in personal issues like marriages, childcare, and parents illnesses."[38] This type of managerial paternalism is still present. Such an employment system meant very low labour mobility and low unemployment. Individuals had high dependence on the enterprise, and hence on the party and the state.

Of significance for subsequent economic calculations and reforms was the fact that the whole system was centrally planned with the government subsidizing, directly or indirectly, most of the costs. Of particular note was the provision of subsidies to support ailing enterprises and the manipulation of supply and prices of goods. These subsidies amounted to as much as 20% of state expenditure throughout the period from 1949–1989.[39] It was this type of support, even in the face of inefficiency and low productivity, that provided the metal for the "iron rice bowl" and which enabled people to keep their jobs and feel secure irrespective of their own performance or that of their enterprise. The assumption came to be made that the 'iron rice bowl' was not conducive to market reform and economic development as envisaged in the "Four Modernizations." The recognized problem of low labour productivity was laid at the door of a system that guaranteed jobs and wages, irrespective of performance, thus emasculating management's efforts to motivate and intensify labour input.

The employment system reforms have amounted, not only to a change in employment relations, but to a fundamental shift in welfare policy and administration. However, the changes wrought have actually resulted in an escalation of welfare needs, and welfare policy "becomes a vital mechanism to mitigate conflicts created by rapid modernizing social changes, high economic growth and market-oriented reforms."[40] Not least of these intensified welfare requirements are those created by rising unemployment and the widening disparities in wealth between employees in different sectors, urban versus rural areas and inter-regionally.[41] And, this is happening as the existing basic system of welfare is being dismantled. The government is responding through a series of additional welfare reforms which cover occupational welfare, rural social security, civil affairs and community services;[42] only the first will be commented on here. The basic strategy with respect to retirement schemes, medical services and unemployment is to have contributory (enterprises and/or employee) schemes with funds entered into a managed trust. This shifts the responsibility away from central government, which they are keen to do in general, moving it into different sectors of society: into neighbourhoods, enterprises and families. In terms of occupational welfare, there is a clear move away from a Leninist model of full state and employer responsibility,[43] and the government is unwilling to shoulder the full burden any longer. But, Leung feels that some people are concerned about this aspect of the reform process, and the potential for social unrest inherent within it, and is sceptical about the early demise of the "iron rice bowl": "... given the abiding importance of occupational welfare to the maintenance of political stability and legitimacy of the CCP, the 'iron rice bowls' will remain largely intact and irreversible."[44]

Despite the enterprise and management reforms, SOE organization and management have still recently been described as "a clan-like structure with a heavy emphasis on informal communication, patriarchal decision making, guaranteed pay, and egalitarian performance criteria based on the hierarchy."[45] Indeed, Boisot has argued that Chinese organizational governance can best be described as fief-like, with a failure to generate formally bureaucratic or market driven systems.[46] Many problems have been identified as resulting from this, both in the Western literature and within China itself. A combination of socialist values and policies, and residual Confucian values are held by some commentators to mean that the system still displays feudalistic elements and high levels of paternalism.[47] Much of this is associated with the *danwei* traditions. The values and attitudes associated with the system persist despite the reforms and attempts to break the "iron-rice bowl."

The Critique of SOEs and the *Danwei* System

This section draws on the first of the research projects we have been involved in. It will be referred to hereinafter as the *jvgrad* [48] study and concerns the expectations and experiences of a group of young Chinese university graduates been recruited to Sino-foreign JVs in Guangdong. It was a longitudinal study with interviews and questionnaires administered immediately on recruitment and on subsequent occasions over close to a three-year period. The process began in late 1991. The recruits were contacted on a convenience basis. Interviews (both group and individual) were conducted with approximately 100 people, but a core group of around 40 provided most of the data used here. All had good educational qualifications, and for the vast majority joining a JV was their first full-time job. Their ages ranged from 21–31 (although most were under 25).

Interviews and survey work in the *jvgrad* project revealed that the respondents had some interesting, mainly negative, conceptions of working for SOEs. Indeed, many indicated that an important reason for seeking JV employment was to avoid some of the negative features they saw as prevalent in domestic enterprises. The essence of these concerns are summarized in the following discussion, which focus on three organizational level issues — motivation and work attitudes, reward-performance relationships and management/leadership style — broadened with material from recent literature.

Beyond the "Tea and Newspaper Syndrome": Motivation and the Work Ethic

Respondents strongly indicated that they perceived a low level of task commitment and a weak work ethic prevailing in SOEs. They claimed that there was no incentive for people to work hard as rewards were not matched to performance, and this was compounded by significant over-manning. As one person graphically put it, "I don't want to spend my time sitting around drinking tea and reading newspapers, which is all that seems to happen in (local) enterprises."

Problems with work motivation, a weak work ethic and poor task orientation in SOEs has been widely commented on in the literature, both overseas[49] and in China.[50] Numerous contributory factors have been discussed, including the existence of the "iron-rice bowl";[51] ineffective reward-performance relationships;[52] improperly devised and administered work quotas;[53] and ineffective ideological/political work.[54] The 1984 policy document "China's Economic Structure Reform" summarized an early government interpretation in broader terms:

> No clear distinction has been drawn between the functions of the government and those of the enterprise; barriers exist between different departments or between different regions; the state has exercised excessive and rigid control over enterprises; no adequate importance has been given to commodity production, the law of value and the regulatory role of the market; and there is absolute egalitarianism in distribution. This has resulted in enterprises lacking necessary decision making power and the practice of "eating out of the same big pot" prevailing in the relations of the enterprises to the state and in those workers and staff members to their enterprises. *The enthusiasm, initiative and creativeness of enterprises and workers and staff members have, as a result, been seriously dampened and the socialist economy is bereft of much of the vitality it should possess.*[55]

However, low productivity should not be attributed only to such factors but also to the fact that China has pursued full-employment policies in part by relying on cheap and inferior technologies that rely on labour intensive methods.[56] In addition, employment policies have resulted in extremely restricted labour mobility which entails not only limited staffing options, but also restricts labour and tends to lock them into a "stifling dependency relationship with their employer."[57]

The following comments about Chinese work attitudes from Western staff in China are indicative of a foreign practitioner perspective. Work attitudes were variously said to be "superficial; not serious; they have little pride in their work; they stress quantity over quality; Chinese are not used to hard work in the workplace; the Chinese go to the workplace to rest and go home to do housework."[58] One expatriate attributes a cause: "Probably due to the political system, most people regard work purely as an act that one has to perform in order to get paid — which they will — regardless of their output."[59] A US manager visiting a Shanghai plant notes many people sleeping and comments "All the offices had beds in them, and they were being used. That shows you something about the work ethic."[60] Similarly, a Hong Kong Chinese human resource manager with considerable experience in China also blames ideological/political dogma: "It's the legacy of the Communist tradition. Whether you work hard or not, you get the same rewards. So no one works."[61] It is most pertinent to note the reiteration of these perceptions by foreign staff by the *jvgrads*. Despite the recent reforms the legacy of the "iron rice bowl" ethos persists.

"To Each According to His Work": Linking Performance and Reward

A contributory factor to this type of work ethos has undoubtedly been the lack of a relationship between reward and performance, so much the linchpin of Western motivational practices. In China, even persistently poor performers are rarely punished, and termination virtually non existent.[62] Despite the reforms, it is proving difficult in practice to roll back the life-time employment/"iron rice bowl" ethos; as Tai Ming Cheung comments: "The government has been unsuccessfully attempting to reform this system since the mid-1980s by introducing fixed-term contract systems and giving factory managers the right to hire and fire."[63] For many in China, the "iron-rice bowl" is still one of the key benefits to stem from the Communist Revolution,[64] and in any case, many of the new labour contracts are for as much as 50 years.[65] Furthermore, as has been cogently argued, the labour contract system has given rise to a two-tier arrangement with certain sectors of the workforce enjoying levels of security that have changed little.[66] Nonetheless, the "iron rice bowl" *is* under pressure, and dismissals and sackings are not as rare as they used to be,[67] even if they still prove very problematic in practice.[68]

Until the recent reform process began, the socialist ideology of economic egalitarianism had been a core aspect of PRC policy and practice since the revolution. It has been argued that this policy-practice nexus has been a most significant and problematic aspect of the reforms. "In a certain sense, the economic reforms taking place in China began by looking at the various types of reward systems and job responsibility systems. The main purpose of these reforms was to alter these systems in such a way as to fulfil people's needs and motivate them to work."[69] The party recognized that the "iron rice bowl" was not conducive to the desired economic growth, especially in terms of work incentives, efficiency and productivity and resolved to dismantle it and alter the nature of employment and the reward system.[70] As Cheung puts it: "Now the egalitarian and need-based security network, 'the iron rice bowl' created during the Maoist period, is considered an impediment to market reform."[71] This was also sharply expressed by an influential commentator in China:

> The primary expression of egalitarianism in labor wages is the fact that many people hold in their hands an "iron rice bowl" and eat from the "same big pot".... Regardless of whether his or her labor attitude is good or bad, regardless of whether his or her contribution is large or small, he or she is entitled to a standard monthly wage.... Under egalitarianism, people are not concerned at all about the results of labour... [the principle of egalitarianism] leads to lowering economic efficiency, which results in a lower level of living and consumption, which in turn further dampens people's labor initiative.[72]

Since the "iron rice bowl" system of enterprise and state paternalism incorporates significant welfare and benefit functions, changing it means a departure from the old policy of "high employment, high welfare and low wages."[73] The "everyone eating from the same big pot" orientation has increasingly been denounced, and new mottoes, such as "more labour, more benefit; less labour, less benefit; no labour, no benefit," and "it is glorious to be rich," begin to surface. A further, encompassing slogan, representing the extent of the intended reforms, is not just "break the 'iron rice bowl'," but "break the three irons": "break the iron chair" (guaranteed posts for managers and administrators), the "iron salary" (the guarantee that wages will not be cut) and the "iron rice bowl."

As the attempt to erode the principle of egalitarianism progresses, it has given way to notions of equity where people are paid, not according to their need, but relative to their performance. The concept of earnings differentials has received increasing endorsement from the government. The *Beijing Review*, back in 1988, reported: "Differences in pay should be widened so as to encourage individual enthusiasm and speed up the development of production."[74] A statement in 1991, that the major policy aim was now "to allow some people to become wealthy first, as part of the goal of common prosperity," reflects the continuing shift in direction.[75] However, there has been some outcry against the "new rich," and support for egalitarian principles is far from dead.[76] There remains much resistance to "breaking the iron rice bowl," both from sections of the labour force and within the party.[77] For many organizations, the principles of pay for performance are barely present, and "Even in large organizations... the top management only receive 4–5 times as much as the typical production worker."[78] Furthermore, incentive bonuses and other payments are often made to the work group and not to individuals, thus people are still rewarded irrespective of their individual effort. "Thus, whilst cash incentives are theoretically possible, in practice they are egalitarian-based, not equity-based."[79]

It has been argued that group incentives and bonuses are not only ideologically-informed but also culturally appropriate given Chinese collectivist and group-centred values. However, Chinese collectivism is familistic and does not readily incorporate abstract collectives, such as work groups or enterprises.[80] Some research in China does suggest that group-based work positively impacts worker performance,[81] but without a clearer link of performance to reward it is unlikely to have the hoped for motivational impact. Workers are still encouraged to work for the country and party, and it is assumed that they will be more motivated to perform well when collectively working toward those ends.[82] As Becker and Yang Gao put it: "... egalitarianism implicitly assumes that individual interests and social interests are one and that individual workers are ... motivated by these larger goals."[83] Prior to 1980, ideological or so-called "spiritual" incentives were deemed to be functional. Ideological encouragement and political training were accompanied by ritualistic awards and non-material incentives such as "Model Worker."[84] Back in 1980 this still seemed to have been impactful since in a survey of factory workers "realization of modernization" was ranked first from a list of ideas or incentives which would motivate them, and a belief in communism was second or third.[85] Such ideological/political motivation techniques are still held by some to be effective and to have a place in the system[86] but are, in reality, much less likely to have a motivational impact in the present work climate. Moral and ideological admonitions are on the decline, and there is a recognition that non-material rewards are insufficient to motivate workers in the desired manner. Amongst sections of the workforce, too, there is more of an individualistic orientation toward their work and economic interests, as the importance ratings of job outcomes by the *jvgrads* shows. They rated aspects of their career development and intrinsic work factors more highly than "opportunity for contributing to society." They also rated "the general public" ninth in importance out of eleven organizational constituents, and "myself" second.

The *jvgrads* gave clear and strong endorsement to the idea that one should be rewarded for performance and on merit, and they were perfectly accepting of differential rewards for different levels of performance. They perceived the espoused move toward this in the SOEs to be far from the reality. They took the still prevailing system, in which rewards and advancement are not based on performance or merit, to be unfair and lamented its consequences. In their view, relationships, political influence and correctness and seniority were more important. Pay for performance systems have not really penetrated into most SOEs, both because of a reluctance to shed the comforting principles of egalitarianism and the security of the "iron rice bowl" and because such systems require more sophistication in work design, work measurement and evaluation: "Despite more recent interest in expanding performance-based reward systems, the implementation... is limited by the absence of a well-developed, even rudimentary performance appraisal system."[87]

As a young, educated élite with good career prospects, they are more willing and able to exploit the opportunities emerging in the new regime and more prepared to accept the risks. In this sense, they are in the vanguard of accepting these new notions, whilst many members of the working community, and indeed the party, remain very suspicious and guarded. Much of the workforce does not readily accept the principle of widely disparate differences in wages.[88] Empirical work suggests some acceptance, but the "equity differential threshold" places tight parameters around what is acceptable.[89] The *jvgrads* clearly felt that performance would not be recognized and rewarded in the SOEs and were worried that, from their point of view, inappropriate criteria would be used to evaluate their performance. This again goes back to the lack of systematic performance management systems which entails that "Workers simply do not accept different evaluations as legitimate, because they appear to be based largely on arbitrary measures."[90] It is this arbitrary and potentially inequitable experience that led the *jvgrads* to seek out the more systematic meritocracy of a JV organization.

The Struggle for Autonomy and Responsibility: Paternalistic Headship and Political Leadership

Weber described the pre-eminent form of dominance in China as patrimonial, under which seemingly absolute power resides with the family patriarch.[91] This tradition, together with reputedly complementary cultural values, such as large power distance,[92] a natural acceptance of hierarchical structuring and in-built legitimization for unequal superior-subordinate relationships,[93] the dutiful fulfillment of role duties, and tendencies toward deference, compliance and conformity to authority,[94] has led to Western commentators depicting Chinese leadership as autocratic. However, this is somewhat inaccurate since the firm power position is ameliorated by other cultural requirements: for leaders to exercise power on behalf of the collective (notably family), not on the grounds of self interest; to maintain harmonious relationships within the group; to display the virtues of human-heartedness, respect, mutual obligation and reciprocity; to exhibit "face" sensitivity; and to uphold a moral character.[95] This gives Chinese leadership a distinctive, complex, dualistic dynamic that has been variously labelled as a "virtuocracy,"[96] "paternalistic headship,"[97] "benevolent autocratic" or "paternalistic."[98]

In the PRC, these cultural traditions are complexly interwoven with the ideological/political values and structures associated with power and authority under the communist system. Enterprise leadership has been embedded in a complex set of interdependent relationships.[99] The roots of this lie in the approximate adoption of Soviet systems of enterprise governance in the early 1950s which located the individual enterprise "within a matrix comprising two administrative lines leading down to two categories of bureaux which relate with state-owned enterprises. Party organs parallel and are embedded in each unit of the structure."[100] There is firstly, then, a dualistic administrative/party structure, and secondly, with central specialist and central industrial ministries, a dualistic administrative arrangement. All have at various times been under different levels of control from the central government, the National People's Congress and the State Council. The current reform measures are only the latest experiment in decentralization. The situation is complicated by the role and functioning of the Trade Unions and by the ideological notion that the means of production are actually owned by the workers.

The current situation of enterprise management is depicted as still being located within an extremely complex network of dependencies.[101] Managers have to cope with these, which include the densely hierarchical arrangements of the dualistic administrative systems with cascading bureau involvement from the central government down to local and community level, the party structure and its organs, the trade union and the Worker's Congress, the employees, as well as suppliers and distributors/customers. Management of each dependency takes place within a framework of a confusingly uncertain mixture of planned and quasi-market transactions, an imperfect and inflexible labour market and continued uncertainties about economic and political direction. These diverse relationships, interests and dependencies are, at the same time, "variously interpreted by the supervisory bureaucracy and have only been moderately clarified by the so-called 'Contract Responsibility System'."[102]

This situation has prompted Walder to point out the "four facts of life" for modern enterprise directors/managers: (1) the need to skillfully manage still important vertical relationships with the government bureaucracy, (2) to maintain workable relationships with party officials and other politicized groupings within the enterprise which is thereby best conceived of as a political coalition, (3) the residual *danwei* orientation in which the enterprise is still a "socio-political community" and not just an economic/productive unit, and (4) the continued requirement to handle non-market transaction relationships, especially in conditions of supply shortages and in securing trade credit.[103]

Contemporary enterprise leadership is thus characterized by persisting authoritarian, but parternalistic styles, apparent increased autonomy and responsibility, but with sustained outside scrutiny and dependencies, and a continuing pattern of change and uncertainty. It is a complex, pluralistic and still politicized environment compounded by the uncertainties of shifts from the securities of central planning and control, to the vagaries of underdeveloped market transactions. Formal systems often cannot be relied upon to deliver resources, and managers are compelled to resort to informal systems and relationships to get what they need. As Boisot and Xing Guo Liang put it: "The firm has become an arena where different interest groups compete for organizational resources in a haphazard way.... An enterprise director is under the constant scrutiny of a supervisory bureaucracy which is both uncoordinated and frequently changing direction — often capriciously — expecting him to follow."[104] Despite the apparent decentralization, state bureaucracies are still a presence to be reckoned with, and the colloquial appellation "mothers-in-law" remains apposite. Enterprise management still lacks institutional legitimacy, both among the workforce and state bureaucracies. Too much managerial autonomy is viewed as potential self-seeking.[105] Managers must somehow strive to meet the interests of both state bureaucracies and the workforce. They tend, if at all possible, to develop highly personalized relationships with hierarchical superiors and key figures in the bureaucracies.

In spite of the welfare, and other reforms, managers still have wider responsibilities than would be the case for Western counterparts.

Expectations and obligations to be involved in social, welfare and interpersonal issues with respect to employees persist. This continued paternalism is reflected in directors being referred to as "father-mother official" (*fu-mu guan*) by subordinates, and there are expectations that he/she "must display a Confucian benevolence towards them at all times and thus get intimately involved in the myriad problems of worker relocation, bonus distribution, education, housing, health and welfare issues."[106] Thus, enterprise managers still have a paternalistic role to fulfill, a key feature of which is its inevitable subjectivity and personalism.[107]

It was this feature of Chinese enterprise leadership that the *jvgrads* reacted to negatively. They characterized the leadership style as autocratic and directive, leading through fear and coercion rather than ability and respect. They also decried the paternalism. As one of them put it: "I don't want a second father at work; I want a manager." SOE employees have little autonomy and are not expected to assume, nor given, responsibility; they are simply told what to do, expected to comply without question and exert only minimal effort in meeting the basic requirements.

SOE systems were also depicted as too rigid and inflexible. Both enterprise systems and staff are considered rule-bound, non-learning and non-adaptive. Individuals are not encouraged to be proactive or change oriented, nor to challenge the *status quo*. Staff become habituated to the passive, unmotivated, responsibility-avoiding cultures of state enterprises. Despite this, the *jvgrads* recognized that high levels of personalism and subjectivity persisted and bemoaned the fact that too much depended on whom you know, relationships and *guanxi*. They had a strong antipathy toward the extensive networks of relationships perceived to be pervasive, intrusive and complex, and indicated that they did not want to expend the inordinate amount of time and energy necessary to ensure that relationship requirements were met.

The avoidance of formality and reliance on personalistic modes of operation is a commonly attributed feature of even overseas Chinese management.[108] Boisot and Xing Guo Liang have, at least in the PRC context, attributed this to the impact of cultural and socio-political values on the codification and dispersion of information. They maintain that there is a disinclination to codify information, and hence dispersion is restricted and contained within personalistic relationship networks. The avoidance of delegation is one consequence of this. It is avoided because managers have low levels of trust with respect to their own organizations, and view administrative systems more as instruments of control than as abstract or supporting systems. In any case, given the importance of personalism and relationships, everyone wants to deal directly with the manager/director, thus restricting effective delegation. Perhaps more significantly, formalization and effective delegation are only really viable where you have routinized, codifiable tasks that can be evaluated according to clear and stable criteria. But, in Chinese enterprises these features are invariably absent, meaning that "working methods are likely to remain much more random and *ad hoc*, and delegation becomes a hazardous enterprise calling for a higher degree of interpersonal trust than exists at present between different hierarchical levels in China."[109]

The *"jvgrads"* also indicated that the trust levels within SOE work units were low as people competed for resources, or access to personal contacts and networks that could lead them to valued resources. Some research in China has confirmed this impression, indicating that the relationship between work unit leaders and workers is poor because workers see that the leader's alignment and loyalty is upward and outward to those who appoint and monitor them, and that they do not have the interests of their group members at heart.[110]

These data suggest a very negative impression of working life in China's SOEs. The accompanying discussion focused on many work-related problems in SOEs as documented in both foreign and Chinese materials. The key concerns addressed related to motivation and the work ethic, performance-reward relationships and the implications of a paternalistic and intrusive leadership style. These problems reveal that much has still to be done at the enterprise level if the broader economic reforms are to be driven by effective and committed work practices from a skilled and motivated work force. It was abundantly clear that the *jvgrads* wanted to avoid these negativities and that was a key reason for them wanting to join a JV. It is their expectations, perceptions and experiences in JVs that we address now.

Critique by Contrast: Working for a Joint Venture

Sino-foreign JVs and, more recently, wholly-owned foreign enterprises in the PRC have grown rapidly over the past decade and have generated considerable interest, especially in the West. For China, JVs represent a controllable form of foreign investment, opportunities for foreign exchange earnings and technology transfer. For the foreign investor, they have increasingly been seen as the most viable mode of entry into the China market.

Much of the research and commentary has focused on the negotiation for, establishment of, and successful operation of Sino-foreign JVs,[111] and particularly on cross-cultural[112] and human resource problems.[113] This has commonly included such obvious things as the language barrier and "culture shock." Additional structural and system problems perceived in China have included: skill shortages (especially managerial); weak and fluid structuring and reliance on personalism; hiring practices and policies; the complexity of relationships with external bodies, especially state bureaucracies; coping with reward differentials; being compelled to over-staff the enterprise; changes and confusions in the regulatory environment; the "one company, two systems" problem;[114] and, inability to effectively discipline or fire staff. Cross-cultural or relationship difficulties have included: differences in communication style; work ethic and motivation differences; the reliance on and complexities of *guanxi*; differences in management style; inter-unit cooperation problems; *face* and respect issues; xenophobism; and, inflexibilities on both sides. Nonetheless, the growth rate of JVs is likely to increase, and they have become a desirable place of employment for increasing numbers of Chinese workers. This was clearly the case with the *jvgrads*, and in this section we focus on their perceptions of working in JVs, especially in comparison to working for SOEs or other Chinese only enterprises.

In the first rounds of interviews with the *jvgrads*, almost immediately after their selection, we discussed their reasons for wanting to join a JV. The motives appear to be broadly twofold: one positive set and one nega-tive. The negative side has been mainly dealt with in the previous section and had to do with their perceptions of local enterprises and the desire to find an employment alternative. For the vast majority, the major attraction was the greater opportunities afforded by JVs, especially in terms of per-sonal and professional learning and development. Many were explicitly interested in learning about Western business and management styles and techniques. Only about 10% made any reference to money or greater earnings potential. The continuing reference to development opportunities in subsequent data leads to the conclusion that this was genuinely the most salient motivating factor. This is important since it reflects a calculation about what they need to do to succeed in the new environment, probably a recognition of the skills deficiencies in the market and as a means of securing a competitive advantage.

Other expectations reveal something of their comparative judgement about working in a JV *vis-à-vis* an SOE. They suggested that they expected to work hard, and by implication, harder than in local enterprises and to be confronted by more interesting and challenging work. It was assumed that they would be given greater levels of responsibility and be able to exercise more initiative. JVs were viewed as meritocracies, with rewards based on performance and administered with fairness and equity. Partly as a consequence of this, they felt that their chances of being promoted more rapidly were enhanced. They fully expected and were mostly accepting of the principle of differential rewards for differential performance. In related, more general terms, they anticipated that JV organizations would be characterized by clearer, more systematic management systems, with formal structures and arrangements, leading to greater effectiveness. They generally expected them to be better organized, more efficient and not so encumbered by intense and complicated personal relationships. This is clearly in contrast to the confusion and personalism they saw as prevalent in SOEs. The view was expressed that JVs would be more performance and result-oriented, and this was welcomed. Furthermore, they felt that JVs would be more characterized by trust and respect of the individual and would better engender a sense of belonging and pride in the company.

There is clearly some idealization in these views, and there are indications that the recruits came to a more realistic view as time passed. Nonetheless, these expectations about the JV are important, not only by virtue of their comparative indications, but also because subsequent satisfaction with the experience of working for the JV may depend upon the extent to which they are met.

A more direct comparison of perceptions of JVs and local enterprises was covered in a questionnaire. Respondents were asked to indicate the extent of their agreement with a set of statements using a 5-point scale (1 = "strongly agree," 5 = "strongly disagree"). The questionnaire was administered twice, once when the recruits had just joined a JV, and a second time about a year later. Table 1 gives the results from this part of the questionnaire.

The first thing to note is that there are few differences in the scores between Time 1 and Time 2, indicating that the expectations held by the recruits on joining a JV were, in the main, confirmed by their experiences of actually working there. There are some differences, which we will comment on shortly, but none are statistically significant. The second

Table 1. Working for a Foreign-managed Company vs. a Chinese Enterprise

Working for a foreign-managed company compared with a local enterprise I would expect...	Time 1 Mean	Time 2 Mean
1 More opportunities for learning and self development	1.1	1.2
2 To do work that is less useful to society	4.4	4.3
3 My individual performance to be recognized and rewarded	1.8	2.0
4 To work harder	1.7	2.1
5 To have a closer relationship with my boss/supervisor	2.8	3.1
6 Promotion to be slower	4.0	3.9
7 Rewards to be given more equitably	2.1	2.5
8 My managers to be less accessible	3.7	3.7
9 To have less discretion and responsibility	4.6	4.5
10 Organizational relationships to be closer	2.1	2.2
11 To be given more interesting and challenging work	1.6	1.7
12 To feel less comfortable in work relationships	3.7	3.8
13 To be criticized more readily when my performance is below standard	2.6	2.9
14 To be faced by more ethical dilemmas	3.4	3.5

general thing to note is that these quantitative scores mirror many of the comments made during the interviews.

More specifically, respondents clearly indicated high expectations of more opportunities for learning and development, confirming the interview data, as do the expectations concerning responsibility and discretion, and interesting and challenging work. Their opinions on these issues barely changed over the course of the year. Two areas where there was a change, although not significant, concerned perceptions of working harder, which declined somewhat, and less certainty about rewards being given on a more equitable basis. In both cases though, they still viewed things as different in the JV. The questionnaire confirmed that they perceived individual performance to be recognized and rewarded more in the JV than the local enterprise, but they became increasingly unsure as to whether there was any difference in the criticism for poor performance. They did, however, continue to believe that promotion opportunities would be better in the JV. In terms of work relationships, they felt that these would be more "comfortable" and "closer" in the JV. They were less sure, and remained so, about the closeness of their relationship with a boss or superior, but interviews suggested a perceived qualitative difference in the relationship between themselves and a JV manager compared to a Chinese manager. Respondents did feel, however, that foreign managers were more accessible. They did not subscribe to the view that working for a market-oriented, capitalistic enterprise meant that the work was less useful to society. With respect to facing ethical dilemmas, they were unsure if there was any difference.

These results are an interesting reflection of how a group of what could be described as China's new élite — young, well-educated, modern in outlook, and ambitious — view their work prospects in the contemporary environment. They are quite disparaging about what they perceive to be the working context in Chinese enterprises, positive about their experiences of working for foreign-managed ones, and quite clear about what they are looking for from their work. Their conceptions of the JV situation are most illuminating when contrasted with the negative conceptions of SOEs discussed earlier. There are distinct aspirations for systematic and transparent management styles and systems as compared with the personalism and opacity they envisage in local organizations. They are also explicit about wanting to have formal appraisal mechanisms which fairly assess performance, are able to differentiate levels of performance and reward accordingly. In addition, a high value is placed upon being able to exercise personal judgement and discretion and on taking responsibility for significant tasks and decisions. Interviews and discussions revealed that this aspect was also seen as in marked contrast to local enterprises.

Questions were also put in the survey and during interviews about their conception of management style and particularly their conception of foreign managers. In terms of desirable managerial skills and competencies, it was apparent that a high value was being placed on both the so-called "soft" and "hard" skills and competencies of management. It was seen as very important that managers had good "people skills," particularly in terms of communication, but also that managers had a sound knowledge and understanding of the business and organizational context and proper mastery of the technical and functional competencies in their areas. There has historically been an emphasis in China on a "hard" conception of management. This in part reflects the vestiges of the Soviet style technical-efficiency and production orientation and a continued view that management can and should be "scientific." This has typically led to a neglect of "soft" skills.[115] The respondents seem to have developed a more balanced view. This was reinforced by responses to a question about the type of knowledge they saw as most essential to managers; the most frequent responses were either in terms of "people" knowledge (with communication and psychology given emphasis) or in terms of "technical" knowledge or knowledge related to particular functional areas.

The same picture emerged from the survey data where we asked for the perceived characteristics of successful middle managers. Items rated as uncharacteristic were "compassionate," "conceited," "forceful," "jealous" and "moody." Only the first of these is worthy of note given the reputed Confucian tradition wherein compassion is a quality of Chinese leadership. In terms of the positive characteristics, the rather vague "has leadership abilities" was the top item, followed by "conscientious" and "adaptable." There were some changes over time, although only one, the increased importance attached to "tact," was statistically significant. Such a change presumably reflects a recognition of managerial realities, that things can only be accomplished through the cooperation of others and that tact is required to secure that. Other notable changes included relative decline in the value of independence and, especially, in aggression and secretiveness. The latter two can be read as indicating a growing maturity and sense of realism. Increases in rank order were apparent on the items "understanding" and "strong personality." It could be suggested that "strong personality" supplants "aggressiveness" as a more workable form of managerial assertion.

Interviews revealed a similar kind of disparagement of the local manager as there had been of the local enterprise, and a similar idealization of the foreign manager. A complicating element here is the employment of ethnic Chinese managers from Hong Kong and elsewhere in some of the JVs. These were often seen as different from both foreign and local Chinese managers. This is significant since it would be a mistake to commit the "similar to me fallacy"[116] of assuming that shared ethnicity, or other presumed commonality, ensures cultural homogeneity and an easy transfer of management style and behaviour. Anecdotal evidence from other sources indicates that non-mainland Chinese have found as much difference and difficulty in managing in China as other "foreigners."

Responses to a set of questionnaire items about the role of foreign managers in a JV were disappointing, with respondents apparently rather cautious about expressing unequivocal opinions: many responses hovered around the scale mid-point (this was a five-point scale, 1 = "strongly agree"; 5 = "strongly disagree"). Nonetheless, there were some subtle, if mostly non-significant, shifts over time. The most notable (and only statistically significant) was the change from agreeing that "Chinese staff must learn to behave like their foreign managers to be effective," to an

Table 2. Perceptions of Foreign Managers

		Time 1 Mean	Time 2 Mean
1	Foreign managers will be unable to understand the situation of local employees	3.17	2.81
2	A local worker would always prefer to discuss personal problems with another Chinese rather than a foreigner	3.03	2.71
3	Foreign managers are too aggressive	2.92	3.03
4	Foreign managers do not care enough about the personal feelings of their subordinates	2.97	3.07
5	A foreign manager cannot be really effective unless he/she becomes fluent in Chinese	2.50	2.61
6	Foreign managers will be more effective with an understanding of Chinese culture and history	4.03	4.07
7	Foreign managers should adapt to local ways of managing subordinates	3.22	3.10
8	Foreign managers will be more effective if they socialize often with Chinese colleagues	3.78	4.03
9	Chinese will be more effective if they socialize often with foreign managers	3.67	4.00
10	Chinese staff must learn to behave like their foreign managers to be effective	3.64	3.07
11	Foreign managers are less skilled at handling interpersonal relations than Chinese	3.00	3.00

undecided position. Any interpretation of this would be purely speculative. They may have felt initially that, as success criteria were controlled by the Western managers, they would need to conform to those criteria. They also came to agree more strongly that Chinese staff needed to socialize often with their foreign managers to be effective. Similarly, the view that foreign managers would benefit from socializing with Chinese colleagues also strengthened. However, there was a slight weakening of the opinion that foreign managers should adapt to local ways of managing, but they remained basically undecided about this. They agreed that foreign managers would be more effective with an understanding of Chinese history and culture, but they never had a strong expectation that foreigners should master the Chinese language.

As already indicated, local managers were often depicted as being too relationship-oriented and personalistic in style. They were, however, seen as less open and accessible compared with Western counterparts. Their unwillingness to delegate was also emphasized. It was further suggested that they were not as enthusiastic or as hard working as either the Hong

Kong Chinese or the Westerner. Western managers were depicted as being: encouraging, supportive and developmental; "smart," well educated, and more professional; and open, sociable and people-oriented. On the negative side, they were also characterized as: too direct and "pushy"; rather strict and "tough"; too results-oriented (contrasted with a perception of Chinese managers being more process-oriented); and sometimes arrogant and rude. Hong Kong managers occupied something of a middle ground and were described as: more practical and task-oriented; more formal but easy to get along with; less direct and critical; more likely to pursue their self-interest; and possessing a more narrow outlook than their Western counterparts. Such perceptions reflect as much about how the *jvgrads* conceive of management and work relationships as it does any objective difference in management style, and are no less significant for that.

The *jvgrads* had a similar disdain for Chinese managers and management style as they did for SOE organizational systems. Although they rather over-glamourized the JV managers, they retained a more favourable view of the foreign manager relative to the local. This again has important implications for the reform process, suggesting that the monumental task of upgrading the managerial skills and talent in the country is urgent and vitally necessary. Enterprise reforms mean little in the end unless there is competent management available to convert the policy intentions into concrete reality and unless professional managers can gain the respect and high level performance from their subordinates. For this group of young Chinese, the JV is perceived to be a much more challenging and rewarding place to work than an SOE. This is encouraging for foreign companies but should be a cause for reflection for those responsible for management education and enterprise reform in China.

Central Meaning of Work Variables: A General Survey

The second piece of research we draw on is a general survey of a large sample of working people in the Beijing area using a translated and modified version of a standard meaning of work (MOW) questionnaire.[117] A stratified sample of enterprises was generated in the Beijing area, with random sampling from within strata, and random sampling at the enterprise level. A wide range of enterprise types and occupations were covered. One thousand questionnaires were administered (sometimes via an interviewer, sometimes left with a group of respondents and collected later), and there were 453 usable returns (a 45% response rate). Sixty per cent of the sample were non-supervisory, 30% managerial and the rest supervisory. Around 60% had secondary school, or vocational training, educational levels or lower, whilst 21.2% had university degrees. About three-fifths were male and two-fifths female. Fifty-four percent were married, and most came from and presently lived in the city or urban area.

The chief focus here is on the central MOW variables. From it we can garner a broad impression of the overall significance of working to people in urban China today. It gives an indication of such key factors as the perceived significance of work relative to people's other life spheres, what aspects of work are important to people, how they define work, and what outcomes they seek from work. We will include comparative data from the original MOW study to help contextualize the China responses.

Work Centrality

As indicated earlier, our MOW model incorporates the central variable of "work centrality." This deals with the centrality of work relative to the person's total view of their life and in relation to the significance to them of other life spheres. It is held to consist of two components: a value orientation toward work as a life role and which concerns levels of involvement, commitment and identification; and a decision orientation, which concerns the choices people make with respect to work as a life sphere and in relation to other life spheres.[118] An overall impression of work centrality is gathered from the response to the question, "How important and significant is working in your total life?" On a 6-point scale (1 = "one of the least important things in my life"; 6 = "one of the most important things in my life"), the Beijing sample scored a mean of 5.3, representing a high work centrality score. More meaningfully perhaps, is the perceived relative importance of work compared with other life spheres. This was tapped by a question asking respondents to allocate 100 points between five life areas: "my leisure," "my community," "my work," "my religion" and, "my family" (see Table 3 below). Unsurprisingly, less than 2% of the points were allocated to "my religion" (similar to responses from Yugoslavia, but much lower than the 14% in the US); and it was the lowest ranked life sphere. The Beijing respondents ranked "work" as the most important life sphere (35.5% allocation) closely followed by "my family" (32.74%). This was a pattern only shared by Japan and the other (then) socialist

Table 3. The Importance of Work Relative to Other Life Spheres

	My leisure	My community	My work	My religion	My family
China	21.0(3)*	9.3(4)	35.2(1)	1.78(5)	32.7(2)
Belgium	24.6(3)	6.0(4)	29.9(2)	4.9(5)	34.7(1)
Britain	22.3(2)	7.8(5)	21.5(3)	8.6(4)	40.1(1)
Germany	22.7(3)	7.3(4)	28.0(2)	5.2(5)	35.7(1)
Israel	18.2(3)	4.5(5)	28.3(2)	4.9(4)	43.9(1)
Japan	19.7(3)	5.3(4)	36.1(1)	3.7(5)	35.1(2)
Netherlands	24.2(3)	7.5(4)	29.6(2)	4.9(5)	33.7(1)
USA	18.1(3)	9.9(5)	24.5(2)	14.0(4)	33.6(1)
Yugoslavia	19.5(3)	7.5(4)	36.7(1)	3.3(5)	35.3(2)

Note: * Rank order is in parenthesis.

state, Yugoslavia. All the others, but one, had "family" first and "work" second — the exception being Britain where "work" drops to third behind "leisure." Together these two sets of responses indicate that work has very high saliency in Chinese people's lives. This is supported by data from the "jvgrad" study where a majority indicated that their career gave them more satisfaction than their "personal or home life" or "other interests."

A further indication of work centrality is provided by the old "lottery question."[119] The original question is: "Imagine that you won a lottery or inherited a sum of money and could live comfortably for the rest of your life without working. What would you do concerning working? 1. Stop working; 2. Continue to work in the same job; 3. Continue to work but with changed conditions." In line with the type of results reported in other countries,[120] only 12.8% of the Chinese respondents said they would give up working: 46.1% would continue but with changed work conditions, whilst 39.1% would remain in their existing job. This is a further indication of high work centrality.

Valued Work Outcomes and Functions

Work clearly has a highly significant general meaning in the lives of these Beijing workers, but what is it about work that they value and find important? This was addressed in the survey by a number of questions. Firstly, respondents were asked to allocate 100 points to a range of statements concerned with what work might mean to them. Table 4 below shows the China scores together with comparative data from the MOW study.

It is unsurprising that all samples gave prime support to the statement

Table 4. Important Work Functions (Mean Points Allocation and Rank)

	Status and prestige	Income	Keeps you occupied	Interesting contacts	Serve society	Interesting and satisfying
China	12.7(5)*	34.5(1)	12.8(4)	14.1(3)	14.4(2)	11.6(6)
Belgium	6.9(6)	35.5(1)	8.7(5)	17.3(3)	10.2(4)	21.3(2)
Britain	10.9(5)	34.4(1)	11.0(4)	15.3(3)	10.5(6)	18.0(2)
Germany	15.7(5)	41.7(1)	16.1(4)	16.8(3)	13.9(6)	19.5(2)
Israel	8.5(6)	31.1(1)	9.4(5)	11.1(4)	13.6(3)	26.2(2)
Japan	5.6(6)	45.4(1)	11.5(4)	14.7(2)	9.3(5)	13.4(3)
Netherlands	4.9(6)	26.2(1)	10.6(5)	17.9(3)	16.7(4)	23.5(2)
USA	11.9(4)	33.1(1)	11.3(6)	15.3(3)	11.5(5)	16.8(2)
Yugoslavia	9.3(6)	34.1(1)	11.7(4)	9.8(5)	15.1(3)	19.8(2)

Note: * Rank order in parenthesis.

"Working provides you with an income that is needed," although the different weighting is noteworthy, and the Chinese response aligns more with a number of Western countries than with Japan. Two things are distinctive about the Chinese responses. Firstly, that work as a means to serve society is second ranked, the highest of all countries (although two do allocate more points to it). Secondly, the very low rating given to work that is "basically interesting and satisfying to you," which they rate last. The former is perhaps unsurprising in a socialist state (note Yugoslavia's rating). There may be some social desirability bias in this type of response, but it may also truly reflect an ideological hegemony. The latter is less easy to interpret, especially given high value placed on "interesting and satisfying work" in the other locations. It seems the respondents are taking a very pragmatic view of work, seeing it mainly as a means of securing needed income and as a way of fulfilling their societal obligations. Job satisfaction and other intrinsic job factors have been significant motivational issues in the West since the Human Relations movement of the 1940s and remain integral to a number of prominent motivation theories. The Western dogma is that intrinsic factors are a significant part of work motivational mechanisms. However, empirical research has generally failed to show a clear relationship between job satisfaction and improved job performance.[121] It may be that the Chinese respondents find no resonance with intrinsic factors and are adopting a more instrumental approach to their work experience.

A related question asked respondents to indicate the importance to them in their work lives of a set of eleven items. The table below shows the top five rated items for China and the other countries.

Table 5. Personal Work Importance Items

	Rank 1	Rank 2	Rank 3	Rank 4	Rank 5
China	pay	good interpersonal relations	good working conditions	opportunities to learn	autonomy
Belgium	interesting work	pay	job security	autonomy	good interpersonal relations
Britain	interesting work	pay	job security	good interpersonal relations	convenient hours
Germany	pay	job security	interesting work	good interpersonal relations	good match
Israel	interesting work	good interpersonal relations	pay	autonomy	opportunities to learn
Japan	good match	interesting work	autonomy	job security	pay
Netherlands	interesting work[i]	autonomy	good interpersonal relations	variety	pay
USA	interesting work	job security	good match[ii]	opportunities to learn	variety
Yugoslavia	interesting work[iii]	good interpersonal relations	pay	opportunities to learn	good match

Notes: i: equal first rank with autonomy;
ii: equal third rank with opportunities to learn;
iii: equal first rank with good interpersonal relations.

The China data reveal a similar pattern to the preceding responses, reflecting a primary instrumental orientation, with pay being the first ranked item. Of the other countries, only Germany has this as the premier choice, the majority rating "interesting work" first — displaying, again, the Western inclination toward intrinsic motivational factors — which does not even appear in the Chinese top five.

The respondents also rank having "good interpersonal relations" highly. It might be tempting to attribute this to the reputed collectivist orientation of Chinese culture, but it may reflect a more micro-political motive. Securing good interpersonal relations may be viewed as a necessity in an organizational environment characterized by high levels of personalism and in which *guanxi* is still a highly significant social mechanism. It is argued that the continued dependency of workers on their work units and the limited alternatives for securing their needs outside of the work environment entail that *guanxi* has taken on even greater significance in the reform period.[122] Furthermore, the uncertainties and ambiguities of the current organizational environment also mean that good relationships are necessary to secure support and obtain resources that are scarce and tightly controlled in the formal system and need to be struggled for via the informal system.

The third ranked item is "good physical working conditions" which does not appear in the top five for any of the others. This obviously reflects the relative state of development in China and the limited resources available for physical amenities. A good working environment is largely taken for granted in Europe and North America, but in China working conditions can still be very poor and so are of concern to people. The high ranking for "opportunities to learn" is noteworthy since our other data sources indicate it to be a significant motivational factor in the present climate. It was, as noted, cited as one of the key reasons for the *jvgrads* wanting to join a JV. The lowest ranked item for the Chinese respondents was, by quite a margin, "variety," another intrinsic factor that for the Chinese appears to have low resonance. Also ranked low were "good opportunities for upgrading or promotion."

A set of responses to another question also reveals the salience of money to the Chinese respondents. They were asked "When you think of your working life, which of the following aspects seem most significant and important to you?" Responses were indicated on a 6-point scale (1 = least significant; 6 = most significant). Table 6 reports the mean and rank scores for China and the MOW countries for which data were available.

As implied, Chinese respondents rated money as the most significant

Table 6. Most Significant Aspects of Working: Means and Rank (in Parenthesis)

	China	Belgium	Germany	Israel	Nether.	US	Yugo.
Tasks	3.9(2)	3.5(4)	3.9(2)	3.9(1)	3.9(1)	3.2(5)	4.2(1)
Company	2.8(6)	2.5(6)	2.5(6)	2.7(6)	2.3(5)	2.9(6)	2.5(6)
Product or service	3.3(4)	3.5(4)	2.8(5)	3.7(3)	3.2(6)	3.8(2)	4.2(1)
Type of people	3.3(4)	3.8(2)	3.7(4)	3.4(5)	3.9(1)	3.8(2)	2.9(5)
Type of occupation	3.7(3)	3.8(2)	3.8(3)	3.6(4)	3.9(1)	3.4(4)	3.4(4)
Money	4.2(1)	3.9(1)	4.3(1)	3.8(2)	3.9(1)	3.9(1)	3.7(3)

Note: Data for Britain and Japan were not reported for this item on the MOW study.

aspect of working; however, they are in line with most of the other countries in this and, indeed, the overall response pattern is not dissimilar from the others and is especially close to Germany. The company they work for is not important to them, and the "type of people" in the work context does not get a very high rating, perhaps belying the presumed Chinese relationship-orientation. Once again it is a very pragmatic picture, with what one earns, the immediate task and the type of occupation being the main preoccupations.

These results, from a sample of Beijing's general working population, contrasts somewhat with the values and attitudes of the young, graduate JV recruits in Guangzhou (although not all were from the Guangzhou area). We have noted that they cited "opportunities for learning" as one of the prime reasons for wanting to join a Sino-foreign JV and it was also the top rated item from a list of personal job outcomes. They also rated "opportunity for career development" as the second most important item, and "opportunity for professional development" highly. There is clearly a much more optimistic and expectant career orientation amongst this group of "new generation" Chinese. It should be noted that these were highly educated young people who had entered the JVs with expectations of moving quickly into managerial positions. Further differences are reflected in the much higher rating they gave to "opportunity for interesting and challenging work" (ranked second among the ten items), and the relatively lower rating of financial reward (ranked fourth), and "opportunity for contributing to society" (ranked sixth). The first indicates an appreciation of intrinsic work factors, and perhaps a wish to avoid the more rigid, routine and less challenging work environments they knew existed in SOEs. The relatively lower rating for financial rewards contrasts with the MOW respondents and is most likely a function of age, more limited responsibilities and youthful enthusiasm for their job and career prospects. The respondents did not endorse the ideological norms of societal contribution as much as those in the wider sample. They displayed a lot of confidence, both in their abilities and future career prospects; partly reflected in giving the lowest rating to job security. Status and recognition, and work as a vehicle for developing friendships, were also of low significance.

Work: Obligation or Entitlement?

The MOW researchers theorized about the types of work-related normative views held within a society. In particular, they were desirous of exploring two specific societal norms concerned with the rights and duties associated with work. Empirical work led them to identify an *entitlement* and an *obligation* norm. The former relates to conceptions about the rights of individuals with respect to work and the work-related responsibilities of organizations and society as a whole in relation to individuals. It includes such norms as "all members of society are entitled to meaningful and interesting work, proper training to obtain and continue in such work, and the right to participate in work/method decisions."[123] The obligation norm relates to the perceived duties of members of society with respect to work. It includes "the notions that everyone has a duty to contribute to society by working, a duty to save for their own future, and the duty to value one's own work, whatever its nature."[124] For the Chinese survey, respondents were asked to indicate their agreement with a set of work-related statements on a 4-point scale: 1 = "strongly disagree"; 4 = "Strongly agree." Table 7 reports the mean scores for the items.

The respondents show variable support, albeit rather weakly, for both entitlement and obligation norms. There is a tendency to score all items within a very tight range, and there may be some response error here. The most strongly supported item is an obligation norm regarding people's

Table 7. Mean Entitlement and Obligation Norm Responses

	Norm	Item	Mean
A	Ent	If a worker's skills become outdated, his employer should be responsible for retraining and re-employment	3.3
B	Obl	It is the duty of every able-bodied citizen to contribute to society by working	3.4
C	Ent	The educational system in our society should prepare every person for a good job if they exert a reasonable amount of effort	3.3
D	Obl	Persons in our society should allocate a large proportion of their regular income toward savings for their future	2.7
E	Ent	When a change in work methods must be made, a supervisor should be required to ask workers for their suggestions before deciding what to do	3.2
F	Obl	A worker should be expected to think up better ways to do his or her job	3.3
G	Ent	Every person in our society should be entitled to interesting and meaningful work	3.1
H	Obl	Monotonous, simplistic work is acceptable as long as the pay compensates fairly for it	2.8
I	Ent	A job should be provided to every individual who desires to work	3.0
J	Obl	A worker should value the work he or she does even if it is boring, dirty or unskilled	3.0

responsibility to contribute to society (item B). This echoes the high rank-ing given to "serve society" in Table 4 and is perhaps an expected endorse-ment of the "commonwealth" ethos induced under a socialist system. The next three items are equally ranked (A, C and F) and consist of two entitlement norms and one obligation norm. In the PRC, citizens have come to expect to be employed and to have secure and stable jobs under the "iron rice bowl" system. All aspects of a person's work are under the control of the state in a macro sense and under the control of the *danwei* in a micro sense. People expect to be prepared for jobs and to have jobs provided. The erosion of the "iron rice bowl" and the threat of dismissal and unemployment are bringing about changes in this ethos, as we noted earlier, but these responses suggest some retention of norms about the right to work and society's obligation to provide the means to employment. However, it should be noted that the item "A job should be provided to every individual who desires work" is less strongly supported, perhaps indicating a recognition that things are changing and the "iron rice bowl" breaking. The support for the notion that workers have an obligation to "think up better ways to do his or her job" is perhaps a little surprising given the reports of low levels of initiative and proactivity on the part of Chinese workers.[125]

The next three items are entitlement norms (E, G, I) which have to do with rights about working and consultation on the job. The lowest rated items are both obligation norms (H, D). These Chinese workers, it seems, are less inclined to endure boring and monotonous work. This is trouble-some, given tendencies for highly specialized job training, fine divisions of labour and limited multi-skilling or rotation. Many jobs in China are designed in ways that involve task simplification, small work cycles, little variety and extensive routinization. The pragmatic attitude toward pay may not be enough to offset a negative reaction to this type of work regime in the long-term. The response to the item about saving is interesting. It could be argued that the question has low resonance in a society where incomes are so low as to severely inhibit saving and state protections mitigate against the need to do so.

This survey provides an overview of what work means to the people surveyed. The results are not generalizable to China as a whole but do say something about values and attitudes associated with work among the working population in the more developed urban centres in China. They indicate that work has a high centrality in people's lives and that they have a rather pragmatic and instrumental orientation toward work, with, however, some residual ideologically-informed orientation. The comparative data have value in revealing some differences in orientation between China and the other countries involved. However, the broad patterns of commonality should also be noted.

Consequences (and Conclusion): Speculations on the Meaning of Work with "Clay Pots" and "Socialist Markets"

Our model indicates that work meaning patterns have expected likely consequences for actual work-related choices, future expectations, motivational states and, ultimately, for job performance and, thus, productive viability. We have little concrete data available to illuminate these consequences. In consequence, we will report limited data from the MOW survey and then comment more speculatively on what the foregoing discussion of work meanings might engender for the future as China continues its reform path.

It has been argued that there are three competing values in China today — traditional Chinese culture, socialism, and development,[126] each of which intersect in the world of work, making for a complex and dynamic environment. What is abundantly clear from the above analysis is that the work context in China is going through some momentous changes, and one would expect that people's experiences of work and the meanings they attach to it are profoundly affected. Profound changes at the macrosocietal level constitute the basic framework for work and work meanings, but some, such as the legislative environment, have a more direct and immediate impact on work. It is, however, changes at the organizational level, themselves shaped by the macro-level changes that have a more forceful impact. Thus, the work environment in China has witnessed radical shifts, particularly in terms of the demise of the *danwei* system, the attempt to break the "iron rice bowl," the restructuring of the labour market, the reform of the welfare system, and changes in the employment relationship — especially in terms of labour contracting and reward-performance relationships. These, and other changes, have altered the organization and conditions of work with the impact being especially acute in the areas of job security, the erosion of the principles of egalitarianism, shifts in leadership autonomy and responsibility, and a more focused attention on performance and productivity and their modes of stimulation and motivation. It would be surprising indeed if these changes did not affect people's perception and experience of work and the meanings they attach to it.

The Changing Context of Work Meanings

The first important general point to make is that the changes are likely to have different effects on different sectors of society. More specifically, the changes will impact upon and be interpreted by different sectors of society in different ways resulting in different work meaning patterns. This was apparent in the analysis when the responses and meanings of the *jvgrads* were contrasted with those of the Beijing sample.

Secondly, in a general way, it is suggested that one consequence of these diverse, sometimes rapid, and in many ways momentous, changes is that collectively they have generated a significantly turbulent and uncertain work environment. This on its own is likely to have an impact on work meanings, possibly generating a pervasive sense of unease and anomie and engendering a good degree of caution in the way people consider their working lives and the type of calculations they make with respect to them. Theories of change processes would suggest that the type of environment currently being experienced in China will generate such uncertainty and result in some resistance to the changes. This is in fact apparent and has been touched on in the preceding discussion.

Another significant effect at the general level is the likelihood that individuals will change their outlook and calculations with respect to work. The attempt to break the "iron rice bowl," the demise of the *danwei*, the restructuring of the welfare system and the insecurities generated by labour contracting, all contribute to a weakening of the dependency relationships between individuals and enterprises, and even between individuals and the state. We can anticipate that people will be compelled to make more individualistic calculations with respect to their working lives, perhaps resurrecting/strengthening the centrality of the family as the core socio-economic unit, with individuals thinking about their work primarily in terms of how it provides economic support to family well-being. For those in possession of scarce and valued skills and abilities, such as the *jvgrads*, the new situation will be welcomed and embraced since they are in a position to take advantage of the opportunities and make individualized calculations that enable them to pursue personally beneficial outcomes. For others, the loss of dependency will more likely be viewed with some trepidation rather than as a freedom of opportunity.

The above issues have a bearing on work centrality. It could be argued that the danwei system implodes life spheres, such that they are all subsumed within the same time-space nexus. The reforms have re-differentiated them, such that family, community, leisure, work and other spheres become more distinct. The changes might lead some to fall back more on the family with less of a tie to the enterprise and less dependence on the state. Work centrality might diminish relative to family for such people. For others, such as the "new rich" and those able to take advantage of new opportunities, the leisure sphere of their life has expanded considerably and is likely to continue to do so. These are new vistas which will affect the values and decisions that bear upon work centrality. However, we expect work to continue to be of high centrality for the majority of the working population for sometime, even if there are subtle shifts in the relative weighting to different life spheres.

In terms of valued work outcomes, one can also witness and predict changes. The Beijing respondents gave high value to material outcomes, and this is not likely to diminish in the near future. The outcomes desired by the *jvgrads* are different. Although the age factor is significant here, it may also presage a gradual strengthening of the value of intrinsic job outcomes as economic conditions improve and become less critical for basic needs and survival. Similarly, concern for the physical working conditions remains high at present but should diminish as wealth increases and enterprises are able to provide resources for improvements. The ideologically-informed outcome of serving society obviously still has value among the working population, but it is weaker among the *jvgrads*. Given the weakening of dependencies, the reliance on material rather than moral incentives, the decline of party influence at the enterprise level and the relative de-politicization of the work-place, we might anticipate a gradual decline in this as a valued work outcome.

The situation with respect to societal norms is less easy to determine and predict. The data showed a mixed response on this issue with perhaps slightly stronger obligation norms than entitlement norms. As jobs and wages loose their guarantees, the issue of work-related rights might strengthen in response. At the same time, the relative easing of political/ideological influence in the work-place and the favouring of more abstractly economic criteria might engender a weakening of the obligation norm. But, this is very speculative and further evidence of a longitudinal nature needs to be adduced before more considered interpretations become possible.

Present Satisfactions, Future Expectations

The survey analysis has dealt with the respondents' subjective expectations about work which are indicative of how satisfied they are with their past and present work experience. Two survey questions concerning attitudes toward their occupation have some bearing on this. Respondents were asked, firstly, "If you were to start all over again, would you choose your occupation or would you choose a different one?" Less than one-third indicated that they would choose the same occupation. A second question asked if they would recommend their occupation to their children. This time more than three-quarters responded that they would not. This is suggestive of some prevalent levels of occupational and job dissatisfaction. These responses were significantly more negative than those of International MOW survey respondents. With the exception of Britain, more than 50% of the respondents of other countries said that they would pursue the same occupation (no data for Belgium and Japan): even for Britain, it was more than 40%. In terms of recommending the occupation to their children, all the other countries were more inclined to do so, and for Israel, the Netherlands and the US it was close to a 60% endorsement (Yugoslavia and Britain gave low endorsements: 26.6% and 37%, respectively — there was no data from Japan, Belgium and Germany).

Driving the Reform Process from the Ground

As stated earlier, the labour contract system, in many ways the linch-pin of the employment and enterprise level reforms, is intended to break the "iron rice bowl" and provide an invigorated environment for performance and productivity enhancements. The loss of lifetime job guarantees, the capacity to make more rational staffing and human resource decisions and a restructured labour market with increased mobility are intended to provide the impetus for more effective worker performance and for enterprise managers to be able to extract greater productivity. There are some significant impediments to this in the implementation. Firstly, as discussed, the contract system is only gradually coming into place and, even where it is in operation, the length of contracts is open to interpretation and, in many cases, offers levels of job security not dissimilar to what existed before. A consequence of this is a two-tier system, with skilled and professional people enjoying relatively privileged contract terms whilst others are treated almost like temporary workers. The meaning of work for these two groups is likely to become substantially different and lead them to make quite different work-related calculations. The intended inducements in performance and productivity terms might prove elusive with respect to the latter group. Secondly, the capacity to make more rational and effective human resource and employment decisions depends upon the willingness and capability of managers to do so. The evidence indicates that management competencies are still at a low level and that personalistic and paternalistic sentiments and relationships continue to prevail. Rational hiring and firing decisions remain difficult in this environment. Furthermore, the information systems and techniques required for the effective management of human resources in the new environment remain impoverished. Thirdly, the tentative movement toward collective bargaining brings a new complexity to the situation and again requires sophisticated mechanisms if it is to prove effective. It will also engender additional competitiveness in the labour market, with some segments of the working population not able to find advantageous outcomes. This will also be a further source of uncertainty and anomie with deflating effects on work motivation.

Related to the above is a further significant change at the enterprise level, that of moving to clearer and impersonal performance-reward relationships. This is also intended to stimulate performance and productivity by doing away with non-contingent rewards. In the West, clear performance-reward relationships have a demonstrated motivational effect and do enhance performance. Again, in China, there are notable impediments to implementation. Firstly, these reforms are a critical challenge to the deep-rooted values of egalitarianism that have been at the heart of the system in the PRC since its inception. The move toward equity-based rewards is welcomed in some quarters, such as the *jvgrads* for example, but it is encountering a lot of resistance in others. Part of the resistance is ideological, but part of it is purely rational-instrumental as some people recognize that they will not benefit materially from such a regime. Secondly, and as with labour contract reform, equity-based performance reward systems require very specific and elaborated systems for their effective administration. We have already noted the relative absence of good performance appraisal systems in China which are a prerequisite for this type of reward regime. Furthermore, performance incentives are tending to be given on a group basis, which may substantially weaken their motivational and performance effects. In the absence of good human resource systems and capable, objective management, the positive effects of these reforms are far from guaranteed, and they may have more negative impacts than positive in the short term.

The reforms have also focused on management and enterprise responsibility and autonomy principles. The intention is to decentralize to the enterprise level and de-couple enterprises from the centre, bureaucratic interference and party control. This is also proving difficult to put fully into place as numerous commentators have indicated. Certainly, SOEs remain politicized entities with complex networks of relationships and dependencies. Decentralization does not, in practice, extend down within enterprises. As the *jvgrads* pointed out, leadership still tends to be autocratic and directive, with little discretion and involvement given to subordinates. Delegation levels are low, and in the current climate there are few incentives to extend them. Managers and enterprise leaders often have low legitimacy coupled with still extensive social and welfare responsibilities. A paternalistic style remains pervasive. From the subordinates point of view, the leadership/management style represents an immediate, interpersonal context shaping their work experience and work meanings. The current scene is not one which encourages a proactive attitude toward work on the part of subordinates, and there is little sense of self-determination. Rather, somewhat passive, reactive postures are the typical response. This further stunts initiative and has a dampening effect upon motivation.

This latter point reflects a general problem with the reform process as it relates to work and the attempt to stimulate productivity and performance. Most of the change initiatives are top-down — they are formulated and implemented from central government and tend to start at the macro-level. Frequently, the changes are monolithic in nature, emanating from the top and imposed uniformly regardless of situational contingencies (although usually after some localized experimentation). The implications on the ground, at enterprise level and in the work lives of individuals, are less well attended to and frequently not thought through or evaluated. There is a need to redress that — to consider bottom-up changes that are grounded in the real problems and relevancies of people at the enterprise level. The broad encompassing changes initiated by the central government are in danger of floundering through not properly resonating with practical problems and concerns at the interpersonal and individual levels. The intended changes of the reforms are only weakly being realized because of deficiencies in the implementation. This chapter has drawn attention to one aspect of that: the impact of the reform changes on work and work meanings. This more micro-level consideration has important implications for the success of the reform process since, if positive work meanings are not engendered, leading to positive work sentiments and appropriate work attitudes, motivations and commitments, then the macro-level reforms are in danger of failing to effectively bring about the desired changes and really invigorating the economy.

The work context in China is certain to continue to evolve and change, and the meaning and experience of work in people's lives will match that. More attention needs to be paid in the reform process to these more micro-level issues within the enterprise. Broad economic reforms and policy changes, and even general enterprise governance and management changes, will assuredly flounder unless people at the work level are able and willing to invest themselves in effective performance. Additional research on the shaping factors of the work context, the meanings and experiences that it generates, and the consequences in terms of motivation, satisfaction and performance would greatly facilitate the targeting of effective changes at the enterprise level and so help to drive the reform process from the bottom-up.

Notes

1. This research includes two projects: one which involved interviews and questionnaire surveys of university graduates recruited by joint venture operations in the Guangdong area (referred to as the "jvgrad" study), and a second consisting of a formal survey of a broad section of working people in Beijing using an established Meaning of Work instrument (referred to as the "MOW" study).

2. See R. H. Hall, *The Sociology of Work* (Thousand Oaks, CA: Pine Forge, 1994); G. Miller, *Its a Living: Work in Modern Society* (New York: St. Martins, 1981); MOW International Research Team, *The Meaning of Work* (London: Academic Press, 1987); P. L. Stewart and M. G. Cantor, *Varieties of Work* (Beverly Hills, CA: Sage, 1982); P. Thompson, *The Nature of Work*, (2nd ed.; Basingstoke: Macmillan, 1989).

3. See P. Joyce, *The Historical Meanings of Work* (Cambridge: Cambridge University Press, 1987); G. Hofstede, *Culture's Consequences: International Differences in Work-related Values* (Beverly Hills, CA: Sage, 1980); MOW International Research Team, ibid.; R. E. Pahl (ed.), *On Work: Historical, Comparative and Theoretical Approaches* (Oxford: Blackwell, 1988).

4. See Notes 2 and 3 above.

5. The research is reported fully in The MOW International Research Team, 1987 (see Note 2).

6. MOW International Research Team, p. 37 (Note 2).

7. Ibid, p. 38.
8. S. Jackson, "Reform of State Enterprise Management in China," *The China Quarterly*, No. 107 (1986), pp. 405–32; M. Xue, "The Problem of Reforming the Economic Management Structure," *Hongqi* (Red Flag), No. 8 (1979), pp. 16–24.
9. Putai Jin, "Work Motivation and Productivity in Voluntarily Formed Work Teams: A Field Study in China," *Organizational Behaviour and Human Decision Processes*, Vol. 54 (1993), pp. 133–55.
10. John Child, *Management in China During the Age of Reform* (Cambridge: Cambridge University Press, 1994); the following discussion of the phases is based on this work.
11. For example Huang Xiang, "On Reform of Chinese Economic Structure," *Beijing Review*, No. 20 (1985), pp. 15–19; C. Riskin, *China's Political Economy: The Quest for Development Since 1949* (Oxford: Oxford University Press, 1987); A. G. Walder, "Factory and Manager in an Era of Reform," *The China Quarterly*, No. 118 (1989), pp. 242–64.
12. A. Hussain, *The Chinese Enterprise Reforms* (London: Research Programme on the Chinese Economy, Paper No. 24, London School of Economics, August 1990).
13. An interpretation based on John Child (Note 10), p. 41 and an assessment of recent events.
14. John Child (Note 6), p. 39; Lee Graf, Masoud Hemmasi, John Lust and Yuhua Liang, "Perceptions of Desirable Organizational Reforms in Chinese State Enterprises," *International Studies of Management and Organization*, Vol. 20 (1/2) (1990), pp. 47–56; I. B. Helburn and J. C. Shearer, "Human Resources and Industrial Relations in China: A Time of Ferment," *Industrial and Labour Relations Review*, Vol. 38 (1984), pp. 3–15.
15. P. Howard, "Rice Bowls and Job Security: The Urban Contract Labour System," *The Australian Journal of Chinese Affairs*, No. 25 (1991), p. 93.
16. Ibid.
17. See M. Korzec, "Contract Labour, the 'Right to Work' and New Labour Laws in the People's Republic of China," *Comparative Economic Studies*, Vol. 30, No. 2 (1988), pp. 117–49.
18. M. Korzec (Note 17); J.C.B. Leung, "Dismantling the 'Iron Rice Bowl': Welfare Reform in the People's Republic of China," *Journal of Social Policy*, Vol. 23, No. 3 (1994), pp. 341–61.
19. Brian Becker and Yang Gao, "The Chinese Urban Labor System: Prospects for Reform," *Journal of Labour Research*, Vol. X, No. 4 (1989), p. 413; P. Howard (Note 15); M. Korzec (Note 17).
20. J.C.B. Leung (Note 18).
21. Ibid., (Note 18) p. 352.
22. Article 1 of the *Labour Law of the People's Republic of China* from an

English translation provided in The Economist Intelligence Unit, *China Hand*, November 1995, Appendix, p. 45.
23. Ibid., Appendix, p. 49.
24. Ibid., Appendix, p. 51.
25. Ibid.
26. Ibid., Appendix, p. 54.
27. State Statistical Bureau report, cited in Lisa Atkinson, "Entertainment Just May Be China's Newest Growth Industry," *The China Business Review*, September–October 1994, pp. 16–22.
28. Lisa Atkinson (Note 27), p. 16.
29. Ibid, p. 20.
30. R. W. Zhao and S. Li, "The Distribution of Income of Chinese Residents: Cities, Villages and Regions," *Reform*, Vol. 2 (1992), pp. 46–58.
31. *Economic Management*, Vol. 2 (1993), pp. 27–34.
32. See John Child (Note 10); Malcolm Warner, "Labour-Management Relations in the People's Republic of China: The Role of Trade Unions," *International Journal of Human Resources Management*, Vol. 2, No. 2 (1991), pp. 205–20.
33. P. Howard (Note 15). The metaphor connotes the more fragile nature of the employment relationship under the reform conditions. Howard extends the metaphor by suggesting that the reforms have given rise to a dual labour force structure under which those with scarce and valued skills enjoy long term contracts that amount to the same type of privlege and security enjoyed by the old "permanent workers." Theirs is a carefully protected "porcelain rice bowl." Others, the vast army of relatively unskilled workers, have been handed an "earthenware rice bowl" — "cheap, easily broken, but easily replaced." See pp. 104–6.
34. R. H. Holton, "Human Resource Management in the People's Republic of China," *Management International Review*, Vol. 30 (1990), pp. 121–36.
35. J.C.B. Leung (Note 18), p. 343.
36. D. A. Abbott, Zhou Zhi and W. H. Meredith, "Married but Living Apart: Chinese Couples Seeking a Better Life," *International Journal of Sociology of the Family*, Vol. 23, No. 1 (1993), pp. 1–10.
37. F. Butterfield, *China: Alive in the Bitter Sea* (London: Coronet, 1982).
38. Jan Borgobjon and Wilfred Vanhonacker, "Modernising China's Managers: The State Education System Is Straining to Adapt to China's Changing Economy," *The China Business Review*, Vol. 19, No. 5 (1992), pp. 12–18.
39. China Statistical Information and Consultancy Service Centre, *China Report (1949–1989)* (Hong Kong: Influxfunds Co. Ltd and Zie Yongder Co. Ltd., 1990), cited in J.C.B. Leung (Note 18).
40. J.C.B. Leung (Note 18).
41. Steven E. Aufrect, "Reform with Chinese Characteristics: The Context of

Chinese Civil Service Reform," *Public Administration Review*, Vol. 55, No. 2 (1995), pp. 175–82.

42. See J.C.B Leung (Note 18).
43. Ibid., p. 452.
44. Ibid., p. 353.
45. I. S. Baird, M. A. Lyles, S. Ji and R. Wharton, "Joint Venture Success: A Sino-U.S. Perspective," *International Studies of Management and Organization*, Vol. 20, Nos. 1 and 2 (1990), pp. 125–34.
46. M. Boisot and J. Child, "The Iron Law of Fiefs: Bureaucratic Failure and the Problem of Governance in the Chinese Economic Reforms," *Administrative Science Quarterly*, Vol. 33 (1988), pp. 507–27; M. Boisot and Xing Guo Liang, "The Nature of Managerial Work in the Chinese Enterprise Reforms: A Study of Six Directors," *Organization Studies*, Vol. 13, No. 2 (1992), pp. 161–84.
47. R. H. Holton, (Note 34); J. A. Wall. "Managers in the People's Republic of China," *Academy of Management Executive*, Vol. 4, No. 2 (1990), pp. 19–32.
48. Refer to Note 1.
49. See O. Laaksonen, *Management in China During and After Mao* (Berlin: De Gruyter, 1988); J. O'Toole, "The Good Managers of Sichuan," *Harvard Business Review*, Vol. 81 (1981), pp. 28–40; Putai Jin (Note 9); O. Shenkar and S. Ronen, "Structure and Importance of Work Goals among Managers in the People's Republic of China," *Academy of Management Journal*, Vol. 30 (1987), pp. 564–76; R. Tung, *Chinese Industrial Society After Mao* (Lexington, Mass: Lexington Books, 1982); A. G. Walder, "Some Ironies of Maoist Legacy in Industry," *The Australian Journal of Chinese Affairs*, No. 5 (1981), pp. 21–38; A. G. Walder, *Communist Neo-Traditionalism: Work and Authority in Chinese Industry* (Berkeley, CA: University of California Press, 1986); X. Yang, "Between State and Society: The Construction of Corporateness in a Chinese Socialist Factory," *The Australian Journal of Chinese Affairs*, No. 22 (1989), pp. 36–60.
50. X. Deng, "Greeting the Great Risk," *Peking Review*, No. 21 (1978), pp. 5–8; Editorial, "Reward and Punishment are Both Needed," *Renmin ribao* (People's Daily), 3 May 1982; D. Wang, "Behavioural Sciences Can Be Used to Improve Worker's Motivation," *Jinji guanli* (Economic Management), No. 7 (1981), pp. 77–78; L. Xu, "Behavioural Sciences and the Reform of Economic Systems," *Jinji guanli*, No. 3 (1981), pp. 57–76; M. M. Yang, *On the Application of Behavioural Sciences to China's Enterprise Management.* In The Policy research Unit (eds), *Political Thought Work Is a Science* (Beijing: The First Ministry of Machine Industry of PRC, 1980).
51. R. H. Holton (Note, 34); M. Xue (Note 8).
52. Editorial (Note 50); S. L. Shirk, "Recent Chinese Labour Policies and the

Transformation of Industrial Organization in China," *The China Quarterly*, No. 88 (1981), pp. 575–93; S. Su and T. Li, "Certain Theoretical Questions Concerning Bonuses," *Renmin ribao*, 2 December 1978; A. G. Walder, "Wage Reform and the Web of Factory Interests" *The China Quarterly*, No. 109 (1987), pp. 22–41.

53. G. Yue, "The Management of Labour Quotas in Industrial Enterprises," *Hongqi* (Red Flag), No. 5 (1978), pp. 78–80.

54. W. Yan, "Award System Cannot Ignore Ideological Work," *Jiefang ribao* (Liberation Daily), 6 January 1979.

55. Communist Party of China, *China's Economic Structure Reform: Decision of the CCP Central Committee* (Beijing: Foreign Languages Press, 1984), pp. 5–6 [our emphasis].

56. P. Howard (Note 15).

57. Ibid, p. 94. See also A. Walder, *Communist Neo-Traditionalism* (Note 49).

58. Cited in J. W. Weiss and S. Bloom, "Managing in China: Expatriate Experiences and Training Recommendations," *Business Horizons*, Vol. 33, No. 3 (1990), pp. 23–29.

59. Ibid, p. 26.

60. Cited in J. R. Engen, "Training Chinese Workers," *Training*, Vol. 31, No. 9 (1994), p. 82.

61. Ibid.

62. R. H. Holton (Note 34); Tai Ming Cheung, "Looking for Work: China Fears Mounting Unemployment Toll," *Far Eastern Economic Review*, Vol. 149, No. 29 (1990), pp. 49–50; P. G. Wilhelm and Ang Xia, "A Comparison of the United States and Chinese Managerial Cultures in a Transitional Period: Implications for Labour Relations and Joint Ventures," *The International Journal of Organizational Analysis*, Vol. 1, No. 4 (1993), pp. 405–26.

63. Tai Ming Cheung (Note 62).

64. M. Warner, "Industrial Relations in the Chinese Factory," *Journal of Industrial Relations*, Vol. 29, No. 2 (1987), pp. 217–32.

65. R. H. Holton (Note 34).

66. P. Howard (Note 15).

67. M. Korzec (Note 17); P. Steidlmeier, "China's Most Favoured-nation Status: Attempts to Reform China and the Prospects for US Business," *Business and the Contemporary World*, Vol. 4, No. 3 (1992), pp. 68–80.

68. Yushi Biah, "Living without the 'Iron Rice Bowl'," *China Daily*, 16 May 1989, p. 2; Li Zhouyan, "Why Enterprise Directors Quit," *China Daily*, 11 February 1989, p. 3; *Far Eastern Economic Review*, Vol. 156, No. 9 (4 March 1993), p. 48.

69. Xu Liancang and Wang Zhongming, "New Developments in Organizational Psychology in China," *Applied Psychology: An International Review*, Vol. 40, No. 1 (1991), pp. 3–14.

70. J.C.B. Leung (Note 18).
71. Ibid, p. 346.
72. L. Zhao, "The Problem of Reforming the Wage System in Our Country," *Chinese Economic Studies*, No. 18 (1985), pp. 38–39.
73. Ibid., p. 343.
74. *Beijing Review*, 15–21 August 1988, p. 4.
75. *Beijing Review*, 15–21 April 1991, p. 5.
76. Holton (Note 34).
77. C. Tausky, "*Perestroika* in the USSR and China: Motivational Lessons," *Work and Occupations*, Vol. 18, No. 1 (1991), pp. 94–95.
78. Holton (Note 34), p. 126.
79. Wilhelm and Xia (Note 62), p. 415.
80. Ibid., p. 411, 413, 415; Holton (Note 34), p. 126.
81. See Xu Liancang and Wang Zhongming (Note 69) and Putai Jin (Note 9).
82. P. C. Early, "East Meets West Meets Midwest: Further Explorations of Collectivistic and Individualistic Work Groups," *Academy of Management Journal*, Vol. 36 (1993), pp. 319–48.
83. Brian Becker and Yang Gao (Note 19), p. 413.
84. John Henley and Nyaw Mee-Kao "The Development of Work Incentives in Chinese Industrial Enterprises: Material Versus Non-Material Incentives," In *Management Reforms in China*, edited by Malcolm Warner (London: Francis Pinter, 1987); M. A. Von Glinow and M. B. Teagarden, "The Transfer of Human Resources Technology in Sino-US Cooperative Ventures: Problems and Solutions," *Human Resource Management*, Vol. 27, No. 2 (1988), pp. 201–29.
85. Xu Liancang and Ling Wenquan, "Survey Research on the Opinion of Chinese Workers," *Kunming Daily*, 22 August 1980 [different rankings for different samples].
86. Chen Wenya, "The Ideological and Political Work — Motivation Approaches to Management in China," *International Journal of Management*, Vol. 9, No. 1 (1988), pp. 28–31.
87. Brian Becker and Yan Gao (Note 19), p. 414.
88. Wang Zhongming, "Managerial Psychological Strategies for Sino-Foreign Joint Ventures," *Journal of Managerial Psychology*, Vol. 7, No. 3 (1992), pp. 10–16.
89. Yu Wen Zhao, "'Chinese' Motivation Theory and Application in China: An Overview," in *Effective Organizations and Social Values*, edited by H.S.R. Kao, D. Singh and Ng Sek Hong (London: Sage, 1995), pp. 117–31.
90. Brian Becker and Yan Gao (Note 19), p. 414.
91. Max Weber, *The Religion of China* (Glencoe, Ill: The Free Press, 1951).
92. G. Hofstede (Note 3).
93. S. G. Redding, *The Spirit of Chinese Capitalism* (Berlin: De Gruyter, 1990).

94. S. G. Redding, ibid.; R. I. Westwood and A. Chan, "Headship and Leadership," in *Organizational Behaviour: Southeast Asian Perspectives*, edited by R. I. Westwood (Hong Kong: Longman, 1992).

95. S. G. Redding, ibid; R. H. Silin, *Leadership Values: The Organization of Large-Scale Taiwanese Enterprises* (Cambridge, Mass: Harvard University Press, 1976); R. I. Westwood and A. Chan, "The Transferability of Leadership Training in the East Asian Context," *Asia Pacific Business Review*, Vol. 2, No. 1, pp. 68–92.

96. Lucian Pye, *Asian Power and Politics* (Cambridge, Mass: Harvard University Press, 1985).

97. R. I. Westwood and A. Chan (Note 95).

98. S. G. Redding (Note 93).

99. J. S. Henley and M. K. Nyaw, "Introducing Market Forces into Management Decision Making in Chinese Industrial Enterprises," *Journal of Management Studies*, Vol. 23 (1986), pp. 635–56.

100. John Child (Note 10).

101. Ibid.

102. M. Boisot and Xing Guo Liang (Note 46), p. 175.

103. A. G. Walder (Note 11).

104. M. Boisot and Xing Guo Liang (Note 46), p. 175.

105. Ibid., p. 169.

106. Ibid., p. 168.

107. Jin Putai (Note 9).

108. See S. G. Redding (Note 93).

109. Max Boisot and Xing Guo Liang (Note 46), p. 175.

110. Jin Putai (Note 9).

111. E.g. I. S. Baird, M. A. Lyles, S. Ji and R. Wharton (Note 45); N. Campbell and J. S. Henley (eds.), *Joint Ventures and Industrial Change in China* (Greenwich, CN: JAI Press, 1991); John Child (Note 10); W. H. Davidson, "Creating and Managing Joint Ventures in China," *California Management Review*, Vol. 29, No. 4 (1987), pp. 77–94; W. H. Newman, "Focused Joint Ventures in Transforming Economies," *The Academy of Management Executive*, Vol. 6, No. 1 (1992), pp. 67–75; M. M. Pearson, *Joint Ventures in the People's Republic of China: The Control of Foreign Direct Investments under Socialism* (Princeton, NJ: Princeton University Press, 1991); S. Stewart (ed.), *Joint Ventures in the People's Republic of China* (Greenwich, CN: JAI Press, 1994).

112. J. Knutsson, "Chinese Commercial Negotiating Behaviour and Its Institutional and Cultural Determinants: A Summary," in *Chinese Culture and Management* (Brussels: Euro-China Association for Management Development, 1986); M. Lockett, "Culture and the Problems of Chinese Management," *Organization Studies*, Vol. 9 (1988) pp. 475–96; L. M. Shore, B. W.

14. Working under the Reforms 423

Eagle and M. J. Jedel, "China-United States Joint Ventures: A Typological Model of Goal Congruence and Cultural Understanding and Their Importance for Effective Human Resource Management," *International Journal of Human Resource Management*, Vol. 4 (1993), pp. 67–83.

113. Cheng Gang, "Chinese Employees in Foreign-Funded Ventures," *Beijing Review*, Vol. 35, No. 46 (1992), pp. 16–22; J. R. Engen (Note 60); Holton, (Note 34); O. Shenkar and Y. Zeira, "Human Resource Management in International Joint Ventures: Directions for Research," *Academy of Management Review*, Vol. 12 (1987), pp. 546–57; M. A. Von Glinow and M. B. Teagarden (Note 84); J. W. Weiss and S. Bloom (Note 58); P. G. Wilhelm and Ang Xia (Note 62).

114. See Wang Zongming (Note 88).

115. Malcolm Warner, "China's Managerial Training Revolution," in Malcolm Warner (ed.), *Management Reforms in China* (London: Francis Pinter, 1987), pp. 73–85.

116. N. J. Adler, *International Dimensions of Organizational Behaviour* (2nd ed.; Boston, Mass: PWS-Kent, 1991).

117. The instrument, and a full report of a large comparative study employing, it is located in: MOW International Research Team (Note 2).

118. R. Dubin, "Central Life Interests: Self Integrity in a Complex World," *Pacific Sociological Review*, Vol. 22 (1978), pp. 405–26.

119. N. C. Morse and R. S. Weiss, "The Function and Meaning of Work and the Job," *American Sociological Review*, Vol. 20 (1955), pp. 191–98.

120. MOW International Research Team, p. 79 (Note 2).

121. M. T. Iaffaldano and P. M. Muchinsky, "Job Satisfaction and Job Performance: A Meta-Analysis," *Psychological Bulletin*, Vol. 97, No. 2 (1985), pp. 251–73.

122. S. E. Aufrect (Note 41).

123. Ibid., p. 94.

124. Ibid., p. 94.

125. See R. H. Holton (Note 34); Putai Jin (Note 9).

126. Suzanne Ogden, *China's Unresolved Issues: Politics, Development and Culture* (Englewood Cliffs, NJ: Prentice-Hall, 1989).

15

China's Demography at the Crossroads

Paul Chun-kuen Kwong

Introduction

In several ways, the year 1995 marked a significant turn in the population development of China. It was to be a year when the 1980 target of population growth for year 2000, 1.2 billion, had been reached five years earlier than planned; when China was scrutinized over thorny issues of gender by women delegates from all over the world; and, when the grave consequences of China's achievement in family planning were re-examined. Although expressing a desire to find alternative ways to manage family planning and migration, population workers, from grassroots personnel to decision makers, are close to exhaustion by the extraneous efforts spent over the last 15 years.

The year was marked by ironies which surfaced in official journals and news reports. For example, while celebrating the 15th anniversary of the establishment of China's family planning and demographic research institutes and journals, staff members of the State Family Planning Commission (SFPC) published the damaging results of a survey in 1993. The findings were severely undermining the validity of fertility statistics published in China since 1982. This kind of scientific fortitude would have been unthinkable 15 years ago, even five years.

Another irony was that, while Western critics were blaming China's leaders (most being male) for the draconian family planning policies that had caused massive numbers of infanticides of infant girls by ancient methods, China's family planning workers (mostly female) at the grassroot level were the actual people who were carrying countless selective abortions (of female foetuses) by modern methods of sex determination. Even more ironic were the irrevocable statistics that showed that the culprits of imbalance in sex ratio were more likely to be college-educated women with urban professional or administrative jobs, not peasant women who could not afford the ultrasound tests.

After a year of awakening and soul searching, China's population workers are at the crossroads on several dimensions: how to reform their family planning programme so it fits better to the new conditions of the market economy; how to reform their research approaches to increase validity of demographic statistics collected from the survey-fatigued populace; and, fundamentally how to genuinely improve the lot of womanhood and motherhood through institutional reforms that aim at community growth rather than individual gain and how to raise self-respect rather than greed.

On Size and Growth

Early Results for 1995

In early February 1996, the State Statistical Bureau (SSB) announced the preliminary results of the one-percent sample survey of the Chinese population that the bureau had conducted at the end of September 1995. It was estimated that China's mainland population on 1 October 1995 was 1,207,780,000, with 616,290,000 males and 591,490,000 females. The crude birth rate of 1995 was 17.12 births per thousand population, and the crude death rate was 6.57 per thousand. The rate of natural increase was thus 10.55 per thousand (1.055%).

The 1.2 Billion Mark

According to the survey results, the population of China increased by 12.71 million people in 1995, about one million per month. At that growth rate, China's total population would have passed the 1.2 billion mark by February 1995. The significance of the 1.2 figure is that it was the "target population size" which had been set for the year 2000 by China's population planners in September 1980. It had been reached five years earlier. Using more realistic fertility rates, Professor Qiao Xiaochun and Mr Mu Guangzhong calculated that the actual date could have been reached four months earlier, in mid-October 1994.[1]

Rate of Growth in 1995

The announced growth rate of 1.06% was much lower than previously expected. Professor Zhang Lingguang of the Chinese Academy of Social Sciences (CASS) and Professor Jiang Zhenghua, deputy director of the SFPC, published as late as June 1995 in a journal of the Chinese Academy of Social Sciences that the natural rate of growth for 1995 would be 13.46 per thousand (1.346%).[2] Compared with the 1.055% rate which was announced in early February 1996, there had been an apparent drop of 22%! What could account for this big gap between them, only eight months apart? A closer examination of various estimates of China's total population would provide some clues.

In the same paper just mentioned, Zhang and Jiang made two projections of the total population. The first projection yielded 1,216.8 million by the end of 1995, while a more optimistic one that assumed lower birth rates yield of 1,215.7 million.[3] In March 1995, an independent projection (also assuming a below-replacement fertility) by Qiao and Mu had expected 1,216.7 million.[4] One would have expected that the survey's total would have fallen between these three figures. However, it turned out to be only 1,211 million,[5] which was respectively 5.8 million (0.48%) and 4.7 million (0.39%) lower than expected. Which one was closer to the truth? It seems that the most probable answer would be the first, being the highest of the four estimates. Moreover, all three figures could have been too low in the first place. As with demographic estimates, like the total fertility rates which have been substantially adjusted upward since announcement, the 1995 population and growth figures too would probably be raised in later years.

Explanations for the Dubious Data

Among several possible explanations, there are three that may account for the shortfall of population implied by the 1995 survey. The first is that the survey might have been inadequate in accounting for the millions of migrants on the move whose unplanned births would have gone under-reported. The second explanation is that the projected population totals were too high due to high birth rates being assumed by the scholars in their projections. The third explanation is that the 1995 survey did not fully capture the actual number of births and of resident population because local officials and the residents had colluded to deceive the surveyors.

While the first explanation, the incomplete coverage of migrants, remains plausible, the extent of its effects remains to be analysed. On the balance of evidence emerging from the recent debates about China's 13-year track record of underreporting in fertility statistics, the second explanation is probably not tenable. Since 1987, China's official total fertility rates (TFRs), when first reported, were consistently low; they were inevitably revised upward in later years.[6] The situation could only have been worse for 1995 because, since 1991, there had been mounting pressures on local cadres and statisticians to fake the birth numbers.[7] Most demographers in China today probably believe that China's actual total fertility rates is above or near the replacement level — 2.2 children per couple.[8] Since the TFRs used in the 1995 projections by the demographers were all below 2.2, it was quite unlikely that their projections of the total population had been too high.

As to the third explanation, the "collusion factor," it has been reported by researchers to account for the incredibly low total fertility rates reported by fertility surveys. Although the 1995 survey was not a fertility survey as such, it contained the fertility questions used in the 1990 census. It had added 15 items to collect valuable socio-economic data. Items especially sensitive to urban households and illegal residents included information about the most recent migration movement and the place of registration of *hukou* (legal residence).[9]

Fears of punishment for harbouring too many illegal residents and for births outside quotas might be the cadre's reason, among others. The seven new items on housing quality and amenities might also have raised anxieties (fearing higher taxes, for example) for rural cadres and households alike in wealthy villages and town which accommodate many guest workers from afar. Some items, such as unemployment, migration and housing quality, might have induced anxieties amongst the cadres and interviewees alike which could have led to collusion and underreporting. In sum, families and cadres could have been pressured to collaborate in concealing the extent of missing births (who are born outside of allotted birth quotas) and missing residents (who do not possess a legal residency).

Demographic Credibility and Integrity

The foregoing assessment of the 1995 survey opens up the sensitive issue of China's "demographic credibility" which, if not solved soon, will erode China's demographic integrity. If demographic integrity does not hold forth, then within a decade, China's quarter-century accomplishments in reducing population growth could sadly resemble one of the past achievements in social experiments, such as the People's Communes, or even the Great Leap Forward, though perhaps to lesser extents than either case. The grave implication of the 22% finding here is that, if true, then the falsification of demographic data has spread from one component (fertility) of China's statistical system to another (migration). Whereas the State Family Planning Commission has since 1982 been the organization most haunted by this issue of credibility in regard to fertility, now the integrity of the venerable institution of the State Statistical Bureau itself is also under threat in regard to both fertility and migration. It was admitted that, although for over a decade, the SSB's annual sample surveys of demographic changes used to be superior to the SFPC's compiled statistics, in recent years (SSB's) birth statistcs have been also obviously (significantly) "underestimated."[10]

If left unchecked, falsification would spread still further, from demographic to social statistics, such as education and welfare. Eventually, falsification could render the entire statistical apparatus of the state useless. The present polity of "governing by command" could then come to a grinding hault. With some misgivings, I would like to point out that the course of development of China's family planning programme has followed what I foresaw 16 years ago. After I made in 1978 a field study of the family planning programme in Doushan commune, Taishan county, Guangdong province, I warned about the latent effects of China's family planning programme as implemented then:

(1) As pent-up demand for more births builds up, violent surges of birth rates could take place (as happened in the mid-1980s due to widespread perception of relaxation of the rules);[11] and,

(2) the danger of the erosion of the authority of government arising from the spread of data falsification from family planning to other areas. What I had not anticipated then was this new phenomenon of cadre-mass collusion to deceive the state.[12]

The quality of fertility data has been deteriorating quickly since 1991. The data had included so much "water content" (errors) that, by 1994, the falsification of data was blamed for "hiding the unplanned births and for being the one big Public Enemy … that has hindered Chinese leaders in scientific decision making, effective monitoring and correct guidance concerning family planning."[13] It took no less a powerful national leader than the General Secretary of the Communist Party, Jiang Zemin, to remind family planning officials gathering at the 1994 Annual Discussion Meeting on the Work of Family Planning that: "Factfinding investigations, plain talks of truth and true statistics reporting must be promoted. Cadres at all levels of government must conduct in-depth investigations to find out the true situation, discover and solve the problems [of falsification] as soon as they occur. Be resolute in order to confirm the true numbers and minimize the extent of fudging or padding data. Do not cheat yourselves or others."[14]

International Aid

Inaccurate fertility statistics have also serious ramifications for international relations. For two decades, China's success in bringing down its birth rate had quickly been admired by governments and international organizations, though human rights objections by the United States to excessive coersion, like forced abortion, had already resulted in funding cuts to family planning assistance for China by multilateral and bilateral sources. Now, a double jeopardy looms large. Soon, foreign aid to China could stop coming because, if China has truly achieved such a low fertility level, then the job of helping China to control its population growth has been done, and so there is no more need to continue the support. Therein, lies a somewhat embarrassing dilemma for various interest groups in the population and family planning field.

The face-saving option would insist on the accuracy of the low fertility statistics even if that resulted in cuts of foreign aids, which though small in comparison to the national budget are greatly needed, if only to maintain valuable foreign contacts and to help consolidating the excellent achievements. Yet, to ask for continuation of aid would require not only admittance to errors made in the underestimation of birth rates, but also painful searches for the causes and courageous efforts to rectify the deficiencies.

Events in 1995 suggest that China has chosen the second option although it is incorrect to attribute admissions of massive falsification entirely to considerations for foreign aid. Unlike the guarded optimistism and self-assuredness that had been prevalent in the population discourse of the past, demographic articles in 1994 and 1995 were characterized by openness without fear, a sense of responsible urgency and traces of despair. The air of openness was also reflected in subtle ways, such as the form of address toward fellow commentators in the population field: following perhaps the international customs, those who did not have professorial, doctoral or official titles were addressed in a report of forum as "Mister," instead of "Comrade."[15]

Unprecedented in the population field for China, journals have printed detailed accounts of the extent of underreporting over time and the deficiencies of existing channels for collecting demographic data. The ingenious ways that the SSB and the SFPC staff have devised to penetrate the webs of "collusion" mentioned above have been graphically described in journals.[16] Finally, criticisms of official policies that have caused the deterioration of data quality have also become sharper and more commonplace.[17]

Sex Ratio at Birth and Selective Abortion

Among various sensitive topics in the demographic field, perhaps the most sensitive one is the sex ratio at birth. It is well known that infant girls have been underreported relative to boys. In almost all of China, except remote regions inhabited by ethnic minorities, male babies have outnumbered female babies by 10% or more. Infanticide of the weaker sex has for many years been a sharp thorn that foreign countries have used to charge China with human rights violation. Chinese demographers have, however, conducted extensive research since 1993 into the extent and causes of the phenomenon of the high sex ratio at birth and have refuted the charges of widespread infanticide of female babies.[18]

By September 1995, when thousands of women converged on Beijing to attend the World Women Conference, Chinese scientists had "converged" onto their target too, a consensus: although female infanticide has never been officially permitted, and although it cannot be ruled out as a cause of imbalance, demographic and hospital records have shown that the high predominance of reported male births could not have been largely due to infanticide.[19] Data on sex ratios at birth in China and Korea for 1982–1989 show that Korea's extent of interference in the "natural" ratios has been much more severe. For example, among third- and fourth-order births, male births exceeded female ones by 19 to 25% in 1986 and 1989 in China, but 31 to 99% in Korea![20] As it is doubtful whether Korea is practising more infanticide than China in the 1980s, one wonders what could have caused the great imbalance of sex ratio in both Korea and China.

As early as 1993, data from the 1990 census had shown the following anomalies. Among first births of 1989, the sex ratio at birth for cities, towns, and villages were about "normal," at 105 to 106 males per 100 females. However, among the third- or higher-birth orders, the ratios was increasing tremendously with the following interesting phenomenon: Whereas in cities there were 36% more males among the third- and higher-order births, in villages there were only 28%.[21] If infanticide had been the principal mode of action to cause such kind of imbalance, then the opposite should have been observed, for the action would have been more easily carried out in villages than in crowded cities. More interestingly, a series of statistical tests have found that higher sex ratios are found among mothers having had more education, "white-collar" jobs and more urban background.[22]

The sex ratio puzzles have been intensively scrutinized in recent years by statisticians and demographers in China and abroad.[23] The more definitive articles are based on the 1990 census returns and hospital records which are of high repute. From the latter category of data, Li Bohua provided an indepth analysis of the plausible causes of the imbalance of the sex ratio. From 1986 to the end of 1991, the Western China Medical University had collected 1.22 million records of hospital births in 29 provinces and municipalities through a national network of centres which monitored birth defects. His conclusions are as follows: (1) the sex ratio at birth (SRB) amongst hospital-delivered births has been steadily increasing since the mid-1980s among urban as well as rural births; (2) the SRB increases rapidly with second- and higher-birth orders; (3) the first major cause for the imbalance in the SRB is "gender specific selective abortion"; (4) the second major cause is "the tendency for mothers (with male foetuses) to deliver the babies in hospitals."

The explanatory model that emerges from Li's article can now be reconstructed thus: Let USD represent Ultrasound Determination of the sex of the foetus, SA be Selective Abortion, HB be Hospital-delivered Births, and SRB be the Sex Ratio at Birth. Then, the two pathways of this simplified model are: Due to gender bias in favour of male offspring, there had been: (1) the more USD, the more SA (of female foetuses), thus the higher the SRB; and (2) the more USD, the higher HB (of male births), thus the higher the SRB.[24]

Spread of the Use of Ultrasound Determination of Foetal Sex

Since 1979, when the first ultrasound device for foetal sex determination was produced in China, USD have been spreading rapidly throughout China. By 1987, there had been 13,000 such devices known to be in existence in hospitals, averaging six devices per county. The largest factory in China that produce such an equipment was able to produce 5,000 pieces in 1991. By 1993, it was reported that " (not only) every county has a B-Ultrasound device; well off district (formerly commune) hospitals and even family planning service stations (at the village level) are equipped with such."[25]

Since it is well known that most abortions are carried out by female staff in hospitals and health stations, and since most aborted foetuses are females rather than males, the ironic inference is that in a male dominated society, "undesirable" female foetuses are selectively aborted by females.

Although none of the family planning policies, the ultrasound devices, and certainly not the health practices are designed with the intent to hurt the female sex, the sad fact remains that more female pregnancies end that way.

On the brighter side, mounting domestic and international pressure has led policy makers to take steps to hault the trend of the kinds of demographic developments discussed so far. For example, laws, regulations and guidelines have been promulgated to reiterate the state's opposition to data falsification and illegal abortions (including sex determination) as the chief official means of fertility reduction.

The community of scholars, too, has exercised its rights as citizens to expose unjust acts and to criticize the current directions of population development.

Demography at the Crossroads

Demography means two things here. The first is the level and trends of population growth and the underlying socio-economic and policy factors; the second is the discipline of population studies, including the community of scholars in family planning and demographic research. This chapter ends with comments on the second meaning, referring thus to the sensitive positions of these scholars.

Whereas almost 40 years ago, demographic economist Professor Ma Yinchu was sacked for using demographic data to oppose Chairman Mao Zedong's population policy, the current generation of scholars has enjoyed more freedom and personal protection than Ma. In fact, the current chairman has agreed with them on the importance of statistical integrity and raising the status of women.[26] The challenge is no longer to admitting past mistakes or to the fear of persecution for blowing the whistle, but searching for new directions.

By "new" directions I understand to be something that deviates from the "old" directions that had been followed by the authorities in the last two decades. The term "deviation" here does not mean a total negation of the previous modes of family planning work; it rather implies a shifting away from existing modes that are characterized by programmatic, command-driven and moral-incentive approaches to models which are structural, demand-induced and material incentive-based approaches. Reforms to the existing system of family planning programmes are preferred to revolutionary replacement of that system which, despite some excesses, had worked well up to the mid-1980s.

In anticipation of the early arrival of the 1.2 billion mark, the 15th anniversary of the full rehabilitation of scientific study of demography and family planning, and the United Nations' Fourth Conference on Women, and the mid-decade (one per cent sample) survey of population growth, demographers and social scientists had worked hard, since 1994, to "take stock" of the demography of the country and the professional health of the discipline of demography itself. Concerning the former, several population and family planning conferences and seminars were held at the "national" level and numerous similar ones at the provincial and local levels.

Noticeable ones held at the national level included: "Thoughts on China's 1.2 Billion People," 20 October 1994,[27] "Academic Seminar on the Problems of and the Counter-measures to the New Problems Arising from the Process of Fertility Decline in China," 25–30 July 1994 (in Beidaihe) and the sequel exactly one year later (in Xiangshan, Beijing).[28]

These three meetings brought into the "mainstream" discourse on population some relatively new concepts that had become fashionable overseas: sustainable socio-economic development, reproductive health, the status of women as the crucial factor in family planning, and the coexistence of enforced and spontaneous mechanisms of fertility decline under conditions of an expanding market economy in China.

Regarding new concepts and directions in family planning in a market economy, two rounds of meetings and forums surrounding the theme were conducted: the "Meeting for the Sharing of Experiences by Grassroots Level Personnel in Family Planning" in November 1994 (in Chongqing, Sichuan) and December 1994 (Beijing demographers and family planning staff).[29] In these meetings, very sharp criticisms of unworkable policies and frank admissions of failures (by the burned-out and demoralized staff) democratically coexisted with views representing "official lines." Despite the great many "1-2-3" or "5-4-3" prefixed programme-names being introduced, the new paradigm of population development has not appeared.[30] The degree of consensus is still high among the experts today that the potential for a "rebouncing surge of fertility" remains dangerously high — any significant change in current fertility policies could be wrongly perceived by parents all over China to be a signal of the abandonment of the long-standing system of family planning. A repeat of the mini baby boom in the mid-1980s could happen again.

At the crossroads, China is waiting for a new roadmap: a new Population Paradigm.

Notes

1. *Renkou yanjiu* (Population Research), March 1995, p. 2.
2. Calculated from *Zhongguo renkuo kexue* (Population Science of China), June 1995, p. 6, Table 5 for 1994 and 1995 year-end population figures and the 1995 projected births and deaths.
3. *Population Science of China*, June 1995, p. 6, Table 5.
4. Qiao Xiaochun and Mu Guangzhong, *Population Research*, March 1995, Table on p. 8.
5. The survey estimated population at 1 October 1995 has been adjusted herein to December 31.
6. Zeng Yi, *Population Research*, May 1995, p. 8, Table 1.
7. Zhang Fengyu, *Population Science of China*, August 1995, p. 63.
8. Zeng Yi, ibid., revised the 1992 TFR figure upward to 2.1 from the incredibly low of 1.52.
9. Items are mentioned in *Population Research*, May 1995, pp. 15–16.
10. See *Population Science of China*, August 1995, p. 62, section 1; *Population Research*, May 1995, p. 11.
11. See Paul Chun-kuen Kwong, "The 1990 Census and the Fertility Policy Debate," in *China Review*, edited by Kuan Hsin-chi and Maurice Brosseau (Hong Kong: The Chinese University Press, 1990), **18**.1–18.26, for possible reasons of a resurgence.
12. Paul Chun-kuen Kwong, "Renkou guihua yu jihua shengyu" (Population Planning and Planned Births), in *Renmin gongshe yu nongcun fazhan: Taishan xian Doushan gongshe jingyan* (People's Commune and Rural Development: The Experience of Doushan Commune, Taishan County), edited by Lee Pui-leung and Lau Siu-kai (Hong Kong: The Chinese University Press, 1981), pp. 1–57.
13. *Population Research*, September 1994, p. 58, first paragraph.
14. Report on Jiang's talk by Wang Hude in *Population Research*, September 1994, p. 58.
15. Compare, for example, the forms of address used in the first and the second "Academic Seminar on the Problems of and the Counter-measures against the New Problems Arising from the Process of Fertility Decline in China," as reported, respectively, in *Population Research*, November 1994, p. 46 and September 1995, p. 55.
16. See for example, *Population Research*, September 1995, p. 30, and May 1995, pp. 27–29.
17. Comprehensive and frank discussions based on a a seminar entitled "An Analytic Seminar on the Causes for and Counter-measures against the Nationwide Inaccuracy of Demographic Data" are summarized in the August 1995 issue of *Population Science of China*, pp. 62–64. Specific aspects of this

serious problem are reported in a fair number of articles in the prestigious journal *Population Research*, September 1994, pp. 34–37; pp. 58–59; November 1994, pp. 22–27; May 1995, pp. 27–29; and, September 1995, pp. 28–31.

18. For example, Jia Wei and Peng Xizhe in *Population Research*, July 1995, p. 19, cited results of research by Zeng Yi, Gu Baochang and Li Yongping to refute T. Hull's infanticide hypothesis.

19. See Li Bohua's analysis of hospital and mass immunization records in *Population Research*, July 1994, pp. 1–9. Census data analysis of child mortality by sex can be found in Tu Ping in *Population Research*, January 1993, pp. 6–13. See also Zeng Yi and others in *Population and Development Review*, 1993, pp. 283–302.

20. Tu Ping in *Population Research*, January 1993, Appendix 2, p. 13. Tu's article which for the first time comprehensively revealed this and other anomalies of China's sex ratio imbalance was voted the best demographic paper for 1993 and 1994. For this excellent paper, Tu got the "Demography Price" of China in 1995.

21. Ibid., see Figure 1, p. 7.

22. Ibid., see Table 1, p. 8.

23. See, for example, my article, "Zhong nan qing nü yu Zhongguo ertong yangyu" (Son Preference, Sex Bias, and the Population Problem of China), in *Xiandai hua yu Zhongguo wenhua yanjiu yantaohui lunwen huibian* (Proceedings of the Conference on Modernization and Chinese Culture), (Hong Kong: Faculty of Social Science and Institute of Social Studies, The Chinese University of Hong Kong, 1985), pp. 41–56.

24. For numerical reference, there were about 60,000 communes and one million villages in China by the early 1980s. The references to the ultrasound devices are found in Tu Ping (see Note 20), p. 11.

25. For Jiang Zemin's comments (see Note 14). See also speeches of Jiang and SFPC Peng Peiyun to the United Nations' Fourth World Conference on Urban in September 1995 (*Population and Family Planning*, No. 5 [1995]).

26. See Note 14.

27. See Note 1, p. 1, and Note 16, p. 46.

28. Reported in *Population Research*, September 1994, pp. 48ff.; and, September 1995, p. 54 ff.

29. *Population Research*, January 1995, p. 45 and p. 72.

30. The new official slogan is *san jie he* (the three-way integration of interests with the work in family planning) — macroscopically, by promoting rural economic development, mesoscopically, by helping peasants to make money and, microscopically, by raising the educational and cultural level of individual family members, especially women. The idea is that, as the market economy expands and money-making opportunities increase, some sort of

spontaneous process of fertility reduction will emerge. That is, when women find it profitable to educate themselves and/or move outside the home for gainful work, they will find ways to control their own fertility. The *san jie he* approach appeared first in 1991 and, in a short time, got the blessing of the central government, replacing another "three-way" slogan called *san wei zhu* (the "Three Imperatives") since 1983. How long will the former slogan last?

Addendum

The following are corrections for chapter 19 in *China Review 1995*:

	p. 19.15 Table 4a Col. 7	p. 19.16 Table 4b Col. 12	p. 19.19 Table 5 Col. 12	p. 19.20 Table 6 Col. 7	p. 19.20 Table 6 Col. 8
	1993	1993	1993	1993	1993
Beijing	45.04	3504	86.9	9.88	14.75
Tianjin	36.68	2114	79.7	17.98	26.84
Hebei	27.16	672	68.6	5.37	8.01
Shanxi	35.60	764	79.1	2.17	3.23
Neimenggu	40.12	876	85.9	2.52	3.76
Liaoning	33.57	1503	78.4	12.14	18.12
Jilin	34.91	916	82.5	6.76	10.09
Heilongjiang	29.92	885	90.3	4.15	6.20
Shanghai	35.90	4020	76.2	33.56	50.09
Jiangsu	37.47	1481	38.5	15.87	23.69
Zhejiang	42.77	1701	35.1	8.19	12.22
Anhui	28.67	476	59.9	5.29	7.89
Fujian	30.93	1009	61.4	52.09	77.74
Jiangxi	27.14	480	64.9	6.30	9.40
Shandong	30.61	957	57.5	13.05	19.48
Henan	27.89	493	63.1	3.98	5.94
Hubei	27.14	624	74.4	8.84	13.19
Hunan	25.94	490	62.9	8.15	12.16
Guangdong	42.80	2088	64.0	31.54	47.07
Guangxi	30.37	539	70.7	21.29	31.78
Hainan	62.19	2000	86.6	29.10	43.43
Sichuan	27.67	488	69.4	6.08	9.07
Guizhou	24.75	296	75.9	2.45	3.65
Yunnan	38.16	650	68.7	2.21	3.30
Tibet	48.50	786	91.2	0.00	0.00
Shaanxi	33.13	592	76.4	6.63	9.90
Gansu	26.10	398	81.0	0.74	1.10
Qinghai	43.43	977	87.2	0.41	0.61
Ningxia	44.34	873	75.3	1.57	2.34
Xinjiang	50.11	1500	88.2	1.26	1.89
China	36.33	961	67.3	13.92	20.78

Index

Note: Roman numerals refer to the pages of "Chronology"; the Arabic numerals to the pages of the main text; the indication "n." directs to the number of the endnote on the given page.

Prepared by Maurice Brosseau